The Earthscan Reader on International Trade and Sustainable Development

Edited by

Kevin P Gallagher
and
Jacob Werksman

Earthscan Publications Ltd
London • Sterling, VA

First published in the UK and USA in 2002 by
Earthscan Publications Ltd

ISBN: 1 85383 887 X paperback
          1 85383 886 1 hardback

Typesetting by Denis Dalinnik, Minsk, Belarus
Printed by Creative Print and Design Wales, Ebbw Vale
Cover design by Andrew Corbett

For a full list of publications please contact:

Earthscan Publications Ltd
120 Pentonville Road
London, N1 9JN, UK
Tel: +44 (0)20 7278 0433
Fax: +44 (0)20 7278 1142
Email: earthinfo@earthscan.co.uk
http://www.earthscan.co.uk

22883 Quicksilver Drive, Sterling, VA 20166–2012, USA

A catalogue record for this book is available from the British Library
Library of Congress Cataloging-in-Publication Data

The Earthscan reader on international trade and sustainable development / edited by
Kevin P. Gallagher and Jacob Werksman.
      p. cm.
   Includes bibliographical references (p.) and index.
   ISBN 1-85383-886-1 (hardback) – ISBN 1-85383-887-X (paperback)
    1. International trade–Environmental aspects. 2. Sustainable development. 3.
   Globalization–Environmental aspects. 4. Foreign trade regulation. I. Gallagher, Kevin,
   1968-II. Werksman, Jacob. III. Earthscan.

   HF1379 .E25 2002
   338.9'27–dc21

                                                                    2002009760

Earthscan is an editorially independent subsidiary of Kogan Page Ltd and publishes in
   association with WWF-UK and the International Institute for Environment and
   Development

Contents

Part I Economic Perspectives

Part II Legal Perspectives

List of Tables, Figures and Boxes

Tables

Figures

Boxes

List of Contributors

James K Boyce

Professor Boyce is author of *The Philippines: The Political Economy of Growth and Impoverishment in the Marcos Era* (University of Hawaii Press, 1993), *Agrarian Impasse in Bengal: Institutional Constraints to Technological Change* (Oxford University Press, 1987), and co-author of *A Quiet Violence: View from a Bangladesh Village* (Zed Press, 1983). He is editor of *Economic Policy for Building Peace: Lessons of El Salvador* (Lynne Rienner, 1996), the product of a study he coordinated on behalf of the United Nations Development Programme. In these books and his related work, Professor Boyce reexamines the organizational and social constraints on economic development. In addition to development economics, Professor Boyce teaches and writes in the field of environmental economics. With a doctorate from Oxford he directs the Political Economy Research Institute's Programme on Development, Peacebuilding and the Environment. Information on this programme can be found at its website: http://www.umass.edu/peri/dpe.html.

Steve Charnovitz

Steve Charnovitz practises law at Wilmer, Cutler & Pickering in Washington, DC. From 1995 to 1999 he was director of Yale University's Global Environment and Trade Study (GETS), which he helped to establish in 1994. From 1991 to 1995 he was policy director of the US Competitiveness Policy Council in Washington, DC, which issued four reports to the US Congress and president. From 1987 to 1991 he was a legislative assistant to the speaker of the US House of Representatives, specializing in trade and tax issues. Before that he was an analyst at the US Department of Labor, where his responsibilities included worker rights in trade negotiations and conducting an evaluation of a human resource development project in Saudi Arabia. He has a BA and Juris Doctor (JD) from Yale University and a Master of Public Policy degree from Harvard University. He is admitted to the Bar in the District of Columbia and New York.

Daniel Chudnovsky

Daniel Chudnovsky is the director of the Center for Research on Transformation (CENIT) in Buenos Aires. He is also a professor of economic development and political economy at the University of Buenos Aires. He has written extensively on trade, industrial restructuring, foreign direct investment and development. Prior to working at CENIT he was an economist at UNCTAD in Geneva and a director of international economics at the Argentine Ministry of Foreign Relations.

Kristin Dawkins

Kristin Dawkins is the director of the Program on Trade and Agriculture for the Institute for Agriculture and Trade Policy. Her work focuses on food security, environmental impacts and intellectual property rights. She travels widely, representing the institute at a broad range of international negotiations and conferences, and has published numerous articles in journals from the US, France, the UK, Germany, Brazil, Malaysia and South Africa. She holds an MA in city planning, specializing in international environmental negotiation, from the Massachusetts Institute of Technology.

David R Downes

David Downes is a senior trade adviser in the Office of the Secretary of the United States Department of the Interior, in Washington, DC. He is also on the adjunct faculty of the American University's Washington College of Law. Previously he was senior attorney at the Center for International Environmental Law (CIEL), also in Washington, before which he practised law with the Washington firm of Steptoe & Johnson. He received his JD in 1988 from the University of Michigan Law School and has a BA in philosophy from the University of Michigan.

Daniel C Esty

As director of the Yale Center for Environmental Law & Policy, Professor Esty holds faculty appointments at the Yale Law School and the Yale School of Forestry and Environmental Studies. He went to Yale in 1994 after eight years in Washington, during which time he served as special assistant to EPA administrator William Reilly, EPA's deputy chief of staff and EPA's deputy assistant administrator for policy, planning and evaluation. He is author or editor of several books, including *Greening the GATT: Trade, Environment, and the Future* (Institute for International Economics, 1994); *Thinking Ecologically: The Next Generation of Environmental Policy* (Yale University Press, 1997); and *Sustaining the Asia Pacific Miracle: Environmental Protection and Economic Integration* (Institute for International Economics, 1994), as well as numerous articles on trade, environmental protection, competitiveness, security, and development issues.

Kevin Paul Gallagher

Kevin Gallagher is a research associate at the Global Development and Environment Institute (GDAE) at the Fletcher School of Law and Diplomacy and Tufts University, in Boston, Massachusetts. GDAE is a research institute dedicated to promoting a new understanding of how societies can pursue their economic goals in an environmentally and socially sustainable manner. He conducts economic research on the relationship between trade, investment and sustainable development in the Western Hemisphere. In additional to his numerous publications and presentations, he has served as an advisor to international institutions, governments and non-governmental organizations.

Andrés López

Andrés López is a researcher at the Center for Research on Transformation in Buenos Aires and a professor on graduate and undergraduate courses at the University of Buenos Aires. His principal areas of research have been in such areas as foreign direct investment, industrial organization and labour markets.

Adil Najam

Adil Najam is an assistant professor at the Department of International Relations and the Center for Energy and Environmental Studies. He holds a PhD from MIT, a BSc from the University of Engineering and Technology in Pakistan, with a specialization in negotiation, global environmental politics, global governance and non-state actors, international negotiation, north–south relations. Professor Najam's work focuses principally on developing countries. He has co-edited (with Lawrence Susskind and William Moomaw) two volumes of *Papers on International Environmental Negotiation* (1993 and 1994, Program on Negotiation, Harvard Law School). He is currently working on a book provisionally titled *Environmental Negotiation in an Unequal World*, (forthcoming, Zed Books). His research has been published in *Environmental Conservation, International Studies, International Environmental Affairs, Population Research and Policy Review, Development Policy Review, and Nonprofit Management and Leadership*. He is a frequent editorial contributor to international environmental periodicals, including *The Earth Times* (New York), *Down to Earth* (New Delhi) and *The Way Ahead* (Karachi).

Eric Neumayer

Dr Neumayer is a lecturer in environment and development, and holds MSCs from Saarbrücken and the LSE, and a PhD from the LSE. An economist by training, his research has focused on sustainable development and monetary measures of resource depletion and environmental degradation. His teaching focuses on neoclassical environmental and ecological economics. His publications include *Weak versus Strong Sustainability: Exploring the Limits of Two Opposing Paradigms*, (Edward Elgar Publishing, 1999) and *Greening Trade and Investment: Environmental Protection without Protectionism*. He is the programme director for the MSc in environment and development at the LSE.

Michael E Porter

Michael E Porter is the Bishop William Lawrence University Professor, based at Harvard Business School. He is a leading authority on competitive strategy and international competitiveness. He received a BSE from Princeton University in 1969, an MBA from Harvard Business School in 1971, and a PhD in business economics from Harvard University in 1973. Professor Porter joined the Harvard Business School faculty in 1973. He is author of 16 books and over 75 articles, most notably *Competitive Strategy: Techniques for Analyzing Industries and Competitors* (Free Press, 1998); *Competitive Advantage: Creating and Sustaining Superior Performance* (Free Press, 1995); *The Competitive Advantage of Nations* (Free Press, 1990); *On Competition* (Harvard Business School Press, 1998); and most recently, *Can Japan Compete?* (Perseus Press, 2000) In addition, he leads the research along with Jeffrey Sachs to create the *Global Competitiveness Report* (World Economic Forum, with CID and GCR), an annual ranking of the competitiveness and growth prospects of countries. In 1994, Professor Porter founded the Initiative for a Competitive Inner City (ICIC), a national organization for which he is now the CEO. More recently, he co-founded and serves as senior adviser to the Center for Effective Philanthropy. In addition, Professor Porter has served as a counsellor on competitive strategy to many companies, and in 1983 was appointed by President Reagan to the president's Commission on Industrial Competitiveness.

Mark Ritchie

Mark Ritchie has been president of the Institute for Agriculture and Trade Policy since 1988. He has spent the last 20 years working to address a wide range of economic, social and environmental issues facing family farms and small towns both in the US and around the world. He grew up in Georgia and Iowa, graduating with honours from Iowa State University in 1971 and from 1972–1976 managed a system of vertically integrated consumer cooperatives in Northern California, with operations ranging from farms to retail outlets. In 1976 he became executive director of the Center for Rural Studies, a San Francisco-based agricultural policy research institute. In 1981 he moved to Minnesota to serve as the research and resource manager of Miller Meester company, one of the nation's largest agriculture-related communications firms. He is a regular columnist for farm and trade publications in the US, Europe, Japan and Canada, and has written and produced two films on agriculture and environment issues.

Nick Robins

Nick Robins is head of research for the Socially Responsible Investment (SRI) team at Henderson Global Investors in London. He joined Henderson's in December 2000 after seven years with the International Institute for Environment and Development (IIED), where he worked as director of the Sustainable Markets Group. During his time at IIED, he worked extensively on issues of global corporate responsibility and sustainable trade. In addition, he acted as an adviser to a range of government bodies, including the Departments for the Environment and International Development in the UK, the Norwegian Ministry of the Environment, the OECD's Environmental Directorate, United Nations Environment Programme (UNEP) and United Nations International Development Organization (UNIDO). Recent publications include *The Reality of Sustainable Trade* (IIED, 2000), *Sustaining the Rag Trade* (IIED, 2000), *Unlocking Trade Opportunities* (IIED, 1997) and *Consumption in a Sustainable World* (IIED, 1998). His articles have also appeared in a number of journals, including *International Affairs, Development, Tomorrow, Resurgence, Greener Management International, Environment and Urbanisation, New Scientist, European Environment* and *The Journal of Sustainable Product Design*. Prior to IIED, he was a special adviser to the European Community's Environmental Directorate working on the preparations and follow-up to the 1992 Earth Summit, and contributed chapters on strategy and innovation to the Business Council for Sustainable Development's landmark report, *Changing Course* (MIT Press, 1992). He has a BA in History (First Class) from Cambridge University, and an MSc in International Relations (Distinction) from the LSE.

Magda Shahin

Magda Shahin holds a PhD in economics from Cairo University. She is deputy assistant minister of foreign affairs for international economic relations in Egypt and assistant professor of international economics at the American Univerisity in Cairo. She has served on the delegation of the Egyptian government to numerous United Nations conferences and as a councillor at the Egyptian Mission to the United Nations in New York. She has also held the post of deputy chief of mission at the Egyptian Mission to the United Nations in Geneva.

David I Stern

David Stern is a research fellow in the ecological economics programme at the Centre for Resource and Environmental Studies of the Australian National University. He holds a PhD in geography, a postdoctoral fellowship at the University of York in the Department of Environmental Economics and Management, a BA in economics and geography, and MSc degrees in geography from the Hebrew University of Jerusalem and the LSE, respectively. His research currently focuses on five areas: global climate change, modelling resource degradation and technical change, ecological economics theory, energy use, pollution and economic development, and the environmental Kuznets curve. His publications include articles in *the Journal of Environmental Economics and Management, Environmental and Resource Economics, Ecological Economics, Energy Economics, Environment and Development Economics, the Journal of Economic Issues, Climatic Change, Nature, World Development*, and other journals and edited books. He was one of the principal organizers of the sixth biennial meeting of the International Society for Ecological Economics that was held in Canberra in July 2000. He is treasurer of the Australia New Zealand Society for Ecological Economics.

Christopher D Stone

Professor Stone is the J Thomas McCarthy Trustee Professor of Law at the University of Southern California Law School. His research interests include: international environmental law and institutions; global resources; precautionary principle; and trade and the environment. He has authored: *Where the Law Ends: The Social Control of Corporate Behavior* (Harper & Row, 1975); *Earth and Other Ethics* (Harper & Row, 1987; paperback, 1988); and *The Gnat is Older than Man: Global Environment and Human Agenda* (Princeton University Press, 1993; paperback, 1995). He teaches classes on property; law, language and ethics; and international environmental law.

Claas van der Linde

Claas van der Linde is on the faculty on the International Management Research Institute of St Gallen University, St Gallen, Switzerland.

Konrad von Moltke

Konrad von Moltke works on international environmental policy, with an increasing focus on the relationship between international economic policy (trade, financial flows, aid and development) and the environment. Most recently he has worked on trade and the environment, the commodities trade in particular. He is senior fellow at the World Wide Fund For Nature in Washington and the International Institute for Sustainable Development in Winnipeg as well as visiting professor at the Institute for Environmental Studies of the Free University Amsterdam.

Jacob David Werksman

Jacob Werksman is a senior lawyer with the Climate Change, and the Trade, Investment and Sustainable Development Programmes at the Foundation for International Environmental Law and Development (FIELD), London. FIELD provides legal advice and assistance to governments, intergovernmental and non-governmental organizations, on all aspects of international economic law and international environmental law at University College London, and has held visiting academic posts at the University of Edinburgh, University of Kent, United Nations University Institute of Advanced Studies and the University of Connecticut Law School.

Lyuba Zarsky

Lyuba Zarsky is director of the Globalization and Governance Program of the Nautilus Institute for Security and Sustainable Development, a non-governmental policy-oriented research and advocacy group. The programme aims to promote environmental sustainability and social justice within market governance in the context of economic globalization, especially in the Asia–Pacific region. She has worked extensively on issues related to trade, investment and the environment, as well as civil society participation and human rights. An economist by academic training, her recent publications include: 'APEC, Globalization, and the "Sustainable Development" Agenda' (*Asian Perspectives*, Vol 22, No 2, 1998); *Energy and the Environment in Asia Pacific: Regional Cooperation and Market Governance* (forthcoming, United Nations University Press); *Stuck in the Mud? Nation-States, Globalisation, and the Environment* (Organisation for Economic Co-operation and Development, Globalisation and Environment: Preliminary Perspectives, 1997). With Simon Tay, she is currently working on a study of the role of civil society in promoting investment in 'clean' industrial technology in Southeast Asia.

List of Acronyms and Abbreviations

AoA	Agreement on Agriculture
AMS	Aggregate Measure of Support
AOC	Appellations d'Origine Contrôlée
APEC	Asia Pacific Economic Cooperation
ASEAN	Association of South East Asian Nations
BTA	border tax adjustment
BTU	British thermal unit
CBD	Convention on Biological Diversity
CDM	Clean Development Mechanism
CFC	chlorofluorocarbon
CIEL	Center for International Environmental Law
CIMMYT	Center for Maize and Wheat Improvement
CITES	Convention on International Trade in Endangered Species of Wild Flora and Fauna
CSCM	Committee on Subsidies and Countervailing Measures (World Trade Organization)
CSIR	Council of Scientific and Industrial Research
CO	carbon monoxide
CO_2	carbon dioxide
CSD	Commission on Sustainable Development
CSE	Centre for Science and Environment
CTE	Committee on Trade and Environment (World Trade Organization)
CVD	countervailing duty
DSP	Dispute Settlement Panel (World Trade Organization)
DSU	Dispute Settlement Understanding
EC	European Community
EEZ	Exclusive Economic Zone
EKC	environmental Kuznets curve
EPA	Environmental Protection Agency
EPZ	export processing zone
EU	European Union
FAO	Food and Agricultural Organization (United Nations)
FCCC	Framework Convention on Climate Change
FDI	foreign direct investment
FSC	Forest Stewardship Council
GATS	General Agreement on Trade in Services
GATT	General Agreement on Tariffs and Trade

GDI	gender-related development index
GDP	gross domestic product
GEMS	Global Environmental Monitoring System
GMO	genetically modified organism
GNP	gross national product
HCFC	hydrochlorofluorocarbon
HDI	Human Development Index
HGDI	Human and Gender-related Development Indexes
ICC	International Chamber of Commerce
ICSID	International Centre for Settlement of Investment Disputes
IISD	International Institute for Sustainable Development
ILO	International Labour Organization
IMF	International Monetary Fund
IPM	Integrated Pest Management
IPR	intellectual property rights
ISCP	International Sustainable Cocoa Program
ISI	import substitution industrialization
ISO	International Organization for Standardization
ITQ	individual tradable quota
IUCN	International Union for Conservation of Nature and Natural Resources
LIDC	low-income developing country
LRTAP	Convention on Long Range Transboundary Air Pollution
MAI	Multilateral Agreement on Investment
MEA	multilateral environmental agreement
MEB	Management Board for Environment and Business
MFN	most favoured nation
MIGA	Multilateral Investment Guarantee Agency
MNC	multinational corporation
NAFTA	North American Free Trade Agreement
NFIDC	net food-importing developing countries
NGO	non-governmental organization
NIE	newly industrializing economy
NO_2	nitrogen dioxide
NO_x	nitrous oxide
NTB	non-tariff barriers
ODS	ozone-depleting substance
OECD	Organisation for Economic Co-operation and Development
PIC	prior informed consent
POPs	persistent organic pollutants
PPM	process or production method
PPP	'purchasing power parity' or 'polluter pays principle'
PSE	producer subsidy equivalents
PTO	Patent and Trademark Office
R&D	research and development
S&T	science and technology

SCM	subsidies and countervailing measures
SHD	Sustainable Human Development
SME	small-to-medium enterprise
SO_2	sulphur dioxide
SPS	sanitary and phytosanitary
TAC	total allowable catch
TBT	technical barriers to trade
TED	turtle excluder device
TREM	trade-related environmental measure
TRIPS	Trade Related Intellectual Property Rights Agreement
UNCED	United Nations Conference on Environment and Development
UNCITRAL	United Nations Commission on International Trade Law
UNCLOS	United Nations Law of the Sea
UNCTAD	United Nations Conference on Trade and Development
UNCTC	United Nations Centre for Transnational Corporations
UNEP	United Nations Environment Programme
URAA	Uruguay Round on Agriculture
USDA	United States Department of Agriculture
VOC	volatile organic compound
WIPO	World Intellectual Property Organization
WTO	World Trade Organization
WWF	World Wide Fund For Nature

The Earthscan Reader on International Trade and Sustainable Development

Dedication

This volume is dedicated to the memory of Eduardo Gitli, the South American economist who understood the importance of taking an integrated approach to globalization and sustainable development

International Trade and Sustainable Development: An Integrative Approach

Kevin P Gallagher and Jacob Werksman

The beginning of this millennium has witnessed an unprecedented opening of the global marketplace. This spread of economic liberalization can also be attributed to the growing number and scope of international negotiations aimed at promoting cross-border trade and investment, and at embedding free-trade ideologies into binding rules and powerful institutions. The previous decade saw, at the global level, the transformation of the General Agreement on Tariffs and Trade (GATT) into a stronger and more encompassing World Trade Organization (WTO). At the regional level, free trade and investment agreements were initiated in Europe, Asia, Africa, Latin America and North America. Since 1990 the value of world trade has tripled, and flows of foreign direct investment have increased by 14 times.

Increased flows of international trade and investment are driving the phenomenon of 'globalization' – the rapid growth and integration of markets, institutions and cultures. The speed of change is too fast for many people to make sense of. An escalating series of protests at the WTO meeting in Seattle in 1999, the Washington meetings of the International Monetary Fund (IMF) and the World Bank in the spring of 2000, the Summit of the Americas meeting in Quebec in April 2001 and the G-8 meeting in Genoa in July 2001, illustrates the breadth and depth of concerns of a growing, but ill-defined, constituency about the potential impacts of an unfettered global marketplace. As the decade closed, for a moment the process paused. Efforts to extend global trade disciplines to the movement of capital, through a Multilateral Agreement on Investment (MAI), and to further broaden the role of the WTO met with resistance and collapsed. Fundamental questions have been raised and answers are being demanded.

Since the collapse of the world trade talks in Seattle, the world's economic ministers have regrouped and managed to launch a new round of trade negotiations. The WTO Ministerial Conference met in Qatar in November 2001 and agreed an ambitious new agenda to further liberalize markets. They also reaffirmed their 'commitment to the objective of sustainable development' and their conviction that:

> the aims of upholding and safeguarding an open and non-discriminatory multilateral trading system, and acting for the protection of the environment and the promotion of sustainable development can and must be mutually supportive.

Procedures have been established within the WTO to identify and debate the developmental and environmental aspects of the negotiations as they proceed. Many remain sceptical of the WTO's institutional and ideological capacity to strike the right balance.

For many environmentalists, each new initiative at promoting economic liberalization raises questions about the potential impact on the Earth's ecosystems and on governments' development choices. They see liberalization as driving the demand for greater consumption of natural resources and as creating pressures to dismantle environmental regulation. A growing, but disparate, scholarly and popular literature has emerged to answer these questions. This volume attempts to present important contributions to this literature. We hope to capture the lessons learned thus far and to guide academics, practitioners, activists and the public at large in the next decade of work on these issues.

The rules, procedures and institutions that comprise the world trading and investment regime, while targeted at promoting the flow of goods, services and capital, also impact political systems, cultures and development. For this reason, no single discipline is fully equipped to analyse these issues alone. To understand trade liberalization the disciplines of economics, law and political science have much to offer. This volume has selected a number of key articles from these disciplines. It is divided into two main parts, 'Economic Perspectives' and 'Legal Perspectives,' accordingly. Many of the articles in both parts address the political and policy aspects of these questions as well. Because we were constrained by the need to bridge disciplinary divides, and by the objective of making this volume accessible to non-specialists, we have chosen articles that are not overly technical in nature. For this reason, many of the 'classic' articles in a given discipline have been omitted. However, most of them appear in the references of the papers included here.

Part I Economic Perspectives[1]

There is an emerging consensus among economists about the relationship between trade and investment liberalization and sustainable development. Without the proper environmental and social policies in place, economic integration can create new problems for nations working to develop their economies in a sustainable manner and can exacerbate existing problems. Unfortunately, in the context of countless other priorities demanded by the liberalization process, many developing countries lack the capacity to institute the necessary social and environmental policies needed to facilitate and balance economic integration.

The chapters in Part I of the volume present a range of papers in economics and political economy on the relationship between economic integration and environmentally sustainable development. This short introduction to the part describes the basic theoretical frameworks that these economists share.

Theoretical Frameworks on the Economics of Trade and Sustainable Development

Economists have begun to develop a broad theoretical framework for analysing the trade and sustainable development relationship. Economic integration has direct and indirect effects on environment and development. The indirect effects are those that need the most attention, and those that economists have focused most on. As an example of direct effects, a recent study of the increasing levels of transportation due to the North American Free Trade Agreement (NAFTA) found that NAFTA trade has directly contributed to air pollution in the five key transportation corridors that link North American commerce. Such pollution is estimated to be 3–11 per cent of all mobile source nitrous oxide (NO_x) emissions in those regions, and 5–16 per cent of all particulate matter emissions (NACEC, 2001b). A second direct effect is the introduction of alien-invasive species through trade. Again, the example of NAFTA is telling, where increased trade flows have accelerated the spread of alien-invasive species leading to 'decreased biological diversity that cost North America millions of dollars' (NACEC, 2001a).

Economic integration can also have indirect effects on sustainable development. Economists have outlined four mechanisms whereby trade and investment liberalization have indirect effects on environment and development: scale, composition, technique and regulatory effects (Grossman and Krueger, 1993). Scale effects occur when liberalization causes an expansion of economic activity. If the nature of that activity is unchanged but the scale is growing, then pollution and resource depletion will increase along with output. Ever-increasing levels of carbon dioxide (CO_2) emissions due to the expansion of the world economy in the 1990s are often cited as examples of scale effects.

Composition effects occur when increased trade leads national economies to specialize in the sectors where they enjoy a comparative advantage. When comparative advantage is derived from differences in regulatory stringency (ie, the pollution-haven effect), then the composition effect of trade will exacerbate existing environmental and social problems in the countries with relatively lax regulations. If 'dirty' or 'socially irresponsible' industries begin to concentrate in nations with standards that are relatively weak, it is feared that a 'race to the bottom' in standard-setting will occur.

The chapter by Zarsky reviews much of the recent research on whether firms in developed countries migrate to developing countries because of lax environmental standards. Zarsky concludes that by and large there has not been the broad shift of dirty production that many had predicted. However, there is a great deal of anecdotal and more recent empirical evidence that supports this hypothesis, thus not ruling out that pollution havens *could* occur. Zarsky, among others, outlines strategies for precautionary measures for pollution-haven prevention (Goodstein, 1998; Neumayer, 2001).

Others have suggested that perhaps we should be looking for pollution havens in the developed world, not the poorer nations. In this volume James Boyce shows how sustainable jute production in Bangladesh and corn production in Mexico have been jeopardized by globalization. In each instance more sustainable practices –

both socially and environmentally – in these two countries have been displaced because the higher pollution costs of synthetic fibres and pesticide-intensive agriculture were not internalized in the prices of their developed country trading partners. Such changes in Mexico have resulted in social displacement, dramatic losses in genetic diversity, higher levels of migration from rural areas and increased pressure on land, aquifers and forests (Nadal, 2000).

Technique effects, or changes in resource extraction and production technologies, can potentially lead to a decline in pollution per unit of output. The liberalization of trade and investment may encourage the transfer of cleaner technologies to developing countries. In 1990 foreign direct investment (FDI) flowing to the developing world was US$44 billion, but reached over US$650 billion in 1998 – while official development assistance continued to hover at close to US$50 billion annually (UNCTAD, 2000). It is argued that these foreign investors often set up operations with modern technologies and management systems that are more advanced, and less polluting, than those that exist locally (Esty and Gentry, 1997).

This possibility of an intriguing 'win–win' solution has its limits, as the chapters by Zarsky and Chudnovsky and López point out. Of all FDI flows in 1998, only 25 per cent went to the developing world. Moreover, three nations – China, Mexico and Brazil – received almost half of the developing world's share (UNCTAD, 2000). These figures suggest that many of the world's poorer nations will not benefit from the possible transfer of cleaner technologies through FDI. Moreover, massive capital flows to the developing countries are not a sustained guarantee; such flows have proven to be erratic and volatile over time. There is also evidence that sometimes FDI comes in the form of outdated, environmentally harmful technology (Esty and Mendelsohn, 1995).

The fourth mechanism whereby trade and investment liberalization affect environment and development is referred to as the regulatory effect. For developing countries, economic integration can crowd out the creation of development-friendly policies and institutions. Michael Finger of the World Bank has estimated that the average developing country needs to spend US$150 million to implement the requirements for just three WTO agreements – the equivalent of one year's development budget for the world's poorer nations. In a discussion of these results, economist Dani Rodrik notes that such commitments entail costly trade-offs in the realm of fiscal and human resources (Rodrik, 2001).

In this volume, Zarsky discusses how economic integration leaves developing countries' social and environmental policies 'stuck in the mud'. She notes that the constraints of competitiveness hinder the capacity and willingness of nations (especially developing countries) to impose any costs on themselves or on domestic producers. Moreover, she adds that those policies that are introduced will be only those that are in force for primary competitors. For developed nations, she argues that competitiveness pressures create a 'regulatory chill', (similar to what Esty calls 'political drag' in another article here) whereby such nations fail to raise the level of standards for fear of capital flight to poorer nations with more lax standards.

This contrasts sharply with the broadly accepted argument that, as economic liberalization increases income levels, newly affluent citizens will demand a cleaner environment. David Vogel (1997) notes that, in the case of the formation of the

European Union (EU) at least, trade liberalization has strengthened the ability of nations to protect environmental and social standards. Importantly, however, he acknowledges that this did not happen automatically. According to Vogel's analysis of the EU, a positive regulatory effect can occur when powerful (often correlating with 'wealthy') nations prod their trading partners to strengthen their policies in the integration process.

Grossman and Krueger (1993) argued that these effects (scale, composition and technique) might combine to form an inverted U-shaped relationship between trade, environment and development – the so-called environmental Kuznets curve in which, first things get worse, then they get better. Early studies suggested that the 'turning point' at which economies would begin to get more environmentally benign was a per capita income of approximately US$5000. These early studies were falsely generalized by policy-makers who prescribed that the environment could wait, since trade-led economic growth would eventually (and naturally) result in environmental improvement.

The chapter by Stern shows how more recent studies have called into question both the specific findings and the broad generalizations of that early work. Among a number of the limitations that he identifies, Stern shows that such relationships were found to be true only for a limited number of pollutants and countries – namely, localized air pollutants in Organisation for Economic Co-operation and Development (OECD) countries. Second, he shows that the range of 'turning-point' estimates are now thought to fall between US$5000 and US$100,000, depending on the pollutant, indicating that environmental degradation could occur for decades before 'turning' around – if it ever does.

Addressing the Need for Properly Crafted Policy

The challenge is to link trade policy with the design of proper social and environmental policies that will help trade to facilitate sustainable development, not hinder it. The chapters by Porter and Neumayer in this volume exhibit innovative ways that governments, industries and citizens have successfully linked social and environmental policy with trade policy. The chapters by Najam and Robins, and by Esty, present frameworks for making these successes more widespread throughout the world economy.

Whether in the form of international treaties, national and local legislation or 'eco-labels' and voluntary standards, a growing number of scholars are beginning to argue that sustainable development policies can enhance competitiveness. The Neumayer chapter and the Porter and van der Linde chapter in this volume discuss state-led international and national forms of regulation. Porter's hypothesis, that regulation-inspired innovation to decrease environmental degradation can lead to reduced costs and therefore increased competitiveness, deserves to be spelled out. Environmental regulation can lure firms to seek ways of increasing resource productivity and therefore reduce the costs of inputs. Such 'innovation offsets' can exceed the costs of environmental compliance. Therefore, the firm that leads in introducing cleaner technologies into the production process may enjoy a 'first-mover advantage' over those industries in the world economy that continue to use more traditional, dirtier production methods. (For a critical rebuttal see Palmer et al, 1995.)

Rhys Jenkins (1998) has offered a synthesis of the Porter hypothesis, arguing that regulation is more likely to lead to 'innovation offsets' under three conditions. Note that each condition requires that a firm has substantial market power in an industry in which there is substantial innovative activity. First, because cost reductions are more likely to occur where new clean technologies are developed rather than in industries that adopt end-of-pipe solutions, the level of research and development (R&D) is likely to be a factor in determining the impact on competitiveness. Second, innovation offsets are more likely in industries or firms that have the ability to absorb environmental costs, which is most often determined by profit margins and firm size. Third, they are more likely to occur in firms that have the ability to pass increased costs on to consumers in the form of higher prices.

As a segue into the second series of chapters in this volume, Daniel Esty outlines how the different goals and subsequent methodologies of economists, trade policy-makers, environmental non-governmental organizations (NGOs), and advocates for sustainable development are key to the many tensions between trade and sustainable development policies in the political arena. Najam and Robins point out that many private firms are also setting their own internal policies for environmental compliance. The car manufacturer, DaimlerChrysler, has begun requiring all of its components' suppliers, many of them from the developing world, that they receive third-party environmental certifications. These authors point to such efforts, in addition to those of citizens and governments, to urge developing countries to make fair trade and sustainable development a 'rallying call'. However, like many of the other authors in this volume, they stress that 'fair trade and sustainable development' means incorporating 'sustainable livelihoods, poverty alleviation, social and environmental justice, and the expansion of ecological and human security'. The chapters that have been chosen for this part of the volume show how changes in trade policy affect sustainable development goals from an economic perspective. They show that trade rules affect trade and investment flows in addition to patterns of development. The norms and disciplines embodied in world trade rules, moreover, can ultimately have impacts that run deeper than economic effects. Such themes are taken up in the next part.

Part II Legal Perspectives

The second half of this volume provides legal and political perspectives on the relationship between the international legal agreements and institutions designed to promote economic liberalization, and the law and policy designed to protect the environment. The economic perspectives in Part I sought to assess the theoretical and empirical question of whether economic liberalization leads to an improvement or to an erosion of environmental quality, and to offer a basis for these two objectives to be reconciled through more rational policy-making.

Challenges for Global Governance

The chapters in Part II acknowledge more directly that governments and the international institutions they have designed have not yet achieved a reconciliation between trade and environmental policies. Instead, the interaction between economic and environmental law described in these chapters illustrates that one government's perception of trade measures taken for the purpose of legitimate environmental protection can be seen by another government as illegitimate economic protectionism. This disjunction of views has become a major challenge for both national and global governance.

As economies rapidly begin to integrate, while cultural and political priorities remain disjoined, where is the most legitimate and effective locus of decision-making? How much can be left to each government to decide and impose unilaterally, and how much must be decided cooperatively at the regional or international level? What decision-making tools, principles and procedures do we agree are adequate to this task? Must, or should, environmental regulators favour environmental objectives in accordance with the 'precautionary principle', or instead be required to demonstrate that they have chosen an environmental regulation that is the least economically restrictive alternative? To what extent should the arguably more 'objective' tests of scientific disciplines be relied on to ferret out protectionism? What role might there be for more 'subjective' disciplines such as ethics and human rights in legitimizing trade measures? How can both trade rules and environmental regulations best take into account the common but differentiated responsibilities and capabilities of developed and developing countries? And when two or more governments fail to resolve their differences, what kinds of procedures and institutions can we trust to provide fair and effective solutions? These and many other questions are addressed by the authors selected in this volume.

Over the past five years, the main locus of intergovernmental debate and rule-making on the trade and environment interface has been the WTO. Most of the contributions contained in this volume focus on the relationship between environmental law and policy and the WTO rules governing the trade in products. However, many economic liberalization agreements share the same basic approach. Whether bilateral, regional or multilateral, they aim to liberalize, promote, protect or regulate transboundary flows of products, services and capital through the international harmonization of economic law and policy. They typically seek to achieve this liberalization by removing barriers to trade and investment, and by prohibiting national measures that directly or indirectly discriminate against products, services, service providers and investors on the basis of country of origin. Therefore, while the detailed analysis contained in these essays focuses on the rules governing trade in products, it should hold lessons that can be generalized to other areas of international commerce.

As has been indicated, the contributions in this part of the volume do not attempt to resolve the debate of whether economic liberalization generally leads to the erosion or the improvement of the environment. Instead, they recognize that the rapid opening of markets can present new and significant challenges to the environmental regulator. Opening markets to a greater volume and variety of products challenges the environmental regulator to anticipate and avoid any additional risks to the environment that the trade in these products may carry. Environmental regulators typically respond to such risks by putting in place trade-related environmental measures (TREMs) which aim directly or indirectly to limit the flow of potentially hazardous products into the importing environment. TREMs that directly limit this flow may include total import bans or restrictions on the quantity of imports. They may include measures that slow down the flow of products by requiring the testing and assessment of risk associated with those products. Direct restrictions on trade may also include the imposition of minimum standards of environmental quality or performance which must be met before the product can enter the market.

Environmental regulators can also indirectly influence the volume of environmentally harmful products entering their domestic market. Environmental taxes on certain products can be used as a means of raising funds for preventing or responding to environmental harm, and, by raising the costs of these products to the consumer, can discourage their purchase. Similarly, government subsidies can lower the production costs of environmentally preferable products in a manner that can provide them with a competitive advantage against similar imported products that have not received a subsidy. Informing consumers of environmental risks associated with certain products through 'eco-labelling' schemes such as those discussed in the chapters by Najam and Robins in Part I, can also be an indirect means of reducing market demand for environmentally harmful products. Because these measures can affect the international trade in the targeted products, they are viewed as TREMs and fall within the scope of measures governed by international trade agreements.

At the same time that international trade agreements promote the volume and variety of imported goods, they can also constrain the environmental regulator's choice of TREM. In the trade context, principles of non-discrimination prohibit governments from applying trade measures that directly or indirectly discriminate between 'like products' on the basis of their country of origin. The WTO Agreements regulating the trade in products seek to liberalize trade through the removal of import bans or market regulations that are more trade restrictive than necessary to achieve an environmental objective. They seek to expose unintentional or 'disguised' protectionism by the application of objective tests and the application of scientific principles that can require the importing country to justify the basis for its environmental regulation.

The North–South Divide?

As Part I, on economic perspectives, closed with a contribution from a lawyer from the North, Part II, on legal perspectives, opens with the contribution of an economist from the South. Shahin's piece details the history, and maps the future, of the 'trade and environment debate' as it has evolved in the rules and institutions of the WTO, and in particular its Committee on Trade and Environment (CTE). Her analysis, from the perspective of both an academic and seasoned trade diplomat, draws out in political terms the tensions between industrialized and developing countries that have been set out in economic terms in Part I. Her discussion focuses on four specific issues that have occupied trade diplomats at the CTE for a number of years: the relationship between multilateral environmental agreements (MEAs) and the WTO; the interaction between the environment and WTO rules on the protection of intellectual property rights; the use of eco-labelling; and the impact of TREMs on the ability of developing countries to access markets. The picture that emerges portrays the WTO's rules and institutions providing a bulwark against green protectionism. While acknowledging the importance of environmental protection, she remains concerned that many TREMs are insensitive to differences in countries' environmental and development priorities, and use market access as an additional economic 'conditionality' for coercing change in developing countries. Raising environmental standards to levels acceptable to all countries must begin instead at the 'grassroots' and requires encouragement through financial and technical assistance, rather than the pressure of economic coercion.

TREMs and PPMs

As Shahin's analysis reveals, environmental regulators often justify their use of TREMs as a means of discouraging activities that threaten environmental resources that lie in the territories of other countries, or that are considered part of the 'global commons', such as the high seas. Sometimes these TREMs have the backing of regional or multilateral environmental agreements designed to protect shared resources (such as the ozone layer) or to promote global environmental objectives (such as the protection of endangered species). Where both the importing and the exporting countries are parties to these environmental agreements, the use of TREMs is relatively uncontroversial. However, in other circumstances TREMs have been imposed unilaterally, without the support of a mutually agreed set of principles or procedures. It is this category of TREMs that require the closest analysis.

Perhaps the simplest TREM with extraterritorial effect is a ban on the import of endangered species, which serves as a direct means of removing market incentives for the destruction of biological diversity in other countries. Importing countries have also sought, however, to discourage environmentally harmful activities abroad by putting in place TREMs linked to the process or production methods (PPMs) of goods that do not have an effect on the physical characteristics of the product itself. These so-called 'non product-related PPMs' have been criticized by free-traders for allowing importing countries to use trade leverage as a means of coercing exporting countries to adopt higher environmental production standards. Developing countries, in particular, have argued that non product-related PPMs are a form of disguised protectionism used by industrialized countries to shield their highly regulated and higher cost domestic industries from competition from abroad. Many have argued that WTO rules against 'indirect' discrimination prohibit distinctions from being drawn between products that are otherwise 'like' on the basis of the manner in which they are produced. They argue that if two products cannot be distinguished based on objective tests, such as their physical characteristics, measures that treat these products in a manner that undermines their competitive relationship are inherently discriminatory. Allowing such measures to stand would invite protectionism based on differences in national regulatory structures, and would undermine the world trading system.

Charnovitz tackles this contentious area of WTO law head-on. Relying on a close analysis of the text of the General Agreement on Tariffs and Trade (GATT) and, in particular, on recent decisions of the WTO Appellate Body, he concludes that the conventional view that trade law prohibits PPMs is 'a myth' in the process of being debunked. His aim is not to construct and defend the absolute right of importers to impose PPM-based TREMs but to show how a correct reading and careful application of trade rules 'may enable new integrative positions that can resolve trade and environment tensions and establish a better framework for preventing inappropriate PPMs'. To achieve this, he must demonstrate in what circumstances PPMs are justifiable as an effective means of achieving legitimate environmental objectives, and answer the real concerns of developing and other countries that unregulated PPMs will undermine their sovereignty and their interests. The approach that emerges suggests that while PPMs are not and should not be prohibited *per se*, it is appropriate that they be passed through the filter of the WTO's 'exceptions' which are designed to exclude trade measures that are arbitrary, unjustifiable or disguised means of protectionism. He offers a number of criteria for 'disciplining' PPMs in a manner that would encourage that PPMs be backed by efforts at multilateral cooperation and be narrowly tailored to achieve their environmental objective. Ultimately, Charnovitz concludes that interpreting WTO law to provide a blanket prohibition on PPMs, in circumstances in which they provide the only effective means for environmental protection, might pose a greater threat to the legitimacy of the trading system than allowing PPMs in limited circumstances. The principles outlined in this contribution may prove a useful guide to governments and activists following the Doha round of trade negotiations.

The contributions in this part then turn to the WTO's specialized rules, developed during the Uruguay Round of trade negotiations, to govern the manner in which countries regulate specific kinds of threats to the environment. The WTO Agreement on Sanitary and Phytosanitary Measures (the SPS Agreement) sets out the disciplines that governments must follow when employing TREMs to protect their domestic environments from risks to human, animal and plant life or health, particularly those risks associated with diseases, pests or toxins. As Charnovitz sets out in his description of the SPS Agreement's eight core disciplines and one exception, this new body of trade law seeks to expose unnecessary trade restrictions and disguised protectionism through the application of scientific principles. The analysis demonstrates the extent to which trade disciplines will require environmental regulators to justify their use of TREMs through a reliance upon scientific risk assessments to provide a rational basis for trade restrictions. Recent WTO Appellate Body jurisprudence allows for an exploration of the interaction between the SPS Agreement's reliance upon science, and the reliance of the environmental regulators on invoking the 'precautionary principle' to justify regulatory action in the face of scientific uncertainty. The adoption in 2000 of the Cartagena Protocol on Biosafety provides an opportunity for a brief, but intriguing discussion of the relationship between the WTO and MEAs that regulate the trade in products associated with certain environmental risks – in this case the potential risks to biological diversity posed by the international trade in living genetically modified organisms (GMOs). This chapter should be read in conjuction with Neumayer's contribution, which discusses the economic relationships between MEAs and the WTO.

Win–Win?

The long-running debates on the relationship between trade rules and environmental protection have spurred a search for opportunities for 'win–win' scenarios in which these often competing disciplines can be viewed as 'mutually supportive'. Stone's contribution and the piece by Ritchie and Dawkins that follows it demonstrate that free-traders and environmentalists may share a common objective in seeking to reduce and remove government subsidies that promote environmentally harmful activity.

The WTO Agreement on Subsidies and Countervailing Measures (SCM) prohibits or discourages the use of direct and specific government support to industry when it promotes exports or causes injury to the domestic industry of another country. Stone plots legal and economic arguments for turning these general rules into a strategy for challenging the widespread use of subsidies that promote the overconsumption of dwindling fisheries resources. The initial insight that trade and environment rules may be 'mutually supportive' is complicated by Stone's observation that while environmentalists and free-traders may join in deploring those subsidies that irresponsibly promote the exploitation of scarce resources, they might disagree on the use of government support for activities viewed as environmentally beneficial. Although the SCM Agreement provides a narrow exception for limited kinds of 'green' subsidies, the trade disciplines were not designed in a manner that was sophisticated enough to take into account and balance environmental concerns in the context of a more ambitious agenda.

Ritchie and Dawkins explore the environmental implications of the WTO Agreement on Agriculture (AoA), a set of rules designed to reduce and remove subsidies within a specific sector of economic activity. This piece was selected for its exploration of the impact that large private commercial interests can have on the shape of trade rules. Ritchie and Dawkins' analysis sets out to debunk the perception that the WTO, if sheltered from the special pleadings of environmental and labour groups, will develop rules that respect free market principles and level the playing-field of international trade. Like Stone, these authors express frustration at the missed opportunity, represented by the AoA, to channel the WTO's powerful rules and institutional influence to achieve win–win solutions that would have made sense from both an economic and an environmental perspective.

Downes' contribution takes the reader outside the WTO rules that directly regulate the trade in products. He sees the potential for a win–win relationship between the WTO Agreement on Trade Related Intellectual Property Rights (TRIPS), its ability to create incentives for the protection of biological resources, and to respect the contribution of traditional knowledge to the development of marketable products. The particular focus of his analysis is to explore ways in which mainstream conceptions of the protection of patent rights could be used to recognize and protect the commercial value of 'traditional knowledge' that informs the resource management techniques of indigenous peoples and farmers, particularly in developing countries. Traditional knowledge has long been recognized by environmentalists as a key component to the protection and sustainable use of biological resources, but has failed to meet standard benchmarks for the protection of intellectual property rights. He notes that the TRIPS disciplines hold the potential both to undermine and to provide new levels of protection for these rights, in a way that could provide economic incentive to prolong traditional approaches, and to ensure that this knowledge is not unjustly appropriated.

Beyond Trade and Environment

In Part I, a number of authors argue that the trade and environment debate should be broadened to include the fundamental development concerns of the South. The final contribution of Part I looks at the implications of the trade and environment debate as it may affect the expansion of liberalization disciplines in other areas of international economic governance.

Von Moltke traces efforts to expand international economic governance to the flow of private investment and questions whether the trade and environment critique holds in the context of international investment agreements. His analysis reveals that in these efforts to promote liberalization in the flow of services and capital, the North–South polarity is reversed. Most developing countries are capital importers rather than capital exporters. As such they are placed in the position of defending their domestic regulation against pressures to open up market access to foreign investment. Strong international investment liberalization regimes, such as that proposed in the negotiations for a multilateral agreement on investment (MAI) could be applied to limit a developing host country's ability to restrict access to its natural resources, or to restrict its discretion to use investment-related measures to channel foreign capital towards environmentally friendly activity. In particular, investor–state dispute settlement procedures can further empower multinational corporations (MNCs) to influence the environmental policies of their host countries by challenging such policies as discriminatory. Von Moltke's analysis, however, does not lead to suggestions against new international rules in this area. Instead he calls for the negotiation of a 'framework' agreement on international investment that protects foreign investors against discrimination, while at the same time rewarding those that channel their investments towards sustainable development objectives.

Toward a More Integrative Approach

Scholars and policy-makers have only been asking questions concerning the relationship between international trade, the environment and development for just over a decade. One thing is clear, it is completely legitimate for nations to pursue trade, environment and development goals in tandem. However, as the authors in this volume reveal, the devil is in the detail: the challenge ahead lies in our ability to design policies and regulations that allow each of these goals to be mutually reinforced. While there are opportunities for 'win–win' solutions, they will require the input and acceptance of a broad range of states and other actors.

We hope this volume can provide the reader with the building-blocks of an integrative approach to these issues. We have included a range of chapters that represent the key debates in law, economics and policy. Such a Reader just five years ago would have looked completely different. In comparing the two, one would notice that the disciplinary lines among the authors in this volume is beginning to blur. In order to make sense of these relationships, scholars and professionals are increasingly incorporating ideas from other disciplines.

The editors hope the readers will find themselves as grateful as we are to the contributors for their assistance in navigating the complex challenges raised by the interface between economic and environmental governance. As none of these contributions was specifically commissioned for this collection, it has been difficult to create a more precise dovetail. Where the pieces overlap, we trust the reader will appreciate the opportunity to revisit the issue from a fresh perspective. Where the views diverge, or even conflict, we hope the reader will be provided with a sufficient basis for reaching their own conclusions as the best way forward.

Note

1   Most economists familiar with this literature will be surprised to see that many of the most well-known articles on this subject are not included in this volume. This is a conscious decision, because many of the best articles are not written in a manner that is accessible to policy-makers and advocates who form the crux of the audience for Earthscan publications. Therefore the editors chose articles that were indeed accessible to a larger policy audience. In most cases then, the authors that were chosen often summarize the arguments most often heard in the more technical literature.

References

Ashford, N, C Ayres, and R Stone (1985) 'Using Regulation to Change the Market for Innovation' *Harvard Environmental Law Review*, Vol 9, No 2, pp419–466

Esty, D and B Gentry (1997) 'Foreign Investment, Globalisation and Environment', *Globalization and the Environment,* Tom Jones (ed) Paris, OECD, Cambridge, MA

Esty, D and R Mendelsohn (1995) *Powering China: The Environmental Consequences of China's Economic Growth*, New Haven, Yale

Fredriksson, P (1999) 'Trade, Global Policy, and the Environment: New Evidence and Issues', *Trade, Global Policy and the Environment,* Per Fredriksson (ed) Washington, World Bank

Goodstein, Eban (1998) *The Trade-off Myth: Facts and Fiction about Jobs and the Environment,* Washington, Island Press

Grossman, G and A Krueger (1993) 'Environmental Impacts of a North American Free Trade Agreement', *Mexico–US Free Trade Agreement,* Peter Garber (ed) Cambridge, MA, MIT Press

Harris, J, T Wise, K Gallagher and N Goodwin (1995) *A Survey of Ecological Economics,* Washington, Island Press

Jenkins, R (1998) 'Environmental Regulation and International Competitiveness: A Review of the Literature', INTECH Working Paper #9801, Maastricht, United Nations University

Nadal, A (2000) *The Environmental and Social Impacts of Economic Liberalization on Corn Production in Mexico,* London, World Wide Fund for Nature, Oxfam

Neumayer, E (2001) *Greening Trade and Investment,* London, Earthscan

North American Commission for Environmental Cooperation (2001a) www.cec.org

North American Commission for Environmental Cooperation (2001b) *North American Trade and Transportation Corridors: Environmental Impacts and Mitigation Strategies,* Montreal, NACEC (www.cec.org)

Palmer, K, W Oates and P Portney (1995) 'Tightening Environmental Standards: The Benefit Cost or the No Cost Paradigm?', *Journal of Economic Perspectives,* Vol 9, No 4, pp119–132

Rodrik, D (2001) 'Trading Illusions', *Foreign Policy,* May/June

Vogel, D (1997) *Trading Up: Consumer and Environmental Regulation in a Global Economy,* Cambridge, Harvard University Press

United Nations Conference on Trade and Development (UNCTAD) (2000) *World Investment Report 2000: Foreign Direct Investment and the Challenge of Development,* Geneva

Part II

Economic Perspectives

2

Stuck in the Mud? Nation States, Globalization and the Environment[1]

Lyuba Zarsky

Introduction

Environmental and resource management is largely the preserve of nation states. Economic globalization, however, constrains the unilateral management capacities of nation states and creates new imperatives on states to cooperate internationally – not only to manage global resources but also to coordinate domestic environmental policies.

This chapter presents the hypothesis that, in the absence of effective multilateralism, economic globalization inhibits innovation in national environmental policy, and thus the rate of improvement in environmental performance. Rather than a 'race to the bottom', heightened competition for global markets causes environmental policy to be 'stuck in the mud'. Nation states are pulled towards environmental policy convergence by market-driven and political pressures, primarily to maintain or gain competitiveness. In the balance and over time, the effect of convergence pressures on the average level of national environmental performance may be positive. Without effective international policy cooperation, however, the terms of convergence will be too low and too slow to point development towards sustainability.

The central challenge of globalization is to raise the terms of policy convergence through effective supranational governance, both global and regional, by states and within the private sector. Good environmental management in the age of globalization also requires new approaches to national policy, approaches in tune with a highly open economy. Far from making nation states irrelevant, globalization makes new and difficult demands on them.

The chapter is organized in four sections. The first develops an analytical framework to show why globalization causes national environmental policy initiatives to be 'stuck in the mud'. The second section examines two illustrative case studies: energy pricing and resource subsidies. The third section explores creative institutional responses to raise the terms of convergence at both supranational and national levels. The final section concludes with some reflections on broader problems of environmental leadership and economic management in a global economy, and makes suggestions towards a further research agenda, including the informational requirements of global environmental policy coordination.

Environmental Management
in the Age of Globalization

Economic globalization is fundamentally changing the nature of environmental management. On one hand, globalization heightens the influence of market forces – most importantly, competition – on the making and enforcement of environmental policy. On the other hand, it subjects national environment policy to the discipline (or chaos) of international economic institutions.

On both counts, the most significant impact of globalization is that it limits the unilateral policy-making capability of nation states. Overcoming these constraints will require strengthening subnational capacities for environmental management on one hand, and, on the other hand, international collective action to build supranational governance capacities. In the age of globalization, nation states face new imperatives to coordinate domestic environmental and resource management policy, as well as to develop new unilateral approaches to the government–market interface. The existing institutional framework for environmental multilateralism, however, is rudimentary at best and its integration with international economic governance nearly non-existent.

The case for international environmental cooperation is usually made in terms of the need to manage global or regional commons and transboundary resources (Young, 1994; Haas et al, 1993).[2] These types of collective-action problems stem from ecological rather than economic interdependence: autarkic as well as open economies would still have to cooperate to establish sustainable utilization regimes for global commons. However, globalization constrains and conditions cooperation by changing the matrix of incentives within and among nations.

The central and specific effects of globalization on environmental management are the new limits on unilateral policy-making in the areas of ecosystem and natural resource management. With increasing global economic integration, domestic economic and social policies affect global prices, market shares and investor expectations – and vice versa. For the large and rich countries of the Organisation for Economic Co-operation and Development (OECD), the reverberations from domestic policy to global markets are greater than for small or poor countries. Even the largest market economies, however, are subject to cost, price and exchange rate pressures imposed by global markets. OECD countries are particularly sensitive to the impact on the market from policies adopted in other OECD countries.

The impact of globalization on environmental management capacities cuts two ways: it constrains governments and it enhances the influence of markets on social and economic outcomes. Markets, in turn, influence environmental performance through technology transfer, changes in the level of demand for environment-intensive goods, substitution effects, 'green' consumerism and other channels. Indeed, in the context of globalization, markets become important vehicles and arenas for the generation and transmission of social norms and behaviours. The nub of the relationship between globalization and environmental management is that globalization changes the character of the government–market interface.

Given this change, the two key questions are: (1) what, in the aggregate, is the likely impact of global market integration on environmental performance, in the current global institutional regime? and (2) what institutional innovations, supranational or national, could significantly raise the level of environmental performance in the context of globalization? The first question is taken up here, the second in the following section.

Convergence in a Global Economy

Market-driven economic globalization creates pressures for countries to become more alike. Convergence trends encompass economic performance, economic policy and social – including environmental – policy.[3]

Convergence trends in economic performance have been studied extensively from both a theoretical and an empirical perspective. With increasing integration of markets, capital will flow towards the economic activities with the highest return. In theory, if all markets – capital, labour, ideas and goods and services – were fully integrated, there would be absolute convergence over time in the performance of key economic indicators such as productivity (output per worker), real wages, rates of return on capital and living standards (Obstfeld and Rogoff, 1996).

In practice, markets are not perfect nor perfectly open. Market imperfections and obstacles generate economic gaps even among fairly homogenous countries such as members of the OECD. Moreover, large and seemingly entrenched gaps between rich/developed and poor/developing countries continue to plague the world economy. Nonetheless, empirical studies suggest that globalization drives a discernible, if less-than-absolute, process of economic convergence both within and between broad categories of 'rich' and 'poor' countries (Williamson, 1996; O'Rourke and Williamson, 1995). These studies are based largely on the 'prior wave' of globalization which took place in the late 19th century.

The hypothesis of this chapter is that market integration also drives policy convergence. The deeper and broader the level of market integration among countries, the greater the tendency towards (economic and social policy) convergence. Moreover, the larger the national market share in global trade and capital, the greater the forces of convergence towards that nation. At a global level, the rich countries of the OECD are the 'large-market' countries as well as the most highly integrated countries. Policy convergence is likely both within the OECD group, as well as, over time, from developing countries towards the OECD.

Market integration impels governments to undertake similar economic policies, especially macroeconomic policies. Obviously, broad international agreement on open market policies is the sine qua non of globalization. Moreover, given technological and communication capabilities, governments would not be able to restrict capital outflows even if they so desired.

But governments also have to keep key aspects of their domestic macroeconomic policies, including interest rates, within bands similar to each other. An interest rate too far below average international rates would spark capital outflows and exchange rate depreciation, triggering or exacerbating domestic inflation. The highly speculative character of unregulated international financial markets aggravates the problem enormously: small changes, or expectations thereof, in interest or exchange rates can ignite huge waves of capital movement.

The market forces of convergence also affect social policy. While theoretical and empirical studies are scarce, historical accounts suggest that the broadest parameter of social policy – the social contract among government, capital, labour and communities – is pulled by global market forces towards sameness. In the period after World War II, the social contract within Western nations was based on full employment and the welfare state. The unravelling of this social contract in the UK and the US generated market pressures on other OECD countries to follow suit (Eichengreen and Kenen, 1994; Boyer and Drache, 1996). It is unlikely that radically different social contract terms among countries, especially OECD countries, would be sustainable in the global economy.

Environmental Policy Convergence

Environmental policy can be seen as part of the social contract. Like other aspects of social governance, environmental policy is subject to international market forces, primarily the forces of competition. Indeed, environmental and resource management policies are especially sensitive to international market forces because such policies are so deeply bound up with the costs of production. The deeper the exposure to international competition, the more the particular resource or environmental management policy is subject to convergence pressures.

There are few empirical studies on how globalization affects national environmental policy formation. An analytical framework suggests that environmental degradation and good environmental management both impose costs. Unless specific policy measures are taken, these costs are not reflected in market prices but are borne socially, either today or in the future. An individual country or company that takes measures to internalize its own local or global environmental costs could be priced out of export markets or lose attractiveness as a production site for domestic or foreign investors.

Even if the change in relative costs is negligible, the fear or threat of such an effect can create policy paralysis. Policy-makers are subject to a wide variety of domestic political economy pressures, in the form of advocacy, lobbying and campaign contributions by international business, as well as by labour and community groups. Political pressures to promote competitiveness intensify as the share of income, both wages and profits, derived from international trade and investment increases.

There are thus strong incentives for the costs to producers imposed by environmental management standards to converge towards those of primary competitors. More subtly, global markets provide incentives for the total costs to business of meeting environmental requirements to converge. Total costs include compliance costs, as well as information, regulatory and other transaction costs. More efficient regulatory regimes may generate a higher level of environmental performance for the same cost.

Among the possible competitors subject to convergence pressures are nations competing for export markets and for overseas investment projects, and to become 'production platforms'; and multinational corporations (MNCs) competing for export markets, government procurement or investment projects. Even wholly domestic firms are subject to convergence pressures if their product markets or inputs are sourced internationally. Moreover, to facilitate trade and investment, policy-makers have a further incentive to harmonize environmental policy in order to reduce transaction costs, ie the costs to business of getting information about environmental requirements and of meeting them. Transnational firms can also reduce learning and management costs by maintaining global standards.

In addition to competitiveness, convergence in environmental product standards is driven by state regulation, especially import requirements by large-market countries. Product standards in OECD and other countries require importers to meet a host of requirements promoting consumer safety and health. The larger the import market, the greater the impact of domestic product standards on international standards. Moreover, OECD policy-makers expressly work to facilitate trade by seeking convergence. Cases where US and European Union (EU) product standards or procedures differ radically, such as eco-labelling, capture a large amount of policy-makers' efforts to find commonality.

Environmental standards for production and resource management are less subject than product standards to policy transmission effects. The World Trade Organization (WTO) prohibits states from unilaterally imposing process and production method (PPM) standards on imports. Eco-labelling standards are controversial in part because they introduce the possibility of discrimination between products on the basis of production processes. Within some regional groupings, such as the EU, policy convergence for both products and PPMs is driven by regional intergovernmental cooperation, as well as by market forces.

Like economic performance, the process of environmental policy convergence is not likely to be absolute or uniform on a global scale. The process called 'globalization' is far from truly global: the overwhelming portion of goods and services are still produced by local producers within countries for domestic markets (Lipsey et al, 1995). Moreover, processes of economic integration are largely regional. And while the North–South divide has been blurred by the emergence of the Newly Industrializing Economies (NIEs), the gap between the OECD countries and all the rest is still glaring (as is the gap between the very poorest and all the others).

Policy convergence is likely to be most pronounced among countries whose markets are the most highly integrated, as well as among those that are the most homogeneous in economic capacity. Among rich countries, environmental product and production standards are therefore likely to converge around an 'OECD average' as well as industry-wide averages for internationally exposed industries.

For developing countries, the primary export markets are OECD countries. Product standards, therefore, are pulled towards the OECD average as export markets become more deeply and broadly integrated with the OECD. The primary competition to act as production platforms, on the other hand, comes from other developing countries. Without regulation, environmental production standards are likely to converge not towards the OECD but towards some kind of NIE or developing country benchmark, at least in the short term. Over time, as the sectoral composition of production becomes more like that in OECD countries, as the environmental management capacities of developing countries improve, or as market forces themselves bring new norms, developing country environmental production standards may be pulled towards the OECD average.

'Stuck in the Mud'? The Constraints of Competitiveness

What will market-driven trends towards environmental policy convergence mean for environmental performance? Some analysts have argued that globalization will generate a 'race to the bottom' in terms of environmental performance standards (Revesz, 1992). The operational dynamic in this framework is competition, especially between high and low standard countries, to act as production platforms. The idea is that the search for higher returns and lower costs will drive international investment towards the low standard countries, while capital outflow and/or the threat of relocation will create pressures to lower standards in high standard countries.

Empirical studies, however, have generally failed to detect any effects of differential environmental management costs on investment–location-of-investment decisions. One exception is a study in progress suggesting that US mining capital relocated investment to Europe during the 1980s to escape the high transaction costs of the US style of 'adversarial legalism' in environmental regulation (Anderson and Kagan, 1996). The study presumes, however, that European standards are no lower than US standards and that investors were attracted by a more efficient, rather than a more lax, regulatory regime. Since the study provides no environmental performance indicators, it is inconclusive as to whether the cheaper regulatory regime in Europe generated the same, better, or worse environmental performance as that in the US.

One reason often cited for the failure to detect 'race to the bottom' effects is that environmental compliance costs in most industries are low and form a small fraction of either investment or operating costs. Given environmental performance indicators (eg greenhouse gas emissions, generation of toxic waste, loss of biodiversity), low environmental compliance costs suggest that industry production costs and hence market prices do not incorporate environmental costs and commitments. In other words, the fact that environmental regulations seem to matter little in investment decisions may be that they are universally low.

The central argument of this chapter is that, rather than triggering a downward spiral, the primary impact of globalization is to keep environmental policy initiatives 'stuck in the mud'. On one hand, the constraints of competitiveness induced by globalization retard the capacity and willingness of *all* nation states to take *any* unilateral measures that impose costs of good environmental management on domestic producers. On the other hand, the pressures of policy convergence mean that measures that *are* taken will only be those in step with primary competitors. The net results are first, that markets become the primary drivers of changes in environmental performance, and second, that environmental managers are pressured to maintain the status quo or to change it only incrementally.

Current relative market prices and patterns of competitive advantage, however, grow out of an institutional context in which environment is mostly out of the equation. The presssures of globalization to maintain the status quo mean that improvements towards environmental performance will be slow. Given the large new demands on global ecosystems posed by rapid economic growth in developing countries, slow progress – even if steady – points towards a pessimistic assessment of the prospects of global sustainability.

Environmental performance, in both OECD and developing countries, in the context of globalization is propelled upward nonetheless by other forces, including consumer trends, industry self-regulation, and advocacy efforts by citizen groups, both internal and external. Moreover, the drive for international competitiveness is itself a two-edged sword: the push to compete in markets can act to undermine inefficient, ecologically damaging national policies such as resource subsidies. For businesses, it can also promote innovation in waste-saving and input-efficient production processes.

Market-driven pressures to be competitive, in short, can enhance as well as retard improvements in environmental performance. In a global economy, crossborder flows of capital, commodities and people promote technological and managerial change. Indeed, over the long run, globalization may be positively correlated with improvements in environmental performance – even taking scale effects into account – as resources are better allocated, environmentally cleaner technologies are disseminated and the environmental standards of the worst performers are pulled gradually upward.

The problem is that, since each nation or firm will be reluctant to take unilateral action that could undermine competitiveness, the average level of environmental performance in the OECD is likely to be low, and, most important, the rate of innovation in improving environmental performance will be slow in all countries. Nation states and businesses are willing to innovate only in incremental ways that increase costs slightly or generate 'win–win' outcomes, improving both competitiveness and environmental performance.

The pressures of competitiveness affect not only the management of domestic resources but also unilateral and collective policy responses to international environmental problems, such as climate change. The greater the potential impact on domestic producers and export markets, the more difficult it is to build political support for policy change – even when the change is fully justified *at a domestic level* economically and/or environmentally.

A market-driven process of convergence is not just low and slow, it is bound to be too blunt as well. Good ecosystem and resource management requires sensitivity to local ecological and social conditions. Diversity of goals and approaches across and within nations will yield better environmental results than uniformity.

Overcoming the problems of uniformity and inertia requires collective action by governments and/or by firms to set broad, common environmental and resource management frameworks that promote continuous improvement in environmental performance. In Europe, the 'common standards' problem was tackled primarily by side payments from more to less powerful nations to bring up their standards (Steinberg, 1996). In the global context, however, gaps between low and high standard countries are much greater, making the potential costs of a 'side-payment' strategy politically problematic. Indeed, most OECD countries have either cut or not increased foreign aid flows in the past decade.

Economic Multilateralism – and Anarchy

Pressures to compete for markets and investment in a global economy constrain nation states from environmental management strategies that impose costs on domestic producers greater than those of primary competitors. The constraints of competition in effect create a 'prisoner's dilemma': if governments were willing to coordinate policy, they could attain greater welfare for all (the same goes for the private sector). Without enforceable coordination, market forces inhibit major initiatives by both governments and businesses to internalize environmental costs.

The 'stuck-in-the-mud' problem is exacerbated by the lack of effective economic multilateralism, especially international monetary management. International financial markets and exchange rates are largely unregulated. The international capital markets are highly developed and offer a long menu of instruments for offshore investment. Large volumes of money can move virtually instantaneously across borders, thanks primarily to electronic transfer and communication capacities. There is little international regulation of global financial markets or coordination of monetary policy. Except for periodic attempts at market intervention by G-7 countries, the global determination of exchange rates is left to international financial markets.[4]

A floating exchange rate regime, combined with increasingly deep and broad international capital markets, creates highly volatile and speculative market behaviour. Expectations of even small changes in domestic interest rates and/or exchange rates can trigger crossborder capital movement. The result is exchange rate volatility and limits on domestic monetary (and thus growth) policies.

Floating exchange rates affect national environmental policy initiatives by heightening domestic sensitivity to competitiveness in two ways. First, they exacerbate the sensitivity of policy-makers and business managers to small differentials in the costs of production – actual or prospective. 'What can comparative advantage mean among developed economies broadly competitive over a wide range of goods when exchange rates can shift by 10 or 20 per cent over a few months?' laments Paul Volcker, who, as head of the Federal Reserve under President Reagan, maintained high US interest rates to keep the dollar strong (Volcker, 1996). Not only does volatility in exchange rates create an unstable climate for both public and private sector decision-making, but any additional volatility (or even predictable change) in business cost structures stemming from environmental management commitments is unwelcome.

Second, floating exchange rates discourage domestic policy-makers from undertaking macroeconomic, especially monetary, policies to promote growth in developed countries. Low-interest rates are the cornerstone of a high-investment, high-growth development path (Keynes, 1964). Unilateral low-interest rate policies, however, spark capital outflow and exchange rate depreciation, thus increasing the value of foreign debt and raising the cost of imports. High interest rates, on the other hand, increase the cost of domestic deficit spending, thus impeding growth-oriented fiscal policies. Low economic growth, in turn, generates high unemployment.

Constraints on growth-oriented domestic macroeconomic policies render domestic policy-makers highly sensitive to social policies – including environmental policies – that could impair competitiveness. In the US, political debates have often centred on what is perceived as a 'jobs versus environment' trade-off. Some studies have demonstrated, persuasively, that 'win–win' strategies are possible, at least for particular sectors like forest products (Repetto, 1995). Nonetheless, in the larger picture, high-employment policies in developed countries are not financially sustainable without moderating the tumultuous and inhibiting effects of volatile and speculative international financial markets. Sustainable, high-employment growth requires policy coordination through a managed international monetary regime (Williamson and Henning, 1994). Without it, political concern over competitiveness and jobs – whether justified or not – will overshadow and stifle unilateral environmental management initiatives.

Energy Prices, Resource Subsidies and Collective Action

The 'stuck-in-the-mud' hypothesis suggests that the pressures of competitiveness keep nation states from taking major unilateral initiatives to improve environmental management if these would entail significant costs for domestic producers. It also predicts that environmental and resource standards will converge around benchmarks set by large-market (primarily OECD) countries for product standards and by primary production-platform competitors for PPMs. The result is that developing country standards are pulled towards OECD standards only gradually and unevenly, and OECD standards improve only gradually. With so much inertia in the system, major innovations to improve domestic environmental management require collective action.

What empirical, historical or even anecdotal evidence might generally support the 'stuck-in-the-mud' hypothesis? While specific studies are lacking, two broad sectors of environmental management policy – energy pricing and resource subsidies – may help to illustrate and generally support the argument.

Energy Prices

In many OECD and developing countries, energy prices incorporate large financial and environmental subsidies. Financial subsidies can be defined as 'economic and fiscal measures with clear budget impacts' which keep prices below market levels or otherwise influence a particular commodity's production or consumption (Runge and Jones, 1996). An environmental subsidy can be defined as any damage to the environment which is external to market prices. The elimination of environmental subsidies through full-cost pricing is a central task of environmental policy.

In the case of prices for fossil fuel-based energy, environmental externalities that constitute subsidies include local air pollution, the effects of climate change due to greenhouse gas emissions, health and environmental damage caused by sulphur emissions in the form of acid precipitation, and marine degradation caused by oil-tanker pollution and accidents. Because environmental subsidies are difficult to quantify, most definitions and estimates of energy subsidies incorporate only direct and indirect financial subsidies. Nonetheless, even with this narrower definition, there is still considerable debate about how precisely to define and quantify subsidies.

Even excluding environmental externalities, energy production and use in many countries are highly subsidized financially, skewing energy prices further away from 'true' costs. In the past few years, especially following the Rio Earth Summit in 1992 and the resulting Framework Convention on Climate Change, many countries have taken or tried to take measures to improve energy pricing. Competitiveness concerns, however, especially within OECD countries, have stymied even modest proposals. In developing countries, heavily subsidized energy prices bolster rapid industrialization strategies and help keep the social peace by assisting workers and the poor.

Within the OECD, the US probably has the highest level of energy subsidies: estimates range from US$5 billion to US$36 billion, depending on how subsidies are defined (Michaelis, 1996). By keeping prices below market levels, subsidies increase demand. The US has the lowest energy prices in the OECD. In 1993, US prices of unleaded gasoline came to 43 per cent of the OECD Europe average; electricity prices in industry were 58 per cent of the OECD Europe average. The US also has the highest emissions of carbon dioxide per dollar of GDP and the second lowest (after Canada) level of energy efficiency, ie input of energy per unit of GDP (OECD, 1996, Figures 5.1 and 5.3; World Bank, 1995, Figure 5.1).

In February 1993, President Clinton proposed a broad-based US energy tax, primarily as an environmental policy initiative to improve energy pricing. The tax was to be levied on the energy content of fuels, with a higher rate for petroleum than for coal or natural gas, or for nuclear energy and hydropower. Non-conventional renewable energy sources were exempted. Because the tax would have applied to energy input rather than electricity output, efficient natural gas technologies would have been favoured over coal for electricity production. The rationale for the Btu (British thermal unit) tax when first proposed was that it would contribute to deficit reduction, decrease environmental degradation, increase energy conservation and efficiency and reduce dependence on foreign oil (Muller, 1995).

Immediately after the proposal was announced, various US companies and industry associations demanded and received special exemptions in the drafting of the tax legislation. The exemptions, however, did not diffuse strong business opposition, especially by the oil industry and the National Association of Manufacturers. The business campaign to defeat the tax proposal was based primarily on the claim – which came to be widely accepted – that the tax would undermine the international competitiveness of US industry, cause widespread job loss and harm fuel-producing regions disproportionately (Hoerner and Muller, 1996).

Estimates of how the proposed tax would actually have affected competitiveness suggest a small or negligible impact on even the most energy-intensive industries. For primary aluminium the tax was estimated to be 2.14 per cent of the value of shipments; for nitrogenous fertilizer, 1.55 per cent; and for industrial inorganic chemicals, 0.94 per cent (Muller, 1995, Table 2). Indeed, Congress subsequently enacted legislation to raise corporate income tax, apparently imposing a greater burden on most businesses than the energy tax would have done. Nevertheless, the business-driven argument about competitiveness won the day: the energy tax legislation was defeated in Congress.[5]

In Australia, the Minister for the Environment proposed a small carbon tax in December 1994. The tax, which came to be known as the 'greenhouse levy', aimed to reduce domestic consumption of fossil fuels, excluding transport fuels. Four-fifths of Australia's electricity is generated with coal, much of it dirty 'brown coal'. Low-sulphur black coal is Australia's most valuable export. The proposed tax rate amounted to US$3 per tonne of carbon, with the revenue targeted for the establishment of an Australian Sustainable Energy Authority to promote energy efficiency and renewable energy.

The greenhouse levy would not have applied to exports of fossil fuels, including coal. Nonetheless, concerns about competitiveness became the central focus of political debate, especially the effects on energy-intensive industries like aluminium. One argument was that the levy would favour the export of raw materials over more labour-intensive value-added industries. However, the levy was so small that its effect on relative electricity prices would have been very slight. A proposal to rebate the levy to energy-intensive industries was strongly – and understandably – opposed by trade advisers (Muller, 1995).

One of the central arguments of the aluminium industry was that, even if the *actual* effect on costs was negligible, the *perceived* effects could skew investment away from Australia and towards low-energy cost countries. The greenhouse levy was described as the 'thin edge of the wedge' which would send a signal about the future direction of Australian energy and environmental policy. If the levy put Australia out of line with competitors, the signal would suggest higher relative costs of production in the long run, if not in response to the particular tax proposal.

Not all proposals for national carbon or energy taxes have failed. Denmark, Finland, the Netherlands, Norway, Sweden and Poland have all adopted carbon/energy taxes. But these exceptions essentially prove the rule. None of the five EU countries has significant domestic coal production and only Denmark uses (imported) coal for electricity production. Finland, Norway and Sweden barely use fossil fuels at all for electricity production. Denmark and Sweden provide substantial tax relief for industry, making competitiveness concerns about domestic costs of production less salient.

On the other hand, the implementation of an EU-wide carbon/energy tax has been postponed, on the grounds that the US, Japan and other trading partners have not adopted similar measures. Instead, the EU will impose a more general energy tax on electricity consumption. To win the support of Europe's powerful, competition-conscious trade unions, the EU has agreed to put the proceeds into an 'employment fund' (Scherp, 1997). In the US, some of the debate over the energy tax focused on the potential benefits to European and other OECD (as well as developing country) competitors of even a small change in US energy costs. In early 1997, the executive council of the AFL-CIO, the largest US trade union group, passed a resolution opposing a pending agreement on climate change because China, Brazil and other rapidly growing developing countries would be exempt from pollution restrictions. The resolution said that such exemptions create an 'uneven playing field' and would 'cause the loss of high-paying US jobs in the mining, manufacturing, transport and other sectors' (Reuters, 1997).

Among developing countries, China, India and the transition economies have the highest rates of direct financial subsidies for energy use. In 1991, China and India subsidized fossil fuels at 26–28 per cent of the world price, transition economies at

40 per cent. Electricity subsidies in 1991 totalled over 40 per cent in China and India and over 50 per cent for the transition economies (World Bank, 1995, Figures 5.1 and 5.2).

These subsidies were designed not to improve export competitiveness but to promote internally oriented, state-directed growth. The result, however, was to promote inefficient power sector technologies. As these economies have opened to the growth opportunities and competitiveness pressures of global markets, energy subsidies have become very expensive. Domestic energy demand has increased greatly, especially in China, helping to promote domestic financial reforms which will generate more private capital internally for energy projects (Razawi, 1997). Development strategies based on linkage with global markets have also increased the availability of external private finance, the transfer of more efficient energy technologies, political pressure from developed countries to reduce subsidies and opportunities to learn about better energy management.

On the other hand, developing countries – especially the 'major developing economies' – are committed to rapid industrialization and compete strongly with each other to serve as production platforms, slowing the subsidy-reform agenda. Moreover, development assistance from the rich countries to improve energy performance has been meagre. Finally, while aimed primarily at industry, energy subsidies are also provided to workers and the poor. While the greatest portion of the benefit from subsidies is captured by the wealthy – who use more energy – the poor still suffer when subsidies are cut. Attempts in the Philippines and elsewhere to cut subsidies have sparked popular uprisings.

Overall, linkage-led growth strategies are likely to move gradually energy prices in developing countries towards a world price. While the environment would benefit, the world price excludes environmental externalities. Better pricing at the global level requires supranational coordination.

Resource Subsidies

The commercial use of resources for export is highly subsidized, both financially and environmentally, in many countries. Resource-intensive sectors involved in international trade which receive high levels of direct and indirect financial subsidies include agriculture, forestry (primarily timber and timber products) and fishing. Direct subsidies embrace a wide range of policy measures: direct payments to producers and input support, especially in agriculture; tax breaks and/or concessional terms for credit or grants, including those for the expansion and modernization of fishing fleets; and trade protectionism, including import constraints and export promotion supports, which are widespread in agriculture and forestry.

Resource-intensive exports are supported by indirect financial subsidies. In forestry, for example, the failure to capture full economic rents on logging concessions is a major source of subsidy for the timber industry and, potentially, for the timber products sector. Quantitative assessment is problematic, since definitions vary and information is scarce. Nonetheless, estimates suggest that low stumpage fees permeate forest policy in both developed and developing countries. Indonesia captured some 20–33 per cent of economic rents from timber concessions in 1993;

Malaysia 35–53 per cent in 1991; and Canada 33–67 per cent in 1979 (Porter, 1996, Figure 1). Low stumpage fees lead to undervaluation and overuse of timber resources.

Indirect financial subsidies are also provided by incomplete property rights, which allow the appropriation of resources without compensation. Coastal shrimp aquaculture, for example, is characterized in most developing countries by a 'slash and burn' style of mangrove swamp exploitation. Shrimp companies, often with ties to local elites, appropriate the mangrove swamps from traditional users for intensive shrimp aquaculture, primarily for export, using a high level of chemical inputs. Once the waters are too polluted to support further harvesting, they are abandoned, leaving local communities deprived of a key resource (Primavera, 1994).

Direct financial subsidies have strongly shaped the marine fisheries sector, leading to overcapitalization of fishing fleets and overfishing. Subsidies are targeted primarily towards fleet modernization, as well as keeping fuel costs below market prices (Porter, 1996).

The largest direct financial subsidies to resource-intensive sectors globally probably accrue to agriculture in OECD countries. The value of direct monetary transfers from governments and consumers to the agricultural sector is measured by producer subsidy equivalents (PSE). In OECD countries, these transfers include market price supports, primarily via border measures to control inputs and outputs; direct payments to farmers; input support, including through capital grants and low interest rates; and agriculture infrastructure projects, including irrigation–water delivery projects. In 1994, the total PSE for the OECD as a whole was US$175 billion (Legg, 1996).

In developing countries, the net financial subsidy to agriculture is generally negative. While most developing countries protect certain 'key' agricultural commodities such as rice, agriculture as a whole subsidizes industrial sectors. At the global level, the rich countries subsidize agriculture and food exports, while the developing industries drain the agricultural sector and subsidize food imports (Lutz, 1992). Agricultural subsidies, in short, distort international trading patterns.

The environmental impacts of financial subsidies in developed countries are well-documented and include water and land pollution from excessive chemical input use, loss of soil productivity through monocultural cropping patterns and non-biological management, and loss of habitat (Faeth, 1991; OECD, 1989). How the skewed trading pattern created by subsidies affects the environment, however, still needs to be studied, especially as developing countries move to liberalize agriculture further. If liberalization means importing heavily subsidized OECD agricultural commodities, then 'free trade' may become a vehicle to disseminate ecologically unsustainable agricultural management practices.

In California, for instance, the production of water-intensive crops like rice is internationally competitive only because of large water subsidies to farmers. The production of rice and other water-intensive crops generates environmental degradation in California and skews crop choices by farmers elsewhere. One study found that the environmental effects of freer agricultural trade with Mexico due to North American Free Trade Agreement (NAFTA) depended crucially on water pricing in California. As long as agricultural water use is subsidized, both Mexico and

California suffer the environmental and financial costs of misallocated production decisions (Feenstra and Rose, 1993).

The unilateral removal of direct financial subsidies would yield net economic and environmental benefits. Why, then, do they persist? In the deep-sea marine fisheries sector, the problem is one of open access and free-riding: the benefits of unilateral action cannot be captured unilaterally and an international management regime is needed.

For resources within domestic boundaries like agricultural lands and fisheries within countries' exclusive economic zones, however, the net benefits can be captured domestically. Nevertheless, there are costs of adjustment due to the loss of competitiveness of existing industries. The costs to particular (typically powerful) domestic interests inhibit domestic policy-makers from undertaking subsidy reform. Moreover, lobbying by special interests finds broad public resonance, given the broader concerns about jobs and competitiveness. And global market integration presents a free-rider problem, with producers in one country unwilling to pay the costs of adjustment that producers in other countries benefit from.

Globalization and the heightened concern about competitiveness which it spawns do not *create* domestic opposition to subsidy reform but give it greater political weight and inhibit unilateral reform efforts. On the other hand, subsidies are expensive in macroeconomic terms, both domestically and externally. The need to be more competitive at an economy-wide level provides incentives to governments for subsidy reform. Collective action would help to overcome the inertia by setting broad policy parameters limiting and eventually eliminating subsidies as legitimate policy instruments within a global trading framework. As a recent OECD workshop on subsidies and the environment concluded: 'Overcoming opposition to subsidy reform will be substantially easier if countries can be convinced to react *together*, rather than *separately*, in reducing subsidies/tax concessions to particular industries or sectors' (Runge and Jones, 1996, p12).

Creative Institutional Responses

Imagine a wondrous new machine, strong and supple, a machine that reaps as it destroys. It is huge and mobile... running over open terrain and ignoring familiar boundaries... [throwing] ... off enormous mows of wealth and bounty while it leaves behind great furrows of wreckage.

Now imagine that there are skilful hands on board, but *no one is at the wheel.* In fact, this machine has no wheel nor any internal governor to control the speed and direction. It is sustained by its own forward motion, guided mainly by its own appetites. And it is accelerating. (Greider, 1997; emphasis added)

Market forces, especially at the global level, are wondrous things. Markets coordinate millions of consumption and production decisions every second. Market-based competition spurs innovation and learning, including rapid changes in technology, and promotes social transformation. Economic interdependence brings people from many cultures and nations into contact, often to undertake common projects. But global markets can also promote undesirable and even dangerous outcomes: social upheaval and inequality within and between countries, which sows seeds of civil and international conflict;[6] cultural homogenization; and degradation of the Earth's life-support systems.

The key to the social impacts of market forces is the institutional structure in which they are embedded. If market forces are like great torrential rains, institutions – with both big and small 'I's' – are the channels and aqueducts that guide them over the land. Or, to use Greider's metaphor of global markets as Terminator-like machines, institutions are the software programs that put someone 'at the wheel'.

Institutional dynamism is the key to overcoming the inertia of global market competition which keeps rapid improvements in environmental and resource management 'stuck in the mud'. Institutional innovation is needed at two levels, supranational and national, to change the ways that states and markets interact in a global economy. At the supranational level, the primary goals of institutional innovation are to increase the average level of environmental performance within OECD countries by enhancing policy coordination, especially for PPMs; and to close the gaps between the OECD and developing countries in both product and production standards by promoting development and capacity-building. At the national level, the primary goal is to enhance the efficiency and reduce the cost of strategies to greatly enhance environmental performance. One of the key ways to do this is to strengthen sub-national capacities for environmental management, at both municipal and provincial levels.

Supranational Governance

The foremost institution governing world trade is the WTO. Since 1991, the WTO or its predecessor, the General Agreement on Tariffs and Trade (GATT), has included environmental issues within its purview, first through a Working Group and, since 1994, through the standing Committee on Trade and Environment (CTE). The hope was that the CTE could build a bridge between rule-making for transparent, non-discriminatory, open – and environmentally sound – trade policies. At the broadest level, the vision was that the CTE would nudge everyone towards a paradigm shift from a negative to a positive understanding of the trade–environment link – that is, away from an emphasis on limiting unilateral state action to protect the trading system, and towards a focus on collective responsibility to promote sustainable trade, investment and economic growth (Zarsky, 1991).

In the event, the CTE has done nothing of the kind, at least for the past two years. Instead, it has focused exclusively on whether (and when) unilateral or multilateral trade restrictions on environmental grounds are permissible. The two issues which have absorbed all its attention – with little result to date – are the so-called 'MEA issue' (trade restrictions within multilateral environmental agreements) and eco-labelling. In the former, the debate revolves around whether there should be a 'safe harbour' in the WTO for trade restrictions within multilateral environmental agreements; and whether powerful nations and blocs, especially the United States and the EU, will eschew unilateral trade measures. On eco-labelling, the central issue is whether 'eco-seal' programmes can raise environmentally unjustified non-tariff trade barriers, requiring the WTO to develop guidelines for national eco-labelling pro-grammes. The central issues, in other words, have revolved around the potential of environmental concerns to restrict trade unduly or unfairly, rather than how trade rules could promote sustainable development.

A spate of studies has arrived at the same assessment: the WTO itself is appar-ently 'stuck in the mud' by its own modus operandi and the status quo. 'In terms of new rules, innovative recommendations or solutions to complex policy conflicts, the Committee on Trade and Environment has failed to deliver', concludes a paper to the US Trade and Environment Policy Project (Cameron and Campbell, 1997). 'The Committee on Trade and Environment has made little progress in resolving most of the difficult issues before it,' concludes David Runnalls, director of the Trade Program of the International Institute for Sustainable Development (IISD) (Runnalls, 1997). According to study by the International Union for Conservation of Nature and Natural Resources (IUCN), 'CTE discussions so far have not focused on finding a synergy between environment and trade as two equal policy objectives. Rather, they have explored how to fit environmental concerns within the framework of the existing trade regime' (Ewing and Tarasofsky, 1996). 'The CTE', concludes an IISD study, 'has addressed its essentially political task in a largely technical man-ner' (IISD, 1996).

There is no doubt that the resolution of technical issues is an important part of the larger trade–environment agenda. Appropriate international guidelines for eco-labelling, for example, entail thorny issues of methodology for evaluating envi-ronmental performance over a product life-cycle and deciding whether environmental marketing claims are scientifically robust. Even on the technical issues, however, the CTE has made little progress.

The OECD Joint Session of Trade and Environment Experts has fared some-what better (Reiterer, 1997). In June 1993, the OECD issued a set of guidelines calling for the environmental review of trade policies and agreements, and vice versa. In May 1995, the Joint Session's Report on Trade and Environment included studies on Environmental Principles and Concepts, Trade Principles and Concepts, and Dispute Settlements in Environmental Conventions. The culmination of two years' work, this report canvassed many of the issues the CTE later examined, but came to broader, deeper conclusions. On the MEA issue, for example, OECD countries took a more pronounced stance on limiting unilateral measures. On eco-labelling, the OECD proposed a seven-step approach to the use of life-cycle analyses, including transparency, adaptation time for trade partners, the use of 'best available science', and special treatment for developing countries. The OECD's role, however, has been primarily that of a think-tank. OECD countries' governments have not yet been willing to take policy initiatives in the OECD context, or even to coordinate their approach in the WTO.

Institutional innovation towards both goals of environmental multilateralism – domestic policy co-ordination and capacity-building – should start with the WTO. First, the organization as a whole needs to affirm its commitment to a 'develop-ment agenda': ways that trade and investment could greatly improve economic and managerial capacities, including those for environmental management, in de-veloping countries. Among other things, this would entail abandoning the idea that the primary goal of trade–environment diplomacy is to enhance the capacities of developed countries for restricting market access on environmental grounds.

Second, the CTE must resolve the issue of its relationship to MEAs and provide clear guidelines to environmental negotiators on the use of trade-restricting measures. Third, environmental issues should not be 'ghettoized' in one particular WTO committee. Policies that affect environmental management are relevant to councils and committees throughout the WTO, and should be evaluated and developed with environmental as well as trade goals in mind. Fourth, the WTO must take up the central issue of managing the trade–environment interface – namely, PPMs. This includes negotiating the elimination of domestic resource management policies, including energy, water, chemical and other subsidies, which both distort trade and engender environmental degradation.

One of the most important innovations at the WTO involves the need to widen and institutionalize the participation of non-state actors, both non-governmental organizations (NGOs) and multigovernmental organizations such as United Nations Environment Programme (UNEP) and the United Nations Conference on Trade and Development (UNCTAD). Transparency and access are crucial, especially in addressing the increasingly interdisciplinary nature of global trade policy, as the mere existence of the CTE makes clear (Cameron and Campbell, 1997). Among the innovations championed by environmental NGOs are the establishment of a right of intervention (eg amicus curiae briefs) in the WTO's Dispute Settlement Understanding and the granting of observer status to NGOs for WTO meetings that are not trade negotiations (Cameron and Campbell, 1997). Greater openness would pave the way for a transition from the narrower trade paradigm of the GATT to the broader policy development role of the WTO. The broadening of perceived institutional identity is central to the task of effective policy coordination.

The WTO may not be up to the task of coordinating joint action to internalize environmental costs, causing at least one analyst to call for a new 'Global Environment Organization' (Esty, 1994). While potentially promising in the long run, the political will for such an organization has not yet materialized. In the short to medium term, regional and plurilateral groupings offer a promising arena for institutional innovation. Regional groups involve fewer negotiating partners than the WTO and are less burdened by its legalistic, rule-bound style. Moreover, economic 'globalization' is in large part a regional phenomenon: in the early 1990s, about 60 per cent of European trade was intra-regional. In East Asia, the figure was about 40 per cent, in South America about 40 per cent and in North America about 35 per cent (S Young, 1994, Table 14.2).

Regional economic organizations, such as the Commission for Environmental Cooperation in North America and the Asia Pacific Economic Cooperation forum (APEC), may provide a vehicle and an incipient model of cooperation and collective action in coordinating environmental policy goals (Zarsky, 1997). The eighteen member economies of APEC span East Asia, Australasia, North America, and Latin America (Mexico and Chile). Both developed and developing countries are within APEC, although generally the developing countries are the world's rapidly industrializing 'star performers'. APEC's *raison d'etre* has evolved since it was formed in 1989 from a loose forum for consultation to a vehicle to implement trade and investment liberalization. It has also embraced environmental, technical and development co-operation as part of its agenda (Zarsky and Hunter, 1997).[7]

Unlike the WTO, APEC is not a negotiating forum but takes practical initiatives based on consensus. The emphasis on consensus suggests that common initiatives are not taken primarily through a process of side payments and threats of sanctions, but on a perception of self-interest, as well as on more subtle forms of political pressure.

The consensus-building approach has been important in gaining regional support for an environmental agenda at APEC and has helped to head off Western tendencies to define environmental issues primarily in terms of their links to market access. Many East Asian countries are deeply concerned about a 'trade–environment' agenda based on market restrictions.

Moreover, a consensus style may increase the likelihood that the initiatives that governments commit to at a regional level will actually be implemented. The problem of implementation has bedevilled multilateral environmental agreements. On the other hand, if there is no external enforcement mechanism, only self-interested initiatives will be undertaken.

The 'APEC way' has promoted a focus on building environmental management capacities, rather than on defining rules and procedures for trade sanctions or any other matter. The capacity-building focus has allowed the environmental agenda to gain rapid momentum, overcoming the political resistance which has plagued other forums, including the WTO.

The APEC model, in short, may eventually generate innovative approaches to environmental policy coordination. The Fisheries Working Group, for example, is considering subsidies as part of a four-year study of market barriers and could potentially build momentum for policy subsidy reform. There are some significant drawbacks to APEC, however. The consensus style derails controversial issues and makes progress slow. A lack of institutional transparency and formal participatory mechanisms inhibits accountability and public input. Some of the most difficult – and significant – issues are still to be resolved, notably the development of a consensus to undertake common policy initiatives, especially on resource management.

Another regional grouping which could help to promote effective international environmental policy coordination is the OECD itself. Its member countries are now negotiating, rather hastily, a Multilateral Agreement on Investment (MAI). As currently conceived, the MAI is designed primarily to promote foreign investor interests by reducing political risk and enhancing the principle of national treatment. There is considerable resistance in developing countries to the broad liberalization which the principle of national treatment implies. The MAI is essentially an 'end run' around the WTO: with the MAI a fait accompli, developing countries are likely to comply either through bilateral agreements with OECD countries or through the WTO.

The rules and principles which shape investment decisions, both domestic and foreign, are crucial for good environmental management. An international investment agreement represents an opportunity to build a global policy framework that encourages investment which enhances good environmental management. This framework could include policy guidelines such as requirements for environmental and social impact assessment prior to undertaking investment projects; commitments by multinational investors to use whichever is the higher between home and host country standards; adherence to international labour and human rights norms; and capacity-building commitments to transfer technology and train local personnel. A group of American environmentalists has called for exceptions to MAI provisions to allow for measures to protect the environment, and the promulgation of mandatory 'environmental readiness criteria' which would have to be met before countries could sign the MAI (CIEL et al, 1997). Another group has called for a broad 'Sustainable Development Investment Agreement' incorporating the principles of Agenda 21 (Earth Council, 1996).

OECD negotiators have offered to incorporate environmental concerns in the MAI by including a 'pollution haven' clause, whereby countries would pledge not to encourage foreign investment by lowering standards. However, as this paper has argued, the main issue is not pollution havens, but competition-induced inertia. The OECD has also offered to append to the MAI its 'Guidelines for Multinational Enterprises'. While this move would be welcome, the voluntary guidelines provide no assurance of effective policy coordination to raise environmental performance: multinational firms operating in OECD countries could undertake some, all, or none of the initiatives that the guidelines encourage.

In addition to dealing with investment, the OECD could encourage movement towards collective action on reducing and eliminating resource subsidies within OECD countries. A 'Multilateral Agreement on Resource Subsidies' would bring benefits to both developed and developing countries, especially if it aimed expressly at sectors in which developing countries suffer the ill-effects of OECD subsidies. The OECD could also promote better energy pricing, both by reducing subsidies and by collectively accepting economic instruments to internalize the environmental costs of energy production and use. The success of OECD initiatives on investment, subsidies or other collective-action environmental issues would be greatly enhanced by provision for regular participation by 'big market economies', including Brazil, Russia, India and China.

In addition to investment and resource management, the OECD could offer its substantial think-tank and convening capabilities for policy coordination on energy pricing. Existing coordination among OECD countries on the use of economic and other instruments to internalize energy costs could help to speed the now-slow climate change negotiations. The OECD could also undertake initiatives to promote capacity-building in developing countries, including financial mechanisms.

Other proposed functional groupings are 'buddy systems' such as joint implementation proposals for the climate change convention. Joint implementation, however, has foundered on the concerns of developing countries that such efforts will retard industrialization, and of environmentalists that they will retard adjustment in developed countries towards lower consumption patterns. Similar proposals might be problematic if they enhanced bloc-like alliances which promoted internal bloc interests.

Innovative institutional approaches are emerging in the private sector, the most significant of which is the Environmental Management System generated by the International Organization for Standardization – ISO 14001. These new voluntary standards provide guidelines for industry on ways to monitor and improve environmental performance. The self-regulation aspect could prompt industry to undertake internal management reforms – especially those that cut costs by increasing energy or input efficiency – which they would not have taken otherwise. Critics fear that the current lack of environmental performance standards reduces the robustness of ISO 14001 and may even allow companies to put a 'green fig leaf' over business-as-usual behaviour (Benchmark, 1995).

The key to the success or failure of ISO 14001 will be the broader regulatory and institutional context in which companies implement it (Roht-Arriaza, 1996). One of its provisions, for example, calls for businesses to comply with all domestic environmental regulations. If these are weak, then companies have no guidelines on how to change, let alone incentives to do so. But if domestic performance expectations are strong, and governments help industries to build management capacities, then ISO 14001 could reach its goal of 'continuous self-improvement'. ISO 14001 also requires international institutional innovation, primarily to develop certification standards and procedures.

A host of attempts at industry self-regulation exist as well. While such initiatives should be welcomed, they, like ISO 14001, need to be nurtured by government regulatory and capacity-building support. There is little evidence that self-regulation has substantially altered business behaviour thus far (UNCTAD, 1996).

Pessimists argue that international policy coordination will founder on the opposition of business, especially multinational corporations. However, the instability and heightened insecurity of global markets, especially the increasing sensitivity to competitors subject to different jurisdictional constraints, suggests that business may generally be more supportive of international than national institutional innovation. 'Despite their supple strengths,' argues William Greider eloquently, 'the great multinationals are, one by one, insecure themselves. Even the most muscular giants are quite vulnerable if they fail to adapt to the imperatives of reducing costs and improving rates of return' (Greider, 1997, p25). Paul Kennedy, the economic historian, chimes in: '*Without* the frameworks established by our international organizations, international business would be lost – only pirates and criminals would flourish. *Within* these frameworks, legitimate enterprise can prosper' (Kennedy, 1996, p35).

National Policy Initiatives

In addition to new imperatives for international policy coordination, globalization creates new limitations on – and opportunities for – unilateral policy initiatives. The central limitation is an emphasis on the efficiency of environmental policy.

The cost-effectiveness of environmental policy can be defined as the improvement in environmental performance per dollar of spending. The more efficient the policy, the greater the benefit for the same level of spending. The greater the fiscal constraint, the more important it is to ensure that policy initiatives are efficient.

While this is theoretically simple, the measurement of environmental performance is complex, both theoretically and quantitatively. A host of think-tanks and other organizations are undertaking work to develop environmental indicators to provide guidance both to policy-makers and business managers (Ditz and Ranganathan,

1996). In the main, policy-makers are operating largely in the dark, often in 'pin-the-tail-on-the-donkey' fashion: one knows that the donkey is out there, but the blindfold makes it hard to find its rear. Nonetheless, the *direction* of environmental performance improvements is generally known and wasteful expenditure can be identified.

One of the most significant innovations to improve efficiency would be the development of 'community partnership' models. These models are based on two key ideas: first, that stakeholders at all levels are legitimate and often creative partners in environmental governance; and second, that local government offers a practical vehicle for broad citizen engagement in environmental management.

Partnerships aim to enhance the role of business in improving internal environmental management, and the role of citizens in monitoring and improving the environmental performance of business, government and other citizens. A public role in monitoring and improving environmental performance would reduce the costs of government enforcement which, in highly adversarial and legalistic contexts like the US, are substantial. In developing countries as well, governments are under severe financial and person-power constraints. Involving businesses and local communities in improving environmental performance is likely to yield faster and broader results than relying on governmental regulatory and enforcement capacities alone.

A key role for national and local government in the 'community partnership' model is to provide training, information and other capacity-building services. For small and medium-sized firms in particular, the root of poor environmental performance is often ignorance of better methods, or lack of money for training or capital improvements. Rather than emphasizing the punitive role of governments, efficiency concerns might point towards government as cheerleader, convenor and facilitator.

In federal systems, the emphasis on efficiency and partnership may justify devolution of environmental management responsibilities to states and cities. However, if such devolution leads to lower environmental performance, it does not necessarily increase efficiency.

Conclusions

This paper has argued that the central challenge of globalization for environmental management is the need for international coordination to manage and raise the terms of policy convergence. It has also offered some rudimentary suggestions for institutional innovations to take on this task.

The problems in moving down this path should not be underestimated. In particular there are three stumbling blocks. The first has to do with leadership. Globalization creates a kind of leadership vacuum. On one hand, globalization makes nation states increasingly interdependent and homogeneous, both creating common problems and making it easier to identify common projects. On the other hand, globalization heightens the sensitivity of the government of each nation state, big and small, to competitiveness and reduces its willingness to suffer costs for the common good.

The problem is especially acute given the constraints on the US. In much of the postwar period, the US has been looked to for leadership in international economic, security and environmental affairs. Still dominant in many markets, the US is none-theless subject to chronic trade and budget deficits and financial market pressures. Since the 1980s, American trade negotiators have often pushed agendas in international institutions which reflect its sectoral trade, rather than its broad strategic interests.

The problem is a structural one: in a global economy without effective multilateral governance, each nation is pressed towards conceiving of economic diplomacy in terms of its own commercial interest. US and EU negotiators often complain bitterly of the reluctance of the other side to take leadership initiatives. Progress towards effective supranational governance will require both greater vision and policy integration within countries (especially OECD countries) and an effective style of collective leadership.

The second problem in achieving effective environmental multilateralism concerns the large global gaps between rich and poor. 'At a global level', argues one analyst, 'the key stumbling block is the problem of inequity. True commitment to 'development' has to be part of the institutional framework of environmental and economic institutions' (Athanasiou, 1996). Besides being a moral imperative, such a commitment by rich countries is needed to move forward the project of multilateral governance.

The third and perhaps most tractable set of problems stems from the informational and analytical requirements of policy coordination. Work is needed to develop – and to standardize – indicators of environmental performance. Further research is needed to develop common definitions and measures of financial subsidies, to analyse the relationship between subsidies and the environment, and to determine where 'double dividends' are possible. Finally, further research is needed on the institutional dynamics of globalization and the environment. This paper has offered some thoughts towards the direction of such research.

Notes

1 From OECD (1997) *Globalization and the Environment, Preliminary Perspectives*, OECD, Paris
2 For global or regional commons like the atomosphere or regional seas, international cooperation is needed to overcome coordination (prisoner's dilemma) and free-rider problems, namely, because individual nation states cannot be excluded from the benefits of investment in sustainable resource utilization, they face an incentive not to pay. Coordination would improve the welfare of all but costs must be apportioned and enforced. For cross-border resources like rivers, nation states have incentives to capture benefits from and slough off externalities on to neighbouring states
3 Globalization also seems to drive countries to be more alike in key social dimensions, especially internal wage and income distribution, at least within the broad categories of 'rich' and 'poor' countries (see Williamson, 1996)

4   EU countries are attempting to establish a European Monetary Union which would keep exchange rates within a certain band
5   The proposed tax also foundered because of its likely distributional impacts, especially those of the gasoline tax (see Krupnick et al, 1993)
6   'It ... appears that the inequality trends which globalization produced prior to World War I were at least partly responsible for the interwar retreat from globalization. Will the world economy of the next century also retreat from its commitment to globalization because of its inequality side effects?' (Williamson, 1996, p31)
7   Environmental priorities at APEC are currently defined to be: 1) clean technology; 2) sustainable urbanization; and 3) sustainable marine environment
8   The 'environmental protection' section of the guidelines exhorts multinational and domestic enterprises to: (1) assess environmental and health consequences of their activites; (2) cooperate with and provide information to competent authorities; and (3) minimize the risk of accidents and environmental damage, and cooperate in mitigating adverse effects. Risk minimization is to be achieved via technology choice, environmental auditing at enterprise level, education and training programmes for employees, contingency plans, equipping and assisting component entities, and supporting public information programmes (OECD, 1997)

References

Andersen, L and R A Kagan (1996) 'Adversarial Legalism, Transaction Costs, and the Industrial Flight Hypothesis', draft paper for Trade and Environment Policy Project, a collaboration of the Berkeley Roundtable on the International Economy, Nautilus Institute for Security and Sustainable Development, and the National Wildlife Federation

Athanasiou, T (1996) *Divided Planet: The Ecology of Rich and Poor*, New York, Little Brown

Benchmark (1995) *ISO 14001: An Uncommon Perspective*, Brussels, European Environment Bureau, November

Boyer, R and D Drache (eds) (1996) *States Against Markets: The Limits of Globalization*, London and New York, Routledge

Cameron, J and K Campbell (1997) 'The CTE: A Renewed Mandate for Change or more Dialogue?', paper presented to a workshop on The Future of the Environment at the WTO, Trade and Environment Policy Project, a collaboration of the National Wildlife Federation, Nautilus Institute for Security and Sustainable Development, and the Berkeley Roundtable on the International Economy, Washington, DC, March

CIEL (Center for International Environmental Law) (1997) Letter to the Hon Charlene Barshefsky, US Trade Representative, 13 February; signatories: Community Nutrition Institute, Defenders of Wildlife, Friends of the Earth, Greenpeace, Institute for Agriculture and Trade Policy, National Wildlife Federation, Sierra Club, World Wide Fund For Nature

Ditz, D and J Ranganathan (1996) *Corporate Environmental Performance Indicators: Bridging Internal and External Information Needs*, World Resources Institute, October

Earth Council (1996) *Proposal for a Sustainable Development Investment Agreement* (SDIA), San José, Costa Rica, August/September

Eichengreen, B and P B Kenen (1994) 'Managing the World Economy Under the Bretton Woods System: An Overview', in P B Kenen (ed), *Managing the World Economy: Fifty Years After Bretton Woods*, Washington, DC, Institute for International Economics

Esty, D C (1994) *Greening the GATT, Trade, Environment, and the Future*, Washington, DC, Institute for International Economics

Ewing, K P and R G Tarasofsky (1996) *The 'Trade and Environment' Agenda: Survey of Major Issues and Proposals From Marakesh to Singapore*, IUCN Environmental Law Centre, Bonn, December

Faeth, P et al (1991) *Paying the Farm Bill: US Agricultural Policy and the Transition to Sustainable Agriculture*, Washington, DC, World Resources Institute

Feenstra, R and A Rose (1993) 'Trade With Mexico and Water Use in California Agriculture', in P Garber (ed), *Mexico–U.S. Free Trade Agreement*, Cambridge, MA, MIT Press, pp189–218

Haas, P M, R O Keohane and M A Levy (1993) *Institutions for the Earth, Sources of Effective Environmental Protection*, Cambridge, MA, MIT Press

Greider, W (1997) *One World, Ready or Not: The Manic Logic of Global Capitalism*, New York, Simon & Schuster

Hoerner, J A and F Muller (1996) 'Carbon Taxes for Climate Protection in a Competitive World', Environmental Tax Program, Center for Global Change, University of Maryland at College Park, June

IISD (International Institute for Sustainable Development) (1996) *The World Trade Organization and Sustainable Development: An Independent Assessment*, Winnipeg, International Institute for Sustainable Development

Kennedy, P (1996) 'The Private Sector, the Nation-State, and International Organizations', *World Economic Affairs*, vol 1, no 1, summer, pp35–39

Keynes, J M (1964) *The General Theory of Employment, Interest and Money*, New York, Harcourt Brace Jovanovich

Krupnick, A J, M A Walls and H C Hood (1993) *The Distributional and Environmental Implications of an Increase in the Federal Gasoline Tax*, Washington, DC, Resources for the Future, September

Legg, W (1996) 'Agricultural Subsidies and the Environment', in *Subsidies and the Environment, Exploring the Linkages*, Paris, OECD, pp117–138

Lipsey, R E, M Blomstrom and E Ramstetter (1995) *Internationalized Production in World Output*, Working Paper 5385, National Bureau of Economic Research, Cambridge, MA, December

Lutz, E (1992) 'Integration of Environmental Concerns into Agricultural Policies of Industrial and Developing Countries', *World Development*, vol 20, no 2, pp241–253

Michaelis, L (1996) 'The Environmental Implications of Energy and Transport Subsidies', in *Subsidies and the Environment, Exploring the Linkages*, Paris, OECD, pp175–192

Muller, F (1995) 'Energy Taxes, The Climate Change Convention and Economic Competitiveness', paper presented to the 3rd International Conference on Social Costs, Ladenburg, 27–30 May

Obstfeld, M and K Rogoff (1996) *Foundations of International Macroeconomics*, Cambridge MA, MIT Press, Ch 7

OECD (1989) *Agricultural and Environmental Policies, Opportunities for Integration*, OECD, Paris

OECD (1996) *Environmental Performance Reviews: United States*, OECD, Paris

OECD (1997) *OECD Guidelines for Multinational Enterprises*, www.oecd.org/daf/cmis/mneguide.htm

O'Rourke, K H and J G Williamson (1995) *Around the European Periphery 1870–1913: Globalization, Schooling and Growth*, Working Paper 5392, National Bureau of Economic Research, Cambridge, MA, December

Porter, G (1996) 'Natural Resource Subsidies, Trade and Environment: The Cases of Forest and Fisheries', paper to Workshop on APEC and the Environment: Innovative Approaches to Trade and Environment in Asia–Pacific, Trade and Environment Policy Project, San Francisco, October

Primavera, J H (1994) 'Shrimp Farming in the Asia–Pacific Region: Environment and Trade Issues and Regional Cooperation', in *Trade and Environment in Asia–Pacific: Prospects for Regional Cooperation,* Workshop Compendium, Nautilus Institute for Security and Sustainable Development, Berkeley, September

Razawi, H (1997) 'Innovative Financing for Environmentally Sustainable Energy Development in Northeast Asia', Nautilus Institute for Security and Sustainable Development, Berkeley, January

Reiterer, M (1997) 'Trade and Environment: Reflections on the Impact of the OECD Joint Session of Trade and Environment Experts on the Report of the WTO Committeee on Trade and Environment (CTE) and the Future Role of the JS', *International Environmental Affairs,* vol 9, no 1, winter

Repetto, R (1995) *Jobs, Competitiveness, and Environmental Regulation: What Are the Real Issues?* Washington, DC, World Resources Institute, March

Reuters (1997) 'Labor Opposes Cutting Pollution in 2000', 22 February, via labornews@igc.apc.org

⚹Revesz, R L (1992) 'Rehabilitating Inter-State Competititon: Rethinking the "Race to the Bottom"', *New York University Law Review,* no 67

Roht-Arriaza, N (1996) 'ISO 14001 in the APEC Context: Uses, Limitations and Policy Alternatives', paper to Workshop on APEC and the Environment: Innovative Approaches to Trade and Environment in Asia–Pacific, Trade and Environment Policy Project, San Francisco, October

Roodman, D M (1996) 'Paying the Piper: Subsidies, Politics, and the Environment', Worldwatch Paper 133, Washington, DC, Worldwatch Institute, December

Runge, C F and T Jones (1996) 'Subsidies, Tax Incentives and the Environment: An Overview and Synthesis', in *Subsidies and the Environment, Exploring the Linkages,* Paris, OECD

Runnalls, D (1997) 'Shall We Dance? What the North Needs to Do to Fully Engage the South in the Trade and Sustainable Development Debate', http://iisd1.iisd.ca/trade/dance.htm

Scherp, J (1997) Comments to Expert Workshop on Globalization and the Environment, Vienna, OECD Environment Directorate, 30–31 January

Serageldin, I and J Martin-Brown (eds) (1996) *Servicing Innovative Financing of Environmentally Sustainable Development,* Environmentally Sustainable Development Proceedings Series no 11, Washington, DC, World Bank, April

Steinberg, R (1996) 'Trade-Environment Rules and Practices: Globalization, Westernization or Regionalization?', paper to Workshop on Innovative Approaches to Trade and Environment in Asia–Pacific, Nautilus Institute and Berkeley Roundtable on the International Economy

UNCTAD (1996) *Self-Regulation of Environmental Management, An Analysis of Guidelines Set by World Industry Associations for their Member Firms,* UNCTAD/DTCI/29 Environment Series No 5, Geneva and New York, United Nations Conference on Trade and Development

Volcker, P (1996) 'Challenges facing the International Monetary System', *World Economic Affairs,* vol 1, no 1, summer, pp32–27

Williamson, J G (1996) *Globalization and Inequality Then and Now: The Late 19th and Late 20th Centuries Compared,* Working Paper 5491, National Bureau of Economic Research, Cambridge, MA, March

Williamson, J and C R Henning (1994) 'Managing the Monetary System', in P B Kenen, *Managing the World Economy, Fifty Years After Bretton Woods,* Washington, DC, Institute for International Economics

World Bank (1995) *Monitoring Environmental Progress, A Report on Work in Progress,* Washington, DC, World Bank, Environmentally Sustainable Development Department, September

Young, O R (1994) *International Governance: Protecting the Environment in a Stateless Society,* Ithaca, New York, Cornell University Press

Young, S (1994) 'Globalism and Regionalism: Complements or Competitors?', in R Garnaut and P Drysdale (eds), *Asia Pacific Regionalism, Readings in International Economic Relations,* Pymble, Australia, Harper Educational, pp179–193

Zarsky, L (1991) *Trade–Environment Linkages and Ecologically Sustainable Development,* Report to Department of Arts, Sports, Environment, Tourism and Territories, Environmental Strategy Branch, Australia, October

Zarsky, L (1997) 'APEC and the Environment: Regional Governance in the Age of Globalization', *Colorado Journal of International Environmental Law and Policy,* summer

Zarsky, L and J Hunter (1996) 'Environmental Cooperation at APEC: The First Five Years', *Journal of Environment and Development,* September

3

Globalization, Foreign Direct Investment and Sustainable Human Development

Daniel Chudnovsky and Andrés López[1]

Introduction

Foreign direct investment (FDI) is generally considered as a driving force in the integration of developing countries into the globalization process that characterizes the world economy. Although most FDI is concentrated in developed countries, developing countries have made the biggest gains in the 1990s in terms of flows of inward FDI: from US$34 billion in 1990 (17 per cent of global inflows) to US$149 billion in 1997 (37 per cent of global inflows). However, a small number of developing countries in Asia and Latin America (notably China and Brazil) have attracted most of the recent flows of FDI.

The majority of the low-income developing countries (LIDCs) – which are defined, for the purpose of the present chapter, as those with a per capita gross domestic product (GDP) of less than US$1000 – have received small, if any, amounts of FDI. Nonetheless, some of the LIDCs have recently received higher inflows (eg Angola, Bangladesh, Uganda and the Republic of Tanzania) and a number of them have significant stocks of FDI in relation to their GDP (although their GDP is often quite low). These countries have generally received resource-seeking FDI in mining and tourism or have export-processing zones, although they may also have received some market-seeking investments.

Since most developing countries are eager to receive FDI, it is not surprising to find that competition among governments to attract increasing FDI inflows has heated up in recent years (Aranda and Sauvant, 1996; Oman, 1998). Developing countries are engaged in this kind of competition because their governments take for granted that FDI is a key instrument to foster growth and competitiveness.

Nonetheless, it is by no means clear that FDI generates more benefits than costs for host countries as is often assumed. In this connection, the main objective of this paper is to examine under what conditions and policy framework FDI may indeed contribute to improve host country's competitiveness and to the fulfilment of Sustainable Human Development (SHD) objectives.

As a contribution to build up a framework for undertaking assessment studies in the countries participating in the United Nations Trade and Development (UNCTAD)/ United Nations Development Programme (UNDP) Global Programme on Globalization, Liberalization and Sustainable Human Development the purposes of the chapter are as follows:

First, to highlight the benefits and costs of FDI in the context of trade liberalization and other structural reforms undertaken in developing countries. Second, to examine the impact of FDI on the growth and SHD processes under three headings: 1) innovative activities and technological spillovers; (2) employment, poverty alleviation and income distribution and (3) environment. Although these issues are strongly related, they are examined one by one for analytical convenience. As a survey of the literature is beyond the scope of this chapter, only a brief examination of the main arguments under discussion is made. In each topic, a concise list of the relevant issues to be addressed in empirical work is presented.

Third, on the basis of the experiences of developed as well as of developing countries some policy options are considered. Instead of paying attention only to those policies aimed at increasing the volume of FDI, as is often done by the investment promotion agencies, the focus is on the set of policies required to develop a competitive domestic enterprise sector and, if possible, to create dynamic knowledge-intensive clusters in which environmentally friendly technologies are used. Policy suggestions are geared not only to enhance the contribution of FDI to growth, competitiveness and SHD, but also to improve the capacity of developing countries and especially of LIDCs to participate in a proactive manner in the regional and international negotiations on a possible multilateral framework for investment.

Finally, a framework for country case studies to shed light on the issues discussed in the chapter is suggested.

Benefits and Costs of Foreign Direct Investment in the Context of Structural Reforms in Developing Countries

Most developing countries made a shift in their economic policy regimes in the last two decades. Leaving behind the regulatory regime that is characteristic of the import substitution industrialization (ISI) stage, these countries have generally liberalized their economies, dismantled their trade barriers and have often privatized their public enterprises. Besides the internal forces, which in each case have operated in this direction, pressures from international financial organizations (like the International Monetary Fund (IMF) and the World Bank) as well as the increasing enforcement of multilateral trade disciplines within the WTO, have been important determinants of this shift as well.

As a key part of the reforms' package, most developing countries have dismantled the restrictions and regulations which were in place on FDI and now are welcoming and competing to attract multinational corporations (MNCs). There are two main reasons for this changing attitude towards MNCs. At the microeconomic level FDI is acknowledged as a potentially powerful instrument for improving the access to international markets, for obtaining the technological and organizational capabilities required for producing and exporting new goods and services, and for fostering backward and forward linkages. In this way, FDI may enhance the international competitiveness of the host country.

At the macroeconomic level, FDI may significantly contribute to financing current account deficits in the balance of payments of host countries. Moreover, since MNCs invest in a country following strategies with long time horizons and objectives and, once installed, have large sunk costs in host countries, FDI is considered as less volatile than portfolio investment and other types of international financial flows. For both reasons, an increasing volume of FDI is often taken as a vital contribution to the development process.

However, neither of these potential benefits should be taken for granted and, perhaps more important, they should be confronted with the costs derived from FDI presence.

As Dunning (1993) states, 'many countries in the world are dependent on MNCs as providers of resources, capabilities and markets, as creators of job and wealth, as suppliers of foreign currency, as stimulators of entrepreneurship and worker motivation, and as raiser of demand expectancies' (p284). But while MNCs are interested in a limited number of private economic goals, nation states have a broader range of economic objectives (gross national product (GNP) growth, full employment, etc) and non-economic objectives (distribution of income and wealth, sovereignty in decision-making, political and cultural identity, environmental protection, etc). Also, whereas MNCs are interested in maximizing global profits or sales, states are interested in maximizing the welfare of their own citizens.

In view of this divergence, some host countries may be worse off as a result of MNCs' activity. They may lose national control over strategic economic sectors, indigenous enterprises may be displaced in certain activities and jobs may be lost, the local environment may suffer, etc. Even if the net benefits are positive, it is possible to assume that the host countries are often not as well off as they could be (Dunning, 1993). As Dunning has clearly pointed out, this implies a difficult counterfactual analysis; in other words, the question to be answered in each case is what would have occurred in the absence of MNCs or in the absence of a set of policies aimed at maximizing the net benefits of MNCs and at building national capabilities.

The contribution of FDI to the economic development of the host country depends not only on its volume but also on its quality. The type of investment, the sector of destination, the kind of assets brought by the MNCs and the role played by the affiliates within the global network of the MNC, are important determinants. At the same time, the characteristics of host countries affect not only the amount and kind of FDI that is attracted, but also its contribution to growth, competitiveness and SHD.

These characteristics include the macroeconomic, trade, competition, sectoral and specific policies towards foreign and domestic enterprises, economic performance (GDP growth, price stability, etc) and structural factors (market size, the availability of natural resources, the quantity and quality of human resources, the physical and technological infrastructure, business ethics, the legal system, etc – see Dunning, 1994). The characteristics of indigenous entrepreneurs (ie the sectors in which they operate, their corporate structures, strategies, innovative capabilities, organizational procedures, risk attitudes, etc) are also a major determinant of FDI contribution.

Although FDI may have a positive role leading to economic diversification and higher exports, generating employment and externalities and strengthening the local system of innovation (see below), it may also have a negative role. This is the case when FDI remains an enclave operation exploiting natural resources with bad environmental practices, when foreign affiliates take advantage of their proprietary assets to crowd out local competitors or to engage in market distorting practices, etc.

Regarding the contribution of FDI to the balance of payments of host countries, it is not only the initial entry of capital that must be considered. Profit flows from FDI operations sooner or later will have a negative impact on the balance of payments. These profits are remitted abroad as dividends and, sometimes, as royalty and interest payments and through transfer pricing of merchandise imports and exports. Moreover, MNCs may have a greater import propensity than local firms, as documented in several studies (Chudnovsky and López, 1998). Thus, in the long term, many FDI projects may have a negative contribution to the balance of payments of host countries.

FDI projects in net export-generating activities and in which the foreign investor repatriates low dividends and reinvests most of the profits within the host country would be the more favourable from this point of view. FDI in non-tradable sectors should be, prima facie, the less favourable ones (South Centre, 1997).

At the same time, doubts have been raised on the fact that FDI is a more stable form of foreign capital inflow. The new developments in financial markets, such as derivatives, and the expansion of existing instruments – for example, hedging – have greatly blurred the distinction between FDI and portfolio investment with respect to the relative stability of these flows. Moreover, profit remittances may be as volatile as portfolio investment flows, especially during an economic crisis (South Centre, 1997).

Notwithstanding these reasonable doubts about the net contribution of FDI to host countries, governments are compelled to compete with each other in order to attract FDI, and a kind of 'prisoner's dilemma' has emerged. While governments have a collective interest in refraining from engaging in bidding wars to attract FDI, individual governments fear that if they refrain from bidding, FDI will be diverted to those countries that offer investment incentives (Oman, 1998). Of course, these incentives – which are mostly fiscal and financial – are part, and often a very significant one, of the costs of attracting FDI, and may imply the diversion of resources from other socially desirable activities (such as education, housing and health).

In sum, FDI can certainly make a positive contribution to growth, competitiveness and SHD in host developing countries, but may have some, and often significant, costs which have to be considered as well. As a consequence, a careful assessment of the impact of FDI must be made in order to design and implement policies – at national as well as at international levels – aimed at enhancing the benefits and reducing the costs of FDI for host countries.

FDI, Growth and Sustainable Human Development: Some Key Issues

The main issues to be addressed in country case studies regarding the impact of MNCs on growth and Sustainable Human Development are examined in this section. Those issues directly involved in the concept of SHD (such as employment, income distribution and environment) are dealt with mostly in relation to technology and innovation since they play, in our view, a crucial role in fostering growth and SHD objectives. At the same time, technology and other innovation-related phenomena represent one of the pillars of competitiveness, at national as well as at the firm's level. The other pillar is, of course, formed by price and cost determinants, which have been dealt extensively in the trade-related literature.

In Appendix 3.1 some statistical exercises regarding the complex relationships between FDI and SHD are shown. Even if the available indicators are too rough and the exercise itself needs to be refined, the main results are worth bearing in mind. On one hand, a positive correlation between FDI and GDP per capita, and human and gender development indicators is apparent, suggesting that a feedback process between Human and Gender-related Development Indexes (HGDI) and FDI growth may have been taking place in the last two decades. On the other hand, FDI seems to have, overall, a negative effect on the environment in host countries. Nonetheless, a cursory examination of the data reveals significant differences among host countries regarding the impact of FDI on SHD indicators.

Thus, to learn more about the causality and dynamics of these relationships, it is important not only to carry out further statistical exercises, but also to go beyond them and examine the pertinent issues at specific FDI and country levels. One dollar of FDI brings different impacts in terms of growth and sustainable development according to the type of FDI, the sector in which it operates and the structural characteristics, development styles and available price and non-price incentives in host countries.

In what follows, a brief discussion regarding the impact of FDI on three main SHD-related issues (technology, employment and income distribution and environment) is made. The objective is to highlight the key questions which should guide country case studies on this matter.

Innovative Activities and Technological Spillovers

All developing countries are dependent on foreign technology. In this sense, many analysts have regarded MNCs as one of the main vehicles, or even the main vehicle, for allowing developing countries to begin to close the gap with the world leaders in technology or at least to be able to keep up in a more open and competitive economic environment.

In many sectors, especially in the most dynamic and knowledge-intensive ones, MNCs have important technological assets. Besides, MNCs are often at the cutting edge in terms of their process and organizational technologies. Hence, the way in which, and the extent to which, developing countries may benefit from the technological advantages of MNCs to foster their social and economic development and enhance their competitiveness are key questions.

Even if most technological inputs can be imported, developing countries have to foster what has been termed a 'social' or 'absorptive' capability (Abramovitz, 1986; Albuquerque, 1997; Dahlman et al, 1987). In other words, developing countries must create a basic endogenous capability to be able to assimilate and take advantage of foreign technology inputs.

This endogenous capability is a crucial element in what has been termed 'structural competitiveness' (OECD, 1992). It is based on the idea that the competitiveness of firms is not only a reflection of successful management and technological practices, but also stems from the strength and efficiency of a national economy's productive structure, the collective learning process associated with innovation and the proper use of human capital.

The empirical evidence shows that those developing countries which have reached a relatively high level of industrialization and of structural competitiveness have done so by building domestic technological capabilities which go beyond those required for choosing, adapting and efficiently using foreign technological inputs. The experience of the most advanced developing economies, and specially those of the Republic of Korea, Taiwan Republic of China, Singapore and Hong Kong (China) indicates that major improvements are possible. New technologies can also be developed by local firms in developing countries while they progress through their learning process. In this way, firms can progressively become 'genuine innovators' (Ernst et al, 1998).

There are four ways in which developing countries can obtain technology from MNCs: through FDI; through joint ventures between domestic firms and MNCs (including what has been termed 'strategic partnerships'); by purchasing technology in contractual form (such as patents, licensing and turnkey contracts); and through reverse engineering, imitation, copying, etc (in this case, without the consent of MNCs). The choice between these four ways, when there is a choice,[2] depends mainly on the type of sector involved, the technological infrastructure of the host country, the availability of skilled domestic human resources and the existence (or absence) of native firms with endogenous innovative capabilities. This chapter will pay attention mainly to FDI, but the other ways of absorbing foreign technology possessed by MNCs should also be partially addressed in the country case studies, as a by-product of the analysis of FDI impacts.

The technological impact of the presence of MNCs should be assessed not only in terms of their direct contribution (ie the technologies they introduce in the host country, the innovative activities they eventually accomplish, etc), but should be mainly related to the following key question: To what extent does the presence of MNCs foster or inhibit the creation and upgrading of the domestic absorption capabilities of host countries?

Through FDI, MNCs may bring to the host country their best technological and organizational practices or, at least, they may introduce technologies and practices which are more up-to-date (although not necessarily more attuned to local conditions or domestic factor prices) than those applied by local firms. Furthermore, MNCs may generate technological spillovers from which indigenous institutions and domestic entrepreneurs can benefit. In this case, the social benefits of MNCs activities are enhanced, since MNCs are not the only ones to enjoy the economic benefits arising from their technological assets.

MNCs may be an important source of spillovers. First, their entry may lead to increasing competition in domestic markets, forcing local firms to enhance their productivity by being more efficient in using existing technologies and, eventually, by adopting new and more efficient technologies. Second, local firms may take advantage of the superior technologies and organizational and management practices of MNCs by imitating them, hiring workers trained by MNCs, or establishing forward and backward linkages with their affiliates (Blomstrom and Kokko, 1997). Finally, if MNCs develop innovative activities in the host country, they could generate significant externalities (through human capital upgrading). It has been suggested also that MNCs may help developing countries, and especially the least developed countries, to foster an entrepreneurial culture. At the same time, cultural barriers, and especially the lack of a 'scientific outlook' in host countries, may help to explain why spillovers from MNCs' operations are often so limited (Buckley and Casson, 1993).

The available evidence on the actual magnitude of this kind of spillover is inconclusive. Even if 'many analyses of the linkages between MNCs and their local suppliers and subcontractors have documented learning and technology transfers that may make up a basis for productivity spillovers... these studies seldom reveal whether the MNCs are able to extract all the benefits that the new technologies or information generate among their supplier firms, so there is no clear proof of spillovers' (Blomstrom and Kokko, 1997, p13), although they readily argue that it 'is reasonable to assume that spillovers are positively related to the extent of linkages'.

Regarding spillovers through the training of workers, Blomstrom and Kokko (1997) assert that there seems to be a definite accumulation of human capital skills among the MNCs' employees, but the extent to which these skills can be appropriated by local firms when these employees move to new jobs is an open question. Although empirical evidence is scattered, most studies suggest that management skills are less firm-specific than technical skills, and can more easily be used in other contexts.

It is well known that MNCs undertake only a small proportion of their research and development (R&D) activities outside their home countries. Although information technology may facilitate greater decentralization of R&D activities, it may also lead to a concentration of such activities in a few developed countries. Whereas in some cases affiliates in developing countries undertake some R&D work, it may well happen that the total expenditure on R&D in the host country may be reduced with the entry of MNCs. For example, an MNC which takes over an existing local firm that used to make significant investments in R&D activities may decide to discontinue these activities since it centralizes them in its home base or in affiliates in developed countries. Even without takeovers, the presence of MNCs may discourage innovative activity in domestic enterprises and induce them to substitute licensing agreements for such activity.

At the same time, MNCs may not necessarily bring their latest technologies to the host countries. This depends, among other things, on the relative price factors, the intensity of competition in the host country market, the requirements of industrial and final customers, and the global strategy followed by MNCs. Nonetheless, FDI is generally regarded as being more conducive to the transfer of modern technologies than other ways of technology transfer such as licensing.

The relationship between FDI and the technological performance of host countries cannot be easily assessed with conventional indicators. If the technological performance through R&D expenditures relative to GDP or through the number of patents granted in the US is measured, the two outstanding cases among developing countries are the Republic of Korea and Taiwan Republic of China, which have relied intensively on foreign technology and have generally not controlled FDI by MNCs. They have mostly used contractual arrangements, joint ventures and reverse engineering. At the same time, there are cases with a high influence of FDI and good technological performance (Singapore), as well as other cases with a relatively low presence of MNCs and poor technological performance (India).

From this complex picture, it can only be concluded that the technological impact of MNCs' activities may be assessed on a case-study basis. On one hand, the type of FDI (ie whether it is market-resource efficiency or asset-seeking), the life-cycle stage of the respective product/sector, the export propensity and the role played by the affiliates in the global corporate network, the mode of entry – greenfield or takeover, with or without a local partner– the country of origin of FDI and the sector in which the firm is doing business have to be taken into account.

On the other hand, the characteristics of the host country have an obvious influence. Increasingly, a key element is the magnitude and quality of what has been termed 'created assets' (human resources, technological and communication infrastructure, etc), which are more prone to attract high-quality FDI. At the same time, as already mentioned, the social or absorptive capability of host countries has a significant role, especially when a dynamic analysis is made. The regulatory and institutional environment, which define the basic price and non-price incentives for firms to compete, and the public policies in force in host countries are obviously key elements as well.

In this sense, the 'system of innovation' framework seems to be a promising way to analyse the impact of FDI on the technological performance of host countries. This relatively recent framework has some weaknesses: it is conceptually diffuse and it is hard to operationalize. However, it has several interesting features: it is holistic and interdisciplinary, it emphasizes the role of history and institutions, it stresses the interactions and interdependence between agents, and it allows the use of different approaches (sectoral, regional or national, even multinational or transnational) (Edquist, 1997). Furthermore, it is similar to the notion of 'structural competitiveness'. In sum, it is a promising research framework for the more systematic and holistic analysis of the interactions between technological and innovative capabilities, and economic and social development.

Even if important adaptations need to be made before applying the system of innovation approach to developing countries (see Albuquerque, 1997), it should be useful as a basic conceptual framework for studying the technological impact of FDI. At the same time, if it is applied in developing countries, the approach itself will be improved and better adapted to the specific conditions of these countries.

There are a number of questions regarding the impact of MNC activity on indigenous technological and organizational assets and skills which empirical studies should address:

1 What kind of product and process technologies do MNCs' affiliates employ in host countries, both in tradable and non-tradable sectors? How much of a gap is there between those technologies and those employed in MNCs' home countries or in their affiliates in developed countries? Has the gap been reduced after trade and FDI liberalization measures? To what extent is the gap due to the relative prices of capital and labour or to non-price factors?

2 Do MNCs' affiliates engage in innovative activities in host countries? If so, what are the characteristics of those activities and the main motivating factors?

3 In what way do MNCs' affiliates interact with different host country science and technology (S&T) institutions?

4 Are there technological partnerships between MNCs and local firms? If so, what are the features and prospects of these kinds of alliances?

5 What kind of technical assistance do MNCs' affiliates provide to their suppliers and customers in the host country?

6 To what extent do MNCs' train and upgrade the technical skills of their labour force? Are there any spillovers from these activities through workers' mobility?

7 Does the presence of MNCs' in LIDCs help to foster the development of an entrepreneurial and innovative culture in local firms and institutions?

Besides their intrinsic relevance, these questions are significant for host countries seeking to put in place a policy framework geared not only to attract more FDI, but also to enhance its quality, increase its social spillovers and contribute to domestic technological capacity-building and national competitiveness.

In this context, it is important to distinguish LIDCs from other developing countries. LIDCs have weak or almost non-existent national systems of innovation; there are few, if any, enterprises with technological capabilities; their S&T institutions are poorly endowed; there is a dearth of skilled human resources, and their manufacturing sector and domestic markets are small. In short, they have not even begun to build the above-mentioned social or absorptive capability that is needed if they are to take advantage of foreign sources of technology.

Almost by definition, FDI should help to reduce the gap with the world leaders in process and product technologies. However, it cannot be expected that MNCs' affiliates will be undertaking significant innovation activities in these countries, and their linkages with domestic firms and local S&T institutions will be generally very weak (especially when MNCs are located in export processing zones (EPZs)). Domestic competitors, if there are any, will find it hard to learn from MNCs' technologies, which are likely to be well beyond their endogenous capabilities.

The technology indicators often employed in developed countries must be adapted if they are to have a meaningful use in developing countries. It is evident that they are totally inappropriate for LIDCs and there are very few studies concerned with the development of S&T indicators suitable for such countries (UNCTAD, 1996). This fact complicates even further the analysis of the technological impact of FDI.

How, then, are we to evaluate this issue? First, it would be advisable to learn about the existence of clusters or networks built around MNCs' activities. At the same time, the impact of MNCs on existing clusters should also be studied. The main objective of this analysis should be to determine whether the presence of MNCs fosters entrepreneurial and innovative attitudes in their suppliers and customers.

Second, the employment of native human resources in jobs which require significant skills and of local engineers and scientists in the labour force of MNCs should be examined. It would also be interesting to learn whether MNCs have any specific policies for training, qualifying and upgrading the skills of local human resources. The mobility of skilled workers is, as mentioned above, one of the possible spillovers from FDI. Since it is plausible to assume that few local existing firms could employ these workers in LIDCs, it would be interesting to know any cases in which workers trained by MNCs have created new enterprises in which they could take advantage of the skills learned in the MNC.

Third, it is important to find out whether the presence of MNCs fosters or inhibits the ability of LIDCs to gain expertise in identifying the technologies which are most suitable to their needs, including 'hard' as well as 'soft' technologies (UNCTAD, 1996).

Finally, the possible existence of differences in the technological performance and in the generation of spillovers for host countries between 'conventional' MNCs and so-called 'Third World' MNCs – a growing phenomenon, especially in some East Asian and Latin American countries (Lall, 1983; Dunning et al, 1997; Narula, 1997) should also be verified.

A different approach is required to analyse the technological impact of FDI in more advanced developing countries. Even if these countries are, in general, far from having a mature national system of innovation, they have generally built an S&T system and have at least some local base of skilled human resources.

Analysing the changes in the technological regimes in Latin America in the 1990s, Katz (1998) suggests some key issues on which empirical studies should be able to shed light. Taking the privatization process, where FDI presence has been very significant, Katz argues that, on one hand, the technological modernization of the infrastructure inherited by new owners has nurtured a number of locally owned firms that are specialized in systems engineering, computer software, etc. On the other hand, privatization has meant a contraction, and even the disappearance, of the domestic R&D infrastructure developed by former state enterprises.

At the same time, MNCs in developing countries, as part of the globalization of their production strategies, have often discontinued local engineering activities in order to adapt and improve the product and process technologies provided by their parent companies. Moreover, the increasing use of imported components may have a negative impact on local firms which were suppliers of MNCs (of course, the same arguments apply when new MNCs take over local existing firms).

Thus, we seem to be witnessing a process of 'creative destruction'. The society's pre-existing human, engineering and technological capabilities are devalued. The new innovation systems seem to rely more on external sources of technology and to be more responsive to the influence of global technological trends. Whether one considers this transition as a good or bad development depends chiefly on the assessment of the quality of the previous technological base, on the extent to which it has been eroded, preserved or transformed, and on the new linkages or spillovers arising from the new productive and innovative strategies by MNCs' affiliates.

In this case, several sectors where the presence of MNCs is widespread should be selected for studies in different countries. It would be advisable to choose sectors with different characteristics – consumer durables (such as cars), a scale-intensive sector (such as petrochemicals) and a high-tech sector (such as electronics or biotechnology) and countries with different structural features, economic policy regimes and levels of development. The study of some activities which have been privatized and are now under foreign control could be relevant as well.

A comparative analysis of the findings of these studies could help us to examine the influence of certain host country characteristics (the public policy framework, the inward or outward orientation of industrial production, the availability and quality of skilled human resources, the technological infrastructure, the existence of domestic firms with competitive capabilities, etc) on the technological performance of MNCs' affiliates, as well as on the effects of the presence of those affiliates on the development of domestic social or absorptive capabilities in developing countries.

Employment, Poverty Alleviation and Income Distribution

Although MNCs employ only 2–3 per cent of the world's workforce (providing approximately 73 million jobs, 12 million of which are located in developing countries), they are particularly important employers in certain sectors and countries. MNCs account for one-fifth of all paid employment in non-agricultural sectors in developed and some developing countries, and are very relevant in capital and technology-intensive manufacturing industries. MNCs may also indirectly generate jobs by establishing backward and forward linkages within host countries; it has been estimated, in the case of a number of developing countries, that at least one or two jobs are generated indirectly for each worker employed by MNCs' affiliates (UNCTAD, 1994).

Overall, the net effect of FDI on the quantity and quality of employment depends on a variety of factors, such as relative labour costs in the host country, the employment elasticity of output in the activities in which FDI is important, the relative importance of greenfield and takeover investments, the creation or displacement of local linkages, the displacement of local firms by MNCs' competition and labour market regulations in host countries. As a consequence, the relationship between MNCs' strategies and employment effects are intricate, although some effects are relatively easy to predict. For example, employment creation should be greater in cases where local labour costs are low, in greenfield investments rather than in takeovers, and in services rather than in manufacturing. In turn, employment is generally reduced when affiliates of MNCs undertake efficiency-seeking investments and switch from stand-alone operations to complex integration strategies.

Things are further complicated since, as stated before, most developing countries have implemented deep structural reforms in recent years, in a context where competition is more intense and globalized, and new technologies and organizational practices are being introduced. In this scenario, both foreign and domestic firms located in developing countries have been under strong pressure to restructure and rationalize their activities. Since affiliates of MNCs have more financial and technological resources than domestic firms to cope with the new situation, foreign firms are likely to have increased their presence. The negative social consequences (greater unemployment and poverty and rising inequality) that may arise from these restructuring processes may be attributed to a growing presence of MNCs, when in reality they are a result of the adjustment process itself and the policies used for that purpose.

Thus, the key question is this: even if the consequence of FDI is the loss of jobs in the host country, what would have happened without, or with less presence of, MNCs? This, in turn, gives room for a second question: what would have happened in that case with or without the implementation of policies aimed to make domestic firms more competitive?

To approach this issue, it is useful to distinguish between tradable and non-tradable sectors. In tradable sectors, trade liberalization in previously protected domestic markets implies new rules for existing firms and opportunities for newcomers. The main strategy to survive and prosper in a more competitive local and international environment is to enhance productivity and improve quality. Some firms may be able to keep up with the changing situation, but other firms may not. This means that unless specific policies for assisting domestic firms to become more competitive are in place jointly with trade liberalization measures, employment is likely to be reduced, or will grow much slower than total production. In this context, the key question is: will an MNC-led restructuring process have more or less deleterious effects on employment as compared with a similar process led by local firms?[3]

If local firms are able to adjust successfully to the new situation as a result of their own or public policies, they could probably expand output and exports and preserve more jobs and, more importantly, they should be able to maintain more domestic linkages with suppliers and subcontractors, some of which would be broken if MNCs relied on their affiliates. On the other hand, it is also possible that local firms would not have survived foreign competition and the number of lost jobs would be even greater than in an MNC-led restructuring process.

In the case of non-tradable sectors, the dynamics will be different according to the sector concerned. In retailing, for example, even if MNCs create a large number of direct jobs, they may also displace many small shops that are unable to compete with hypermarkets and supermarkets. In tourism, MNCs may have a more positive effect on employment, since they generally contribute to the creation of a previously non-existent infrastructure (such as hotels, transport car rental).

All these arguments show that caution is needed when it comes to the analysis of the impact of FDI on employment. Both a proper definition of the issues to be studied and the methodology to be employed is required, taking into account the specific conditions of host countries and the type of FDI involved in each case. Nevertheless, some comments are in order.

LIDCs have a significant surplus of labour engaged in low-productivity or subsistence activities. An essential feature of the development process is that part of this labour force is gradually hired in the 'modern' sector of the economy. This may mean that 'hidden' unemployment decreases and, eventually, real wages begin to rise. MNCs' entry may accelerate this process and that is one of the reasons why so many countries compete for the attraction of FDI. In this context, almost by definition, MNCs provide jobs to individuals who otherwise would have no source of income or would earn very low incomes. Furthermore, it is very likely that these jobs will be related to export activities.

However significant this contribution may be, it would be advisable to learn about other potential, more 'qualitative' contributions of MNCs to the long-term development goals of host countries. This implies the analysis of: the wage structure and wage/profit ratio in MNCs' affiliates; the skill and gender composition of their labour force; the extent to which MNCs' affiliates meet their needs for skilled human resources through expatriates from their home countries or other affiliates, and whether there is a gradual displacement of expatriates in favour of local personnel; and the indirect employment effects of MNCs' presence through subcontractors, suppliers, repair and maintenance.

One of the mechanisms preferred by developing countries to attract FDI is the establishment of EPZs. According to the International Labour Organization (ILO) (1998), some 27 million people work in nearly 850 EPZs worldwide. An increasing number of governments are considering establishing EPZs in their countries and competing with each other by granting incentives to potential (and generally foreign) investors. Many of these EPZs are located in countries with a GNP per capita of less than US$1000 – for example, in Africa (mostly in Kenya), Central America (eg Honduras) and Asia (notably in China where 124 EPZs were operating in 1997), although surprisingly, the US is the country where there are the most EPZs (213).

Even when the objective of EPZs is to contribute to economic development and employment creation, labour and social problems are widespread, especially when labour standards are not enforced. In turn, the generation of employment through FDI in EPZs has limitations, both in terms of the kinds of jobs generated and the sustainability of those jobs, given that, as labour costs increase, FDI in EPZs often relocates to other countries (UNCTAD, 1994).

These considerations raise a number of questions: What is the standard of the working conditions in EPZs, especially for women? To what extent do MNCs' affiliates employ not only unskilled domestic labour, but also qualified workers? What has been the 'life-cycle' of FDI in EPZs? What happens when real wages begin to rise and the host country begins to lose its comparative advantages over other locations?

Another issue is the role that MNCs might play in promoting or inhibiting employment discrimination and sex segregation in developing countries. In this connection, Buckley and Casson (1993) have pointed out the impact of MNCs on labour markets and their potential to lead or reinforce the dualist tendencies in many societies. For example, the tradition of subservience to despotic authority can sometimes be exploited by MNCs searching for cheap unskilled labour that is easily disciplined by intimidation. Women and children accustomed to absolute paternal authority may become useful factory or plantation employees.

Besides paying attention to the attitude of MNCs towards gender discrimination in host countries, it would also be advisable to learn about the possible relationships between the existence of overt gender discrimination and certain aspects of the national culture of the home country of the MNC (see Lawler, 1995). At the same time, it would be useful to learn about cases where FDI has been attracted to a host country by the existence of a labour force accustomed to paternal authority.

In more advanced developing countries, growing FDI inflows have often been part of the results of structural reform packages which have had a significant impact on productive activities. Labour markets have been deeply affected by these processes, which have had major impacts on employment rates, wage structures, the demand for skilled and unskilled labour, poverty and income distribution.

Since there are so many causes and effects behind recent trends, to examine the specific influence of MNCs on the changes in labour markets and social development conditions is clearly impossible. Hence, a more focused approach to the impact of FDI on these issues through case studies is required. As a result of privatization and deregulation, MNCs have been able to acquire assets in public utilities and industries and services in which the involvement of foreign private capital was once either prohibited or restricted. The impact of these changes on employment, wages, working conditions, training and industrial relations can be assessed through relevant case studies. A sectoral or 'cluster' approach could be useful as well, perhaps including tradable as well as non-tradable sectors.

Regarding income distribution and poverty alleviation, there are clearly many different factors that have a significant influence on them besides FDI. In fact, probably the main impact of FDI on this matter is its effects in terms of employment.

Nonetheless, besides their direct impact on income distribution through their wage and employment policies, MNCs may have significant indirect effects arising from their production and pricing strategies and their oligopolistic behaviour. The direct impact of MNCs on income distribution may be examined by the evolution of productivity and wages paid to different categories of workers and, if data are available, through the ratio between the wages paid by those firms and the profits which they earn. If possible, such data should be compared with income distribution trends in the areas where the foreign firms are located.

MNCs may have a significant influence on income distribution and welfare more indirectly, when they introduce new products or services, or new processes for making existing products or services in the host country. Thus, they may affect consumption styles as well as the relative access of the different segments of the population to the products or services they supply. This influence may be positive or negative, depending, for example, on the pricing and advertising strategy of an MNC which is introducing a new product that may have significant consequences on the health or nutrition levels of the population of the host country.

While the entry of foreign firms may increase competition in domestic markets and benefit industrial and personal consumers with lower prices or higher quality products and services, it may also lead to a more concentrated supply structure and restrictive business practices which worsen income and assets distribution. Although in the sector of tradables a more concentrated supply structure may be disciplined through competing imports, to counteract the adverse welfare effects of a growing supply concentration in both tradable and non-tradable sectors, a well-designed and implemented domestic competition policy is required. Since this is not the case in most developing countries, the indirect effects of FDI on welfare and income distribution are unlikely to be very positive. Indirect effects can only be examined through case studies, but, unfortunately, data to assess these effects are very difficult to obtain.

Environment[4]

The effects of FDI on the environment in developing countries have been assessed in quite a different manner in the past than in the present. From being accused of investing in developing countries to take advantage of lax environmental regulations and hence being responsible for many environmental problems in such countries, MNCs are increasingly considered nowadays as leaders in the introduction of good environmental management practices and in the diffusion of environmentally sound technologies in developing countries.

While the evidence in support of both arguments is limited, there is no doubt that many MNCs have the potential of being a more conducive agent for introducing environmentally sound technologies. However, their actual environmental management would depend on the age of the facilities, the presence of sunk costs, the host country environmental regulations and degree of enforcement, the availability of pollution-prevention technologies and the global environmental policies of the MNC in question.

The traditional position suggested the existence of 'pollution havens' in developing countries to attract more FDI, since MNCs could be interested in escaping from countries with high environmental standards.

Despite the popularity of this argument, there is little evidence of the existence of such pollution havens. Most investment decisions are not made on the basis of environmental criteria. As environmental costs represent less than 2 per cent of the GDP in the industrialized countries, it is difficult to imagine that they have any significant weight in location decisions.

Furthermore, countries which operate transparent and efficient environmental programmes are often quite successful in attracting new investment. Countries with high environmental standards are the major producers and exporters of most environmentally sensitive goods and have the highest living standards. If anything, the imposition of higher environmental standards seems more likely to generate a technological response than to lead to capital mobility (OECD, 1998).

However, in particular sectors, such as chemicals, oil, steel, mining or cement, the costs of complying with more stringent environmental regulations might be greater and therefore might play a more significant role in the decision-making process. In these sectors there is a common fear that some developing countries may use lower environmental standards to attract new FDI, and that by lowering their environmental standards, or by just not raising them, some countries could gain competitive advantages over others.

There is also some tendency for certain types of firms in specific industries to seek cost relief related to environmental parameters. This tendency will be highest in those industries whose products are undifferentiated and which are most subject to small (and environment-based) cost differences. Although the fear of a general 'race to the bottom' in environmental standards, based on competitiveness concerns, may be somewhat exaggerated, there are a few sectors of the economy in some countries where such a race may well be taking place, but this does not seem to be the general case (OECD, 1998).

Regarding the present position, it has increasingly been argued that FDI can facilitate access to environmentally sound technologies that might result in a technology-based improvement for the host country's environment. Furthermore, FDI may lead to some standardization of technologies used across countries and may also promote the diffusion of environmentally friendly technologies through the expansion of environmental goods and services (OECD, 1998).

As some MNCs are at the frontier in research on, and the application of, pollution-prevention technologies, their affiliates may play a positive role in diffusing these technologies in developing countries. Pollution-prevention measures have economic as well as environmental advantages over more conventional solutions ('end-of-pipe' treatments). According to many observers, pollution-prevention technologies may not only be less costly than end-of-pipe treatment. They may also generate, in some cases, additional monetary benefits. Hence, it comes as no surprise that they have been warmly received in developing countries, where social problems such as poverty or unemployment can only be mitigated in a context of sustained and sustainable economic growth. The idea is, thus, to shift from a corrective approach to a preventive one in environmental management.

The development of an innovatory capability to find preventive solutions for pollution problems in the productive sector should be, therefore, a key element in making this fundamental change (Chudnovsky et al, 1997) and an integral part of any policy framework aimed at developing a national system of innovation.

In so far as MNCs move from end-of-pipe towards pollution-prevention environmental management approaches, they may not only employ pollution-prevention technologies in their affiliates in developing countries, but they may also influence the environmental management of their affiliates' suppliers, competitors and customers, both by setting an example and by introducing their own environmental standards. Furthermore, the parent companies may also provide local engineers and technical staff with training in pollution-prevention technologies and practices and waste minimization (O'Connor and Turnham, 1992; UNCTAD, 1993).

In this sense, a key question is whether MNCs follow the same environmental standards applied in their home country when operating abroad (regardless of the host country's own environmental regulations), and if their affiliates in developing countries may or may not impose those standards on their suppliers and subcontractors.

There are several examples of MNCs which apply the same environmental standards in affiliates operating abroad as in their home country, but these tend to be corporations operating in several industrial and service branches,[5] rather than those involved in the exploitation of the natural resources. In fact, the liberalization of FDI may encourage some MNCs to rely on the export of domestic natural resources without due regard to the limits of sustainability.

Furthermore, MNCs generally do not employ in developing countries the same technologies they use in their headquarters or in their affiliates in developed countries. A survey of 80 MNCs (Levy, 1995) found that the adoption of cost-effective and environmentally friendly practices such as pollution prevention or 'eco-efficiency' had no significant relationship with environmental performance. These findings leave MNCs open to the charge that they avoid costly environmental investments and perhaps engage in 'window-dressing' in their environmental practices.

Even when MNCs do impose codes of conduct on their affiliates abroad, these codes may not be requested of their suppliers or subcontractors. As many MNCs no longer own and operate the plants in which some components of their products are being made, they subcontract the production of some goods and act as global distributors. This decoupling has prompted MNCs to assert that they are not responsible for the environmental conditions or wage levels in factories that manufacture parts of their products (Kolodner, 1994). Nevertheless, some companies do impose codes of conduct on their subcontractors, which can have a positive spillover on local conditions. Such codes of conduct may go beyond environmental issues to cover also ethical, health and safety standards.

Bearing all these points in mind, it is important to pay attention to the situation in LIDCs where environmental priorities and FDI characteristics differ widely from the other developing countries. LIDCs are generally resource-based, with a weak industrial sector and with large proportions of the population living in conditions of extreme poverty. The environmental problems confronting LIDCs generally belong to the 'brown agenda' – ie, problems mostly generated by poverty, and which represent a threat to human health and life: lack of drinking water and sewage systems, pollution of water flows, erosion of soil resources and deforestation (mainly as a result of the use of wood for fuel).

Therefore, researchers analysing the effects of FDI on the environment in the LIDCs need to be aware of the environmental conditions prevailing in the country in question, and to take into account not only strictly environmental problems, but also issues related to social and economic development, such as sanitary conditions, education and poverty indicators.

Environmental regulations in developing countries tend to be more lax, in general, than in developed countries. This fact should be taken into account when studying the relationship between FDI and the environment in these countries. As previously stated, low environmental standards and poor levels of enforcement may become an incentive for investment decisions in certain sectors, such as mining and other resource-based activities. Thus, the regulatory environmental framework and its enforcement should also be taken into account in any assessment on this subject.

As already mentioned, most FDI directed to LIDCs is resource-seeking. As local regulations are less strict and less strictly enforced than in MNCs' home countries, the environmental impact of MNCs' operations to a great extent depend on the age of the facilities, on their own environmental performance and the imposition of standards and codes of conduct not only in affiliates but also on their suppliers and subcontractors.

If MNCs apply higher environmental standards in their operations than those required by local regulations, or even simply comply with such regulations, there might be a positive spillover, not only on the environment and social welfare of the host country, but also on the technological upgrading of national firms and competitors. But as this is not always the case, special attention should be given to the way that MNCs operate, taking into account working conditions and the way that natural resources are harvested. MNCs may have a negative social development impact through 'resource degradation'.

The mining sector provides a good case study for the analysis of the relationship between FDI and the environment in LIDCs. Mining is considered a highly polluting activity, largely because the environmental impacts of mining are often dramatic and obvious. The main environmental impacts of mining are: surface and underground water pollution, air pollution, solid waste, loss of flora and fauna habitats due to excavation and the damaging effects on human health and buildings of noise and vibration (UNCTAD, 1997b).

Government regulations covering new mining projects are relatively recent in most countries and, indeed, do not exist in many developing countries. The absence of legislation can result in environmentally harmful operations in many mining sites in developing countries, not to mention poor working conditions and safety standards. Moreover, although some developing countries have adopted administrative regulations related to products, technology or emissions standards, in many cases these regulations have proved to be legally or practically unenforceable, to be technically difficult to monitor and generally to have an insufficient deterrent effect (UNCTAD, 1997b).

Since mining implies only a temporary use of the land, there is one issue of special concern to developing countries related to the mineral sector's sustainability that should be taken into account: the rehabilitation, restoration and reclamation of mining sites. Rehabilitation refers to the processes where unavoidable impacts on the environment are repaired, and suggests returning the site to a stable and permanent use in accordance with a pre-mine plan. These processes include revegetation with native species and the restitution of topsoil (Clark, 1997). Restoration denotes returning to the conditions existing prior to mining activities, if possible, whereas reclamation is a less stringent concept implying that land disturbed by mining activities should be returned to the approximate pre-mine use when economically and technically feasible (Marsh, 1997). The conditions under which MNCs may engage in these kinds of activities should be included in studies of the mining sector.

The logging sector may also be a good case to study in analysing the relationship between FDI and the environment. Although deforestation in many LIDCs is a result of the use of fuel wood and the conversion of forest into cropland, there are cases where MNCs' operations have been devastating. Some examples of this can be found in MNCs' contribution to deforestation in Gabon or the Congo where they control, respectively, 90 per cent and 77 per cent of commercial logging. Such logging activities entail negative externalities such as the rapid run-off of rainwater, leading to flooding and the loss of topsoil (Kolodner, 1994).

However, some changes may be occurring in MNCs' practices, partly because of increasing public pressure but also as a result of the growing implementation of environmental management systems and internal or external environmental audits by many corporations. There are also conditionalities for credit access aimed at ensuring good environmental practices that are being required by international finance institutions and commercial banks, putting extra pressure on MNCs to improve their environmental performance. It is important to verify how these recent changes are applied in actual operations in LIDCs, especially in new undertakings.

When studying the impact of FDI on the environment in more advanced developing countries, other factors should be taken into account. As income rises, some environmental problems are likely to be attenuated, and eventually disappear, while others increase. In the first group are the problems associated with the lack of infrastructure, such as sewage systems and the supply of drinking water. In the second group are the environmental problems related to higher levels of development and industrialization, such as industrial emissions, toxic waste and urbanization.

It is also possible that there will be greater demands for environmental quality at higher income levels. As income rises, more pressure for environmental regulations may appear, demanding more environmental protection and higher levels of enforcement. Pressure for more stringent environmental regulations may also occur at the international level, where industrialized countries demand the implementation of international environmental standards as a way of preventing the creation of pollution havens and eventual losses in the international competitiveness of their own products.

In industrialized countries, the diffusion of pollution-prevention technologies plays a crucial role in improving the environmental performance of the production sector without lowering its competitiveness. Special attention should thus be paid to this issue and to the role played by MNCs' affiliates in this respect. At the same time, there is a crucial need to develop the knowledge and expertise to handle technological change among local firms to take advantage of environmental spillovers from MNCs' affiliates and to accomplish the organizational changes required if they are to move towards pollution-prevention technologies.

This analysis should be made for both resource-seeking investments (eg mining) and market-seeking investments. In both cases, it would be useful to compare, where appropriate, the environmental management systems and performance of MNCs' affiliates and those of local firms, as well as internal-market oriented investments and export-oriented ones. Again, a key issue is whether MNCs' affiliates are 'environmental islands' or whether they diffuse their environmental systems and technologies to their suppliers, customers and competitors.

Policy and Institutional Framework for Enhancing the Contribution of FDI to Development

In recent years, restrictions on FDI have been substantially reduced in the majority of countries. As stated before, many governments have also implemented incentive regimes designed to attract FDI. Since incentives can be more easily manipulated by governments than other factors which influence investment decisions, the 'incentives-led' competition for FDI makes some sense (Aranda and Sauvant, 1996).

This competition for FDI is not necessarily bad in itself. The problem is the form that it assumes in many cases. Host governments are often only interested in the quantity of FDI, paying little, if any attention to the externalities which it generates or to its impact on income distribution or the environment, for example. Furthermore, there has been criticism of the use of incentives as the predominant tool for attracting FDI.

Even if 'rules-based competition' may appear as a better alternative for attracting FDI, since it gives less room for bribery and corruption, this kind of competition includes a broad and heterogeneous group of government actions which could include the lowering of standards regarding workers' rights or environment protection – with obvious negative effects in terms of SHD – but also the signing of regional integration treaties or the strengthening of judicial systems (Oman, 1998).

Different surveys on this issue suggest that there are more influential determinants of FDI attraction – namely, host market size and rate of growth, physical and communications infrastructure, and the quality of human resources – than fiscal or financial incentives. These other determinants of FDI are especially important when governments are trying to attract high-quality FDI, from which substantial externalities could be obtained in terms of employment, human resources upgrading, value-added exports, technology and the enhancement of environmental performance. It is acknowledged, however, that incentives can be important in the margin, when MNCs are choosing among a short list of fairly similar alternative locations in a given country.

Nonetheless, there seem to be some successful examples of a promotional policy for FDI based on fiscal and financial incentives. The first step in designing policies to attract and enhance the contribution of FDI in developing countries is to study the preconditions for this success, and the modalities and objectives of the instruments implemented. The example of Ireland is useful in this respect. From the 1980s onwards, Ireland's FDI policy was based on: (1) selecting leading, high value-added industries (electronics, software, medical instruments, financial services, etc); (2) creating specialized industrial clusters in designated locations; and (3) promoting links with domestic firms (UNCTAD, 1998). The FDI policy included, among other things, grants for establishing R&D facilities. At the same time, fiscal and financial incentives were not the only factors in attracting FDI; education and training efforts were fostered by the Irish Government to upgrade the qualifications of the labour force.

As for the East Asian 'tigers', Lall (1997) illustrates the different policy approaches followed with regards to FDI and describes some cases in which a policy for guiding or selecting FDI has been successfully implemented. Singapore has probably the world's highest reliance on FDI. The Singaporean Government has intervened to guide MNCs to higher valued-added activities and has developed an educational structure designed to provide the technical skills required for such activities. Besides financing R&D expenditure by private firms, the government has also established an impressive technological and scientific infrastructure in the targeted sectors.

Taiwan Republic of China offers an example of an approach to FDI which has also tried to benefit from the technological capabilities of MNCs. The promotion of linkages with domestic firms, especially small and medium enterprises (SMEs), has been one of the elements of this policy. The strategy also targeted industries where domestic capabilities were insufficient, but which were considered strategic by the government.

Of course, these kinds of intervention are prone to failure as well. From an institutional point of view, they not only involve the capacity to identify desirable objectives, design the instruments to attain them and implement the policies, but they also require monitoring of the results of the policies and the authority to discipline private firms when their performance does not fulfil the objectives of the policy. They also often imply, especially when complex incentives packages are involved, policy coordination at various levels of government. Another danger is that excessive competition for FDI could result in an excessive transfer of rents to MNCs (Aranda and Sauvant, 1996; Haaland and Wooton, 1998). These arguments reveal the need for a cautious balance between the costs and benefits of these kinds of policies.

To accomplish this task, profound institutional transformations are needed in most developing countries, and especially in LIDCs. In this sense, it has been suggested that developing countries should move from incentives-based towards rules-based competition, without impairing their domestic labour or environmental standards (Oman, 1998). This suggestion also makes sense considering that rules-based competition may not only benefit MNCs, but may also enhance the country's structural competitiveness and significantly contribute to SHD objectives.

This institutional capacity-building should be the first step in designing new FDI policies to attract FDI and maximize the potential benefits which MNCs can offer. Besides the need for this kind of institution-building, developing countries must take into account the evolving international policy framework. The Agreement on Trade-related Investment Measures and other agreements within the framework of the WTO constrain the use of some policy instruments, but they leave some options open for developing countries and especially for LIDCs.

Regarding a possible multilateral agreement on investment (MAI), Ganesan (1998) has suggested that developing countries, if they decide to take part in the negotiation of an MAI, or a similar kind of multilateral instrument, must try to ensure that it takes adequate care of their developmental, as well as political and social, needs and concerns. One of the key issues requiring the special attention of developing countries is that of performance requirements and investment incentives. Developing countries must try to preserve some flexibility so that they can employ some instruments which could be helpful for their developmental needs. This implies that, at least for some time, this group of countries should be exempted from some of the clauses of any MAI.

For that objective to be attained, developing countries face the difficult task of preparing for long collective negotiations which will place an extra burden on them as they work towards institutional transformation. International technical assistance could help developing countries to strengthen their capacity to evaluate and negotiate the options which are best suited to their interests.

A Framework for Policy-related Country Studies

Since most developing countries have been actively trying to attract FDI and, at the same time, have implemented structural reforms programmes which include trade liberalization, state enterprises privatization, capital account liberalization, etc, the microeconomic analysis of FDI cannot be isolated from the macroeconomic and sectoral changes that the country studies will deal with as well.

Taking into account the focus of the UNCTAD/UNDP programme for which this chapter has been prepared, FDI is a convenient entry point to examine the impact of macroeconomic and sectoral changes upon domestic enterprise development, employment and environment.

The arguments presented in this chapter call for a systemic approach to analyse the relationship between FDI and growth and Sustainable Human Development. Thus, instead of analysing each topic separately (competitiveness, technology, employment, environment, etc), they should be jointly approached in the country case studies. At the same time, a dynamic, historical and institutional analysis of the impact of FDI is required.

The main issues to be addressed in country studies *before, during and eventually after* the key structural reforms have been implemented are as follows:

- The contribution of FDI to host country structural competitiveness in terms of increasing the number of export items or providing more value added to actual exports (both at product level and at main clusters), backward and forward linkages and/or growing imports (capital goods, intermediate products, consumer goods).
- The impact of FDI-related technology transfer both on affiliates technological capabilities and on domestic enterprise and institutions innovatory capabilities. If possible, the case studies will compare FDI-related technology transfer with other forms of technology transfer such as licensing agreements, consultancy and engineering services.
- The direct and indirect impact of different forms of FDI on employment creation or reduction and on gender issues, as well as its impact on income distribution.
- The environmental management practices of foreign affiliates, the factors accounting for the adoption of environmentally friendly technologies and the spillover effects on domestic suppliers, competitors and clients.

An analysis of the policy framework within which MNCs have been doing business in the host country is crucial in any attempt to determine the actual impact of FDI on growth and SHD. In this connection, it is not only the impact of macroeconomic policies, trade and FDI liberalization and privatization that should be assessed. Specific policies to assist domestic firms and especially SMEs in adapting to the new rules, the enforcement of environmental regulations, training and human resource development programmes and the technology policies in force should also be examined. Furthermore, the institutional framework within which policy is designed, applied and enforced should be taken into account especially.

As mentioned above, for host countries to reap most of the potential benefits which could arise from the presence of MNCs, a social or absorptive capability is needed. Empirical evidence shows, in turn, that this capability is often insufficient in most developing countries. Thus, the policy agenda must include several instruments aimed at creating or enhancing this capability.

Fostering domestic entrepreneurship is a key issue in this respect. For MNCs to develop linkages with local suppliers or to generate spillovers which could be reaped by subcontractors, customers or competitors, it is essential that local enterprises have the human resources, skills and capabilities required to take advantage of these spillovers or to qualify as a supplier for MNCs' affiliates.

In this respect, instruments geared towards enhancing the technological, marketing and productive capabilities of domestic firms (especially those of SMEs) are a crucial component of any policy towards MNCs, if this policy is to go beyond merely attracting FDI and try to maximize its net social benefits in host countries.

There are few, if any, historical examples of FDI-led development strategies (Singapore being the exception that proves the rule). Even if SMEs' growth is obviously a key element in any successful development story, most countries that were latecomers to industrialization have a handful of domestic conglomerates with a key presence in the domestic economy, and which have often themselves become MNCs. Fostering domestic entrepreneurship implies, thus, not only a policy on SMEs, but also, especially in medium- or high-income developing countries, nurturing these domestic conglomerates which can be not only suppliers and customers, but also partners and competitors for MNCs.

Developing a social or absorptive capability includes many additional issues that deserve to be studied as such and hence are beyond the scope of this exercise. The education and training of human resources is obviously a key element. A good S&T domestic infrastructure is also needed. Institution-building and the creation or development of markets such as capital markets are also crucial.

On the basis of the actual impact of MNC operations, the current policy and institutional framework, the potential opportunities offered by the host country and the policy experiences of other countries, specific recommendations for governments to increase the growth and Sustainable Human Development impact of FDI and foster national capabilities should be made a part of the country studies.

The policy recommendations should be formulated in the light of the conditions under which different horizontal and sectoral policies have worked in selected developed and developing countries or territories (such as Ireland, Singapore or Taiwan Republic of China) to strengthen the competitiveness and technological capabilities of domestic enterprises, and to increase the spillovers effects of MNCs' presence in the host country. The kinds of policies that host countries should put in place in order to achieve these objectives and the institutional capacity-building required to overcome the failures of coordination and government intervention should be assessed in each case.

Such an approach could serve not only to improve public policies in LIDCs, but also to orient the requirements for international cooperation, especially regarding the institutional capacity-building objectives, and the position which developing countries should take in international forums where policies towards MNCs are discussed and negotiated.

To make the proposed studies operational, they should be concentrated on a few key sectors in which FDI has been important in the past. It would be particularly useful, where possible, to study the same sectors in at least two countries, so that a comparative analysis is possible. Country case studies should involve not only

LIDCs, but also more advanced developing countries with a record of successful FDI-related policies, since in this way LIDCs may learn from the experience and public policies applied in more advanced countries. Thus, it would be plausible to choose pairs of countries (a country in the LIDC group and a more advanced developing country) which share some basic characteristics – geographic location, culture, language, etc.

Country case studies should begin with a brief overview of the economy in terms of the level of development, productive and social structure, recent macroeconomic evolution and basic economic policy framework, with special emphasis on trade and investment regimes and any recent changes in them. Basic data on the evolution and composition of exports and imports and indicators of the revealed comparative advantage should be provided. It would also be important to collect a broad range of indicators as well as to review the available evidence on key social, environmental, technological and developmental issues, although it is well known that such information is scarce in developing countries, and especially in LIDCs (in Appendix 3.2 a summary of the main data and information required is presented).

Country case studies should focus on the most significant operations of MNCs in each case. EPZs, mining projects and tourism are obvious candidates in LIDCs. In medium- or high-income developing countries, mining could be a plausible alternative in some cases. Some manufacturing activities as well as the evolution of some privatized public utilities sectors should also be included. The findings of these studies would be useful for LIDCs, since they would allow those countries to anticipate the problems and opportunities they are likely to face in their economic development process.

Data should be compiled on the various aspects of how FDI and MNCs have affected and may sustain the competitiveness of the sector, including market orientation, technological development, organization of production and the development of linkages. The international configuration of the industries/services pertinent to the cases studied should be examined, and a profile of leading MNCs and their investment strategies should be presented.

Appendix 3.1 FDI and SHD: Some Statistical Tests[6]

It is worth examining the general information available on FDI and growth and Sustainable Human Development indicators in developing countries to see if any relationship between those indicators can be detected. To do this, a sample of 88 developing countries was prepared, for which FDI stock, Human and Gender-related Development Indexes (HDI and GDI respectively) and environmental indicators are available; tax havens and transition economies were excluded from the sample.[7] We are fully aware of the limitations of these data – since, for example, FDI stock is not always adequately measured – and of the criticisms which have been raised about HDI and GDI. Thus, the following results should be taken cautiously, and only as a first step of a possible research programme which may complement country case studies.

When the sample was classified according to the importance of FDI stock in GDP, the data suggest a positive correlation between FDI and HDI and GDI levels. At the same time, a higher FDI weight seems to be positively associated with worsening environmental performance, as measured by the energy intensity of GDP, the CO_2 emissions per capita and the deforestation rate (see Table 3.1).

If developing countries are divided into two groups according to whether their per capita GDP is above or below US$1000, the picture for LIDCs is the same as that for all developing countries (Table 3.2a). For the rest of the developing countries, there also seems to be a positive association between FDI and GDI and HDI, although these indicators are very similar for the three groups. In terms of the impact of FDI on the environmental performance, the pattern is difficult to discern, since the three indicators suggest different results (Table 3.2b).

It can also be observed, taking the sample as a whole, as well as the figures in which the LIDCs are separated from the rest of the developing countries, that those countries with higher FDI weighting, also have higher levels of GDP per capita (Tables 3.1 and 3.2).

If a Spearman rank correlation test is applied to these data, it is possible to reject the null hypothesis – which states that there is no association between FDI weight and GDP per capita, GDI and HDI levels – in the case of LIDCs. The null hypothesis can also be rejected for the whole sample in the cases of FDI, GDI and HDI association. However, the null hypothesis cannot be rejected in any of the three cases when high and medium-income developing countries are considered.

Table 3.1 *Main FDI and Sustainable Human Development indicators for developing countries/territories (1997)*

	No of countries/ territories	GDP per cap	HDI	GDI	GDP per unit of energy	CO_2 emissions per cap	Defor- estation rate
Above 20%[1]	27	3985	0.645	0.599	3.40	3.90	1.29
Between 10% and 20%[2]	22	1790	0.597	0.569	3.60	1.26	1.09
Below 10%[3]	39	3366	0.547	0.507	4.91	1.34	1.24

1 Angola, Bolivia, Chad, Chile, Congo, Costa Rica, Egypt, Equatorial Guinea, Fiji, Gabon, Gambia, Guyana, Hong Kong (China), Indonesia, Jamaica, Malaysia, Mexico, Nigeria, Panama, Papua New Guinea, Saudi Arabia, Singapore, Togo, Trinidad and Tobago, Tunisia, Viet Nam and Zambia
2 Barbados, Botswana, Brazil, Brunei, Burkina Faso, Cameroon, China, Colombia, Dominican Republic, Ecuador, Ghana, Guatemala, Honduras, Lebanon, Lesotho, Malawi, Mozambique, Nicaragua, Niger, Oman, Paraguay, Rwanda, Thailand and Yemen
3 Algeria, Argentina, Bangladesh, Burundi, Benin, Central African Republic, Côte d'Ivoire, El Salvador, Ethiopia, Guinea, Guinea-Bissau, Haiti, Jordan, India, Kenya, Kuwait, Madagascar, Mali, Mauritius, Morocco, Myanmar, Nepal, Pakistan, Peru, Philippines, Qatar, Republic of Korea, Senegal, Sri Lanka, Syrian Arab Republic, Turkey, United Republic of Tanzania, Uganda, United Arab Emirates, Uruguay, Venezuela and Zimbabwe

Source: UNCTAD (1997a and 1998); World Bank (1998); and UNDP (1998)

Table 3.2 *Main FDI and Sustainable Human Development indicators for developing countries/territories (1997)*

(a) Countries with GDP per capita below U$S1000

Indicators	Countries with FDI/GDP		
	Below 10%[1]	*Between 10% and 20%*[2]	*Above 20%*[3]
GDP per capita	390	423	505
HDI	0.371	0.437	0.440
GDI	0.353	0.421	0.430
GDP per unit of energy	7.294	4.367	4.525
CO_2 emissions per capita	0.255	0.544	0.589
Deforestation rate	0.760	0.845	1.100

1 Angola, Bolivia, Chad, Guyana, Gambia, Nigeria, Pakistan, Papua New Guinea, Republic of Congo, Togo, Vietnam and Zambia

2 Cameroon, China, Ghana, Honduras, Lesotho, Malawi, Mozambique, Nicaragua, Niger, Rwanda and Yemen

3 Central African Republic, Côte d'Ivoire, Bangladesh, Benin, Burundi, Burkina Faso, Ethiopia, Guinea, Guinea-Bissau, Haiti, India, Kenya, Madagascar, Mali, Myanmar, Nepal, Senegal, Sri Lanka, Tanzania, Uganda and Zimbabwe

(b) Countries/territories with GDP per capita above U$S1000

Indicators	Countries/Territories with FDI/GDP		
	Below 10%[1]	*Between 10% and 20%*[2]	*Above 20%*[3]
GDP per capita	5729	3156	6377
HDI	0.745	0.757	0.780
GDI	0.709	0.703	0.714
GDP per unit of energy	2.433	2.738	2.629
CO_2 emissions per capita	2.833	2.075	5.793
Deforestation rate	1.767	1.438	1.562

1 Algeria, Argentina, El Salvador, Jordan, Kuwait, Mauritius, Morocco, Philippines, Peru, Korea, Syria, Turkey, United Arab Emirates, Uruguay and Venezuela

2 Barbados, Botswana, Brazil, Colombia, Dominican Republic, Ecuador, Guatemala, Lebanon, Oman, Paraguay and Thailand

3 Chile, Costa Rica, Egypt, Equatorial Guinea, Fiji, Gabon, Hong Kong (China), Indonesia, Jamaica, Malaysia, Mexico, Panama, Singapore, Saudi Arabia, Trinidad and Tobago, and Tunisia

Source: UNCTAD (1997a and 1998), World Bank (1998) and UNDP (1998)

Regarding environmental performance, the only indicator for which the null hypothesis can be rejected is that based on CO_2 emissions per capita (Table 3.3).

When the impact of FDI growth on Sustainable Human Development indicators is estimated for the period 1980–1995, there seems to be a positive association between FDI growth and improving HDI indicators for LIDCs, as shown in Table 3.4a;[8] it should be emphasised that those countries with higher FDI growth also had higher levels of HDI at the beginning of the period (1980). At the same time, higher FDI growth seems to be associated not only with higher CO_2 emissions, but

Table 3.3 *Correlation tests between FDI and main Sustainable Human Development indicators*

	Countries with GDP per capita		Total
	Above US$1000	*Below US$1000*	
GDP per capita			
r^2	0.13	0.31	0.19
Sample size	44	44	88
Decision[2]	Do not reject Ho	**Reject Ho**	Do not reject Ho
HDI			
r^2	0.18	0.38	0.25
Sample size	44	43	87
Decision	Do not reject Ho	**Reject Ho**	**Reject Ho**
GDI			
r^2	0.13	0.36	0.23
Sample size	44	43	87
Decision	Do not reject Ho	**Reject Ho**	**Reject Ho**
GDP per unit of energy			
r^2	−0.09	−0.15	−0.16
Sample size	37	38	75
Decision	Do not reject Ho	Do not reject Ho	Do not reject Ho
CO_2 emissions per cap			
r^2	0.35	0.47	0.36
Sample size	37	39	76
Decision	**Reject Ho**	**Reject Ho**	**Reject Ho**
Deforestation rate			
r^2	−0.04	0.26	0.10
Sample size	37	39	76
Decision	Do not reject Ho	Do not reject Ho	Do not reject Ho

1 Spearman rank correlation test: $r_S = 1 - (6\Sigma d_i^2)/[n(n^2 - 1)]$
d_i = range y_i − range x_i
y_1 = FDI/GDP (1995)
x_1 = gdp per capita, HDI, etc
2 Ho: no correlation exists between ranges
Level of significance: 0.05

also with greater energy efficiency. In the case of medium- and high-income developing countries, those with low or medium FDI growth are those where the HDI indicators have grown faster. They are also those countries where environmental performance seems to have been deteriorating more rapidly, especially in terms of CO_2 emissions per capita and deforestation (Table 3.4b).

Taken as a whole, these findings suggest a positive correlation between FDI and GDP per capita, HD and GD indicators, at least for the group of LIDCs. At the

Table 3.4 Evolution of sustainable human development and FDI indicators for developing countries/territories (1980–1995)

(a) Countries with GDP per capita below US$1000

Growth of FDI/GDP	HDI			GDP per unit of energy			CO_2 emissions per capita			Defor rate
	1980	1995	% growth	1980	1995	% growth	1980	1995	% growth	1990–95
High growth[1]	0.303	0.432	42	3.13	3.97	27	0.68	0.80	19	0.85
Medium growth[2]	0.296	0.401	36	5.75	4.86	–15	0.30	0.32	8	1.01
Low growth[3]	0.275	0.380	38	7.58	7.39	–3	0.26	0.28	4	0.76

1 Growth of more than 15 per cent: Angola, Chad, China, Gambia, Lesotho, Nigeria, Pakistan, Papua New Guinea, Congo, Vietnam and Zambia
2 Growth of between 5 and 15 per cent: Bolivia, Cameroon, Ghana, Guinea-Bissau, Honduras, Malawi, Mozambique, Nicaragua, Niger, Tanzania, Rwanda, Togo, Uganda, Yemen
3 Growth of less than 5 per cent: Bangladesh, Benin, Burkina Faso, Burundi, Central African Republic, Ethiopia, Guinea, Haiti, India, Kenya, Madagascar, Mali, Myanmar, Nepal, Senegal, Sri Lanka, Côte d'Ivoire, Zimbabwe

(b) Countries/territories with GDP per capita above US$1000

Growth of FDI/GDP	HDI			GDP per unit of energy			CO_2 emissions per capita			Defor rate
	1980	1995	% growth	1980	1995	% growth	1980	1995	% growth	1990–95
High growth[1]	0.646	0.790	22	2.76	2.56	–7	4.87	5.46	12	1.35
Medium growth[2]	0.561	0.722	29	2.91	2.40	–17	1.47	2.08	42	1.77
Low growth[3]	0.618	0.786	27	2.76	2.89	5	2.25	3.21	43	1.88

1 Growth of more than 10 per cent : Brazil, Chile, Costa Rica, Egypt, Ecuador, Gabon, Hong Kong, Indonesia, Jamaica, Malaysia, Mexico, Oman, Saudi Arabia, Singapore, Trinidad and Tobago, and Tunisia
2 Growth of between 5 and 10 per cent: Colombia, Dominican Republic, Guatemala, Jordan, Morocco, Panama, Paraguay, Peru, Philippines, Turkey, Thailand, United Arab Emirates and Venezuela
3 Growth of less than 5 per cent: Algeria, Argentina, Barbados, Botswana, El Salvador, Kuwait, Lebanon, Mauritius, South Korea, Syria and Uruguay
Source: UNCTAD (1997a and 1998), World Bank (1998) and UNDP (1998)

same time, a negative correlation between FDI and environmental indicators appears, which seems to be particularly strong when CO_2 emissions are considered.

However, no causal relationship can be deduced from these findings. They do not indicate, for instance, whether FDI contributes in a positive manner to HD or whether higher HD indicators attract more FDI. Nonetheless, it is interesting to observe that FDI growth has been higher in the group of countries where, at the beginning of the period under analysis, HDI levels were, on average, higher. This suggests that a feedback process between HDI and FDI growth may have been taking place.

Appendix 3.2 Basic Information Required for Country Case Studies

- *Host economy's structure:* GDP rate of growth; GDP per capita evolution; sectoral composition of GDP; most dynamic productive branches in recent years; sectoral competitiveness levels; relevant domestic clusters or networks.
- *Foreign trade:* export and import rates of growth and volumes; sectoral composition of exports; share of resource-based and/or environmentally sensible exports; imports composition; geographic pattern of foreign trade.
- *Information on FDI:* country of origin of foreign firms; FDI sectoral destination; greenfield investments and takeovers; FDI by newcomers and by existing firms; impact of FDI on the balance of payments (exports, imports, profit remittances, intracompany loans, etc).
- *Factors that attract FDI inflows:* size and rate of growth of the domestic market; economic and political stability; cost and availability of natural resources; exchange rate regimes; cost and quality of human resources; transport, communication and technological infrastructure; trade and FDI regimes; regional trade agreements; privatization of state enterprises; export processing zones; sectoral or regional policies; fiscal or financial incentives for FDI.
- *Labour and social issues:* wages structure; rates of employment and unemployment; labour market inequality (labour and capital shares in value-added, skilled and unskilled labour force earnings, gender differentials); income distribution; rates of poverty; child labour; labour standards; presence of precarious or informal forms of employment.
- *Environment:* basic environmental indicators (air pollution, water contamination, hazardous waste, solid waste, etc); in the case of LIDCs, indicators and information on deforestation and on the environmental impacts of mining activities should receive special attention.
- *Technology and innovation:* imports and, if available, local production of machinery and equipment by type of machinery and sector of destination; payments for licences and fees and consultancy services; patents and trade mark applications and registrations; data and information about innovative activities by national or foreign firms as well as about the activities of S&T institutes. For further mapping of the national systems of innovation, it would be important to collect information

on: employment (by skills and sex) and turnover of research institutions; enrolment levels in secondary and tertiary education; numbers of university graduates in different disciplines; brain drain; labour-force composition in private firms (unskilled vs skilled workers, technical and scientific personnel, etc).

- *Sectoral information:* production, sales, exports, imports and apparent consumption; employment (of different skills and gender); investment; environmental management and emissions; regional location; productivity levels (by size and type of the ownership of the firm).

Notes

1   CENIT, Buenos Aires. Comments from the participants at the Experts meeting held in Geneva in February 1999 are gratefully acknowledged. The usual caveats apply

2   MNCs may be reluctant to engage in arm's-length technology transfer or to associate with domestic firms. As for reverse engineering or copying, the international legal framework seems to have been moving for many years towards a more stringent enforcement of intellectual and industrial property rights

3   In their restructuring process, domestic firms should certainly rely on foreign technological and organizational inputs (see below), which may include the non-controlling participation of MNCs

4   The useful research assistance of Sebastian Rubin in this section is acknowledged

5   Even in these sectors, only the largest MNCs operate with the same environmental production standards in all their locations, to preserve the corporate image and to avoid the possibility of being sanctioned in their home countries (Jha and Teixeira, 1994)

6   The useful research assistance of Silvana Melitsko in preparing the material of this section is acknowledged.

7   Transition economies are excluded because of the lack of data.

8   When the Spearman rank correlation test was applied to these data, it was not possible to reject the null hypothesis

References

Abramovitz, M (1986) 'Catching up, Forging Ahead, and Falling Behind', *Journal of Economic History,* June

Albuquerque, E (1997) 'National Systems of Innovation and non-OECD Countries: Notes about a Rudimentary and Tentative "Typology"', paper presented at the Annual Conference of the European Association for Evolutionary Political Economy (EAEPE), Athens, November

Aranda, V and K P Sauvant (1996) *Incentives and Foreign Direct Investment*, UNCTAD, Current Studies, Series A, No 30, Geneva

Blomstrom, M and A Kokko (1997) 'How Foreign Investment Affects Host Countries', World Bank, International Trade Division, Policy Research Working Paper 1745

Buckley, P and M Casson (1993) 'Multinational Enterprises in Less-developed Countries: Cultural and Economic Interactions', in S Lall (ed) *Transnational Corporations and Economic Development,* United Nations Library on TNCs, vol 3, London, Routledge

Chudnovsky, D, A López and V Freylejer (1997) 'Environmental Management in Argentine Industry: the Diffusion of Pollution Prevention Measures', Final Report of the Project on Competitiveness, Technological Innovation and Sustainable Development: Case Studies in the Argentine Manufacturing Sector, IDRC/North South Center of the University of Miami/ Avina Foundation

Chudnovsky, D and A López (1998) 'La Inversión Directa Extranjera en la Argentina en los Años 1990: Tendencias, Determinantes y Modalidades', in Argentina, Ministerio de Relaciones Exteriores, Comercio Internacional y Culto, *Argentina de Cara al Mundo III,* Buenos Aires

Clark, I (1997) 'Rehabilitation of Mining Sites', in *Environmental Policies, Regulations and Management Practices in Mineral Resources Development in Asia and the Pacific,* United Nations, Mineral Resources Assessment, Development and Management Series, vol 2

Dahlman, C, B Ross-Larson and L Westphal (1987) 'Managing Technological Development: Lessons from the Newly Industrializing Countries', *World Development,* vol 15, no 6

Dunning, J (1993) *Multinational Enterprises and the Global Economy,* Addison-Wesley, Wokingham, England

Dunning, J (1994) 'Re-evaluating the benefits of foreign direct investment', *Transnational Corporations,* vol 3, no 1

Dunning, J, R Van Hoesel and R Narula (1997) 'Third World Multinationals Revisited: New Developments and Theoretical Implications', Discussion Papers in International Investment and Management, no 227, University of Reading, UK

Edquist, C (ed) (1997) *Systems of Innovation: Technologies, Institutions and Organizations,* London, Pinter

Ernst, D, T Ganiatsos and L Mytelka (1998*) Technological Capabilities and Export Success in Asia,* Routledge, London

Ganesan, A V (1998) 'Strategic Options Available to Developing Countries with Regard to a Multilateral Agreement on Investment', Geneva, UNCTAD Discussion Paper no 134

Haaland, J and I Wooton (1998) 'International Competition for Multinational Investment', paper presented at the Conference on Competition and Industrial Policies in Open Economies, Bergen, May

ILO (1998) 'Labour and Social Issues Relating to Export Processing Zones', International Labour Organization, Geneva

Jha, V and A P Teixeira (1994) 'Are Environmentally Sound Technologies the Emperor's New Clothes?' Geneva, UNCTAD, Discussion Paper no 89

Katz, J (1998) 'Structural Reforms and Technological Behaviour. The Sources and Nature of Technological Change in Latin America in the 1990s', paper presented at the seminar on 'The Economics of Industrial Structure and Innovation Dynamics', INTECH, Lisbon, October

Kolodner, E (1994) 'Transnational Corporations: Impediments or Catalysts of Social Development?', Occasional Paper no 5, World Summit for Social Development, United Nations Research Institute for Social Development

Lall, S (1983) *The New Multinationals. The Spread of Third World Enterprises,* London, Wiley/ IRM

Lall S (1997) 'East Asia', in J Dunning (ed), *Governments, Globalization and International Business,* Oxford, Oxford University Press

Lawler, J (1995) 'Multinational Firms, National Culture, and Gender-based Employment Discrimination', working paper, Institute of Labor and Industrial Relations, University of Illinois

Levy, D (1995) 'The Environmental Practices and Performance of Transnational Corporations', *Transnational Corporations*, vol 4, no 1

Marsh, B (1997) 'Successful Reclamation', in *Environmental Policies, Regulations and Management Practices in Mineral Resources Development in Asia and the Pacific*, United Nations, Mineral Resources Assessment, Development and Management Series, vol 2

Narula, R (1997) 'The Role of Developing Country Multinationals in the Acquisition of Industrial Technology in Nigeria', *Science, Technology and Development* , vol 15, no 1

O'Connor, D and D Turnham (1992) 'Managing the Environment in Developing Countries', OECD Development Centre, Paris, Policy Brief No 2

OECD (1992) *Technology and the Economy: The Key Relationships,* OECD, Paris

OECD (1998) 'Foreign Direct Investment and the Environment: An Overview of the Literature', mimeo, prepared for the Negotiating Group on the Multilateral Agreement on Investment, OECD, Paris

Oman, C (1998) 'Policy Competition and Foreign Direct Investment', draft, OECD Development Centre, Paris

South Centre (1997) 'Foreign Direct Investment, Development and the New Global Economic Order. A policy brief for the South', South Centre, Geneva

UNCTAD (1993) 'Report of the Workshop on the Transfer and Development of Environmentally Sound Technologies', Technology Programme, Geneva, UNCTAD

UNCTAD (1994) *World Investment Report 1994: Transnational Corporations, Employment and the Workplace*, New York and Geneva (UNCTAD/DITC/10), United Nations publication, sales no E. 94.II.A.14

UNCTAD (1996) *Fostering Technological Dynamism: Evolution of Thought on Technological Development Processes and Competitiveness: A Review of the Literature*, Geneva, UNCTAD

UNCTAD (1997a) *World Investment Report 1997: Transnational Corporations, Market Structure and Competition Policy*, New York and Geneva, United Nations publication, sales no E. 97. II. D.10

UNCTAD (1997b) 'Management of Commodity Resources in the Context of Sustainable Development: Governance Issues for the Mineral Sector', report by the UNCTAD secretariat

UNCTAD (1998) *World Investment Report 1998. Trends and Determinants*, United Nations publication, sales no E. 98.II D. 5, New York and Geneva

UNDP (1998) *Human Development Report, 1998,* New York

World Bank (1998) *World Development Report, 1998*, New York

4

The Globalization of Market Failure?[1]

James Boyce

Introduction

The economic case for trade liberalization rests on its capacity to extend the reach of the market's fabled invisible hand. As trade barriers are lowered and the world market grows more integrated, producers reallocate land, labour and capital to those economic activities in which they enjoy a comparative advantage, and away from the production of goods and services that now can be more cheaply obtained from others. The result is a larger economic pie, which in principle – if seldom in practice – can benefit all concerned.

With the globalization of the market, however, comes a globalization of market failures, due to the fact that prices do not capture 'external' costs and benefits to third parties. Say that country A produces corn more cheaply than country B, but in so doing generates more pollution. In the absence of countervailing policies, trade liberalization will cause production to shift from country B to country A, with a corresponding increase in pollution and its external costs. Similarly, if producers in country B generate higher positive externalities than those in country A – for example, via the conservation of crop genetic diversity – trade liberalization will erode the supply of these benefits. In both cases, the happy ending of a bigger pie – once the external costs and benefits are counted – can no longer be taken for granted. Whether the social gains from trade liberalization will exceed the social losses from the attendant market failures is an empirical question, one which cannot be answered by theoretical fables.

This chapter considers the impact of trade-driven market failures on sustainable agriculture. By sustainable agriculture I do not refer solely to 'traditional' farming in developing countries, but also to 'modern' farming: both are important to sustaining the supply of food and fibre for current and future generations. Moreover, the boundary between them is increasingly fuzzy as both traditional and modern agriculture evolve and interact through time.

I focus on two important types of market failures. The first is the displacement of natural fibres by synthetic substitutes, resulting from competition in which the higher pollution costs associated with the latter are not internalized in world prices. The second is the erosion of crop genetic diversity, arising from the fact that markets do not reward farmers for their provision of this public good. Section 2 discusses the displacement of natural fibres by synthetics, illustrated by the competition between jute and polypropylene. Section 3 discusses of the erosion of crop genetic diversity, illustrated by the impact of the North American Free Trade Agreement (NAFTA) on Mexican maize farmers. Finally, Section 4 considers some policy implications of the globalization of market failure.

Natural Fibres versus Synthetic Substitutes: The Case of Bangladeshi Jute

Since World War Two, renewable natural raw materials, including cotton, jute, wool, sisal and rubber, have lost international markets to synthetic substitutes. Between 1963 and 1986 substitution by synthetics is estimated to have reduced the consumption of natural raw materials in the industrialized countries by almost half.[2] While the production and consumption of natural raw materials are by no means free of negative environmental impacts, the environmental costs associated with the production and consumption of synthetics typically are considerably larger.

The production of many natural raw materials is concentrated in developing countries (the 'South'), while the production of synthetic substitutes is concentrated in the industrialized countries (the 'North'). Hence the competition between natural raw materials and synthetics pits relatively clean producers in the South against relatively dirty producers in the North – the opposite of what is commonly assumed in discussions of the environmental impacts of North–South trade. The competition between jute and polypropylene is a case in point.

Jute is the second most important natural fibre in world trade after cotton. It has two main end-uses: burlap (also known as hessian) cloth and carpet backing. In recent decades, jute consumption in the industrialized countries has contracted sharply in the face of competition from synthetics. Between 1970 and 1992 the annual jute imports of North America and Western Europe plummeted from 1 million to 52,000 metric tonnes (Thigpen et al, 1987; IJO, 1993). Over the same period the real price of jute declined by roughly 70 per cent.[3]

Bangladesh accounts for roughly 80 per cent of world jute exports (FAO, 1994, p233). With a per capita income of US$220 per year, Bangladesh ranks among the poorest countries in the world. Jute-related activities in agriculture, manufacturing and trade affect the livelihoods of about 25 million Bangladeshis – roughly a quarter of the country's population (World Bank, 1992). Jute cultivation requires 50 per cent more labour per hectare than rice, the principal alternative crop (Hye, 1993). The decline of the international jute market has therefore hit the incomes of some of the world's poorest people.

Polypropylene (PP), the main synthetic substitute for jute, is manufactured primarily in the North, although newly industrializing countries, including Korea, China and Brazil, have now entered the industry. The US is the world's largest producer, followed by Japan (United Nations, 1993). PP producers include multinational firms such as Exxon, Hoechst, Hyundai Petrochemical and Shell (Johnson, 1990).

The price advantage that permits PP to capture and retain the erstwhile markets for jute has been fairly modest. In 1990 the wholesale price ratio of jute to synthetic cloth in New York was 1.35; its average over the preceding decade was 1.42 (World Bank, 1992, p12). The incorporation of environmental costs into the prices of PP and jute could substantially alter this ratio.

The major environmental impacts of PP manufacture are from air pollution and energy consumption. Air pollutants generated in PP production include particulates, sulphur oxides, nitrogen oxides, carbon monoxide and volatile organic compounds, total emissions of which are estimated at 127kg per tonne of PP (Tellus Institute, 1992, p9T-6). In addition, PP production emits smaller amounts of other toxic air pollutants, including ammonia, benzene, biphenyl, ethylbenzene, lead, methane, toluene and xylene (ibid).

Energy use in the production of PP cloth is estimated at 84 gigajoules/tonne, at least six times the energy requirement for production of jute cloth (Braungart, 1992, p89). Carbon dioxide (CO_2) emissions in the PP production process are estimated at 3.7 tonnes per tonne of fibre (ibid, p91). The long-term environmental effects of additions to atmospheric CO_2 derived from fossil carbon remain uncertain, but they include impacts on agriculture, forestry, biodiversity and a rise in sea level. By virtue of its low-lying deltaic terrain, Bangladesh is among the countries that stand to be most adversely affected by the latter (Pearce et al, 1995).

Polypropylene is not biodegradable. Its recycling potential is limited by the use of additives in the production process, and by mixture with other plastics in the collection process (leading to 'downcycling' – reuse in products of inferior quality). At the end of the product life-cycle, PP disposal therefore incurs the costs of landfill storage, incineration or litter. As much as 6 per cent of PP cloth, by weight, is comprised of chemical additives, including stabilizers, colouring pigments and flame retardants (Braungart, 1992, pp66–75). These contain heavy metals, including chromium, copper, lead, nickel and zinc, which also ultimately enter the waste stream (ibid, p66).

The environmental impacts of jute production are relatively modest by comparison. Jute growers use some chemical fertilizer, but not very intensively. Most apply no pesticides at all to the crop. The flooded fields in which jute ripens support diverse fish populations, which play a critical role in the Bangladeshi diet (especially in the diets of the poor). Hence the fact that jute can be grown without reliance on pesticides is an important environmental plus.

Like all plants, jute absorbs CO_2 from the atmosphere when it grows and returns it when it decays. Atmospheric CO_2 is the most important of the greenhouse gases implicated in global warming. Jute thus provides a temporary environmental benefit: it sequesters carbon while in use. The transport and milling of the fibre, and the production and transport of inputs for the crop, generate some CO_2 emissions, but these amount to less than one-sixth of those generated in PP manufacture (Braungart, 1992, pp89–90).

The most serious negative environmental impacts of jute production probably arise in the process known as retting, when the jute stalks are submerged for three to four weeks in ponds where anaerobic microbial decomposition loosens the fibre in the inner bark. Retting causes transitory deterioration in water quality, including oxygen depletion, which can harm gill-breathing fish. The decomposition products are non-toxic, however, and these enhance soil fertility (Alam, 1993, p362). Retting releases methane, a potent greenhouse gas, in quantities that have yet to be measured; technologies to capture the methane for use as biogas fuel are still at an experimental stage.

Environmental impacts in the manufacturing stage of jute production arise primarily from energy consumption, the production of fibre wastes and pollution from dyes. Energy use in jute production is estimated at up to 14 gigajoules/per tonne (Braungart, 1992, p89). Jute dust waste produced during processing amounts to roughly 2 per cent of the fibre, some of which is burned for energy (ibid, p35). Only a small fraction of jute fabrics – around 1–2 per cent – is dyed, but effluent samples from jute-dyeing processes show releases of heavy metals (ibid, pp34, 39).

Jute is biodegradable: at the end of the product life-cycle it decomposes in the soil. Residues from mineral oils used to soften the fibre may persist; conversion to the use of vegetable oils for this purpose would ensure rapid and complete biodegradation (Braungart, 1992, p38).

Several further positive side-effects of jute warrant mention. The edible leaves of the plant provide a cheap (often free) source of food for the poor, and the jute stalks, left after the fibre is stripped away, are a renewable source of cooking fuel and building material. The high labour intensity of jute cultivation also can be regarded a social benefit in a land where agricultural labourers are among the poorest of the world's poor.

To date there have been no comprehensive attempts to evaluate the full range of environmental impacts of jute and PP in economic terms. Elsewhere (Boyce, 1995), however, I have performed exploratory valuations for three major impacts: air pollution, carbon dioxide emissions and solid waste disposal. Table 4.1 summarizes the results, showing how internalization of these costs would affect the relative price of jute and polypropylene.

Air pollution has the greatest impact. The calculations in Table 4.1 include only the high-volume pollutants (particulates, sulphur oxides, nitrogen oxides, carbon monoxide and volatile organics), and not the other toxic air pollutants released in smaller quantities in PP manufacture. The monetary values used to translate these

Table 4.1 *Effect of internalization of environmental costs on relative price of jute and polypropylene*

	Prices ($/1000 yd²)		Price ratio (jute/PP)
	Jute	PP	
Market price (1990)	240	178	1.35
Prices internalizing PP air pollution costs only	240	224	1.07
Prices internalizing CO_2 costs only	242	182	1.33
Prices internalizing non-biodegradable disposal costs only	240	180	1.33
Prices internalizing all of the above	242	230	1.05

Source: Boyce (1995)

emissions into costs are derived from the average values adopted by policy-making agencies in the US as a whole; these are considerably below those used in densely populated and highly polluted regions such as southern California. Carbon dioxide emissions are here valued at US$50 per tonne of carbon.[4] No account is taken of the positive benefit provided by carbon sequestration in jute, on the grounds that in the long run this carbon returns to the atmosphere via biodegradation. Disposal costs at the end of the product life-cycle are based on average tipping fees at landfills in the US.[5]

A more complete analysis of the environmental costs of jute and PP would incorporate other impacts, including the effects of fertilizer run-off and retting on water quality in the case of jute; the impact of methane emissions during jute retting; the impacts of the heavy metals and other chemical additives used in the manufacturing processes of PP and jute; and the impact of other toxic air pollutants emitted in PP production. If, as seems likely, the most economically important of these are the costs associated with emissions of toxic pollutants, due to the use of chemical additives (the quantity of which is greater in PP) and to the other air pollutants released in PP production, then internalization of these costs would further lower the jute/PP price ratio.

The price advantage that has enabled polypropylene to displace jute so dramatically in world markets therefore rests, in no small measure, on the failure of market prices to reflect environmental costs. Correction of this market failure would benefit not only the global environment, but also some of the world's poorest people, the jute growers and agricultural labourers of Bangladesh. The absence of corrective policies, on the other hand, benefits some of the world's largest corporations. The paucity of international attention to the environmental implications of the displacement of natural fibres by synthetics may reflect the power disparities between their producers.

Genetic Diversity: The Case of Mexican Maize

Some five millennia ago, the ancestors of the Mayan farmers in what are now Mexico and Guatemala achieved what must rank, in terms of its cumulative impact on human well-being, among the great technological advances of history: the domestication of maize. Over time, the cultivation of maize spread among the indigenous peoples of the Americas, and with the arrival of the Europeans, it expanded across the globe. Yet the crop's historic centre of origin has remained its centre of genetic diversity, in keeping with the association first postulated in the 1920s by the great Russian botanist, N I Vavilov (Vavilov, 1992).

No worldwide inventory of genetic diversity in maize (or other crops) exists. An indicator of its geographical distribution, however, can be derived from the holdings of the world's most comprehensive gene banks. The number of accessions from a given country, normalized for differences in acreage, provides a rough index of genetic diversity. Although not a perfect measure – gene-bank collections are uneven across countries and some accessions are duplicates – this can provide a useful first approximation.

Table 4.2 presents data on accessions held at the world's premier maize research institute, the International Center for Maize and Wheat Improvement (CIMMYT), near Mexico City. Mexico accounts for about one-third of the gene bank's 13,000 holdings, and the country ranks highest on the diversity index. Guatemala, with only 2.5 per cent of the maize acreage of the US, accounts for almost 14 times as many varieties.

Scientists call the hilly, rain-fed maize plots of south-central Mexico and Guatemala 'evolutionary gardens,' or 'gardens of chaos' (Wilkes, 1992). Here the maize plant continues to evolve under the full pressure of natural selection. As the climate changes, and as new strains of insect pests and plant diseases evolve, the interaction between nature and human purpose in these plots yields a stream of new varieties adapted to the new conditions. The campesino (peasant) farmers of the region thus not only maintain a vast stock of maize varieties, but also manage an on-going flow of new varieties.

Maize is the number one crop in Mexico and the US. In the US it covers one-seventh of the arable land; in Mexico is covers nearly one-third. With average yields of 7.4 metric tonnes per hectare (mt/ha), the US produces roughly 200 million mt of maize annually on roughly 300,000 farms. Mexico, with average yields of 2.0 mt/ha, produces roughly 14 million mt on 2.7 million farms (see Table 4.3). Most US maize is used as animal feed; most Mexican maize is consumed directly by humans.

US production techniques differ dramatically from those of the Mexican campesinos. Half-a-dozen varieties account for almost half of the US maize acreage, and only a few hundred, many of them closely related, are available commercially. With so much area under so few varieties, the US maize crop is highly vulnerable to insect and disease epidemics, as was dramatically illustrated when leaf blight destroyed one-fifth of the nation's harvest in 1970 (Walsh, 1981). To keep ahead of rapidly evolving pests, plant breeders must release a constant stream of new varieties; for this reason, the average commercial lifespan of a maize variety in the US

Table 4.2 *Maize diversity in selected countries*

Country	Number of accessions at CIMMYT	Maize acreage (1992–94 average, 1000 ha)	Genetic diversity index*
Mexico	4,220	7,536	289.8
Brazil	2,508	12,992	146.3
Guatemala	590	709	82.4
Argentina	152	2,430	14.7
United States	43	28,047	2.0
China	25	20,821	1.3
India	4	6,052	0.3
Philippines	3	3,240	0.3
Nigeria	1	1,567	0.1

Source: Boyce (1996)

* Genetic diversity index = $V/A^{0.3}$, where V = number of accessions and A = acreage

Table 4.3 *Corn agriculture in Mexico and the US*

	Mexico	US
Production		
Area (million hectares)	7.3	27.1
Share in total cropland (%)	31.7	14.4
Yield (metric tonnes/ha)	2.0	7.4
Output (million mt)	14.6	201.5
Number of farms (million)	2.7	0.3
Input use		
Area fertilized (%)	70	97
Area under hybrids (%)	33	100
Area irrigated (%)	15	80
Area treated with herbicides (%)	NA	96
Area treated with insecticides (%)	NA	29
Tractors/farm worker	0.02	1.5
Varietal diversity		
Number of varieties available	5000	454
Share of top six varieties (% of area)	NA	43

NA = not available
Source: Boyce (1996)

is only seven years (Duvick, 1984, p164). The ultimate raw material for this varietal relay race is the maize germ plasm originating from the evolutionary gardens of traditional agriculture.[6]

Ninety-six per cent of US maize acreage is treated with herbicides, and about one-third with insecticides. Comparable data are not available for Mexico, but pesticide usage in maize farming there is considerably lower, particularly among small farmers.[7] The herbicides and insecticides applied to US maize have resulted in widespread contamination of groundwater. A survey conducted by the US Environmental Protection Agency (1990) found that atrazine, the most widely used herbicide in cornfields, was present in the water of one in every 60 community water systems and in one in 140 private wells nationwide.[8]

By the price standard of the market, the US produces maize more 'efficiently' than Mexico. When the North American Free Trade Agreement (NAFTA) was being negotiated, US maize cost about US$110 per tonne at the border, while in Mexico maize farmers received US$240 per tonne (Scott, 1992). The Mexican government has long restricted maize imports to protect domestic farmers. This protection is now being phased out over a 15-year period under the terms of NAFTA. The controversial nature of this move within Mexico is reflected by the fact that this is the slowest phase-out of protection for any commodity under the agreement.[9]

The price advantage of US maize has four sources: (1) natural factors – notably, better soils, more regular rainfall and a killing frost that limits pest populations in the US corn belt; (2) farm subsidies that reduce the US market price; (3) the exclusion from market prices of environmental costs such as groundwater contamination, which is of greater importance in the US, where agrochemical use is more intensive, than in Mexico; and (4) the failure of market prices to value the maintenance of genetic diversity by Mexican maize farmers.

NAFTA will not completely eliminate maize production in Mexico. Large-scale Mexican growers on the best soils, many of whom use US-style production techniques – including commercial hybrid varieties, irrigation and intensive agrochemical applications – probably will be able to compete successfully. And very small-scale growers producing solely for their own household consumption might be less sensitive to the market price.[10]

NAFTA is likely to result in a substantial contraction of Mexico's maize acreage in the years ahead, however, as imported US maize displaces domestic production. Much of the abandoned maize land will be converted into cattle pastures, requiring far less labour. Estimates of the number of Mexican maize farmers who will be displaced by US imports vary widely. Relatively conservative estimates predict that hundreds of thousands of campesinos will migrate to Mexican cities (and perhaps to the US) as a result. Upper-end predictions of the number of migrants run as high as 15 million people – one-sixth of the Mexican population.[11]

The extent of campesino displacement could be mitigated by government measures to support the 'modernization' of maize production and diversification to other crops (de Janvry, Sadoulet and Gordillo de Anda, 1995). In a similar vein, Levy and van Wijnbergen (1995) advocate a programme of public investment in land improvements, notably irrigation, to offset losses to Mexican maize farmers. Such support would represent a marked departure from the policy trends of recent years, which have seen cutbacks in marketing, credit and technical assistance services for small farmers. Even if such policies were forthcoming, however, they would not necessarily arrest the erosion of genetic diversity in maize; indeed, they could accelerate it.

In the face of this prospect, only limited comfort can be drawn from the fact that seed samples of many Mexican maize varieties are stored at CIMMYT and several gene banks around the world. It would be difficult to overstate the value of these *ex situ* (off-site) collections. But they do not provide a satisfactory substitute for on-the-ground, *in situ* genetic diversity for three reasons.

First, the gene banks are not completely secure. Accidents happen; so do wars. The seeds must be stored under controlled temperature and humidity conditions, and periodically regenerated by planting to harvest new seed. The world's largest maize germ-plasm collection is at the Vavilov Institute in St Petersburg; the second largest is in Belgrade (Plucknett et al, 1987, p120). Today the viability of the seeds in both collections is an open question. Even in relatively wealthy and stable countries such as the US, plant breeders routinely lament the inadequate funding for seed collection maintenance from financially strapped governments. Irreplaceable material in gene banks has already been lost as a result of human error and mechanical failures. At CIMMYT, for example, maize collections from the 1940s were lost (Wade, 1974, p1187); 'back-up copies' of Mexican maize at the US National Seed Storage Laboratory in Fort Collins, Colorado, were destroyed, as well (Raeburn, 1995, pp62–63).

Second, many genetic attributes of crop varieties can be identified only by growing them in micro-habitats similar to those from which they originated. For example, the fact that a particular Mexican maize variety has a gene which enables it to withstand droughts at four-week intervals will not be apparent unless the plant is grown under those specific conditions. The alternative of expressing such genetic attributes in laboratory growth chambers is extremely costly.

Finally, even if it were possible to establish perfectly secure gene banks (which it is not), these could at best store only the existing stock of genetic diversity at any point in time. The on-going process of evolution, which gave us this diversity and which continues to yield a flow of new varieties, cannot be stored in the bank; it can happen only in the field. Plant breeders can develop new crosses from the existing genetic stock, but they cannot replace the flow of new raw material from the evolutionary gardens.[12]

None of this implies that *ex situ* gene banks are unnecessary. On the contrary, the world needs more gene banks, better funding for them, and more investment in professional training for plant breeders whose knowledge is an essential complement to the gene banks (Wilkes, 1992). Modern plant breeding has played a central role in the rapid growth in world food output in the past 50 years. Moreover, as recent experiences in Nicaragua and Cambodia have shown, *in situ* biodiversity is also vulnerable to losses – due to wars, among other causes – and in these cases *ex situ* collections provide crucial back-up copies (Plucknett et al, 1987, p94). But while necessary, *ex situ* collections are not sufficient to sustain the genetic diversity on which long-term world food security ultimately rests. The gene banks are vital complements to *in situ* biodiversity, but not substitutes for it.

The competition between Mexican and US maize thus entails both positive and negative externalities. The positive externality – the conservation and evolution of crop genetic diversity – is generated south of the border. The negative externalities arising from intensive agrochemical use are concentrated north of the border, although they also characterize 'modern' Mexican maize farming. Under free trade, the Mexican campesinos who generate positive externalities sell at prices that fail to internalize the full social benefit of their production, while US producers sell at prices that fail to internalize the full social cost. The resulting double market failure not only undermines sustainable rural livelihoods in Mexico, but also jeopardizes the long-term sustainability of this key food crop worldwide.

Policy Implications

With the increasing integration of world markets comes a corresponding need for international policy responses to market failures. Unilateral measures by individual governments can have only limited impacts on trade-driven market failures. To confront such problems as the erosion of crop genetic diversity and the displacement of renewable natural raw materials by pollution-intensive synthetic substitutes, multilateral initiatives are necessary.

Such initiatives could advance the goal of sustainable agriculture, with 'sustainability' understood to mean maintaining the production of food and fibre that is sufficient to meet the needs of current and future generations worldwide. By this definition, sustainable agriculture implies neither the worldwide hegemony of 'modern' agriculture nor a romantic return to 'traditional' agriculture. Instead, the world needs both high-productivity, low-diversity 'modern' farming *and* low-productivity, high-diversity 'traditional' farming (and intermediate technologies that combine the two). Productivity is vital for world food security in the short run and for diversity for world food security in the long run.

In the absence of corrective policies, the market rewards only short-run productivity as measured by price. One limitation of this myopic objective was noted by Schumpeter (1976, p83):

> A system – any system, economic or otherwise – that at every point in time fully utilizes its possibilities to the best advantage may yet in the long run be inferior to a system that does so at *no* point in time, because the latter's failure to do so may be a condition for the level of speed of long-run performance.

The role of crop genetic diversity in long-run agricultural performance illustrates Schumpeter's point.

In the discussions of trade and the environment at such multilateral forums as the United Nations Conference on Trade and Development (UNCTAD) and the World Trade Organization (WTO), it is often assumed that negative externalities are more prevalent in the South, while in the North, tougher regulations have led to a greater internalization of environmental costs.[13] The threat of 'environmental dumping' – exports at prices below the full cost of production, including the social costs of pollution – is therefore viewed primarily as a route by which Southern producers may win markets at the expense of their Northern competitors.

The examples discussed in this chapter illustrate the opposite possibility: international trade can result in the displacement of relatively clean and sustainable Southern production by environmentally more costly and less sustainable Northern production. Indeed, if one reflects on the history of international commerce since the Industrial Revolution, it is arguable that the main direction of environmental dumping has been from North to South.

Southern governments have been slow to call for policies that would help them to translate the comparative *environmental* advantages of their farmers into comparative *economic* advantages. In the case of jute, for example, the main response to the challenge from synthetics has been an effort to diversify into new end-uses for the natural fibre. Little serious attempt has been made to defend jute's position in its traditional end-use markets on the basis of its lower environmental costs. In the case of maize, the Mexican government is actually dismantling the quotas, tariffs and price supports that provided some protection to Mexican farmers, reflecting both the government's embrace of neoliberal ideology and the declining political clout of the country's campesinos.

Yet the governments of the developing countries have an opportunity to move beyond a defensive posture in trade negotiations – in which they are cast as the international laggards in environmental protection – to a more positive stance as proponents of sustainable agriculture. They can draw support for this stance from the international environmental movement and, in particular, from citizens in the

North who bear the environmental costs of pollution-intensive production. A genuine 'greening of world trade' could help to secure the livelihoods of some of the poorest people in the world today – the small farmers and agricultural labourers of developing countries – as well as the well-being of future generations worldwide.

Notes

1   I wish to thank M Asaduzzaman, Stephen Brush, Peter Dorman, Andrew Klemer, J Mohan Rao, James Scott and H Garrison Wilkes for comments on earlier versions of this chapter. I also thank seminar participants at the University of California, Riverside, the University of Massachusetts, Amherst, Yale University and the Third Biennial Meeting of the International Society for Ecological Economics for useful discussions. Research for this study was supported by a Faculty Research Grant from the University of Massachusetts, Amherst. I am grateful to Roohi Prem Baveja, Kevin Cahill, Nasrin Dalirazar, and Mariano Torras for research assistance

2   Based on calculations by Maizels (1992, p189; 1995, p108), who reports that substitution reduced the developed market-economy countries' consumption of natural raw materials by 2.9 per cent per year from 1963–1965 to 1971–1973, 0.9 per cent per year from 1971–1973 to 1978–1980, and 1.2 per cent per year from 1978–1980 to 1984–1986

3   The nominal price of raw jute was US$299 per tonne in 1972 (World Bank, 1992, p12) and US$277 per tonne in 1992–1993 (IJO, 1993, p4). The real price trend is here calculated using the US producer price index as a deflator

4   Dixon and Mason (1994) summarize various damage cost estimates, ranging from US$5.3–$50 per tonne of carbon in the decade 1991–2000 and rising to US$6.8–$120 per tonne in the following decade. Pearce et al (1995, p68) report similar estimates

5   This can be regarded as a lower-bound estimate in so far as (1) landfill costs are higher in more densely populated countries; (2) landfills are publicly subsidized; (3) landfills generate negative externalities; and/or (4) the improper disposal of PP is common and this generates higher environmental costs than disposal in landfills

6   Plant breeders rely heavily on selected 'elite' breeding lines for the production of new hybrids. The traditional 'landraces' from the farmers' fields provided the original genetic material in these lines, and landraces continue to be used as the main source for introducing greater diversity into them. For discussion, see Duvick (1984)

7   A 1994 survey of ejido maize producers in Mexico found that only 35 per cent used herbicides, insecticides or fungicides. For small farmers (cultivating less than 2ha), medium farmers (2–10ha), and large farmers (more than 10ha), the shares using any of these pesticides were 15 per cent, 34 per cent and 51 per cent, respectively (calculated from data reported by Secretaría de Reforma Agraria, 1995, pp5.17 and 5.19)

8   In 1994, citing concerns about human cancer risks and the effects on aquatic organisms, the US Environmental Protection Agency (1994) launched a Special Review of atrazine and two closely related herbicides

9   Mexican resistance to US corn imports was one of the most difficult issues in the negotiation of NAFTA's agriculture chapter. In return for the 15-year phase-out, Mexico agreed to allow the immediate duty-free import of up to 2 million tonnes of US corn per year (Thurston and Negrete, 1992)

10 De Janvry, Sadoulet and Gordillo de Anda (1995) cite survey data that indicate that roughly half of ejido maize growers do not produce market surpluses and conclude that neglect of this fact has caused other studies to overstate the labour displacement likely to result from NAFTA. Even among these growers, however, some households may shift to cheap imported corn to meet consumption needs, resulting in the further contraction of maize acreage

11 Estimates prepared for the World Bank indicate that in the first five years of NAFTA, between 145,000 and 300,000 farmers could abandon their land (DePalma, 1993). José Luis Calva (1992, p35) of the National Autonomous University of Mexico predicted that total rural out-migration, including family members, could reach 15 million people. For other estimates, see Levy and Wijnbergen (1991), Robinson et al (1991) and Harvey and Marblestone (1993)

12 For further discussion of the need and potential for *in situ* conservation of crop genetic resources, see Prescott-Allen and Prescott-Allen (1982), Altieri and Merrick (1987), and Brush (1992, 1995)

13 Some authors (for example, Grossman and Krueger, 1995) find evidence of an 'environmental Kuznets curve', whereby total pollution at first rises and then declines as per capita income grows. Chapter 5 offers evidence that changes in the distribution of power, rather than income alone, explain declines in pollution

References

Alam, A (1993) 'Jute Retting and Environment', in *Improved Retting and Extraction of Jute and Kenaf,* Proceedings of Regional Workshop held at Research Institute for Tobacco and Fiber Crops, Malang, Indonesia, 1–6 February 1993, Rome, Food and Agriculture Organization of the United Nations; and Dhaka, International Jute Organisation, pp362–371

Altieri, M A and L C Merrick (1987) '*In situ* Conservation of Crop Genetic Resources through Maintenance of Traditional Farming Systems', in *Economic Botany,* vol 41, no 1, pp86–96

Boyce, J K (1995) 'Jute, Polypropylene, and the Environment: A Study in International Trade and Market Failure', in *Bangladesh Development Studies,* no 13, pp49–66

Boyce, J K (1996) 'Ecological Distribution, Agricultural Trade Liberalization, and *in situ* Genetic Diversity', *Journal of Income Distribution,* vol 6, no 2, pp263–284

Braungart, M (1992) 'Jute and Polypropylene: Environmentally Intelligent Products? Comparative Impact Assessment', October, Hamburg, Environmental Protection Encouragement Agency

Brush, S (1992) 'Farmers' Rights and Genetic Conservation in Traditional Farming Systems', *World Development,* vol 20, no 11, pp1617–1630

Brush, S (1995) '*In situ* Conservation of Landraces in Centers of Crop Diversity', *Crop Science,* no 35, pp346–354

Calva, J L (1992) *Probables Efectos de un Tratado de Libre Comercio en el Campo Mexicano*, Mexico City, Fontamara

De Janvry, A, E Sadoulet and G Gordillo de Anda (1995) 'NAFTA and Mexico's Maize Producers', *World Development,* vol 23, no 8, pp1349–1362

DePalma, A (1993) 'Mexicans fear for corn, imperiled by free trade', *The New York Times,* 12 July

Dixon, J A and J Mason (1994) 'Global Warming: Measuring the Costs', World Bank, Environmentally Sustainable Development Vice Presidency, Dissemination Note No 4, February, Washington, DC, World Bank

Duvick, D N (1984) 'Genetic Diversity in Major Farm Crops on the Farm and in Reserve', *Economic Botany,* vol 38, no 2, pp161–78

Food and Agriculture Organization of the United Nations (1994) *Trade Yearbook 1993,* FAO, Rome

Grossman, G M and A B Krueger (1995) 'Economic Growth and the Environment', *Quarterly Journal of Economics,* no 110, pp353–377

Harvey, N and J Marblestone (1993) 'Emptying the Fields? NAFTA and Mexican Agriculture', *Brown Foreign Affairs Journal,* vol 6, no 1, pp2–10

Hye, S A (1993) 'Review on Labour and Employment', in M Asaduzzaman and K Westergaard (eds), *Growth and Development in Rural Bangladesh: A Critical Review,* Dhaka, University Press Ltd, pp261–406

International Jute Organisation (IJO) (1993), 'Review of Jute Situation and Policies Affecting Jute Production and Trade', International Jute Council 20th Session, 3–5 November 1993, Dhaka, Bangladesh

Johnson, E (1990) 'Polypropylene: Action Plan', *Chemical Engineering,* May, pp30–37

Levy, S and S van Wijnbergen (1991) 'El Maíz y el Acuerdo de Libre Comercio entre México y los Estados Unidos', *El Trimestre Económico,* vol 58, no 4, pp823–862

Levy, S and S van Wijnbergen (1995) 'Transition Problems in Economic Reform: Agriculture in the North American Free Trade Agreement', *American Economic Review,* vol 85, no 4, pp738–754

Maizels, A (1992) *Commodities in Crisis: The Commodity Crisis of the 1980s and the Political Economy of International Commodity Prices,* Oxford, Clarendon Press

Maizels, A (1995) 'The Functioning of International Markets for Primary Commodities: Key Policy Issues for Developing Countries', in United Nations Conference on Trade and Development (UNCTAD), *International Monetary and Financial Issues for the 1990s: Research Papers for the Group of Twenty-Four,* vol V, New York and Geneva, United Nations

Pearce, D W , W R Cline, A N Achanta, S Fankhauser, R K Pachauri, R S J Tol and P Vellinga (1995) 'The Social Costs of Climate Change: Greenhouse Damage and the Benefits of Control', draft, April

Plucknett, D L, N J H Smith, J T Williams and N M Anishetty (1987) *Gene Banks and the World's Food,* Princeton, Princeton University Press

Prescott-Allen, R and C Prescott-Allen (1982) 'The Case for *in situ* Conservation of Crop Genetic Resources', *Nature and Resources,* vol 18, no 1, pp15–20

Raeburn, P (1995) *The Last Harvest: The Genetic Gamble That Threatens to Destroy American Agriculture,* New York, Simon & Schuster

Robinson, S, M E Burfisher, R Hinojosa-Ojeda and K E Thierfelder (1991) 'Agricultural Policies and Migration in a US–Mexico Free Trade Area: A Computable General Equilibrium Analysis', Working Paper No 617, December, Berkeley, University of California, Department of Agricultural and Resource Economics

Schumpeter, J (1976) *Capitalism, Socialism and Democracy,* (5th edn), London, George Allen & Unwin

Scott, D C (1992) 'Trade Deal with the United States Puts Many Mexican Farmers at Risk', *Christian Science Monitor,* 4 November, p10

Secretaría de Reforma Agraria (1995) 'El Sector Ejidal en la Agricultura Mexicana: Impacto de las Reformas', mimeo

Tellus Institute (1992) *Tellus Institute Packaging Study*, Boston, Tellus Institute and Council of State Governments

Thigpen, M E, P Marongiu and S R Lasker (1987) 'World Demand Prospects for Jute', World Bank Staff Commodity Working Paper No 16

Thurston, C W and I Negrete (1992) 'Mexico Yields on Corn Quota; Farm Accord Near', *Journal of Commerce*, 15 July, p1A

United Nations (1993) *Industrial Statistics Yearbook 1991. Volume II: Commodity Production Statistics 1982–1991*, New York, United Nations

United States Environmental Protection Agency (EPA) (1990) 'National Pesticide Survey: Atrazine', Washington, DC, EPA, Office of Water and Office of Pesticides and Toxic Substances

United States Environmental Protection Agency (EPA) (1994) 'EPA Begins Special Review of Triazine Pesticides', *EPA Environmental News*, Release 279, 10 November

Vavilov, N I (1992) *Origin and Geography of Cultivated Plants*, Cambridge, Cambridge University Press

Wade, N (1974) 'Green Revolution (II): Problems of Adapting a Western Technology', *Science*, no 186, 27 December, pp1186–1192

Walsh, J (1981) 'Genetic Vulnerability Down on the Farm', *Science*, no 214, 9 October, pp161–164

Wilkes, H G (1992) *Strategies for Sustaining Crop Germplasm Preservation, Enhancement, and Use*, Washington, DC, Consultative Group for International Agricultural Research, Issues in Agriculture, no 5, October

World Bank (1992) *Bangladesh: Restructuring Options for the Jute Manufacturing Industry*, Report No 10052-BD, 25 February

5

Progress on the Environmental Kuznets Curve?

David I Stern

Introduction

The environmental Kuznets curve (EKC) hypothesis proposes that there is an inverted U-shape relation between various indicators of environmental degradation and income per capita. This has been taken to imply that economic growth will eventually redress the environmental impacts of the early stages of economic development and that growth will lead to further environmental improvements in the developed countries. Far from being a threat to the environment in the long-term, as argued by Meadows et al (1972) and Meadows et al (1992) among others, economic growth is necessary in order for environmental quality to be maintained or improved. This is an essential part of the sustainable development argument as put forward by the World Commission on Environment and Development (1987) in *Our Common Future*. The EKC is named after Kuznets (1955) who hypothesized that the relationship between a measure of inequality in the distribution of income and the level of income is an inverted U-shape curve. An example of an estimated EKC is shown in Figure 5.1.

Proponents of the EKC hypothesis argue that at very low levels of economic activity environmental impacts are generally low, but as development proceeds the rates of land clearance, resource use and waste generation per capita increase rapidly. However, 'at higher levels of development, structural change towards information-intensive industries and services, coupled with increased environmental awareness, enforcement of environmental regulations, better technology, and higher environmental expenditures, result in levelling off and gradual decline of environmental degradation' (Panayotou, 1993). Thus there are both proximate causes of the EKC relationship – changes in economic structure or product mix, changes in technology and changes in input mix, as well as underlying causes such as environmental regulation, awareness and education. These effects act to counteract or exaggerate the gross impact of economic growth or the scale effect.

The EKC theme was promoted by the World Bank's *World Development Report 1992* (IBRD, 1992). The authors noted that: 'The view that greater economic activity inevitably hurts the environment is based on static assumptions about technology, tastes and environmental investments' (p38), and that: 'As incomes rise, the demand for improvements in environmental quality will increase, as will the resources avail-

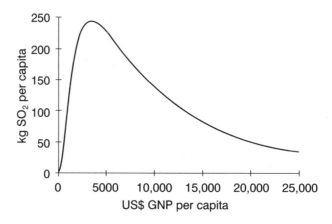

Figure 5.1 *Environmental Kuznets curve for sulphur (Panayotou, 1993)*

able for investment' (p39). Others have expounded this position even more forcefully: 'there is clear evidence that, although economic growth usually leads to environmental degradation in the early stages of the process, in the end the best – and probably the only – way to attain a decent environment in most countries is to become rich' (Beckerman, 1992).

These views have been countered by critics of the EKC concept (eg Arrow et al, 1995; Stern et al, 1996). The main arguments against the EKC are: much of the empirical evidence is weak and statistical techniques inappropriate, the static relationship between rich and poor countries does not necessarily tell us about dynamics as countries experience economic growth, and EKC relationships have been found for only a subset of indicators – growth might improve some but would lead to worsening levels of others. In addition, even where EKC relationships might hold true, projections (Stern et al, 1996; Selden and Song, 1994) show that global levels of environmental impacts are likely to rise over the next few decades.

In the several years since Grossman and Krueger's (1991) path-breaking study, a large literature has developed that reports EKC estimates and discusses their implications. This chapter reviews that literature. The question I ask in order to evaluate the contributions is: 'Do developments in the literature represent advances in terms of our knowledge about the existence of such relations, in our understanding of their determinants and implications, and in the methods used to investigate them?'

There have been four main types of contributions to the literature: estimation of 'basic' EKCs, studies of the theoretical determinants of the EKC, studies of the empirical determinants of the EKC and critique of EKCs. The chapter is organized so that theoretical studies that build on the basic background discussed above are reviewed in the next section, followed by a survey of the estimates of basic EKCs. These sections are followed by a review of the critiques of these basic EKCs and their interpretation. The fifth section surveys studies that have examined empirical determinants of the EKC, while the final two sections of the paper examine whether progress is being made in our understanding of the EKC and suggest directions for further research.

Theoretical Determinants of the EKC

A number of papers have built on the heuristic theory of the EKC described in the previous section to relate mathematically plausible assumptions about technology and preferences to the shape of the time path of environmental impacts.

Lopez (1994) provides a theoretical analysis of environment–growth relationships at a fairly high level of generality. His model has two production sectors, weak separability between pollution and the conventional factors of production, constant returns to scale, quasi-fixed inputs of capital and labour, exogenous technical change, and exogenous output prices. Preferences are a function of revenue, pollution and the output price vector. If producers pay a zero or fixed pollution price, then increases in output unambiguously result in increases in pollution in this system, irrespective of the features of the technology or preferences. However, when producers pay the social marginal cost of pollution, then the relation between emissions and income depends on the properties of the technology and preferences. If preferences are homothetic, increasing output again results in increasing pollution. However, when preferences are non-homothetic, as is likely in reality (Pollak and Wales, 1992), the response of pollution to growth depends on the elasticity of substitution in production between pollution and the conventional inputs, and the degree of relative risk aversion – ie the rate at which marginal utility declines with rising consumption of produced goods.[1] The faster marginal utility declines and the more substitution is possible in production, the less pollution will tend to increase with production. For empirically reasonable values of these two parameters, pollution may increase at low levels of income and fall at high levels – the inverted U. The role of pollution prices seems to be critical. Pollutants such as sulphur dioxide (SO_2) which are subject to control in many countries might have effective prices that are close to being optimal. Inverted U-shape EKCs have been found for these pollutants. On the other hand, the effective price of carbon dioxide (CO_2) is probably far from optimal and this pollutant appears to have a monotonic EKC. Also, in the latter case the elasticity of substitution is probably lower and the apparent damage less evident to consumers, both implying a higher turning point. Lopez also constructs a model for deforestation, where, as might be expected, if the stock effects of the forest on agricultural production are internalized, then growth results in less deforestation and vice-versa.

Selden and Song (1995) derive an inverted U curve for the optimal path of pollution using Forster's (1973) growth and pollution model. The latter model is similar to Lopez's model but assumes a priori that utility is additively separable in consumption and pollution. It corresponds therefore to Lopez's non-homothetic preferences case. Optimal abatement is zero until a given capital stock is achieved, whereafter it rises sharply at an increasing rate. As a result, the optimal pollution path is an inverted U in the capital stock.

While Lopez (1994) and Selden and Song (1995) both develop models based on infinitely lived agents, John and Pecchenino (1994) and John et al (1995) develop models based on overlapping generations (McConnell, 1997). In these models, the externality of pollution is, therefore, only partially internalized. Also pollution is generated in these latter models by consumption rather than production activities. All these models can generate inverted U-shape curves under appropriate conditions. McConnell (1997) develops a model of consumption pollution.[2] He uses this model to argue that there is no defining role for the income elasticity for environmental quality in the EKC model. While a higher elasticity will lead, *ceteris paribus,* to a faster reduction in pollution, pollution can decline even if the elasticity is non-positive.

In summary, it seems fairly easy to develop models that generate EKCs under appropriate assumptions. The challenge would appear to be to find empirical evidence as to which of these stories, if any, is more plausible.

Basic EKCs

In this section I survey studies whose primary purpose is to estimate the relationship between environmental impact indicators and GDP. Several of these studies also examined the effects of possible conditioning variables such as trade intensity, but that was a secondary focus of these papers.

The first empirical EKC study appears to have been the National Bureau of Economic Research (NBER) working paper by Grossman and Krueger (1991)[3] that estimated EKCs as part of a study of the potential environmental impacts of the North American Free Trade Agreement (NAFTA). They estimated EKCs for SO_2, dark matter (fine smoke) and suspended particles (SPM) using the Global Environmental Monitoring System (GEMS) data set. This data set is a panel of ambient measurements from a number of locations in cities around the world. Each regression involves a cubic function of PPP (purchasing power parity) per capita gross domestic product (GDP) and various site-related variables, a time trend, and a trade intensity variable. The turning points for SO_2 and dark matter are at around US\$4,000–\$5,000 while the concentration of suspended particles appeared to decline even at low-income levels. Both the time trend and the trade intensity variables had a significant negative coefficient in the SO_2 regression, while neither the time trend nor the trade variable was significant in the equation explaining the concentration of dark matter. The time trend was significant in the suspended particles regression, but again the trade variable was insignificant. At income levels over US\$10,000–\$15,000 Grossman and Krueger's estimates show increasing levels of all three pollutants. Although economic growth at middle-income levels would improve environmental quality, growth at high-income levels would be detrimental. This result may either reflect the type of phenomenon raised by Pezzey (1989) (see below) or simply be the result of an inappropriate functional form – ie a dependent variable in levels rather than logs.

Shafik and Bandyopadhyay's (1992)[4] study was particularly influential as the results were used in the 1992 World Development Report (IBRD, 1992). They estimated EKCs for ten different indicators: lack of clean water, lack of urban sanitation, ambient levels of suspended particulate matter, ambient sulphur oxides, change in forest area between 1961 and 1986, the annual observations of deforestation between 1961 and 1986, dissolved oxygen in rivers, faecal coliforms in rivers, municipal waste per capita and carbon emissions per capita.

They used three different functional forms: log-linear, log-quadratic and, in the most general case, a logarithmic cubic polynomial in PPP GDP per capita, a time trend and site-related variables.[5] In each case the dependent variable was untransformed. Lack of clean water and lack of urban sanitation were found to decline uniformly with increasing income and over time. Both measures of deforestation were found to be insignificantly related to the income terms. River quality tends to worsen with increasing income. Shafik and Bandyopadhyay suppose that this is because the external costs imposed by this form of pollution may decline as water supply systems improve. The two air pollutants, however, conform to the EKC hypothesis. The turning points for both pollutants are found for income levels of between US$3000 and US$4000. The time trend is significantly positive for faecal coliform and significantly negative for air quality. Finally, both municipal waste and carbon emissions per capita increase unambiguously with rising income. The broader range of indicators examined by Shafik and Bandyopadhyay shows a much more ambiguous picture of the relationship between environment and development than indicated by Grossman and Krueger's more limited study.

Subsequent studies have tended to: use pollution emissions data rather than ambient concentrations, include population density as an explanatory variable for a number of indicators, calculate future projections based on the estimated EKCs and investigate further indicators such as energy use.

Panayotou (1993, 1995) estimated EKCs for SO_2, NO_x (nitrous oxide), SPM and deforestation. The three pollutants are measured in terms of emissions per capita on a national basis. Data for developing countries were estimated from fuel use and fuel mix data. Deforestation is measured as the mean annual rate of deforestation in the mid-1980s, plus unity. In contrast to most other studies, Panayotou employs only cross-sectional data and GDP is in 1985 US dollars converted at market exchange rates. The fitted equations for the three pollutants are logarithmic quadratics in income per capita. For deforestation, Panayotou fits a translog function in population density and income per capita, with the addition of a dummy variable for tropical countries. All the estimated curves are inverted Us which conforms to the result for these variables in the other studies. For the sample mean population density, the turning-point for deforestation is US$823 per capita. Deforestation rates were significantly greater in tropical countries. Deforestation was also higher in countries with higher population densities. For SO_2 emissions the turning-point is around US$3000 per capita (see Figure 5.1), for NO_x around US$5500 per capita and for SPM around US$4500. The market exchange rates used by Panayotou tend to lower the income levels of developing countries and raise those of the developed countries (apart from the US) relative to the PPP values. Despite this, the turning-points for the pollutants are in a similar range to those reported by Grossman and Krueger, and Shafik and Bandyopadhyay, probably because Panayotou uses emissions per capita rather than ambient concentrations.

Selden and Song (1994) estimated EKCs for four airborne emissions series: SO_2 NO_x, SPM and CO (carbon monoxide) on longitudinal data from World Resources (WRI, 1991). These primarily represent developed countries. I concentrate on the results they present for a fixed-effects model, including a population density variable. The authors suggest that in countries with low population densities there will be less pressure to adopt stringent environmental standards and emissions from transportation will be higher. The estimated turning-points are all very high compared to the three studies discussed above: SO_2, US\$8709; NO_x, US\$11,217; SPM, US\$10,289; and CO, US\$5963. Selden and Song suggest that this is because ambient pollution levels are likely to decline before aggregate emissions. The paper also contains projections for these pollutants for the next few decades, which show a monotonic increase in global emissions.

Holtz-Eakin and Selden (1995) estimate quadratic EKCs for CO_2 emissions on panel data confirming the very high (US\$35,000 in a levels regression – US\$8 million in a logarithmic regression) turning-points for this pollutant found by Shafik (1994). They utilize a wide range of diagnostic tests and statistics. They also produce projections for emissions over the next century under a number of different assumptions and a convergence-based economic growth model. Schmalensee et al (1995) also look at CO_2 and make projections using a more extensive version of the Holtz-Eakin and Selden database. The innovation is the use of a spline regression in place of the conventional polynomials. The spline estimate has ten piecewise segments. Carbon elasticities with respect to income are negative for both the segment associated with the lowest level of income and that associated with the highest level of income (below PPPUS\$(1985) 629 and above PPPUS\$(1985) 9799) but positive for middle-income levels. This shows declining per capita carbon emissions with rising income well within the sample range. The time effects from the fixed effects estimator show rising emissions from 1950 to 1980 with no increase thereafter. Despite the inverted U-shape curve, emission projections using Intergovernmental Panel on Climate Change (IPCC) population and economic growth assumptions show a more rapid rise in emissions than assumed by the IPCC.

Horvath (1997) estimates an EKC for energy use per capita for a sample of 114 countries using cross-sectional and longitudinal data. Per capita energy use is increasing with rising per capita income. As suggested by Stern et al (1996) and Suri and Chapman (1997), energy use might serve as an indicator of overall environmental impact.

Cole et al (1997) add a number of novel indicators to those examined in previous studies, including specific transport emissions for SO_2, SPM, NO_2 and total energy use, nitrates in water, chlorofluorocarbons (CFC) emissions, traffic volumes and methane. Again, local pollutants had inverted U-shape curves, as did CFCs. Traffic volumes, nitrates and methane did not have within-sample turning-points.

Cropper and Griffiths (1994) estimate three regional (Africa, Latin America and Asia) EKCs for deforestation using panel data for 64 countries over a 30-year period. The dependent variable is the negative of the percentage change in forest area between two years. The independent variables in each regression are: rural population density, percentage change in population, timber price, per capita GDP, percentage change in per capita PPP GDP, square of per capita PPP GDP, a dummy variable for each country and a time trend. Neither the population growth rate nor the time trend was significant in either Africa or Latin America, and the price of tropical logs was insignificant in Africa. Otherwise the coefficients in these regressions were significantly different from zero. None of the coefficients in the Asian regression were significant. For Africa the turning-point is US$4760 and for Latin America it is US$5420. These levels are very much higher than those from either Panayotou's (1993) or Shafik and Bandyopadhyay's (1992) results. Antle and Heidebrink (1995) estimate EKCs for afforestation and national parks on cross-sectional data. They find a U-shape curve for both indicators (ie, an inverted U for environmental impact) with turning-points of US$2000 and US$1200 1985 respectively – a result closer to that of Shafik and Panayotou. The use of panel data by Cropper and Griffiths might be the cause of their higher estimated turning points.

Komen et al (1997) and de Bruyn (1997) estimate EKC's for dependent variables that do not directly reflect environmental quality or pollution emissions but instead factors that might drive those outcomes. Komen et al (1997) estimate an EKC for public research and development (R&D) expenditures on environmental protection in a group of Organisation for Economic Co-operation and Development (OECD) countries. The main result of the paper is that the elasticity of these expenditures with respect to income is approximately unity. The authors recognize that public expenditures are only a small part of the total environmental R&D expenditures. Also, R&D is only a small part of the total expenditure on environmental protection and may or may not actually result in improved environmental quality. Nonetheless, this is one of the links in an investigation of the empirical determinants of the EKC. De Bruyn (1997) estimates a regression of sulphur emission-reduction targets for 2000 from 1990 levels for the Convention on Long Range Transboundary Air Pollution (LRTAP) countries and the US. It is found that greater cuts are related to higher levels of income, but a dummy variable for former Communist countries (which are all low income) is also related to larger cuts, and income explains only 13 per cent of the total variance.

Critique of the EKC

Identification of Problems

Stern et al (1996), Arrow et al (1995), Ekins (1997), Pearson (1994), and Ansuategi et al (1996) provide a series of reviews and critiques of the EKC studies. Rothman (1996, 1997) reviews the critiques, and numerous articles in special editions of *Ecological Economics* (1995), *Environment and Development Economics* (1996) and *Ecological Applications* (1996) discuss the Arrow et al (1995) paper.

Stern et al (1996) identified seven major problems with some of the basic EKC estimates and their interpretation: (a) the assumption of unidirectional causality from growth to environmental quality and the reversibility of environmental change; (b) the assumption that changes in trade relationships associated with development have no effect on environmental quality; (c) econometric problems; (d) ambient concentrations versus emissions; (e) asymptotic behaviour; (f) the mean–median income problem; and (g) the interpretation of particular EKCs in isolation from EKCs for other environmental problems. Most of the other criticisms can be fitted into this framework. The remainder of this section reviews these problems, integrating the insights from other critiques and indicating where progress has been made in empirical studies since the writing of Stern et al (1996).

Simultaneity and irreversibility

The EKC hypothesis derives from a model of the economy in which environmental damage is reversible and there are special assumptions regarding the impact of environmental damage on growth. For example, in the McConnell (1997) and Ansuategi et al (1996) models, consumption pollution affects output negatively, but neither abatement activities nor production itself generate any pollution. In the Lopez (1994) pollution model, pollution does not affect production. In the absence of feedback to production or irreversibilities, uncontrolled economic growth would maximize economic output and environmental quality in the long-run. But, given such feedback and/or irreversibility, attempting to grow fast in the early stages of development, when environmental degradation is rising, may prove unsustainable. There is clear evidence of this from many developing countries (Barbier, 1994).

Generally, the economy and its environment are jointly determined (Perrings, 1987). Estimating single equation relationships by ordinary least squares where simultaneity exists produces biased and inconsistent estimates. In practice, this criticism is most likely to be of relevance for samples, including very poor countries where land degradation and the like are having a current impact on GDP (Barbier, 1994) and for regressions where the dependent variable is a general indicator, such as energy use whose increase enables broad economic growth. The simultaneity issue was directly addressed by Cole et al (1997) and Holtz-Eakin and Selden (1995) who used Hausman tests for regressor exogeneity. They found no evidence of simultaneity.

Trade and the EKC

Several of the early EKC studies included trade variables. These variables were indicators of openness to trade rather than measures of actual physical trade. Whereas *ceteris paribus* openness might be expected to reduce environmental damage in both developing and developed countries (Grossman and Krueger, 1991), trade itself is likely to increase impacts in developing countries and reduce them in the developed countries. This may be one of the determinants of the EKC relationship (see discussion of Suri and Chapman, 1997). The Hecksher–Ohlin trade theory suggests that, under free trade, developing countries would specialize towards the production of goods that are intensive in the factors that they are endowed with in relative abundance: labour and natural resources. The developed countries would specialize towards human capital and manufactured capital-intensive activities. Part of the reduction in environmental degradation levels in the developed countries and increases in environmental degradation in middle-income countries may reflect this specialization (Lucas et al, 1992; Hettige et al, 1992; Suri and Chapman, 1997). Environmental regulation in developed countries might further encourage polluting activities to gravitate toward the developing countries (Lucas et al, 1992; Ekins et al, 1994).

These effects would exaggerate the apparent decline in pollution intensity with rising income along the EKC. In our finite world the poor countries of today would be unable to find further countries from which to import resource-intensive products as they themselves become wealthy. When the poorer countries apply similar levels of environmental regulation, they will face the more difficult task of abating these activities rather than hiving them off to other countries (Arrow et al, 1995; Stern et al, 1996). Several papers have now attempted to capture the effects of actual trade flows (see below).

Econometric problems

As discussed above, there are a number of simultaneity issues that make identification of alternative structures difficult, if not impossible, within a single equation ordinary least squares (OLS)/generalized least squares (GLS) framework and especially using cross-section data.[6] Also, none of the early EKC studies presented diagnostic statistics of the regression residuals. Stern et al (1996) raised the issue of heteroscedasticity that may be important in the context of cross-sectional regressions of grouped data. Schmalensee et al (1995) found that regression residuals from OLS were heteroscedastic, with smaller residuals associated with countries with higher total GDP and population, as predicted by Stern et al (1996). Ekins (1997) points out that even for the same pollutant, different researchers have found different results by investigating different data sets, using different functional forms (eg logarithmic versus levels) and different estimation techniques. This seems to indicate that the relationship, if any, is fragile.[7]

Ambient concentrations versus emissions

Data on environmental problems are notoriously patchy in coverage or poor in quality. Those studies that have attempted to estimate the EKC have faced these problems. The available data are not necessarily the appropriate data on which to base policy conclusions. Grossman and Krueger, and Shafik and Bandyopadhyay both used ambient pollution data from urban areas. This is appropriate in as far as the effects on human health in urban areas is concerned. However, the estimated EKC relationship can be misleading in projecting the expected change in the acid burden from nitrogen and sulphur oxide emissions on natural and agricultural ecosystems. As is well known, societies tend to go through a process of increasing and then falling urban population densities and concentrations of population as they develop (see Stern, 1992, for references). The concentration of pollution sources is therefore also likely to go through a similar process. Declining ambient concentrations of pollutants do not mean necessarily that the overall pollution burden is declining. Many more studies have now been carried out using emissions data. As predicted, EKC estimates based on emissions show much higher turning-points than do ambient concentration EKCs.

Asymptotic behaviour

Economic activity inevitably implies the use of resources. By the laws of thermodynamics, the use of resources inevitably implies the production of waste. Regressions that allow levels of indicators to become zero or negative are inappropriate, except in the case of deforestation where afforestation can occur.[8] This restriction can be applied by using a logarithmic dependent variable. De Bruyn and Opschoor (1994) present evidence that the 'delinking' of GDP from material use in the 1970s and early 1980s was partially reversed in the late 1980s. Pezzey (1989) proposes that the optimal level of environmental degradation may be monotonically increasing with the level of development. Initially, property rights are not established and environmental degradation increases more rapidly than the optimal rate. As environmental degradation and the level of development increase, property rights are established and the level of environmental degradation declines until it 'catches up' to the optimal path and the increase in environmental degradation recommences. As total impacts cannot tend eventually to zero in the very long run (Common, 1995), then rising income, if it could be sustained, would inevitably mean rising degradation. Various results that use cubic regressions find that pollution rises again at high-income levels (eg Grossman and Krueger, 1991). However, none of these studies used logarithmic dependent variables (see Table 5.1), so the cubic term might be modelling a slow decline in pollution and an asymmetric EKC that would be better captured using a logarithmic dependent variable.

Mean versus median income

Some studies show that EKC estimates for a number of indicators – SO_2 emissions, NO_x and deforestation – peak at income levels around the current world mean per capita income. So a cursory glance at the available econometric estimates might lead one to believe that, given likely future levels of mean income per capita, environmental degradation should decline. This interpretation is evident in the 1992 World Bank Development Report (IBRD, 1992). However, income is not normally distributed but very skewed, with much larger numbers of people below mean income per capita than above it. Therefore, it is median rather than mean income that is the relevant variable. This means that assuming that the EKC relationship is valid, global environmental degradation is set to rise for a long time to come (Stern et al, 1996; Ekins, 1997; Selden and Song, 1995). On the other hand, some other studies (eg Cropper and Griffiths, 1994; Selden and Song, 1994) found much higher turning-points for some of these indicators, which reduces the chance of this misinterpretation.

Aggravation of other environmental problems

It is clear that the levels of many pollutants per unit of output in specific processes have declined in the developed countries over time with increasingly stringent environmental regulations and technical innovations. However, the mix of effluent has shifted from sulphur and nitrogen oxides to carbon dioxide and solid waste, so that aggregate waste is still high and per capita waste may not have declined. Economic activity is inevitably environmentally disruptive in some way (see above). Satisfying the material needs of people requires the use and disturbance of energy flows and materials. The enhanced greenhouse effect is one of the most serious threats to global sustainability (Common, 1995), but almost no one suggests that an inverted U-shaped curve applies for the greenhouses gases[9] nor for energy use per capita

(Suri and Chapman, 1997). EKCs for global pollutants with long-term costs and perhaps for some resource stocks tend to be monotonically increasing, while those with local impacts tend to have the inverted U-shape (Arrow et al, 1995). Therefore, even if economic growth could greatly lower the current rates of per capita emissions of other pollutants and deforestation in developing countries, it would be likely to increase these countries' contribution to global warming. Estimation of EKCs for total energy use are an attempt to capture environmental impact whatever its nature (eg Suri and Chapman, 1997).

Suggestions for Alternative Approaches

In their concluding comments, Stern et al (1996) argued that:

> If econometric studies are to provide a basis for projections of future trends, they will need to take the form of structural models, rather than reduced form equations of the EKC type. Such models would also have the potential to inform policy choices, which EKC results do not. We believe that a more fruitful approach to the analysis of the relationship between economic growth and environmental impact would be the examination of the historical experience of individual countries, using econometric and also qualitative historical analysis. (p1159)

There have been no attempts to estimate structural models or to test the theoretical models discussed previously. However, there have been several studies of individual countries. Vincent (1997) examines the experience of Malaysia and Carson et al (1997) look at variation across US states, while de Bruyn et al (1997) examine the experience of four OECD countries (see below). Unruh and Moomaw (1997) use a qualitative historical approach and testing for structural breaks in regressions to look at events in individual countries around the oil price shocks (see below). Vincent (1997) compared Selden and Song's predictions for a country with the income level of Malaysia, with the actual data for Malaysia with mixed results. In particular, sulphur emissions fell sharply in the 1980s rather than rising as predicted. This was due to a sudden shift to power generation using domestic natural gas. Ambient measurements of total suspended particulates and various water-pollution indicators are available for about 15 years for most of the states of peninsular Malaysia whose income levels vary widely but overlap temporally due to rapid economic growth. All the indicators show rising monotonic or insignificant relations with income and population density. Shafik (1994) and Grossman and Krueger (1991) both found declining concentrations over this income range. Carson et al (1997) argue that a study of a single country eliminates the problems associated with comparing data from different countries. The richest US states have more than double the income of the poorest. The variation among US counties is even greater. On the other hand, institutional factors and other variables are fairly common across the states. All EKCs for a variety of pollutants for both US states and counties were declining in income. This relationship was significant even when industrial employment mix variables were added to the regression. As mining and mineral processing are very capital-intensive activities, this is not so surprising and perhaps gross product originating on an industry basis should have been used. It turns out that the poorest US states such as Louisiana, West Virginia, New Mexico, Utah, etc are often states with important resource extraction and processing industries, while the richest states such as Connecticut, New Jersey, Massachusetts and New York are states with an orientation towards the service sector and high-tech industries. Trade specialization among these states might explain even more of the variation in emissions across states than worldwide trade specialization might explain variation in emissions among countries.

Pearson (1994) reiterates the points in Stern et al's (1996) critique, but emphasized the need for empirical work to investigate the determinants of the EKC relationship in terms of structural change, policy variables, etc, even if in a single equation framework. This is the direction in which most of the recent literature seems to be moving. As will be seen below, although recent EKC studies have looked at the role of additional explanatory variables, in most cases this has not been a systematic effort to explain the underlying determinants of the EKC relationship, but rather each study examines separately the role of possible conditioning variables in influencing the EKC relationship. Although these studies are interesting and useful as initial explorations, there is the danger of omitted variables bias.

Empirical Determinants of the EKC

Many of the most recent EKC studies have focused on examining possible determinants of the EKC relationship or on investigating the impact of various conditioning variables on the EKC relationship. A few studies claim to have achieved a decomposition of the EKC. Unruh and Moomaw (1997) and Moomaw and Unruh (1997) argue instead that historical events trigger reductions in emissions across countries at varying levels of income.

Conditioning Variables

Trade

Rock (1996) estimates regressions where the dependent variables are two indicators of toxic intensity of GDP also used by Lucas et al (1992). The equations include a quadratic function in income per capita, the share of manufacturing in GDP and four different indicators of trade orientation. A separate regression was estimated for each of the latter indicators. The inverted U-shape is present and pollution is rising with the share of manufacturing in GDP. A dummy variable for closed versus open economies shows that closed economies had lower toxic intensities of GDP, while the growth rate of exports and the growth rate of the share of exports in GDP are both positively related to the pollution indices.

Liddle (1996) examines changes in the consumption/production ratio of various metals and paper in the OECD countries. In most cases there is no clear trend. This result would be evidence against a major role for trade in determining the EKC. In contrast to Liddle, Suri and Chapman (1997) argue for an important role for trade in generating the EKC relationship. They show that the ratio of manufacturing exports to manufacturing imports has increased in many developing countries, while it has decreased in many developed countries. They estimate an EKC for energy use per capita for the period 1970–1991 for 34 countries, ranging from Bangladesh to the US in income levels. The EKC is a logarithmic quadratic with the addition of the following variables: M/MFG – imports of all manufactures as a share of domestic manufacturing production; X/MFG – exports of all manufactures as a share of domestic manufacturing (MFG) production; and MFG/GDP – share of manufacturing in GDP. The estimates indicate an inverted U (turning-point more than US$50,000) with the expected signs for the auxiliary variables, but only the coefficient for X/MFG among the auxiliary variables is significant. Exclusion of the quadratic term results in all the coefficients being significant, showing that these variables covary strongly with squared GDP per capita. A number of variant models are also estimated. A model with an interaction term M GDP/MFG investigates whether the effect of imports on lowering energy use is greater as income rises. This seems to be the case and the M/MFG coefficient falls to zero. A third version with a dummy variable for high-income countries in the interaction term provides a better fit. This is the best evidence so far that trade effects are one of the causes of the flattening or downward slope of the EKC, but this result was not found for a different sample of countries with carbon dioxide as the dependent variable (Cooke, 1997).

Rothman (1997) argues that one way to avoid the trade issue is to look at the environmental impacts generated by consumption rather than by the production activities in a country. To this end he estimates EKCs for expenditure on different categories of consumption goods. Only expenditure on food, beverages and tobacco shows an inverted U-shape within the sample range of income. The other categories of expenditure are monotonically increasing, including a number of resource intensive categories such as rent, fuel and power. The data are calculated on the basis of international PPP prices, but there is no guarantee that the prices of individual commodities within groups reflect their environmental impact or that the impact from a dollar's worth of each good consumed in the developed countries is equal to that in the developing countries.

Political freedom

Torras and Boyce (1996) look at how various indicators of democracy may influence the formation of preferences and mediate between private preferences and public policy. They estimate cubic EKCs using the GEMS data analysed by Grossman and Krueger (1994) and data on access to safe water and access to sanitation at the national level from the Human Development Report. In addition, the following variables are included in the regression: the Gini coefficient of income distribution,[10] literacy, an index of civil liberties and control variables similar to those used by Grossman and Krueger. On the whole, coefficients for the three 'democracy' indicators have the expected negative sign and are significant, especially for the developing countries. Literacy and rights have a more consistent effect than the Gini index, possibly reflecting difficulties in measuring and comparing this index across countries. For the three atmospheric pollutants from the GEMS data, the significance of the income terms declines when the democracy variables are added, showing that they explain variation previously modelled by the EKC relationship. The pattern is mixed for the other dependent variables.

3, *Density of economic activity*

Kaufmann et al (1997) and Shukia and Parikh (1992) examine the influence of the spatial intensity of economic activity (GDP/area) and city size, respectively, on ambient concentrations. Kaufmann et al (1997) use ambient SO_2 concentrations for a panel of mostly developed and middle-income countries (but including China) between 1974 and 1989. The estimated equation is:

$$C_{jt} = \alpha + \beta_1 (Y/P)_{jt} + \beta_2 (Y/P)^2_{jt} + \beta_3 (P/A)_{jt} + \beta_4 (Y/A)^2_{jt} + \beta_5 (S/GDP)_{jt} + \beta_6 t + \varepsilon_{jt} \quad (1)$$

where Y/P is GDP per capita, Y/A is GDP per area and S/GDP is steel exports as a percentage of GDP which is intended to capture the effects of trade. The authors argue that this approach is superior to including population density as an RHS variable because the impact of population density would be expected to vary with the level of income per capita. Increases in density would have less impact when overall emissions were low than when they were high. This could be easily addressed instead by simply putting all variables in logarithms, including the dependent variable, or using the multiplicative approaches of Panayotou (1993) or Vincent (1997). In (1) the elasticity of emissions with respect to Y/P is in fact dependent on Y/A as the area of individual countries are fixed and therefore national Y/A cannot be held constant as Y/P increases:

$$\frac{\partial C_j}{\partial (Y/P)_j} = \beta_1 + 2\beta_2 (Y/P)_j + \beta_3 (P/A)_j + 2\beta_4 (Y/P)_j (P/A)^2_j \quad (2)$$

The model is estimated for both national average levels of Y/A and city specific levels of Y/A. The authors find that concentrations are a U-shape function of income per capita and an inverted U-shape function of income per area. The former result is obviously diametrically opposed to the standard EKC results for sulphur dioxide concentrations. However, the signs of the parameters in (2) are $\beta_1 < 0$, $\beta_2 > 0$, $\beta_3 > 0$, $\beta_4 < 0$. This implies a reverse-shape N cross-section as Y/P is increased – so that at high-income levels emissions are declining. Similar results are reported by Panayotou (1997) who claims that the GDP per area variable represents 'scale'.

Shukia and Parikh (1992) were primarily interested in the relationship between city size and ambient pollution levels for SO_2, particulates, and smoke. Using cross-sectional data from WRI (1989) they found that pollution rose with city size. However, when they added GDP per capita and its square to the regression, an inverted U was found with respect to city size. The EKC relationship holding city size constant was, however, U-shaped, although few coefficients are significant at conventional levels except for those in the particulates regression. This finding is similar to the results of Kaufmann et al (1997) and Panayotou (1997).

M\ *Economic structure*

Westbrook (1995), Suri and Chapman (1997), Rock (1996), Panayotou (1997) and Cooke (1997) all examine aspects of the output structure. Westbrook and Cooke both estimated models for CO_2 emissions and used a systematic breakdown of GDP into three or four major sectors. Suri and Chapman and Rock looked at the influence of the share in GDP of manufacturing on energy consumption and pollution intensity respectively.

Westbrook (1995) used a panel of 56 developing countries between 1971 and 1991. The omission of developed countries restricts generality, but many other EKCs omit developing or low-income countries instead. Of most interest is a regression of log emissions per capita on GNP per capita and its square, and the shares of GNP in agriculture and services. All the coefficients in the regression are significantly different from zero. The income relationship is an inverted U and, as would be expected, the signs of the industrial structure coefficients are negative, reflecting the lower emissions of agriculture and services relative to the industrial sector. The implication is that although industrial structure is a significant explanatory factor, other factors also contribute towards the inverted U relationship. Cooke's (1997) results (including both developed and developing countries) are very similar, and Suri and Chapman (1997) and Rock (1996) also find a positive coefficient for manufacturing. Panayotou (1997) finds similar results for the GEMS SO_2 data set.

EKC Decompositions

A few studies have attempted to decompose the EKC relationship into a number of more fundamental underlying components such as structural change, growth, scale, price and other effects. De Bruyn et al (1997) estimate the following regression individually for West Germany, the Netherlands, UK and US for groups of 17–29 observations over the period 1960–1993:

$$\Delta \ln E_{jt} = \beta_{0j} \Delta \ln Y_{jt} + \beta_{1j} + \beta_{2j} \ln Y_{jt-1} + \beta_{3j} \Delta \ln P_{jt} + \varepsilon_{jt} \qquad (3)$$

for CO_2, NO_x and SO_2, E is emissions, Y is income and P are energy prices. They interpret β_{0j} in terms of the scale effect. If $\beta_{1j} < 0$ and $\beta_{2j} = 0$, then they would attribute the declining emissions to exogenous technical change. If, however, $\beta_{2j} < 0$, then they would attribute the change to structural change and increased R&D efforts as income levels rise. β_{3j} would be expected to be less than unity in absolute value. In the cases examined, β_{0j} is positive and, except in one case, significant. β_{1j} is mostly zero or negative. β_{2j} is zero or negative and more significantly so for NO_x and for all three pollutants in Germany. β_{3j} is insignificant except for CO_2 in the US. Therefore, they conclude that structural change related to the income level is of importance. They argue that the decline in pollution seen in developed countries since the early 1970s is due to the slow rate of economic growth during this period. The on-going effects of the level of income in reducing pollution has not been overcome by the effects of growth in raising it. They also calculate the economic growth rates that are compatible with zero emissions growth, holding energy prices constant. For CO_2 these are 1.8 per cent in the UK and the Netherlands, 2.9 per cent in Germany and 0.3 per cent in the US where the price effect has had most influence in reducing emissions. Zero emissions growth rates are much higher for the other two pollutants, but lowest for the UK which has the least effective legislation.

This model can also be interpreted as a type of error correction model (see Cuthbertson et al, 1992), although there is no tendency to return to an equilibrium between income and emissions if emissions are perturbed by exogenous shocks. The price and growth effects have the effect of permanently shifting the emissions–income relationship. When $Y_{jt-1} = \exp(-\beta_{1j}/\beta_{2j})$ and growth and price inflation are zero, there is no tendency for emissions to change. Below this, income-level emissions tend to increase irrespective of the growth rate and above this level they tend to decline. The interpretation of β_{1j} and β_{2j} as technical and structural change parameters is therefore problematic.

De Bruyn (1997) carries out a Divisia index number decomposition (Ang, 1994) of SO_2 emissions in West Germany and the Netherlands for the 1990s. The method requires sector-by-sector emissions on the same basis as national accounting data and therefore will be difficult to apply elsewhere. The results indicate only a small role for structural change in reducing emissions.

Panayotou (1997) also claims to carry out a decomposition of the EKC. He estimated a cubic regression (with some cross-product terms dropped) of ambient concentrations of SO_2 on GDP per capita, GDP per square kilometre, industry shares, population density, the growth rate of GDP and a quality of institutions variable. GDP per square kilometre is supposed to represent scale, industry shares, structural change and GDP per capita – a pure income effect. The growth rate and population density terms are additional variables which are not seen as part of the decomposition per se. He argues that faster growth, higher population density, greater scale and industrialization worsen levels of pollution, while income and institutional variables can offset this deterioration. The abatement effect is, in fact, tenuous as although SO_2 concentrations fall with rising income up to about US$15,000 per capita (market exchange rates), they rise with income at higher levels. This latter effect is statistically significant. This 'decomposition' is problematic as it mixes both proximate and underlying causes of the EKC and yet omits some important variables such as trade flows or orientation.

Historical Events

Unruh and Moomaw (1997) and Moomaw and Unruh (1997) argue that the EKC theory that income reduces emissions is incorrect and instead reductions in emissions have been triggered by specific events such as the 1973 oil crisis. As an example, they find that the transition to lower per capita emissions of CO_2 can happen at varying income levels and tends to happen fairly abruptly. In particular, the major changes in countries as different as Spain and the US happened shortly after the oil price shocks of the 1970s. Moomaw and Unruh (1997) test for the existence of a structural break in 1973 in time series, cross-section and panel CO_2-income regressions. In general, emissions per capita decline as income per capita rises after 1973 and rise as a function of income per capita before 1973. But these countries were selected on the basis that visual inspection of the EKC plot shows evidence of a structural break around 1973. Given this sampling bias, statistical testing adds very little.

Progress on the EKC?

There are several promising signs in recent EKC papers. In particular, there is a concentration on investigating empirical determinants of the EKC. Also, four studies have looked at historical events (Unruh and Moomaw, 1997) or estimated EKCs for individual countries (Vincent, 1997; de Bruyn et al, 1997; Carson et al, 1997). Econometric practice does not seem to have improved (see below). In particular, the paper by Cole et al (1997) claims to address the statistical, issues raised by Stern et al (1996) such as investigating the simultaneity issue in a statistical sense. However, the deeper issues of irreversibility raised by Arrow et al (1995) have not been addressed adequately. EKCs for energy use have been estimated addressing the issue of the shifting nature of environmental impact. The different natures of EKCs and impact projections seems to be better understood than was shown by the World Bank Development Report in 1992 (eg Rothman, 1997). Differences between EKCs for ambient concentrations and emissions have also been discussed extensively.

Econometric technique is one aspect of the many studies that can be summarized quantitatively. Table 5.1 summarizes the key points concerning the econometric techniques used by the 25 studies that employ econometrics. The studies vary in terms of the type of data that they use. De Bruyn et al (1997) estimate separate time series regressions for each country hence the appropriateness of OLS, national currencies and the omission of a cubic term. The Vincent study is for the states of Malaysia and the Carson et al study for US states – hence the use of the national currency. Of the other studies, only the Schmalensee et al (1995) study uses all of what I consider the more sophisticated techniques (Stern et al, 1996). Table 5.2 summarizes these data in terms of the proportion of studies using the more sophisticated techniques. In the entire sample, use of panel data and fixed effects, or GLS estimation, are the most widely adopted techniques, while testing of cubic terms is the least adopted. Adoption of all the techniques, except the use of logarithmic-dependent variables, has increased from the pre-1997 sample to the post-1997 sample. The use of logarithmic-dependent variables as opposed to a dependent variable in levels declined between the two time periods. There is certainly an increase in sophistication over time.

Conclusions

There has been progress in understanding the scope and determinants of the EKC in the last few years and some progress in methods of investigation. Evidence continues to accumulate that the inverted U-shape relation only applies to a subset of impacts and that overall impact, perhaps approximately indicated by per capita energy use (Suri and Chapman, 1997), rises throughout the relevant income range. The current crop of studies shows surprisingly little interest in looking at whether impacts begin to rise again at high-income levels for those indicators where a mid-income turning-point has been identified.

Table 5.1 *Econometric techniques*

Authors	Date	Data type	Estimation technique	Dependent variable	Exchange rate	Cubic term	Regression diagnostics
Antle and Heidebrink	1995	C-S	OLS	Levels	Market	No	No
Carson et al	1997	C-S	OLS, GLS, non-parametric fit	Levels	National current	NA	Discussed but not presented
Cole et al	1997	Panel, C-S	FE/GLS, OLS	Logs and levels	PPP	No	*
Cropper and Griffiths	1994	Panel	FE	ΔLogs	PPP	No	No
de Bruyn et al	1997	Time series	OLS	ΔLogs	National currency	NA	Yes
de Bruyn	1997	C-S	OLS	Logs	Market	No	Yes
Grossman and Krueger	1991	Panel	RE	Levels	PPP	Yes	No
Holtz-Eakin and Selden	1995	Panel	FE	Logs and levels	PPP	No	*
Horvath	1997	Longitudinal	FE	Levels	PPP	Yes	No
Kaufmann et al	1997	Panel	OLS, FE, RE	Levels	PPP	No	Yes
Komen et al	1997	Panel	OLS, FE, RE, AR	Levels	PPP	No	Yes
Liddle	1996	Panel	FE	Logs and levels	PPP	No	Durbin-Watson
Moomaw and Unruh	1997	Time series, C-S and panel	OLS, FE	Levels	PPP	Yes	No
Panayotou	1993	C-S	OLS	Logs	Market	No	No
Panayotou	1997	Panel	FE/RE	Levels	Market	Yes	Yes
Rock	1996	C-S	OLS	Levels	Market	No	No
Rothman	1997	C-S	OLS	Levels	PPP	No	No

Authors	Date	Data type	Estimation technique	Dependent variable	Exchange rate	Cubic term	Regression diagnostics
Schmalensee et al	1995	Panel	FE, spline regression	Logs	PPP	NA	Yes
Selden and Song	1994	Panel	OLS, FE, RE	Levels	PPP	No	Yes
Shafik	1994	Panel, C-S	FE	Levels	PPP	Yes	No
Shukla and Parikh	1992	C-S	OLS	Levels	Market	No	No
Suri and Chapman	1997	Panel	FE, AR	Logs	PPP	No	No
Torras and Boyce	1996	Panel	OLS	Levels	PPP	Yes	No
Vincent	1997	Panel	FE, RE	Levels	National currency	Yes	Yes
Westbrook	1995	Panel	FE, RE	Logs	Market	No	No

Notes: C-S: cross-section, OLS: ordinary least squares, GLS: generalized least squares, FE: fixed effects, RE: random effects, AR: autocorrelation correction applied, PPP: purchasing power parity, *: results available from authors

Table 5.2 *Summary of econometric techniques*

Time period	Panel or longitudinal data	FE, RE, GLS	Logarithmic-dependent variable	PPP exchange rate	Cubic term	Regression diagnostics
All studies	71%	71%	40%	68%	32%	48%
Pre-1997	67%	67%	46%	58%	18%	33%
1997	75%	75%	33%	80%	45%	62%
Number of relevant studies	24	24	25	22	22	25

Note: For each variable the figure is the per cent using the technique in question of all the relevant papers

Knowledge has advanced furthest in terms of understanding the determinants of the EKC. It is clear that structural change and technological progress are of importance. Torras and Boyce (1996) show the importance of 'democracy' – a variable that is also a correlate of development – in lowering emissions. There is, however, increasing evidence that the EKC is partly determined by trade relations. If this is so, the poorest countries of today will find it more difficult than today's developed countries to reduce the environmental impact as income rises. Some studies present more disaggregated evidence that is of interest in evaluating the performance of individual countries and the influence of particular events. Change may occur quite rapidly in crisis periods such as the oil price shocks of the 1970s or the CFC negotiations of the 1980s. Some of the empirical relationships that have been uncovered may not be robust – although this is not yet known – the issue of omitted variables bias has not been adequately raised.

Despite such progress we know little about other issues. There has not been any explicit empirical testing of the theoretical models surveyed on pp93–94. De Bruyn et al (1997), de Bruyn (1997) and Panayotou (1997) have attempted to decompose the EKC into proximate causes. However, the de Bruyn (1997) study is very limited in scope in terms of countries and time periods studied and neither de Bruyn et al (1997) nor Panayotou (1997) carry out a rigorous and systematic decomposition. *Need more rigorous +systematic*

Acknowledgements

I thank the authors of the Boston ISEE Conference papers and Dale Rothman for making copies of those papers available to me. Charles Perrings provided me with preprints of the papers in the special issue of *Environment and Development Economics* on the EKC. Charles Perrings, Mick Common, Dale Rothman and three anonymous referees made very useful comments on draft versions of this chapter.

Notes

1   This specific result depends on a CES revenue function. For other aggregators the path could depend on further parameters
2   A similar model is developed by Ansuategi et al (1996)
3   The paper was later published as Grossman and Krueger (1994). See also Grossman and Krueger (1995)
4   See also Shafik (1994)
5   Shafik and Bandyopadhyay (1992) also carried out a number of additional regressions, adding various policy variables such as trade orientation, electricity prices, etc. The results of these are rather ambiguous and are not reported in Shafik (1994)
6   The majority of studies use panel data (Table 5.2)
7   See Levine and Renelt (1992) for a possible approach to investigating this problem.
8   For some pollutants one could imagine future technologies where emissions are essentially zero, eg for sulphur dioxide. A 100 per cent efficient pollutant recovery process is either physically infeasible or just uneconomic given the energy and material expenditures involved. So eliminating sulphur dioxide emissions means that no metals would be processed from sulphate ores using technologies that generate sulphur gases and no coal or oil, etc would be burnt. Such a state of technology is way off in the future, so the average impact will not be zero for some time to come. The marginal impact can well be negative at least for a range of incomes until abatement costs start rising sharply. From then on total impact will again start to rise. Also, all services require large expenditures of energy and materials so that a shift to the consumption of services will only partially aid in averting an upturn in environmental impacts
9   Schmalensee et al (1995) present results showing a within-sample turning-point for the carbon dioxide EKC. This paper is discussed on p99 above
10 The Gini coefficient is a measure of a nation's income inequality. Those coefficients closest to 1 are the most unequal

References

Ang, B W (1994) 'Decomposition of Industrial Energy Consumption: The Energy Intensity Approach', *Energy Economics,* no 16, pp163–174
Ansuategi, A, E B Barbier and C A Perrings (1996) 'The Environmental Kuznets Curve', paper presented at the USF Workshop 'Economic Modelling of Sustainable Development: Between Theory and Practice', Free University, Amsterdam, November. Authors at Department of Environmental Economics and Environmental Management, University of York
Antle, J M and G Heidebrink (1995) 'Environment and Development: Theory and International Evidence', *Economic Development and Cultural Change,* no 43, pp603–625
Arrow, K, B Bolin, R Costanza, P Dasgupta, C Folke, C S Holling, B-O Jansson, S Levin, K-G Mäler, C Perrings and D Pimentel (1995) 'Economic Growth, Carrying Capacity, and the Environment', *Science,* no 268, pp520–521

Barbier, E B (1994) 'Natural Capital and the Economics of Environment and Development', in A Jansson, M Hammer, C Folke and R Costanza (eds) *Investing in Natural Capital: The Ecological Economics Approach to Sustainability*, New York, Columbia University Press

Beckerman, W (1992) 'Economic Growth and the Environment: Whose Growth? Whose Environment?', *World Development*, no 20, pp481–496

Carson, R T, Y Jeon and D R McCubbin (1997) 'The Relationship Between Air Pollution Emissions and Income: US Data', *Environment and Development Economics*, vol 2, no 4, pp433–450

Cole, M A, A J Rayner and J M Bates (1997) 'The Environmental Kuznets Curve: An Empirical Analysis', *Environment and Development Economics*, vol 2, no 4, pp401–416

Common, M S (1995) *Sustainability and Policy: Limits to Economics*, Cambridge, Cambridge University Press

Cooke, K (1997) 'An Empirical Investigation of the Relationship Between Economic Development and Carbon Dioxide Emissions', Masters research essay, National Centre for Development Studies, Australian National University, Canberra

Cropper, M and C Griffiths (1994) 'The Interaction of Population Growth and Environmental Quality', *American Economic Review*, no 84, pp250–254

Cuthbertson, K, S G Hall and M P Taylor (1992) *Applied Econometric Techniques*, Ann Arbor, MI, University of Michigan Press

de Bruyn, S M (1997) 'Explaining the Environmental Kuznets Curve: Structural Change and International Agreements in Reducing Sulphur Emissions', *Environment and Development Economics*, vol 2, no 4, pp485–503

de Bruyn, S M and J B Opschoor (1994) 'Is the Economy Ecologizing?', Discussion Paper TI 94-65, Tinbergen Institute, Free University, Amsterdam

de Bruyn, S M, J C J M van den Bergh and J B Opschoor (1997) 'Economic Growth and Emissions: Reconsidering the Empirical Basis of Environmental Kuznets Curves', *Ecological Economics*, special issue on EKC

Ekins, P (1997) 'The Kuznets Curve for the Environment and Economic Growth: Examining the Evidence', *Environment and Planning A*, no 29, pp805–830

Ekins, P, C Folke and R Costanza (1994) 'Trade, Environment and Development: The Issues in Perspective', *Ecological Economics*, no 9, pp1–12

Forster, B A (1973) 'Optimal Capital Accumulation in a Polluted Environment', *Southern Economic Journal*, no 39, pp544–547

Grossman, G M and A B Krueger (1991) 'Environmental Impacts of a North American Free Trade Agreement', National Bureau of Economic Research Working Paper 3914, NBER, Cambridge, MA

Grossman, G M and A B Krueger (1994) 'Environmental Impacts of a North American Free Trade Agreement', in P Garber (ed) *The US–Mexico Free Trade Agreement*, Cambridge, MA, MIT Press

Grossman, G M and A B Krueger (1995) 'Economic Growth and the Environment', *Quarterly Journal of Economics*, no 112, pp353–378

Hettige, H, R E B Lucas and D Wheeler (1992) 'The Toxic Intensity of Industrial Production: Global Patterns, Trends, and Trade Policy', *American Economic Review*, vol 82, no 2, pp478–481

Holtz-Eakin, D and T M Selden (1995) 'Stoking the Fires? CO_2 Emissions and Economic Growth', *Journal of Public Economics*, no 57, pp85–101

Horvath, R J (1997) 'Energy Consumption and the Environmental Kuznets Curve Debate', Department of Geography, University of Sydney, Sydney, NSW

International Bank for Reconstruction and Development (IBRD) (1992) *World Development Report 1992: Development and the Environment*, New York, Oxford University Press

John, A and R Pecchenino (1994) 'An Overlapping Generations Model of Growth and the Environment', *Economic Journal*, no 104, pp1393–1410

John, A, R Pecchenino, D Schimmelpfennig and S Schreft (1995) 'Short-lived Agents and the Long-lived Environment', *Journal of Public Economics,* no 58, pp127–141

Kaufmann, R K, B Davidsdottir, S Garnham and P Pauly (1997) 'The Determinants of Atmospheric SO_2 Concentrations: Reconsidering the Environmental Kuznets Curve', *Erological Economics,* special issue on the EKC

Komen, M H C, S Cerking and H Folmer (1997) 'Income and Environmental R&D: Empirical Evidence from OECD Countries', *Environment and Development Economics,* vol 2, no 4, pp505–515

Kuznets, S (1955) 'Economic Growth and Income Inequality', *American Economic Review,* no 49, pp1–28

Levine, R and D Renelt (1992) 'A Sensitivity Analysis of Cross-country Growth Regressions', *American Economic Review,* no 82, pp942–963

Liddle, B T (1996) 'Environmental Kuznets Curves and Regional Pollution', paper presented at the 4th biennial conference of the International Society for Ecological Economics, Boston University, Boston, MA

Lopez, R (1994) 'The Environment as a Factor of Production: The Effects of Economic Growth and Trade Liberalization', *Journal of Environmental Economics and Management,* no 27, pp163–184

Lucas, R E B, D Wheeler and H Hettige (1992) 'Economic Development, Environmental Regulation and the International Migration of Toxic Industrial Pollution: 1960–1988', in P Low (ed) *International Trade and the Environment,* World Bank Discussion Paper no 159, Washington, DC

McConnell, K E (1997) 'Income and the Demand for Environmental Quality', *Environment and Development Economics,* vol 2, no 4, pp383–399

Meadows, D H, D L Meadows and J Randers (1992) *Beyond the Limits: Global Collapse or a Sustainable Future,* London, Earthscan

Meadows, D H, D L Meadows, J Randers and W Behrens (1972) *The Limits to Growth,* New York, Universe Books

Moomaw, W R and G C Unruh (1997) 'Are Environmental Kuznets Curves Misleading Us? The case of CO_2 Emissions', *Environment and Development Economics,* vol 2, no 4, pp451–463

Panayotou, T (1993) 'Empirical Tests and Policy Analysis of Environmental Degradation at Different Stages of Economic Development', Working Paper WP238, Technology and Employment Programme, International Labour Office, Geneva

Panayotou, T (1995) 'Environmental Degradation at Different Stages of Economic Development', in I Ahmed and J A Doeleman (eds) *Beyond Rio: The Environmental Crisis and Sustainable Livelihoods in the Third World,* London, Macmillan

Panayotou, T (1997) 'Demystifying the Environmental Kuznets Curve: Turning a Black Box into a Policy Tool', *Environment and Development Economics,* vol 2, no 4, pp465–484

Pearson, P J G (1994) 'Energy, Externalities, and Environmental Quality: Will Development Cure the Ills it Creates?', *Energy Studies Review,* no 6, pp199–216

Perrings, C A (1987) *Economy and Environment: A Theoretical Essay on the Interdependence of Economic and Environmental Systems,* Cambridge University Press

Pezzey, J C V (1989) 'Economic Analysis of Sustainable Growth and Sustainable Development', Environment Department Working Paper no 15, World Bank, Washington, DC

Pollak, R A and T J Wales (1992) *Demand System Specification and Estimation,* New York, Oxford University Press

Rock, M T (1956) 'Pollution Intensity of GDP and Trade Policy: Can the World Bank be Wrong?' *World Development,* no 24, pp471–479

Rothman, D S (1996) 'Basic Economic Indicators', in L Roberts et al (eds) *World Resources: A Guide to the Global Environment,* New York, Oxford University Press

Rothman, D S (1997), 'Environmental Kuznets Curves – Real Progress or Passing the Buck? A Case for Consumption-based Approaches', *Ecological Economics,* special issue on the EKC

Schmalensee, R, T M Stoker and R A Judson (1995) 'World Energy Consumption and Carbon Dioxide Emissions: 1950–2050', Sloan School of Management, Massachusetts Institute of Technology, Cambridge, MA

Selden, T M and D Song (1994) 'Environmental Quality and Development: Is There a Kuznets Curve for Air Pollution?', *Journal of Environmental Economics and Environmental Management,* no 27, pp147–162

Selden, T M and D Song (1995) 'Neoclassical Growth, the J Curve for Abatement and the Inverted U Curve for Pollution', *Journal of Environmental Economics and Environmental Management,* no 29, pp162–168

Shafik, N (1994) 'Economic Development and Environmental Quality: An Econometric Analysis', *Oxford Economic Papers,* no 46, pp757–773

Shafik, N and S Bandyopadhyay (1992) 'Economic Growth and Environmental Quality: Time Series and Cross-country Evidence', Background Paper for the World Development Report 1992, World Bank, Washington, DC

Shukia, V and K Parikh (1992) 'The Environmental Consequences of Urban Growth: Cross-national Perspectives on Economic Development, Air Pollution, and City Size', *Urban Geography,* no 12, pp422–449

Stern, D I (1992) 'Population Distribution in an Ethno-ideologically Divided City: The Case of Jerusalem', *Urban Geography,* no 13, pp164–186

Stern, D I, M S Common and E B Barbier (1996) 'Economic Growth and Environmental Degradation: The Environmental Kuznets Curve and Sustainable Development', *World Development,* no 24, pp1151–1160

Suri, V and D Chapman (1997) 'Economic Growth, Trade and Energy: Implications for the Environmental Kuznets Curve', *Ecological Economics,* special issue on the EKC

Torras, M and J K Boyce (1996) 'Income, Inequality, and Pollution: A Reassessment of the Environmental Kuznets Curve', *Ecological Economics,* special issue on the EKC

Unruh, G C and W R Moomaw (1997) 'An Alternative Analysis of Apparent EKC-type Transitions', *Ecological Economics,* special issue on the EKC

Vincent, J R (1997) 'Testing for Environmental Kuznets Curves within a Developing Country', *Environment and Development Economic,* vol 2, no 4, pp417–431

Westbrook, T (1995) 'An Empirical Examination of the Relation Between Carbon Dioxide Emissions and Economic Development, and Carbon Dioxide Emissions and Economic Structure', MSc dissertation, Department of Environmental Economics and Environmental Management, University of York, York, UK

World Commission on Environment and Development (1987), *Our Common Future,* Oxford, Oxford University Press

WRI (1989) *World Resources 1988–89,* World Resources Institute, Washington, DC

WRI (1991) *World Resources 1990–91,* World Resources Institute, Washington, DC

6

Towards a New Conception of the Environment–Competitiveness Relationship

Michael E Porter and Claas van der Linde

The relationship between environmental goals and industrial competitiveness has normally been thought of as involving a trade-off between social benefits and private costs. The issue was how to balance society's desire for environmental protection with the economic burden on industry. Framed this way, environmental improvement becomes a kind of arm-wrestling match. One side pushes for tougher standards; the other side tries to beat the standards back.

Our central message is that the environment–competitiveness debate has been framed incorrectly. The notion of an inevitable struggle between ecology and the economy grows out of a static view of environmental regulation, in which technology, products, processes and customer needs are all fixed. In this static world, where firms have already made their cost-minimizing choices, environmental regulation inevitably raises costs and will tend to reduce the market share of domestic companies on global markets.

However, the paradigm defining competitiveness has been shifting, particularly in the last 20–30 years, away from this static model. The new paradigm of international competitiveness is a dynamic one, based on innovation. A body of research first published in *The Competitive Advantage of Nations* has begun to address these changes (Porter, 1990). Competitiveness at the industry level arises from superior productivity, either in terms of lower costs than rivals or the ability to offer products with superior value that justify a premium price.[1] Detailed case studies of hundreds of industries, based in dozens of countries, reveal that internationally competitive companies are not those with the cheapest inputs or the largest scale, but those with the capacity to improve and innovate continually. (We use the term innovation broadly, to include a product's or service's design, the segments it serves, how it is produced, how it is marketed and how it is supported.) Competitive advantage, then, rests not on static efficiency nor on optimizing within fixed constraints, but on the capacity for innovation and improvement that shift the constraints.

This paradigm of dynamic competitiveness raises an intriguing possibility: in this chapter, we will argue that properly designed environmental standards can trigger innovation that may partially or more than fully offset the costs of complying with them. Such 'innovation offsets', as we call them, can not only lower the net cost of meeting environmental regulations, but can even lead to absolute advantages over firms in foreign countries that are not subject to similar regulations.

Innovation offsets will be common because reducing pollution is often coincident with improving the productivity with which resources are used. In short, firms can actually benefit from properly crafted environmental regulations that are more stringent (or are imposed earlier) than those faced by their competitors in other countries. By stimulating innovation, strict environmental regulations can actually enhance competitiveness.

There is a legitimate and continuing controversy over the social benefits of specific environmental standards, and there is a huge benefit-cost literature. Some believe that the risks of pollution have been overstated; others fear the reverse. Our focus here is not on the social benefits of environmental regulation, but on the private costs. Our argument is that whatever the level of social benefits, these costs are far higher than they need to be. The policy focus, then, should be on relaxing the trade-off between competitiveness and the environment rather than accepting it as a given.

The Link from Regulation to Promoting Innovation

It is sometimes argued that companies, by the very notion of profit seeking, must be pursuing all profitable innovations. In the metaphor that economists often cite, US$10 bills will never be found on the ground because someone would have already picked them up. In this view, if complying with environmental regulation can be profitable, in the sense that a company can more than offset the cost of compliance, then why is such regulation necessary?

The possibility that regulation might act as a spur to innovation arises because the world does not fit the Panglossian belief that firms always make optimal choices. This will hold true only in a static optimization framework where information is perfect and profitable opportunities for innovation have already been discovered, so that profit-seeking firms need only choose their approach. Of course, this does not describe reality. Instead, the actual process of dynamic competition is characterized by changing technological opportunities coupled with highly incomplete information, organizational inertia and control problems reflecting the difficulty of aligning individual, group and corporate incentives. Companies have numerous avenues for technological improvement and limited attention.

Actual experience with energy-saving investments illustrates that in the real world, US$10 bills are waiting to be picked up. As one example, consider the 'Green Lights' programme of the Environmental Protection Agency (EPA). Firms volunteering to participate in this programme pledge to scrutinize every avenue of electrical energy consumption. In return, they receive advice on efficient lighting, heating and cooling operations. When the EPA collected data on energy-saving lighting upgrades reported by companies as part of the Green Lights programme, it showed that nearly 80 per cent of the projects had paybacks of two years or less (DeCanio, 1993). Yet only after companies became part of the programme and benefited from information and cajoling from the EPA, were these highly profitable projects carried out. This chapter will present numerous other examples of where environmental innovation produces net benefits for private companies.[2]

We are currendy in a transitional phase of industrial history where companies are still inexperienced in dealing creatively with environmental issues. The environment has not been a principal area of corporate or technological emphasis, and knowledge about environmental impacts is still rudimentary in many firms and industries, elevating uncertainty about innovation benefits. Customers are also unaware of the costs of resource inefficiency in the packaging they discard, the scrap value they forgo and the disposal costs they bear. Rather than attempt to innovate in every direction at once, firms in fact make choices based on how they perceive their competitive situation and the world around them. In such a world, regulation can be an important influence on the direction of innovation, either for better or for worse. Properly crafted environmental regulation can serve at least six purposes.

First, regulation signals companies about the likely resource inefficiencies and potential technological improvements. Companies are still inexperienced in measuring their discharges, understanding the full costs of the incomplete utilization of resources and toxicity, and conceiving new approaches to minimize discharges or eliminate hazardous substances. Regulation rivets attention on this area of potential innovation.[3]

Second, regulation focused on information-gathering can achieve major benefits by raising corporate awareness. For example. Toxics Release Inventories, which are published annually as part of the 1986 Superfund reauthorization, require more than 20,000 manufacturing plants to report their releases of some 320 toxic chemicals. Such information-gathering often leads to environmental improvement without mandating pollution reductions, sometimes even at lower costs.

Third, regulation reduces the uncertainty that investments to address the environment will be valuable. Greater certainty encourages investment in any area.

Fourth, regulation creates pressure that motivates innovation and progress. Our broader research on competitiveness highlights the important role of outside pressure in the innovation process, to overcome organizational inertia, foster creative thinking and mitigate agency problems. Economists are used to the argument that pressure for innovation can come from strong competitors, demanding customers or rising prices of raw materials; we are arguing that properly crafted regulation can also provide such pressure.

Fifth, regulation levels the transitional playing-field. During the transition period to innovation-based solutions, regulation ensures that one company cannot gain position opportunistically by avoiding environmental investments. Regulations provide a buffer until new technologies become proven and learning effects reduce their costs.

Sixth, regulation is needed in the case of incomplete offsets. We readily admit that innovation cannot always completely offset the cost of compliance, especially in the short term before learning can reduce the cost of innovation-based solutions. In such cases, regulation will be necessary to improve environmental quality.

Stringent regulation can actually produce greater innovation and innovation offsets than lax regulation. Relatively lax regulation can be dealt with incrementally and without innovation, and often with 'end-of-pipe' or secondary treatment solutions. More stringent regulation, however, focuses greater company attention on discharges and emissions, and compliance requires more fundamental solutions, like reconfiguring products and processes. While the cost of compliance may rise with stringency, then, the potential for innovation offsets may rise even faster. Thus the *net* cost of compliance can fall with stringency and may even turn into a net benefit.

How Innovation Offsets Occur

Innovation in response to environmental regulation can take two broad forms. The first is that companies simply get smarter about how to deal with pollution once it occurs, including the processing of toxic materials and emissions, how to reduce the amount of toxic or harmful material generated (or convert it into saleable forms) and how to improve secondary treatment. Molten Metal Technology, of Waltham, Massachusetts, for example, has developed a catalytic extraction method to process many types of hazardous waste efficiently and effectively. This sort of innovation reduces the cost of compliance with pollution control, but changes nothing else.

The second form of innovation addresses environmental impacts while simultaneously improving the affected product itself and/or related processes. In some cases, these 'innovation offsets' can exceed the costs of compliance. This second sort of innovation is central to our claim that environmental regulation can actually increase industrial competitiveness.

Innovation offsets can be broadly divided into product offsets and process offsets. Product offsets occur when environmental regulation produces not just less pollution, but also creates better performing or higher quality products, safer products, lower product costs (perhaps from material substitution or less packaging), products with higher resale or scrap value (because of ease in recycling or disassembly) or lower costs of product disposal for users. Process offsets occur when environmental regulation not only leads to reduced pollution, but also results in higher resource productivity such as higher process yields, less downtime through more careful monitoring and maintenance, materials savings (due to substitution, reuse or recycling of production inputs), better utilization of by-products, lower energy consumption during the production process, reduced material storage and handling costs, conversion of waste into valuable forms, reduced waste-disposal costs or safer workplace conditions. These offsets are frequently related, so that achieving one can lead to the realization of several others.

As yet, no broad tabulation exists of innovation offsets. Most of the work done in this area involves case studies, because case studies are the only vehicle currently available to measure compliance costs, and both direct and indirect innovation benefits. This chapter is not the place for a comprehensive listing of available case studies. However, offering some examples should help the reader to understand how common and plausible such effects are.

Innovation to comply with environmental regulation often improves product performance or quality. In 1990, for instance, Raytheon found itself required (by the Montreal Protocol and the US Clean Air Act) to eliminate ozone-depleting chlorofluorocarbons (CFCs) used for cleaning printed electronic circuit boards after the soldering process. Scientists at Raytheon initially thought that complete elimination of CFCs would be impossible. However, eventually they adopted a new semi-aqueous, terpene-based cleaning agent that could be reused. The new method proved to result in an increase in average product quality, which had occasionally been compromised by the old CFC-based cleaning agent, as well as lower operating costs (Raytheon, 1991, 1993). It would not have been adopted in the absence of environmental regulation mandating the phase-out of CFCs. Another example is the move by the Robbins Company (a jewellery company based in Attleboro, Massachusetts) to a closed-loop, zero-discharge system for handling the water used in plating (Berube, Nash, Maxwell and Ehrenfeld, 1992). Robbins was facing closure due to violation of its existing discharge permits. The water produced by purification through filtering and ion exchange in the new closed-loop system was 40 times cleaner than city water and led to higher quality plating and fewer rejects. The result was enhanced competitiveness.

Environmental regulations may also reduce product costs by showing how to eliminate costly materials, reduce unnecessary packaging or simplify designs. Hitachi responded to a 1991 Japanese recycling law by redesigning products to reduce disassembly time. In the process, the number of parts in a washing-machine fell 16 per cent and the number of parts on a vacuum cleaner fell 30 per cent. In this way, moves to redesign products for better recyclability can lead to fewer components and thus easier assembly.

Environmental standards can also lead to innovation that reduces disposal costs (or boost scrap or resale value) for the user. For instance, regulation that requires the recyclability of products can lead to designs that allow valuable materials to be recovered more easily after disposal of the product. Either the customer or the manufacturer who takes back used products reaps greater value.

These have all been examples of product offsets, but process offsets are common as well. Process changes to reduce emissions frequently result in increases in product yields. At Ciba-Geigy's dyestuff plant in New Jersey, the need to meet new environmental standards caused the firm to re-examine its wastewater streams. Two changes in its production process – replacing iron with a different chemical conversion agent that did not result in the formation of solid iron sludge and process changes that eliminated the release of potentially toxic product into the wastewater stream – not only boosted yield by 40 per cent but also eliminated wastes, resulting in annual cost savings of US$740,000 (Dorfman, Muir and Miller, 1992).[4]

Similarly, 3M discovered that in producing adhesives in batches that were transferred to storage tanks, one bad batch could spoil the entire contents of a tank. The result was wasted raw materials and high costs of hazardous waste disposal. 3M developed a new technique to run quality tests more rapidly on new batches. The new technique allowed 3M to reduce hazardous wastes by 10 tonnes per year at almost no cost, yielding an annual savings of more than US$200,000 (Sheridan, 1992).

Solving environmental problems can also yield benefits in terms of reduced downtime. Many chemical production processes at DuPont, for example, require start-up time to stabilize and bring output within specifications, resulting in an initial period during which only scrap and waste is produced. Installing higher quality monitoring equipment has allowed DuPont to reduce production interruptions and the associated wasteful production start-ups, thus reducing waste generation as well as downtime (Parkinson, 1990).

Regulation can trigger innovation offsets through substitution of less costly materials or better utilization of materials in the process. For example, 3M faced new regulations that will force many solvent users in paper, plastic and metal coatings to reduce their solvent emissions by 90 per cent by 1995 (Boroughs and Carpenter, 1991). The company responded by avoiding the use of solvents altogether and developing coating products with safer, water-based solutions. At another 3M plant, a change from a solvent-based to a water-based carrier, used for coating tablets, eliminated 24 tonnes per year of air emissions. The US$60,000 investment saved US$180,000 in unneeded pollution-control equipment and created annual savings of US$15,000 in solvent purchases (Parkinson, 1990). Similarly, when federal and state regulations required that Dow Chemical close certain evaporation ponds used for storing and evaporating wastewater resulting from scrubbing hydrochloric gas with caustic soda, Dow redesigned its production process. By first scrubbing the hydrochloric acid with water and then caustic soda, Dow was able to eliminate the need for evaporation ponds, reduce its use of caustic soda and capture a portion of the waste stream for reuse as a raw material in other parts of the plant. This process change cost US$250,000 to implement. It reduced caustic waste by 6000 tonnes per year and hydrochloric acid waste by 80 tonnes per year, for a saving of US$2.4 million per year (Dorfman, Muir and Miller, 1992).

The Robbins Company's jewellery-plating system illustrates similar benefits. In moving to the closed-loop system that purified and recycled water, Robbins saved over US$115,000 per year in water, chemicals, disposal costs and laboratory fees, and reduced water usage from 500,000 gallons per week to 500 gallons per week. The capital cost of the new system, which completely eliminated the waste, was US$220,000, compared to about US$500,000 for a wastewater treatment facility that would have brought Robbins' discharge into compliance only with current regulations.

At the Tobyhanna Army Depot, for instance, improvements in sandblasting, cleaning, plating and painting operations reduced hazardous waste generation by 82 per cent between 1985 and 1992. That reduction saved the depot over US$550,000 in disposal costs, and US$400,000 in material purchasing and handling costs (PR Newswire, 1993).

Innovation offsets can also be derived by converting waste into more valuable forms. The Robbins Company recovered valuable precious metals in its zero discharge plating system. At Rhône-Poulenc's nylon plant in Chalampe, France, diacids (by-products that had been produced by an adipic acid process) used to be separated and incinerated. Rhône-Poulenc invested Fr76 million and installed new equipment to recover and sell them as dye and tanning additives or coagulation agents, resulting in annual revenues of about Fr20.1 million. In the US, similar by-products from a Monsanto Chemical Company plant in Pensacola, Florida, are sold to utility companies who use them to accelerate sulphur dioxide removal during flue gas desulphurization (Basta and Vagi, 1988).

A few studies of innovation offsets do go beyond individual cases and offer some broader-based data. One of the most extensive studies is by INFORM, an environmental research organization. INFORM investigated activities to prevent waste generation – so-called source reduction activities – at 29 chemical plants in California, Ohio and New Jersey (Dorfman, Muir and Miller, 1992). Of the 181 source-reduction activities identified in this study, only one was found to have resulted in a net cost increase. Of the 70 activities for which the study was able to document changes in product yield, 68 reported yield increases; the average yield increase for the 20 initiatives with specific available data was 7 per cent. These innovation offsets were achieved with surprisingly low investments and very short payback periods. One-quarter of the 48 initiatives with detailed capital cost information required no capital investment at all; of the 38 initiatives with payback period data, nearly two-thirds were shown to have recouped their initial investments in six months or less. The annual savings per dollar spent on source reduction averaged US$3.49 for the 27 activities for which this information could be calculated. The study also investigated the motivating factors behind the plant's source-reduction activities. Significantly, it found that waste-disposal costs were the most often cited, followed by environmental regulation.

To build a broader base of studies on innovation offsets to environmental regulation, we have been collaborating with the Management Institute for Environment and Business on a series of international case studies, sponsored by the EPA, of industries and entire sectors significantly affected by environmental regulation. Sectors studied include pulp and paper, paint and coatings, electronics manufacturing, refrigerators, dry-cell batteries and printing inks (Bonifant and Ratcliffe, 1994; Bonifant 1994a, b; van der Linde, 1995a, b, c). Some examples from that effort have already been described here.

A solid body of case study evidence, then, demonstrates that innovation offsets to environmental regulation are common.[5] Even with a generally hostile regulatory climate, which is not designed to encourage such innovation, these offsets can sometimes exceed the cost of compliance. We expect that such examples will proliferate as companies and regulators become more sophisticated and shed old mindsets.

Early-mover Advantage in International Markets

World demand is moving rapidly in the direction of valuing low-pollution and energy-efficient products, not to mention more resource-efficient products with higher resale or scrap value. Many companies are using innovation to command price premiums for 'green' products and open up new market segments. For example, Germany enacted recycling standards earlier than in most other countries, which gave German firms an early-mover advantage in developing less packaging-intensive products, which have been warmly received in the marketplace. Scandinavian pulp and paper producers have been leaders in introducing new environmentally friendly production processes, and thus Scandinavian pulp and paper equipment suppliers such as Kamyr and Sunds have made major gains internationally in selling innovative bleaching equipment. In the US, a parallel example is the development by Cummins Engine of low-emissions diesel engines for trucks, buses and other applications in response to US environmental regulations. Its new competence is allowing the firm to gain international market share.

Clearly, this argument only works to the extent that national environmental standards anticipate and are consistent with international trends in environmental protection, rather than break with them. Creating expertise in cleaning up abandoned hazardous waste sites, as the US Superfund law has done, does little to benefit US suppliers if no other country adopts comparable toxic waste clean-up requirements. But when a competitive edge is attained, especially because a company's home market is sophisticated and demanding in a way that pressures the company to further innovation, the economic gains can be lasting.

Answering Defenders of the Traditional Model

Our argument that strict environmental regulation can be fully consistent with competitiveness was originally put forward in a short *Scientific American* essay (Porter, 1991; see also van der Linde, 1993). This essay received far more scrutiny than we expected. It has been warmly received by many, especially in the business community. But it has also had its share of critics, especially among economists (Jaffe, Peterson, Portney and Stavins, 1993,1994; Oates, Palmer and Portney, 1993; Palmer and Simpson, 1993; Simpson, 1993; Schmalensee, 1993).

One criticism is that while innovation offsets are theoretically possible, they are likely to be rare or small in practice. We disagree. Pollution is the emission or discharge of a (harmful) substance or energy form into the environment. Fundamentally, it is a manifestation of economic waste and involves the unnecessary, inefficient or incomplete utilization of resources, or resources that are not used to generate their highest value. In many cases, emissions are a sign of inefficiency and force a firm to perform non-value-creating activities such as handling, storage and disposal. Within the company itself, the costs of poor resource utilization are most obvious in incomplete material utilization, but are also manifested in poor process control which generates unnecessary stored material, waste and defects. There are many other hidden costs of resource inefficiencies later in the life-cycle of the product. Packaging discarded by distributors or customers, for example, wastes resources and adds costs. Customers bear additional costs when they use polluting products or products that waste energy. Resources are also wasted when customers discard products embodying unused materials or when they bear the costs of product disposal.[6]

As the many examples discussed earlier suggest, the opportunity to reduce cost by diminishing pollution should thus be the rule, not the exception. Highly toxic materials such as heavy metals or solvents are often expensive and hard to handle, and reducing their use makes sense from several points of view. More broadly, efforts to reduce pollution and maximize profits share the same basic principles, including the efficient use of inputs, the substitution of less expensive materials and the minimization of unneeded activities.[7]

A corollary to this observation is that scrap or waste or emissions can carry important information about flaws in product design or the production process.

A recent study of process changes in 10 printed circuit-board manufacturers, for example, found that 13 of 33 major changes were initiated by pollution-control personnel. Of these, 12 resulted in cost reduction, 8 in quality improvements and 5 in the extension of production capabilities (King, 1994).

Environmental improvement efforts have traditionally overlooked the systems cost of resource inefficiency. Improvement efforts have focused on *pollution control* through better identification, processing and disposal of discharges or waste, an inherently costly approach. In recent years, more advanced companies and regulators have embraced the concept of *pollution prevention,* sometimes called source reduction, which uses material substitution, closed-loop processes and the like to limit pollution before it occurs.

But although pollution prevention is an important step in the right direction, ultimately companies and regulators must learn to frame environmental improvement in terms of *resource productivity, or* the efficiency and effectiveness with which companies and their customers use resources.[8] Improving resource productivity within companies goes beyond eliminating pollution (and the cost of dealing with it) to lowering true economic cost and raising the true economic value of products. At the level of resource productivity, environmental improvement and competitiveness come together. The imperative for resource productivity rests on the private costs that companies bear because of pollution, not on mitigating pollution's social costs. In addressing these private costs, it highlights the opportunity costs of pollution – wasted resources, wasted efforts and diminished product value to the customer – not its actual costs.

This view of pollution as unproductive resource utilization suggests a helpful analogy between environmental protection and product quality measured by defects. Companies used to promote quality by conducting careful inspections during the production process and then by creating a service organization to correct the quality problems that turned up in the field. This approach has proven misguided. Instead, the most cost-effective way to improve quality is to build it into the entire process, which includes design, purchased components, process technology, shipping and handling techniques, and so forth. This method dramatically reduces inspection, rework and the need for a large service organization. (It also leads to the often-quoted phrase 'quality is free'.) Similarly, there is reason to believe that companies can enjoy substantial innovation offsets by improving resource productivity throughout the value chain instead of through dealing with the manifestations of inefficiency like emissions and discharges.

Indeed, corporate total quality management programmes have strong potential also to reduce pollution and lead to innovation offsets.[9] Dow Chemical, for example, has explicitly identified the link between quality improvement and environmental performance by using statistical process control to reduce the variance in processes and lower waste (Sheridan, 1992).

A second criticism of our hypothesis is to point to the studies finding high costs of compliance with environmental regulation, as evidence that there is a fixed trade-off between regulation and competitiveness. But these studies are far from definitive.

Estimates of regulatory compliance costs prior to the enactment of a new rule typically exceed the actual costs. In part, this is because such estimates are often

self-reported by industries who oppose the rule, which creates a tendency to inflation. A prime example of this type of thinking was a statement by Lee Iacocca, then
vice-president at the Ford Motor Company, during the debate on the 1970 Clean Air
Act. Iacocca warned that compliance with the new regulations would require huge
price increases for cars, force US car production to a halt after 1 January 1975 and
'do irreparable damage to the US economy' (Smith, 1992). The 1970 Clean Air Act
was subsequently enacted and Iacocca's predictions proved to be wrong. Similar dire
predictions were made during the 1990 Clean Air Act debate; industry analysts
predicted that burdens on the US industry would exceed US$100 billion. Of course,
the reality has proved to be far less dramatic. In one study in the pulp and paper
sector, actual costs of compliance were US$4.00–5.50 per tonne compared to origi-
nal industry estimates of US$16.40 (Bonson, McCubbin and Sprague, 1988).

Early estimates of compliance cost also tend to be exaggerated because they
assume no innovation. Early cost estimates for dealing with regulations concerning
the emission of volatile compounds released during paint application held everything else constant, assuming only the addition of a hood to capture the fumes from
paint lines. Innovation that improved the paint's transfer efficiency subsequently
allowed not only the reduction of fumes but also paint usage. Further innovation in
water-borne paint formulations without any volatile organic compound (VOC) re-
leasing solvents made it possible to eliminate the need for capturing and treating the
fumes altogether (Bonifant, 1994b). Similarly, early estimates of the costs of complying with a 1991 federal clean air regulation calling for a 98 per cent reduction
in atmospheric emissions of benzene from tar-storage tanks used by coal-tar distillers initially assumed that tar-storage tanks would have to be covered by costly gas
blankets. While many distillers opposed the regulations, Pittsburgh-based Aristech
Chemical, a major distiller of coal tar, subsequently developed an innovative way
to remove benzene from tar in the first processing step, thereby eliminating the
need for the gas blanket and resulting in a saving of US$3.3 million instead of a
cost increase (PR Newswire, 1993).

Prices in the new market for trading allowances to emit sulphur dioxide (SO_2)
provide another vivid example. At the time the law was passed, analysts projected
that the marginal cost of SO_2 controls (and, therefore, the price of an emissions
allowance) would be in the order of US$300–600 (or more) per ton in Phase I and
up to US$1000 or more in Phase II. Actual Phase I allowance prices have turned
out to be in the US$170–250 range and recent trades are heading lower, with Phase
II estimates only slightly higher (after adjusting for the time value of money). In case
after case, the differences between initial predictions and actual outcomes – especially after industry has had time to learn and innovate – are striking.

Econometric studies showing that environmental regulation raises costs and
harms competitiveness are subject to bias, because net compliance costs are over-
estimated by assuming away innovation benefits. Jorgenson and Wilcoxen (1990),
for example, explicitly state that they did not attempt to assess public or private
benefits. Other often-cited studies that focus solely on costs, leaving out benefits,
are Hazilla and Kopp (1990) and Gray (1987). By largely assuming away innovation
effects, how could economic studies reach any other conclusion than they do?

Internationally competitive industries seem to be much better able to innovate in response to environmental regulation than industries that were uncompetitive to begin with, but no study measuring the effects of environmental regulation on industry competitiveness has taken initial competitiveness into account. In a study by Kalt (1988), for instance, the sectors where high environmental costs were associated with negative trade performance were ones such as ferrous metal mining, non-ferrous mining, chemical and fertilizer manufacturing, primary iron and steel and primary non-ferrous metals, industries in which the US suffers from dwindling raw material deposits, very high relative electricity costs, heavily subsidized foreign competitors and other disadvantages that have rendered them uncompetitive, quite apart from the environmental costs.[10] Other sectors identified by Kalt as having incurred very high environmental costs can actually be interpreted as supporting our hypothesis. Chemicals, plastics and synthetics, fabric, yarn and thread, miscellaneous textiles, leather tanning, paints and allied products, and paperboard containers all had high environmental costs but displayed positive trade performance.

A number of studies have failed to find that stringent environmental regulation hurts industrial competitiveness. Meyer (1992, 1993) tested and refuted the hypothesis that US states with stringent environmental policies experience weak economic growth. Leonard (1998) was unable to demonstrate statistically significant offshore movements by US firms in pollution-intensive industries. Wheeler and Mody (1992) failed to find that environmental regulation affected the foreign investment decisions of US firms. Repetto (1995) found that industries heavily affected by environmental regulations experienced slighter reductions in their share of world exports than did the entire American industry from 1970 to 1990. Using US Bureau of Census Data of more than 200,000 large manufacturing establishments, the study also found that plants with poor environmental records are generally not more profitable than cleaner ones in the same industry, even controlling for their age, size and technology. Jaffe, Peterson, Portney and Stavins (1993) recently surveyed more than 100 studies and concluded there is little evidence to support the view that US environmental regulation had a large adverse effect on competitiveness.

Of course, these studies offer no proof for our hypothesis, either. But it is striking that so many studies find that even the poorly designed environmental laws presently in effect have little adverse effect on competitiveness. After all, traditional approaches to regulation have surely worked to stifle potential innovation offsets and imposed unnecessarily high costs of compliance on industry. Thus, studies using actual compliance costs to regulation are heavily biased towards finding that such regulation has a substantial cost.[11] In no way do such studies measure the potential of well-crafted environmental regulations to stimulate competitiveness.

A third criticism of our thesis is that even if regulation fosters innovation, it will harm competitiveness by crowding out other potentially more productive investments or avenues for innovation. Given incomplete information, the limited attention that many companies have devoted to environmental innovations and the inherent linkage between pollution and resource productivity described earlier, it certainly is not obvious that this line of innovation has been so thoroughly explored that the marginal benefits of further investment would be low. The high returns evident in the studies we have cited support this view. Moreover, environmental investments represent only a small percentage of overall investment in all but a very few industries.[12]

A final counterargument, more caricature than criticism, is that we are asserting that any strict environmental regulation will inevitably lead to innovation and competitiveness. Of course, this is not our position. Instead, we believe that if regulations are properly crafted and companies are attuned to the possibilities, then innovation to minimize and even offset the cost of compliance is likely in many circumstances.

Designing Environmental Regulation to Encourage Innovation

If environmental standards are to foster the innovation offsets that arise from new technologies and approaches to production, they should adhere to three principles. First, they must create the maximum opportunity for innovation, leaving the approach to innovation to industry and not the standard-setting agency. Second, regulations should foster continuous improvement, rather than locking in any particular technology. Third, the regulatory process should leave as little room as possible for uncertainty at every stage. Evaluated by these principles, it is clear that US environmental regulations have often been crafted in a way that deters innovative solutions or even renders them impossible. Environmental laws and regulations need to take three substantial steps: phrasing environmental rules as goals that can be met in flexible ways; encouraging innovation to reach and exceed those goals; and administering the system in a coordinated way.

Clear Goals, Flexible Approaches

Environmental regulation should focus on outcomes, not technologies.[13] Past regulations have often prescribed particular remediation technologies – like catalysts or scrubbers to address air pollution – rather than encouraging innovative approaches. American environmental law emphasized phrases like 'best available technology', or 'best available control technology'. But legislating as if one particular technology is always the 'best' almost guarantees that innovation will not occur.

Regulations should encourage product and process changes to better utilize resources and avoid pollution early, rather than mandating end-of-pipe or secondary treatment, which is almost always more costly. For regulators, this poses a question of where to impose regulations in the chain of production from raw materials, equipment, the producer of the end product, to the consumer (Porter, 1985). Regulators must consider the technological capabilities and resources available at each stage, because it affects the likelihood that innovation will occur. With that in mind, the governing principle should be to regulate as late in the production chain as practical, which will normally allow more flexibility for innovation there and in upstream stages.

The EPA should move beyond the single medium (air, water, and so on) as the principal way of thinking about the environment, towards total discharges or total impact.[14] It should reorganize around affected industry clusters (including suppliers and related industries) to better understand a cluster's products, technologies and total set of environmental problems. This will foster fundamental rather than piecemeal solutions.[15]

Seeding and Spreading Environmental Innovations

Where possible, regulations should include the use of market incentives, including pollution taxes, deposit-refund schemes and tradable permits.[16] Such approaches often allow considerable flexibility, reinforce resource productivity and also create incentives for ongoing innovation. Mandating outcomes by setting emissions levels, while preferable to choosing a particular technology, still fails to provide incentives for continued and ongoing innovation, and will tend to freeze the status quo until new regulations appear. In contrast, market incentives can encourage the introduction of technologies that exceed current standards.

The EPA should also promote an increased use of pre-emptive standards by industry, which appear to be an effective way of dealing with environmental regulation. Pre-emptive standards, agreed to with EPA oversight to avoid collusion, can be set and met by industry to avoid government standards that might go further or be more restrictive on innovation. They are not only less costly, but allow faster change and leave the initiative for innovation with industry.

The EPA should play a major role in collecting and disseminating information on innovation offsets and their consequences, both here and in other countries. Limited knowledge about opportunities for innovation is a major constraint on company behaviour. A good start can be the 'clearing-house' of information on source-reduction approaches that the EPA was directed to establish by the Pollution Prevention Act (PPA) of 1990. The Green Lights and Toxics Release Inventories described at the start of this chapter are other programmes that involve collecting and spreading information. Yet another important initiative is the EPA programme to compare emissions rates at different companies, creating methodologies to measure the full internal costs of pollution and ways of exchanging best practices and learning on innovative technologies.

Regulatory approaches can also function by helping to create demand pressure for environmental innovation. One example is the prestigious German 'Blue Angel' eco-label, introduced by the German government in 1977, which can be displayed only by products meeting very strict environmental criteria. One of the label's biggest success stories has been in oil and gas heating appliances: the energy efficiency of these appliances improved significantly when the label was introduced, and emissions of sulphur dioxide, carbon monoxide and nitrogen oxides were reduced by more than 30 per cent.

Another point of leverage on the demand side is to harness the role of government as a demanding buyer of environmental solutions and environmentally friendly products. While there are benefits to government procurement of products, such as recycled paper and retreaded tyres, the far more leveraged role is in buying specialized environmental equipment and services.[17] One useful change would be to alter the current practice of requiring bidders in competitive bid processes for government projects to bid only with 'proven' technologies, a practice sure to hinder innovation.

The EPA can employ demonstration projects to stimulate and seed innovative new technologies, working through universities and industry associations. A good example is the project to develop and demonstrate technologies for super-efficient refrigerators, which was conducted by the EPA and researchers in government, academia and the private sector (United States Environmental Protection Agency, 1992). An estimated US$1.7 billion was spent in 1992 by the federal government on environmental technology research and development (R&D), but only US$70 million was directed towards research on pollution prevention (US Congress, Office of Technology Assessment, 1994).

Incentives for innovation must also be built into the regulatory process itself. The current permitting system under Title V of the Clean Air Act Amendments, to choose a negative example, requires firms seeking to change or expand their production process in a way that might impact air quality to revise their permit extensively, *no matter how little the potential effect on air quality may be.* This not only deters innovation, but drains the resources of regulators away from timely action on significant matters. On the positive side, the state of Massachusetts has initiated a programme to waive permits in some circumstances or to promise an immediate permit, if a company takes a zero-discharge approach.

A final priority is new forums for settling regulatory issues that minimize litigation. Potential litigation creates enormous uncertainty; actual litigation burns resources. Mandatory arbitration or rigid arbitration steps before litigation is allowed, would benefit innovation. There is also a need to rethink certain liability issues. While adequate safeguards must be provided against companies that recklessly harm citizens, there is a pressing need for liability standards that more clearly recognize the countervailing health and safety benefits of innovations that lower or eliminate the discharge of harmful pollutants.

Regulatory Coordination

Coordination of environmental regulation can be improved in at least three ways: between industry and regulators, between regulators at different levels and places in government, and between US regulators and their international counterparts.

In setting environmental standards and regulatory processes to encourage innovation, substantive industrial participation in setting standards is needed right from the beginning, as is common in many European countries. An appropriate regulatory process is one in which regulations themselves are clear, who must meet them is clear, and industry accepts the regulations and begins innovating to address them, rather than spending years attempting to delay or relax them. In our current system, by the time that standards are finally settled and clarified, it is often too late to address them fundamentally, making secondary treatment the only alternative. We need to evolve towards a regulatory regime in which the EPA and other regulators make a commitment that standards will be in place for, say, five years, so that industry is motivated to innovate rather than adopt incremental solutions.

Different parts and levels of government must coordinate and organize themselves so that companies are not forced to deal with multiple parties with inconsistent desires and approaches. As a matter of regulatory structure, the EPA's proposed new Innovative Technology Council, being set up to advocate the development of new technology in every field of environmental policy, is a step in the right direction. Another unit in the EPA should be responsible for continued re-engineering of the process of regulation to reduce uncertainty and minimize costs. Also, an explicit strategy is needed to coordinate and harmonize federal and state activities.[18]

A final issue of coordination involves the relationship between US environmental regulations and those in other countries. US regulations should be in sync with regulations in other countries and, ideally, be slightly ahead of them. This will minimize possible competitive disadvantages relative to foreign competitors who are not yet subject to the standard, while at the same time maximizing export potential in the pollution-control sector. Standards that lead world developments provide domestic firms with opportunities to create valuable early-mover advantages. However, standards should not be too far ahead of, or too different in character from, those that are likely to apply to foreign competitors, for this would lead industry to innovate in the wrong directions.

Critics may note, with some basis, that US regulators may not be able to project better than firms what type of regulations, and resultant demands for environmental products and services, will develop in other nations. However, regulators would seem to possess greater resources and information than firms for understanding the path of regulation in other countries. Moreover, US regulations influence the type and stringency of regulations in other nations, and as such help to define demand in other world markets.

Imperatives for Companies

Of course, the regulatory reforms described here also seek to change how companies view environmental issues.[19] Companies must start to recognize the environment as a competitive opportunity, not as an annoying cost or a postponable threat. Yet many companies are ill-prepared to carry out a strategy of environmental innovation that produces sizeable compensating offsets.

For starters, companies must improve their measurement and assessment methods to detect environmental costs and benefits.[20] Too often, relevant information is simply lacking. Typical is the case of a large producer of organic chemicals that retained a consulting firm to explore opportunities for reducing waste. The client thought it had 40 waste streams, but a careful audit revealed that 497 different waste streams were actually present (Parkinson, 1990). Few companies analyse the true cost of toxicity, waste, discharges and the second-order impacts of waste and discharges on other activities. Fewer still look beyond the out-of-pocket costs of dealing with pollution to investigate the opportunity costs of the wasted resources or forgone productivity. How much money is going up the chimney? What percentage of inputs are wasted? Many companies do not even track environmental spending carefully or subject it to evaluation techniques typical for 'normal' investments.

Once environmental costs are measured and understood, the next step is to create a presumption for innovation-based solutions. Discharges, scrap and emissions should be analysed for insights about beneficial product design or process changes. Approaches based on the treatment or handling of discharges should be accepted only after being sent back several times for reconsideration. The responsibility for environmental issues should not be delegated to lawyers or outside consultants except in the adversarial regulatory process, or even to internal specialists removed from the line organization, residing in legal, government or environmental affairs departments. Instead, environmental strategies must become a general management issue if the sorts of process and product redesigns needed for true innovation are even to be considered, much less be proposed and implemented.

Conclusion

We have found that economists as a group are resistant to the notion that even well-designed environmental regulations might lead to improved competitiveness. This hesitancy strikes us as somewhat peculiar, given that in other contexts, economists are extremely willing to argue that technological change has overcome predictions of severe, broadly defined environmental costs. A static model (among other flaws) has been behind many dire predictions of economic disaster and human catastrophe: from the predictions of Thomas Malthus that population would inevitably outstrip food supply; to the *Limits of Growth* (Meadows and Meadows, 1972) which predicted the depletion of the world's natural resources; to *The Population Bomb* (Ehrlich, 1968) which predicted that a quarter of the world's population would starve to death between 1973 and 1983. As economists are often eager to point out, these models failed because they did not appreciate the power of innovations in technology to change old assumptions about resource availability and utilization.

Moreover, the static mindset that environmentalism is inevitably costly has created a self-fulfilling gridlock, in which both regulators and industry battle over every inch of territory. The process has spawned an industry of litigators and consultants, driving up costs and draining resources away from real solutions. It has been reported that four out of five EPA decisions are currently challenged in court (Clay, 1993, cited in US Congress, Office of Technology Assessment, 1994). A study by the Rand Institute for Civil Justice found that 88 per cent of the money paid out between 1986 and 1989 by insurers on Superfund claims went to pay for legal and administrative costs, while only 12 per cent were used for actual site clean-ups (Acton and Dixon, 1992).

The US and other countries need an entirely new way of thinking about the relationship between environment and industrial competitiveness – one closer to the reality of modern competition. The focus should be on relaxing the environment-competitiveness trade-off rather than accepting and, worse yet, steepening it. The orientation should shift from pollution control to resource productivity. We believe that no lasting success can come from policies that promise that environmentalism will triumph over industry, nor from policies that promise that industry will triumph over environmentalism. Instead, success must involve innovation-based solutions that promote both environmentalism and industrial competitiveness.

Acknowledgements

The authors are grateful to Alan Auerbach, Ben Bonifant, Daniel C Esty, Ridgway M Hall, Jr, Donald B Marron, Jan Rivkin, Nicolaj Siggeltow, R David Simpson and Timothy Taylor for extensive valuable editorial suggestions. We are also grateful to Reed Hundt for on-going discussions that have greatly benefited our thinking.

Notes

1   At the industry level, the meaning of competitiveness is clear. At the level of a state or nation, however, the notion of competitiveness is less clear because no nation or state is, or can be, competitive in everything. The proper definition of competitiveness at the aggregate level is the average *productivity of* industry or the value created per unit of labour and per dollar of capital invested. Productivity depends on both the quality and features of products (which determine their value) and the efficiency with which they are produced

2   Of course, there are many non-environmental examples of where industry has been extremely slow to pick up available US$10 bills by choosing new approaches. For example, total quality management programmes only came to the US and Europe decades after they had been widely diffused in Japan, and only after Japanese firms had devastated US and European competitors in the marketplace. The analogy between searching for product quality and for environmental protection is explored later in this chapter

3   Regulation also raises the likelihood that product and process in general will incorporate environmental improvements

4   We should note that this plant was ultimately closed. However, the example described here does illustrate the role of regulatory pressure in process innovation

5   Of course, a list of case examples, however long, does not prove that companies can always innovate or substitute for careful empirical testing in a large cross-section of industries. Given our current ability to capture the true costs and often multifaceted benefits of regulatory-induced innovation, reliance on the weight of case study evidence is necessary. As we discuss elsewhere, there is no countervailing set of case studies that shows that innovation offsets are unlikely or impossible

6   At its core, then, pollution is a result of an intermediate state of technology or management methods. Apparent exceptions to the resource productivity thesis often prove the rule by highlighting the role of technology. Paper made with recycled fibre was once greatly inferior, but new deinking and other technologies have made its quality better and better. Apparent trade-offs between energy efficiency and emissions rest on incomplete combustion

7   Schmalensee (1993) counters that NO_x emissions often result from thermodynamically efficient combustion. But surely this is an anomaly, not the rule, and may represent an intermediate level of efficiency

8   One of the pioneering efforts to see environmental improvement this way is Joel Makower's (1993) book, *The E-Factor: The Bottom-Line Approach to Environmentally Responsible Business*

9   A case study of pollution prevention in a large multinational firm showed those units with strong total quality management programmes in place usually undertake more effective pollution-prevention efforts than units with less commitment to total quality management. See Rappaport (1992), cited in US Congress, Office of Technology Assessment (1994).

10 It should be observed that a strong correlation between environmental costs and industrial competitiveness does not necessarily indicate causality. Omitting environmental benefits from regulation and reporting obvious (end-of-pipe) costs, but not the more difficult to identify or quantify innovation benefits, can actually obscure a reverse causal relationship: industries that were uncompetitive in the first place may well be less able to innovate in response to environmental pressures and thus be prone to end-of-pipe solutions whose costs are easily measured. In contrast, competitive industries capable of addressing environmental problems in innovative ways may report a lower compliance cost

11 Gray and Shadbegian (1993), another often-mentioned study, suffers from several of the problems discussed here. The article uses industry-reported compliance costs and does not control for plant technology vintage or the extent of other productivity-enhancing investments at the plant. High compliance costs may well have been borne in old, inefficient plants where firms opted for secondary treatment rather than innovation. Moreover, US producers may well have been disadvantaged in innovating, given the nature of the US regulatory process – this seems clearly to have been the case in pulp and paper, one of the industries studied by the Management Institute for Environment and Business (MEB)

12 In paints and coatings, for example, environmental investments were 3.3 per cent of total capital investment in 1989. According to Department of Commerce (1991) data (self-reported by industry), capital spending for pollution control and abatement outside of the chemical, pulp and paper, petroleum and coal, and primary metal sectors made up just 3.15 per cent of the total capital spending in 1991

13 There will always be instances of extremely hazardous pollution requiring immediate action, where imposing a specific technology by command and control may be the best or only viable solution. However, such methods should be seen as a last resort

14 A first step in this direction is the EPA's recent adjustment of the timing of its air rule for the pulp and paper industry so that it will coincide with the rule for water, allowing industry to see the dual impact of the rules and innovate accordingly

15 The EPA's regulatory cluster team concept, under which a team from relevant EPA offices approaches particular problems for a broader viewpoint, is a first step in this direction. Note, however, that of the 17 cluster groups formed, only 4 were organized around specific industries (petroleum refining, oil and gas production, pulp and paper, printing), while the remaining 13 focused on specific chemicals or types of pollution (US Congress, Office of Technology Assessment, 1994)

16 Pollution taxes can be implemented as effluent charges on the quantity of pollution discharges, as user charges for public treatment facilities, or as product charges based on the potential pollution of a product. In a deposit-refund system, such product charges may be rebated if a product user disposes of it properly (for example, by returning a lead battery for recycling rather than sending it to a landfill). Under a tradable permit system, like that included in the recent Clean Air Act Amendments, a maximum amount of pollution is set and rights equal to that cap are distributed to firms. Firms must hold enough rights to cover their emissions; firms with excess rights can sell them to firms who are short

17 See Marron (1994) for a demonstration of the modest productivity gains likely from government procurement of standard items, although in a static model

18 The cluster-based approach to regulation discussed earlier should also help to eliminate the practice of sending multiple EPA inspectors to the same plant who do not talk to one another, make conflicting demands and waste time and resources. The potential savings from cluster- and multimedia-oriented permitting and inspection programmes appear to be substantial. During a pilot multimedia testing programme called the Blackstone Project, the Massachusetts Department of Environmental Protection found that multimedia inspections required 50 per cent less time than conventional inspections – which at that time accounted for nearly one-fourth of the department's operating budget (Roy and Dillard, 1990)

19 For a more detailed perspective on changing company mindsets about competitiveness and environmentalism, see Porter and van der Linde (1995) in the *Harvard Business Review*

20 Accounting methods that are currently being discussed in this context include 'full cost accounting', which attempts to assign all costs to specific products or processes, and 'total cost accounting', which goes a step further and attempts both to allocate costs more specifically and to include cost items beyond traditional concerns, such as indirect or hidden costs (like compliance costs, insurance, on-site waste management, operation of pollution control and future liability) and less tangible benefits (like revenue from enhanced company image). See White, Becker and Goldstein (1991), cited in US Congress, Office of Technology Assessment (1994)

References

Acton, Jan Paid and Lloyd S Dixon (1992) 'Superfund and Transaction Costs: The Experiences of Insurers and Very Large Industrial Firms', Santa Monica, Rand Institute for Civil Justice

Amoco Corporation and United States Environmental Protection Agency (1992) 'Amoco-US EPA Pollution Prevention Project: Yorktown, Virginia, Project Summary', Chicago and Washington, DC

Basta, Nicholas and David Vagi (1998) 'A Casebook of Successful Waste Reduction Projects', *Chemical Engineering,* 15 August, no 95, pp11, 37

Berube, M, J Nash, J Maxwell and J Ehrenfeld (1992) 'From Pollution Control to Zero Discharge: How the Robbins Company Overcame the Obstacles', *Pollution Prevention Review,* spring, vol 2, no 2, pp189–207

Bonifant, B (1994a) 'Competitive Implications of Environmental Regulation in the Electronics Manufacturing Industry', Management Institute for Environment and Business, Washington, DC

Bonifant, B (1994b) 'Competitive Implications of Environmental Regulation in the Paint and Coatings Industry', Management Institute for Environment and Business, Washington, DC

Bonifant,.B and I Ratcliffe (1994) 'Competitive Implications of Environmental Regulation in the Pulp and Paper Industry', Management Institute for Environment and Business, Washington, DC

Bonson, N C, Neil McCubbin and John B Sprague (1988) 'Kraft Mill Effluents in Ontario', report prepared for the Technical Advisory Committee, Pulp and Paper Sector of MISA, Ontario Ministry of the Environment, Toronto, Ontario, Canada, 29 March, Section 6, p166

Boroughs, D L and B Carpenter (1991) 'Helping the Planet and the Economy', *US News & World Report,* 25 March, no 110, pp11, 46

Clay, Don (1993) 'New Environmentalist: A Cooperative Strategy', *Forum for Applied Research and Public Policy,* spring, no 8, pp125–128

DeCanio, Stephen J (1993) 'Why Do Profitable Energy-Saving Investment Projects Languish?', paper presented at the Second International Research Conference of the Greening of Industry Network, Cambridge, Mass

Department of Commerce (1991) 'Pollution Abatement Costs and Expenditures', Washington, DC

Dorfman, Mark H, Warren R Muir and Catherine G Miller (1992) *Environmental Dividends: Cutting More Chemical Wastes,* New York, INFORM

Ehrlich, Paul (1968) *The Population Bomb,* New York, Ballanrine Books

Freeman, A Myrick, III (1985) 'Methods for Assessing the Benefits of Environmental Programs', in A V Kneese and J L Sweeney (eds) *Handbook of Natural Resource and Energy Economics,* vol 1, Amsterdam, North-Holland, pp223–270

Gray, Wayne B (1987) 'The Cost of Regulation: OSHA, EPA, and the Productivity Slowdown', *American Economic Review,* vol 77, no 5, pp998–1006

Gray, Wayne B and Ronald J Shadbegian (1993) 'Environmental Regulation and Productivity at the Plant Level', discussion paper, US Department of Commerce, Center for Economic Studies, Washington, DC

Hartwell, R V and L Bergkamp (1992) 'Eco-Labelling in Europe: New Market-Related Environmental Risks?', *BNA International Environment Daily,* Special Report, 20 October

Hazilla, Michael and Raymond J Kopp (1990) 'Social Cost of Environmental Quality Regulations: A General Equilibrium Analysis', *Journal of Political Economy,* vol 9, no 4, pp853–873

Jaffe, Adam B, Peterson, S Portney, Paul and Stavins, Robert N (1993) 'Environmental Regulations and the Competitiveness of US Industry', Economics Resource Group, Cambridge, Mass

Jaffe, Adam B, S Peterson, Paul Portney and Robert N Stavins (1994) 'Environmental Regulation and International Competitiveness: What Does the Evidence Tell Us', draft, 13 January

Jorgenson, Dale W and Peter J Wilcoxen (1990) 'Environmental Regulation and US Economic Growth', *Rand Journal of Economics,* summer, vol 21, no 2, pp314–340

Kalt, Joseph P (1988) 'The Impact of Domestic Environmental Regulatory Policies on US International Competitiveness', in Spence, A M and H Hazard (eds) *International Competitiveness,* Cambridge, Mass, Harper & Row, Ballinger, pp221–262

King, A (1994) 'Improved Manufacturing Resulting from Learning-From-Waste: Causes, Importance, and Enabling Conditions', working paper, Stern School of Business, New York University

Leonard, H Jeffrey (1998) *Pollution and the Struggle for World Product,* Cambridge, UK, Cambridge University Press

Makower, Joel (1993) *The E-Factor: The Bottom-Line Approach to Environmentally Responsible Business,* New York, Times Books

Marron, Donald B (1994) 'Buying Green: Government Procurement as an Instrument of Environmental Policy', mimeo, Massachusetts Institute of Technology

Massachusetts Department of Environmental Protection (1993) Daniel S Greenbaum, Commissioner, interview, Boston, 8 August

Meadows, Donella H and Dennis L Meadows (1972) *The Limits to Growth,* New York, New American Library

Meyer, Stephen M (1992) *Environmentalism and Economic Prosperity: Testing the Environmental Impact Hypothesis.* Cambridge, Mass, Massachusetts Institute of Technology

Meyer, Stephen M (1993) *Environmentalism and Economic Prosperity: An Update,* Cambridge, Mass, Massachusetts Institute of Technology

National Paint and Coatings Association (1992) *Improving the Superfund: Correcting a National Public Policy Disaster,* Washington, DC

Oates, Wallace, Karen L Palmer and Paul Portney (1993) 'Environmental Regulation and International Competitiveness: Thinking About the Porter Hypothesis', Resources for the Future, Working Paper 94-02

Palmer, Karen L and Ralph David Simpson (1993) 'Environmental Policy as Industrial Policy', *Resources,* summer, no 112, pp17–21

Parkinson, Gerald (1990) 'Reducing Wastes Can Be Cost-Effective', *Chemical Engineering,* July, vol 97, no 7, p30

Porter, Michael E (1985) *Competitive Advantage: Creating and Sustaining Superior Performance,* New York, Free Press

Porter, Michael E (1990) *The Competitive Advantage of Nations,* New York, Free Press

Porter, Michael E (1991) 'America's Green Strategy', *Scientific American,* April, p168

Porter, Michael E and Claas van der Linde (1995) 'Green and Competitive: Breaking the Stalemate', *Harvard Business Review,* September–October

PR Newswire (1993) 'Winners Announced for Governor's Waste Minimization Awards', 21 January, State and Regional News Section

Rappaport, Ann (1992) 'Development and Transfer of Pollution Prevention Technology Within a Multinational Corporation', dissertation, Department of Civil Engineering, Tufts University, May

Raytheon Inc. (1991) 'Alternate Cleaning Technology', Technical Report, Phase II, January–October

Raytheon Inc. J R Pasquariello, Vice President Environmental Quality; Kenneth J Tiemey, Director Environmental and Energy Conservation; Frank A Marino, Senior Corporate Environmental Specialist (1993) interview, Lexington, Mass, 4 April

Repetto, Robert (1995) 'Jobs, Competitiveness, and Environmental Regulation: What are the Real Issues?', Washington, DC, World Resources Institute

Roy, M and L A Dillard (1990) 'Toxics Use in Massachusetts: The Blackstone Project', *Journal of Air and Waste Management Association,* October, vol 40, no 10, pp1368–1371

Schmalensee, Richard (1993) 'The Costs of Environmental Regulation', Massachusetts Institute of Technology, Center for Energy and Environmental Policy Research, Working Paper 93-015

Sheridan, J H (1992) 'Attacking Wastes and Saving Money ... Some of the Time', *Industry Week,* 17 February, vol 241, no 4, p43

Simpson, Ralph David (1993) 'Taxing Variable Cost: Environmental Regulation as Industrial Policy', Resources for the Future, Working Paper ENR93-12

Smith, Zadury A (1992) *The Environmental Policy Paradox,* Englewood Cliffs, NJ, Prentice Hall

United States Environmental Protection Agency (1992) 'Multiple Pathways to Super Efficient Refrigerators', Washington, DC

US Congress, Office of Technology Assessment (1994) 'Industry, Technology, and the Environment: Competitive Challenges and Business Opportunities', OTA-ITE-586, Washington, DC

van der Linde, Claas (1993) 'The Micro-Economic Implications of Environmental Regulation: A Preliminary Framework', in *Environmental Policies and Industrial Competitiveness,* Paris, Organisation of Economic Co-operation and Development, pp69–77

van der Linde, Claas (1995a) 'Competitive Implications of Environmental Regulation in the Cell Battery Industry', Hochschule St Gallen, St Gallen

van der Linde, Claas (1995b) 'Competitive Implications of Environmental Regulation in the Printing Ink Industry', Hochschule St Gallen, St Gallen

van der Linde, Claas (1995c) 'Competitive Implications of Environmental Regulation in the Refrigerator Industry', Hochschule St Gallen, St Gallen

Wheeler, David and Ashoka Mody (1992) 'International Investment Location Decisions: The Case of US Firms', *Journal of International Economics,* August, no 33, pp57–76

White, A L, M Becker and J Goldstein (1991) 'Alternative Approaches to the Financial Evaluation of Industrial Pollution Prevention Investments', prepared for the New Jersey Department of Environmental Protection, Division of Science and Research, November

7

WTO Rules and Multilateral Environmental Agreements

Eric Neumayer

This chapter looks at the potential conflicts between multilateral environmental agreements (MEAs) and World Trade Organization (WTO) rules. Most of this potential originates in the use of trade measures by MEAs, which is why they are the major focus of this chapter. However, substantive provisions, not related to trade measures, in the Convention on Biological Diversity might also clash with the Trade Related Intellectual Property (TRIPS) Agreement, which forms one of the WTO agreements, and are therefore dealt with here as well.

Potential Conflicts because of Trade Measures in MEAs

Theoretical Considerations on the Role of Trade Measures in MEAs

Trade measures in MEAs fulfil three functions. First, they can be used to deter internal and external free-riding; second, they can mitigate problems with so-called emissions leakage; and finally, they can be used to further directly the objectives of an MEA in restricting trade in specified substances or species. These three functions will now be examined.

Economists have examined the strategic incentives that countries face with respect to internal and external free-riding in international environmental cooperation, and have developed the concepts of self-enforcing and renegotiation-proof agreements.[1] What does this mean? Many environmental problems are truly international or global. They cannot be tackled by a single country alone – hence international cooperation is needed for a solution. But whereas environmental policy can use the enforcing power that sovereign nation states ideally have within their territory, in general international environmental policy cannot take recourse to a supranational authority with enforcing powers. The affected countries are confronted with a basic prisoner's dilemma, in the following sense: the countries have an interest in, say, reducing emissions or reducing the over-harvesting of an exhaustible natural resource and all the countries would be better off with international environmental cooperation, but each and every one of them also has an incentive to free-ride on the others' efforts

Example of Moratorium of Whaling

and to enjoy the benefits of abatement or harvest limitations without incurring any costs of emissions or harvest reduction. (In the following I will speak of emissions only for expositional ease, but the argument applies to any form of environmental degradation.)

Therefore, MEAs normally have to deter *external* free-riding – ie, they have to deter countries that would benefit from emissions reduction from not signing up to the agreement and staying outside. Equally, they have to deter *internal* free-riding – ie, they have to deter signatory countries from not complying with the requirements of the agreement. What is important is that the mechanism employed to achieve deterrence has to be self-enforcing in the sense that a recourse to an external enforcement agency is not feasible: no country can be forced to sign an agreement and signatories cannot be forced to comply with the agreement.

One of the mechanisms that could potentially achieve such deterrence is trade measures. Before coming to this point, let us first examine, however, what the problems are if trade measures (or a similar mechanism) were unavailable. Then the only variable left to a country is the amount of pollution it emits. Hence, the only mechanism left is to threaten not to undertake any emissions reduction in order to deter external free-riding or to decrease emissions by less than that required by the agreement in order to punish non-compliant countries and to deter internal free-riding. This threat has to be credible in the sense that it is in the interest of the threatening country (or countries) actually to execute the threat whenever other countries try to free-ride. In other words, a threat cannot be credible if a country is worse off after executing the threat than it would be without execution. Non-credible threats cannot deter because potential free-riders will anticipate that they could get away with free-riding without being punished. Moreover, an agreement that establishes such a mechanism to deter free-riding has to be renegotiation-proof. This means that the threat has to be credible also in the sense that the threatening country (or countries) must be better off actually executing the threat than refraining from execution and renegotiating a new agreement with the free-riding country (or countries). Agreements that are not renegotiation-proof cannot deter because potential free-riders will anticipate that they could strike another deal after free-riding and could therefore get away without being punished.

What are the consequences of the requirements of self-enforcement and renegotiation-proofness on international environmental cooperation? If trade measures (or a similar mechanism) are unavailable, then one basic result holds: a self-enforcing and renegotiation-proof agreement will either consist of only a small subset of affected countries or, if many countries are parties to the agreement, the gains from cooperation relative to the non-cooperative equilibrium are very small. In other words, large-scale cooperation will either not take place as only a few countries will sign the agreement or, if it does take place, it is virtually irrelevant as the agreed cooperation improves only marginally on what would have been achieved by unilateral action in the absence of the agreement.[2] Cooperation is either narrow (instead of wide) or shallow (instead of deep).

This result leads to pessimistic expectations about the solution to an environmental problem for which international cooperation is most needed. For example, in cases where the benefits to be gained from emissions abatement are high and the

costs are low (for example, ozone-depleting substances), the end result that cooperation will either be narrow or, if it is wide, it will not be deep, matters little as
countries have big incentives to solve the problem unilaterally. The same might even
be true if the benefits of emissions abatement are relatively low, as long as the costs
are low as well. Similarly, in cases where the benefits of abatement are low and the
costs are high, the end result of the economic theory of international environmental cooperation is insignificant as even the full cooperative outcome would achieve
little because of the high costs involved. The cases for which the end result is really
relevant are those where the benefits of emissions abatement are high, but so are
the costs (for example, greenhouse gas emissions). These are exactly the cases for
which finding the solution to environmental problem will demand the widest and
deepest cooperation (Barrett, 1991, pp14ff).

What is the intuitive reason for this rather pessimistic result? In order to deter
free-riding, an agreement must specify that the non-free-riding countries are permitted to increase their emissions relative to an agreement without free-riding in order
to punish other free-riders for not decreasing their emissions at all (external free-
riding) or by not as much as requested by the agreement (internal free-riding). In
order to deter free-riding, the damage to the potential free-rider caused by the
increase in emissions must be greater than the potential benefit from free-riding.
The wider and deeper the cooperation is, the higher the benefit is from free-riding,
so that the damage to the potential free-rider must also increase in order to deter
free-riding. The problem is, however, that the bigger the damage is to the potential
free-rider, the bigger the damage is to the punishing countries themselves as well.
This self-inflicted damage due to the emissions increase limits the punishment that
is available for free-rider deterrence. It must not hurt the punishing countries more
than the damage caused by the free-riding, otherwise it will not be credible as the
potential free-rider knows that it is not in the best interest of the punishing countries to execute the punishment. ✳✳✳

What is more, there must be no incentive for the punishing countries and the
free-riders to renegotiate the agreement and strike another deal. For this condition
to hold, the punishment must not be too great or the damage to the free-riding
country will be great, as will be its incentive to renegotiate another agreement. For
these two reasons the credible punishment that is available cannot be very substantial, which means that it cannot deter much free-riding. Because external free-riding
can be deterred only to a small extent, free-riding is ubiquitous and the number of
countries participating in an agreement is small. Alternatively, because internal free-
riding can be deterred only to a small extent, an agreement can improve little relative
to the non-cooperative equilibrium in order to keep the incentives for non-compliance small, if the number of signatories is large.

Trade measures are a way of overcoming the negative effects of the requirements of self-enforcement and renegotiation-proofness in the field of international
environmental cooperation. Barrett (1997b) shows how linking a multilateral environmental agreement with trade can promote cooperation. Trade measures are a
more credible threat to deter free-riding than an increase in emissions because, according to Barrett, trade measures mainly harm the free-rider, whereas an emissions
increase considerably harms the punisher as well.[3] Hence, with trade measures free-

riding can be deterred more effectively as a more substantial punishment becomes credible, so wider and deeper cooperation can be achieved as a self-enforcing and renegotiation-proof equilibrium.[4]

Another problem that can be addressed by restrictive trade measures is so-called leakage, which describes the phenomenon that a decrease in emissions by the participants to an agreement is counteracted by an increase of emissions by non-members. Such an increase can be a deliberate decision by the free-riding countries. Because the decrease in emissions by the participants lowers the marginal social damage of emissions by the non-participants, their 'non-cooperative' self-interest response is to let their emissions rise. These non-members will therefore usually find it in their own best interest to increase emissions deliberately. However, this is just part of the story. The other reasons why emissions of non-participants might rise are more subtle and can hardly be traced back to a deliberate policy by these countries to exploit the emissions reductions of others. To understand this point, take the example of carbon dioxide (CO_2) emissions. If a subset of all countries – for example, only developed countries and transition countries as with the Kyoto Protocol – agrees on limiting their CO_2 emissions, then production of carbon-intensive goods and services becomes relatively more expensive in these countries. The comparative advantage in these goods and services shifts to the non-participating countries that increase their production of carbon-intensive goods and services. Similarly, some especially carbon-intensive industries might migrate from signatory to non-signatory countries. Also, the reduction in demand for fossil fuels due to the limitation of CO_2 emissions by the participants to the agreement will lower world fossil fuel prices, which increases demand for fossil fuels in non-member countries. All of these feedback mechanisms lead to an increase of emissions by non-participants quite involuntarily – ie, without the participating countries being able to blame the non-members for deliberately exploiting their emissions reduction. How significant leakage would be depends on the underlying assumptions about the number of countries that form an agreement, the size of reduction in emissions and the instruments that are used to achieve a reduction of emissions. Econometric estimates show that leakage could be anywhere between around 5 per cent and 30 per cent.[5] In any case, leakage potentially can be an important obstacle for MEAs and trade measures imposed on non-members can help to mitigate the problem.

The deterrence of internal and external free-riding, as well as the mitigation of leakage, are not the only purposes for which trade measures are used, however. In some MEAs, as will be discussed in the next section, restrictions on trade in specified substances or species is the very objective of the MEA, rather than an instrument to deter free-riding. This will always be the case when trade itself is considered to be endangering the preservation of species (Convention on International Trade in Endangered Species of Wild Flora and Fauna – CITES) and biodiversity (Convention on Biological Diversity) (CBD)), or endangering human life and health (Basel Convention, Rotterdam Convention and the Agreement on Persistent Organic Pollutants (POPs)). Let us now turn, therefore, to how trade measures and the threat of trade measures have been used in actual MEAs.

Trade Measures in Practice

Maybe surprisingly, these theoretical considerations notwithstanding, the vast majority of MEAs do not contain any trade measures. A 1994 survey revealed that while many of the then 180 international treaties and other agreements on environmental matters contained trade-related aspects, only 18 actually employed trade measures (WTO, 1994). However, in seven of the most important MEAs, discussed below, trade measures play a prominent role and those measures are bound to play a major role in future amendments to the Kyoto Protocol for the reduction of greenhouse gas emissions.

The Montreal Protocol

The aim of the Montreal Protocol on Substances that Deplete the Ozone Layer is to phase out ozone-depleting substances (ODSs) – ie, substances responsible for the thinning of the ozone layer in the stratosphere which filters out ultraviolet radiation. The major ODSs covered by the Protocol – the so-called controlled substances – are chlorofluorocarbons (CFCs) and halons. As of 2000, 175 countries have ratified the Montreal Protocol, which gives it almost universal support. Only five countries were WTO members but not parties to the Protocol.

The Protocol's major trade provisions are contained in its Article 4. It bans imports (Article 4.1) and exports (Article 4.2) of controlled substances between parties and non-parties of the Protocol, unless the non-parties can demonstrate that, in spite of not being formally a party to the Protocol, nevertheless they comply with its obligations (Article 4.8). Article 4.3 also bans the import of products containing controlled substances from non-parties. In principle, Article 4.4 of the Protocol even provides the possibility to ban or restrict the import from non-parties of products made with, but not containing, controlled substances. However, such restrictions were soon deemed infeasible by the parties to the Protocol. These provisions were therefore never made operational and it must be regarded as highly unlikely that they would ever become operationalized.[6]

One problem that countries are faced with is the illegal trade in ODSs. To contain this problem, the Montreal Amendment to the Montreal Protocol, which at the time of writing has been ratified by 37 nations and brought into force in November 1999, introduces a mandatory licensing system for the import and export of ODSs from 2000 onwards, with developing countries enjoying the possibility of delaying the introduction of such a licensing system for methyl bromide and hydrochlorofluorocarbons (HCFCs) until 2002 and 2005 respectively.

Have all these trade provisions been effective in bringing about multilateral environmental cooperation? As an answer to this question depends on counter-factual evidence, there cannot be an unambiguous answer as we cannot know what would have happened if the trade provisions had not existed. Furthermore, it is next to impossible to separate the effects of the threat of trade measures (sticks) from the effects that the promise of financial assistance for developing countries (carrots) contained in Article 10 of the Protocol had on encouraging the participation of the developing world. Many experts agree, however, that the threat of trade restrictions against non-parties has been important in bringing about almost universal participation (see, for example, French, 1994, p62; Brack, 1996, p55; Barrett, 1997b, p346; OECD, 1997).

The Convention on International Trade in Endangered Species of Wild Fauna and Flora (CITES)

CITES is not an MEA with trade among many other provisions. Rather, its very aim is to restrict the international trade in endangered species. At the time of writing, the Convention has been ratified by 138 countries, of which only 10 were WTO members but not parties to the Convention.

CITES' major trade provisions are as follows. Appendix I names species (around 600 animals and 300 plant species) that are threatened with extinction and whose trade for commercial purposes is generally prohibited with few exceptions (Article III). Appendix II names a further 4000 animals and 25,000 plant species that might become threatened with extinction if their trade is not regulated. Their export is only allowed if the exporter has acquired an export permit from the state of export, testifying that the export will not be detrimental to the survival of that species, that the specimen has not been obtained in contravention of the protection laws of the exporting state, and that any living specimen will be so prepared for transport that the risk of injury, damage to health or cruel treatment is minimized (Article IV). Similar to the Montreal Protocol, trade in the species listed in Appendix II and, in rare circumstances, even in Appendix I is possible with non-parties if these countries can demonstrate that they comply fully with the Convention (Article X). If a party fails to comply with the Convention's obligations, it can lose its right to be treated as a party and can be treated essentially as a non-party.

Experts' assessment of the effectiveness of CITES and therefore on the trade provisions contained therein are mixed (OECD, 1999, p22). Crocodilians and elephants are the cases where CITES might have significantly helped to improve their conservation. It has been less effective with respect to, for example, rhinoceros and tiger species, and has been indifferent with respect to the conservation status of some other species (ibid). Martin (2000, p30) comes to the rather sobering conclusion that 'if the convention is benefiting species then, even after careful study, it has not been demonstrated'. Unlike the Montreal Protocol, CITES does not contain substantial financial assistance to help developing countries comply with the Convention, which has been regarded as one of the major reasons for the poor implementation of species trade-control systems in these countries and consequently substantial illegal poaching and trafficking (OECD, 1999, p26). Another shortcoming is that CITES is unbalanced in regarding the international trade in wildlife all too often as a threat to preservation rather than as a means to raise the preservation value of endangered species if it is properly regulated (Martin, 2000; 't Sas-Rolfes, 2000). Complete trade bans often merely raise the value of illegal trafficking and render stringent controls more difficult.[7]

The Basel Convention

Similar to CITES, restrictions on trade are at the heart of the Basel Convention on the Control of Transboundary Movements of Hazardous Wastes and Their Disposal. It aims to 'ensure that the management of hazardous wastes and other wastes including their transboundary movement and disposal is consistent with the protection of human health and the environment whatever the place of disposal' (preamble). At the time of writing, the Convention has been ratified by 136 countries, but not by the US, which has signed but not ratified the Convention. Some 28 countries were WTO members but not parties to the Convention.

The major trade provisions of the Basel Convention are as follows. Trade in hazardous waste is subjected to a comprehensive control system which is based on the principle of prior informed consent (PIC). This means that a country can only export these materials to another country if it has gained the prior written consent from the importing country and all transit countries (Article 6). Trade in these materials with non-parties is prohibited (Article 4:5) unless agreements with these non-parties have been concluded which 'do not derogate from the environmentally sound management of hazardous wastes and other wastes as required by this Convention' (Article 11:1). A party has the right to ban the entry or disposal of foreign hazardous waste in its territory (Article 4:1). Furthermore, an amendment to the Convention generally bans trade in these materials between so-called Annex VII (OECD countries) and non-Annex VII countries. However, at the time of writing, this amendment had been ratified by only 20 countries and it is unclear whether it will reach the necessary ratifications to enter into force (cf Krueger, 1999, pp106–108).

Similar to CITES, the Basel Convention does not contain any substantial provisions for financial assistance to developing countries to assist them in implementing their obligations. This has been regarded as one of the major reasons for the poor implementation of hazardous waste trade-control systems in these countries and the consequent substantial illegal trading, which will become exacerbated once the amendment to the Convention banning trade between OECD and non-OECD countries comes into force (ibid, pp27ff).

In terms of effectiveness, Krueger (1999, p62) suggests that 'in as far as the goal was to eliminate the worst forms of hazardous waste dumping on developing countries, the trade restrictions of the Convention can generally be deemed a success'. However, it is unclear to what extent the trade measures were necessary to achieve this effect, for, as Krueger (ibid) suggests:

> By publicizing and condemning the practice of exporting hazardous wastes for final disposal to poor countries, the Basel Convention arguably put a great deal of political pressure on exporting countries to stop this practice. In this way, the creation of a Convention that changed the norms of international practice was perhaps as effective as the actual trade measures themselves.

Furthermore, it is unclear what the effect of the Basel Convention has been on the overall amount of transboundary hazardous waste movements as reliable data are practically non-existent (OECD, 1999, p24). It could well be that the Convention has also deterred some transboundary movements which would have actually been in the environmental interest – for example, movements to environmentally preferable recycling or waste-disposal facilities in other countries (ibid). The notification requirements could lead to a more environmentally sound management of transboundary movements of hazardous waste, but much depends on how effectively it will be administered.

The Rotterdam Convention

The Convention on the Prior Informed Consent Procedure for Certain Hazardous Chemicals and Pesticides in International Trade (Rotterdam Convention) was adopted and opened for signature in Rotterdam in September 1998. It is an MEA in pursuance of Chapter 19 of Agenda 21 on 'Environmentally sound management of toxic chemicals, including prevention of illegal international traffic in toxic and dangerous products'.[8] Its objective is 'to promote shared responsibility and cooperative efforts among Parties in the international trade of certain hazardous chemicals in order to protect human health and the environment from potential harm and to contribute to their environmentally sound use' (Article 1). It needs to be ratified by 50 countries and is not in force yet.

Annex III of the Convention specifies the chemicals that are subject to the Prior Informed Consent (PIC) procedure (initially, Annex III encompasses 30 chemicals). This means that a country may only export one of these chemicals to another country if it has sought and received the PIC of the importing country. Furthermore, the exporting country has the duty to provide for 'labelling requirements that ensure adequate availability of information with regard to risks and/or hazards to human health or the environment, taking into account relevant international standards' (Article 13:2). This applies to all chemicals listed in Annex III, all chemicals banned or severely restricted in the exporting country's territory (Article 13:2) as well as to all chemicals subject to environmental or health labelling requirements (Article 13:3). Exports of chemicals, the use of which are banned or severely restricted in the exporting country's territory, are subject to laborious information requirements for export notification as laid down in Annex V of the Convention.

Countries need not give their consent to import Annex III chemicals. According to Article 10 of the Convention, each party has the right not to consent to import or merely consent to import, subject to specified conditions, any of the chemicals contained in Annex III. However, if a country decides to ban imports or consent to import only under specified conditions, then according to Article 10:9 it has to 'simultaneously prohibit or make subject to the same conditions' the import of the chemical from any other country and the domestic production of the chemical for domestic use. In other words, a country cannot ban or severely restrict imports of a chemical from one country but not another, or to ban or severely restrict imports of a chemical but not domestic production.

The Agreement on Persistent Organic Pollutants

In December 2000, in Johannesburg, 122 countries concluded negotiations on a multilateral Agreement on Persistent Organic Pollutants (POPs Agreement). Formally signed in 2001 will enter into force once it has been ratified by at least 50 countries. The objective of the agreement is the eventual elimination of eight POPs: aldrin, chlordane, dieldrin, endrin, heptachlor, hexachlorobenzene, mirex and toxaphene. The use of another four POPs becomes severely restricted: dichlorodiphenyltrichloroethane (DDT) for use against malaria, dioxins, furans, and polychlorinated biphenyls (PCBs).

POPs are considered of special danger to human health and the environment as they are persistent and can accumulate in the environment, and therefore can be passed on from one generation to the next. Article D of the agreement allows the importation of the relevant POPs only for the purpose of environmentally sound disposal or for a specified use permitted explicitly by the agreement. Exportation is only allowed for the same purposes and only to either parties to the agreement or to non-parties that can document that they comply with the provisions of the agreement.

The Convention on Biological Diversity

The Convention on Biological Diversity (CBD), which was one of the few tangible results of the United Nations Conference on Environment and Development in Rio de Janeiro in 1992, has as its objectives 'the conservation of biological diversity, the sustainable use of its components and the fair and equitable sharing of the benefits arising out of the utilization of genetic resources' (Article 1). As of 2000, it had 177 parties – that is, practically universal membership, with the notable exception of the US which has signed but not ratified the Convention. Only three countries are WTO members but not parties to the Convention.

The CBD does not provide explicitly for trade measures, but it can have important trade implications in restricting access to genetic resources: 'Recognizing the sovereign rights of States over their natural resources, the authority to determine access to genetic resources rests with the national governments and is subject to national legislation' (Article 15:1). However, parties 'shall endeavour to create conditions to facilitate access to genetic resources for environmentally sound uses by other Contracting Parties and not to impose restrictions that run counter to the objectives of this Convention' (Article 15:2). Access should be 'on mutually agreed terms' (Article 15:4) and 'subject to prior informed consent of the Contracting Party providing such resources' (Article 15:5).

The Cartagena Protocol on Biosafety

Living modified organisms, better known as genetically modified organisms (GMOs), represent a special threat to biodiversity as they represent an exogenously introduced disturbance of the existing ecosystems and, in some cases at least, can mutate, migrate and procreate. Furthermore, GMOs, which are directly used as food or feed, can pose a potential danger to human or animal health. The use of GMOs therefore needs to be controlled, which is the objective of the Cartagena Protocol on Biosafety. It was finalized in Montreal in January 2000, was signed by 81 countries at the time of writing and needs the ratification of 50 countries to become effective.

The Cartagena Protocol comes under the CBD, Article 19:3 of which calls on parties to consider 'the need for and modalities of a protocol setting out appropriate procedures, including, in particular, advance informed agreement, in the field of the safe transfer, handling and use of any living modified organism resulting from biotechnology that may have adverse effect on the conservation and sustainable use of biological diversity'. The Cartegena Protocol does just that. It would be beyond the scope of this chapter to provide a comprehensive analysis of the Protocol, which can be found in Cosbey and Burgiel (2000), Swenarchuk (2000) and Falkner (2000). Suffice it to say here that the single most important element of the Protocol is an advance informed agreement procedure similar to the prior informed consent mechanism of the Rotterdam Convention. The country of potential import can put conditions on the import or even ban the import. However, many types of GMOs are not subject to this procedure:

- Pharmaceuticals addressed by other relevant international agreements or organizations (Article 5).
- GMOs in transit to another country (Article 6:1).
- GMOs destined for contained use (Article 6:2).
- GMOs intended for direct use as food or feed, or for processing (Article 7:2).
- GMOs that have been declared 'not likely to have adverse effects on the conservation and sustainable use of biological diversity, taking also into account risks to human health' by a decision of the Conference of the Parties (Article 7:4).

Critics of GMOs invoke a whole range of reasons for their opposition, including environmental, ethical, spiritual and religious reasons (see, for example, Institute of Science in Society, 1999a, b; Lappé and Bailey, 1999). Their supporters, on the other hand, do not fail to mention that GMOs might also help to overcome hunger in the developing world. African scientists, for example, are therefore divided over whether or not to support modern biotechnology (ICTSD, 2000b). Critics counter that hunger is not a problem of insufficient food supply, but of the inequitable access to food resources. Again, it would be vastly beyond the scope of this chapter to provide an assessment of these arguments. Instead, we will concentrate in this chapter on the potential for conflict between the Protocol and the WTO system.

The Kyoto Protocol and potential follow-up conventions

In its current form the Kyoto Protocol, which sets up obligations for so-called Annex 1 countries (Organisation of Economic Co-operation and Development (OECD) countries and the economies in transition in Eastern Europe, including the Russian Federation) to reduce emissions of greenhouse gases, does not contain substantial trade provisions. In the words of Brack, Grubb and Windram (2000, p127): 'It is almost an exaggeration to say that the non-compliance provisions of the climate change regime are in their infancy – they are not really yet developed that far.' Article 17 of the Protocol employs so-called emissions trading provisions as part of the flexibility mechanisms contained in the Protocol, which means that countries and potentially private entities as well can trade emissions reduction obligations with each other. Once the specifics of the emissions trading system have been decided upon, pertinent questions will be asked regarding whether the emissions trading system will fall under WTO rules and the disciplines contained therein – for a good discussion of these aspects see Brack, Grubb and Windram (ibid, pp117–123).

As of 2000, the Protocol has not come into force yet, with unlikely prospects of this ever happening (see Barrett, 1998). The problem is that US ratification is far from assured. As non-ratification by the US would potentially deter other countries from ratifying the Protocol as well, this, together with the fact that 55 countries comprising at least 55 per cent of emissions must ratify, could well mean that the Protocol will never formally come into force. This need not render it irrelevant, however, as often countries obey international obligations they have signed up to even though these obligations never became formally binding via ratification. Only the future will tell.

Trade measures in MEAs and WTO rules: Do they conflict?

No World Trade Organization member has ever challenged any trade measure that another WTO member had purportedly undertaken in compliance with an MEA. Hence, no relevant WTO case law and no binding interpretation exists – as yet. Nevertheless, one can examine whether trade provisions in MEAs appear to clash with WTO rules. The answer is, as will be discussed below, that they might do, as the potential for conflict clearly exists.

Most MEAs with explicitly mandated or permitted trade provisions restrict trade between parties and non-parties, or even trade between parties. These restrictions might violate the general most favoured nation treatment obligation in the General Agreement on Tariffs and Trade (GATT) Article I. If these restrictions take the form of import or export bans, export certificates or access restrictions rather than duties, taxes or other charges, they might violate the general elimination of quantitative restrictions obligation in GATT Article XI. If countries in alleged pursuance of or compliance with MEAs applied regulations or taxes differently to imported than to domestically produced goods and services, they might also violate their national treatment obligation contained in GATT Article III. If they applied product standards or sanitary or phytosanitary measures that affected domestic and foreign producers differently, they might violate their Technical Barriers to Trade (TBT) or Sanitary and Phytosanitary measures (SPS) Agreement obligations. However, the trade provisions contained in MEAs that appear to violate one or the other GATT obligations, can still be considered WTO consistent if they are covered by the general exceptions of GATT Article XX or similar provisions in one of the other WTO agreements. In the following, we will look first only at the Montreal Protocol, CITES, the Basel Convention and the CBD, the most relevant MEAs in force. After that, we will take a closer look at the Cartagena Protocol, which plays a special role due to its far-reaching embracement of the precautionary principle.

The Montreal Protocol, CITES, the Basel Convention and the CBD

The ozone layer, as well as endangered species and biodiversity (genetic resources), constitute an exhaustible natural resource in the meaning of Article XX(g). The article further demands that trade measures 'are made effective in conjunction with restrictions on domestic production or consumption', which is true for the Montreal Protocol, the CBD and the Basel Convention. However, problems could arise with respect to CITES as its provisions for the regulation of domestic wildlife use, contrary to its provisions for the regulation of international wildlife trade, are rather rudimentary. Trade measures must also 'relate to' the conservation of an exhaustible natural resource, which has been interpreted by the GATT/WTO dispute settlement as 'primarily aimed at' such conservation (see pl22). All three MEAs should pass this test as their very aim is the conservation of an exhaustible natural resource. However, a problem could arise if a WTO panel narrowly interprets the objective of trade measures, especially in the Montreal Protocol and the CBD, as merely broadening the participation of countries in deterring free-riding, rather than directly protecting an exhaustible resource. Could these trade measures, then, still be considered 'primarily aimed at' conservation?

All four MEAs furthermore purport to protect either human, animal or plant life or health in the meaning of Article XX(b). The article requires further that trade measures are 'necessary' for such protection, which has been interpreted by the GATT/WTO dispute settlement as requiring that 'no alternative measures either consistent or less inconsistent' with WTO rules exist (see pl24). This requirement could potentially pose an insurmountable hurdle for all four MEAs. Could taxes or transferable emissions permits have phased out ODSs as effectively and rapidly as the trade restrictions contained in the Montreal Protocol? Could direct harvest and wildlife-management regulations prevent the extinction of endangered species similarly to the trade restrictions contained in CITES? Are trade restrictions really necessary to prevent environmental and health damage from transborder shipments of hazardous waste? Even accepting the validity of 'limited capabilities of the developing countries to manage hazardous wastes and other wastes' (preamble of the Basel Convention), is a complete ban on the trade in hazardous waste between OECD and non-OECD countries really necessary? Are there really no less GATT-inconsistent measures for the preservation of biodiversity than restrictions on access to genetic resources? Would less GATT-inconsistent measures need to be as effective as the trade restrictions to be considered alternatives? It would be beyond the scope of this book to attempt to answer these questions. Suffice it to say here that it is open to debate at least whether the trade measures contained in the four MEAs could pass the 'necessity' test of Article XX(b).

If trade measures in MEAs are covered by one of the exceptions in Article XX(b) or XX(g), they must still pass the requirements set by the preamble of the article. This seems to be rather easy with respect to the requirement that these measures are not applied in a manner that would constitute 'a disguised restriction on international trade', as the four MEAs are explicit and rather transparent in their provision for trade restrictions (least so the CBD, however). It is more doubtful, but still arguable, that they are 'not applied in a manner which would constitute a means of arbitrary or unjustifiable discrimination between countries where the same conditions prevail'. This clause is usually interpreted by GATT/WTO panels as the requirement to balance carefully the environmental objectives of the trade measures with the trade rights of negatively affected WTO members. As all four MEAs have very widespread multilateral support, it can be argued that the international community of nation states has given its blessing to the objectives contained in the MEAs and to the trade measures they employ. Furthermore, the Montreal Protocol, CITES and the Basel Convention do not discriminate against non-parties as such, as these can still enjoy all the trade benefits of parties if, in spite of the remaining non-parties, they comply with the substantial obligations of the agreement. The CBD does not have such a provision for non-parties. However, its almost universal membership means that the number of non-parties is very small indeed. From this perspective, one could argue that the trade measures in all four MEAs would have a good chance to pass the preambular test of Article XX.

So far we have focused on trade measures between parties, and either non-parties or non-complying parties as specifically mandated or explicitly allowed by the MEAs. It has been shown that while the potential for WTO inconsistency clearly exists, it is far from clear that these measures actually are WTO inconsistent. Things are different with respect to the measures an MEA party might undertake without a specific mandate or permission contained in an MEA. Such a country could still argue that while these measures are not specifically mandated or allowed for by an MEA, they are undertaken nevertheless in pursuance of and compliance with mandated MEA obligations. Whether these would pass scrutiny for WTO consistency is much less clear and cannot be answered in general as the answer very much depends on the concrete measures undertaken and the manner in which they were applied.[9]

That countries like to invoke MEAs at times in justification for clearly protectionist measures can be seen by two cases. In the United States, prohibition of imports of tuna and tuna products from Canada was justified, inter alia, as furthering the objectives of the Inter-American Tropical Tuna Commission and the International Convention for the Conservation of Atlantic Tunas (GATT, 1983, paragraph 3.10). In Canada, measures were introduced affecting exports of unprocessed herring and salmon, and the state in its submissions referred to international agreements on fisheries and the United Nations Convention on the Law of the Sea (GATT, 1987b, paragraph 3.39).

The Cartagena Protocol on Biosafety

The major potential for conflict between the Cartagena Protocol on Biosafety and the WTO system does not lie in its trade measures as such, but in the Protocol's explicit and repeated embracing of the so-called precautionary principle in the body of the Protocol. Article 1 of the Protocol proclaims that the objective of the Protocol is 'in accordance with the precautionary approach contained in Principle 15 of the Rio Declaration on Environment and Development'. Article 10:6 gives considerable significance to the principle:[10]

> Lack of scientific certainty due to insufficient relevant scientific information and knowledge regarding the extent of the potential adverse effects of a living modified organism on the conservation and sustainable use of biological diversity in the Party of import, taking also into account risks to human health, shall not prevent that Party from taking a decision, as appropriate, with regard to the import of the living modified organism in question...

The reader should recall that the precautionary principle is not explicitly but only indirectly referred to in the SPS Agreement. Also, it can only be invoked in provisional suspension of the requirement to perform a risk assessment (see p30). With regard to these two important aspects, the Cartagena Protocol considerably differs from the SPS Agreement. Herein also lies the potential for conflict as the following hypothetical scenario shows: a country which is a member of the WTO and a party to the Cartagena Protocol bans the import of GMOs without sufficient scientific information for a risk assessment, but invoking the precautionary principle. The exporting country, which is a WTO member, but not a party to the Protocol, regards these trade measures as violating the other country's obligations under the SPS Agreement as no risk assessment is provided and challenges the measures before a WTO panel.

Given this potential for conflict, parties have fought hard over how the relationship between the Protocol and the WTO system would be spelled out in the Protocol. Those who are major exporters of GMOs and regard the precautionary principle with suspicion as they fear that it will be used to restrict imports of GMOs, were gathered in the so-called Miami Group (Argentina, Australia, Canada, Chile, the US and Uruguay). The Miami Group wanted to include an article in the main body of the Agreement, stating that nothing in the Protocol would affect the parties' rights and obligations under other existing international agreements, which basically meant the WTO Agreements. Such a clause is actually included in the CBD's Article 22:1 which states that 'the provisions of this Convention shall not affect the rights and obligations of any Contracting Party deriving from any existing international agreement, except where the exercise of those rights and obligations would cause a serious damage or threat to biological diversity'.

Most other countries and environmentalists rejected this approach as they regarded it as a subordination of the Protocol under a trade agreement.[11] In the end stood a compromise that merely restates the conflicting views on the issue and that followed the precedent set by the Rotterdam Convention on the Prior Informed Consent Procedure for Certain Hazardous Chemicals and Pesticides in International Trade. The Miami Group had to accept that a relevant text was merely included in the less binding preamble, but pushed through the formulation that 'this Protocol shall not be interpreted as implying a change in the rights and obligations of a Party under any existing international agreement'. However, the very next paragraph confirms the view of all other countries and environmentalists that 'the above recital is not intended to subordinate this Protocol to other international agreements'. Thus, a potential for conflict clearly exists and, given the massive export interests of GMO-producing countries from the Miami Group, it seems only a question of time until a dispute before the WTO is initiated.

How can this conflict be resolved? The heart of the problem lies in the SPS Agreement's unsatisfactory dealing with insufficient scientific evidence. I have argued in detail elsewhere why the SPS Agreement needs to be reformed, to the effect that the precautionary principle becomes fully and directly incorporated and is invokable not only provisionally. Doing so would remove the major potential for conflict between the Cartagena Protocol and the WTO Agreements so that both could coexist in mutual support.

Reconciling Trade Measures in MEAs and WTO Rules

Given that the potential for conflict between the trade provisions in MEAs and WTO rules exists, it is pertinent to examine different options for dealing with this potential.

Wait and see

The easiest way to deal with the potential for conflict is to do nothing for the time being and to embark on policy reform only if it was found to be necessary in the future.

Assessment: No trade provision contained in MEAs has ever been challenged before GATT/WTO. Even if it was, a panel or the appellate body might still uphold the provisions, as argued above. The most likely potential future dispute will not be about mandated or specifically allowed trade provisions, however, but about measures, not demanded or specifically allowed, but undertaken by a country in alleged pursuance of and compliance with an MEA. But even in this case it might be best to wait and see how a WTO panel and the appellate body would rule. If it turned out that in either case these came to the conclusion that is unsatisfactory from an environmental perspective, one could still have recourse to one of the other options analysed below. This wait-and-see approach is therefore very much influenced by the idea that something that is not obviously broken does not need fixing.

Wait and see is the preferred option of the vast majority of developing countries (WTO, 1996), but is regarded as inadequate by most developed countries (for example, Canada, 1999; European Communities, 1999; Norway, 1999), with the possible exception of the US (BNA, 2000). Always suspicious towards the developed countries' inclination to protect themselves against cheaper imports from poorer countries, they see the more far-reaching options discussed below as potentially biased against their trading rights in their de facto effects, if not in their design. On the other hand, many observers have spoken out against the wait-and-see approach. WWF (1996, p10), for example, suggests that the wait-and-see approach 'calls for political reinforcement of the current uncertainties and trade biases of the WTO and thus of their potential "chill" effect on the use of environmentally effective trade measures in MEAs'.

I would concede that the wait-and-see approach does not solve the conflict. On the other hand, the conflict so far exists merely potentially and wait and see is the best way to find out whether the conflict will actually materialize. In as far as a dispute between parties and non-parties to an MEA is more likely to arise before the WTO than a dispute between the parties to an MEA (where countries can use the consultation and, if existent, the dispute-settlement facilities of the MEA), the likelihood of a WTO challenge is very small indeed. As noted above, with the exception of the Basel Convention there is only a handful of countries that are not parties to these arguably most important MEAs, but members of the WTO. Furthermore, for many countries non-ratification has other reasons than opposition to the MEA and might still come about as time passes by. Maybe more importantly still, the vast majority of countries that are WTO members but not parties to one of the four MEAs are small and very poor developing countries that have not so far initiated any dispute before the WTO and are highly unlikely to do so regarding trade provisions contained in one of the MEAs.[12]

Furthermore, it might be the only option realistically available. As will be discussed below, all other options need the approval of most, if not all developing countries' WTO members, and they strongly favour the current status quo. I will also argue in favour of amending the GATT to provide an MEA exception clause along the blueprint given by the North American Free Trade Agreement (NAFTA). This could be achieved in the next round of trade negotiations if developed countries can convince the developing countries of the benefits of such an approach (or bribe them with concessions in other areas to concord). Until then, the best and indeed the only option is to wait and see.

Require environmental experts on panels and appellate bodies

A second option slightly beyond the wait-and-see approach is to change the composition of WTO panels and appellate bodies so that in any potential future dispute involving the trade provisions of MEAs, one or more of the panellists must have explicit expertise in environmental matters in addition to expertise in international trade law. This proposal addresses, at least with respect to MEAs, a common concern shared by many: that trade lawyers with no particular expertise in environmental matters decide on environmentally related disputes. The hope would be that with the infusion of environmental expertise, the panel might come to decisions that take environmental aspects better into account.

Assessment: To require environmental experts on panel and appellate bodies is neither necessary nor sufficient for solving conflicts between trade provisions in MEAs and WTO rules. Already panels have the right to seek information from outside expert groups (Dispute Settlement Understanding, Article 13) and they actually do so. The panel in the shrimp/sea turtle case, for example, has confronted five environmental experts with an exhaustive list of investigating questions (WTO, 1998). This, together with the possibility of environmental NGOs to submit position papers, so-called *amicus curiae* briefs, as explicitly allowed for by the appellate body in the shrimp/sea turtle case, should guarantee the sufficient provision of environmental expertise. Furthermore, in past dispute settlements it does not appear that decisions that were regarded by some as environmentally unfriendly were taken because of a lack of environmental expertise, but rather because of a specific legal interpretation of the WTO rules.

Certification by MEA secretariat

MEAs could be designed so that their secretariats have the option to certify trade measures undertaken by countries in alleged pursuance of or compliance with an MEA (Marceau, 1999, p150). The idea is that such certification could serve as further evidence in a potential future dispute that the trade measure is genuinely undertaken for the alleged objective.

Assessment: This seems to be a good idea that can lead to some further clarification should a future dispute arise. However, this option stops a long way short of reconciling the conflict itself.

Restricting access to the WTO dispute settlement

The Understanding on Rules and Procedures Governing the Settlement of Disputes (Dispute Settlement Understanding (DSU)) could be amended to the effect that countries that are members both of an MEA and of the WTO are either required to settle their dispute via the dispute settlement mechanism of the MEA, and would therefore be prohibited from entering the WTO dispute settlement process, or they would be required to try to exhaust the possibilities of an MEA dispute settlement first before they have recourse to the WTO dispute settlement. The European Union (EU) seems to be in favour of such an approach (European Communities, 2000). Amendment of the DSU can only be undertaken by consensus, however (Article X:8 of the Agreement Establishing the WTO).

Assessment: This option is not very helpful for two reasons. First, the dispute settlement in MEAs is usually institutionally weak with no streamlined timetable and no enforcement mechanism via retaliatory and cross-retaliatory trade sanctions as existent in the WTO system. Some MEAs do not even have provisions for a dispute settlement. WTO members might therefore be more than hesitant to forgo their right to challenge trade measures before the WTO either completely or until the dispute settlement mechanisms of the relevant MEA are exhausted. Second, and more importantly, this option can only apply to cases where both countries are members of both the WTO and the relevant MEA. A future dispute can also arise between two countries where only one country is a member of the MEA and imposes trade measures on the other country as a non-party to the MEA. As non-parties cannot challenge a trade measure before the MEA, they would automatically have to challenge the measure before the WTO.

Temporary waiver

Article IX:3 of the Agreement Establishing the WTO provides for the temporal waiving of WTO obligations, which could be used to waive certain obligations with respect to trade provisions in MEAs. Waiving decisions should normally be taken by consensus, otherwise by a three-fourths majority. A waiver must be temporary with a fixed date of termination and is allowed in exceptional circumstances only (Article IX:4).

Assessment: A temporary waiver is a non-option as it would not really solve any conflict. It does not provide any security or permanence. It is ad hoc and unpredictable (Schoenbaum, 1997, p283; Rutgeerts, 1999, p84).

Interpretative statement

According to Article IX:2 of the Agreement Establishing the WTO, the Ministerial Conference and the General Council of the WTO 'have the exclusive authority to adopt interpretations of this Agreement and of the Multilateral Trade Agreements'. An interpretation becomes adopted if it gains the support of three-fourths of WTO members. For example, in 1996 the EU had put forward a proposal for an interpretation of Article XX(b) so that, under certain conditions, a trade measure undertaken by a country in pursuance of an MEA would automatically be regarded as 'necessary' in the meaning of the article and would therefore merely have to pass the test of the preamble to Article XX (WTO, 1996, p5).[13] The conditions were that the 'MEA was open to participation by all parties concerned with the environmental objectives of the MEA, and reflected, through adequate participation, their interests, including significant trade and economic interests' (ibid).

Switzerland in a later submission went one step further in suggesting that such trade measures should be exempted from the scrutiny of Article XX entirely, including the chapeau (Switzerland, 2000). This submission was probably influenced by the importance that WTO panels and appellate bodies had put on the chapeau of Article XX in the meantime.

Assessment: An interpretative statement to GATT articles has the important advantage over the amendment of GATT articles discussed below that it does not need ratification. However, it is somewhat unclear how far-reaching an interpretative statement can be. This is because Article IX:2 of the Agreement Establishing the WTO states that the paragraph allowing interpretative statements 'shall not be used in a manner that would undermine the amendment provisions in Article X'. Even the EU proposal might be contested by many as calling for an amendment to GATT Article XX rather than an interpretation. To be on the safe side, it seems therefore much more appropriate to go the way via amending GATT articles if substantive change is required.

Amendment to GATT

The most far-reaching option is to amend the GATT. A proposal for amendment needs a two-thirds majority and has effect only for those members who have accepted the amendment (Article X:3 of the Agreement Establishing the WTO).[14] The amendment would need ratification by the accepting countries (Wold, 1996, p916). GATT could be amended in a number of ways – for example:

- Brack (1996, p82), without embracing the suggestion, considers the introduction of a 'sustainability clause' which would set out 'agreed principles of environmental policy – such as the polluter pays principle and the precautionary principle – against which trade measures can be judged'.
- Several countries have proposed the establishment of a number of pre-specified ex ante requirements for an MEA to be granted exception from WTO obligations (see WWF, 1996 and WTO, 1996). These requirements were supposed to be more or less binding and were regarded with suspicion by environmental NGOs such as the World Wide Fund For Nature (WWF) as they would introduce 'new criteria, guidelines, or legal tests that are grounded in trade, not environment, policy considerations' (WWF, 1996, p10). WWF, for its part, has called for a general exception for MEAs without providing any detailed proposal, however (ibid, pp29ff).
- Hudec (1996, pp120–142) has proposed a new exception to Article XX which would introduce a two-tier approach modelled on the existing Article XX(h), which excepts international commodity agreements. According to this proposal, in its

first part such a new exception would lay down pre-specified criteria as to the substance, structure and negotiating procedure that an MEA would need to fulfil to qualify for the exception. In its second part, the new exception would allow the submission of any MEA to WTO members for approval and the granting of the exceptional status, which would be possible whether or not the criteria in the exception's first part were met or not. Similarly, Housman and Zaelke (1995, pp324–327) suggest a number of criteria for an MEA to be protected from challenge before the WTO.

- A similar suggestion, but one going one step beyond the GATT amendment, is to conclude a special agreement on trade-related environmental measures (TREMs) (suggested, for example, by Cosbey, 1999). In its chapter on MEAs, the TREMs Agreement would have to specify 'what constitutes an MEA under the agreement, how different types of trade measures should be treated, and what types of complementary measures must be applied under what circumstances' (ibid, p5). Brack (2000, pp294–296) has put forward a similar idea for a WTO Agreement on MEAs which would need to specify a definition of an MEA and of trade measures, and would need to put down rules for a dispute settlement.

- A final possibility to amend GATT is to introduce an MEA exception clause in following the blueprint set NAFTA's Article 104 which governs the relationship to environmental and conservation agreements. Its first paragraph states that 'in the event of any inconsistency between this Agreement and the specific trade obligations set out in' CITES, the Montreal Protocol, the Basel Convention and two further bilateral agreements between NAFTA partners 'such obligations shall prevail to the extent of the inconsistency, provided that where a Party has a choice among equally effective and reasonably available means of complying with such obligations, the Party chooses the alternative that is the least inconsistent with the other provisions of this Agreement'. Its second paragraph opens the possibility for the inclusion of further future MEAs in stating that 'parties may agree in writing to modify Annex 104.1 to include any amendment to an agreement referred to in paragraph 1, and any other environmental or conservation agreement'.

Assessment: The 'sustainability clause' will mitigate, but will not solve the conflict. The Agreement Establishing the WTO already contains a commitment to sustainable development in its preamble. Article 31:3(c) of the Vienna Protocol on the Law of Treaties requires to take into account other 'rules of international law applicable to the partners' and it is standard practice of panels and appellate bodies to take international environmental principles, such as the polluter pays principle, into account.

To establish pre-specified criteria that MEAs must comply with in order to qualify for the exception of GATT obligations is, in my view at least, inferior to an MEA exception clause following the blueprint given by NAFTA. The exact wording of these criteria will be highly contested and open to interpretation. The criteria necessarily need to be kept non-specific. For example, it would not make much sense to specify the exact number of parties or the range of interests to be represented as this would have to differ from MEA to MEA. Equally contested will be who has the right to decide on whether the criteria are fulfilled.

The much clearer and cleaner approach is to state explicitly which MEAs are exempted. This could take the form of either an environmental side agreement (a special agreement or an MEA code in WTO language) or the form of a simple MEA exception clause in a renegotiated GATT.[15] During the next round of trade negotiations the CBD, CITES, the Basel Convention and the Montreal Protocol, including their amendments, could be exempted explicitly. The same holds true for other MEAs with similar widespread international participation. What about future MEAs? To require consensus for inclusion of a future MEA might be appropriate for an agreement like NAFTA with only three partners. It would be too demanding for the WTO, however. I would suggest that other MEAs also become exempted if three-fourths of WTO members are in favour. Such a decision rule would ensure that no MEA is exempted if the majority of developing countries, the major proponents of the wait-and-see approach, is not in favour. On a case-by-case basis countries could decide whether they regard the MEA in question to be satisfactory on such criteria as the number of parties, the range of interests represented or the existence of a fair compromise between trade measures (sticks), and financial and technological assistance (carrots) to grant them exemption from WTO obligations.

Against such a proposal, Caldwell (1994, p192) raises the fear that an MEA exception clause might reinforce 'the perception, particularly frustrating to the environmental community, that the GATT and the goals of liberalized trade it represents have priority over all other concerns'. This misses the point, however, as an MEA exception clause actually gives precedence to MEAs over the GATT. It is therefore the environmental objective of the exempted MEAs that has priority over GATT's goals of liberalized trade, not vice versa.

It should be noted that for those MEAs that do not become explicitly exempted by WTO members, no presumption is implied that measures taken in their pursuance could be challenged successfully before the WTO. Those trade measures could still be justified under GATT Article XX or other provisions in one of the WTO Agreements, and the normal rules of dispute resolution would apply. Also, should a WTO panel or an appellate body ever find a trade measure taken in pursuance of an MEA in violation of WTO rules, there would be enormous pressure on countries to exempt the MEA in retrospect. Non-exemption of an MEA at some point of time therefore does not leave the MEA without any protection from being challenged before the WTO.

Conclusion

If, as suggested above, the potential for a clash between trade measures employed in MEAs and WTO rules exists, then it will be just a matter of time until a country will challenge such a measure. When this will be is difficult to say. It could well be in the near future, but it could also be that nothing happens for at least another decade. Even if a measure became challenged, it is far from clear that a WTO dispute panel or appellate body would find the measure in conflict with WTO rules. Obviously, much depends on the concrete measure and its design, but, as suggested above, there are good arguments to presume that such a panel or body might find the measure to be covered by one of the environmental exceptions contained in GATT Article XX. It is reasoning such as this that makes the wait-and-see approach so attractive. Most, especially developing, countries therefore support this approach.

In spite of its attractiveness, the wait-and-see approach does not provide a solution, however. It is an unimaginative and short-sighted approach. Instead I would submit that we need to be more anticipative and seek a more long-term solution. Such a solution is the MEA exception clause proposed above. It is simple and clear, leaving very little room for ambiguity. As it would need the consent of the vast majority of developing countries, it cannot be denounced as biased against their interest. Combined with the possibility for specific trade measures undertaken by countries to become certified by MEA secretariats, it offers the best policy option to reconcile trade measures in existing and future MEAs with WTO rules.

Potential Conflicts between Substantive CBD Provisions and the TRIPS Agreement

It is contested whether some of the substantive provisions of the CBD, discussed above, might clash with Article 27:3(b) of the TRIPS Agreement. The reader should recall that this article allows the patentability of 'non-biological and microbiological processes' and calls upon WTO members to 'provide for the protection of plant varieties[16] either by patents or by an effective *sui generis[17]* system or by any combination thereof.'

Most developed countries and their business groups argue that there is absolutely no reason to presume that the TRIPS Agreement clashes with the objectives of the CBD, which are 'the conservation of biological diversity, the sustainable use of its components and the fair and equitable sharing of the benefits arising out of the utilization of genetic resources' (CBD Article 1) (ICTSD, 1998). A position paper of the International Chamber of Commerce (ICC) makes this point very succinctly: 'It is ICC's position that both the CBD and TRIPS are important international conventions, equally binding on their numerous signatories. They deal with different topics. They are fully consistent with each other and must both be fully implemented by their signatories.' Those who hold this position argue that the availability of patents provides the right incentives for companies to invest into research for making pharmaceutical or agricultural use of biological diversity. The ensuing rise in the value of biodiversity would render the preservation and sustainable use of biodiversity more worthwhile relative to activities that would lead to its destruction. Furthermore, developed countries' companies would be more willing to share the use of relevant technologies with developing countries if their intellectual property rights are protected.

Critics, among them most developing countries and many environmentalists, argue that the TRIPS Agreement is in conflict with the spirit, if not the letter, of the CBD. Their major separate, but interrelated, arguments are as follows:

- The TRIPS Agreement is practically silent on the 'fair and equitable sharing of the benefits arising out of the utilization of genetic resources' as enshrined in Article 1 and, with special reference to making use of the knowledge, innovations and practices of indigenous and local communities, in Article 8(j) of the CBD (IISD and UNEP, 2000, p55). The fear is that developed countries' companies will appropriate the lion's share of the benefits from genetic resource use if they are granted patents on modifications that are sufficient to be considered a new and inventive step, and are capable of industrial application as required by Article 27:1 of the TRIPS Agreement – a phenomenon that critics regard as 'bio-piracy' (CUTS, 1997). Cosbey (1999) asserts that 'there has been a steady and substantial transfer of resources from South to North as the valuable products of informal innovation have been appropriated cost-free'.
- It is feared that, in the agricultural field, the patentability of non-biological and microbiological processes would lead to restrictions on the transfer of technology to developing countries, which would run counter to the provisions for access to and the transfer of technology for developing countries in Article 16 of the CBD.[18]
- It is feared that the patentability of non-biological and microbiological processes would lead to a concentration of market power in the hands of a few companies from the developed world and to the domination of monocultures in the crops supplied by these companies, as farmers rush away from their traditional varieties to use standardized high-yielding crops. This could threaten the biodiversity of cultivated species (IISD and UNEP, 2000, p56).
- It is also feared that the TRIPS Agreement is biased against the traditional innovations of farmers. As Cosbey (1999) points out: '... by most interpretations there will be no protection for the varieties produced by informal innovation – by farmers selecting for desired characteristics generation after generation'. This is often referred to as the neglect by the TRIPS Agreement of so-called farmers' rights as opposed to breeders' rights.
- Lastly, if patents are granted in very broad terms, this might counteract its supposed effect of encouraging research and development. As IISD and UNEP (2000, p57) note: 'Patents have been granted, for example, for such broad categories as sunflower seeds with high oleic acid content. To the extent that such a patent stifles innovative research into improved ways of producing high oleic acid sunflowers, strong intellectual property rights protection defeats one of its main avowed goals.' The granting of very broad patents might also lead to highly problematic consequences on equity. Cosbey (1999) quotes the Director-General of the International Plant Genetic Resources Institute as stating the following concern: 'The granting of patents covering all genetically engineered varieties of a species, irrespective of genes concerned or how they were transformed, puts in the hands of a single inventor the possibility to control what we grow on our farms and in our gardens.'

A review of Article 27:3(b) of the TRIPS Agreement is currently under way under the auspices of the WTO as part of the so-called built-in negotiating agenda from the Uruguay Round Agreements and as explicitly called for in the article.

Developed countries argue that this obligatory review should be confined to assess whether countries, especially developing countries, have provided the patents or effective *sui generis* systems for the protection of plant varieties. Many developing countries have not yet provided either patents or *sui generis* systems, however. As a minimum demand, they have called for an extension of the deadline, which for developing countries was 1 January 2000 (2006 for the 29 so-called least developed WTO members). Given the fact that the Seattle meeting has not led to any conclusion on this contested matter, WTO members have found a so-called gentlemen's agreement which says that non-implementation will not be challenged before the WTO until further negotiations find a way out of the deadlock (ICTSD, 2000a).[19] However, the US has made it clear that it will only see itself bound to this agreement with respect to developing countries who encounter real problems in implementation and not with respect to developing countries who want an extension of the deadline because ultimately they do not want the implementation of the provisions at all (ibid).

But non-implementation seems to be the ultimate goal of developing countries who want the substance of the article itself to be addressed in its review and ultimately want to get rid of its provisions (ICTSD, 1998). Kenya (on behalf of the African Group, but representative for the vast majority of developing countries) has demanded that the review process 'should clarify that plants and animals as well as microorganisms and all other living organisms and their parts cannot be patented, and that natural processes that produce plants, animals and other living organisms should also not be patentable' (Kenya, 1999, p4). It also seeks explicit clarification of the article so that it does not contravene the CBD (ibid, p5). More specifically, it wants the insertion of a footnote to Article 27:3 (b) allowing countries to pass laws that provide for:

1   the protection of the innovations of indigenous and local farming communities in developing countries, consistent with the Convention on Biological Diversity ...;
2   the continuation of the traditional farming practices, including the right to save, exchange and save seeds, and sell their harvest;
3   the prevention of anti-competitive rights or practices which will threaten the food sovereignty of people in developing countries ...

The case of the CBD is somewhat unique in that it is the only one so far in which it is one of the WTO Agreements which is in potential conflict with an MEA, rather than the other way around. The reader should note that, similar to the case of GMOs, many critics reject the patentability of any form of life for much more general reasons than a potential clash with CBD obligations, including environmental, ethical, spiritual and religious reasons (see, for example, Institute of Science in Society, 1999b and Indigenous People's Statement, 1999). It would be vastly beyond the scope of this chapter to assess these arguments. Here, I will therefore not make a judgement on the appropriateness or otherwise of allowing the patentability of any form of life. Instead I will confine myself to assessing if this particular article of the TRIPS Agreement is in conflict with the CBD.

I would argue that this is not the case. That the TRIPS Agreement is silent on an equitable sharing of the benefits of biodiversity use does not mean that the patent or *sui generis* systems to be enacted could not include rules that lead to such an equitable sharing. Even the ICC (1999) admits that if equitable sharing of the benefits from inventions that make use of indigenous knowledge does not take place, this could reasonably be called 'biopiracy'. Similarly, just because the TRIPS Agreement does not contain an explicit reference to the preservation of biodiversity does not mean that the patent or *sui generis* systems to be enacted could not be designed in a way that promotes biodiversity preservation. It is true that Article 16:3 of the CBD subjects patents and other intellectual property rights 'to national legislation and international law in order to ensure that such rights are supportive of and do not run counter to its objectives'. However, those who see a clash with the TRIPS Agreement often seem to forget that this agreement also allows members to:

> exclude from patentability inventions, the prevention within their territory of the commercial exploitation of which is necessary to protect order public or morality, including to protect human, animal or plant life or health or to avoid serious prejudice to the environment, provided that such exclusion is not made merely because the exploitation is prohibited by their law (Article 27:2).[20]

Furthermore, the fact that Article 27:3(b) of the TRIPS Agreement allows developing countries to provide an 'effective *sui generis* system' as an alternative to patents should give these and other countries some leeway to design these systems to their benefit and to the benefit of biodiversity preservation. They are not required to accede to the International Convention for the Protection of New Varieties of Plants (UPOV Convention), an existing *sui generis* system, which critics argue is biased towards developed countries' interests (for more detail on this Convention, see Cosbey, 1999 and Dutfield, 2000). In conclusion, therefore, as mentioned above, one might reject the provisions in Article 27:3(b) of the TRIPS Agreement for many other reasons, but there is no a priori reason to presume that this article is to be revoked because it clashes with the CBD.[21]

Notes

1   The major contributions are Barrett (1990, 1991, 1994a, 1994c, 1997a, 1997b); Carraro and Siniscalco (1993); Endres and Finus (1998); Finus and Rundshagen (1998a, 1998b).

2   Cooperation can be wider and deeper if the emissions abatement is characterized by fixed costs, so that the average costs fall over a certain range of abatement, or if the emissions abatement creates positive technological externalities, so that abatement by one country reduces the abatement costs of other countries – see Heal (1994).

3   A necessary condition is, however, that the trade measures are executed by a minimum number of countries and not just by one country alone (Barrett

1997b, p347). Indeed, cooperating countries that fail to execute trade sanctions against free-riders might themselves face trade measures.

4   Trade measures are cheaper than transfer payments as they do not impose any costs as long as the deterrence of free-riding is successful.

5   For an overview, see Smith (1998).

6   In addition to these explicit trade measures addressed at non-parties, parties to the Montreal Protocol might enact a number of measures in compliance with the Protocol, which can have relevant effects on the trade with other parties. These include, for example, quantitative restrictions on the imports of, and excise taxes on ODSs, and restrictions on the import of ODS technologies.

7   Furthermore, CITES is biased towards mammals and especially to the ones that humans find 'attractive' at the expense of the relative neglect of endangered nonmammals (Webb, 2000). Interestingly, Metrick and Weitzman (1996) have found the same bias for the US Endangered Species Protection Act.

8   Agenda 21 was concluded at the United Nations Conference on Environment and Development (UNCED) in Rio de Janeiro in 1992.

9   One test case could have been the Chilean ban on the trans-shipments of sword-fish (see Neumayer, 2001, p138), but it never went before a panel.

10 Similarly, Article 11:8 for the special case of living modified organisms intended for direct use as food or feed, or for processing.

11 For a general critique of this approach, see Saladin (1999).

12 The most conspicuous exception being, of course, the United States, a non-party to both the CBD and the Basel Convention.

13 Because the proposal was never formally submitted to the Committee on Trade and Environment (CTE), it is called a 'non-paper' in WTO nomenclature.

14 Amendments to GATT Articles I and II need consensus (Article X:2).

15 Note that such a clause would need to be outside GATT Article XX and would therefore not be subject to its chapeau requirements.

16 Plant varieties are improved versions of plants through breeding techniques with the purpose of making them stable and uniform (South Centre, 1997, p28).

17 That is, a system specifically designed for a specific type of intellectual property. One such *sui generis* system is the International Convention for the Protection of New Varieties of Plants (UPOV Convention).

18 Note, however, that even the CBD demands that 'such access and transfer shall be provided on terms which recognize and are consistent with the adequate and effective protection of intellectual property rights' (Article 16:2).

19 Note that many provisions other than Article 27 have also not been implemented yet by developing countries and that the gentlemen's agreement covers all nonimplementation issues, not just those with respect to Article 27. On 1 May 2000 the United States announced that it would initiate two disputes against developing countries which are non-related to Article 27 of the TRIPS Agreement (ICTSD, 2000h).

20 In the absence of relevant WTO case law on Article 27 of the TRIPS Agreement, it is unclear whether a panel would apply the same restrictive interpretation to the term 'necessary' as meaning 'least trade restrictive' as panels have interpreted the similar formulation of GATT Article XX(b).

21 One last remark: Critics of the patentability provisions contained in Article 27:3(b) sometimes seem to forget that this article actually provides countries with the discretion to explicitly exclude certain life forms from patentability. This is true for all plants and animals as well as all essentially biological processes for the production of plants or animals. It is also true for all non-genetically modified micro-organisms found in nature.

References

Barrett, S (1990) 'The Problem of Global Environmental Protection', *Oxford Review of Economic Policy,* vol 6, no 1, pp68–79

Barrett, S (1991) 'Economic Analysis of International Environmental Agreements: Lessons for a Global Warming Treaty' in OECD (ed) *Responding to Climate Change: Selected Economic Issues,* Paris, OECD

Barrett, S (1994a) 'Self-enforcing International Environmental Agreements', *Oxford Economic Papers,* vol 46, no 5, pp878–894

Barrett, S (1994b) 'The Biodiversity Supergame', *Environmental and Resource Economics,* vol 4, no 1, pp111–122

Barrett, S (1997a) 'Heterogeneous International Environmental Agreements' in Carlo Carraro (ed) *International Environmental Negotiations – Strategic Policy Issues,* Cheltenham, Edward Elgar

Barrett, S (1997b) 'The Strategy of Trade Sanctions in International Environmental Agreements', *Resource and Energy Economics,* vol 19, no 4, pp345–361

Barrett, S (1998) 'Political Economy of the Kyoto Protocol', *Oxford Review of Economic Policy,* vol 14, no 4, pp20–39

BNA (2000) 'WTO Rules Allow Parties to Forgo Rights in Multilateral Environment Pacts', *Environment Reporter,* vol 31, no 11, 17 March, Washington, DC, Bureau of National Affairs

Brack, D (1996) *International Trade and the Montreal Protocol,* London, Earthscan and Royal Institute of International Affairs

Brack, D (2000) 'Environmental Treaties and Trade: Multilateral Environmental Agreements and the Multilateral Trading System', in Gary Sampson and W Bradnee Chambers (eds) *Trade, Environment, and the Millennium,* Tokyo, United Nations University Press

Brack, D, M Grubb and C Windram (2000) *International Trade and Climate Change Policies,* London, Earthscan and Royal Institute of International Affairs

Caldwell, D Jake (1994) 'International Environmental Agreements and the GATT: An Analysis of the Potential Conflict and the Role of a GATT "waiver" Resolution', *MD Journal of International Law & Trade,* vol 18, pp173–198

Canada (1999) *Canadian Approach to Trade and Environment in the New WTO Round – Communication from Canada,* WT/GC/W/358, Geneva, World Trade Organization

Carraro, C and D Siniscalco (1993) 'Strategies for the International Protection of the Environment', *Journal of Public Economics,* vol 52, no 3, pp309–328

Cosbey, A (1999) *The Sustainable Development Effects of the WTO TRIPS Agreement: A Focus on Developing Countries,* Winnipeg, International Institute for Sustainable Development, online available at http://www.ictsd.org

Cosbey, A and S Burgiel (2000) *The Cartagena Protocol on Biosafety: An Analysis of Results – an IISD Briefing Note,* Winnipeg, International Institute for Sustainable Development

CUTS (1997) *TRIPS, Biotechnology and Global Competition,* Jaipur, CUTS Centre for International Trade, Economics and Environment

Dutfield, G (2000) *Intellectual Property Rights, Trade and Biodiversity: Seeds and Plant Varieties,* London, Earthscan

Endres, A and M Finus (1998) 'Renegotiation-proof Equilibria in a Bargaining Game over Global Emission Reductions – Does the Instrumental Framework Matter?' in N Hanley and H Folmer (eds) *Game Theory and the Environment,* Cheltenham, Edward Elgar

European Communities (1999) *EC Approach to Trade and Environment in the New WTO Round – Communication from the European Communities,* WT/GC/W/194, Geneva, World Trade Organization

European Communities (2000) *Resolving the Relationship between WTO Rules and Multilateral Environmental Agreements – Submission by the European Community,* WT/CTE/W/170, Geneva, World Trade Organization

Falkner, R (2000) 'Regulating Biotech Trade: The Cartagena Protocol on Biosafety', *International Affairs,* vol 76, no 2, pp299–313

Finus, M and B Rundshagen (1998) 'Toward a Positive Theory of Coalition Formation and Endogenous Instrumental Choice in Global Pollution Control', *Public Choice,* vol 96, nos 1–2, pp145–186

Finus, M and B Rundshagen (1998b) 'Renegotiation-proof Equilibria in a Global Emission Game when Players are Impatient', *Environmental and Resource Economics,* vol 12, no 3, pp275–306

French, Hilary F (1994) 'Making Environmental Treaties Work', *Scientific American,* vol 271, no 6, pp62–65

GATT (1983) *United States – Prohibition of Imports of Tuna and Tuna Products from Canada,* Panel report, adopted on 22 February 1982, L/5198, BISD 29, Geneva, World Trade Organization

GATT (1987) *Canada – Measures Affecting Exports of Unprocessed Herring and Salmon,* Panel Report, adopted on 22 March 1988, BISD 35S/98, Geneva, World Trade Organization

Heal, G (1994) 'Formation of International Environmental Agreements', in Carlo Carraro (ed) *Trade, Innovation, Environment,* Dordrecht, Kluwer

Housman, R and D Zaelke (1995) 'Mechanisms for Integration', in R Housman, D Goldberg, B van Dyke and D Zaelke (eds) *The Use of Trade Measures in Select Multilateral Environmental Agreements,* Nairobi, United Nations Environment Programme

Hudec, R E (1996) 'GATT Legal Restraints on the Use of Trade Measures Against Foreign Environmental Practices', in J N Bhagwati and R E Hudec (eds) *Fair Trade and Harmonization,* vol 2, Cambridge, Mass, MIT Press

ICC (1999) *TRIPS and the Biodiversity Convention: What Conflict?,* Paris, International Chamber of Commerce

ICTSD (1998) 'Discussion Launched on TRIPS Article 27.3(b) Review but Relationship with Biodiversity Convention Remains Unclear', *BRIDGES between Trade and Sustainable Development Monthly Review,* vol 3, no 6, p7

ICTSD (2000a) 'Prospects for New Round Depend on Flexibility', *BRIDGES Weekly Trade News Digest,* vol 4, no 12, 28 March

ICTSD (2000b) 'African Convention Parties to Address Traditional Knowledge and Agricultural Trade', *BRIDGES between Trade and Sustainable Development Monthly Review,* vol 4, no 3, pp9ff

IISD and UNEP (2000) *Environment and Trade: A Handbook,* Winnipeg and Nairobi, International Institute for Sustainable Development and United Nations Environment Programme

Indigenous People's Statement (1999) *Indigenous People's Statement on the Trade-related Aspects of Intellectual Property Rights (TRIPS) of the WTO Agreement,* Geneva

Institute of Science in Society (1999a) *Open Letter from World Scientists to All Governments,* Milton Keynes, Institute of Science in Society

Institute of Science in Society (1999b) *Why Patents on Life-forms and Living Processes should be Rejected from TRIPS – Scientific Briefing on TRIPS Article 27.3 (b),* Milton Keynes, Institute of Science in Society

Kenya (1999) *The TRIPS Agreement – Communication from Kenya on Behalf of the African Group,* WT/GC/W/302, Geneva, World Trade Organization

Krueger, J (1999) *International Trade and the Basel Convention,* London, Earthscan and Royal Institute of International Affairs

Lappé, M and B Bailey (1999) *Against the Grain: The Genetic Transformation of Global Agriculture,* London, Earthscan

Marceau, G (1999) 'A Call for Coherence in International Law: Praises for the Prohibition Against "Clinical Isolation" in WTO Dispute Settlement', *Journal of World Trade,* vol 33, no 5, pp87–152

Martin, R B (2000) 'When CITES works and when it does not' in Jon Hutton and Barnabas Dickson (eds) *Endangered Species, Threatened Convention: The Past, Present and Future of CITES, the Convention on International Trade in Endangered Species of Wild Fauna and Flora,* London, Earthscan, pp29–37

Metrick, A and M L Weitzmah (1996) 'Patterns of Behavior in Endangered Species Preservation', *Land Economics,* vol 72, no 1, pp1–16

Norway (1999) *Trade and Environment – Communication from Norway,* WT/GC/W/176, Geneva, World Trade Organization

Neumayer, E (2001) *Greening Trade and Investment: Environmental Protection without Protectionism,* London, Earthscan Publications

OECD (1997) *Experience with the Use of Trade Measures in the Montreal Protocol on Substances that Deplete the Ozone Layer,* Paris, Organisation for Economic Co-operation and Development

OECD (1999) *Trade Measures in Multilateral Environmental Agreements: Synthesis Report of Three Case Studies,* COM/ENV/TD(98)127/FINAL, Paris, Organisation for Economic Co-operation and Development

Rutgeerts, A (1999) 'Trade and Environment: Reconciling the Montreal Protocol and the GATT', *Journal of World Trade,* vol 33, no 4, pp61–86

Saladin, C (1999) *WTO 'Supremacy Clause' in the POPs Convention,* Working Paper, Washington, DC, Center for International Environmental Law

Schoenbaum, T J (1997) 'International Trade and Protection of the Environment: The Continuing Search for Reconciliation', *American Journal of International Law,* vol 91, no 2, pp268–313

Smith, C (1998) Carbon Leakage: An Empirical Assessment Using a Global Econometric Model', in J Köhler (ed) *International Competitiveness and Environmental Policies,* Cheltenham, Edward Elgar

South Centre (1997) *The TRIPS Agreement: A Guide for the South,* Geneva, South Centre

Swenarchuk, M (2000) *The Cartagena Biosafety Protocol: Opportunities and Limitations,* mimeo, Toronto, Canadian Environmental Law Association

Switzerland (2000) *Clarification of the Relationship Between the WTO and Multilateral Environmental Agreements – Submission by Switzerland,* WT/CTE/W/168, Geneva, World Trade Organization

't Sas-Rolfes, M (2000) 'Assessing CITES: Four Case Studies', in J Hutton and B Dickson (eds) *Endangered Species, Threatened Convention: The Past, Present and Future of CITES, the Convention on International Trade in Endangered Species of Wild Fauna and Flora,* London, Earthscan, pp69–87

Webb, G W (2000) 'Are all Species Equal? A Comparative Assessment', in J Hutton and B Dickson (eds) *Endangered Species, Threatened Convention: The Past, Present and Future of CITES, the Convention on International Trade in Endangered Species of Wild Fauna and Flora,* London, Earthscan

Wold, C (1996) 'Multilateral Environmental Agreements and the GATT: Conflict and Resolution?', *Environmental Law,* vol 26, no 3, pp841–921

WTO (1994) 'Trade Measures for Environmental Purposes taken Pursuant to Multilateral Environmental Agreements: Recent Developments', Note by the Secretariat, PC/SCTE/W/3, Geneva, World Trade Organization

WTO (1996) *Report (1996) of the Committee on Trade and Environment,* WT/CTE/1, Geneva, World Trade Organization

WTO (1998) *United States – Import Prohibition of Certain Shrimp and Shrimp Products,* Panel Report, WT/DS58/R, Geneva, World Trade Organization

WWF (1996) *Trade Measures and Multilateral Environmental Agreements: Backwards or Forwards in the WTO?* Gland, World Wide Fund For Nature

8

Seizing the Future: The South, Sustainable Development and International Trade

Adil Najam and Nick Robins

'Would you tell me, please, which way I ought to go from here?'
'That depends a good deal on where you want to get to,' said the Cat.
'I don't much care where ...' said Alice.
'Then it doesn't matter which way you go,' said the Cat.
'... so long as I get somewhere,' Alice added as an explanation.
'Oh, you're sure to do that,' said the Cat, 'if you only walk long enough.'
Lewis Carroll, *Alice's Adventures in Wonderland*

The Dual Crisis

The inability of the third ministerial meeting of the World Trade Organization (WTO) held in Seattle in late 1999 to agree on a mandate for a new round of negotiations represents a profound crisis not only for the international trade community, but also for those supporting the shift to sustainable development. While the Seattle challenge to the trade community is self-evident, the threat to the sustainable development agenda is perhaps less obvious. Yet Seattle can be seen as the outcome of a decade-long fraying of the sustainable development bargain struck at the Rio Earth Summit in 1992. For all the strategies and action plans generated, the global sustainable development policy community stands accused of failing to introduce the changes necessary to break the remorseless trends towards the increasing marginalization of the world's poor and the mounting degradation of the natural resource base.[1] The representative of Pakistan probably spoke for many in the South at the April 2000 session of the UN Commission on Sustainable Development when he pointed out that developing countries have begun to mistrust the entire concept of sustainable development, which they feel is consistently 'viewed through the prism of the environment', its social and economic aspects and equity concerns largely forgotten.[2]

It is clearly dangerous to interpret the current stalemate exclusively in terms of a simplistic bipolar world of antagonisms between a rich North and a poor South.[3] Indeed, differences between the US and Europe lay at the heart of the most controversial disputes during the 1990s. Nevertheless, many of the blockages to future progress on sustainable development – especially within the trade arena – can be traced to this persistent global fault-line between North and South.[4] It is not just that the post-industrial economies of the North have broken their pledge to provide new and additional assistance for environmental protection and economic development in the emerging South. Over US$700 billion worth of trade barriers still confront exports from developing economies to the Organisation for Economic Co-operation and Development (OECD), and agreed measures to liberalize key sectors, such as textiles, have generally been sluggishly implemented by the industrialized world.[5] But more than this, neither North nor South has managed to design a positive strategy for making international commerce an engine of rising prosperity, social justice, open governance and environmental regeneration – in other words, for sustainable trade.

As a result, the preambular commitment to sustainable development in the WTO agreement, and the repeated statements about making trade, environment and development 'mutually supportive', remain essentially hollow. In many ways, the urgent global conversation on trade and sustainable development has yet to start. Most policy discussions still quarantine issues of 'trade and environment' apart from those of 'trade and development', thus preserving a pre-Brundtland outlook on both the global economy and the fundamental nature of the global environmental *problematique.*[6] What is missing most from the fractured debate is a strategic sense of the real world outcomes that all sides wish to see realized over the short, medium and long terms. Instead, the situation is dominated by tactical trench warfare over procedures, the inevitable outcome of a situation lacking firm foundations built on trust and shared analysis. As Lavanya Rajamani has observed, 'at the root of the dissonance between the North and the South on the trade – environment issue is a series of enduring perceptions.'[7] From the perspective of the South, an embedded sense of inequity, powerlessness and marginalization in international affairs keeps developing countries persistently wary of the North. Equally, in the North, a lingering sense of responsibility as 'custodians' of world order – which harkens back at least to the dynamics of the Cold War and probably to colonization – fosters a sense of disdain for the South's motivations.[8]

The tragedy of the 1990s lies in the failure to address and resolve these underlying tensions. Indeed, many core perceptions (and misperceptions) have become more, not less, entrenched over the past decade. For example, prevailing Southern views of Northern intentions in linking trade and environment are now more aggressive than ever in their accusation of 'green protectionism'. Similarly, the feeling that developing countries simply do not care about basic labour and environmental norms continues to fuel powerful pressures in Europe and North America.

It could be argued that this hardening of the policy arteries is to a large extent due to the absence of a clear and forceful vision from the WTO and its member states that honestly confronts the opportunities, tensions and dilemmas that international trade poses for sustainable development. Both the proponents of pure trade liberalization without any integration of sustainability and the supporters of the primacy of environmental or labour rights have compelling programmes for achieving their ends. Yet those who see world trade as a necessary engine for sustainable development have still to develop the same clarity of purpose.[9] As it is the South that stands to benefit most from a world where sustainable development is realized, the challenge is how it can seize control of the agenda and turn it to its advantage.[10]

This chapter seeks to begin defining a pathway for the South out of the deadlock. It begins by reviewing the South's current strategy towards trade and the environment, and arguing that there are compelling reasons for a shift in perspective. It then turns to the realities facing Southern producers in global markets, as sustainability factors become integrated into supply-chain programmes. The article then looks forward and presents a set of scenarios describing different ways of tackling the trade and sustainable development dynamic. It concludes by identifying some of the critical ingredients for a new proactive approach, and suggesting that fair and sustainable trade could become a new rallying call for the South.

The South after Seattle

For the past decade, developing countries have been, and remain, wary of movement on global trade and environment policy, which they view as suspect for being a guise for Northern agendas of green protectionism.[11] There is, of course, merit to the Southern concern: industrialized countries have exhibited a tendency to coopt environmental concerns for what seem (at least to Southern observers) like protectionist purposes. For example, careful analysis of the classic tuna – dolphin dispute between Mexico and the US reveals that it was the economic interests of American canneries, rather than environmental concerns, that played the determining role in the introduction of trade barriers to Mexican tuna.[12] Overall, Anil Agarwal and his colleagues at the Centre for Science and Environment (CSE) in India have argued that 'the increasing internationalization of trade [has] led to the emergence of the global consumer, and the birth of a selective global conscience'. As a result, they argue, 'the dividing line between actions motivated by genuine environmental concerns, and those which are a guise for protectionism in trade [has] narrowed'.[13]

Yet, for the very same reasons, the South cannot afford to ignore the link between trade and environment indefinitely. From the perspective of real politics, the ever-increasing number of environment-related disputes before the WTO are evidence that this link is becoming more pronounced, not less. From the perspective of trade realities, the market is increasingly making the link whether policy-makers do so or not. From the perspective of sustainable development, there are deep substantive connections between the two areas and lasting progress on either front is dependent on the other; we are beginning to realize that a healthy environment is as important to a healthy economy as the latter is to the former. Sooner rather than later, developing countries will have to confront the inescapable interconnectedness of trade, environment and their development ambitions.

The events at Seattle look set to force the pace. Largely unnoticed amid the attention focused on street demonstrations was the fact that the developing country agenda was snubbed by both Northern policy-makers and Northern environmental groups. According to the *Guardian*, 'developing countries were bullied, sidelined from the negotiations and patronised' in a setting that Shridath Ramphal, former secretary-general of the Commonwealth, described as 'neocolonialist'.[14] There is a very clear sense in the post-Seattle world that environmental activists in the North will push ever more aggressively for the imposition on trade rules of explicit environmental provisions, with little attention to the implications for the world's poorest. It is now evident that the groups most assertively campaigning for such environmental conditionalities – which to the South seem very much like a recipe for 'green protectionism' – are the ones that define 'the environment' most narrowly and have the least understanding of Southern concerns and realities.

Moreover, the South has allowed itself to be seen as the scapegoat for the policy deadlock on trade and environment. At Seattle, developing country governments were widely portrayed as 'anti-environmental' and certainly as the main hurdle to any integration of trade, environment and development. While some observers in the North have been suggesting this more politely, environmental activists and the media were far more blunt in lambasting the South as the 'villain' in the story.[15] For example, in a 'curtain-raiser' to the Seattle negotiations, a story in the *Seattle Times* described developing countries as being concerned with seeking trade niches such as 'specializing in producing pollution-intensive goods, exporting natural resources or manufacturing products that use low-wage labour, where workers, perhaps children, repetitively perform some menial task'.[16] The *Baltimore Sun* went further in expressing its disdain for the Southern position, lamenting that 'few developing countries see either labour rights or human rights as anything they need to be concerned with'. In expressing its anguish at India's refusal to be part of a US-sponsored study on setting global labour standards, the article declaimed caustically, 'One would think that at least India ("the world's largest democracy") would get it... Most of the multinational corporations are American, and they're the ones that go in and exploit foreign labor. What good does that do Third World countries? Not to mention the jobs it costs here'.[17]

On one hand, such accounts highlight how misunderstood the Southern position is in the North. On the other hand, branding the developing countries as the 'bad guys' of trade and environment has also had an indirect spin-off for those industrialized countries that are no more, or even less, interested in integrating trade and environment concerns. The South's guaranteed opposition to change has enabled these industrialized countries to point to developing country intransigence as an excuse for their own inaction. As a result, the South has a major image restoration exercise before it. Developing countries now have to demonstrate – through word and through action – that they are not anti-environmental, but simply have different priorities, focusing more on issues of environmental justice, sustainable livelihoods and sustainable development more broadly. This more nuanced realization is evident, for example, in former South African president Nelson Mandela's reminder that 'there can be no refusal to discuss matters such as labour standards, social issues and the environment, but equally all must be prepared to listen carefully before judgements are made. On a note of greater caution he added that 'if developing countries feel that there is nothing to gain except further burdens, then it will prove difficult to deal with these crucial matters'.[18]

The challenge to the South in a post-Seattle world, therefore, is both stark and clear. It has to confront the reality that it is now increasingly difficult, if not impossible, to keep trade discussions delinked from the environment.[19] Experience shows that the developing countries have been consistently unsuccessful throughout GATT (General Agreement on Trade and Industry)/WTO history in attempting to use the threat of their non-participation to influence outcomes on issues that are of high interest to key industrialized countries. If the developed countries are indeed bent on including a set of environmental clauses in WTO rules, they are likely to impose them one way or the other, sooner or later. Reportedly, the ASEAN (Association of South East Asian Nations) countries asserted their position on process or production methods (PPMs) in relation to environmental impacts with great brevity and finality: 'not now, not never!'[20] The architects of this adamant position seem to have got half of their wish – but only half, and not for long.

If developing countries participate proactively in trade discussions and focus on putting forward alternative proposals on how to incorporate environmental issues into international trade regimes, they will at least have some chance of shaping the final outcome. By opting to remain 'out of the loop' at this formative juncture, they risk being reduced to mere spectators. Some of the core positions adopted by the South may also need to be reviewed. For example, developing country delegates have tended to take a somewhat curious position that sounds as if they are 'against' multilateral environmental agreements (MEAs) – because they are wary of unnecessary environmental conditionalities – and 'for' free trade. The position is curious because, in general, international environmental regimes have been far more accommodating than trade agreements in providing differential, and preferential, treatment to developing countries. For very understandable reasons, developing country governments tend to take trade negotiations much more seriously than environmental negotiations. Yet, as the 1999 *Trade and Development Report* of the United Nations Conference on Trade and Development (UNCTAD) stressed, 'developing countries have striven hard, and often at considerable cost, to integrate more closely into the world economy, but have had few gains, because of the deep seated imbalances in economic power and systemic biases in the international trading and financial system'.[21] The track record suggests that developing countries get at least a more sympathetic hearing within environmental regimes – and in key instances it is the South that has been the *demandeur* for restrictions on trade to serve environmental goals, notably in the case of biosafety.[22] Indeed, developing countries can defend their interests better in fora seeking 'sustainable development' than in those advocating unadulterated trade liberalization.

Looking back, the position adopted by developing countries up to now has been one of trying to stall any movement on trade and environment issues in the WTO. Although the motivations for doing so are understandable, this (non-)strategy has backfired. On one hand, it has allowed industrialized countries to use developing countries as scapegoats. On the other hand, the developing countries have effectively removed themselves from a position where they could influence the emerging discussion on the subject and steer it in a relatively South-friendly direction. Looking forward, the time is right for the South to adopt a more positive and proactive approach and to begin building a strategy on the basis of an explicit vision rooted in the South's sustainable development interests. The need to do so, and to do so in haste, is greater than ever before. The decision whether or not to engage in the trade and environment debate is now, in effect, beyond the control of Southern (or even Northern) governments. For international markets are already making the decision for them – not because of the WTO, but in spite of the WTO.

Confronting Market Realities

The contrast between policy paralysis and market dynamism is one of the most striking features of the trade arena in recent years. Time and again, the market has proved itself more agile and responsive than governments to concerns about the sustainability of today's patterns of trade. For Professors Bhattacharyya and Mago of the Indian Institute of Foreign Trade, 'environmental consciousness has to be considered as part of the globalization process, and any future international trading strategy has to take this factor into account'.[23] Yet the market can be a cruel and blunt instrument and current initiatives have often demonstrated severe governance and equity gaps that only public policy can resolve.[24]

What seems increasingly clear is that market-led globalization is rendering some of the core assumptions that guide trade policy – notably the primacy of the nation-state as the decision-making unit – less and less useful as a guide on how to achieve sustainable development. As more and more economic activity is channelled through transnational corporations and outsourced along international value chains, so some of the traditional approaches to linkages between trade and sustainability are becoming de facto obsolete. For example, the stipulation by importing countries of social or environmental standards for PPMs is regarded as anathema in policy circles, being seen as a fundamental challenge to national sovereignty. Yet the incorporation of PPMs – for quality and, increasingly, sustainability factors – into contractual arrangements lies at the heart of the supply-chain management programmes of some of the world's leading corporations in the motor car, electronics, food and forestry sectors.

While cases of mandatory PPMs are relatively few in the environmental field, the number and variety of market instruments is immense, ranging from corporate codes of conduct through sector-based certification schemes to industry-wide initiatives. Supermarket retailers in the UK, for example, do not just specify the quality of the food they import or the level of pesticide residues in the final product; they also require producers to abide by detailed integrated crop management standards and controls on the use of genetically modified organisms (GMOs), thereby specifying methods of production that many would regard as illegal for the UK government to demand under WTO rules.[25] Equally, major car-makers, such as DaimlerChrysler are starting to require all their suppliers to achieve third-party registration to an environmental management system based on the ISO14001 standard. Just like the French army in its reliance on the fixed defences of the Maginot Line to deter invasion in 1940, so many governments today appear to be upholding sovereignty on PPMs, while fast-moving corporations and non-governmental organizations (NGOs) cut around their flanks and capture the prize. In the words of Rafael Wong, executive vice-president of the Favorita Fruit Company in Ecuador, the first banana producer to receive certification under the Rainforest Alliance's Better Banana scheme, 'in five years from now, there will be no access to international markets for companies that do not show this respect for the environment. It is becoming fundamental to international trade'.[26]

The driving forces for the integration of sustainability factors into trading relations are many and complex. In most cases, the reasons are defensive – to avoid damage to brand reputation from negative media coverage and civil society pressures. In fact, some of these initiatives amount to a new form of 'civic regulation' whereby NGOs are essentially controlling corporate access to markets in key areas such as labour standards, forest practices and genetic modification. For example, frustrated with the failure of governments to introduce a legally binding convention to control global deforestation, the World Wide Fund For Nature (WWF) launched the Forest Stewardship Council (FSC) in 1993. The FSC is one of a new breed of multi-stakeholder standard-setting bodies set up to fill the vacuum left by global policy paralysis. By establishing a common set of criteria for good forest management and harnessing the purchasing power of major timber buyers, the FSC has helped to galvanize international timber markets. Over 20 per cent of the UK timber trade is now covered by FSC certification and Forest Trade Networks have been established in more than ten countries to stimulate demand for certified timber products.

In the case of cocoa, it is the major chocolate manufacturers themselves that have taken the initiative to tackle some of the major social, economic and environmental constraints facing the sector.[27] Launched by the American Cocoa Research Institute, the International Sustainable Cocoa Program (ISCP) represents a corporate response to the severe challenge to future output posed by declining commodity prices which fail to give sufficient incentives for farmers to continue growing cocoa and to do so in sustainable ways. Its aim is to encourage 'an assured and sustainable supply of cocoa cultivated in a way that makes a positive contribution to the tropical rainforest environment and the income of the smallholder farmer'.[28] Understandably, perhaps, producer countries and others have expressed some suspicion about the initiative, fearing that the chocolate makers are interested solely in maintaining or expanding production so as to keep prices down. In addition, the programme has focused largely on improving production methods rather than on changing the terms of trade to favour smallholder producers along the lines of the 'fair trade' movement. Nevertheless, the ISCP provides a foundation for a more broadly based initiative, involving importing and exporting governments, civil society and the private sector – one of the emerging 'global public policy networks' that are evolving to fill some of the governance gaps created by globalization.[29] In the case of cocoa, new multi-stakeholder mechanisms are needed to move beyond ineffective commodity agreements to finance the public goods – such as biodiversity conservation and sustainable rural livelihoods – that market approaches cannot deliver.

Certainly, integrating sustainability into international supply chains can generate new trade opportunities for those developing country producers that are able meet the standards. Producers can win access to new markets or secure and perhaps expand market share in existing areas. Price premia may be available – notably where there is a gap between demand for sustainable products and available supply. Thus, when India's largest textile producer obtained the Ecotex standard for its products in 1995, it gained an 8–10 per cent price advantage and its market grew by a tenth in the first year.[30] Furthermore, companies can earn powerful internal productivity benefits from investing in improved labour practices and resource use. For Syed Naved Hussain, the chief executive officer of Beximco Textiles, one of Bangladesh's leading enterprises, 'the goals of rapid economic progress and high social and environmental standards can and must be achieved simultaneously'.[31] And there are some important instances where effective demand from consumers, notably for organic food, is a positive force for new export opportunities.[32] But, as with the internet, it is the business-to-business (B_2B), rather than the business-to-consumer relationship that is the most significant market driver for sustainable trade.

Yet these market-led measures can prove a double-edged sword for sustainable development, bringing technical improvements at the expense of wider setbacks. Serious concerns are emerging about the systemic exclusion of developing country voices from corporate as well as international standard-setting. While it is largely capacity constraints that are holding back developing country participation in institutions, such as the International Organization for Standardization (ISO), corporate codes of conduct are private and often confidential documents that suppliers have little chance of influencing. Trade liberalization is also creating a 'buyers' market' in many sectors central to developing country export prospects, with an increasing concentration of market power on the demand-side and an expansion of the supply base in the South.[33] As a recent competition inquiry into UK supermarkets concluded, unfair practices towards suppliers – both domestic and international – are widespread, with the result that 'suppliers are likely to invest and spend less on new product development and innovation, leading to lower quality and less consumer choice.'[34] In these conditions, social and environmental requirements are simply imposed on suppliers, often at the same or lower price for the finished product. Even B&Q, a UK home-improvement retailer at the forefront of demands for FSC-certified timber, recognizes that this imposition model can often undermine trust between buyers and suppliers.[35]

Signs are emerging, however, that the South's traditional position as price and standard taker is now shifting. Producers realize that prospering in liberalizing markets means moving up the value chain and capturing some of the benefits currently accruing to traders and retailers in the North – and that high social and environmental performance is one lever by which to achieve this. Bangladeshi textile and garment exporters agreed recently, for example, that they should develop their own code of conduct to enable them to negotiate from a position of strength with foreign buyers.[36] Similarly, clothing exporters in the 'T-Shirt City' of Tirupur in south India have also concluded that the scale of market requirements and local pressures for better performance necessitates the development of their own 'sustainable brand'.

Central to a proactive Southern strategy for sustainable trade would be ways of reinforcing such 'bottom-up' initiatives to counter the governance and equity downsides to the current suite of voluntary initiatives. But the need for a more active public policy response goes further. By their very nature, voluntary initiatives are limited to those sectors and countries where there are sufficient public expectations and demands to prompt corporate action. There is no guarantee, therefore, that the coverage will be either comprehensive or durable. Export sectors with frequent serious social and environmental impacts have yet to be targeted by civil society, and public pressure to change practices can fade as well as intensify. As a result, 'the archaic – perhaps anarchic – nature of civil regulation means that it will not be sufficient on its own to deliver a system of democratic governance for sustainable development.'[37] The responsibility for filling these gaps thus falls on makers of public policy, a challenge that the trade community has hitherto ducked, but one that offers many opportunities for innovation.

Envisioning the Future: Scenarios for 21st Century Trade

Whatever view is taken of the future, it is likely that the sustainable development imperative – maintaining ecological integrity, enhancing economic well-being and ensuring social justice – will become even more pronounced than it is today. The pressures of expanding global output, growing populations, climbing inequality and destructive patterns of production and consumption are all pushing up against the boundaries of governance systems programmed for a different age. The policy inertia on sustainable development is real, even palpable. Yet there is no reason why it should be so, every reason why it must not be so, and at least some signs of hope that we will reawaken to the imperative – either out of choice or compulsion – sooner rather than later.

Policy-makers who have argued that the public (particularly in wealthy countries) is not ready to make the changes necessary for sustainable development appear to be out of step with their own constituencies. While the shift in public opinion is slow, there is evidence that it is happening. For example, the Gallup International Millennium Survey across 60 countries found universal frustration over government management of environmental issues, and a near-consensus that protection of the environment is ultimately more important than economic growth.[38] Equally, the business community, although still uneasy with the concept of sustainability, is beginning to look seriously at the opportunities embedded in it.[39] For example, when a group of major multinational corporations came to survey the future agenda in 1999, they concluded that 'sustainability will be the dominant business paradigm in the future. Investing in sustainable opportunities is low risk. Furthermore, it is an inevitable investment for the company that wishes to be still in business in 15–25 years time.'[40]

In the age of globalization, the trade arena has become the lightning rod for these pressures, aspirations and expectations. If policy-makers are to move beyond the stalemate at Seattle, a resolution of the entangled issues of trade, environment and development will be essential. Seattle changed things fundamentally, not by resolving the issue but by making its further postponement impossible. One of the central problems it highlighted was the unwillingness of the trade regime to confront (or admit to) the underlying mental maps and assumptions that guide the diverse array of actors. Although the breakdown at Seattle was a surprise for many, it can be explained largely by the inability of the trade establishment to entertain properly, or even acknowledge, the viewpoints of those traditionally marginalized by the system, notably developing country governments, local communities, environmental activists and labour unions.

If sustainable development can be seen as an 'arrow of history' that will (or should, even must) shape the future of trade, then a critical first step for a new strategy would be to sketch out the possible worlds that could emerge, given where we are today and given the directions in which different actors are pushing the discourse. One way to do this is through scenario planning, a tool increasingly used by decision-makers to understand better both their ways of seeing the world and the blind spots that constrain their vision.[41] Different actors can each see only part of the system at any one time, and in the especially complex world of international trade, scenarios can model key assumptions and thus identify inconsistencies, dilemmas – and gaps: what we simply do not know.[42]

Critical to the success of scenario planning for trade and sustainable development is the development of a range of alternative futures that all present *plausible* routes to sustainable development. Arguably, one can construct a virtually infinite number of scenarios for the future of trade and sustainable development. But scenario exercises are most useful with a *limited number* of competing visions that can be kept in the mind simultaneously as a tool for reflection. Looking back at the competing interests that exploded at Seattle and forward to the choices ahead, at least three dominant visions of tomorrow can be identified; each seeks synergy, even fusion, between the goals of international trade and of sustainable development, yet each traces a very different path.[43]

The first could loosely be termed the *trading up* scenario, which sees the global market as the primary agent of innovation towards sustainable trade.[44] It draws on the existing range of supply-chain initiatives and builds on the emergence in the South of new, globally excellent producers who integrate social and environmental factors into their export and innovation strategies. Its proponents place their faith in market transactions and envision a future where social and environmental improvement is racheted up through self-interest, as globally aware and connected consumers demand ever higher standards of corporate performance. The shift from the industrial to the network economy, trading in services rather than goods, also places a premium on resource productivity and the fostering of human capital. In this world, corporations would join with civil society actors and governments in ad hoc alliances to solve specific trade and environment problems, but will firmly resist pressures for the environmental regulation of trade.[45] This world is realist in persuasion and individualist in outlook: the complexity and diversity of viewpoints makes reaching intergovernmental global agreements on trade and sustainable development impossible. The problem of fairness in these market-driven solutions remains unresolved, as does their limited coverage. But supporters of this approach would point to the historical failure of governments – either to remove perverse subsidies or to implement basic regulations – as a reason for not trusting them as the primary agents of change.

A different vision of the future is offered by what we call *the global integration* scenario. In this world, a premium would be placed on new forms of intergovernmental agreement and regulation as the source of innovation for sustainable trade.

This is the vision of those who see a reformed international trading regime, based on existing but revitalized institutions, emerging from the ashes of Seattle. The scenario imagines the first decade of the 21st century being dominated by a reappraisal of the need for regulation to deliver the public goods that the global market cannot produce. It posits a world where governments respond to the operational flaws in the current portfolio of international institutions through a package of measures that resolve today's nagging but eminently resolvable questions of coordination (for example, between the WTO and MEAs). The centrepiece of such a world would be a grand global bargain between North and South which would emerge from an appreciation and acceptance of each other's differential agendas and the common stake in sustainable trade. Specifically, it could be structured around agreements for resource transfers or new forms of governance of commodity chains to finance sustainable production and return value to the producer.[46] This world is internationalist in persuasion and statist in outlook: the globe is too large a place and too complex a system to be left rudderless, either to the whims of the market or to the social fashions of the idealists. The ultimate outcome of such a vision would be a rescue of the nation-state through the sharing of sovereignty, and the effective quieting of competing claims to authority over trade from corporations and civil society.

Both of these scenarios are quite familiar, representing accentuations of the dominant visions of how trade, environment and development can be reconciled: either through the market or the state. Where the conventional debate has been blinkered, however, is in not considering a third vision of the future, a more communitarian perspective on the underlying goals and mechanisms of international trade, which emerged on the global stage at Seattle. What we call the 'new protectionism' scenario is driven by a citizen revolt in North and South against the inability of governments and corporations to deal with the costs of globalization through mere managerial responses.[47] This is the vision of those who wish for the 'spirit of Seattle' to rise once again, with a driving imperative of protecting the livelihoods of those who are marginalized by the current trade regime: developing countries, local communities threatened by new forms of export production, producers in vulnerable sectors and fragile environments. This is a world that seeks a fundamental reversal of the burden of proof: rather than wait for social and environmental benefits to 'trickle down', proponents of international commerce would have to demonstrate that all social and environmental costs are dealt with *prior to* trading taking place. Central to this world is the democratic renewal of both the institutions that govern trade and the agents that carry it out. Power is dispersed away from international institutions, nation-states and corporations, with an emphasis on community control and local self-rule as primary tools to uphold human rights and new transnational networks as the key means of global coordination.[48] To be 'protected' in this vision of the world, are not just markets, but livelihoods; not just national economies, but social as well as natural resilience. The currency of discourse and decision-making is that of emergent global social norms and processes of shaming laggards, rather than market transactions or negotiated legal regimes. This world is egalitarian in persuasion and communitarian in outlook: the purpose of globalization is not to homogenize but to connect. The goal is not to submit blindly to a single universal identity, but to actualize common aspirations (includ-

Table 8.1 *Three scenarios of sustainable trade: a comparison of key features*

	Trading up	Global integration	New protectionism
Primary agent	The market (the merchant)	The state (the prince)	Civil society (the citizen)
Champions	Cutting-edge producers, retailers, consumers	International institutions and national governments	Community-based organizations and NGOs
Change mechanism	Supply-chain innovation spurred by demand dynamics	Intergovernmental agreements and international regulation	Democratic renewal and localization
Decision 'currency'	Market transactions	International bargaining	Social norms and shaming
Outlook	Individualist	Statist	Communitarian
Challenge to the South	Understanding and shaping market dynamics	Building negotiating and institutional capacity	Involving excluded groups in decision-making
Slogan	'The race to the top!'	'A new sustainable trade order'	'Protect the local globally'

ing the environmental and developmental) without letting go of variety and diversity. It is a vision that is open to criticism for seeming anarchic. However, its champions are likely to stress that democracy is always a messy affair, but a worthy goal nonetheless.

The three visions of how international trade and sustainable development may be harmonized are described here in a necessarily abridged fashion and a detailed exposition of the nuances of each is beyond the mandate of this chapter; however, a summary comparison of the key features of each is presented in Table 8.1. There is no suggestion of either prediction or preference in this exposition. It is not our intent, nor would it be useful, to prop any of them up as the embodiment of either 'hell' or 'heaven' in terms of sustainable trade. Indeed, each can ultimately turn out to be either.

The future will, of course, be different from any one of these scenarios, containing elements of all as well as totally new ingredients. Some might argue that the most desirable picture of tomorrow will be a combination of all three, and the most likely would be a mere continuation of the all-too-familiar world-without-vision that was on display at Seattle. This would be a world where neither market dynamics, nor international policy, nor citizen action is able to shift world trade on to a sustainable path – a world, in effect, continuing in the status quo of directionless muddle.

Be that as it may, the goal of the scenario exercise here is not to predict the future that *will be,* but to envision the futures that *could be.* It is in the act of envisioning the 'futures possible', as opposed to the 'future probable', that we take the first steps towards outlining the elements of the strategy that could take us from where we are to where we want to be, and could be. If our analysis is correct, and the pressures and demands for sustainable development are set to grow – not least in the South itself – then policy-makers must now begin thinking seriously about how each of these worlds might impact on them and how they might best prepare. The next section will briefly review these questions from the particular perspective of the developing countries of the South.

The Challenge for the South

Each of the scenarios poses a somewhat different set of challenges and opportunities for developing countries. By testing their current policy positions against these scenarios, we see key starting points for a proactive strategy on trade and sustainable development begin to emerge.

The challenge in the *trading up* world is that of understanding and shaping the complex dynamics of global markets. For the South to succeed in this world, developing country policy-makers would need to place far greater emphasis on, and invest far more effort in, understanding the real dynamics that are driving international markets. Preconceptions – either of a host of untapped 'green trade' opportunities that await them or of the barrage of unseen 'green barriers' that threaten them – would have to be discarded. Replacing this would be a more nuanced appreciation of the more complex terrain ahead: one where opportunities exist, but need to be nurtured; one where threats lurk, but can be avoided. To navigate in such a terrain, national trade agencies will need to consider how to provide new forms of support to their private sector. Central to this would be the engendering of new partnerships to start shaping the sustainability requirements within supply chains in the interests of the South – with an ultimate vision of seeing a shared coevolution of such standards by all stakeholders along the chain.

A future dominated by the *global integration* scenario would primarily expose the readiness of governments in the South to take on a more assertive role. Remaining reactive to international pressures, as the South has done up to now, would merely serve as an invitation to further marginalization. For the South, the fundamental challenge of such a world is the challenge of capacity. Chronic imbalances in the numbers of personnel available for trade talks are already a serious constraint on the South. Designing a new generation of trade and sustainable development deals would stretch these resources further. This means that the South should place a premium on ensuring that the current vogue for 'capacity building on trade and environment' really results in expanded capabilities and not in already overstretched officials and experts being siphoned into yet more workshops and seminars. Of critical importance in preparing for such a world is building indigenous negotiating and institutional capacity within trade institutions (governmental as well as nongovernmental, public as well as private) in developing countries – capacity, not simply to *understand* what is happening in international policy, but to *influence* it. A number of avenues could be pursued. On a national level, it will be critical to improve the understanding, interaction and sharing of analysis between trade, environmental and other negotiators as a way of helping different domestic constituencies to appreciate other perspectives and priorities. For the South collectively, capacity could be pooled possibly through a 'South secretariat' or regional centres of excellence, where staff could be seconded to develop skills and experience.[49]

The *new protectionist* future would pose an especial threat to traditional intergovernmental and international market approaches to managing trade. The challenge to the South in such a world is the challenge of meaningfully involving, and empowering, its own excluded groups and working with them in forging transnational alliances with others who seek similar goals. Transparency, democracy and inclusion would be the watchwords of such a world. Governments, but particularly those of developing countries, who have so closely guarded their fortified enclaves of influence in trade regimes by denying popular participation and transparency in decision-making, would be pushed to reach accommodation with the new forces of global democracy, openness and inclusion. The demand of civil society for a greater voice in trade policy, both at the national level and internationally, is already becoming an inescapable part of the wider trend to political liberalization. More importantly, it could prove to be a major asset for the South in reclaiming the moral high ground, notably within the sceptical North, which has successfully used the developing world as a scapegoat for its own inaction. Within the WTO itself, considerable sensitivity and ingenuity are now required to turn an inward-looking club into a network that responds effectively to the fast-changing realities of global markets and rising popular expectations, particularly those in the South. This opening to civil society could also involve thoughts of new alliances with pro-development forces in the North. Here, the Jubilee 2000 campaign to cancel Third World debt is instructive. One of the reasons for the (limited) success of the campaign was its ability to link the moral demand for debt removal with the positive targeting of the proceeds to poverty reduction. A similar linkage now needs to be made between trade liberalization in critical sectors such as agriculture and textiles and the promotion of sustainable development in the South. In preparing for such a world, the key step for the South is to give voice to its own excluded and disempowered communities, for it is in giving them voice that the South would find its own voice in the world of tomorrow.

From the above outline emerge some of the primary ingredients of what might be termed the South's 'no regrets' policy for trade and sustainable development:

1 supporting the private sector to help shape emerging market rules, so that issues of equity and governance are incorporated;
2 building domestic institutional and negotiating capacity for trade policy, so that new deals can be led from the South; and
3 giving voice and space to civil society as a key partner in trade policy, both to reflect marginalized communities and also to help recapture the moral high ground.

An important fourth action point, which may be one of the principal lessons of Seattle, is that future battles will be fought not only in the texts being negotiated by the WTO, but also in the courts of international public opinion. The South's case for sustainable development is strong and ethically rooted, and could be powerfully deployed to cultivate public support among transnational civil society. Developing countries need to make clear that their stance is not 'against' the environment, but 'for' sustainable development.[50] These are not idle priorities suitable only for a distant future, but would also help the South to deal with today's threats and opportunities, even if the current muddle continues.

Reorienting Trade

At the root of the current trade and environment deadlock lies a vacuum concerning the ultimate goal of the trade regime. As Mark Halle has convincingly argued, 'the time is right for the WTO to articulate its end-purpose and that end-purpose should be sustainable development'.[51] To date, the South has stumbled through international trade negotiations, not only without a strategy, but also without a defining vision. Sustainable development, and therefore sustainable trade, can be – and must be – the basis of the South's vision. This 'reorientation' of the international trade imbroglio can best, and maybe only, come from the developing countries. They, after all, are those who are most uncomfortable with the status quo and those who have the most to gain from a world that is structured around norms of sustainable development.[52] Just as it would be folly to be bullied into agreements that do not serve the South's interests, it would be even sadder to refuse options linking trade and sustainable development that benefit the South's own citizens and their environments just to spite the North.

The opportunity facing the South is to convert the 'trade and environment' debate into a 'trade and sustainable development' debate; and the challenge is to accentuate the opportunities that it provides while deflecting the threats. From the perspective of the Southern policy-maker, the easy option is to opt out of the trade and environment debate on the grounds that it is driven by narrow Northern agendas that are potentially a guise for green protectionism. The more difficult, but clearly advisable option is to become actively engaged in the discussion and change the terms of the debate by calling for a sustainable and fair trade agenda – one that places the trade and environment discourse within the broader framework of sustainable livelihoods, poverty alleviation, social and environmental justice, and the expansion of ecological and human security. Essentially, the South needs to call the North's bluff and test whether the rich world's often pious commitment to sustainable development is more then simple rhetoric. Here, lessons could be learned from the North's own process of trade liberalization, notably the European Union's (EU's) Internal Market programme. Unlike the measures adopted under GATT and the WTO, the EU accompanied the removal of trade barriers with substantial financial transfers to peripheral countries to build the necessary capacity and infrastructure to cope with open markets. While often no friend of sustainability, these Structural and Cohesion Funds have proved successful at stimulating growth – notably in the case of the 'Celtic Tiger' Ireland that now has per capita income levels approximating those of its old rival the UK.

This paper has charted three possible scenarios of how this might take place. While the ultimate goal is the same for all three, each takes a very different path, has very different proponents and offers distinct sets of challenges to the developing countries. Although we have only just begun to explore the challenges that these visions of the future pose for the South, it is already clear that they point us towards what could be the first ingredients of the South's 'no regrets' agenda for trade and sustainable development: encouraging the private sector to help shape market rules; ensuring high-quality capacity-building for public policy; and involving civil society as a key partner in trade policy. These are steps that will not only prepare the developing countries for whichever world may come, but will advance their sustainable development interests in the meantime. By no means will this approach be cost- or risk-free, but neither is the current situation.

If sustainable development is to become the organizing focus of the international trade regime, then at some point, 'sustainable trade' will have to replace 'free trade' as the grand rationale for our efforts. For the early advocates of GATT, the ultimate and non-negotiable goal – to be reached through small steps – was to create a world in which all trade was 'free'. The new goal, equally non-negotiable at its core, must be the creation of a world where all trade is seen as a part of the larger sustainable development enterprise. Whether this reorientation of trade takes place, and whether the South takes a hand in shaping the process to its needs, will be the central question for the coming years.

Acknowledgements

This article draws on the authors' recent research work, as well as numerous discussions and collaborations over a number of years with a range of individuals, including Tariq Banuri, Jennifer Biringer, Emmanuel Boon, Beatrice Chaytor, Aaron Cosbey, Richard Dewdney, Paul Ekins, Tom Fox, Mark Halle, Ulrich Hoffmann, Saleemul Huq, Shahrukh Rafi Khan, Ritu Kumar, Caroline Lucas, Nick Mabey, Ricardo Melendez Ortiz, Sarah Roberts, David Runnalls, Mohammed Saqib, Penny Urquhart, Konrad Von Moltke and Rene Vossenaar. The authors alone, however, are responsible for all opinions and judgements.

Notes

1   See UNEP (2000) *Global Environment Outlook 2000,* Earthscan, London; UNDP (2000) *Human Development Report* 2000 Oxford University Press, Oxford
2   See 'CSD reveals unchanged positions on agriculture, trade and sustainable development', *Bridges* vol 4, no 4, International Centre for Trade and Sustainable Development, Geneva, May 2000
3   For a useful summary of the issues, see *Is there really a North–South Split on Trade and Environment?*, WWF International, Gland, November 1999

Najam Adil (1995) 'An environmental negotiation strategy for the South', *International Environmental Affairs* vol 7, no 3, 1995, pp249–287

5   *Trade and Development Report 1999* (1999) UNCTAD, Geneva
6   The report of the World Commission on Environment and Development (WCED) released in 1987 is generally referred to by the name of its chair, Gro Harlem Brundtland, former Prime Minister of Norway: *Our Common Future: Report of the World Commission on Environment and Development,* Oxford University Press, New York
7   Rajamani, Lavanya (2000) *Developing Country Resistance to Linking Trade and Environment: The Perceptions of Inequity and the Politics of Autonomy,* Global and Environment Trade Study: North–South Series, No 1, August, www.gets.org/gets/library
8   See Thomas, Caroline (1987) *In Search of Security: The Third World in International Relations,* Lynne Rienner, Boulder, CO; Najam, Adil (1994) *The case for a South secretariat in international environmental negotiation,* Program on Negotiation, working paper 94–98, Program on Negotiation at Harvard Law School, Cambridge, MA
9   For one of the first attempts to outline a compelling perspective on trade and sustainable development, see the International Institute on Sustainable Development's Statement on Trade and Sustainable Development, 2000, at http://iisd.ca/trade/
10 See Najam, Adil (2000) 'Trade and environment after Seattle: a negotiating strategy for the South', *Journal of Environment and Development*, Vol 9, No 4, pp405–425
11 See Nath, Kamal (1997) 'Trade, environment and sustainable development', in V Jha, G Hewison and M Underbill (eds) *Trade, Environment and Sustainable Development: A South Asian Perspective*, Macmillan, London, pp15–20; Shahin, M (1998) 'Developing country perspective', in D Brack (ed), *Trade and Environment: Conflict or Compatibility?* Earthscan/Royal Institute of International Affairs, London, pp150–163; South Centre (1998) *The WTO Multilateral Trade Agenda and the South* South Centre, Geneva; Youssef, H (1998) *Special and Differential Treatment for Developing Countries in the WTO,* Trade Working Paper No 2, South Centre, Geneva
12 Koerber, Achim (2000) 'The green protectionism hypothesis: why everybody loves Flipper', in Peider Koenz, (ed), *Trade, Environment and Sustainable Development: Views from sub-Saharan Africa and Latin America,* UNU/ICTSD, Tokyo/Geneva
13 Agarwal, Anil, Narain, Sunita and Sharma, Anju (eds) (1998) *Green Politics,* Centre for Science and Environment, New Delhi, p258
14 Coates, Barry (1999) 'Friends fall out,' *Guardian* (Society), 8 December, p4
15 Whalley, J (1990) 'Trade and environment, the WTO, and the developing countries', in R Z Lawrence, D Robrik and J Whalley (eds), *Emerging Agenda for Global Trade: High Stakes for Developing Countries,* Policy Essay No 20, Overseas Development Council, Washington, DC, pp81–98; Uimonen, P (1999) 'The environmental dilemmas of the World Trade Organization', in J J Schott (ed), *Launching New Global Trade Talks: An Action Agenda,* special report No 12

Institute for International Economics, Washington, DC, pp111–132: Von Moltke, K (1999) 'Trade and the environment: the linkages and the polities', paper presented at Roundtable on Trade and Environment, Canberra, 25 August

16 Anderson, C Leigh and Hennes, David A (1999) 'Why WTO? The progress report', *Seattle Times,* 28 November, pB13

17 Ivins, Molly (1999) 'Clashing heads at WTO talks', *Baltimore Sun,* 30 November, p19A

18 See 'LDCs call for market access, debt promises fulfilled', *Bridges Weekly Trade News* Digest, ICTSD, Geneva, Vol 3, No 19, 25 May 1999, available at http://www.ictsd.org/html/newsdigesl.htm

19 See, for example, Whalley, 'Trade and environment'; Uimonen, G P 'The environmental dilemmas of the World Trade Organization', pages 111–132 in J Schott (ed), *Launching New Global Trade Talks: An Action Agenda,* Special Report 12, Institute for International Economics, Washington, DC; Von Moltke, K (1999) 'Trade and the environment: the linkages and the politics', presented at Roundtable on Trade and Environment, Canberra, 25 August; Sampson, G (1999) *Trade, the Environment, and the WTO: A Policy Agenda,* ODC Policy Paper, Overseas Development Council, Washington, DC; Brack (ed), *Trade and Environment*

20 See Griffith, Andrew (1997) 'Market access and environmental protection: a negotiator's point of view', Department of Foreign Affairs and International Trade, Canada; quoted in Agarwal et al (eds) *Green Politics;* South Centre, *The WTO Multilateral Trade Agenda and the South,* p275

21 UNCTAD, *Trade and Development Report* 1999, pV

22 See Cosbey, Aaron and Burgiel, Stas (2000) *The Cartagena Protocol on Biosafety: An Analysis of Results,* IISD briefing note, IISD, Winnipeg, February

23 Bhattacharyya, B and Mago, L D (1998) *Trade and Environment Issues in the WTO: Indian Experience,* Indian Institute of Foreign Trade, New Delhi

24 See Roberts, Sarah and Robins, Nick (2000) *The Reality of Sustainable Trade,* International Institute for Environment and Development, London

25 See Robins, Nick, Roberts, Sarah and Abbot, Jo (1999) *Who Benefits?* IIED, London

26 Quoted in World Bank (2000) *Environment Matters: Annual Review,* Washington, DC

27 Fox, Tom (2000) *Sustainable Cocoa: The Demand Side Perspective,* IIED, London

28 See American Cocoa Research Institute, www.acri-cocoa.org/acri

29 Reinicke, Wolfgang H and Deng, Francis (2000) *Critical Choices,* International Development Research Centre, Ottawa

30 Robins, Nick and Roberts, Sarah (1997) *Unlocking Trade Opportunities,* IIED, London

31 Quoted in Nick Robins (2000) 'Victims or Victors?', *Tomorrow,* Vol 3, No 10, May/June, Tomorrow Publishing, Stockholm

32 *Organic Food and Beverages: World Supply and Major European Markets* (1999) UNCTAD/WTO International Trade Centre, Geneva

33 Von Moltke, Konrad, Kuik, Onno, van der Grijp, Nicolien, Salazar, Chito, Banuri, Tariq, Mupimpila, Christopher, Inman, Crist, Mesa, Nathalia, Oleas, Reyna, de los Santos, Juan José (1998) *Global Product Chains: Northern Consumers, Southern Producers and Sustainability,* UNEP, Geneva

34 *Supermarkets: A Report on the Supply of Groceries from Multiple Stores in the United Kingdom,* Vol I: *Summary and Conclusions* (2000) Competition Commission, London, October

35 *Being a Better Trading Neighbour* (1999) B&Q, London

36 See report of the 'Finding New Synergies' workshop hosted by the Bangladesh Textile Mills Association and the Commonwealth Science Council, January 2000, on http://www.commonwealthknowledge.net

37 Bendell, Jem (2000) 'Civil regulation: a new form of democratic governance for the global economy', in Jem Bendell (ed), *Terms of Endearment: Business, NGOs and Sustainable Development,* Greenleaf Publishing, Sheffield

38 Quoted in *Rights of Exchange: Social, Health, Environmental and Trade Objectives on the Global Stage,* London: Cabinet Office, Performance and Innovation Unit, 2000, p33

39 See Najam, Adil (1999) 'World Business Council on Sustainable Development: the Greening of Big Business or a Greenwash?' *Yearbook of International Co-operation on Environment and Development, 1999/2000,* Earthscan, London, pp65–75

40 The Performance Group and Consortium Partners (Deutsche Bank, Electrolux, Gerling, ICI, Monsanto, Unilever and Volvo), *Sustainable Strategics for Value Creation: Reflections from a Learning Journey* (Oslo, 1999)

41 See, for example, WBCSD, *Exploring Sustainable Development: WBCSD Global Scenarios 2000–2050,* available at http: www.wbcsd, also Hammond, Allen (1998) *Which World? Scenarios for the Twenty-first Century,* Island Press, Washington, DC

42 See General Consultative Forum, *Vision 2020: Scenarios for a Sustainable Europe,* European Commission, November 1996. Some governments in the North, such as the British, are starting to use scenarios to underpin longer-term perspectives on trade; see Performance and Innovation Unit, *Rights of Exchange*

43 These three scenarios, and the paths they encompass, reflect the predominant worlds of the prince, the merchant and the citizen. See Najam, Adil (1996) 'Understanding the third sector: revisiting the prince, the merchant, and the citizen', *Nonprofit Management and Leadership* Vol 7, No 2, pp203–219; Nerfin, Marc (1986) 'Neither prince nor merchant: citizen – an introduction to the third system', in K Ahooja-Patel, A G Drabek and M Nerfin (eds) *World Economy in Transition,* Pergamon, Oxford, pp47–59

44 The term 'trading up' is borrowed from David Vogel (1995) *Trading Up: Consumer and Environmental Regulation in a Global Economy,* Harvard University Press, Cambridge, MA

45 This notion of 'ad hoc alliances' is at the heart of the WBCSD's Jazz Scenario for Sustainable Development, in WBCSD, *Exploring Sustainable Development*

46 For an overview of one specific mechanism proposed to internalize environmental costs into international trade, see Kox, Henk (1998) 'International

commodity related environmental agreements: a way to promote sustainable production of primary commodities', *Bridges,* Vol 2, No 7, ICTSD, Geneva, October

47 The 'new protectionism' term is taken from Lang, Tim and Hines, Colin (1993) *The New Protectionism,* Earthscan, London. See also Hines, Colin (2000) *Localization,* Earthscan, London

48 See Shiva, Vandana, Jafri, Afsar H and Bedi, Gitanjali (1997) *Ecological Cost of Globalization: the Indian Experience,* Research Foundation for Science, Technology and Ecology, New Delhi

49 See Najam, *The Case for a South Secretariat in International Environmental Negotiation*

50 We are very grateful to Dr Tariq Banuri for this insight (personal communication)

51 Halle, Mark *Seattle and Sustainable Development,* IISD WTO Series, International Institute for Sustainable Development, Winnipeg, Canada, available at http://www.iisd.ca/pdf/seattleandsd.pdf

52 See Najam, 'An environmental negotiation strategy for the South'; 'Trade and environment after Seattle'

9

Bridging the Trade–Environment Divide

Daniel C Esty

Introduction

Perceived conflict between trade liberalization and environmental protection can be traced to a number of issues. Some tensions relate to the environmental Kuznets curve and whether economic growth yields environmental benefits. Other concerns arise from efforts to address transboundary externalities and disputes over the role of trade measures as an environmental enforcement tool. Another set of issues centres on the risk of a race-towards-the-bottom regulatory dynamic and the limits of legitimate comparative advantage. This chapter argues that, in an ecologically and economically interdependent world, trade and environmental policies are inescapably linked as a matter of descriptive reality and normative necessity.

Protection: for free traders, this word represents the consummate evil. For environmentalists, it is the ultimate good. Of course, for the trade community, 'protection' conjures up dark images of Smoot and Hawley while the environmental camp sees clear mountain streams, lush green forests and piercing blue skies. One cannot blame all the tensions at the trade–environment interface on linguistic differences, but these competing perspectives are emblematic of a deep clash of cultures, theories and assumptions.

Trade officials often seek to limit efforts to link trade and environmental policy-making, and sometimes to prohibit such efforts altogether. In this regard, the narrow focus and modest efforts of the World Trade Organization's (WTO's) Committee on Trade and Environment are illustrative.[1] The launch of negotiations for a Free Trade Area of the Americas with an express decision to exclude environmental issues from the agenda provides an even starker example of the trade community's hostility toward serious environmental engagement. Economists have been prominent among those arguing that pollution control and natural resource management issues are best kept out of the trade policy-making process (Cooper, 1994; Bhagwati, 1999). Other economists, however, have tried to set trade policy-making in a broader context and to build environmental sensitivity into the international trading system (Runge, 1994; Rodrik, 1997; Summers, 2000).

In fact, there is no real choice about whether to address the trade and environment linkage; its existence is a matter of fact. The only choice is whether the policies put in place to respond will be designed openly, explicitly and thoughtfully, with an eye to economic and political logic, or implicitly and without systematic attention to the demands of good policy-making. This chapter seeks to explain why trade liberalization and environmental protection appear to be in such tension and to push economists to explore more aggressively what economic theory and practice might do to address the concerns being raised.

Trade and Environmental Linkages

Potential Conflicts Between Domestic Regulations and Trade

In recent years, the focus of trade liberalization has shifted from lowering tariffs, which have come down considerably around the world, to the elimination of non-tariff barriers to trade (Jackson, 1992). Since many kinds of domestic regulations can potentially be non-tariff barriers, the extent and impact of the market access commitment and other regulatory disciplines negotiated in the trade domain has expanded.

A number of the most prominent international trade disputes in the last decade have concerned the clash between domestic regulations and trade rules. In the well-known tuna-dolphin case, the US banned Mexican tuna imports because the fishing methods resulted in incidental dolphin deaths. In 1991, Mexico obtained a General Agreement on Tariffs and Trade (GATT) panel decision declaring the US to be in violation of its GATT obligations for imposing such a ban. In the on-going beef hormone dispute, the European Union (EU) has refused to adjust its 'no added hormones in beef' food safety standards despite a series of WTO rulings that its regulations had no scientific foundation and were in contravention of the rules of international trade. And the US sanctions against Thai shrimp caught using methods that killed endangered sea turtles were recently deemed to be GATT-illegal. Trade and environment friction can be found outside the World Trade Organization (WTO) as well. Witness the enormous effort that the EU has put into harmonizing environmental standards over the past several decades (Vogel, 1994).

There is no end in sight to 'trade and environment' cases. If anything, the number of disputes seems to be rising (Sampson, 2000). As global economic integration intensifies, so does the potential for conflict (Lawrence et al, 1996; Dua and Esty, 1997). Public health standards, food safety requirements, emissions limits, waste management and disposal rules, packaging and recycling regulations, and labelling policies all may shape trade flows. And trade disciplines may affect national-scale environmental efforts, especially to the extent that dispute settlement procedures are used to challenge pollution control or natural resource management programmes. Thus, while fear-mongering about lost 'sovereignty' (Perot, 1993; Wallach and Sforza, 1999) can be dismissed, the suggestion that trade liberalization constrains regulatory flexibility rings true. With new issues like biotechnology and climate change emerging, the potential for significant and divisive battles between trade policy and regulatory choices – including environmental rules – looms large.

Increasing Trade, Economic Growth and Environmental Risks

The literature on the interaction between economic growth and pollution points to what has been called an environmental 'Kuznets curve'. The Kuznets curve is an inverted-U relationship which shows that environmental conditions tend to deteriorate in the early stages of industrialization and then improve as nations hit middle-income levels, at a per capita GDP of about US$5000–8000 (Grossman and Krueger, 1993, 1995; Shafik and Bandyopadhyay, 1992; Seldon and Song, 1994). Since the primary purpose of liberalizing trade is to increase economic growth, trade unavoidably affects the level of environmental protection through its impact on the Kuznets curve.

1   A first concern stemming from the Kuznets curve is that air and water pollution problems tend to worsen in the early stages of development. Many developing countries are living through the part of the Kuznets curve in which environmental conditions deteriorate.

2   A second concern is that even if expanded trade and economic growth *need not* hurt the environment, there is no guarantee that it *will not* (Harbaugh et al, 2000; Hauer and Runge, 2000). The effects of economic growth on trade can be broken down into three effects. 'Technique' effects arise from the tendency towards cleaner production processes as wealth increases and trade expands access to better technologies and environmental 'best practices'. 'Composition' effects involve a shift in preferences toward cleaner goods. 'Scale' effects refer to increased pollution due to expanded economic activity and greater consumption made possible by more wealth (Grossman and Krueger, 1993; Lopez, 1994). Thus, the claim that growth improves the quality of the environment can be rephrased as a claim that, above a certain level of per capita income, technique and composition effects will outweigh scale effects. Empirical evidence on the relative sizes of these effects is limited. But at least some of the time, it appears that expanded trade may worsen environmental conditions (Antweiler, Copeland and Taylor, 1998).

3   Finally, the odds that increased trade will have net negative environmental impacts rise if resources are mispriced (Anderson, 1995; Panayotou, 1993). Around the world, many critical resources like water, timber, oil, coal, fish, and open space are underpriced (or overpriced) (World Bank, 1997; Earth Council, 1997). Even the WTO acknowledges in its most recent 'Trade and Environment Special Report' that expanded trade can exacerbate pollution harms and natural resource management mistakes in the absence of appropriate environmental policies (Nordstrom and Vaughan, 1999).

Transboundary Externalities

Transboundary pollution spillovers make attention to trade–environment linkages a matter of normative necessity as well as descriptive reality. Perhaps the most-discussed issues involve emissions of ozone-layer depleting chlorofluorocarbons (CFCs) and greenhouse gases, which threaten global climate change. But recent advances in tracing the movement of pollutants have also demonstrated long-distance impacts from particulates (Grad, 1997), sulphur dioxide and other precursors of acid rain (Howells, 1995), DDT and other pesticides (Lawler, 1995; Rappaport et al, 1985), mercury and other heavy metals (Fitzgerald, 1993), and bioaccumulative toxics (Francis, 1994). Other transboundary issues involve rules governing shared resources such as fisheries in the open ocean and biodiversity.

The need to control transboundary externalities makes trade–environment linkages essential from the point of view of good economic policy-making. After all, uninternalized externalities not only lead to environmental degradation, but also threaten market failures that will diminish the efficiency of international economic exchanges, reduce gains from trade and lower social welfare. National governments, no matter how well intended, cannot address unilaterally inherently international problems such as climate change or fisheries depletion. A functioning Global Environmental Organization, operating in parallel with the trading system, might be a 'first-best' policy option in response to these challenges (Esty, 2000a). But no such regime exists. Thus, the WTO, along with regional trade agreements, cannot avoid some shared responsibility for managing ecological interdependence.

The Political Economy of Trade Liberalization

Taking environmental issues seriously must also be understood as a political necessity for free traders. Forward momentum in the trade realm is difficult to sustain (Bergsten, 1992). In this regard, the trade community cannot risk diminishing further the already narrow coalition in favour of freer trade, especially in the US. Dismissing environmental concerns, which results in broad environmental community opposition to trade agreements, generates unnecessary and avoidable political resistance to liberalized trade (Esty, 1998a).

Certain environmentalists will always be opposed to trade liberalization because they adhere to a 'limits to growth' philosophy. But the environmental community is not monolithic nor uniformly protectionist. Many mainstream environmentalists believe in 'sustainable development' and will support freer trade if they feel that pollution and natural resource management concerns are being taken seriously. For example, the congressional vote in favour of the North American Free Trade Agreement (NAFTA) depended critically on the fact that a number of environmental groups came out in favour of the agreement, which translated into support from politicians who define themselves as both pro-free trade and environmentally oriented trade (Audley, 1997). Concomitantly, the several recent failures to obtain a majority for new fast-track negotiating authority can be attributed to this swing group voting against the legislation because the proposals lacked environmental credibility (Destler and Balint, 1999).

In practice, moreover, there is no empirical support for the suggestion that environmental linkages detract from trade agreements or trade liberalization. The

NAFTA often considered the 'greenest' trade pact ever, contains a number of en-
vironmental elements and was adopted with an Environmental Side Agreement.
There is no evidence that these provisions have in any way diminished the post-
NAFTA US–Canada–Mexico trade flows (Araya, 2001; Hufbauer et al, 2000).

One might argue that this political analysis has little to do with the economist's
role in the trade and environment debate. To the contrary, if the arguments of
economists become disconnected from the reality of political pressures and policy
imperfections, then economic logic is unlikely to prevail in trade policy-making.

The Arguments for Separating Trade and Environmental Policy

While many 'no linkage' economists and trade officials understand the arguments
for taking up environmental issues in the trade context, they fear a scenario in
which protectionist wolves find their way into the trading system in environmental
sheep's clothing (Bhagwati, 1988; Subramanian, 1992).[2] The sight at the 1999
WTO Ministerial Meeting in Seattle of green activists marching arm-in-arm with
avowed protectionists confirmed for many, especially in the developing world, the
suspect motives of those advancing the environmental agenda. A related argument
for keeping the environment out of the WTO turns on the fear that trade liberalization will grind to a halt under the weight of environmental burdens. Why, ask trade
economists, must trade measures be used to enforce multilateral environmental
agreements? Shouldn't environmental policy problems be solved with environmental
policy tools? Those who wish to separate trade and environmental policy-making also
fear that high-income countries will impose lofty environmental standards on low-
income countries, depriving them of one aspect of their natural comparative advantage and subjecting them to trade barriers if they fail to perform up to developed
country standards (Bhagwati, 1999; 2000).

But while these worries have some basis in reality, they do not provide a persuasive justification for a complete separation of trade and environmental policies.
Certainly, environmentalism should not be used as a cover to disguise trade barriers. And the tactical partnerships of some environmental groups have undoubtedly
been misguided. Certainly, better environmental regulation at both the national and
global levels could markedly reduce trade–environment tensions.[3] Certainly, global-
scale environmental efforts should not mean a reduction in the standard of living
for people in low-income countries.

But these are not arguments for ignoring the inescapable linkages between trade
and the environment. They are arguments for trying to integrate trade and environmental policies in sensible ways. The next three sections discuss key areas for
research and policy analysis that could help to narrow the divide between trade and
environmental policy goals and practices. The next section focuses on strengthening the foundations of environmental policy, while the following sections focus on
the issues of economic theory and trade policy.

Strengthening Environmental Policy Foundations

A battle rages among environmentalists over how best to address (and even understand) environmental challenges. Many environmentalists support the concept of 'sustainable development' (WCED, 1987) and believe that economic growth, if managed properly, can support environmental improvements. A significant number of environmental advocates remain committed, however, to a 'limits to growth' paradigm in which trade liberalization contributes to more economic activity and therefore more pollution and unsustainable consumption of natural resources (Meadows et al, 1972; Daly, 1993). But even those who find the promise of sustainable development attractive worry that, in practice, environmental policy tools are not up to the pressures of globalization.

Economists are likely to have little in common with the advocates of lower consumption levels, especially when the burdens of such a policy choice would fall most heavily on those in the poorest countries of the world. But economists can play a role in answering certain persistent environmental research and policy questions which, in turn, could help to expand the common ground between free-traders and environmentalists.

Clarifying Concerns about Sustainable Development

Sustainable development has proved hard to define and even harder to put into practice. It is clear that poverty can force people to make short-term choices that degrade the environment, like cutting down nearby trees for firewood despite the likelihood of future soil erosion. But the hope that trade liberalization will lead to economic growth that will alleviate poverty and generate resources for environmental investments sometimes seems to rely on a tenuous chain of events that may well unravel under real-world conditions.

It is useful to discuss these issues in terms of the inverted-U Kuznets curve discussed earlier, which shows a general pattern of increasing environmental degradation up to a certain level of per capita gross domestic product (GDP) and environmental improvements beyond that point. Environmentalists will always be worried about societies that are living through the portion of the Kuznets curve where growth is accompanied by environmental degradation, even if it can be shown that people are receiving other welfare gains. Economists could, however, significantly bridge the gap with green groups if they were to find ways to reduce the duration and intensity of environmental deterioration as low-income countries grow to middle-income ones. Economists might also confirm that ignoring pollution altogether until middle-income levels are reached is a serious policy mistake. Some environmental investments (eg protecting drinking-water or siting polluting factories downwind of urban areas) have such high benefit–cost ratios that even the poorest countries should undertake them.

As regards the portion of the Kuznets curve in which growth and environmental quality are both improving, many mainstream environmentalists express concerns that either rising wealth or increased population will drive up consumption in ways that undermine prospects for sustainable development. Both economic theory and recent empirical evidence could help to assuage these apprehensions. Development economists have demonstrated that population growth diminishes with wealth. Economists might do more to demonstrate that poverty alleviation is critical for population control, which, in turn, offers significant potential environmental benefits. More generally, the economics field has had little to say about how to minimize scale effects and maximize the chances that growth will improve environmental quality.

Finally, certain environmental harms do not appear to diminish with increases in income. Carbon dioxide (CO_2) emissions, for instance, continue to rise, albeit at a decreasing rate, as GDP per capita goes up. It may be that, even for carbon dioxide emissions, the downward portion of the environmental Kuznets curve would be reached at some income level, but no society yet seems to have achieved the exalted wealth required. If or until that occurs, economists could gain credibility by agreeing that wealth is not an environmental cure-all.

The common theme in this discussion is that the Kuznets curve need not be destiny. The present shape, as estimated from historical experience, reflects a political economy interaction between trade, growth and the environment. Trade has a positive effect on the environment (and perhaps a net welfare benefit more broadly) only if environmental policy advances alongside trade liberalization (Anderson, 1992, 1995; Esty, 1994). However, institutional failures in the environmental realm often mean that the requisite strengthening of environmental performance in parallel with trade liberalization may not occur (Chichilnisky, 1994; Zhao, 2000). In this regard, economists should take more seriously the need to find policy strategies that lead to a shorter and flatter Kuznets curve.

Disciplining Free-riders

Economists and environmental policy-makers generally agree on the wisdom of enforcing the 'polluter pays' principle which holds that those who cause environmental degradation should bear the costs. But as a matter of policy, this goal remains elusive. While economists have demonstrated the value of market-based environmental strategies, by and large they have not managed to convince the environmental and political worlds that pollution fees, emissions allowances or other economic incentives will work in practice. Environmental policy remains underdeveloped in terms of economic sophistication and largely mired in 'command and control' approaches. The collapse of the international negotiations over climate change, in part because of disputes over how far to go in using market mechanisms, demonstrates the persistence within the environmental policy community of anti-economics sentiment.

Figuring out how to enact policies that embody the polluter pays principle becomes even more difficult when the scope of the environmental harm is broader than the vista of the regulators. Dua and Esty (1997) argue that 'super-externalities', which spill beyond the defined jurisdiction of regulatory authorities in either space or time, aggravate the collective action problem.[4] A small number of scholars have looked at the spatial distribution of issues in the trade domain (Krugman, 1991; Bloom and Sachs, 1998), and at the geographic dimensions of the trade and environment problem (Hauer and Runge, 2000; Esty, 1994), but more work needs to be done in the realm of economic geography.

Transboundary environmental spillovers create the risk of allocative inefficiency and market failure in the international economy. Some mechanism for promoting collective action and for disciplining free-riders is therefore required (Baumol and Oates, 1988). Whether free-traders like it or not, trade measures are one potential candidate for this function. Admittedly, trade sanctions are imperfect, costly to those who impose them and may backfire. But at least in some cases, trade penalties have worked (Brack, 1996; Barrett, 1997). Moreover, better tools to discipline free-riders in the international environmental domain do not seem readily available. As environmentalists point out, the weakness of the extant global environmental regime cannot be wished away nor dismissed as irrelevant to the question of how environmental goals get squared with the trade liberalization agenda.

There are a number of issues to be investigated which could shed light on the use of trade policy as a tool for enforcement of environmental standards. First, refined theory on the use of trade measures to support environmental cost internalization in the international realm is needed, advancing the preliminary analyses of Charnovitz (1993), Chang (1995) and Barrett (1997). Second, more work to find ways to strengthen the international environmental regime, which could relieve the pressure on the WTO to play a major environment role, would be useful (Esty, 1994; 2000a). Such work might build on efforts to investigate the political economy of environmental protection (for example, Keohane, Revesz and Stavins, 1998). Third, the advantages and disadvantages of policy linkages need to be explored more fully. Concerns are sometimes expressed that if trade policy becomes entangled with environmental policy, either or both sets of policies may be unable to advance. Yet the potential benefits of cross-issue policies and trade-offs have been demonstrated repeatedly (Haas, 1958; Carrero and Siniscalco, 1994). Finally, those who wish to limit the trade system's role in enforcing multilateral environmental agreements would find their case greatly strengthened if they could point to workable alternative enforcement mechanisms.[5]

Refining Trade Theory

Environmental perspectives on trade often clash with the settled views of economists. Frequently, the problem reflects a degree of economic misunderstanding by those in the environmental community. But often there is a kernel (or more) of truth in the environmental position with which the economic community has failed to grapple. In these areas, there are intriguing research opportunities for economists.

Level Playing Fields

Environmentalists often worry that expanded trade will lead to competitive pressures that will push down environmental standards. They fear a regulatory 'race towards the bottom' as jurisdictions with high environmental standards relax their rules so as to avoid burdening their industries with pollution-control costs higher than competitors operating in low-standard jurisdictions. Thus, they call for harmonization of pollution-control regulations at stringent levels, the imposition of 'eco-duties' on those with sub-par rules or other policy interventions to 'level the playing field'.

Economists point out that the existence of divergent circumstances, including variations in societal preferences about the optimal level of environmental protection, is what makes gains from trade possible. If environmental rules vary because of differences in climate, weather, geography, existing pollution levels, population density, risk preferences, level of development or other 'natural' factors, the variation in standards should be considered welfare-enhancing and appropriate. Clearly, a sweeping presumption in favour of uniform standards fails to grasp the insight of comparative advantage and makes no sense (Burtless et al, 1998). More generally, economists tend to find arguments in favour of regulatory harmonization in a context of economic integration unpersuasive (Bhagwati, 1996; 2000).

Diversity in circumstances generally makes uniformity less attractive than standards tailored to the heterogenous conditions that exist (Mendelsohn, 1986; Anderson, 1995) – but not always. Divergent standards across jurisdictions may impose transaction costs on traded goods that exceed any benefits obtained by allowing each jurisdiction to maintain its own requirements. Sykes (1995; 1999) has demonstrated that market forces will tend, over time, to eliminate such problems. Vogel (1994) argues, in fact, that upwards harmonization (a 'race to the top') often occurs. But this logic only applies to product standards, and standards that relate to production processes or methods are not subject to the same market pressures.

Some theoretical work has been done to try to understand the different harmonization dynamics (Bhagwati and Hudec, 1996; Esty and Geradin, 1998). But more would be useful, as would empirical evidence on what happens to environmental standards in the process of trade liberalization. For example, how often do free-trade agreements include commitments to lower environmental standards and how often to higher standards.

Environmentalists also fear that the rules of international trade are biased against their interests. They believe that within the trading system – both WTO and regional trade agreements – free-trade principles always trump other policy goals such as environmental protection. Some recent analyses suggest that such a tilt in GATT jurisprudence might once have existed, but is now less pronounced (Charnovitz, 2000; Wofford, 2000). Efforts to illuminate the facts might diminish fears that trade liberalization runs roughshod over environmental issues. Some efforts have been made in this regard (Trachtman, 2000; Burtless et al, 1998), but more would be welcome.

Psychological Spillovers and Ethical Preferences

Most economists acknowledge, at least in theory, that transboundary pollution externalities need to be addressed, but economists tend to be sceptical about claims of psychological spillovers (Blackhurst and Subramanian, 1992; Cooper, 1994).

What are we to make of complaints about environmental degradation in China or campaigns to save the rainforest? As long as the harms are localized, shouldn't environmental policy choices (even 'mistakes') in other jurisdictions be accepted? Maybe so from a perspective of economic theory, but most people do not see the world this way. The fact that Chinese workers produce goods under adverse environmental conditions is not celebrated, even if the low standards in China translate into cheaper products in export markets. Why not?

Perhaps economists assume a utilitarianism that is oversimplified. Sen (1977) and others have noted the narrow behavioural assumptions on which most of economics builds, ignoring human realities such as the existence of interdependent welfare functions. In fact, many people consider themselves, at least to some extent, to be part of a global community. In addition, economists may accept too readily as a given that the policy choices in places like China are locally optimal and do not stop to ask whether Chinese environmental standards truly reflect the will of the people.[6] By gliding past 'choice of public' questions (Esty, 1996), economists simplify their models but diminish the policy traction of their arguments.

Environmentalist concerns about extraterritorial policy choices frequently seem to be paternalistic or even imperialistic. Green groups often think that they know better than the people or governments of other countries, especially developing countries, what constitutes the 'right' environmental standard or policy programme. Economists have been quick to condemn those who 'are keen to impose their own ethical preferences on others, using trade sanctions to induce or coerce acceptance of such preferences' (Bhagwati, 1993).

But trade, like any realm of human endeavour, cannot exist without base-line rules, defined by community standards and values. One such set of rules concerns what constitutes a fair and legitimate basis for comparative advantage. From 19th-century British hesitation about trading with the slave-holding American South to Article XX(e) of the GATT, which permits trade restrictions on products made by prison labour, the international trading system has always circumscribed the bounds of acceptable commercial behaviour.

The issue becomes one of line drawing. When is a divergent policy in another jurisdiction just a 'choice', worthy of respect and acceptance in a world of diversity? When does it become a violation of moral minimum standards that should not be abided?

A conservative answer here would be that when environmental harms are purely local in scope, then preservationist demands from abroad are overreaching. In such a case, trade policy should not be the primary tool for international environmental policy, and instead environmental advocates should find a way to pay for their preferences in other countries. But if localized environmental harms are vast and there is reason to doubt whether the will of the people is being fairly represented, it makes sense to leave open the possibility that international pressure for a cleaner environment may be justified.

Is There a Race Towards the Bottom?

Economists have strongly rejected suggestions that country-versus-country competitiveness pressures degrade environmental standards.[7] They argue that the idea that jurisdictions with low environmental standards will become pollution havens, luring industries from high-standard jurisdictions and triggering a back-and-forth downward spiral in environmental standards finds little basis in theory (Revesz, 1992; Drezner, 2000) and lacks empirical support (Kalt, 1988; Low and Yeats, 1992; Repetto, 1995). For example, it does not appear that US pollution control standards have dropped in the aftermath of NAFTA or the various rounds of GATT and WTO negotiations over time.

But the real concern is not about a race literally to the bottom. Rather, the concern arises from the possibility that economic integration will create a regulatory dynamic in which standards are set strategically with an eye on the pollution-control burdens in competing jurisdictions. The result may be a 'political drag' that translates into suboptimal environmental standards in some places.[8] These effects might involve not only weakened environmental laws, but perhaps more importantly, environmental standards not strengthened as much as they would otherwise have been or environmental enforcement cases not brought.

The evidence here is by no means as one-sided as economists have generally come to believe. Some recent empirical studies find races to the bottom (Mani and Wheeler, 1999; van Beers and van den Bergh, 1997). Moreover, a growing theoretical literature, largely published in law journals, suggests that if the market in 'locational rights' is flawed, regulatory races toward the bottom may occur (Klevorick, 1996; Engel and Rose-Ackerman, 2001; Esty and Geradin, 2001). A mismatch between the scope of pollution harms and the jurisdiction of regulators, as well as information gaps or technical deficiencies in the regulatory process, or public choice distortions (such as the fact that politicians may be more influenced by highly visible job effects and may overlook more subtle environmental impacts) may lead jurisdictions to set their environmental standards too low (or too high) (Esty, 1996). And once a trade competitor has deviated from optimal regulatory levels, a welfare-maximizing government may benefit by strategically adjusting its own environmental standards.

Within economics, the welfare effects of interjurisdictional regulatory competition have been carefully analysed (Fischel, 1975; Oates and Schwab, 1988). However, the application of the theory to the race-towards-the-bottom question in the international trade and environment context has only recently begun to get attention (Levinson, 1997; Fredriksson and Millimet, 2000). New work is beginning to specify those settings in which regulatory competition will improve outcomes and when some degree of harmonization (not necessarily uniform standards) will improve results.[9]

The Development and Evolution of Trade Policy-making

Advances in both the procedures and substantive rules of the international trading system could help to alleviate some trade–environment tensions. A good bit of the environmentalist animosity towards freer trade arises from the closed process by which trade liberalization has historically proceeded and the sense that any expression of environmental concerns, no matter how valid, would not be taken seriously. The WTO, like GATT before it, has usually done its business through negotiations between governments. Mechanisms for participation by non-governmental organizations (NGOs), including environmental groups and other elements of civil society, have been limited. But the obscure nature of the process and the attempt to channel all political debate to the national level has created an image of the WTO as a star chamber or 'black box' where insiders take advantage of their access to the levers of power.

The closed nature of the system had a logic; it shielded the trade regime from special interest manipulation and 'capture' (Bhagwati, 1988; Subramanian, 1992). But the organization's future now depends on it becoming more transparent. Beyond building public understanding and acceptance, a more open WTO policy-making process has other virtues. Notably, NGOs provide critical 'intellectual competition' for both national and intergovernmental decision-makers (Esty, 1998b). In presenting alternative perspectives, data, policy analyses and options, these NGOs force officials to explain and justify their policy choices. There remains, however, work to be done to find ways to maximize the benefits of the interchange while limiting the risk that access will give special interests undue power to manipulate or block outcomes. In this regard, the learning from public choice theory may be helpful.

Economists could also help the trade community to modernize the WTO's substantive rules on a basis of greater analytic rigour. In this regard, several issues stand out at the trade–environment interface.

First, the reliance on a distinction between product standards imposed on imports (generally acceptable) and production process or methods restrictions (generally unacceptable) makes little sense in a world of ecological interdependence.[10] How things are produced matters. Production-related externalities cannot be overlooked. For example, semi-conductors manufactured using CFCs destroy everyone's ozone layer. Where multilateral environmental agreements are in place, such as the 1987 Montreal Protocol phasing out CFCs, trade rules should be interpreted to reinforce the agreed-upon standards. Indeed, such a principle can be found in Article 104 of NAFTA.

A recrafted trade principle that accepts the legitimacy of environmental rules aimed at transboundary externalities would eliminate the risk of the trade regime providing cover for those shirking their share of global responsibilities. A number of economists, including some who have been sceptical about trade–environment linkages, have now come around to view that trade rules must not permit free-riding on global environmental commitments (Cooper, 2000; Bhagwati, 2000). But how this agreement in principle should be translated into actual trade policies has not been clarified. Economists are in a good position to think through the efficiency and equity implications of the issues and options.

Another opportunity for updating of the trade system centres on the traditional rule that, when trade and environment principles clash, only the 'least GATT-inconsistent' environmental policies are acceptable. Such an approach lacks balance because clever policy-makers can *always* come up with a possible policy alternative that is less trade restrictive. A more neutral decision rule would focus on whether the environmental standards are arbitrary, unjustifiable or a disguised restriction on trade.

Such a principle seems to be emerging in recent WTO dispute settlement cases, notably the 1998 shrimp turtle Appellate Body decision (Wofford, 2000).

Final Thoughts

A traditional piece of received wisdom about trade policy-making is that more can be accomplished by operating in a closed 'club system' beneath the radar of public scrutiny rather than through open debate (Keohane and Nye, 2001). Whether this hypothesis was ever correct is now moot. The WTO has gained a very high profile and it will never again be able to operate in the policy shadows (Esty, 2000b). When the trade agenda was perceived to be narrow and technical, the trade regime's performance was of interest only to the trade cognoscenti. But today the WTO's work has much broader impacts and the trade agenda encompasses non-tariff barriers and other issues which impinge on commercial and governmental activities beyond the trade domain. Thus, where once the WTO's legitimacy turned on its capacity to produce good results from a trade perspective, the organization is now subject to much wider scrutiny. If the WTO is to play its designated role as one of the key international organizations managing economic interdependence, it must find a new centre of gravity (Schott, 2000).

Going forward, the WTO's authority and public acceptance will have to be founded on a more democratic basis and on a refined ability to reflect the political will of the global community. Such a transformation entails a commitment to transparency and an open trade policy-making process that provides access to NGOs across the spectrum of civil society. The WTO's future legitimacy requires a more robust trade and environment dialogue, not artificial separation of these policy-making realms. Special interest lobbies will have to be disciplined by exposure and argument, not exclusion (Esty, 1998b).

Environmental rules cannot be seen as simply pollution control or natural resource management standards; they also provide the ground-rules for international commerce and serve as an essential bulwark against market failure in the international economic system. Building environmental sensitivity into the trade regime in a thoughtful and systematic fashion should be of interest, therefore, to the trade community as well as to environmental advocates. In working towards a world of effective environmental protection that is simultaneously free of trade protectionism, economists could play a substantial role.

Notes

1 For a full review of the WTO Committee on Trade and Environment's work, see http://www.wto.org/WT/CTE

2 Some trade officials, however, seem not to have learned their economics very well. Many of the comments of the trade leaders who spoke at the WTO's 1999 'Trade and Environment Symposium' reflected serious deficiencies in the understanding of core principles, such as the implications of externalities or the

Olsonian logic of collective action. See, for example, the speech of de la Calle (WTO, 1998)

3 The momentum for a revitalized international environmental regime, perhaps including a new Global Environmental Organization to serve as a counterpart and counterbalance to the WTO, seems to be building (Esty, 1994; Ruggiero, 1999; Barrett, 2000; Jospin, 2000)

4 Issues that cross jurisdictional boundaries create a risk of 'structural' failure in the regulatory cost-benefit calculus (Esty, 1996). Related problems arise with long-term environmental issues in which there is a risk of market failure because future citizens are not present to cast their 'market votes'. Some thinking has gone into how to manage problems with long-term horizons (Cline, 1993; Revesz, 1999). But if economic theories are to be persuasive to environmentalists, they will have to deal explicitly with the broader set of issues such as threshold effects, non-linear cost curves, and irreversibility (eg species destruction)

5 The suggestion that there should be more use of carrots (financial rewards for compliance) and less of sticks (trade measures) may be useful in some circumstances. But in other cases, transboundary pollution spillovers represent a serious infringement on property rights, making a 'victim pays' strategy inappropriate (Esty, 1996)

6 A number of economists (Sachs, 1998; Sen, 1999) and others (Esty and Porter, 2000) have begun to argue that a society's underlying legal, political and economic structure critically affects economic growth trajectories, environmental performance and other variables. The extent to which economic and trade theory even applies in a nation may therefore depend on these structural conditions

7 Economists see any such pressures that emerge as mere market-clearing or 'pecuniary' effects, not real externalities that distort allocative efficiency (Baumol and Oates, 1988). Interestingly, the legal literature leans in a different direction on this point. Elliott, Ackerman and Millian (1985), for example, explain that real economic externalities will arise if the scope of the cost-bearers and beneficiaries of regulation are not coterminous

8 In many instances, the result will be lower standards. But note that, where NIMBYism is pervasive, strategic behaviour may create pressures for suboptimally high standards as a way of discouraging local development (Levinson, 1997)

9 For a recent study, drawing on the work of economists, lawyers, political scientists and business professors, and looking at this issue across regulatory domains (environment, labour, tax, banking) and economic integration experiences (US versus EU versus WTO), see Esty and Geradin (2001)

10 A potentially ground-breaking WTO decision in the asbestos case has shown more sensitivity regarding restrictions based on process and production methods (WTO, 2001)

References

Anderson, Kym (1992) 'The Standard Welfare Economics of Policies Affecting Trade and the Environment', in Kym Anderson and Richard Blackhurst (eds) *The Greening of World Trade Issues,* Ann Arbor, University of Michigan Press, pp25–48

Anderson, Kym (1995) 'Environmental and Labor Standards: What Role for the WTO?', in Anne O Krueger (ed) *The WTO as an International Organization,* Chicago, University of Chicago Press

Anderson, Kym and Richard Blackhurst (1992) 'Trade, the Environment and Public Policy', in Kym Anderson and Richard Blackhurst (eds) *The Greening of World Trade Issues,* Ann Arbor, University of Michigan Press, pp3–18

Antweiler, Werner, Brian R Copeland and M Scott Taylor (1998) 'Is Free Trade Good for the Environment?', National Bureau of Economic Research, Working Paper, no W6707 (August)

Araya, Monica (2001) 'Trade and Environment Lessons from NAFTA for the FTAA', in Carolyn Deere and Daniel C Esty (eds) *Trade and Sustainability in the Americas: Lessons from NAFTA*

Audley, John (1997) *Green Politics and Global Trade: NAFTA and the Future of Environmental Politics,* Washington, Georgetown University Press

Barrett, Scott (1997) 'The Strategy of Trade Sanctions in International Environmental Agreements', *Resource and Energy Economics,* vol 19, no 4, pp345–361

Barrett, Scott (2000) 'Trade and Environment: Local Versus Multilateral Reforms', *Environment and Development Economics,* no 5, pp349–359

Baumol, William J and Wallace E Oates (1988) *The Theory of Environmental Policy,* Cambridge, Cambridge University Press

Beckerman, Wilfred (1992) 'Economic Growth and the Environment: Whose Growth? Whose Environment?', *World Development,* no 20, pp481–496

Bergsten, C Fred (1992) 'The Primacy of Economics', *Foreign Policy,* summer, no 87, pp3–24

Bhagwati, Jagdish (1988) *Protectionism,* Cambridge, MIT Press

Bhagwati, Jagdish (1993) 'The Case for Free Trade', *Scientific American,* November, pp42–49

Bhagwati, Jagdish (1996) 'Trade and Environment: Does Environmental Diversity Detract from the Case for Free Trade?', in Jagdish Bhagwati and Robert Hudec (eds) *Fair Trade and Harmonization: Prerequisites for Free Trade?,* Cambridge, MIT Press

Bhagwati, Jagdish (1999) 'Third World Intellectuals and NGOs Statement Against Linkage', letter drafted by Bhagwati and signed by several dozen academics, circulated on the Internet; copy on file with author

Bhagwati, Jagdish (2000) 'On Thinking Clearly About the Linkage Between Trade and the Environment', *Environment and Development Economics,* vol 5, no 4, pp485–496

Bhagwati, Jagdish and Robert Hudec (eds) *Fair Trade and Harmonization: Prerequisites for Free Trade?,* Cambridge, MIT Press

Blackhurst, Richard L and Arvind Subramanian (1992) 'Promoting Multilateral Cooperation on the Environment', in Kym Anderson and Richard L Blackhurst (eds) *The Greening of World Trade Issues,* Ann Arbor, University of Michigan Press

Bloom, Dave E and Jeffrey Sachs (1998) 'Geography, Demography, and Economic Growth in Africa' (revised) CID/HIID Working Paper, October, available online at http//www2.cid.harvard.edu/cidpapers/brookafr.pdf

Brack, Duncan (1996) *International Trade and the Montreal Protocol,* London, Chatham House

Burtless, Gary et al (1998) *Globaphobia: Confronting Fears About Open Trade,* Washington, Brookings Institution

Carrero, C and D Siniscalco (1994) 'Policy Coordination for Sustainability', in Goldin and Winters (eds) *The Economics of Sustainable Development,* Cambridge, Cambridge University Press, pp264–282

Chang, Howard F (1995) 'An Economic Analysis of Trade Measures to Protect the Global Environment', *Georgetown Law Journal,* no 83, pp2131–2213

Charnovitz, Steve (1993) 'Environmentalism Confronts GATT Rules', *Journal of World Trade,* April, vol 27, no 2, pp37–52

Charnovitz, Steve (2000) 'World Trade and the Environment: A Review of the New WTO Report', *Georgetown International Environmental Law Review,* vol 12, no 1, pp523–541

Chichilnisky, Graciela (1994) 'North-South Trade and the Global Environment', *American Economic Review,* September, vol 84, no 5, pp851–875

Cline, William R (1993) *The Economics of Global Warming,* Washington, Institute for International Economics

Cooper, Richard N (1994) *Environment and Resource Policies for the World Economy,* Washington, Brookings Institution

Cooper, Richard N (2000) 'Trade and the Environment', *Environment and Development Economics,* vol 5, no 4, pp501–504

Daly, Herman E (1993) 'The Perils of Free Trade', *Scientific American,* November, pp51–55

Destler, I M and Peter J Balint (1999) *The New Politics of American Trade: Trade, Labor and the Environment,* Washington, Institute for International Economics

Drezner, Daniel W (2000) 'Bottom Feeders', *Foreign Policy,* November/December, vol 29, no 6

Dua, André and Daniel C Esty (1997) *Sustaining the Asia Pacific Miracle: Environmental Protection and Economic Integration,* Washington, Institute for International Economics

Earth Council (1997) *Subsidizing Unsustainable Development,* Vancouver, Earth Council

Elliott, E Donald, Bruce A Ackerman and John C Millian (1985) 'Toward a Theory of Statutory Evolution: the Federalization of Environmental Law', *Journal of Law Economics and Organization,* autumn, vol 1, no 2

Engel, Kirsten and Susan Rose-Ackerman (2001) 'Environmental Federalism in the United States: The Risks of Devolution', in Daniel C Esty and Damien Geradin (eds) *Regulatory Competition and Economic Integration: Comparative Perspectives,* Oxford, Oxford University Press

Esty, Daniel C (1994) *Greening the GATT: Trade, Environment and the Future,* Washington, Institute for International Economics

Esty, Daniel C (1996) 'Revitalizing Environmental Federalism', *Michigan Law Review,* vol 93, no 3, pp570–653

Esty, Daniel C (1998a) 'Environmentalists and Trade Policymaking', in Alan W Deardorff and Robert M Stern (eds) *Constituent Interests and U.S. Trade Policies,* Ann Arbor, University of Michigan Press

Esty, Daniel C (1998b) 'NGOs at the World Trade Organization: Cooperation, Competition or Exclusion', *Journal of International Economic Law,* vol 1, no 1, pp123–148

Esty, Daniel C (2000a) 'Global Environment Agency will take Pressure off WTO', *Financial Times,* 13 July

Esty, Daniel C (2000b) 'Environment and the Trading System: Picking up the Post-Seattle Pieces', in Jeffrey J Schott (ed) *The WTO After Seattle,* Washington, Institute for International Economics

Esty, Daniel C and Damien Geradin (1998) 'Environmental Protection and International Competitiveness: A Conceptual Framework', *Journal of World Trade,* vol 32, no 3, pp5

Esty, Daniel C and Damien Geradin (2001) 'Regulatory Competition', in Daniel C Esty and Damien Geradin (eds) *Regulatory Competition and Economic Integration: Comparative Perspectives,* Oxford, Oxford University Press

Esty, Daniel C and Michael E Porter (2000) 'Measuring National Economic Performance and Its Determinants', in Michael E Porter, Jeffrey D Sachs, et al (eds) *The Global Competitiveness Report 2000,* New York, Oxford University Press

Fischel, William A (1975) 'Fiscal and Environmental Considerations in the Location of Firms in Suburban Communities', in Edwin S Mills and Wallace E Oates (eds) *Fiscal Zoning and Land Use Controls,* Lexington, MA, Lexington Books, pp119–174

Fitzgerald, William F (1993) 'Mercury as a Global Pollutant', *The World and I,* 8 October, pp192–223

Francis, B Magnus (1994) *Toxic Substances in the Environment,* New York, John Wiley

Fredriksson, Per G and Daniel L Millimet (2000) 'Strategic Interaction and the Determination of Environmental Policy and Quality Across the US States: Is there a Race to the Bottom?' (unpublished working paper)

Fredriksson, Per (ed) (2000) *Trade, Global Policy, and the Environment,* World Bank Discussion Paper no 402, Washington, World Bank

Grad, Franklin P (1997) *Treatise on Environmental Law,* New York, M Bender

Grossman, Gene M and Alan B Krueger (1993) 'Environmental Impacts of a North American Free Trade Agreement', in Peter M Garber (ed) *The Mexico–US Free Trade Agreement,* Cambridge, MIT Press, pp13–56

Grossman, Gene M and Alan B Krueger (1995) 'Economic Growth and the Environment', *Quarterly Journal of Economics,* vol CX, no 2, pp353–377

Haas, Ernst B (1958) *The Uniting of Europe: Political, Social and Economic Forces,* Stanford, Stanford University Press

Harbaugh, William, Arik Levinson and David Wilson (2000) 'Re-examining the Empirical Evidence for an Environmental Kuznets Curve', National Bureau of Economic Research (NBER), Working Paper no 7711 (May)

Hauer, Grant and C Ford Runge (2000) 'Transboundary Pollution and the Kuznet's Curve in the Global Commons', (unpublished manuscript)

Howells, Gwyneth P (1995) *Acid Rain and Acid Waters,* New York, E Horwood

Hufbauer, Gary C et al (2000) *NAFTA and the Environment: Seven Years Later,* Washington, Institute for International Economics

Jackson, John (1992) *The World Trading System: Law and Policy of International Economic Relations,* Cambridge, MIT Press

Jospin, Lionel (2000) 'Development Thinking at the Millennium', speech to the Annual Bank Conference on Development Economics (World Bank), Paris, 26 June

Kalt, Joseph (1988) 'The Impacts of Domestic Environmental Regulatory Policies on US International Competitiveness', in A Michael Spence and Heather A Hazard (eds) *International Competitiveness,* Cambridge, Ballinger, pp221–262

Keohane, Nathaniel, Richard L Revesz and Robert N Stavins (1998) 'The Choice of Regulatory Instruments in Environmental Policy', *Harvard Environmental Law Review,* vol 22, no 2, pp313–367

Keohane, Robert O and Joseph S Nye (2001) 'The Club Model of Multilateral Cooperation and the World Trade Organization: Problems of Democratic Legitimacy', in Robert O Keohane and Joseph S Nye (eds) *Efficiency, Equity and Legitimacy: The Multilateral Trading System at the Millennium,* Cambridge, Harvard University Press

Klevorick, Alvin K (1996) 'The Race to the Bottom in a Federal System: Lessons from the World of Trade Policy', *Yale Law and Policy Review* and *Yale Journal on Regulation* (Symposium Issue), no 14, pp177–186

Krugman, Paul R (1991) *Geography and Trade,* Cambridge, MIT Press

Lawler, Andrew (1995) NASA Mission Gets Down to Earth, *Science,* 1 September, pp1208–1210

Lawrence, Robert, et al (1996) *A Vision for the World Economy,* Washington, Brookings Institution

Levinson, Arik (1997) 'A Note on Environmental Federalism: Interpreting some Contradictory Results', *Journal of Environmental Economics and Management,* no 33, pp359–66

Lopez, Ramon (1994) 'The Environment as a Factor of Production: The Effects of Economic Growth and Trade Liberalization', *Journal of Environmental Economics and Management,* no 27, pp163–184

Low, Patrick and Alexander Yeats (1992) 'Do Dirty Industries Migrate?', in Patrick Low (ed) *International Trade and the Environment,* World Bank Discussion Paper 159, Washington, World Bank

Mani, Muthukumara and David Wheeler (1999) 'In Search of Pollution Havens? Dirty Industry in the World Economy 1960–1995', in Per G Fredriksson (ed) *Trade, Global Policy and the Environment,* Washington, World Bank, pp115–127

Meadows, Donella H et al (1972) *The Limits to Growth,* New York, Universe Books

Mendelsohn, Robert (1986) Regulating Heterogeneous Emissions, *Journal of Environmental Economics and Management,* December, vol 13, no 4, pp301–313

Nordstrom, Hakan and Scott Vaughan (1999) *Special Studies: Trade and Environment,* Geneva, World Trade Organization

Oates, Wallace E and Robert M Schwab (1988) 'Economic Competition Among Jurisdictions: Efficiency Enhancing or Distortion Inducing?', *Journal of Public Economics,* vol 35, no 1, pp333–362

Panayotou, Theodore (1993) *Green Markets: The Economics of Sustainable Development,* San Francisco, ICS Press

Perot, Ross (1993) *Save Your Job, Save Our Country: Why NAFTA Must Be Stopped Now!,* New York, Hyperion

Rappaport, R A et al (1985) '"New" DDT Inputs to North America Atmospheric Deposition', *Chemosphere,* no 14, pp1167–1173

Repetto, Robert (1995) *Jobs, Competitiveness and Environmental Regulation: What are the Real Issues?,* Washington, World Resources Institute

Revesz, Richard L (1992) 'Rehabilitating Interstate Competition: Rethinking the "Race-to-the-Bottom" Rationale for Federal Environmental Regulation', *New York University Law Review,* December, no 67, pp1210–1254

Revesz, Richard L (1999) 'Environmental Regulation, Cost-Benefit Analysis and the Discounting of Human Lives', *Columbia Law Review,* May, no 99, pp941–1017

Rodrik, Dani (1997) *Has Globalization Gone Too Far?,* Washington, Institute for International Economics

Ruggiero, Renato (1999) 'Opening Remarks to the High Level Symposium on Trade and the Environment', speech at the WTO High Level Symposium on Trade and the Environment, Geneva, Switzerland, 15 March

Runge, C Ford (1994) *Freer Trade, Protected Environment: Balancing Trade Liberalization and Environmental Interests,* New York, Council on Foreign Relations

Sachs, Jeffrey (1998) 'Globalization and the Rule of Law', Yale Law School Occasional Papers, 2nd series, no 4

Sampson, Gary P (2000) *Trade, Environment and the WTO: The Post-Seattle Agenda,* Washington, Johns Hopkins University Press

Schott, Jeffrey (2000) 'The WTO After Seattle', in Jeffrey Schott (ed) *The WTO After Seattle,* Washington, Institute for International Economics, pp3–40

Seldon, Thomas M and Daqing Song (1994) 'Environmental Quality and Development: Is There a Kuznets Curve for Air Pollution Emissions?', *Journal of Environmental Economics and Management,* September, vol 27, no 2, pp147–152

Sen, Amartya K (1977) 'Rational Fools', *Philosophy and Public Affairs,* vol 6, no 4, pp317–344

Sen, Amartya K (1999) *Development as Freedom,* New York, Knopf

Shafik, Nemat and Sushenjit Bandyopadhyay (1992) 'Economic Growth and Environmental Quality: Time Series and Cross-Country Evidence', Background Paper prepared for World

Bank, *World Development Report 1992: Development and the Environment,* New York, Oxford University Press

Subramanian, Arvind (1992) 'Trade Measures for Environment: A Nearly Empty Box?', *World Economy,* vol 15, no 1, pp135–152

Summers, Lawrence (2000) Speech to the Confederation of Indian Industry, 18 January, Bombay

Sykes, Alan O (1995) *Product Standards for Internationally Integrated Goods Markets,* Washington, Brookings Institution

Sykes, Alan O (1999) 'Regulatory Protectionism and the Law of International Trade', *University of Chicago Law Review,* no 66, pp1

Trachtman, Joel (2000) 'Assessing the Effects of Trade Liberalization on Domestic Environmental Regulation: Towards Trade-Environment Policy Integration', in *Assessing the Environmental Effects of Trade Liberalization Agreements: Methodologies,* Paris, OECD

van Beers, Cees and Jeroen C J M van den Bergh (1997) 'An Empirical Multi-Country Analysis of the Impact of Environmental Regulations on Foreign Trade Flows', *Kyklos,* vol 50, no 1, pp29–46

Vogel, David (1994) *Trading Up: Consumer and Environmental Regulation in a Global Economy,* Cambridge, Harvard University Press

Wallach, Lori and Michelle Sforza (1999) *Whose Trade Organization: Corporate Globalization and the Erosion of Democracy,* Washington, Public Citizen

Wofford, Carrie (2000) 'A Greener Future at the WTO: The Refinement of WTO Jurisprudence on Environmental Exceptions to the GATT', *Harvard Environmental Law Review,* vol 24, no 2, pp563–592

World Bank (1997) *Expanding the Measure of Wealth: Indicators of Environmentally Sustainable Development,* Washington, World Bank

World Commission on Environment and Development (WCED) (1987) *Our Common Future,* Oxford, Oxford University Press (commonly known as the 'Brundtland Report')

World Trade Organization (WTO) (1998) High Level Symposium on Trade and Environment, Proceedings available online (visited 12 October 2000) at http://www.wto.org/english/tratop_e/envir_e/hlspeech.htm

World Trade Organization (WTO) (2001) *Report of the Appellate Body on Measures affecting asbestos and asbestos-containing products,* AB-2000-11 (WTO/DS/135/AB/R/ 12 March, 2001)

Zhao, Jinhua (2000) 'Trade and Environmental Distortions: Coordinated Intervention', *Environmental and Development Economics,* October, vol 5, no 4, pp361–376

Part III

Legal Perspectives

10

Trade and Environment:
How Real is the Debate?

Magda Shahin

Globalization and liberalization are the twin processes marking the beginning of the 21st century. Today, we are confronted with maxims such as 'Making Globalization Social and Green'[1] or 'Globalization with a Human Face'. A myriad of new standards is in the making to handle the devastating effects of globalization on developed and developing countries alike. Yet, without a doubt, developed countries are the front-runners. Green consumers, healthy consumers and safe consumers are now in the driving sear. Today, trade wars are erupting even between the US and the European countries on genetically altered crops and modified food, threatening trade and investment flows, accounting for more than US$2000 billion annually and providing 14 million jobs on both sides of the Atlantic.[2] What are the underlying motives? Are they truly anxiety and concern for food safety, the environment, morality and concern for humankind?' Or are these kinds of trade wars driven by world hegemony and by commercial interests with billions of dollars at stake? Is linking trade to environment a justified concern with genuine environmental goals?' Or are additional protection measures at play? Where do the developing countries fit into all this, with their resource constraints, poor information flows and lack of scientific knowledge?

Background

The relationship between trade and environment is complex and critical. It is over-burdened with suspicion and strained by misunderstandings that need to be addressed and clarified. To that end, it is appropriate to go back as far as the issuing of the Brundtland Report in the mid-1980s. Brundtland, the prime minister of Norway at that time, chaired a group of eminent personalities. In her famous report, she drew the attention of the international community to the interface between environment and development in the newly introduced phrase 'sustainable development'. When introduced at the 39th General Assembly in 1985, it was met with a great deal of scepticism on the part of developing countries in general. The notion of sacrificing today's development to preserve the environment for the development of future generations was viewed with resentment and misgivings. It took the international community several years and a huge effort to work out a smooth relationship between development and environment and to establish close linkages between them.

This culminated in an Agreement at the United Nations (UN) Conference on Environment and Development (UNCED) held in Rio de Janeiro in 1992. The Agreement has established fundamental principles to be observed and specific measures to be undertaken for the attainment of environmental goals, all framed in a detailed programme of action: Agenda 21. Some of the key principles of the Rio Declaration are particularly pertinent to our discussion:

- The right to development must be fulfilled so as to meet equitably the developmental and environmental needs of present and future generations (Principle 3).
- Eradicating poverty is an indispensable requirement for sustainable development (Principle 5).
- States have common but differentiated responsibilities with regard to promoting sustainable development (Principle 7).
- There should be a diffusion and transfer of technologies (Principle 9).
- States should cooperate to promote a supportive and open international economic system that would lead to economic growth and sustainable development in all countries (Principle 12).[3]

Agenda 21 set out specific measures on trade; in particular, the promotion of 'an open, non-discriminatory and equitable multilateral trading system that will enable all countries – in particular, the developing countries – to improve their economic structures and improve the standard of living of their populations through sustained economic development'.[4] In addition, a range of measures was agreed for the transfer of technology and the provision of new and additional financial resources to the developing countries for the implementation of the programme. Hence Agenda 21 set the basic principles as well as the overall framework within which the international community shoulders its burden of responsibility and has to work in order to protect, preserve and enhance the environment together with the development process, particularly in developing countries.

Nevertheless, in parallel to that event and far away in Geneva, while trade representatives were busy negotiating the Uruguay Round Agreements of the soon to be World Trade Organisation (WTO), environmentalists were determined to integrate environment in the trade debate. Their intentions and motives were questioned at a time when the Rio Conference had just been concluded successfully. Were developed countries thinking of backtracking on the commitments and obligations they had agreed to within the framework of the UN Conference? Were developing countries justified in their apprehensions about the trade debate? Were these apprehensions legitimate? It did not take long for such doubts to be proved well founded. In addition to the persisting divisions in the ongoing debate in the WTO, the lack of progress in the mid-term review of the Rio Programme of Action in New York in 1997 was yet further proof of the doubts and suspicions aired by developing countries. There has been obvious, and regrettable, backtracking on the obligations undertaken by the developed countries, especially with regard to improving market access for developing country exports, the transfer of technology and the provision of new and additional resources. (With regard to financial resources, it was estimated that the developing countries would require US$125 billion, in the form of grants and concessions, from the international community to implement the activities specified in Agenda 21. This requirement remains unmet.) Moreover, in the view of many developing countries, developed countries are in effect retreating from the holistic approach to sustainable development agreed at Rio. Their focus is now on unilateral measures and on environmental conditionalities attached to trade and investment. This trend is inimical to the attainment of both developmental and environmental goals.[5]

The Trade and Environment Debate in the WTO

Although initially developing countries resisted debating the trade environment relationship in the WTO, they came to an agreement reluctantly towards the end of the Uruguay Round. A decision was issued at the Marrakesh Ministerial Conference (1994) to that effect. A Committee on Trade and Environment was established to cool the heat created by the non-governmental organisations (NGOs) and to allow for a smooth signing and ratification of the Uruguay Round Agreements and the creation of the WTO. Dealing with the relationship between trade and environment in the WTO has gone through various phases, at some points being a leading priority in the framework of the WTO work, at other times being less attractive and thus occupying a lower profile. At no time were developing countries the *demandeurs*: on the contrary, they succumbed to pressure on many occasions. In all this, the central question remained how to bring the trade and the environmental systems closer together without undermining either system, knowing that they are not necessarily always compatible. In fact, the two regimes are often even in conflict. The environmental regime allows for measures that go beyond a country's borders for the sake of protecting the environment, whereas such a measure would amount to a flagrant violation of WTO rules and regulations that do not allow for extraterritorial measures. The problem goes even further. Today we see growing concern by environmental groups at the national level forcing the issue of *national sovereignty* against the country's obligations to abide by WTO judgements. A case in point is the well-known dispute regarding 'Import Prohibition of Certain Shrimp and Shrimp Products' between the US on one hand and Thailand, India, Pakistan and Malaysia on the other hand. Unhappy with rulings on the matter by the WTO dispute settlement panel and the Appellate Body, a coalition of US environmental groups raising the issue of national sovereignty succeeded in winning a ruling from the US Court of International Trade that went against the WTO panel. There is no doubt that this ruling from the Court of International Trade will handicap US efforts to comply with the WTO panel and Appellate rulings.[6] The environmentalists believe that the US is compromising its national sovereignty for the sake of its international obligations.

Today, after five years of intensive discussion and learning about the relationship between trade and environment, many continue to have mixed feelings about how to go about this relationship. Traders and environmentalists have many a time stood helpless and perplexed in front of this conundrum, which turns on how to accommodate environmental concerns in trade policy without tampering with the trade rules. Striking a balance between the need for governments to protect and preserve the environment on one hand, and avoiding the usage of environmental measures as a new trade protection measure on the other hand, remains a sensitive and highly controversial issue.

It was only after long and informed reasoning that many realized beyond a doubt that the two systems could not remain under the same roof because their objectives vary as well as their methods of implementation. That does not mean, however, that trade and environment are not mutually supportive. In many instances they are. Nevertheless, all the efforts to incorporate environment within the WTO system were to no avail. Based on this, Renato Ruggiero, the outgoing WTO Director-General, was brave enough to come up with a solution, which is – to my mind – straightforward and simple. He explained that all we need is a multilateral rules-based system (similar to that of the WTO) for environment – a World Environment Organization to the institutional and legal counterpart to the WTO. Such a proposal has been put forward on a number of occasions, the last being the High Level Symposium on Trade and Environment in the WTO on 15 March 1999.[7] There has been agreement with this viewpoint. 'Indeed, nothing would advance "trade and environment" harmony more than the creation of a Global Environmental Organization to work alongside the WTO,' wrote Daniel C Esty of Yale University in his presentation to the High Level Symposium.[8]

Realizing the immense difficulties involved in resolving the trade and environment relationship and easing the tension that had developed in the WTO in this regard, the European Commission proposed a high-level 'political' conference to bring trade and environment ministers together in the WTO. Because the debate in the WTO seemed burdened with suspicion and scepticism, developing country representatives in Geneva felt that the timing was not propitious, especially in the light of the fact that many issues remained unsolved in this relationship. In their mind, this needed further technical work before it could be brought to a political forum. Together with developed country delegations, they agreed after long deliberations to turn the high-level 'political' conference into a non-official, non-conclusive symposium involving a wider spectrum of the public, notably NGOs and academia, in a brainstorming session with a view to airing all positions, including those of civil societies.

It is astonishing that, in spite of the general view that further work needs to be undertaken on all items of the agenda of the Committee on Trade and Environment (CTE), predetermined positions are still taken. Such positions continue to press for amending the WTO rules to accommodate environment or call for the legitimization of the processes and production methods approach in the GATT system, irrespective of the wide-ranging and serious implications for developing countries and their methods of production. In addition, little tribute is paid to the concerns of developing countries in general. Market access and the new environmental conditions are key in this respect. The pretext that competition among nations is creating downward pressure on environmental standards is causing new protectionist measures to be arbitrarily imposed. The debate has revolved around these and other issues for the past few years. Developing countries have defended their interests and stood firm for positions that today might warrant more explanation and definition. The next phase of negotiations will be not less but certainly more controversial, and developing countries will again have to defend their positions aggressively.

The Basis of the WTO Trade/Environment Debate

It is worth noting that the trade and environment debate in the WTO is set within a consensual framework and based on three essential premises. These I would call the three Cs: Consistency with the level of development; the Competence of the world trading system and allaying fears of additional Conditionality. Let me elaborate further.

First, no one denies the importance assigned to the protection and preservation of the environment in the Preamble of the Marrakesh Agreement Establishing the World Trade Organization.[9] But it is equally true that the Preamble emphasized that this should be done in a manner that is consistent with the needs and concerns of countries at different levels of economic development. What is of significance here is that the importance accorded to environment was not absolute, but linked to countries' levels of development. I could even argue that priority was given to development, because the protection and preservation of the environment can be achieved only to the extent that this is consistent with the level of development.

It is not difficult to draw a comparison between the WTO Preamble and Rio Principle 7, cited earlier, concerning the common but differentiated responsibilities of states with regard to promoting sustainable development. This principle was the anchor for the UNCED. It accepted that the Northern countries had a greater responsibility for meeting the costs of adjustment because of their larger role in environmental degradation as well as their economic capacity to absorb more costs. The developing countries still needed to grow and develop (sustainably, of course) to meet their people's needs. The North also made a commitment to provide adequate financial resources and technology transfer to facilitate the South's transition to sustainable development.[10]

Secondly, the Marrakesh Ministerial Decision on Trade and Environment[11] was clear in setting the terms of reference for WTO work on trade and environment. The fourth paragraph of the Preamble stipulates that the coordination of policies in the field of trade and environment should be done without exceeding the competence of the multilateral trading system. Again of utmost significance here is that the negotiators were adamant that the 'competence of the multilateral trading system' is limited to trade policies and those aspects of environmental policies that may result in significant trade effects for its members.

Thirdly, in order to allay any possible fears of a new 'green conditionality' attached to market access opportunities, thus nullifying the benefits accruing from trade liberalization within the context of the Uruguay Round, the 1996 Singapore Ministerial Report on Trade and Environment[12] stressed the following:

1   the WTO is not an environmental protection agency and it is assumed that the WTO itself does not provide an answer to environmental problems;
2   environmental problems require environmental solutions, not trade solutions;
3   no blank cheque for the use of trade measures for environmental purposes;
4   trade liberalisation is not the primary cause of environmental degradation, nor are trade instruments the first-best policy for addressing environmental problems;
5   GATT/WTO agreements already provide significant scope for members to adopt national environmental protection policies, provided that they are non-discriminatory;
6   secure market access opportunities are essential to help developing countries work towards sustainable development;
7   increased national coordination as well as multilateral cooperation are necessary to address trade-related environmental concerns adequately.

It is worth stressing that the first WTO Ministerial Conference was keen to elucidate the reality of the relationship and its rightful stance in the multilateral system. It was clear from the ongoing debate at the time that there was no quarrel with depicting the WTO as an environment-friendly organisation. In fact, the GATT allows for any action to be taken at the national level to protect the environment, provided it is in compliance with its basic rules and regulations. Article XX ('General Exceptions'),[13] the Agreement on Technical Barriers to Trade (TBT)[14] and the Agreement on the Application of Sanitary and Phytosanitary Measures (SPS)[15] are all cases in point: they give each country the right to set the level of protection that it deems appropriate on environment, provided it does not act against the basic principles of the WTO as stipulated by Article I ('Most-Favoured-Nation Treatment') and Article III ('National Treatment'). In addition, it should not constitute an unnecessary barrier to trade. I should emphasize that the 'Trade and Environment' Report adopted at the first Ministerial Conference remains as valid as ever and constitutes the backbone of the ongoing debate on trade and environment. However, one issue that developing countries were keen to elucidate was that the report does not represent a legal instrument, and hence does not alter or touch on the rights and obligations of WTO members.

I shall now turn to a few of the specific issues that were subject to intensive debate at the CTE. I start with the interrelationship between multilateral environment agreements and the WTO, followed by the complex relationship between the Agreement on Trade-related Intellectual Property Rights (TRIPS) and environment. I then deal with eco-labelling as a life-cycle analysis and the problem of process and production methods. Finally, I address market access and competitiveness as prime issues of interest to developing countries in the trade and environment debate.

Some Specific Issues in the Debate

The Relationship between Multilateral Environment Agreements and the WTO

The relationship between the provisions of the multilateral trading system and trade measures for environmental purposes, including those pursuant to multilateral environmental agreements (MEAs), was a topic that was extensively debated and subject to the most controversy. In spite of the long and tedious discussions throughout the previous five years or so, little rapprochement, if any, was achieved. Views on a number of issues were and remain wide apart; the definition of MEAs, Article XX, the issue of process and production methods, the effectiveness of trade restrictions and whether they were the most appropriate instruments to advance environmental policies are but a few of these issues.

The relationship between the multilateral trading system and the multilateral environmental agreements raised numerous difficulties and controversies. These ranged from issues of hierarchy and compatibility between the two entities to the comprehensive framework of the MEAs, which combine a mixture of incentives and trade measures to deal with environmental externalities. In the framework of MEAs, positive measures – such as improved marker access, capacity-building, additional finance, and access to and transfer of technology – were considered to be effective instruments to assist developing countries to meet multilaterally agreed environmental targets. This was in sharp contrast to the much-disputed effectiveness of trade measures applied as sanctions under the purview of the WTO. The scope for trade measures pursuant to MEAs under WTO provisions and their unilateral application to address environmental problems that lie outside a country's national jurisdiction led to wide disagreement and were strongly contested.

In this debate, developing countries had to defend themselves on a number of fronts. First, developing countries continued to argue against developed countries' intentions of arming the WTO with additional power to protect the environment because this would have the effect only of elevating trade measures, ie sanctions, to be considered as priority tools for the environment. This would undermine the international consensus reached on a whole range of positive measures negotiated at length within the framework of the multilateral environmental agreements. Isolating the trade measures would not serve the purpose and could prove to be detrimental to the environment because they deprive developing countries of an assured source of resources. Such resources could be directed, among other things, towards the protection of the environment. Furthermore, in order to determine the necessity and effectiveness of the trade measures, these would have to be assessed together with other measures in a holistic framework, such as the one provided for by the multilateral environmental agreements. Countries cannot press for the use of trade measures just because they are less expensive and hence more appealing to politicians, without weighing the pros and cons of such usage in an objective and comprehensive manner. On the contrary, MEAs should provide developing countries with the 'carrot' to entice them to comply with their obligations under such agreements, if – as proclaimed – the ultimate goal is to preserve and protect the environment.

Secondly, regarding the issue of hierarchy, at the Singapore Ministerial Conference of the WTO in December 1996,[16] developing countries succeeded in undermining the attempts by developed countries to give the MEAs superiority over the WTO's settlement of disputes. The underlying reasons were clear: developing countries refused the dominance of environmental considerations, as advocated in the MEAs, over the WTO Dispute Settlement Understanding (DSU) as guided by the key principles of the trading system – notably, most favoured nation and national treatment – as well as the rejection of unilateral measures. Developing countries felt that on no account should they give up or weaken their inalienable rights to have recourse to the WTO DSU by giving primacy to settling disputes through the MEA. That did not mean, however, that MEAs were disregarded. They remain a viable option for disputants to settle their disputes, if they so wish.

The repeated attempts by the European Commission to reinterpret or even add an amendment to the WTO rules that would prioritize environment or make it an exception through what they would like to perceive as an 'environmental window' were doomed to failure. Developing countries have stood firm against any amendments to the WTO rules in order to legitimize inconsistent trade measures in the WTO. They insisted that any effort to reopen the WTO rules would mean imposing environmental conditionality on trade and would give sufficient ground for unilateral measures that would amount to protectionism and the restriction of market access under the disguise of protecting the environment. It was also recognized that, in principle, trade measures taken pursuant to MEAs were not to be challenged by the WTO membership because the majority are also members of the MEAs. Furthermore, trade measures within the MEAs – as multilaterally agreed on – were tolerated, and many of them were even pushed by developing countries themselves. This was the case with the Basel Convention and the Prior Informed Consent Convention on Hazardous Chemicals.

It is surprising that voices are still raised in favour of effecting substantive changes in the GATT. The first of these would involve amending Article XX on the pretext that, as it is currently applied, it gives prominence to trade goals over environmental ones. In my view this is the wrong way to look at things. The WTO's main concern is implementing trade goals. It is entitled to rectify any wrong-doings in the area of trade, but it is not within the competence of the organization or its trade representatives to deal with issues going beyond trade and trade-related issues, be they environment, human rights, child labour or other social issues. In addition, it has been stated that Article XX is flexible enough to accommodate legitimate environmental concerns. It was precisely with this in mind that negotiators stressed the competence of the multilateral trading system in the fourth paragraph of the Preamble of the Marrakesh Ministerial Decision on Trade and Environment.

Another substantive amendment to the current GATT structure that would facilitate peace between the trade and environment camps would involve the recognition by GATT that, in an ecologically interdependent world, *how* things are produced is often as important as *what* is produced. In particular, environmental standards that relate to processes and production methods (PPMs) cannot always be rejected and

judged indiscriminately to be violations of GATT.[17] However, accepting the introduction of PPMs in GATT/WTO would amount to the imposition of a country's
domestic environmental values or policies on other countries. As environmental
standards and PPMs are based on values that differ from one society to another, it
would be difficult to internationalize PPMs and require all countries to follow the
same production methods. On the other hand, we have to distinguish between environmental standards that are product-related, such as disposal and handling, with
which I have no quarrel, and non-product-related standards, which do not affect the
final product.

The risks of setting and accepting ecological standards for PPMs in GATT today
are twofold. First, these standards would most likely be the ones used in developed
countries, thus allowing environmental standards to be easily manipulated for protection purposes. Second, setting ecological standards for PPMs could be used as
an opening for over-stretching the concept in the future and taking it as a precedent
to incorporate, other non-trade-related goals, such as labour standards, human rights,
good governance and all sorts of other domestic pressures that have hardly any relationship with the WTO.

The *Shrimp–Turtle* Dispute

It is worth referring briefly to the *Shrimp–Turtle* dispute. In this case, the two rulings
(by the dispute settlement panel as well as by the Appellate Body) are precedent-
setting. The dispute was the first concerning a trade embargo based solely on
domestic environmental legislation forced by the US as the only country that interprets Article XX so broadly as to allow for extraterritorial measures to protect the
environment beyond its territories. It was obvious from the very beginning that the
issue at stake was not a trade measure mandated by an MEA (in this case the Convention on International Trade in Endangered Species of Wild Fauna and Flora
[CITES]), but a measure to address a global environmental concern applied unilaterally by one country.

For the US, the case involved the right of WTO members to take measures
under Article XX (b) and (g)[18] of GATT 1994 to conserve and protect natural resources, as reaffirmed and reinforced by the Preamble to the WTO Agreement. For
the complainant, it was a case about the imposition of unilateral trade measures
designed to coerce other members to adopt environmental policies that mirrored
those in the US. The US based its entire defence on Article XX which allows countries to take measures contrary to GATT obligations when such measures (a) are
necessary to protect human, animal or plant life or health; (b) relate to the conservation of exhaustible natural resources.

In this case, the US argued that a trade measure was necessary because sea
turtles were threatened with extinction and the use of turtle-excluder devices on
shrimp nets was the only way effectively to protect them from drowning in shrimp
nets. The panel, however, stressed the WTO's preference for multilaterally negotiated solutions.[19] Furthermore, the panel focused its analysis on the headnote or
'chapeau' of Article XX which requires legitimate trade restrictions to be applied 'in
a manner, which would not constitute a means of arbitrary or unjustifiable discrimination between countries where the same conditions prevail or a disguised restriction

on international trade'. The panel found that interpreting the chapeau in a way that would allow importing countries to restrict market access according to exporters' adoption of 'certain policies, including conservation policies' would mean that 'GATT 1994 and the WTO Agreement could no longer serve as a multilateral framework for trade among Members'. Such an interpretation, the panel felt, could lead to 'conflicting policy requirements' because exporting countries would need to conform with different domestic policies in importing countries, thus threatening the 'security and predictability of trade relations' under WTO agreements. It therefore drew the conclusion that 'certain unilateral measures, insofar as they could jeopardize the multilateral trading system, could not be covered by Article XX'.[20]

The panel reaffirmed the logic of developing countries that the WTO cannot be made responsible for safeguarding all kinds of different interests. This would give leeway to members to pursue their own trade policy solutions unilaterally, thus reinstating power politics. This would certainly amount to an abuse of Article XX exceptions, as the panel put it, and thus threaten the preservation of the multilateral trade system based on consensus and multilateral cooperation. It is worth recalling at this juncture that to do away with a power-based system and replace it with a rule-based one was an essential objective of the seven-year Uruguay Round of negotiations, which hardly anyone would want to give up today.

Without much ado, the Appellate Body also concluded that the US measure was 'unjustifiably discriminatory'.[21] In its ruling, the Appellate Body was more cautious and less blunt than the panel. Trying to find some 'political' justification for the US measure, it characterized the ban 'as an appropriate means to an end', although its application was at fault. It attributed the unjustifiable nature of the discrimination to the failure of the US to pursue negotiations for consensual means of protecting and conserving sea turtles, resulting in the 'unilateral' application of its trade measure. The Appellate Body further agreed that the US had applied the measure in an 'arbitrary and discriminatory' manner between countries where the same conditions prevail, contrary to the requirements of the chapeau of Article XX. The application was discriminatory in giving a longer grace period to Caribbean countries than to Asian nations, in nor transferring technology to them on similar terms, in its lack of transparency, etc.

The Appellate Body then stressed that it had not decided that the sovereign nations that are members of the WTO cannot adopt effective measures to protect endangered species, such as sea turtles; 'Clearly, they can and should'.[22] It stressed that protection and preservation of the environment are of significance to WTO members, provided that 'they [sovereign states] act together bilaterally, plurilaterally or multilaterally, either within the WTO or in other international forums'. Finally the Appellate Body decided that, 'although the measure of the US in dispute in this appeal serves an environmental objective that is recognized as legitimate under paragraph (g) of Article XX of GATT 1994, this measure has been applied by the US in a manner which constitutes arbitrary and unjustifiable discrimination between Members of the WTO, contrary to the requirements of the chapeau of Article XX.[23]

Although the US ambassador to the WTO hailed the Appellate Body's ruling as a success for the US position, a similar sense of victory was neither felt nor expressed by US environmental NGOs which, as mentioned earlier, had brought the case to the US Court. The Appellate Body ruling, in my view, does not amount to a reversal of the panel ruling, as some would like to have it, but rather falls under what the Singapore Ministerial meeting attempted to elucidate. GATT/WTO agreements do provide significant scope for national environmental protection policies, provided they are not discriminatory in nature. Moreover, countries should seek joint and not unilateral action. This is how, I believe, the Appellate Body findings and conclusions should be regarded. This decision is an attempt not to overturn the consensus reached in the WTO CTE, but rather to strengthen it. In fact, the Appellate Body pronounced itself clearly against WTO-inconsistent trade measures applied unilaterally to address extrajurisdictional environmental problems. It thus underlined what WTO members had succeeded in injecting into the factual part of the Singapore report. It was explicitly mentioned that 'all delegations except one'[24] stated that they consider that the provisions of GATT Article XX do not permit a member to impose unilateral trade restrictions that are otherwise inconsistent with WTO obligations for the purpose of protecting environmental resources that lie outside its jurisdiction. In any event, arguments in favour of reinterpreting Article XX to address environmental concerns (as put forcefully by those who want to see Article XX amended or reinterpreted) for fear of the trend by the Appellate Body to expand, on its own, the meaning of Article XX, remain void. There is no doubt that neither the Appellate Body nor the panels are entitled to attempt to interpret the WTO rules. *Interpretation of the rules is the sole right of the membership.*

The Environment and Trade-related Intellectual Property Rights

The relationship between environment and trade-related intellectual property rights (TRIPS) is yet another example of the underlying conflict in the WTO between the urge to protect the environment on one hand and the tools made available for such an objective in the framework of the TRIPS Agreement on the other hand. Here the case is quite the reverse. The TRIPS Agreement as negotiated and pushed for by the developed countries has proved to be unfriendly to the environment. In fact, reading carefully through the TRIPS Agreement, one cannot fail to realize that environmental concerns did not really occupy a priority at the negotiating table then. It has become clear only over the past few years that a number or provisions in the TRIPS Agreement go against the objectives of Agenda 21 and the various multilateral environmental agreements with regard to access to and transfer of technology to help maintain and protect the environment. The outcry came first from NGOs engaged in development and environment in developed and developing countries alike.

India was one of the few countries that, at an early stage in the work of the CTE, recognized the real problem in reconciling intellectual property protection, as laid down in the TRIPS Agreement, with the objectives and provisions on transfer of technology incorporated in some of the MEAs.[25] It failed, however, to summon the necessary backing on the part of the developing countries on this topical issue. The primary reason was the complexity of the issue itself. Hardly any developing countries were grabbed by this difficult and composite relationship because they were still struggling with other outstanding commitments emanating from the Uruguay Round. Coping with the various provisions of the TRIPS Agreement was not a priority because they felt they had ample time until the transitional period expired.

As we get closer to the implementation of the TRIPS Agreement and with environment looming as a topic in the Millennium Round, developing countries ought to look more seriously at this issue. Let me hasten to say that at no point in my argument should it be taken that developing countries are trying to back-pedal on their commitments. Nonetheless it remains a fact that the TRIPS Agreement as negotiated was put in a very narrow context and with limited objectives, ie to lay down minimum standards for the protection of the owner, the titleholder and the patentee, conferring on them exclusive rights. This goes against a whole myriad of legitimate and valid concerns: topping the list are socio-economic and developmental issues, the environment, technology transfer, and fair and open competition. It is no secret that, for these as well as other reasons, developing countries remained inimical to such an agreement until the eleventh hour. It was only under pressure of the 'Single Undertaking' commitment that they were obliged to accede to it.

Addressing the relationship between the TRIPS Agreement and environment, the CTE focused in its deliberations on two main issues:

1   the generation of access to, and transfer of environmentally sound technologies, and
2   the contradiction between the TRIPS Agreement and the Convention on Biological Diversity.

With regard to the first issue, the question concerns what happens if TRIPS put such technologies beyond the reach of developing countries. This would undoubtedly have a negative impact on the environment and on the stringent efforts developing countries are making to cope with the environmental requirements. It is true that Article 7 of the TRIPS Agreement stipulates that patenting should encourage the promotion of technological innovation and the transfer and dissemination of technology, to the mutual advantage of producers and users, that is and in a manner conducive to social and economic welfare. This, however, has not yet materialized owing to the fact that developing countries are still benefiting from the transitional period of the implementation of the Agreement. Nor has any empirical evidence sustained this argument so far. Hence, the question remains how TRIPS link up with the objective of facilitating access to and the transfer of technology 'on fair and most favourable terms'[26] to assist in the conservation of the environment and to promote sustainable development.

As for the relationship between the TRIPS Agreement and the Convention on Biological Diversity (CBD), this heads the list of concerns of developmental and environmental NGOs in the North as well as in the South. The contradiction between TRIPS and the CBD is not implicit. There are doubts about the compatibility of the various provisions of the TRIPS Agreement with the clear objectives of the Convention as it relates to the conservation and sustainable use of genetic resources. The underlying disparity between the timely transfer of relevant biotechnology as agreed in the CBD and Article 33 of TRIPS, which provides for a term of protection of at least 20 years, remains a point of contention and a source of serious concern. This concern will grow for developing countries as their obligation to fully implement TRIPS was phased in in 2000. The relationship between TRIPS and the CBD will be a focus for negotiation under the Doha Development.

It was only alter the conclusion of the TRIPS Agreement and after its adoption within the framework of the Uruguay Round that questions regarding the compatibility between TRIPS and the CBD started to surface. Equitable sharing of the benefits arising out of the utilization of the knowledge systems of indigenous communities and fair trade-offs between access to genetic resources and the transfer of technology remain the essence of the CBD, as agreed notably in Articles 15 and 16 of the Convention.[27] However, concerns were expressed about the negative impact of TRIPS in the fields of agriculture, nutrition and healthcare because they would inevitably lead to an extension of the monopoly control of transnationals over production and distribution in these vital areas for developing countries. Moreover, the TRIPS Agreement does not try to curb the commercial exploitation of genetic resources or deal with the sharing on a fair and equitable basis of the benefits arising out of the patenting of genetic resources. Much has been said with respect to the usage and applicability of' Article 31(k) of the TRIPS Agreement regarding compulsory licensing for the public domain, as permitting the necessary flexibility. With all the strings attached to this article, however, the question arises whether it truly serves the purpose of facilitating access to and transfer of technology, including biotechnology, on fair and most favourable terms, as stipulated by Article 16.2 of the Biodiversity Convention. This issue undoubtedly requires more in-depth study.

Because of these fundamental controversies and whether or not environment becomes an issue in the next multilateral trading round or is mainstreamed in the various agreements, environment will have to be an integral part of any review process of the TRIPS Agreement. The different available alternatives should be weighed and carefully studied. Three main options, which set the framework for the overall trade and environment debate, come to mind:

1   to agree on the relevance of Article XX as a general exception in the context of the TRIPS Agreement when specifically addressing biodiversity and the sustainable use of genetic resources;
2   to decide whether the TRIPS Agreement or the Convention would prevail in the event of a dispute and how it would work out between parties and non-parties to either; and
3   to keep the issue open, to be addressed and settled on an ad hoc basis by panels in the event of a dispute.

It is worth stressing at this juncture that developmental and environmental NGOs from the North as well as from the South latched on to the issue that developing countries should have been tackling in depth much earlier. Their views should not be neglected, otherwise developing countries might at some point find themselves on the defensive and be confronted with the same kind of arguments raised against the TRIPS Agreement – namely, that it was negotiated entirely out of the public view; it might then perhaps be too late. The recent failure of the lengthy negotiations on the Multilateral Agreement on Investment in the Organisation for Economic Co-operation and Development (OECD) is a case in point. It clearly denotes the strength and skills of environmental NGOs and, if they feel sidelined, TRIPS could be next in turn.

Eco-labelling

Eco-labelling is another highly controversial issue. Compared with other voluntary standards, such as packaging, labelling or even recycling requirements, it has attracted much attention in the trade and environment debate in the WTO. In spite of the fact that it was discussed extensively prior to the Singapore Ministerial Conference as well as in the framework of the review process of the Agreement on Technical Barriers to Trade, hardly any decision has materialized to date. The issue has raised a number of practical, conceptual and systemic problems. It might sound strange and be difficult to comprehend, but the more the debate is focused on the core of the issue at hand, the more the gap between the various views widens.

The complexity of the issue arises from the fact that eco-labelling schemes are based on life-cycle analysis, which involves PPMs. In other words, eco-labelling is interested in the product during its entire life-cycle: the sourcing of raw materials, production, consumption and disposal. This approach requires, in and of itself, large amounts of information when products or materials are imported, which may cause enormous practical problems, especially for developing countries.[28] In addition, specific PPM-related criteria based on domestic conditions and priorities in the importing country may be less appropriate in other countries. Whereas there is no question that each country has the right to institute domestic regulations on eco-labelling, the concern is that it should not be used for protectionist purposes – applied by some countries selectively to products that are imported or that compete with their own products.

The principal fear of developing countries in dealing with the issue of eco-labelling in the WTO is that an attempt will be made to extend the coverage of such labelling – even though voluntarily – to non-related PPMs. They fear not only the whole range of implications for their exports that such an extension would produce, but more the systemic problem it raises in the WTO. It would amount to writing new rules for a system that has so far served the international community and the world trading system well. The problem of subjecting eco-labelling to WTO rules and disciplines lies in the conflict that would arise with the product-based rules of the GATT/WTO trading system. Discriminating between 'like products' and making market access conditional on complying with PPMs, thus legitimizing unincorporated PPMs, which are not product-related, would upset the entire multilateral trading system and would have devastating effects, in particular on developing country exports.

Developing countries have recognized that what is being put into question – through using eco-labelling as a litmus test – is the basic criteria and characteristics that have so far governed the multilateral trading system. Through eco-labelling, the WTO would become more and more deeply involved in the realm of domestic policy and intervention from the outside would be allowed to set national priorities. On this basis, most developing countries have insisted that eco-labelling is inconsistent and should not be accommodated within the WTO system. This was strongly supported by the fact that the negotiating history of the TBT Agreement upheld their view that unincorporated PPMs were not covered by the Agreement.[29] While admitting the role that equivalence and mutual recognition could play in helping them meet the requirements of foreign schemes, they insisted that accommodating unincorporated PPMs would amount to creating scope for the extraterritorial imposition of national standards. This, they felt, would have significant consequences for the trading system as a whole.[30]

Furthermore, as stated earlier and as emphasized by the Preamble of the WTO Agreement, environmental objectives should be *consistent* with the level of development. The prevention of product differentiation on the basis of unincorporated PPMs allows countries to set standards, whether environmental or otherwise, that are appropriate for their level of development. In other words, it allows countries to trade their developmental needs against their needs for environmental protection in a manner that is consistent with how they themselves value these needs (and not on the basis of how others value them for them).[31]

What I would like to add here is that the debate in the CTE on eco-labelling schemes has triggered a similar heated debate between environmentalists and business groups. The former have criticized what they consider to be the narrow perspective of international trade rules, noting that PPMs are fundamental to minimizing the environmental impact of a product during its life-cycle. Business groups see trade rules that distinguish between products solely on the characteristics of end products as relevant and appropriate. Like many developing countries, they view the introduction of PPMs into the trade debate as the beginning of a slippery slope, where loosely related production factors would become the basis for trade barriers.

Lastly, it is essential to recall Principle 11 of the Rio Declaration in this context, which stipulates that environmental standards, management objectives and priorities should reflect the environmental and developmental context to which they apply. The standards applied by some countries may be inappropriate and of unwarranted economic and social cost to other countries, in particular developing countries.[32] Accordingly, the disciplining of eco-labelling schemes should be on the basis of equivalencies and mutual recognition, where each country sets its standards according to its own values, as stipulated by Agenda 21. The aim of harmonizing or internationalizing PPMs on the basis of any set of multilateral guidelines is in contradiction to what the international community agreed upon unanimously in Agenda 21. What is even more risky is that such an attempt would be detrimental to the trading system, at a time when all countries are embracing and respecting its rules.

Market Access and Competitiveness Aspects of the Trade/Environment Debate

One cannot address the interface between trade and environment without looking at the market access and competitiveness aspects of this relationship. These aspects tended to be underplayed and even overlooked at the beginning of the debate, for the obvious reasons stated earlier. It is needless to reiterate that the whole debate was triggered by developed countries targeting specific issues of concern to themselves. As developing countries gradually became aware of the underlying reasons and objectives of this debate, they rightly pushed issues of their own to the fore. It should be stressed, however, that this move by developing countries was on no account aimed at eventually achieving trade-offs. On one hand, their refusal to amend or reinterpret Article XX or to introduce non-related PPMs was based on systemic principles, which cannot be subjected to bargaining because this would alter the very essence of the system. On the other hand, the purpose of bringing in market access and competitive concerns was to add balance to the lopsided debate and put it in its proper perspective.

From the very beginning the debate on this issue was set in a North–South context. This has harmed rather than helped the debate advance. False allegations continue to be made by firms in countries with high environmental standards and high costs of compliance that they are often undercut by competition from companies based in countries with less strict regulation and lower costs. In theory, this could lead to entire industries departing for countries with lower standards, the so-called 'pollution havens'. So far, however, there is no evidence of this happening. The reverse – that high environmental standards were a factor in location decisions or have led to the relocation of industry – has also not occurred on a large scale.

The debate on market access from the perspective of developing countries tends to be twofold. They want to ensure first that existing market access conditions are not eroded by emerging environmental requirements and second that additional market access – through what can be perceived as win–win situations – will help to promote environmental protection and sustainable development. In this context developing countries have tried to concentrate on identifying sectors of export interest to them. These could be textiles and clothing, leather, footwear, furniture and other consumer goods, and other labour-intensive sectors, where environmental measures could affect existing market access opportunities and thus possibly nullify or impair the Uruguay Round results. In fact, empirical studies, mostly done by the UN Conference on Trade and Development (UNCTAD), show that the sectors of interest to developing countries are those most affected by environmental standards often set unilaterally by the importing governments. Such standards negatively influence developing countries' market access, even though the environmental effects of, say, textile production might mainly be local and do not affect the final characteristics of the product. In addition, there are few – if any – transboundary externalities.

Furthermore, UNCTAD's studies have also demonstrated that small and medium enterprises (SMEs) in developing countries have encountered difficulties in complying with environmental policies emerging in the above-mentioned sectors. Such policies have had significant effects on the competitiveness of SMEs in developing countries and have in many instances acted as barriers to trade. A number of reasons have been cited, among them are the following:

- The possibility of compensating for the loss of competitiveness in some sectors by gains in others is higher in economies that are diversified and dynamic, which are not necessarily the main characteristics of developing countries' economies.

- Developing country exporters are normally price-takers because they compete on price rather than on non-price factors such as technology and ideas. Consequently, any environmental requirement resulting in cost increases reduces export competitiveness. Nevertheless it may vary from one industry to another as well as among developing countries at different stages of development and with varying capability to integrate innovative approaches.
- The problems of adjustment are higher for SMEs in developing countries, especially as they are important players in the export promotion strategy for sectors such as textiles, clothing and footwear. Thus the need to examine the possible conflict between the export promotion strategies of developing countries and the need to comply with environmental requirements and their effects on competitiveness becomes all the more relevant.
- The variable cost component of complying with environmental standards is higher in some sectors than in others. Again, evidence has shown that it is higher in sectors of interest to developing countries, especially leather and footwear, as well as textiles and garment sectors. For example, in leather tanning, the cost of the chemicals required to meet international standards is approximately three times the cost of conventional chemicals.[33]

Two additional topics are germane to the market access and competitiveness debate: the internalization of environmental costs, and charges and taxes for environmental purposes. Although these topics are not new and have in fact been debated at length, they remain contentious and difficult, especially if the idea is to add them to the trading agenda.

The concept of internalization remains difficult to adopt in GATT on the grounds that it interferes with the efficiency of the comparative advantage principle, which is central to the free trading system. The tendency to consider the lack of internalization as a kind of implicit subsidy, that would be actionable under GATT/WTO is a non-starter. Furthermore, environmental externalities are in principle not distinguishable from other factors, such as education, infrastructure and social policy that contribute to the comparative advantages and thus competitiveness edge of an economy. Are we to conclude that the costs of all these factors are to be integrated in production processes under the auspices of the multilateral trading system? The internalization of environmental costs by domestic producers in no way conflicts with GATT principles. However, it becomes problematic under GATT if countries start implementing trade policies on the basis of whether or not foreign producers have internalized their environmental costs. GATT would be more concerned with the trade-distorting or discriminatory effect of such a policy, and with its necessity and effectiveness, rather than with its environmental objectives.

As for charges and taxes for environmental purposes, no one can deny the validity and effectiveness of imposing taxes as such. But what is occurring here is the imposition of taxes on a phenomenon that is not quantitative. Forcing producers to incorporate environmental externalities by imposing taxes on products made with polluting processes is based on the assumption that the costs to the polluting firm and the damage caused by the pollution are known. Moreover, if this is true at the national level, it can only be more complex and difficult if an importing country aims at adjusting such costs at its borders by imposing border tax adjustments on its 'like' imports. In addition, the question of what would be an appropriate tax for pollution that would be accepted internationally is still open.

Border tax adjustments (BTAs) should pass the necessity and effectiveness test to find out how pertinent they are to the environment, before even debating how to impose them at the border. The effectiveness of BTA is doubted and even contradicts the view, widely acknowledged by developing and developed countries alike, that environmental problems should be addressed at source. So how can a tax imposed on final products, as a BTA, be effective for problems that should be dealt with as far upstream in the production process as possible?[34] As rightly pointed out by UNCTAD, it is generally better if the tax is levied on the production and extraction process causing the environmental problems rather than on the resulting product. In other words, a tax levied internally by the producing country would be more effective at dealing with environmental problems at their source. GATT neither prohibits nor prevents a country from pursuing a policy of taxation or regulation with regard to environmental protection as long as these policies apply only to its domestic consumers and producers. In fact, one can even go one step further. For BTA on imports to pass the compatibility test in GATT, it has to meet the following conditions:

1　the tax is product related;
2　the imported product has not been taxed in the country of origin, to avoid double taxation;
3　the imported product has caused transboundary pollution and the polluting input was not consumed domestically.

Similarly to their stance on process and production methods in eco-labelling, developing countries insist that there should be an explicit reference to addressing charges and taxes that relate only to products or product characteristics that are covered by WTO provisions. In any event, the environmental effectiveness and potential trade effects of levying environmental taxes and charges, particularly on market access and competitiveness, remain questions open for debate.

Before concluding, let me state that no one can deny the fact that the relationship between trade and environment has been debated extensively in the WTO. This has undoubtedly helped to clarify the status of this relationship in the framework of the organization and to shape positions in response to the underlying motives and objectives. Today, even before settling this complex relationship, other more difficult and cumbersome issues are emerging, such as linking trade to labour standards. Although from the very beginning such an inclusion has met with strong objections, it will continue to be pushed in the WTO mainly by the US – for obvious reasons, which neither time nor space permit to be addressed here. One thing is clear, however. Developing countries have to stand firm on their positions on trade and environment as regards changing the rules. Such a move would only serve as a prelude to the integration of the 'social clause' in the WTO, which has wider implications for developing countries and should be of more serious concern.

Conclusion

The Seattle Ministerial Conference in December 1999 and the Doha Ministerial Conference in 2001 have together provided a turning point in the trade and environmental debate. As the trade and environment debate moves to the WTO's formal negotiating agenda, one thing remains clear. A great deal of work and education continue to be needed before drawing conclusions or reaching the stage of negotiating rules and disciplines, not to mention changing the rules, as some would like to happen. The trade and environment relationship continues to be an area prone to difficulties, complexities and, most of all, sensitivities. Throughout this chapter I have tried to show that so far the CTE has worked within a consensual framework. To try to tamper with this framework in order to incorporate additional objectives will necessitate a new consensual framework. The attempts by the international community to forward some alternatives remain in the very early stages and will need further in-depth study. The following are a few of the options:

1   The debate will continue in the CTE as part of the Doha Development Agenda negotiations, with a view to bringing the two ends closer together. This option is unlikely to achieve results because, in the view of many people, the CTE has exhausted the debate.
2   The so-called 'Ruggiero' option presented earlier: a World Environment Organization to be the counterpart to the WTO. This is a pragmatic and likely workable option in view of the difficulties encountered so far, although it is still resisted by mainly developed countries and their NGOs. Some developed countries – notably, the EU countries, Norway, Switzerland and Canada – continue to believe that the WTO, with its strong and enforceable dispute settlement mechanism, is an appealing instrument for policy-makers, particularly in the field of environment. Many NGOs continue to be convinced that the trading systems should provide the necessary flexibility for the sake of the environment, which is undoubtedly their priority.
3   Mainstreaming environment in the various agreements, such as Agriculture, TRIPS, Textiles and Clothing, and others. The degree of complexity and controversy inherent in this option, which is still to be tested, is difficult to anticipate. However, care should be taken because this option carries with it the inherent risk of doing away with the sensitive balance carefully negotiated in the CTE between issues of interest to developing and developed countries alike, thus thwarting the possibility of trade-offs, if any. With this option, the issues of market access would be spread thinly over different agreements, leaving the two topics of concern to developed countries, ie the relationship between trade and environment and PPMs, to be negotiated separately.

In spite of tremendous efforts not to label the trade and environment debate as a North–South issue, these have hardly borne fruit. No one can deny that there is evidence of a conflict between developed and developing countries, which will continue and deepen unless the existing doubts about linking environmental interests with protectionism dissipate. *The challenge is to separate protectionism from environment.* The environment cannot be safeguarded and enhanced through trade sanctions. Benefiting the environment must be through access to technology, increased awareness, financial resources and access to markets, without which developing countries will find it extremely difficult to generate the resources necessary to protect their domestic environments and the global commons.

Let me conclude by stating how Rubens Ricupero, the Secretary-General of UNCTAD, perceives the trade environment relationship:

> Trade and Environment are two poles in a dialectical thesis, where the resulting synthesis should conciliate the two ends. Unlike many would like to believe, linking trade to environment does not come as something natural. To reconcile these two ends necessitates tremendous efforts – and not without sacrifices – where environment should not be treated as a late consideration or an afterthought.[35]

The way to deal with environmental problems is to go to their roots and integrate environment in the decision-making process from the very beginning. This requires the provision of the necessary technology and making available the required financing, knowledge and expertise for the preservation and protection of the environment.

Acknowledgements

Although I am indebted to René Vossenaar, UNCTAD, and Doaa Abdel Motaal, WTO, for their valuable comments and suggestions, which have sharpened the exposition, I wish to exonerate them from any responsibility for the final product. This chapter is my own responsibility and is not meant to reflect Egypt's position.

Notes

1   *Herald Tribune,* 15 March 1999
2   Stuart E Eizenstat, US Undersecretary of Stare for Economic Affairs, 'Why We Should Welcome Biotechnology', *Financial Times,* 16 April 1999
3   Rio Declaration on Environment and Development, United Nations Conference on Environment and Development, Rio de Janeiro, June 1992
4   'Report of the United Nations Conference on Environment and Development', Rio de Janeiro, 3–14 June 1992, Chapter 1, Objectives 2.9(a), p3
5   'Trade and Environment: A Developing Countries' Perspective', a paper presented by the Dominican Republic, Egypt, Honduras and Pakistan to the WTO High Level Symposium on Trade and Environment, 15–16 March 1999
6   'Legal Wrangle Engulfs US Shrimp Dispute', *Financial Times,* 14 April 1999
7   Opening remarks by Renato Ruggiero to the WTO High Level Symposium on Trade and Environment, 15 March 1999

8 Daniel C Esty, 'Economic Integration and Environmental Protection: Synergies, Opportunities and Challenges', Yale University, 6 March 1999 (draft presented to the WTO High Level Symposium)

9 GATT, *The Results of the Uruguay Round of Multilateral Trade Negotiations. The Legal Texts,* 1994, p6

10 Khor, Martin (1999) 'Trade, Environmental and Sustainable Development: A Developing Country View of the Issues Including in the WTO Context', paper presented to the WTO High Level Symposium on Trade and Environment, 15 March

11 Final Act Embodying the Results of the Uruguay Round of Multilateral Trade Negotiations, signed Marrakesh, 15 April 1994

12 WTO CTE, *Report (1996) of the Committee on Trade and Environment,* WT/CTE/1, 12 November 1996

13 Article XX ('General Exceptions') gives ample opportunity to use measures to protect (a) public morals, (b) human, animal or plant life or health, etc. The chapeau of the Article stipulates that these measures should not be applied in a manner that would *constitute a means of arbitrary or unjustifiable discrimination between countries where the same conditions prevail or a disguised restriction on international trade*

14 The Agreement on Technical Barriers to Trade deals basically with technical regulations and international standards, including packaging, marking and labelling requirements, and procedures for assessment of conformity. It further makes sure that these regulations and standards should not constitute a means of arbitrary or unjustifiable discrimination between countries where the same conditions prevail or there is a disguised restriction on international trade

15 The Agreement on the Application of Sanitary and Phytosanitary Measures forms an integral part of the Agreement on Agriculture. It reaffirms in its Preamble that no member should be prevented from adopting or enforcing measures necessary to protect human, animal or plant life or health. These measures are subject to the requirement that they are not applied in a manner that would constitute a means of arbitrary or unjustifiable discrimination between members where the same conditions prevail or there is a disguised restriction on international trade

16 The 1996 Singapore Ministerial Conference was the first ministerial meeting of the WTO

17 Esty, 'Economic Integration', op cit

18 Article XX (b) (g) stipulates that any country subject to the requirement that such measures are not applied in a manner that would constitute a means of arbitrary or unjustifiable discrimination could take measures: (b) necessary to protect human animal, or plant life or health; (g) relating to the conservation of exhaustible natural resources if such measures are made effective in conjunction with restrictions on domestic production or consumption

19 *United States Import Prohibition of Certain Shrimp and Shrimp Products,* Report of the Panel, WT/DS58 R, 15 May 1998, paras 278–300

20 Ibid

21 *United States Import Prohibition of Certain Shrimp Products, Appellate* Body Report, WT/DS58/AB/R, adopted 6 November 1998.

22 Ibid, para 185
23 Ibid
24 It is no secret that the 'one' delegation was the US
25 Non-paper by India Agreement to the Committee on Trade and Environment, The Relationship of the TRIPS Agreement to the Development, Access and Transfer of Environmentally Sound Technologies and Products', 20 June 1996
26 This is a term used in some MEAs and is of particular interest to developing countries because it is interpreted by many of them as meaning 'on preferential and non-commercial terms', Indian non-paper, op cit
27 Article 15 emphasized the sovereign rights of states over their natural resources. It further stresses that access to genetic resources is to take place on terms that are environmentally sound and on a mutually agreed basis, and to be subject to prior informed consent of the party providing the resources, unless otherwise determined by that party. Article 16 implies a central role for access to and transfer of technology in the conservation and sustainable use of biodiversity resources. It further stipulates that such transfer of technology shall be provided on favourable terms, including concessional and preferential treatment as mutually agreed
28 Vossenaar, R and Mollerus, R (1996) 'Eco-labelling and International Trade: Possible Effects on Developing Countries', UNCTAD, ITC/233/IB/96-II-TP
29 *Negotiating History of the Coverage of the Agreement on Technical Barriers to Trade with Regard to Labelling Requirements, Voluntary Standards, and Processes and Production Methods Unrelated to Product Characteristics,* WT/CTE/W/10 and G/TBT/W/11, 29 August 1995
30 Report (1996) of the Committee on Trade and Environment, op cit, p233
31 Ibid, p230
32 This should also apply to ISO schemes, especially ISO-14001, because their unbiased formation is highly doubted by many developing countries. Such schemes cannot be forced into the WTO as internationally agreed ones, as long as developing countries in practice remain outside the effective frame of decision-making in such standard-setting bodies and organizations
33 UNCTAD (1995) 'Environmental Policies, Trade and Competitiveness: Conceptual and Empirical Issues', TD/B/WG.6/6, 29 March
34 Ibid
35 Ricupero, Rubens (1997) UNCTAD Workshop, Vietnam, July

11

Solving the Production and Processing Methods (PPMs) Puzzle

Steve Charnovitz

Introduction

One of the most knotty issues of the 'trade and environment' debate is the use of trade measures linked to the production process. These are called PPMs. It is often alleged that the rules of the World Trade Organization (WTO) prohibit PPMs. In response, many environmentalists say this shows that the trading system interferes with ecological protection. Conflicting views about PPMs have been one of the biggest barriers to reducing tensions between the WTO and environmentalists.

PPMs can be appropriate instruments of environmental policy. The World Charter for Nature, approved by the United Nations General Assembly in 1982, calls on governments to 'Establish standards for products and manufacturing processes that may have adverse effects on nature, as well as agreed methodologies for assessing these effects'.[1] Even the WTO Agreement on Agriculture – in prescribing criteria for domestic support measures that remain exempt from reduction – states that payments under environmental programmes must be dependent on specific conditions such as 'conditions related to production methods or inputs'.[2] So long as a country applies PPMs only to domestic producers, no other country will complain.

The conflict occurs because governments seek to apply PPMs to imported products. A government that does so is signalling that it cares about conditions outside of its own borders. Of course, this may not be the only motivation behind a PPM. A government that has imposed a regulatory burden on its domestic producers may seek to impose a similar burden on foreign producers so they do not gain a competitive advantage. PPMs may also constitute disguised protectionism.

The use of externally directed PPMs is an inevitable by-product of globalization and of the increased recognition that activities in one country can impinge on the environment in another. Thus PPMs are not likely to be extinguished. If anything, they will probably be used more in the future than in the past.

Nevertheless, the use of PPMs and the debate surrounding them continue to be a puzzle. Both sides of the debate are convinced that they are in the right, and little common ground has been found in the past several years. A central disagreement is whether rules of the General Agreement on Tariffs and Trade (GATT) prohibit PPMs per se, or whether they are permitted in certain circumstances.

This chapter takes one step toward 'Solving the PPM Puzzle'. The thesis advanced here is that if governments share the same understanding of the legal status of PPMs in the WTO, then it would be easier to move forward with agreements for supervising the use of externally directed PPMs. Right now governments do not share the same legal understanding. This has led to an inside-out debate that cannot possibly go forward. Without a common understanding about the legal status of PPMs it has been impossible even to hold a meaningful dialogue on how to curb PPM excesses.

As will be shown below, a widespread myth exists that the WTO forbids PPMs. If this were true, it would put the WTO at odds with environmental regulation. Happily, it is not true. The WTO does not categorically prohibit the application of a PPM to an imported product. The WTO's Shrimp–Turtle decision of 1998 clarified trade rules on this point.[3] Ironically, turtles remained a flash-point with the public in late 1999 when some of the anti-WTO protestors in Seattle dressed up as turtles.[4]

This chapter proceeds in the following way. Following this introduction, there is an explanation of what PPMs are and an exploration of when they might be justifiable. The taxonomy of PPMs is also set out. Next follows a careful examination of the relevant WTO case-law on the issue of PPMs. Using the taxonomy set out on pp233–235, a Restatement of the WTO Law of PPMs is given. This information is then tied together to show how a correct legal reading may enable new integrative positions that can resolve trade and environment tensions and establish a better framework for preventing inappropriate PPMs. The chapter ends with a brief conclusion.

This chapter only addresses environmental PPMs. The legal and policy conclusions reached here are not necessarily transferable to other kinds of PPMs, such as labour, human rights or animal welfare restrictions. This point is noted at the start to deal with the inevitable complaint that countenancing environmental PPMs would lead to a slippery slope of less justifiable PPMs.

One possible weakness of this chapter is that it is written by a United States national who might be perceived as taking a Northern, big economy perspective. On pp250–254, however, the chapter suggests ways of disciplining and managing PPMs so that they will not undermine the interests of developing countries. As will be noted, many PPMs have been designed and implemented in ways that are unfair to economic actors in developing countries who are struggling to export.

What are PPMs and When Are They Justifiable?

The term PPM means 'processes and production methods'. It originated in the Tokyo Round Agreement on Technical Barriers to Trade and referred to standards aimed at the production method rather than product characteristics.[5] During the 1990s, the connotation of PPM expanded beyond that origin. Now PPM refers to any trade measure or any domestic regulation or tax that distinguishes products by looking beyond perceptible characteristics. For example, a law prohibiting the sale of fish caught using a drift-net is a PPM. By contrast, a law prohibiting the sale of fish below a prescribed size is not a PPM.)

A custom has developed of dividing PPMs into two categories – product-related and non-product-related.[6] Product-related PPMs are used to assure the functionality of the product or to safeguard the consumer who uses the product. The best example is in the area of food safety where regulators rely on process-based sanitary rules so as to avoid having to test the salubrity of the final product (which could destroy its market value). Such PPMs help to assure that consumers receive a product at the anticipated quality level. Thus, they are *related* to the product. By contrast, the non-product-related PPM is designed to achieve a social purpose that may not even matter to the consumer. For example, prohibiting the use of a drift-net to catch fish may achieve a public goal, but has no effect on the fish as such or on the nutritional and gustatory functionality for the consumer. Thus, such PPMs are denoted as non-product-related.[7]

Although this related/unrelated distinction is not stated explicitly in WTO rules, it appears to be followed in two agreements. The Agreement on Technical Barriers to Trade (TBT) defines a covered regulation as a document which 'lays down product characteristics or their *related* processes and production methods ...'.[8] This would seem to suggest that TBT covers the product-related PPMs, and excludes the others.[9] The Agreement on the Application of Sanitary and Phytosanitary Measures (SPS) defines covered measures broadly, including those referring to 'processes and production methods'.[10] But because SPS applies only to measures seeking to protect life or health *within* the territory of the importing country, the typical non-product-related PPM would be excluded by this geographic limitation'.[11] For example, regulations referring to the humane treatment of a farm animal used to make meat for export would be a non-product-related PPM and thus not covered by SPS.

The related/unrelated distinction is popular with commentators, but is flawed. It is used for its simplicity and because that distinction can help to explicate WTO rules. This chapter will use it too. Yet before doing so I want to point out that the distinction is not as clear as it may seem. To start with, the assertion of unrelatedness is too strong. Since any PPM is employed with reference to a product, categorizing it as 'unrelated' or 'non-related' is a misnomer.[12]

A deeper problem is the assumption that consumer preferences can be neatly divided between the functionality of the product itself and broader concerns. To be sure, the blindfolded consumer will not be able to tell whether the fish on the dinner plate was caught using a drift-net. Yet in the real world, consumers do not have blindfolds on. Once a consumer suspects that the fish was caught with a drift-net, it may taste different to her. Indeed, she may not want to eat it at all. It will be simply impossible to convince the sovereign consumer that her concerns about unsustainable fishing practices are not related to the fish itself.)

Another problem with the related/unrelated distinction occurs with regulations that have multiple purposes. For example, a ban on genetically modified food might be used to address the alleged ecological impact on agriculture, or the human health impact of consumption. So the same regulation might be both product-unrelated and product-related.

Still another difficulty is that for some PPMs, the product is the process. The best example is a regulation specifying a minimum amount of recycled content. Such a regulation defines the product and also mandates a production process that uses recycled inputs. Yet recycled newsprint may be indistinguishable from virgin newsprint and will be used in the same way by the consumer.[13] So is this PPM product-related?

Notwithstanding these conceptual dilemmas, this chapter will follow the custom of categorizing PPMs as being either product-related or non-product-related, and will focus on the non-product-related environmental PPMs. We will explore why they are used and what the trade regime should do about them.

Why PPMs are Needed

The popular and simplistic view that the non-product-related PPMs are ill-conceived and should be forbidden by the WTO is unjustified. The drift-net fishing example is just one of a wide array of concerns that consumers may have about the externalities of production. Various terms are used to describe this – like the social profile of a product or its ecological footprint, or its embedded values. And for a consumer to have these concerns may be rational. Consumers in one country can be affected by the production methods used in another. And they may logically ask their governments to take action and to work together to manage this interdependence.

The need for doing so is not a new idea, and certainly not a new idea to the Graduate Institute. As Professor William Rappard explained in 1925: 'Little by little the boundaries of what is held to be solely within the domestic jurisdiction of individual states are receding and the realm of what is governed by international law is expanding'.[14] Rappard's point is that a state's domestic jurisdiction over an issue may not be exclusive and does foreclose a broader community interest and jurisdiction over what transpires within a state. Rappard's insight is especially applicable to environmental policy, where many irritants flow across political borders.

From the beginning of international environmental law, PPMs unrelated to the product have been employed by governments. For example, a 1925 treaty between Mexico and the US set up an International Fisheries Commission to conserve marine life in the Pacific Ocean and committed the parties to refuse the landing of any fish taken in violation of the Commission's regulations'.[15] A 1931 treaty between Denmark and Sweden to protect migratory birds forbade the use of nets for catching seabirds and prohibited the sale or transport of such birds when caught in nets'.[16] Even when they obtain treaties, governments will use trade measures to promote treaty compliance. For instance, in 1950 the US enacted a law prohibiting the import of whale products taken in violation of the Whaling Convention.[17] These examples serve to demonstrate the historical point that governments use PPMs to promote changes in foreign practices inimical to the international interest. Regulatory prescriptions regarding the production process are an inherent part of environmental policy.

Because the environment regime has successfully produced many important treaties during the past three decades, there is sometimes a tendency to believe that any significant transborder environmental problem will engender a treaty that will obviate unilateral PPMs. This was a common theme in the criticism of PPMs throughout the 1990s which assumed that countries like the US were choosing national action over equally available multilateral action. But the reality is that effective, broad-membership treaties are difficult to achieve. Furthermore, treaty-making negotiations sometimes succeed because leading countries have manifested a willingness to act alone if necessary, a process called 'policy-forging' unilateralism by Laurence Boisson de Chazournes.[18]

In their introductory essay to *The Greening of World Trade Issues* in 1992, Kym Anderson and Richard Blackhurst framed the issue properly. They said that 'If all countries participated in all international environmental agreements, there would be nothing more to add'.[19] Yet as Anderson and Blackhurst and the other authors recognized in that seminal volume, many environmental problems are not addressed by treaties with universal participation.[20]

The protection of migratory sea turtles is a good example of a long-recognized problem for which international legislation has been slow in developing. As early as 1924, the Pan-Pacific Food Conservation Conference declared that 'prompt action is necessary to save the marine turtles of various countries from commercial, if not actual extinction ...'.[21] In 1979, the World Conference on Sea Turtle Conservation called for international and national fishery commissions to 'promulgate regulations requiring the use of gear which precludes the capture of sea turtles ...' and for the UN Environment Programme and the Food and Agriculture Organization to make US technology for turtle-safe shrimping available to world fishing fleets.[22] In 1989 the US Congress directed the Secretary of State to initiate negotiations as soon as possible with all foreign governments who have nationals engaged in commercial fishing that may adversely affect sea turtles.[23] Yet it was not until 1996 that governments succeeded in negotiating a treaty on sea turtle conservation, and this did not occur until the US government had embargoed shrimp imports from countries whose vessels were not using turtle excluder devices (TEDs).[24]

Of course, environmental negotiations will not always need the catalyst of trade measures. Most environmental treaties were achieved without any inducement by trade measures. But trade measures can sometimes be useful to address the problem of free-riders. For example, the Montreal Protocol on Ozone prohibits trade in controlled substances with non-parties (unless they are in full compliance with the Protocol's control measures).[25] This provision is considered to be an important factor in eliciting the wide membership of this treaty.[26]

When the first-best option of multilateral cooperation is unavailable, an affected government may consider using a trade PPM to address transborder problems indirectly. Precisely because it is so indirect, such a PPM will be less than fully efficient. But the most efficient measures are only available to a government with prescriptive jurisdiction over the production process. So if the producing country's government fails to use the regulatory instruments at its disposal, other affected country governments may be left with only inefficient or blunt instruments.[27] In deciding whether to use such a PPM, a government may consider not only the immediate impact but also the demonstration effect of acting to address an environmental problem.

The earliest recognition of this quandary in international environmental affairs involved bird-hunting. In the early 20th century, millions of birds were being killed for their plumage. Bird protection groups in the UK sought a ban on feather imports, but were opposed on the grounds that this would not necessarily safeguard birds in other countries. One essayist responded to this claim eloquently in 1909 by saying that:

> ... if the importation into our country is stopped, other Governments may follow suit. Representations to foreign countries are much more likely to be effectual if made by a Government, which has had the courage of its convictions, and has already put its principles into practice.[28]

By 1917, the UK took action to ban the importation of bird plumage. Similar action in other countries cut down traffic in birds and led to changes in fashion that reduced demand for feathers.[29]

Some commentators have suggested that it is illegitimate for a government to apply environmental PPMs to imports because that seeks to force changes in practices occurring in other countries. If this were true, then it would also be true for product-related PPMs, such as food-safety rules that work by eliciting changes in production practices in other countries. The same concern would also apply to simple product standards – for example, motor-car safety requirements that regularly induce foreign manufacturers to adapt their assembly lines.[30] The WTO itself contains 33 pages of textile tariff classifications, some of which create fine categories that may encourage producers to qualify their products for one rather than the other.[31] Since such normal standard-setting cannot possibly be illegitimate, the initial premise must be faulty. The fact that a government regulation in country A will induce businesses in countries B and C to change their behaviour does not render A's regulation illegitimate.

Because environmental PPMs are employed to correct market failure, they can increase global economic efficiency when well designed. But not every country will necessarily be better off. Trade measures taken for environmental purposes can cause adverse economic effects on exporting countries.

Policy-makers using PPMs need to be sensitive to how much burden is being shifted to target countries. It may be useful to regularize the examination of the costs imposed by PPMs to the least developed countries.

Yet one needs to keep this in perspective. The biggest impediment to market access for developing countries are *undisguised* protectionist measures in industrial and other developing countries. The complaints about PPMs are highly disproportionate to their relative adverse impact on developing countries, in comparison to all of the other practices that constrain their exports. Indeed, it is a sad irony that developing country governments devote so much time to complaining about environmental PPMs (which provide some social benefits through the correction of market failure) while giving less attention to commercial barriers in agriculture and textiles (which do not correct market failure).

Of course, any PPM – product related or not – should be subjected to scrutiny by the WTO to see if it is protectionist.[32] This inquiry needs to be carried out in a sophisticated manner. The fact that domestic producers may want foreign producers to be subject to harmonized environmental PPMs may be a warning signal of protectionist intent, but is not itself conclusive. The key question to ask is whether there is an environmental rationale for the importing country government to be concerned about production practices in the exporting country. If not, then the effort to prescribe equivalent PPMs in other countries in order to level the playing-field is probably protectionist. In many instances, however, the importing country will have an environmental reason to want other countries to take comparable action to safeguard a shared natural resource.

Let me summarize this chapter so far. Governments use environmental PPMs in treaties and national law in order to achieve conservation or anti-pollution goals.[33] PPMs aimed at foreign governments are indirect and thus will always be inefficient, but resort to such PPMs may be better than doing nothing in the absence of multilateral cooperation. It is wrong to assort that governments should mind their own business environmentally. It is also wrong to assert that PPMs are illegitimate because they may induce changes in foreign production practices. Even the simplest product standard can do that.

Generalizing about non-product-related PPMs is challenging because they come in many different forms. The next section will introduce a taxonomy that is the key to solving the PPM puzzle. The debate on PPMs has made little progress in ten years because it jumbles up too many different kinds of measures.

A Taxonomy of PPMs

PPMs can be divided into two main types – (1) the How Produced standard and (2) the (Foreign) Government Policy standard. The How Produced standard looks at the processing method used in making the product. For example, a law banning the importation of drift-net-caught fish is a how-produced PPM.[34] The Government Policy standard looks at the foreign government's laws or regulations regarding the production process or at its enforcement of them. For example, a law banning the importation of fish from any country that permits drift-net fishing is a government policy PPM.[35] Both types of PPM train on the methods used for mining, harvesting, manufacturing, packaging and transporting.[36]

In using the term 'standard', I mean its everyday connotation of an instruction that is binding. Thus, the usage here differs from the definition of 'standard' in the TBT Agreement which refers to product characteristics or product-related PPMs with which compliance is not mandatory.[37] By contrast, in the TBT definitions, a regulation is 'mandatory'. I am not using the term 'regulation' for two reasons. First, while some environmental PPMs are regulations applied equally to foreign and domestic products, many PPMs are import bans that do not come within the scope of TBT. Second, the term 'regulation' may connote a jurisdiction to prescribe or mandate, but this does not fit PPMs which set conditions for entry or sale which the exporter may decide to meet or not to meet. If it does not meet them, no disadvantage is incurred other than an inability to sell to the PPM-applying country.

A standard prescribing *where* a product must be produced is not a PPM. For example, a US law that bans fish (and all other) imports from Cuba is an embargo rather than a PPM. Sometimes import laws blend 'where' and 'how' standards.

A where-produced standard can be disguised as a how-produced standard by using origin-neutral language that pertains only to a particular country. Consider, for example, the most well-known PPM before the tuna–dolphin case. That was the German law of 1904 providing a tariff reduction for 'large dappled mountain cattle or brown cattle reared at a spot at least 300 meters above sea level and which have at least one month's grazing each year at a spot at least 800 meters above sea level'.[38] That is a how-produced PPM that is non-product related. It is a classic example of how origin-based protectionism can be disguised as a how-produced standard.[39]

A standard prescribing eligible producers or importers can be viewed as a subset of a how-produced standard, but may not always be classified as a PPM. 'For example, a law that bans fish imports from a producer owned by a pariah government can be considered an import control rather than a PPM. Nevertheless, in setting out a PPM taxonomy, we will need to take account of the Producer Characteristics standard. This is so for two reasons: First, in prescribing attributes of a producer or its contractual relations, the importing government can seek to accomplish policy purposes similar to what might be sought using a how-produced or a government-policy PPM. Second, much of the trade law jurisprudence that seems applicable to PPMs involved measures based on producer characteristics. So the producer characteristics standard will be treated here as a PPM.

Although this chapter looks at environmental PPMs, one should note that the suggested taxonomy applies to other PPMs too. For example, in July 2000, the World Diamond Congress took action to address the problem of 'conflict diamonds' which fund terrorism in Africa.[40] The Congress recommended that governments enact laws to prohibit imports of diamonds from countries that have not enacted red-line legislation which requires that diamond imports be sealed and registered. This is a standard based on the foreign government's policy, not on how a particular diamond was mined or on whether it is being mined or sold by rebel forces.

In presenting this PPM taxonomy. I am suggesting that form matters. My thesis is that the how-produced standard is preferable to the (foreign) government policy or producer characteristics standards. In the following section, I will show that the how-produced standard may be more WTO-consistent than the other two. At this time, no GATT or WTO dispute panel has ruled against a how-produced standard utilized for an environmental purpose.

The government policy standard has numerous faults. First, it is coercive in that it dictates environmental policies to foreign governments. Second, it penalizes private economic actors who may be doing everything right environmentally, but whose exports remain blocked because its environmental behaviour is not mandated by law. Third, the government policy standard is unfair because it is more available to large than to small countries. Fourth, the government policy standard can engender irreconcilable conflicts because two importing countries might impose inconsistent policy standards on an exporting country government.

By contrast, the how-produced standard operates similarly to a simple product standard. It does not coerce governments.[41] It does not penalize economic actors who are willing to assure that their exports meet the importing country standard. Small countries can use such standards because they will almost always find willing suppliers. So the how-produced standard will never cause as much trade tension as the government policy standard does. Thus, if environmental PPMs are needed, they should be written in the how-produced form rather than the government policy form.

The how-produced standard can be a proportionate and measured response to a situation where importing from the other country can exacerbate an environmental problem. When a government allows the importation of fish caught with a drift-net, the importing country signals that such odious practices are acceptable for future trade, and so exporting country producers may continue to use them. But when a country bans such fish, it signals its objections to that method of production and makes it less profitable. Private economic actors will then have a new incentive to improve their environmental behaviour.

To be sure, a how-produced PPM may be less effective than a government policy standard, and that could be unsatisfactory to environmental regulators.[42] But this lower effectiveness needs to be balanced against the disadvantages to environmental policy of being heavy-handed. It is one thing for country A to specify a PPM for the fish that it imports from country B. It is quite another for country A to say that it will not import any fish from B unless *all* of B's fish are caught in the prescribed way. Environmentalists must not forget that any PPM applied to imports is an indirect measure and is thus inferior to attaining appropriate regulations in other countries. Treating country B unfairly may make it harder to convince B's government and stakeholders to cooperate on the environment.

In summary, this section has explained why PPMs are needed and presents a taxonomy of them. The government policy standard is contrasted with the how-produced standard and the latter is shown to be a more reasonable approach. In the next section, we will look at how international trade law treats different types of PPM.

The WTO Law of PPMs

This section will analyse how WTO rules supervise PPMs applied to imports. The focus will be on non-product-related environmental PPMs. Thus, it will not be necessary to look at the SPS and TBT agreements. Instead, the main focus will be on the GATT.

Many commentators have contended that the GATT does not permit importing governments to make distinctions based on the production process. For example:

> The most fundamental problem with Article XX is that it makes the legitimacy of environmental regulations turn on what is produced, not how it is produced. Specifically, GATTs existing rules focus on the concept of 'like products', barring environmental discrimination against imports that are physically similar to domestic products, no matter how damaging the production process used to make or obtain the good.[43]

> [GATT] Article XX only examines what is produced and not how it is produced, without explicitly mentioning this fact. Trade cannot be restricted on the basis of different environmental PPMs.[44]

In other words, PPM requirements are permissible under the GATT law basically to absorb 'consumption externalities' rather than 'production externalities': the latter should be dealt with by the producing, exporting country.[45] (Shinya Murase, Academy of International Law, 1995)

The WTO agreements are interpreted to say two important things. First, trade restrictions cannot be imposed on a product purely because of the way it has been produced. Second, one country cannot reach out beyond its own territory to impose its standards on another country.[46]

The trade community has emphasized repeatedly that discrimination between 'like' products based solely on method of production should find no place in trade rules.[47] (Sir Leon Brittan, European Commission, 1998)

. . . [T]he WTO rules generally prohibit distinguishing among non-product-related Production and Processing Methods (PPMs).[48]

One of the basic principles of the WTO is that member countries may not discriminate between 'like products'. This has hitherto normally been interpreted as preventing discrimination between goods on the basis of how they are produced.... To allow discrimination on the basis of production and processing methods, there would have to be a reinterpretation of the crucial term 'like product'.[49]

As part of its core non-discrimination principles, the GATT requires that 'like products' be treated the same by the importing country and distinctions based on 'production processes or methods' are generally prohibited.[50]

And, we noted, WTO law does not allow countries to discriminate against like products, whatever their different environmental impacts. This prohibition makes little environmental sense. The way a product is produced is one of the three central questions for an environmental manager....[51]

Yet is all that really true? Certainly, the text of the GATT does not forbid national regulations, taxes, tariffs or import bans based on the production process. On the contrary, the GATT allows governments to discriminate against imports made in prohibited ways. Thus, governments can take customs action against an imported article made using a subsidy or whose producer prices it too low, or whose producer does not have the requisite intellectual property licenses.[52] The consumer may not agree with his government that these methods of production should be attacked with trade measures. The subsidized, low-cost imported fish will taste as good as the higher cost domestic fish. But the GATT permits governments to impose PPMs of this sort anyway, even though the behaviour being complained about has no effect on the product as such.

Even without explicit language, however, GATT rules may still prohibit environmental PPMs. As noted above, many commentators take this position. Over the years, the GATT Secretariat has taken both sides of the debate. When it first addressed the matter in 1971, the Secretariat explained that:

> A *shared resource*, such as a lake or the atmosphere, which is being polluted by foreign producers may give rise to restrictions on trade in the *product of that process* justifiable on grounds of the public interest in the importing country of control over a *process* carried out in an adjacent or nearby country.[53]

Twenty years later, after environmental concerns grew in importance, the GATT Secretariat shifted its position. Now it asserted that 'In principle it is not possible under GATT's rules to make access to one's own market dependent on the domestic environmental policies or practices of the exporting country'.[54] This negative view was reaffirmed by WTO Director General Renato Ruggiero in 1997 who slated in a speech that:

> What a country cannot do under WTO rules, however, is apply trade restrictions to attempt to change the processes and production methods – or other policies – of its trading partners. Why? Basically because the issue of production and process methods lies within the sovereign jurisdiction of each country'.[55]

Three years later, the WTO Secretariat continues to insist that PPMs violate trade rules.[56]

The WTO Secretariat's characterization of the rule against PPMs is similar to what many trade law commentators contend. The quotations above were selected to show how widespread the view is that PPMs are illegal under trade rules.[57] This list is balanced in containing commentators who favour the WTO's anti-PPM stance and those who oppose it.[58]

Fortunately, these legal assessments are wrong. The GATT case-law on PPMs is nuanced and does not point to a prohibition on the use of such environmental instruments. This will be explicated below.

The structure of GATT obligations is as follows: A PPM could be inconsistent with GATT Article I (most favoured nation or MFN) or GATT Article III (national treatment) or GATT Article XI (elimination of quantitative restrictions). If so, it would be reviewed under the General Exceptions in Article XX when there is an applicable exception.

The relationship between the GATT disciplines and Article XX is subject to different interpretations. One school of thought is that GATT Articles I, III, and XI impose *disciplines* on governments and that GATT Article XX provides exceptions to those disciplines. Whether a national measure is in conformity with the GATT can only be determined by looking at *both* the disciplines and the exceptions in tandem. Viewed in this way, when there is a measure that fails to provide national treatment, it should not be called a GATT violation merely because it violates Article I; a determination of GATT status requires a review of Article XX too. As Richard J McLaughlin has noted with respect to Article XX, governments 'have an expectation that they will be able to restrict trade in order to conserve exhaustible natural resources or to protect the health of humans, animals, and plants'.[59]

The other school of thought is that GATT Articles I, III and XI grant (or define) a *right* of a WTO member country to have the exports of its nationals accepted by other WTO member countries. Viewed in this way, the Article I, III or XI 'rights' of the exporter will need to be weighed against the Article XX rights of the importer to rely upon one of the listed exceptions. Acting inconsistently with Article I constitutes a GATT violation, but it might be excused by Article XX.

The WTO Appellate Body leans toward the latter school. In the US Gasoline case, the Appellate Body held that 'If those [Article XX] exceptions are not to be abused or misused, in other words, the measures falling within the particular exceptions must be applied reasonably, with due regard both to the legal duties of the parties claiming the exception and the legal rights of the other parties concerned'.[60] In the US Shrimp–Turtle case, the Appellate Body stated that

> ...WTO Members need to maintain a balance of rights and obligations between the right of a Member to invoke one or another of the exceptions in Article XX, specified in paragraphs (a) to (j), on the one hand, and the substantive rights of the other Members under the GATT 1994, on the other hand. Exercise by one Member of this right to invoke an exception, such as Article XX(g), if abused or misused, will, to that extent, erode or render naught the substantive treaty rights, in, for example, Article XI:1, of other Members.[61]

The Appellate Body did not explain why Article XI:1 provides a 'substantive' right, while Article XX does not. More fundamentally, the Appellate Body does not explain how Article XI:1 confers a 'right' on any government. In the Japan Alcoholic Beverages case, the Appellate Body alludes to the 'sheltering scope' of Article III, which suggests that Article III shelters measures from GATT review by conferring a right to undertake them.[62] But Article III is not a shield; it is a sword against discrimination.

By using the language of rights, the Appellate Body muddles GATT law and weakens the General Exceptions in Article XX. If the exporting country has a WTO 'right' to have its exports accepted, then there will be tendency to interpret Article XX narrowly and begrudgingly so as not to interfere with that putative right. In characterizing Article XI as substantive, while implying that Article XX is not, the Appellate Body positions them at different levels and makes it easier for panels to forget the overriding injunction of Article XX which provides that subject to certain requirements, 'nothing' in the GATT shall be construed to prevent the adoption or enforcement of listed measures. An exporting country that faces an environmental trade measure may feel more justified in challenging the measure if it believes that GATT Articles I, III and XI are detachable from Article XX.

A recent decision by a WTO arbitral panel, in the Brazil Aircraft case, continues down the path of minimizing Article XX. In that case, the panel had to interpret item (k) of Annex I to the Agreement on Subsidies and Countervailing Measures (SCM). To simplify item (k), it contains a rule and an exception. Looking at item (k), the panel said that 'A possible *justification* under item (k), like a justification under Article XX of the GATT 1994, does not change the legal nature of the measure'.[63] While this may be a good analysis for the SCM Agreement, it is a troublesome analysis for the GATT because a justification of a measure under Article XX does change its legal nature. Thus, an environmental measure that violates GATT Article III, and might therefore violate the GATT, will have its legal nature transformed if it can be justified under Article XX. Unfortunately, under current WTO jurisprudence, the implications of Article XX can be characterized differently. It is said that if an environmental trade measure violates Article III, it violates the rights of the exporting country, and perhaps even violates the GATT, but is nevertheless tolerated because of Article XX.

This issue of orientation is noted at the start because it may facilitate understanding of the PPM jurisprudence as presented below. The first section will consider GATT Article I; the next section Article III and the last section Article XX. A PPM-based import ban will violate Article XI – just as a non-PPM import ban would – and so the Article XI case-law has not directly addressed PPMs.

Article I

GATT Article I:1 (General Most-Favoured-Nation (MFN) Treatment) provides that with respect to customs duties, taxes, regulations and import rules, any advantage or favour granted by a Party to any product shall be accorded immediately and unconditionally to the 'like' product of all other parties. What this means is that a WTO member government cannot discriminate by treating the product of one WTO member country better than the like product of another member country. The decision as to whether two products are 'like' will often be pivotal since Article I does not prohibit differential treatment of unlike products.

One of the earliest GATT decisions considered whether a PPM violated Article I. The case was 'Belgian Family Allowances' in 1952.[64] At issue was a Belgian tax on imports purchased by local government bodies. The 7.5 per cent tax was used for the family allowance programme in Belgium which was otherwise funded by employer taxes. Not every country was subject to the import tax, however. An exemption was available for countries that imposed an employer tax for family allowances similar to Belgium's tax. The two plaintiff governments, Denmark and Norway, complained that the tax violated Article I because an exemption had been given to Sweden but not to them. The panel sided with the plaintiffs but on broader grounds. Since Belgium had granted the exemption to some GATT parties, the panel reasoned, Article I required that it grant the exemption to every other GATT party *regardless* of whether a government had a family allowance system similar to that of Belgium.[65]

To reframe this case, Belgium was levying a PPM tax on other countries based on a (foreign) government policy standard. In the panel's view, the nature of an exporting country's family allowance programme was 'irrelevant', to GATT Article I, which did not permit discrimination based on that factor.[66] Because Belgium did not claim an Article XX exception, the case ended with the finding of the MFN violation.

No other Article I cases involving non-product-related PPMs ensued before the advent of the WTO. In a 1981 decision, a panel considered a product-related PPM and found that the distinction was not enough to prevent two similar products from being deemed 'like'.[67] At issue was whether different methods of cultivation and processing of coffee beans justified different tariff classifications for various types of unroasted coffee. The panel said no.

The WTO has considered two GATT Article I disputes involving PPMs, both about motor cars. In the Indonesia Automobile case, Japan, the European Communities and the US complained that Indonesia applied higher customs duties and sales taxes to imported products when the exporting manufacturer did not utilize a sufficient amount of Indonesian parts and personnel.[68] In the Canada case, Japan and the European Communities complained that Canada provided an import duty exemption for an eligible corporation conditioned on its having a manufacturing presence and sufficient value-added in Canada.[69] In both cases, the panels found a violation of GATT Article I. No Article XX exception was invoked.

In the Indonesia automobile decision, the panel held that under Article I, an advantage 'cannot be made conditional on any criteria that is not related to the imported product itself'.[70] Elaborating on this point, the panel stated that 'In the GATT/WTO, the right of Members cannot be made dependent upon, conditional on or even affected by any private contractual obligations in place'.[71] To reframe this case Indonesia was levying a PPM lax and tariff based on producer characteristics and domestic content, and that was deemed an MPN violation.

In the Canada automotive decision, the panel held that Article I was being violated, but adopted a more nuanced interpretation of the Article I discipline. Specifically, the panel said: 'We therefore do not believe that ... Article I:1 must be interpreted to mean that making an advantage conditional on criteria not related to the imported product itself is per se inconsistent with Article 1:1, irrespective of whether and how such criteria relate to the origin of the imported products'.[72] In other words, the panel suggested that truly origin-neutral conditions might be permissible under Article I. The panel took care to distinguish the holdings in the Belgian Family Allowances and Indonesia automobile cases, both of which it viewed as relating to origin-based discrimination. In the instant case, the panel concluded that the conditions were not origin-neutral, so Article I was being violated. On appeal, the Appellate Body upheld the panel's finding of the Article I:1 violation and did not address the panel's interpretive point.

Here is a summary of the case-law showing how GATT Article I addresses PPMs. A government policy standard violates MFN because it is origin-contingent.[73] A producer characteristics standard was held a violation in the Indonesia and Canada automobile cases, but the latter panel suggested that PPMs are not per se violations of MFN. No how-produced standard has yet been reviewed under Article I.

Article III

GATT Article III (National Treatment) contains disciplines for domestic taxation and regulation. Under Article III:2, imported products shall not be subject to taxes of any kind in excess of those applied to like domestic products. Under Article III:4, imported products shall be accorded treatment no less favourable than that accorded to like products of national origin. In addition, Article III:1 provides that internal taxes and regulations affecting the internal sale, transportation, distribution or use of products, 'and internal quantitative regulations requiring the mixture, processing or use of products in specified amounts or proportions, should not be applied to imported or domestic products so as to afford protection to domestic production'.

It is sometimes alleged that the drafters of Article III did not contemplate PPMs or, if they did intended to disallow them. Yet the text of Article III suggests otherwise. As noted above, Article III:1 addresses regulations requiring the mixture or processing of products, but states only that it should not afford protection to domestic production. The implication is that mixture or processing regulations that do not afford protection to domestic production are not prohibited. This interpretation is confirmed by looking at other provisions in Article III that address mixture and processing. For example, Article III:5 prohibits mixture/processing regulations linked to domestic content. Article III:7 prohibits mixture/processing regulations that seek to allocate proportions among external sources of supply. If all mixture/processing regulations were prohibited, then why would Article III have three prohibitions aimed at particular kinds of mixture/processing regulations?

Suppose that a government had a regulation prohibiting the sale of lumber unless at least 95 per cent of its weight came from sustainably harvested timber. This how-produced PPM would specify a minimum proportion for processing. Written in this way, such a measure would not seem a per se violation of Article III.

Nevertheless, as shown below, panels adjudicating Article III have objected to PPMs, in the few cases where PPMs were reviewed. Under the GATT, there were four cases, all against the US. Under the WTO, only two cases have arisen, but other decisions bear on how Article III will be applied to PPMs.

The earliest GATT decision came in 1991 and is known as the first Tuna–Dolphin decision.[74] At that time, the US imposed an import ban on tuna from countries that did not have a regulatory regime to protect dolphins comparable to the US regime. Mexico, one of the embargoed countries, complained that this law violated Article III. The US import ban was a government policy standard that looked at Mexico's laws. (Indeed, it went further than that by requiring Mexico to keep its overall dolphin-killing rate no more than 25 per cent higher than the US' annual rate.)[75] The panel ruled that Article III 'covers only those measures that are applied to the product as such', and so the US measure regarding dolphins did not fit Article III because this PPM 'could not possibly affect tuna as a product'.[76] The panel went on to say that if the US measure were covered by Article III, it would constitute a violation because the US treatment to Mexico cannot be predicated on whether or not the incidental taking of dolphins by Mexican vessels corresponds to that of US-flag vessels. This judgement was not adopted by the GATT Council and thus has no legal status. When the matter was debated before the Council in 1992, the European Commission argued that adoption of the Tuna–Dolphin report was 'a necessary first step in clarifying the relationship between environmental policies and GATT provisions'.[77]

In the next case – US Alcoholic Beverages – Canada complained about an excise tax credit in the state of Minnesota for small beer breweries whether domestic or foreign.[78] The panel held that beer from micro-breweries is a like product to beer from large breweries, and so a tax that distinguished the two violated Article III:2.[79] The tax credit was a producer characteristics PPM.

The second Tuna–Dolphin decision came next and it too was not adopted. Its holding was similar to that of the first Tuna–Dolphin panel. The second panel held that Article III did not apply to laws 'related to policies or practices that could not affect the product as such ...'[80]

The last pre-WTO decision was US Automobile Taxes and it too was not adopted. The European Communities lodged several complaints, one of which was that the US Corporate Average Fuel Economy (CAFE) regulation violated Article III:4 because it was based on a fleet averaging method that treated domestic and foreign-made cars separately. The panel ruled that 'Article III:4 does not permit treatment of an imported product less favourable than that accorded to a like domestic product, based on factors not directly relating to the product as such'.[81] Thus, fleet averaging itself violated Article III because it was 'based on the ownership or control relationship of the car manufacturer' and therefore 'did not relate to cars as products'.[82]

The first WTO case, US Gasoline, considered a PPM regulation for petrol pollution. Venezuela and Brazil complained that the regulation (which required reduction from a pollution base-line) was discriminatory because it assigned foreign producers a standard base-line while giving domestic refiners an individual base-line. Because foreign petrol was generally higher polluting, the assignment of a standard base-line required some of those producers to undertake greater reductions in polluting ingredients than if they had been given an individual base-line. The US regulation was undoubtedly a violation of national treatment but in so finding, the panel issued a broad decision that built on the US Alcoholic Beverages and Automobile Taxes decisions. Noting that the US regulation had been defended on the ground that data from foreign producers was unverifiable, the panel held that Article III:4 'does not allow less favourable treatment dependent on the characteristics of the producer and the nature of the data held by it'.[83] This holding was not appealed.

The second WTO case was Indonesia Automobile. The panel found an Article III:2 violation because the tax measures were based on nationality and origin 'or other factors not related to the product itself ....'[84] This was similar to the panel's ruling on Article I.

The Japan Alcoholic Beverages panel did not consider a PPM, but in rejecting the so-called 'aim-and-effect' test, its holding would seem to implicate all PPMs as GATT Article III violations. Aim-and-effect was a treaty interpretation developed in GATT case-law and commentary during the 1990s which sought to define product likeness in a way that prevented Article III from unnecessarily infringing on national regulatory autonomy'.[85] As the US Alcoholic Beverages panel explained in 1992, 'once products are designated like products, a regulatory product distinction, eg, for standardization or environmental purposes, becomes inconsistent with Article III even if the regulation is not *applied so as to afford protection to domestic production*'.[86] Nevertheless, the first time this test was invoked in the WTO, in Japan Alcoholic Beverages, the panel rejected such a test in Article III:2 in favour of an analysis of the physical and functional likeness of two products.[87] The Appellate Body upheld the panel on this point and in a later decision (Bananas) stated its rejection of 'aim-and-effect' explicitly.[88] Although it was not propounded as a way to defend PPMs, the aim-and-effect test could have provided a doctrinal basis for distinguishing two otherwise like products that differ only in their conformity to the PPM. Without the aim-and-effect test, a PPM-compliant domestic product may be easily deemed a 'like' product to a PPM-non-compliant imported product. If so, an Article III violation will ensue when government action denies the imported product an equal opportunity to be sold in the domestic market.

The most recent Article III decision came in the European Communities Asbestos case. In response to a complaint by Canada, the panel found that a French ban on asbestos violated Article III:4 because a Canadian asbestos fibre was a like product to non-imported substitute fibre that was permitted. In a surprising decision, the panel held that the risk to human health or life could not be a factor in determining whether two products were 'like' under Article III because that would allow a government 'to avoid the obligations in Article XX ....'[89] This was not a PPM decision: the French ban was based on the dangers of the product to the user. But if this new interpretation is upheld, it would make it even harder to defend a PPM against an Article III challenge.

In summary, the textual ambiguities in Article III are being resolved in a way that is unfavourable to PPMs. A producer characteristics standard was held a violation in US Alcoholic Beverages, US Automobile Taxes, US Gasoline and Indonesia Automobile. The first Tuna–Dolphin decision suggested that a government policy standard would violate Article III if Article III were applicable. No how-produced standard has been tested, but WTO jurisprudence points to the likelihood that such a standard would be deemed a national treatment violation.

It is interesting to note that in a recent article, Robert Howse and Donald Regan contend that the text of Article III provides no support for the product/process distinction or the proposition that Article III prohibits all process measures. The authors contrast origin-neutral process measures (which would include how-produced standards as defined here) with country-based measures (which would include government policy standards as defined here) and say that while Article III prohibits the country-based measure, it does not prohibit origin-neutral measures that distinguish products according to their production process. In their view, WTO panels remain free in applying Article III to consider the aim and effect of a regulatory PPM in order to determine the legality of differential treatment of PPM-compliant and non-compliant products.[90]

Article XX

GAIT Article XX lists ten exceptions to GATT disciplines. These exceptions are '[s]ubject to the requirement that such measures are not applied in a manner that would constitute a means of arbitrary or unjustifiable discrimination between countries where the same conditions prevail, or a disguised restriction on international trade....' This requirement is now known as the 'chapeau'. Two of the exceptions would be available for environmental measures – paragraph (b) for measures 'necessary to protect human, animal or plant life or health', and paragraph (g) for measures 'relating to the conservation of exhaustible natural resources if such measures are made effective in conjunction with restrictions on domestic production or consumption'. Article XX will be central to an analysis of PPMs because, as discussed above, many PPMs will violate Articles I, III, or XI.

The first Article XX PPM case was United States Automotive Spring Assemblies in 1983. In this case, Canada complained about an import exclusion order against certain automotive spring assemblies produced in violation of a valid US patent and without a licence from the patent holder. The panel ruled that the exclusion order was necessary under the Article XX(d) exception and met the terms of the chapeau.[91]

In the Tuna–Dolphin cases, two panels held that the PPM-based import bans did not qualify for an Article XX exception. The first decision addressed the import ban of tuna from Mexico. The panel asserted that Article XX(b) did not cover such an 'extra-jurisdictional' measure to safeguard dolphins outside the US. According to the panel, if Article XX(b) were applied in this way, the importing government 'could unilaterally determine the life or health protection policies from which other contracting parties could not deviate without jeopardizing their *rights* under the General Agreement'.[92] The second decision focused on the intermediary import ban of tuna from certain European countries. This tuna was being barred because the implicated governments had not prohibited the importation of tuna from Mexico (or other countries targeted by the US embargo). As the US import ban was predicated on the policy of the European tuna-consuming countries, it was a government policy standard. Reviewing the import ban under Article XX(g), the panel pointed out that tuna imports were prohibited 'whether or not the particular tuna was harvested in a manner that harmed or could harm dolphins ....'[93] The primary embargo had the same fault, said the panel, and both types of embargo 'were taken so as to force other countries to change their policies with respect to persons or things within their own jurisdiction', and therefore did not meet the terms of XX(g)'.[94] The panel declined to interpret Article XX(g) in a way that would permit such a measure because 'the balance of rights and obligations among contracting parties, in particular the right of access to market, would be seriously impaired'.[95] Note that the panel assumes that the Netherlands Antilles has a 'right of access' to the US market that has independent valence in interpreting Article XX.

The second panel seemed to be trying to correct the overreaching by the first panel, but the second decision was too ambiguous to be a guidepost. One leading GATT commentator, Robert Hudec, read the decision as saying that the US law was a GATT violation because of its coercive design, but that a rewritten law barring imports of fish caught by dolphin-unsafe methods could be justified under Article XX'.[96] Yet other commentators read the decision as prohibiting all PPMs directed at foreign countries.

In US Automobile faxes, the panel held that the fleet averaging method could meet the requirements in paragraph (g) of Article XX.[97] As noted above, fleet averaging violated GATT's national treatment discipline because the US regulation was dependent on factors not directly relating to the product as a product. But Article XX(g) does not preclude such factors, according to the panel. Despite this favourable holding, the panel ruled that another feature of the US measure – separate foreign fleet accounting – prevented the US measure from qualifying under Article XX(g). To reframe this holding, the panel ruled that Article XX could potentially permit a producer characteristics PPM. The GATT Council did not adopt this decision, however.

In the US Gasoline case, the Appellate Body concluded that the US base-line rule fit within the terms of paragraph (g), but found that its application violated the Article XX chapeau'.[98] This was the first adopted decision that an environmental PPM could fit within one of the Article XX exceptions. The measure at issue was a producer characteristics PPM. The marketability of the petrol depended on the foreign or domestic status of the producer and on achieving reductions from an assigned base-line. (It should be noted that none of the parties of the dispute characterized this measure as a PPM.)

In complying with the WTO decision, the US government changed its regulation to allow foreign refiners the option of applying for and using an individual base-line.[99] The ability to sell petrol would still be based on producer characteristics, but the discrimination against foreign producers was removed. To assure compliance, foreign refiners had to agree to a set of enforcement measures, including unannounced inspections by US regulators. Under the new regulation, the ability to sell a particular gallon of petrol depends on whether the producer has met its base-line requirements. Thus, petrol from one producer could be barred while identical petrol from another producer is permitted.

The US Shrimp–Turtle case involved an import ban on shrimp from countries that did not have a turtle conservation regime comparable to that of the US.[100] The US law is complex: it blends a how-produced standard, a government policy standard and a review of the actual performance of the foreign shrimping fleet in safeguarding turtles. At the time of the case, most of the complaining countries – India, Malaysia, Pakistan and Thailand – were under a shrimp embargo linked to a requirement that they enforce comprehensive requirements regarding the use of turtle-excluder devices by their fishing vessels. Thus, in this adjudication, the US measure was framed as a government policy standard.

The WTO panel held that the import ban could not be justified by Article XX. In particular, the panel declared that the scope of Article XX did not extend to measures that condition market access on the adoption of particular conservation policies by the government seeking access for its nationals.[101] The panel was troubled by the fact that the US government was requiring the plaintiff countries to adopt prescribed policies for *all* production, not just for exports to the US. The panel found this situation unacceptable because if the US did this, so could other countries, and if the unilateral requirements were inconsistent, 'it would be impossible for exporting Members to comply at the same time with multiple conflicting policy requirements'.[102] The panel contrasted such a regulation with a ban on the import of products made by prison labour. That ban applies only to the products of such labour, not to the exporting country's *policy* on prison labour. In summarizing its holding, the panel explained that its decision did 'not imply that recourse to unilateral measures is always excluded, particularly after serious attempts have been made to negotiate....'[103]

The Appellate Body upheld the panel's conclusion that the US import ban violated the GATT, but modified the reasoning substantially. Unlike the panel, the Appellate Body found that the import ban did fit within the scope of Article XX and was provisionally justified by XX(g).[104] Specifically, the Appellate Body stated that the 'means and ends relationship' of banning shrimp imports and protecting turtles was 'close and real' and the trade measure used was 'not disproportionately wide in its scope and reach ....'[105] Nevertheless, the US measure was flawed, the Appellate Body said, because the measure failed to meet the requirements of the Article XX chapeau. One major flaw was that the US certification process 'does not allow for any inquiry into the appropriateness of the regulatory programme for the conditions prevailing in those exporting countries'.[106] Other flaws included inflexibility in administrative determinations and no opportunity for the embargoed country government to appeal.[107] To reframe the point, the Appellate Body seems to be saying that it is not necessarily a GATT violation to impose a government policy PPM on exporting countries, but in doing so the regulator must be sensitive to the conditions in each country, and the administrative process must meet minimum standards of transparency and procedural fairness. This result does not conflict with Belgian Family Allowances, which was not an Article XX case. But the new ruling shows a more sophisticated consideration of discrimination not present in the Belgian Family Allowances judgement.

The Appellate Body also noted critically that the US was not a party to the Law of the Sea treaty or to the Convention on Biological Diversity, and thus was not making use of the international cooperative mechanisms that did exist.[108] Furthermore, according to the Appellate Body, the US government had not sought to negotiate a treaty with affected countries before imposing the import embargo.[109] The US government admitted this to some extent, but pointed out that its subsequent efforts to negotiate a treaty were spurned by the Asian country plaintiffs.

Although the Appellate Body did not say that the shrimp–turtle PPM was GATT-legal, the inferences in the decision are affirmative for PPMs. The lower panel had asserted that this kind of PPM fell outside the scope of Article XX and the Appellate Body reversed that conclusion. Then the Appellate Body found that the import ban fitted paragraph (g), but failed to comply with the chapeau. Had the Appellate Body believed that the GATT prohibits non-product-related PPMs. then it could have said that in one sentence. The fact that the Appellate Body reviewed the PPM carefully and gave specific criticisms of how the US government was applying the law demonstrates that PPMs are potentially justifiable under Article XX. Although not all PPMs will be covered by a GATT General Exception, environmental PPMs will be.

In complying with the WTO decision, the US Department of State revised its regulation to provide more due process to foreign governments and to permit shrimp imports so long as the shrimp were harvested by vessels using turtle excluder devices.[110] In other words, the US government shifted the implementation of the statute from a government policy standard to a how-produced standard. Although this shift may not have been proper under US law,[111] the new policy remains in force. In autumn 2000, Malaysia asked the WTO Dispute Settlement Body to consider whether the US compliance meets WTO requirements.[112]

The Asbestos case does not involve a PPM, but it was the first ruling by a WTO panel that an import measure could be justified by Article XX(b). In applying this exception, the panel held that a health measure could be deemed 'necessary' under this provision if there were not other measures consistent (or less inconsistent) with the GATT that could achieve the defendant government's health policy objectives.[113] This clarified that the application of Article XX(b) does not utilize a least-trade-restrictive test.[114] This arduous test had been one of the recommendations of Agenda 21 which states that 'Should trade policy measures he found necessary for the enforcement of environmental policies, certain principles and rules should apply ... [including] the principle that the trade measure chosen should he the least trade-restrictive necessary to achieve the objectives.[115] So in this respect, the WTO is greener than Agenda 21.

In summary, the Article XX exceptions apply to PPMs. Indeed, no adopted GATT or WTO decision has suggested that PPMs are outside the scope of Article XX. The decisions in the WTO Gasoline and Shrimp–Turtle cases against the environmental measure did not turn on its PPM status. Although the Shrimp–Turtle panel criticized the coerciveness of a government policy standard, the Appellate Body in Shrimp–Turtle did not perceive this regulatory approach as legally fatal. None of the environmental cases has involved a how-produced standard. The first review of such a standard may occur in the impending examination of US compliance in the Shrimp–Turtle dispute.

Restatement of the Law

For environmental PPMs, the most important WTO law is found in GATT Article XX and can be restated as follows: The WTO/GATT does not prohibit environmental PPMs *as such.* PPM-based import bans may be inconsistent with GATT Articles I, III or XI, but if undertaken for an environmental purpose, such measures may qualify for an Article XX exception. Both the government policy standard and the producer characteristics standard are potentially justifiable under Article XX, and will receive scrutiny as to procedural fairness and environmental justification. A how-produced standard has not been tested and should present a diminished problem under GATT law.

In its two Article XX environmental decisions, the Appellate Body breathed life into the Article XX chapeau which can serve as a bulwark against unfair and protectionist measures.[116] The rigorous chapeau review in Shrimp–Turtle may develop as a key foundation of the new law of PPMs.

This chapter is focused on environmental PPMs, but the question arises whether the same conclusion – that the WTO does not prohibit environmental PPMs – applies to other kinds of PPMs. For example, what would be the legal status of an import ban on a rug made by indentured children, or on fur from a country that permits leg hold traps, or on pharmaceuticals tested on animals?[117] The answer is not clear. In Shrimp–Turtle, the Appellate Body saw a 'nexus' between the locus of the environmentally harmful shrimping and the US interest in conserving migratory sea turtles.[118] Such a nexus should be easy to find for environmental issues when the two litigant countries share an ecosystem. But for other issues, the required nexus may not exist.

It should also be noted that PPMs address only one part of the product cycle, and the legal conclusions presented here might not be applicable to regulations that extend beyond production. For example, importation can be made contingent on a variety of post-production practices. Goods that are stolen, expropriated, mislabelled or packaged in certain ways might be stopped at the border. Similarly, importation can be contingent on how a product is to he used or how it is to be disposed.[119] Importation can also be contingent on whether exportation is legal in the country of export. Note that the common feature in all of these requirements is that two otherwise like products are treated differently.

Although this paper addresses only regulations on import, many of the same legal issues arise in export regulations. For example, an export ban on hazardous waste to countries that are not parties to a treaty would be a violation of GATT Article XI that would be tested under Article XX.

In conclusion, this section has explicated the WTO law of PPMs and demonstrated the falsity of the myth that PPMs are illegal under the WTO. The following section will discuss the implications of that insight for making progress in resolving trade and environment tensions.

Debunking the Myth and Moving Forward

The argument that environmental PPMs violate the WTO has not had the intended effect. Rather than stamping out PPMs, it has prevented a reasoned discourse about how to distinguish appropriate from inappropriate PPMs. Little is being done to deal with the root causes of such trade restrictions.

Without any agreement on PPMs governments have found it harder to move ahead on any of the other elements of the trade and environment work programme at the WTO. For example, many commentators and governments have suggested that the first priority should be to address the use of trade measures in multilateral environmental agreements (MEAs). Yet since some of these measures are PPMs, the confusion about their legal status spills over into the debate about MEAs.

When negotiators do not share a common legal understanding about the subject of a negotiation that will tend to impede a successful resolution. It is hard to bargain in the shadow of the law when stakeholders have widely divergent views on what the law is. Because the governments most opposed to PPMs believe (incorrectly) that they are illegal, they have adopted an implacable and adversarial stance toward PPMs that may undermine settlement of conflicts.

But it is not just governments opposed to PPMs who are victims of the myth that PPMs are illegal. Some of the governments that recognize the need for PPMs are also confused about WTO law. Therefore, these governments tend to frame their proposals as amending or interpreting GATT to permit multilateral PPMs. Yet because WTO decision-making is consensual, such an amendment will be impossible, and the lack of receptivity reinforces the perception that 'trade and environment' issues are irresolvable.

The divergent views about the status of PPMs has undermined support for the WTO. Developing country officials – who may believe the myth that the WTO prohibits PPMs – perceive the continued use of PPMs by the US as proof that the WTO remains power-based rather than rule-based. Proponents of using environmental PPMs may view the WTO negatively because it may rule against such laws in favour of commercial interests.[120] This is bad for the trade regime, since alienated environmentalists will undermine public support for the WTO. But the schism between environmentalists and the trading system is also bad for environmental policy. Until the status of PPMs is properly understood, many environmentalists are not going to pay much attention to the ways that WTO rules and trade itself can promote opportunities for better environmental policy. Therefore, win–win opportunities may be missed.

If stakeholders shared a common understanding of the WTO law of PPMs, it might be possible to begin to bridge the gap between expectations and reality between commerce and conservation, and between the sovereignty of the producer and the sovereignty of the consumer. When a foreign environmental practice has an adverse environmental impact at home, the WTO cannot blindly demand that consumers accept foreign products of that process in the interest of promoting greater trade. What the WTO can do, however, is to erect effective disciplines for assuring that PPMs have an environmental justification and are applied in a reasonable manner. The current implementation of Article XX is not ideal. Yet replacing it with something better will not be easy because the topic of PPMs is emotionally charged. The proponents of PPMs should admit that they sometimes impose global costs and the opponents should admit that PPMs sometimes generate global benefits.

The next two sections make suggestions for disciplining and managing PPMs. Disciplines are needed to screen out improper PPMs. Better global management is needed to resolve the transborder problems that give rise to PPMs.

Disciplining PPMs

We need effective disciplines against ill-conceived environmental PPMs applied to imports. The worst abuse is a protectionist PPM, which should be prohibited. So should PPMs that discriminate in an arbitrary or unjustifiable way. International rules should strongly discourage PPMs that prescribe inappropriate policies and PPMs that impede intergovernmental cooperation. Some of these factors are within the competence of the trade regime, while others will require interregime cooperation.

It is often said that a key distinction is multilateral versus unilateral PPMs. Yet this distinction can be misleading because in reality there are many different shades of multilateralism. A treaty can require a PPM – for example, the Montreal Protocol on Ozone forbids the importation of controlled substances from states that are not a party to the Protocol (or have not agreed to be bound by it).[121] A treaty can authorize a PPM – for example, the Wellington Convention on Driftnets states that each party may take measures consistent with international law to prohibit the importation of fish caught using a drift-net.[122] A treaty can authorize trade measures in response to actions that undermine the treaty – for example, the Anadromous Stocks Convention directs the parties to take appropriate measures to prevent trafficking in anadromous fish taken in violation of the Convention.[123] Furthermore, the Commission administering an environmental treaty can authorize non-product-related PPMs. For example, on several occasions the International Commission for the Conservation of Atlantic Tunas has recommended that parties take 'non-discriminatory trade restrictive measures' on specified fishery products from listed countries that are adjudged to be violating the Convention.[124] All of these examples might be called multilateral, but they are also unilateral (except for the first) because the PPM-using country is encouraged but not required to use the trade measure. Moreover, under some of the treaties, the trade action is or can be directed at non-parties, so it is not consensually based.

Despite these complexities, the degree of multilateral approval for the PPM ought to be a factor in evaluating its appropriateness. If several countries are applying the PPM, it is much less likely to be protectionist or arbitrary. On the other hand, an environmental treaty can also signal disapproval of a PPM or even pre-empt unilateral action against parties in compliance with the treaty.[125] For example, the Inter-American Convention for the Protection and Conservation of Sea Turtles directs Parties to act in accordance with GATT Article XI with respect to the subject matter of the Convention.[126] This seems to imply no import bans since Article XX is not mentioned.

When unilateral PPMs are under review GATT Article XX will often be the decisive law. If product Y is banned to safeguard a resource Z, the WTO will need to analyse the facts related to both Y and Z. For example, in the Shrimp–Turtle case, the Appellate Body considered shrimping regulation, turtle conservation and how shrimping affected turtles. Had the US government banned widgets from countries that did not require turtle-safe shrimping, then the Appellate Body's analysis would have been different.[127]

In scrutinizing PPMs, the WTO needs to assess the validity of the environmental purpose underlying the trade measure. As the Appellate Body pointed out in US Gasoline, WTO member governments retain 'a large measure of autonomy to determine their own policies on the environment ...'[128] But the WTO does not have to tolerate an economic motivation for imposing a PPM on imports.[129] For example, it is one thing for the US to demand that the shrimp it imports be caught in a turtle-safe way so as to safeguard turtles. Yet it is an entirely different matter to seek to 'level the playing-field' by insisting the foreign producers use the same production practice so as to offset any difference in environmental costs. This latter motivation should not be shielded by GATT's Article XX.

The WTO will never be able to prevent all PPMs, but it can discourage the most troublesome ones. The government policy standard should be disfavoured because it is coercive and because it abides origin-based discrimination. The producer characteristics standard should be disfavoured because such a standard is too easy to tilt against foreign producers. Thus, if a unilateral PPM is to be used, it should be crafted as a how-produced standard that can be aimed directly at the odious production practice.

In calling for the government policy standard to be disfavoured, I am not calling for it to be outlawed. There may be circumstances when a how-produced standard is impractical. For example, when raw materials are co-mingled in production, there may be no way to enforce a how-produced PPM. A how-produced standard may also prove to be unsuccessful.[130] One can easily imagine a scenario whereby the how-produced standard does not prevent the environmental damage, but instead only reallocates the product.[131] For example, in a dispute like shrimp–turtle, the turtle-safe shrimp could be shipped to countries that insist on it while the more haphazardly caught shrimp is shipped elsewhere (at a lower price).

In that scenario, should the WTO permit a more coercive trade measure that might cure the problem? The Shrimp–Turtle panel answered with a categorical 'no', and in my view went too far.[132] Yet the legal hurdle for a unilaterally determined government policy standard ought to be set high. It will rarely be reasonable for one government to require that another government adopt a particular law as a condition for trade.

In addition to examining the PPM itself, the WTO should also examine why it was invoked and how it is applied. The Appellate Body decisions in US Gasoline and Shrimp–Turtle lay down helpful markers for steps that should be taken to attain multilateral cooperation and to accord due process to the exporting country. Some commentators have been critical of these requirements, particularly as they relate to treaty-making. For example, Lakshman Guruswamy contends that the Shrimp–Turtle decision 'constitutes a violation of the principle of state sovereignty by attempting to second-guess the manner in which the United States should have conducted treaty negotiations'.[133] Virginia Dailey argues that the language of Article XX should not be interpreted to require governments to attempt to negotiate a treaty as a precondition for using a trade measure.[134] In my view, prior efforts to negotiate a treaty can be relevant to an Article XX review, but the adjudicator should look at the actions of the exporting country too.

Although better disciplines for PPMs can emerge through WTO adjudication, some of the criteria suggested above are not in GATT Article XX and should not be read into the text. Thus, rather than relying on interpretation, it would be better for the WTO to negotiate new rules so that all governments could participate in this exercise. (Moreover, the opportunities for law-making through interpretation are limited by the content and flow of the cases.) Such negotiations could bring to bear other solutions – for example, capacity building for environmental management – that would require action outside the WTO.

Managing PPMs

PPMs are not a syndrome they are a symptom. While it is easy to criticize PPMs as a manifestation of eco-imperialism, that is too simplistic an explanation. PPMs are a symptom of dysfunctions in international environmental governance. Among the biggest problems are poor stewardship of the global commons, lack of accountability for transborder environmental harms and free-riding in efforts to achieve treaties. PPMs are an inevitable response to independent countries at different stages of development and enlightenment who share the same planet. Addressing these root causes would not only obviate many PPMs, but could also improve prospects for economic growth and environmental protection.

The world needs better environmental governance. To boost membership in treaties, rich countries should make more funding and technical assistance available. To improve compliance, treaties need better developed non-compliance mechanisms that use civil society participation as one means of putting pressure on governments to comply. For many issues, however, a treaty might not be achievable. In those circumstances, concerned governments and private actors should put more emphasis on market-based mechanisms such as product labels and certifications, corporate codes and seals, and monitoring processes.

Although the WTO is not responsible for environmental protection, it should become an ally to the various international organizations that do have an environmental mandate. Just before he retired in 1999. WTO Director-General Ruggiero gave a thoughtful speech here at the Graduate Institute in which he said:

> [W]e need to look at the policy challenges we face as pieces of an interconnected puzzle. We can no longer treat human rights, the environment, development, trade, health, or finance as separate sectoral issues, to be addressed through separate policies and institutions.[135]

I could not agree more with this reflection. The WTO needs to work more closely with the UN Environment Programme, the governing conferences of multilateral environmental treaties, the World Health Organization, and other UN agencies. Authority exists for this in Article V:1 of the WTO Agreement which provides that the 'General Council shall make appropriate arrangements for effective cooperation with other intergovernmental organizations that have responsibilities related to those of the WTO'.

To improve management of PPMs the following steps should be taken:

1   The WTO should promote greater transparency of PPMs. This might be done through the Trade Policy Review Mechanism (or through another subsidiary body) with input from relevant international organizations. A WTO review of a particular PPM – written outside the context of dispute settlement – might give some impetus to reform within the authoring government. We should not assume that the only way to get a government's attention is to convict it of a WTO violation.

2   A new trade and environment conflict is often a signal of inadequate environmental cooperation. The WTO could seek to relay that signal to the appropriate multilateral environmental institutions. Analogously, if the environment regime sees a way in which trade negotiations might exacerbate or control an environmental problem, it should communicate that to the WTO.

3   The WTO should look for opportunities to coordinate its technical assistance on trade with the technical assistance on the environment being sponsored by other international agencies. By doing so, the WTO might encourage better coordination between the trade and environmental officials in participating countries.

4   The WTO needs to clarify its disciplines regarding labelling. PPM labelling offers a potential avenue to avoid trade restrictions by leaving the choice up to retailers and consumers.[136] This is a market-friendly response and should not be discouraged by the WTO.

Finally, although steps like these will help, new trade and environment disputes are almost inevitable. When they occur, the WTO Director-General should be more active in offering mediation and conciliation services.[137] In some cases like Shrimp–Turtle, both sides were partly right and partly wrong. That dispute should have been settled (or prevented) with the US giving help to the complaining countries to improve shrimping practices.[138] Another idea – authored by Gabrielle Marceau – is for the WTO to establish an Environmental Monitoring Body. This body would seek a solution to trade and environment conflicts short of formal dispute settlement.[139] The composition of such a body could include experts from industry and NGOs.

Conclusion

An environmental PPM is not illegal under WTO rules. Whenever it violates GATT Articles I, III or XI, the PPM will be reviewed under GATT Article XX(b) or (g) and the chapeau to the article. With respect to the chapeau, the Appellate Body has explained that the line of legality 'moves as the kind and the shape of the measures at stake vary and as the facts making up specific cases differ'.[140] Thus, the WTO legality of a PPM will depend both on its implementation and its environmental rationale.

The myth that PPMs are illegal under the WTO has had three unfortunate effects. First, it has undermined the WTO in the public's perception. In his careful study of trade-related environmental measures in 1995, Howard Chang warned of these dangers:

> The creation of barriers to environmental protection in the name of free trade has eroded respect for GATT institutions in particular and political support for free trade in general. ... The GATT panels were understandably concerned about the potential for protectionist abuse of Article XX. Their crude but sweeping rules against trade restrictions, however, make no attempt to distinguish between legitimate environmental concerns and protectionism, and in the process do the cause of free trade a great disservice: the political backlash against free trade may also fail to make the same distinction.[141]

Ironically, the GATT jurisprudence on Article XX has improved substantially since 1995.[142] But the public may not be aware of that. The second negative effect is that the divergence of views on the legality of PPMs has undermined any potential progress in the ongoing work of the WTO Committee on Trade and Environment. Even without being on the formal agenda, the issue of PPMs colours many of the other issues, such as the use of trade measures in environmental treaties. The third repercussion is that without a shared understanding of the legal base-line, it is impossible to develop new disciplines to prevent inappropriate PPMs.

By debunking the PPM myth and by exploring why PPMs are used, this chapter points the way to the next stage in analysis which is to recognize PPMs as a symptom of governance dysfunction and to act accordingly to address the root causes of conflict. Not all recourse to PPMs will be justifiable. But sometimes governments may use PPMs because that is the only way to respond to a global or transborder environmental harm occurring in another country. In those situations, the right role for the WTO may be to stand aside and permit the PPM. Outside the WTO there will be a need for international environmental institutions to step in with technical assistance and other efforts to spur environmental cooperation. In the end PPMs may be less important for what they accomplish through trade than for what they reveal about the interface between trade, the environment, and international law.

Notes

1   World Charter for Nature. UN Doc A/RES/37/7, 9 November, 1982, para 21(b)
2   Agreement on Agriculture, Annex 2, para 12(a), reprinted in *World Trade Organization, The Legal Texts, The Results of the Uruguay Round of Multilateral Trade Negotiations*
3   Bruce Neuling, 'The Shrimp-Turtle Case: Implications for Article XX of GATT and the Trade and Environment Debate', 22 *Loyola of Los Angeles International and Comparative Law Review* 1 (1999). Despite its formal name that gives no mention of the turtles, this matter is widely known as the Shrimp–Turtle case. Even the WTO website notes this shorthand designation. Robert Howse calls it the Turtles Panel. For his critique of the panel report, see Robert Howse, 'The Turtles Panel. Another Environmental Disaster in Geneva', 32, *Journal of World Trade* 73 (October 1998)
4   Joan Lowy, 'Protesters Have Long List of Complaints Against World Trade Group', *Chattanooga Free Press*, 2 December 1999, pA7
5   Agreement on Technical Barriers to Trade (1979), GATT, BISD 26S/8, para 14.25
6   OECD Secretariat, 'Processes and Production Methods (PPMs): Conceptual Framework and Considerations on Use of PPM-Based Trade Measures', OCDE/GD(97)137. This study presents an analytical framework for PPMs
7   Another term used is unincorporated PPMs meaning that the characteristics of the process do not become part of the product
8   WTO Agreement on Technical Barriers to Trade, Annex I, para 1 (emphasis added)
9   See 'Negotiating History of the Coverage of the Agreement on Technical Barriers to Trade with Regard to Labelling Requirements, Voluntary Standards, and Processes and Production Methods Unrelated to the Product Characteristics', WTO Doc G/TBT/W/11, 29 August 1995, paras 131, 146
10 Agreement on the Application of Sanitary and Phytosanitary Measures, Annex A, para 1
11 Ibid, para 1. It is conceivable for a non-product-related PPM to be covered by SPS. For example, a measure forbidding the use of a pesticide in foreign agriculture, not because it is harmful to the consumer but because wind blows the pesticide across the border into the importing country and hurts its agriculture, would be covered by SPS
12 Appleton, Arthur E (1998) 'Telecommunications Trade: Reach Out and Touch Someone?', 19 *University of Pennsylvania Journal of International Economic Law*, pp209, 216
13 Thomas, J Christopher (1992) The Future: The Impact of Environmental Regulations on Trade, 18 *Canada-United States Law Journal*, pp383, 389–390 (discussing newsprint standard)
14 Rappard, William E (1925) 'International Relations as Viewed from Geneva', p127, Rappard was the co-founder and longtime Director of the Graduate Institute

15 Convention to Prevent Smuggling and for Certain Other Objects, 23 December 1925, US–Mexico, 48 LNTS 444, arts 10–12 (no longer in force)
16 Agreement regarding certain provisions for UNTS the Protection of Migratory Game-Birds, 9 October 1931, Denmark–Sweden, 126 UNTS, p259, art 1
17 16 USC §916c(a)
18 Boisson de Chazournes, Laurence (2000) 'Unilateralism and Environmental Protection: Issues of Perception and Reality of Issues', *European Journal of International Law*, No 11, pp315, 317, 325
19 Anderson, Kym and Blackhurst, Richard (1992) 'Trade, the Environment and Public Policy', in *The Greening of World Trade Issues*, 3, 20 (Anderson and Blackhurst (eds))
20 The earliest analysis that has come to my attention of the difficulty in attaining an environmental treaty is: Charles Edward Fryer, 'International Regulation of the Fisheries of the High Seas', 28, *Bulletin of the Bureau of Fisheries*, No 28, pp91, 95
21 *Mid-Pacific Magazine*, No 29, pp182–183, January 1925
22 Biology and Conservation of Sea Turtles, Proceedings of the World Conference on Sea Turtle Conservation. November 1979 (Karen A Bjorndal (ed) 1981), p582
23 PI, pp101–162 §609(a)(2)
24 Inter-American Convention for the Protection and Conservation of Sea Turtles, 1 December 1996, Senate Treaty Doc 105–148. US embargoes on shrimp began in 1991. US Customs Service memorandum regarding Importation of Shrimp from Suriname, 2 May 1991
25 Montreal Protocol on Substances that Deplete the Ozone Layer, 16 September 1987 and as adjusted thereafter, art 4, available at www.unep.org/ozone/mont_t.htm
26 Brack, Duncan (1996) *International Trade and the Montreal Protocol*, pp54–58
27 Regulatory action may not be efficient for the producing country. For example, a hypothetical electorate might place little value on sea turtles and therefore that government may be justified in taking no action to regulate shrimp harvesting
28 Holte MacPherson, A (1909) *Legislation for the Protection of Birds*, p29
29 See generally Robin W Doughty, *Feather Fashions and Bird Preservation* (1975)
30 For example, in 2001 the US will require that car boots have inside releases. This new standard will surely force foreign carmakers to redesign their products
31 Agreement on Textiles and Clothing, Annex. Some of these categories read like PPMs (eg 5702.10)
32 Blank, Daniel P (1996) 'Target-Based Environmental Trade Measures: A Proposal for the New WTO Committee on Trade and Environment', 15 *Stanford Environmental Law Journal*, No 61, p119
33 Lee, James R (2000) *Exploring the Gaps. Vital Links Between Trade, Environment and Culture*, p174
34 No such law exists in the US, but federal law bars the import of tuna that is not 'dolphin safe' which until recently was defined in relation to the method of harvesting. 16 USC § 1417(a)(1), (d) (1998)

35 US law provides for an import ban in certain circumstances of fish and sport fishing equipment from countries whose governments have not agreed to terminate large-scale drift-net fishing by nationals beyond the exclusive economic zone. 16 USC § 1826a(b)

36 Thus, banning the importation of fish caught with a drift-net is different from banning the importation of widgets as a sanction to induce the other country to stop drift-net fishing practices

37 Agreement on Technical Barriers to Trade, *supra* note 8, Annex 1, para 2

38 League of Nations, Memorandum on Discriminatory Tariff Classifications (1927), League Doc CECP 96, p8

39 Robert E Hudee (2000) 'Like Product': The Differences in Meaning in GATT Articles I and III, in *Regulatory Barriers and the Principle of Non-discrimination in World Trade Law,* pp103, 109–111 (Thomas Cottier and Pelros C Mavroidis (eds))

40 Burkhalter, Holly (2000) Deadly Diamonds, *Legal Times,* 11 September, p74. See also Parker, Andrew (2000) Pledge on Action to Curb Sales of 'Conflict Diamonds', *Financial Times,* 27 October, p8

41 Howse, Robert and Regan, Donald (2000) 'The Product/Process Distinction An Illusory Basis for Disciplining "Unilateralism" in Trade Policy', *European Journal of International Law,* No 11, pp249, 277

42 See Chang, Howard F (1995) 'An Economic Analysis of Trade Measures to Protect the Global Environment', *Georgetown Law Journal,* pp2131, 2177–2185

43 Esty, Daniel C (1994) *Greening the GATT,* Institute for International Economics, pp49–51. In correspondence with the author, Esty states that this passage represented the prevailing reading of the GATT in 1994, but that since then, a more refined reading of Article XX has emerged in WTO case-law

44 Schlagenhof, Markus (1995) 'Trade Measures Based on Environmental Processes and Production Methods', Swiss government, *Journal of World Trade,* pp123, 138, December

45 Murase, Shinya (1995) 'Perspectives from International Economic Law on Transnational Environmental Issues', Academy of International Law, *Recueil des Cours,* No 253, pp287, 339

46 World Trade Organization, Trading into the Future Introduction to the WTO, p47 (1998). The same text remains on the WTO website as of November 2000

47 'Vice President Brittan Calls for More Coherence in Trade and Environmental Policy', *European Union News,* 23 March 1998

48 Wallach, Lori and Sforza, Michelle, (1999) 'Whose Trade Organization?', *Public Citizen,* p174 (footnote omitted)

49 House of Lords, Select Committee on European Communities, The World Trade Organization: The EU Mandate After Seattle, 13 June 2000, paras 223–24

50 Elliott, Kimberly Ann (2000) '(Mis)Managing Diversity: Worker Rights and US Trade Policy, 5 *International Negotiation* 97, p120, Institute for International Economics (2000)

51 UN Environment Programme and International Institute for Sustainable Development, *Environment and Trade, A Handbook,* p43 (2000)

52 GATT, arts VI, XVI, XX(d)

53 GATT, 'Industrial Pollution Control and International Trade, *GATT Studies in International Trade,* No 1, July 1971 (emphasis added)

54 'Trade and the Environment', in GATT, *International Trade,* No 1, pp90–91, at 23

55 Renato Ruggiero, 'A Shared Responsibility: Global Policy Coherence for our Global Age', December 1997, available on WTO website

56 See WTO, *infra* note 46

57 In his treatise of 1989 John Jackson suggests that the Article XX exceptions imply a focus on the product itself, and not on the production process. But he goes on to add that it might be possible to argue the contrary and that the issue has not been squarely posed in dispute settlement. John Jackson, *The World Trading Systems,* p209 (paperback edition, 1992)

58 Of course, a vocal minority of commentators deny that the WTO prohibits PPMs. For example, see Howse and Regan, *supra* note 41

59 McLaughlin, Richard J (1999) 'Sovereignty, Utility, and Fairness: Using US Takings Law to Guide the Evolving Utilitarian Balancing Approach to Global Environmental Disputes in the WTO', *Oregon Law Review,* No 78, pp855, 938

60 United States – Standards for Reformulated and Conventional Gasoline, Report of the Appellate Body [hereinafter Appellate Body Gasoline Report], 29 April 1996, WT/DS2/AB/R, at 22. In its interpretation of GATT Article XX(g), the Appellate Body declared that this exception ('relating to the conservation of exhaustible natural resources') 'may not be read so expansively as seriously to subvert the purpose and object of Article III:4'. Appellate Body Gasoline Report, ibid at 18. This conclusion seems questionable. The purposes of objects of Article III are already reflected to the appropriate extent, in the Article XX chapeau which excludes a measure that would constitute a 'disguised restriction' in international trade

61 United Slates – Import Prohibitions of Certain Shrimp and Shrimp Products, Report of the Appellate Body [hereinafter Appellate Body Shrimp-Turtle Report], 12 October 1998, WT/DS58/AB/R, para 156 (emphasis added). See also para 159 (discussing the 'competing rights' under Articles XI and XX)

62 Japan–Taxes on Alcoholic Beverages, Report of the Appellate Body, 4 October 1996, WT/DS8/AB/R, at 20

63 Brazil – Export Financing Programme for Aircraft – Recourse to Arbitration by Brazil under Article 22.6 of the DSU and Article 4.11 of the SCM Agreement, Decision by the Arbitrators, 28 August 2000, para 3.39. Article XX was not an issue in this case, so this analogy is dicta

64 Belgian Family Allowances, GATT, BISD IS/59

65 Ibid paras 3, 6

66 Ibid para 3

67 Spain – Tariff Treatment of Unroasted Coffee, GATT, BISD 28S/102, para 4.11

68 Indonesia – Certain Measures Affecting the Automobile Industry, Report of the Panel [hereinafter Indonesia Automobile Panel Report], 2 July 1998, WT/DS54/R. This case was not appealed

69 Canada, Certain Measures Affecting the Automotive Industry, Report of the Panel [hereinafter Canada Automotive Report], 11 February 2000, WT/DS/139/R

70 Indonesia Automobile Panel Report, *supra* note 68, para 14.143

71 Indonesia Automobile Panel Report, *supra* note 68, para 14.145

72 Canada Automotive Report, *supra* note 69, para 10.24. See also paras 10.29, 10.30

73 It is interesting to note that in 1927, the Swedish delegation to the World Economic Conference pointed out that the MFN principle might be evaded by an unfounded distinction (between similar kinds of goods) such as the 'measures taken by the authorities of the exporting State'. League of Nations. 1 Report and Proceedings or the World Economic Conference, pp235–236 (1927), League Doc. C.356.M.129.1927.II

74 See Thaggert, Henry L (1994) 'A Closer Look at the Tuna–Dolphin Case: "Like Products" and "Extrajurisdictionality" in the Trade and Environment Context', in *Trade and the Environment: The Search for Balance,* No 1, p69 (James Cameron et al (eds))

75 This is not a producer characteristics standard because no solitary producer can meet it on its own. It is also not a how-produced standard since the import ban is countrywide

76 United States – Restrictions on Imports of Tuna [hereinafter Tuna–Dolphin 1 Report), GATT. BISD 39S/155, paras 5.14, 5.15 (not adopted)

77 Minutes of meeting held on 18 February 1992, GATT Doc. C/M/254, at 23

78 United States – Measures Affecting Alcoholic and Malt Beverages [hereinafter US Alcoholic Beverages Report], GATT. BISD 39S/206. This was only one of numerous complaints in the case. For purposes of its decision the panel assumed that the Minnesota tax credit was available to Canadian producers. Ibid para 5.19

79 Ibid. From the report of the case, the US Trade Representative made little effort to defend Minnesota's law

80 United States – Restrictions on Imports of Tuna [hereinafter Tuna–Dolphin II Report], 16 June 1994, 33 ILM 842. para 5.8 (not adopted)

81 United States – Taxes on Automobiles [hereinafter US Automobile Taxes Report], 29 September 1994, CATT Doc. DS31/R, para 5.54 (not adopted)

82 Ibid para 5.55

83 United States – Standards for Reformulated and Conventional Gasoline, Report of the Panel [hereinafter Gasoline Panel Report], 29 January 1996, WT/DS2R, para 6.11

84 Indonesia Automobile Panel Report, *supra* note 68. para 14.112

85 Robert E Hudec (1998) 'GATT/WTO Constraints on National Regulation: Requiem for an "Aims and Effects" Test', *International Lawyer*, No 32, p619. One intellectual foundation of this test can be found in a paper by two GATT Secretariat officials in 1989. See Roessler, Frieder (2000) 'The Constitutional Function of the Multilateral Trade Order', in *The Legal Structure, Functions, & Limits of the World Trade Order. A Collection of Essays* by Frieder Roessler, pp109, 127–130

86 US Alcoholic Beverages Report, *supra* note 78, para 5.72

87 Japan – Taxes on Alcoholic Beverages, Report of the Panel, 11 July 1996, WT/DS8/R, para 6.17. One stated reason for doing so was that if protection of

health could be accomplished without violating Article III that could 'circumvent' Article XX which requires governments to show that a health measure is necessary. The panel did not explain why non-violation of Article III circumvents Article XX

88 See European Communities – Regime for the Importation, Sale and Distribution of Bananas, Report of the Appellate Body, 9 September 1997, WT/DS27/AB/R, para 241 (making clear that the Appellate Body had rejected this test)

89 European Communities – Measures Affecting Asbestos and Asbestos Containing Products, Report of the Panel, 18 September 2000, WT/DSH5/R, para 8.1 30. This decision is now under appeal

90 Howse and Regan, *supra* note 41, pp264-268. In a paper that predates some of the recent WTO jurisprudence, two commentators suggested that when based on broadly shared consumer preferences, PPM distinctions might not violate Article III. Marco Bronckers and Natalie McNelis, 'Rethinking the 'Like Product' Definition in GATT 1994: Anti-Dumping and Environmental Protection', in *Regulatory Barriers and the Principle of Non-discrimination in World Trade Law, supra* note 39, pp345, 376–377

91 United Slates – Imports of Certain Automotive Spring Assemblies, GATT, BISD 30S/107, paras 55–56, 59–61. GATT Article XX(d) provides an exception for measures necessary to secure compliance with laws or regulations which are not inconsistent with the provisions of the GATT, including those relating to customs enforcement, the enforcement of certain monopolies, the protection of patents, trademarks and copyrights, and the prevention of deceptive practices

92 Tuna–Dolphin 1 Report, *supra* note 76, para 5.27 (emphasis added). As many commentators noted, this point was circular since Mexico's rights to have its tuna accepted by the US could not be determined independently of application of Article XX. The panel made a similar ruling regarding Article XX(g)

93 Tuna–Dolphin II Report, *supra* note 80, para 5.23

94 Tuna–Dolphin II Report, *supra* note 80, para 5.24. The panel uses the term 'countries' as a synonym for governments

95 Ibid para 5.26

96 Robert E Hudec (1996) GATT Legal Restraints on the Use of Trade Measures Against Foreign Environmental Practices, in *Fair Trade and Harmonization*, No 2, pp95, 119, 151 (Jagdish N Bhagwati and Robert E Hudec (eds))

97 US Automobile Taxes Report, *supra* note 81, paras 5.65–5.66

98 Appellate Body Gasoline Report, *supra* note 60, pp13–29

99 Regulation of Fuels and Fuel Additives: Baseline Requirements for Gasoline Produced by Foreign Refiners, *Federal Register*, No 62, 45.533 (1997). This rule was challenged in US court in part on the argument that the US Environmental Protection Agency should not have considered US obligations under the WTO in administering the statute. The court upheld the Agency's statutory interpretation. Warren Corporation v EPA, 159 F.3d pp616, 624

100 All four of the plaintiff countries had a turtle conservation regime in place. Indeed, two of them (India and Pakistan) had imposed unilateral trade bans on endangered sea turtles before the adoption in 1973 of the Convention on International Trade in Endangered Species of Wild Fauna and Flora (CITES).

United States – Import Prohibitions of Certain Shrimp and Shrimp Products, Report of the Panel (hereinafter Shrimp-Turtle Panel Report], 15 May 1998, paras 3.4, 3.11

101 Ibid, paras 7.26, 7.45, 7.50, 7.51

102 Shrimp-Turtle Panel Report, *supra* note 100, para 7.45. The panel's important point deserves more attention. Suppose that country A forbids the importation of shrimp from countries that do not require the use of a turtle excluder device (TED) while country B forbids the importation of shrimp from countries that do not require the use of a turtle untrapping device (TUD). In that hypothetical, economic actors in country C would not be able to sell simultaneously to A and B. One can make the hypothetical more troublesome by assuming that A is the leading producer of TEDs and B is the leading producer of TUDs

103 Ibid para 7.61 Caron, David D and Trüeb, Hans Rudolf (1998) 'Protecting Trade and Turtles: The WTO and the Coherency of International Law', *Translex* 3.5, December

104 Appellate Body Shrimp-Turtle Report, *supra* note 61, paras 121, 141, 145, 140. The Appellate Body found that the US measure was made effective in conjunction with a restriction on domestic production (harvesting) of shrimp – ie the domestic PPM and imported-product PPM were applied evenhandedly. Ibid para 144

105 Ibid para 141

106 Ibid para 165

107 Ibid paras 177–182

108 Ibid para 171

109 Ibid paras 166, 171

110 Notice of Proposed Revisions to Guidelines for the Implementation of Section 609 of Public Law 101–162 Relating to the Protection of Sea Turtles in Shrimp Trawl Fishing Operations, 64 *Federal Register* 14,481 (1999)

111 Brevetti, Rossella (2000) 'State Department Considers Options After Court Ruling on Shrimp Import Ban', *BNA Daily Report for Executives*, 18 August, pA-8

112 'Malaysia Poised to Fight US Turtle Protection After Talks with US', *Inside US Trade*, 6 October 2000, p12

113 European Communities – Measures Affecting Asbestos and Asbestos Containing Products, *supra* note 89, paras 8.173, 8.179, 8.183, 8.199, 8.204, 8.206. Furthermore, the panel suggests that each government can determine what level of risk it wants to assure. Ibid para 8.175 n 119.

114 The judgement of the US Gasoline Panel also suggests a least-GATT-inconsistent rather than a least-trade-restrictive test. Gasoline Panel Report, *supra* note 83, para 6.24

115 Earth Summit Agenda 21, para 2.22(i)

116 See Chang, *supra* note 42, at 2172. 2208 (noting that the Article XX chapeau contains clauses designed to prevent abuse of the Exceptions)

117 See eg Adelle Blackett, Whither Social Clause? Human Rights, Trade Theory and Treaty Interpretation, 31 *Columbia Human Rights Law Review* 1 (1999); Royal Society for the Prevention of Cruelty to Animals. *WTO-Food for Thought-Farm Animal Welfare and the WTO* (1999)

118 Appellate Body Shrimp–Turtle Report, *supra* note 61, para 133

119 For example, in the US, there is a high tariff on hand-woven wool fabrics, but no tariff when such fabrics are to be used or sold by a religious institution. Harmonized Tariff Schedule of the US, subheading 9810.00.20

120 Fugazzotto, Peter and Steiner, Todd (1998) *Slain by Trade. The Attack of the World Trade Organization on Sea Turtles and the US Endangered Species Act*

121 Montreal Protocol on Substances that Deplete the Ozone Layer, *supra* note 25, arts 4.1, 4.9. This is a government policy standard

122 Convention for the Prohibition of Fishing with Long Driftnets in the South Pacific Ocean, 24 November 1989, 29 ILM 1454, art 3(2)

123 Convention for the Conservation of Anadromous Stocks in the North Pacific Ocean, 11 February 1992, US Senate Treaty Doc 102–130, art III:3

124 For example, see the ICCAT Resolution for an Action Plan to Ensure the Effectiveness of the Conservation Program for the Atlantic Bluefin Tuna, transmitted 23 January 1995

125 See Howse, Robert 'Managing the Interface between International Trade Law and the Regulatory State: What Lessons Should (and Should Not) Be Drawn from the Jurisprudence of the United States Dormant Commerce Clause', in *Regulatory Barriers and the Principle of Non-discrimination in World Trade Law*, *supra* note 39, pp139, 151

126 Inter-American Convention for the Protection and Conservation of Sea Turtles, *supra* note 24, art XV:2

127 Under Article XX(g), there would be a highly tenuous 'means and ends' relationship between shrimp and widgets. See *supra* note 105. Under the Article XX chapeau, a widget ban might constitute arbitrary discrimination. Why widgets rather than trifles?

128 Appellate Body Gasoline Report, *supra* note 60, p30

129 Kirgis, Frederic L, Jr (1972) 'Effective Pollution Control in Industrialized Countries: International Economic Disincentives, Policy Responses and the GATT', *Michigan Law Review*, pp859, 901–902

130 The issues presented in this paragraph arise out of a discussion with Robert Hudec, but the conclusion is mine

131 Chang, *supra* note 42, p2179

132 See Shrimp–Turtle Panel Report, *supra* note 100, paras 7.44–7.45

133 Guruswamy, Lakshman (2000) 'The Annihilation of Sea Turtles: World Trade Organization Intransigence and US Equivocation', *Environmental Law Reporter*, No 30, pp10261, 10267

134 Dailey, Virginia (2000) 'Sustainable Development: Reevaluating the Trade Vs. Turtles Conflict at the WTO', *Journal of Transnational Law and Policy*, No 9, pp331, 377

135 Ruggiero, Renato (1999) 'Beyond the Multilateral Trading System', April, available on WTO website

136 Of course, a consumer may want to free-ride by buying the less expensive product without the label. So a label alone may not be an optimal response to economic externalities, Chang, *supra* note 42, p2177

137 See Understanding on Rules and Procedures Governing the Settlement of Disputes, art 5.6

138 See Stilwell, Matthew (1999) 'Applying the EPTSD Framework to Reconcile Trade, Development and Environmental Policy Conflicts', Expert Panel on Trade and Sustainable Development Working Paper, September 1999, pp11–15

139 Marceau, Gabrielle (1999) 'A Call far Coherence in International Law. Praises for the Prohibition Against "Clinical Isolation" in WTO Dispute Settlement', *Journal of World Trade*, No 32, pp87, 148–149, October

140 Appellate Body Shrimp–Turtle Report, *supra* note 61, para 159

141 Chang, *supra* note 42, p2209

142 Wofford, Carrie (2000) 'A Greener Future at the WTO: The Refinement of WTO Jurisprudence on Environmental Exceptions to GATT', *Harvard Environmental Law Review*, No 21, p563

12

The Supervision of Health and Biosafety Regulation by World Trade Rules

Steve Charnovitz

The Agreement on the Application of Sanitary and Phytosanitary Measures (SPS) – which is part of the organic law of the World Trade Organization (WTO) – can affect the ability of governments to provide health and ecological protection.[1] Governments that are members of the WTO must follow SPS rules in enacting legislation and implementing regulations that come within the scope of the agreement. These rules have been criticized by consumer and environmental groups for undermining public health.[2]

This chapter has three parts. Part 1 reviews the operation of the SPS Agreement. Part 2 examines two important policy issues – the precautionary principle and product labelling. Part 3 looks briefly at the new Cartagena Protocol on Biosafety. The overall conclusion is that while there are legitimate concerns about whether SPS interferes too much in health policy, it is too soon to seek major revisions in it.

Operation of the SPS Agreement

Concerns about unjustified sanitary measures go back many decades. This problem was examined by the League of Nations with a view toward using science to determine the validity of trade bans. No multilateral discipline ensued until 1947, however, when the General Agreement on Tariffs and Trade (GATT) was established. Although GATT rules were intended to prohibit sanitation-based import bans that were disguised restrictions to trade, these rules were hardly ever tested.[3] Instead, a GATT Standards Code was written in 1979 and when that proved inadequate, a new effort to draft a separate SPS Agreement was begun in the late 1980s.

SPS builds on the GATT in many ways. Perhaps the most important addition is the discipline on domestic measures.[4] Under the GATT, a domestic health standard impeding an import was held only to the principle of 'national treatment'. So long as the import was treated no less favourably than the domestic product, it did not matter how flimsy the justification was for the domestic standard. As will be explained below, SPS subjects non-discriminatory domestic measures to supervision whenever they affect trade. Because SPS has more stringent disciplines than GATT, the health exception in GATT Article XX(b) is not available to a government as a defence in an SPS lawsuit.[5]

As of January 2000, three SPS judgements have been handed down by WTO panels and the Appellate Body.[6] In all three cases, the defendant government employing the health measure lost. Two of the disputes involved 'sanitary' measures focusing on food safety and on fishery ecology. One dispute involved 'phytosanitary' measures focusing on agricultural disease.

The first case was 'EC Measures Concerning Meat and Meat Products (Hormones)'.[7] Here, the US and Canada complained against a European Commission ban (begun in 1989) on the importation of meat produced from cattle that had been injected with or fed growth hormones. The Commission had banned the use of six growth hormones in Europe in order to promote food safety and sought to keep out foreign meat produced with such hormones. The rationale for the ban was that the hormones might be carcinogenic. The WTO Appellate Body ruled against the European Union in January 1998 and an arbitrator gave the Commission 15 months to bring its law into conformity with SPS rules. In mid-1999, the US and Canada imposed trade retaliation against the European Union for failing to lift the import ban against meat produced using growth hormones.[8]

The second case was 'Australia – Measures Affecting the Importation of Salmon'.[9] Here Canada complained against an Australian ban (begun in 1975) on the importation of fresh, chilled or frozen salmon (ie, not heat-treated). Australia had enacted this ban to prevent the introduction of exotic pathogens not present in Australia. The WTO Appellate Body ruled against Australia in October 1998 and an arbitrator gave Australia eight months to bring its regulation into conformity with SPS rules. Australia has issued a new regulation, but Canada claims that it is inadequate and is seeking authority from the WTO to retaliate against Australia.

The third case was 'Japan – Measures Affecting Agricultural Products'.[10] Here the US complained about a Japanese phytosanitary measure (begun in 1950) that banned imports of apples, cherries, nectarines and walnuts potentially infested with coddling moth. In 1987, Japan had provided for lifting this ban subject to certain quarantine and fumigation requirements which call for each variety of fruit to be individually tested. It was this separate testing requirement that provoked the WTO dispute. The Appellate Body ruled against Japan in February 1999. Thereafter, Japan agreed to bring its regulation into conformity with SPS rules by the end of 1999.

The victory by plaintiffs in these three longstanding disputes will surely lead to more such cases in the future. Already in the WTO pipeline are cases regarding a French ban on asbestos and a US subnational import ban on Canadian cattle and grain. Disputes may also be looming on issues such as antibiotics in animals and genetically modified (GM) organisms.[11] Even when the substance being regulated is unquestionably harmful (eg dioxin), disputes can occur over whether the regulatory response is broader or longer lasting than necessary.

Overview of SPS

SPS is a trade agreement, not a health agreement. Although the Preamble to SPS takes note of a desire by governments to improve human and animal health, SPS targets only the overuse of national health regulation. Governments do not violate SPS by permitting exports unsafe for the foreign consumer.

Consider food safety, for example. Even though world food trade is very important economically and nutritionally, SPS contains no minimum standard for food safety or for applying science to the food production process. In other words, although a government can violate SPS by using poor science to impose food safety regulation, a government cannot violate SPS by neglecting science in *failing* to impose adequate food safety regulation.

SPS rules apply only to sanitary and phytosanitary measures as defined in the agreement.[12] In broad terms, SPS pertains to laws that protect against exposure to pests (eg insects and weeds), disease-carrying organisms, disease-causing organisms, disease-carrying animals or plants, and to additives, contaminants and toxins in food and feedstuffs. For example, protection against pesticide residues in fruit is covered by SPS because that is a contaminant. Protection against the entry of exotic species is covered if they cause disease or are pests. On the other hand, many health or environmental risks are not covered. For example, a law regulating the entry of drugs or cigarettes will usually not come within the terms of SPS. Protection against a (real or imagined) human health risk from bioengineered processed products is apparently not covered by SPS because genetic modification is not listed in the above categories.[13] But the risk that bioengineered seeds might spread pests is covered by SPS because the 'spread of pests' is a listed SPS risk.[14]

There has been considerable confusion about what it means for a product to be covered by SPS. If SPS applies to a particular risk, then governments must not undertake health regulation prohibited by SPS rules. If SPS does not apply to a particular risk, then governments have no SPS obligations for that product or process. That does not mean that governments are prevented from regulating that risk.[15] Rather, it means that the WTO will review such regulation under less onerous rules in the Agreement on Technical Barriers to Trade (TBT) or the GATT. The TBT Agreement does not supervise any measure covered by the SPS Agreement.[16]

It should be noted that the SPS Agreement pertains only to health standards applied to imports. Thus, it would not be an SPS violation for a country to impose an unscientific domestic ban (eg on a pesticide residue) so long as it did not apply that standard to imports. Of course, this retained autonomy is unlikely to prevent trade conflict. Governments do not typically impose a health standard on domestic production and yet legally permit imports that do not meet that standard. It should also be noted that the SPS Agreement pertains only to risks within the territory of the importing country.[17]

Before turning to the SPS rules, it may be helpful to discuss briefly the burden of proof and the standard of review. As is typical in lawsuits, the initial burden lies with the plaintiff government lodging the complaint which must establish a clear (ie prima facie) case of inconsistency with SPS rules. Once that occurs, the defendant government utilizing the health measure has the burden to bring forward evidence and arguments to refute the allegation that it is violating a WTO rule. The standard of review dictates whether the panel should be deferential to the regulatory authorities of the defendant country imposing the health measure. In 'Hormones', the Appellate Body rejected the European Union's (EU's) arguments for deference and instead stated that the role of the panel is to make an 'objective assessment of the facts' relying on the evidence as presented by governments and outside experts.[18]

SPS Disciplines

The complex SPS rules can be abridged into eight disciplines and one exemption. This section will briefly discuss these rules drawing from the language of SPS and, when available, WTO case-law. It should be noted that SPS is a comprehensive agreement containing many requirements that are not discussed.

The first SPS discipline is the science requirement.[19] SPS Article 2.2 states that governments 'shall ensure that any sanitary or phytosanitary measure is applied only to the extent necessary to protect human, animal or plant life or health, is based on scientific principles, and is not maintained without sufficient scientific evidence'.[20] In 'Agricultural Products', the Appellate Body interpreted this provision to require 'a rational or objective relationship between the SPS measure and the scientific evidence'.[21] The panel and Appellate Body concluded that Article 2.2 was being violated because Japan could not show that the quarantine and fumigation used for one variety of fruit or nut would be inadequate for other varieties.

Although it is often averred that the SPS Agreement requires governments to use 'sound science',[22] that term does not appear anywhere in the SPS Agreement. In omitting this term, the agreement remains unclear as to what extent panels may discount questionable scientific findings presented by a government. So far, no panel has been faced with such a decision. But a dispute will surely arise where a government presents a scientific study for an SPS measure that is then challenged by other scientists as being a poorly conducted study. It seems likely that future WTO panels will seek to weigh competing studies in the manner that many national courts do.

A second SPS discipline is the requirement for a risk assessment. Analysts looking for coherence within the WTO might view this discipline as part of a new pro-competitive regulatory thrust of world trade rules. At a sufficient level of abstraction, there is a common thread between the WTO requirements to protect intellectual property,[23] to administer services regulations 'in a reasonable, objective and impartial manner'[24] and to utilize a risk assessment. The common thread is the articulation of appropriate government regulatory practices.

SPS Article 5.1 requires governments to ensure that their sanitary and phytosanitary measures are 'based on an assessment, as appropriate to the circumstances, of the risks to human, animal or plant life or health'. This requirement has proven to be of central importance in enforcing the SPS Agreement. It was litigated in all three WTO disputes and thus there is now a small body of case-law. In all three disputes, the defendant government was found to be in violation of Article 5.1.

What is a risk assessment? The SPS Agreement explains that a risk assessment can be either (1) the evaluation of the likelihood of entry, establishment or spread of a pest or disease or (2) the evaluation of the potential for adverse effects on human or animal health arising from the presence of additives, contaminants, toxins or disease-causing organisms in food, beverages or feedstuffs.[25] In interpreting this provision, the Appellate Body seems to be saying that while an adequate assessment must evaluate the probability of risk, it does not have to make a monolithic finding.[26] Thus, a risk assessment that presented both a 'mainstream' and a 'divergent' scientific view could be an adequate assessment.[27] Moreover, there is no requirement that a risk assessment be expressed as a quantitative conclusion.[28]

Box 12.1 *The SPS Agreement: Obligations*

Basic obligations (Article 2)	'Specific application'* (Articles 3, 5, 7, 8)
Applied 'only to the extent necessary to protect' humans, animals or plants	Is in conformity with existing international standards, guidelines or recommendations *or*
'Based on scientific principles'	Scientific justification rationally based on risk assessment *and*
'not maintained without sufficient evidence'	Not more trade restrictive than required *and*
'not arbitrarily or unjustifiably discriminate/where identical or similar conditions prevail' [NT and MFN]	Complies with transparency and procedural obligations in Annexes B and C
'shall not be applied in a manner which would constitute a disguised restriction on international trade'	*Japanese Varietals AB, para 82.

Source: Foundation for International Environmental Law and Development (1999)

According to the Appellate Body, a risk assessment must find evidence of an 'ascertainable' risk.[29] The Appellate Body has stated that it will not be sufficient for governments to impose regulations simply on the basis of the 'theoretical' risk that underlies all scientific uncertainty.[30] For example in 'Salmon', the Appellate Body agreed with the panel that the analysis conducted by the Australian Government was not a proper risk assessment because it lent too much weight to 'unknown and uncertain elements'.[31] On the other hand, there is no minimally sufficient magnitude of risk that regulators must ascertain.[32] Adding this up, the Appellate Body appears to be saying that a risk assessment can still be acceptable even if it points to an extremely small risk.

The central importance of a risk assessment was made clear in 'Hormones'. In that dispute, there was considerable evidence that the use of hormones as a growth promoter was safe. Yet most of this evidence assumed that the hormones would be used in accordance with 'good veterinary practice'.[33] Thus, if hormones were misused in fattening animals, the available evidence did not demonstrate the safety of eating such meat.

This lacuna did not prevent the EU from losing the case, however.[34] Even while admitting that hormone abuse could constitute a health risk, the Appellate Body faulted the European Commission for not having a risk assessment of such potential abuse. Although some commentators suggest that SPS only prohibits import bans on products that have been proven safe, this episode shows that SPS disciplines can disallow a health regulation aimed at a potentially unsafe practice when no risk assessment exists.

Once the existence of an adequate risk assessment is shown, the panel must then consider whether the health measure is 'based on' this assessment. The Appellate Body reads 'based on' as a substantive requirement. In the first SPS case (Hormones), the panel sought to impose a procedural requirement that the defendant government should actually rely on the risk assessment. The panel then undertook an administrative law analysis of the EU's decision-making process. This approach had the effect of excluding new scientific evidence that arose during the course of WTO review. In an important ruling, the Appellate Body rejected this attempt to incorporate rule-making-type obligations into SPS.

The Appellate Body has been a bit unclear on how this 'based-on' test operates. Within the same decision, it said that the risk assessment must 'sufficiently warrant', 'sufficiently support', 'reasonably warrant', 'reasonably support' or 'rationally support' using the health measure, and that there must be an 'objective relationship' or a 'rational relationship' between the risk and the measure.[35] This test was first implemented in the Hormones case, where the panel and Appellate Body found that the thin EU risk assessment did not rationally support banning the importation of meat produced with growth hormones.[36]

The Appellate Body noted that an expert consulted by the panel had testified that one out of every million women would get breast cancer from eating meat produced with growth hormones.[37] But the Appellate Body dismissed this testimony from Dr George Lucier of the (US) National Institute of Environmental Health Sciences, noting that Lucier's opinion was not based on studies that he had conducted and that his views were 'divergent' from the other views received by the panel. It is unclear whether the Appellate Body dismissed Lucier's opinion as scientifically unsound, or adjudged a one-in-a-million risk to be unimportant.

The SPS Agreement does not direct panels to apply benefit–cost analysis.[38] Thus, so long as a governmental measure is based on an adequate risk assessment, the fact that the measure's cost exceeds its benefit would not constitute a violation of SPS. Looking ahead, there will probably be attempts by litigant governments to impose an economic test on defendant governments via Article 2.2. Even in its first SPS decision, the Appellate Body noted that promoting international trade and protecting human health were 'sometimes competing' interests.[39]

The third core SPS discipline is the requirement for national regulatory consistency. Article 5.5 states that 'With the objective of achieving consistency' in levels of protection against health risks, a government 'shall avoid arbitrary or unjustifiable distinctions in the levels it considers to be appropriate in different situations, if such distinctions result in discrimination or a disguised restriction on international trade'. This is the most controversial SPS rule because it supervises a government's choice of a 'level' of health protection to be pursued.[40]

The Appellate Body has confirmed that there are three elements to an Article 5.5 violation. First, the defendant government must be seeking different levels of health protection in 'comparable' situations. In Salmon, the Appellate Body explained that situations are 'comparable' when there is a common risk of entry or spread of one disease of concern.[41] For example, health regulations on salmon (for consumption) may be compared to regulations on herring (for bait) because both salmon and herring can cause the same health risk. The second element is that the differences in the government's intended level of protection must be 'arbitrary or unjustifiable'. This can be found if the risks are commensurate but the level of protection is different. The third element is that the health measure embodying these differences result in discrimination or a disguised restriction on international trade. In the disputes so far, the first two elements have been more easily shown.[42] So it is the third element on which many cases will hinge.

In Salmon, the Appellate Body makes five arguments for concluding that the Australian health measure constituted discrimination or a disguised restriction on trade.[43] It will be useful to examine the Appellate Body's analytical approach because the five arguments do not prove much. The first two arguments are mere bootstrapping; the Appellate Body points to the lack of a risk assessment (discussed above with Article 5.1) and to the different levels of health protection being sought for salmon and herring. The third argument is that there was a 'substantial' difference in the levels of health protection pursued. The fourth argument is that an Australian Government draft report in 1995, which would have been tolerant of salmon imports, was revised in the final report of 1996.[44] The fifth argument is that Australia lacks strict internal controls on salmon equivalent to what it imposes at the border.

This judicial approach is confounding in its analytical weakness and in its potential for mischief. Accusing a government of trade discrimination or a disguised trade restriction is a serious charge that should not be hurled lightly. As the Australian representative explained to the Appellate Body, it should not be a violation of the WTO for a government to change a recommendation between a draft and a final report.[45] Similarly, it should not be a WTO violation for a government to lack internal health controls on commerce equivalent to border controls. Yet according to the Appellate Body, such possibly innocent acts can aggregate into a SPS violation.[46] The mistake the Appellate Body makes is to assume that the incoherence of Australia's policy is motivated by protectionism. This puts the WTO in the odd position of being intolerant of irrational government policy in matters of public health while continuing to tolerate 'lose–lose' government trade policies such as tariffs and quotas.

A government convicted of violating Article 5.5 has two choices if it wants to comply. It can upwardly harmonize its chosen level of health protection or it can downwardly harmonize. Thus, although it would not be correct to say that Article 5.5 promotes downward harmonization, there is that potential and therefore the implementation of SPS decisions should be closely monitored.

The fourth core SPS discipline is the least trade restrictiveness requirement. Article 5.6 states that governments shall ensure that their sanitary and phytosanitary measures 'are not more trade-restrictive than required to achieve their appropriate level' of protection. To prove a violation, there must be an alternative measure, reasonably available, that is significantly less restrictive to trade.[47] So far, the WTO has found no Article 5.6 violation.

In two cases, the panels held that Article 5.6 was being violated, but both decisions were reversed on appeal. Nevertheless, these Appellate Body rulings contain some important interpretations of Article 5.6 which will be noted briefly. One is that governments are obligated to determine and reveal their chosen level of protection to WTO panels so that SPS rules can be applied.[48] Another is that in analysing an alternative measure, panels will consider whether it matches the intended level of protection, not the level of protection actually achieved by the SPS measure that is the target of the WTO lawsuit.[49] Another is that the complaining country must show that the alternative measure exists.[50] In other words, a panel may not posit the alternative based on the advice of experts. A key issue for the future will be how Article 5.6 is applied to domestic measures.

The fifth SPS discipline, Article 2.3, forbids measures that arbitrarily or unjustifiably discriminate between countries where identical or similar conditions prevail. It also states that SPS measures shall not be applied in a manner 'which would constitute a disguised restriction on international trade'. This provision has not yet been independently invoked in finding an SPS violation.[51]

The sixth SPS discipline is the requirement to use international standards. Article 3.1 states that governments 'shall base' their SPS measures on international standards, where they exist, except as otherwise provided.[52] As this provision links with others in a very confusing skein of obligations and exceptions, this Article will seek only to give a summary of this part of the SPS Agreement. International standards are the standards drafted by organizations such as the Codex Alimentarius Commission for food safety, the International Office of Epizootics for animal health, and the International Plant Protection Convention for plant health. When such standards do not exist, Article 3.1 has no effect.

When international standards do exist, a government has three choices: (1) use a higher standard in order to pursue a higher level of health protection, (2) use a lower standard, or (3) conform its SPS measure to the international standard. By conforming to the international standard, a government would gain a presumption in the WTO that its measure complies with the SPS rules. This presumption would be rebuttable, however. Some analysts have suggested that governments would have a greater incentive to use international standards if they were truly a 'safe harbour' from being challenged as SPS violations. Other analysts have criticized benchmarking to standards drafted in closed processes. For example, in February 2000, the Transatlantic Consumer Dialogue declared that 'governments should only recognize or be involved in harmonization activities negotiated in open, accountable democratic fora, with clear avenues for public input and transparent methods of rulemaking and recordkeeping'.

If a government chooses to pursue a level of health protection lower than the international standard, then it too must meet other SPS requirements. But it would not have to justify the deviation from international standards, even for its exports. The government need only assert that the lower standard results from its chosen level of protection. It should also be noted that a government of a country exporting food that fails to meet international health standards has no obligation to notify importing countries.[53]

The seventh SPS discipline involves the recognition of equivalence. Article 4.1 requires the government of an importing country to accept an SPS regulation by an exporting country as equivalent to its own, if the exporting country's government can objectively demonstrate that its health regulation achieves the level of protection chosen by the importing country government. This provides a valuable opportunity for exporting countries that often face impenetrable regulatory systems in importing countries.[54]

The eighth SPS discipline regards approval and inspection procedures. SPS Article 8 and Annex C require such procedures to be undertaken and completed 'without undue delay'.[55] This provision has not yet been the subject of dispute settlement.

In addition to these eight SPS disciplines, there is one other core SPS provision – Article 5.7 regarding provisional measures. The provision states that '[I]n cases where relevant scientific evidence is insufficient,' a government may 'provisionally adopt sanitary or phytosanitary measures on the basis of available pertinent information'. In such circumstances, the government is required to obtain additional information necessary for a more objective assessment of risk and to review the SPS measure within a reasonable period of time. This provision provides a qualified exemption from SPS Article 2.2.

The first country to invoke Article 5.7 was Japan in the Agricultural Products case. In an important decision, the panel suggested that it was up to the US (the plaintiff) to establish that Japan had not complied with Article 5.7.[56] But on the facts before it, the panel rejected Japan's claim and was upheld by the Appellate Body which stated that Japan had not obtained information for an objective assessment as to whether different fruit varieties manifest dissimilar quarantine effects. Japan had also failed to review its measure within a reasonable period of time.[57]

A discussion of Article 5.7 provides a good window for introducing the Precautionary Principle which is relevant to this provision and also relevant to SPS as a whole. As articulated in the Rio Declaration on Environment and Development (Principle 15), it states that 'where there are threats of serious or irreversible damage, lack of full scientific certainty shall not be used as a reason for postponing cost-effective measures to prevent environmental degradation'.[58] In the Hormones dispute, the EU chose not to invoke Article 5.7 as a defence.[59] Instead, the EU sought to justify its failure to follow Article 5.1 by calling attention to the Precautionary Principle which it characterized as a rule of customary international law. The panel responded that even if it was part of customary international law, the Precautionary Principle would not override Article 5.1, particularly since the Precautionary Principle had been incorporated into Article 5.7.[60]

The Appellate Body agreed with this conclusion and offered some additional observations about the Precautionary Principle.[61] First, it expressed uncertainty as to whether the Precautionary Principle had crystallized into a general principle of customary international environmental law. Second, it found that outside of environmental law – in other words, health law – the status of the Precautionary Principle awaits more authoritative formulation. Third, it stated that the Precautionary Principle had not been written into the SPS Agreement as a ground for justifying a measure that otherwise violates SPS. Fourth, it said that the Precautionary Principle 'finds reflection' in SPS Article 5.7, but that this provision does not exhaust the relevance of the Precautionary Principle for SPS.[62] Fifth, the Appellate Body counsels panels considering whether 'sufficient scientific evidence' exists to bear in mind that responsible, representative governments commonly act from perspectives of prudence and precaution where risks are irreversible. The Appellate Body counterbalances this point, however, by stating that the Precautionary Principle does not by itself relieve a panel from applying principles of treaty interpretation. What all these dicta add up to must await clarification in future cases.

As noted above, Article 5.7 states that when relevant scientific evidence is insufficient, governments may provisionally adopt SPS measures on the basis of available pertinent information. Future adjudications will determine how insufficient evidence can be and still justify an SPS measure. It is also unclear whether Article 5.7 provides an exemption to other SPS disciplines beyond Article 2.2.

Appraisal of SPS Dispute Settlement

SPS dispute settlement is providing good results for producers in exporting countries. Three long-standing complaints have been brought to the WTO and been adjudicated in favour of the exporter. At the end of 1999, none of these decisions have been complied with, but such compliance may ensue. Champions of SPS claim that no health interests have been sacrificed because the overruled import bans were unjustified. But until new imports enter, no one can know for sure.

Resolving the legal dispute is not equivalent to resolving the health dispute. Suppose that Australia complies with the WTO ruling, allows in Canadian salmon, and then suffers a huge loss from foreign salmon disease. Who would bear the cost of the WTO panel being wrong about the danger of alien pathogens? Not the panel, surely. Not the Canadian exporter. Not the WTO. No, it would be Australians who would suffer that cost. Right now, defendant countries like Australia have nothing to gain from SPS litigation and plaintiff countries like Canada have nothing to lose.[63]

It should also be noted that the SPS Agreement – which was largely initiated by the US government – favours those countries that have a surfeit of administrative procedures. Governments that can produce a voluminous risk assessment, show that it was considered by regulators and document each step of the regulatory process will probably do better as SPS defendants than countries with thinner regulatory structures. This may be one reason why no case has been lodged against the US even though there are numerous US regulations that keep out foreign agricultural products.

Although most SPS disciplines need extended observation before one can draw any conclusion, it is not too soon to begin drawing conclusions about Article 5.5, the requirement for regulatory consistency in levels of health protection being sought. In conducting an examination of national policy-making, an SPS panel is bound to provoke public concern about the loss in regulatory autonomy. The stringency of SPS Article 5.5 can be seen by comparing it to US commerce clause and European Community (EC) internal market jurisprudence.[64] While an odd exception may exist, facially neutral regulations are not struck down either in Europe or the US for being more stringent than regulations applied in comparable situations.

Precautionary Principle and Labelling

In this section, two of the most controversial topics in SPS law are discussed. First, there is an examination of the ambiguities of the Precautionary Principle and how it relates to SPS. Second, the topic of labelling, particularly as it relates to GM products, is reviewed.

Precautionary Principle

As noted above, the Appellate Body held that the Precautionary Principle finds reflection in SPS Article 5.7 which states that where scientific evidence is insufficient, governments 'may provisionally adopt sanitary or phytosanitary measures on the basis of available pertinent information'. Article 5.7 provides leeway to an interventionist-minded government worried about unknown risk. At this early stage of SPS adjudication, there is no reason to conclude that the existing language in Article 5.7 is inadequate to the problem of uncertain science.

Nevertheless, Article 5.7 is viewed as insufficient from two sides. Consumer groups and the European Commission say that the Precautionary Principle should be written into this Article, or perhaps more broadly into the WTO Agreement.[65] The word 'provisionally' is also objected to because it suggests that precautionary measures should be time-limited. On the other side, business groups view Article 5.7 as a potential loophole that allows trade restrictions with no scientific basis.

One problem with incorporating the Precautionary Principle into SPS is that there is no single authoritative statement of the principle.[66] The various intergovernmental renditions of the Principle differ on key elements. For example, the World Charter for Nature of 1982 states that:

> Activities which are likely to pose a significant risk to nature shall be preceded by an exhaustive examination; their proponents shall demonstrate that expected benefits outweigh potential damage to nature, and where potential adverse effects are not fully understood, the activities shall not proceed.[67]

This seems to be directed at individual economic activity and mandates a benefit–cost analysis. In 1990, the Bergen Declaration on Sustainable Development used the term 'precautionary principle' and states the idea as:

> Where there are threats of serious or irreversible damage, lack of full scientific certainty should not be used as a reason for postponing measures to prevent environmental degradation.[68]

The Bergen Declaration seems to be directed at collective environmental measures and proposes that they go forward in the absence of full scientific certainty. Measures to prevent environmental degradation could be inhibitory (eg government regulations) or promotional (eg government subsidies).

The most well-known formulation came in the Rio Declaration of 1992. Denoted as the 'precautionary approach', it states that:

> Where there are threats of serious or irreversible damage, lack of full scientific certainty shall not be used as a reason for postponing cost-effective measures to prevent environmental degradation.[69]

This provision seems to be directed at environmental measures and mandates that cost-effective action not be postponed while awaiting more scientific information. Like all versions of the Precautionary Principle, it provides guidance in situations of scientific uncertainty. According to James Cameron, a leading legal expert on the Principle, when scientific certainty is present, measures to prevent harm are 'preventative', not precautionary.[70]

It is unclear what cost-effective means in this context. In weighing benefits against costs, does it calculate the benefit based on a 'worst-case' assumption or on a 'best-guess' assumption?[71] In 1998, the European Commission formulated guidelines for the application of the Precautionary Principle which state that 'Measures based on the precautionary principle must include a cost/benefit assessment....'[72] This accords with the views of one prominent environmental analyst who explains that 'It is critical to recognize that the precautionary principle is meaningless without a robust analysis of the economic aspects of its application in particular cases'.[73] But the basic question of how future benefits are to be estimated and discounted has not been settled.

Incorporating the Rio Declaration precautionary approach into SPS would constitute a major change because, as presently interpreted, SPS does not mandate reliance on benefit–cost analysis.[74] SPS permits governments to impose very costly controls so long as there is some minimal risk being avoided. Although the Precautionary Principle might loosen SPS in allowing regulation without 'full scientific certainty', such loosening would be limited by a new requirement for a cost-effectiveness finding. Thus, contrary to the assumption of some consumer advocates, adding the Precautionary Principle to SPS would not necessarily make it easier for governments to justify bans on hormones or GM products.[75]

There is no one official rendition of the Precautionary Principle. Some commentators exclude the cost–benefit test. For instance, the WTO Secretariat (1999) states that the Precautionary Principle calls for caution 'to ensure safety margins against possibly irreversible damage'.[76] Another interpretive issue involves the allocation of the burden of proof in a regulatory process.[77] For example, the Wingspread Statement (1998) on the Precautionary Principle says that 'When an activity raises threats of harm to human health or the environment, precautionary measures should be taken even if some cause and effect relationships are not fully established scientifically. In this context the proponent of an activity, rather than the public, should bear the burden of proof'.[78] The advocacy group Public Citizen (1999) states the principle as 'potentially dangerous substances must be proven safe before they are put on the market'.[79] Both the Wingspread and Public Citizen formulations seek to put the onus on the producer rather than on the regulator. The World Charter for Nature (1982) also seems to do so.

If there is any principle underlying the Precautionary Principle, it is that collective decision-makers should exercise caution regarding private activities that may engender irreversible environmental effects. Government intervention is counselled to retard such activities. In highly regulated systems, this can mean governmental inaction.

One little-noted characteristic of SPS rules is that they apply in the same way to national regimes where:

(A) private activities are prohibited unless the proponent shows them to be safe, and
(B) private activities are permitted unless a regulator shows them to be unsafe and hence prohibits them.

While there are probably no governments that are pure Type A or B,[80] governments differ widely in their regulatory approach to risk. Yet SPS is procrustean in requiring evidence of risk before a product can be regulated (other than provisionally). Even regulatory *inaction* – refusing to approve a new product – is a governmental measure if there is an underlying law which prohibits activities unless they are permitted.

The Precautionary Principle has a different impact on Type A and B countries. Consider the following example: Suppose a regulator wants to be very cautious about the bioengineering practice of blending fish genes into fruit and decides to wait 20 years (ie one human gestational cycle) of innocuous use elsewhere before granting approval for such genetically modified (GM) products. Assuming that GM products come within the SPS jurisdiction, SPS rules would seem to disallow such extreme risk aversion – if 20 years is too long to be 'provisional'. This example shows that Type A countries may have a harder time complying with SPS than Type B countries.

This situation has led many environmentalists to call for a change in the burden of proof in WTO/SPS proceedings. Under present rules, the US can prevail by showing that the EU's hormone ban is not based on a risk assessment. The rules could be changed to require the US to prove that the banned hormones are safe.

The tightness of SPS rules is only one aspect of the broader debate about the Precautionary Principle. Proponents have a much broader goal than taking the WTO's thumb off national regulators. The goal seems to be to fortify national regulation against technological change. It would be interesting to run a simulation of a 'strong' Precautionary Principle and apply it to the major innovations of the 20th century such as nuclear fission, lasers, jet engines, contact lens, antibiotics, etc. Would the Precautionary Principle have slowed these down?

Product Labelling

SPS rules are unclear regarding mandatory product labelling. In its definition of SPS measures, the Agreement includes 'packaging and labelling requirements directly related to food safety'. The implication is that other labelling requirements are not supervised by SPS. For example, labelling for general consumer information would seem to be supervised, if at all, by other WTO agreements such as Technical Barriers to Trade (TBT) and GATT.[81] But no panel has yet clarified this point. Some legal analysts have suggested that a labelling requirement for meat produced with added hormones would violate WTO rules.[82] Many developing country governments argue that eco-labelling requirements are inconsistent with WTO rules.[83]

Within civil society, there is strong support for labelling. Recently, Consumers International stated that 'Measures to support informed choice should not be undermined by the WTO; for example, the labelling of genetically modified foods should not be threatened by WTO rules'.[84] Recognizing the adage that 'you are what you eat', many consumers seek information not only about the salubriousness of food, but also the ethics of its production.

The biggest labelling conflict involves genetic modification. Many governments are already implementing labelling requirements (eg the EU and Japan) or are moving towards them (eg Australia). Indeed, in 1999 a UN Development Programme study urged that every country should demand transparency and labelling of transgenic products.[85] But some governments, such as the US and Canada, have resisted the labelling movement.[86] According to the US Trade Representative:

> In the United States, companies are not required to label products simply because they are produced through biotechnology. The United States believes that such labelling is unnecessary, in the absence of an identified and documented risk to safety and health.[87]

In general, factual product labels are a market-friendly measure. Providing consumers with additional information empowers them to make choices according to their own self-interest. Although a labelling requirement is coercive when the manufacturer would prefer not to disclose the information,[88] labelling compares favourably with the alternative of banning a product. In the long-run, labelling may prove beneficial to the GM industry by enabling a gradual build-up of consumer confidence regarding the safety of genetic modification.

It may be true that gratifying consumer inquisitiveness with unnecessary information will turn counterproductive if consumers make irrational choices with that information. But even so, it is hard to see how the WTO can call factual food labelling unnecessary when the WTO permits governments to require labels disclosing the country of origin.[89] The WTO would put itself in peril by attempting to restrict GM labelling.[90]

Cartagena Protocol on Biosafety

In January 2000, an intergovernmental conference approved a Protocol on Biosafety to the Convention on Biological Diversity.[91] A similar effort a year earlier had ended in deadlock, and it appears that the new willingness of governments to compromise resulted from a more conciliatory stance by industry and a desire by governments to avoid another failure like WTO Seattle Ministerial. The Biosafety treaty has many important facets far beyond the scope of this article and the discussion here will focus on implications for the SPS agreement, the precautionary principle, and labelling.

The Biosafety Protocol is an environmental treaty with the stated objective of '... ensuring an adequate level of protection in the field of the safe transfer, handling and use of living modified organisms resulting from modern biotechnology ....'[92] Living organisms are defined as 'any biological entity capable of transferring or replicating genetic material, including sterile organisms, viruses and viroids.[93] Living modified organisms (LMOs) are defined as living organisms that possess a novel combination of genetic material obtained through the use of modern biotechnology.[94] Thus, for example, raw grain shipped to a food producer is an LMO, while the content of canned goods made by the producer is not an LMO. Pharmaceuticals for humans are excluded from the Protocol.[95]

The treaty sets up a system to regulate international trade of LMOs. For LMOs intended to be introduced into the environment (eg planted), the treaty provides a prior informed consent procedure and declares that a Party may prohibit such imports following a risk assessment.[96] The treaty further provides that 'Lack of scientific certainty ... shall not prevent that party from taking a decision, *as appropriate* ... in order to avoid or minimize such potential adverse effects'.[97] For LMOs intended for direct use as food, feed, or processing, the treaty declares that a Party may take a decision on imports under a domestic regulatory framework, or if it is a developing or transition country, may regulate imports following a risk assessment.[98] Such import decisions are subject to the same guidance about a lack of scientific certainty.[99] The treaty also directs that 'Measures based on a risk assessment shall be imposed to the extent necessary to prevent adverse effects ...' of LMOs.[100]

The treaty includes provisions regarding the minimum documentation needed for the transboundary movement of LMOs. When intended to be introduced into the environment or held in contained use. LMOs are to be clearly identified.[101] When intended for use as food, feed or processing, the requirements are less strict; the package need only say that it 'may contain' LMOs.[102] Detailed requirements for this are to be developed by the Conference of the Parties.

The drafters sought to make the Biosafety treaty compatible with SPS, and it appears that they succeeded. To the extent that the Biosafety treaty requires a trade measure – most notably in declaring that measures based on a risk assessment shall be imposed to the extent necessary to prevent adverse effects[103] – this would seem to be potentially consistent with SPS Articles 2.2 and 5.1. To the extent that the Biosafety treaty permits national discretion in using trade measures in the absence of scientific certainty, this would seem to be potentially consistent with SPS Article 5.7. Furthermore, action taken pursuant to the Biosafety treaty may be an international standard privileged under SPS Article 3.2 which would give an import ban or a label a presumption of consistency with the SPS disciplines in Articles 5.5 and 5.6.

Disputes about a national measure taken pursuant to the Biosafety treaty could, of course, be brought to the WTO, but there is no reason to think that a WTO panel would rule against an import ban or label that meets the terms of the Biosafety treaty. Looking ahead, the key issue is whether the dispute procedure of the Convention on Biological Diversity (CBD) will be utilized to make these judgements in an environmental context rather than relegating them to the WTO to be made in a trade context. Unlike the WTO dispute procedures which have compulsory jurisdiction, the CBD procedures depend upon prior consent of the parties before going to arbitration or submitting the dispute to the International Court of Justice'.[104] But if the CBD arbitration or adjudication takes place, it seems likely that the WTO would grant deference to it.[105]

The Biosafety Protocol employs a fairly strong version of the Precautionary Principle with no mention of cost-effectiveness. Yet it does state that decisions will be taken 'as appropriate'.[106] It is unclear whether this is meant to incorporate a proportionality test.

Conclusion

In its first five years, the SPS Agreement has been used by governments to challenge foreign trade barriers that may not be necessary. With the exception of a few rough spots, the process has worked reasonably well. Nevertheless, there are grounds for worry that the new SPS Agreement endangers public support for the trade regime. As European Trade Commission Pascal Lamy admitted recently, the SPS Agreement 'was not primarily conceived with consumers in mind'.[107]

In adjudicating SPS complaints, the WTO may gain a reputation as a naysayer to health and safety regulation. Every time it declares an SPS measure to be WTO-illegal, there will be consumers who lament a perceived loss in health security. Already there are many NGOs around the world who oppose the WTO because they believe that it privileges trade over a healthy environment. The WTO rules on food safety were one of the chief targets for protestors at the WTO Ministerial Conference in Seattle.

The debate over the precautionary principle has helped to clarify the difficulty of imposing science-based rules on national regulatory processes that routinely balance science against social values. The drafters of SPS thought it would be flexible enough to accommodate all legitimate health concerns. And perhaps it is. But the drafters did not foresee that the process of international supervision would become so controversial among consumers.

The Biosafety Protocol is significant because it establishes new environmental rules that cut through some of the uncertainty in SPS. By achieving a treaty that appears to balance trade and environmental concerns, the governments have taken an important step to head off GM-related disputes that could undermine the WTO.[108] A similar approach could be used for other health and environmental concerns in the years ahead.

Acknowledgements

The views expressed are those of the author only. Portions of this study appeared in *Trade, Environment, and the Millennium* (1999). The author wishes to thank Bill Davey for his helpful comments

Notes

1   See Agreement on the Application of Sanitary and Phytosanitary Measures (here in after SPS Agreement)
2   See, eg Lean, Geoffrey (1999) 'The hidden tentacles of the world's most secret body', *The Independent* (London), 18 July, p13; Wallach, Lori and Sforza, Michelle (1999) Whose *Trade Organization? Corporate Globalization and the Erosion of Democracy*, Public Citizen, Inc, especially chapters 2 and 3. See also the full page

advertisement in the *New York Times*: 'Warning–Bioinvasion', *New York Times*, 20 September 1999, pA11 (stating that trade threatens biodiversity and calling for a de-emphasis on global trade and travel)

3   See World Trade Organization, Vol 1 *Guide to GATT Law and Practice*, p565 (1995) (discussing the drafting history of GATT Article XX which anticipated consultation with international scientific agencies)

4   Domestic measures regulate activities within a country and may be applied similarly to imported products. By contrast, a trade measure applies only to imported products

5   See Agreement Establishing the World Trade Organization, Annex 1A, General Interpretative Note

6   SPS rules are enforced in WTO dispute settlement. If a WTO member government believes that another member is utilizing a health measure in violation of SPS rules, it can lodge a complaint to the WTO. A panel will be appointed to hear testimony from the plaintiff and defendant governments and then render a decision. After the panel hands down its decision, it may be appealed to the WTO Appellate Body (as the first three SPS cases were). The Appellate Body then delivers a final decision within 90 days. If the defendant government loses the case, it is asked by the WTO Council to bring its SPS measure into conformity with whatever SPS rule it was found to violate. If the government does not do so within a specified period of time, the WTO Council may authorize the complaining country to impose trade retaliation on the scofflaw government. In all three SPS cases, the panels consulted scientific experts to reach a decision

7   'EC Measures Concerning Meat and Meat Products (Hormones)', Report of the Panel, WT/DS26 and WT/DS48; modified by Report of the Appellate Body, AB-1997-4, 16 January 1998 (hereinafter Appellate Body Hormones Decision)

8   'US, Canada Name Final EU Imports Targeted for Duties in Beef Dispute', *World Food Regulations Review*, No 9, pp13, 14 (September 1999)

9   'Australia – Measures Affecting the Importation of Salmon', Report of the Panel, WT/DS18; modified by Report of the Appellate Body, AB-1998-5, 20 October 1998 (hereinafter Appellate Body Salmon Decision)

10 'Japan – Measures Affecting Agricultural Products', Report of the Panel, WT/DS76; modified by Report of the Appellate Body, AB-1998-8, 22 February 1999 (hereinafter Appellate Body Agricultural Products Decision)

11 'US Considers Filing WTO Complaint Over EU Barriers to GMO Trade, USTR Says', BNA Daily Report for Executives, 25 June 1999, pA-2

12 SPS Annex A, para 1. See Ag-Biotech Forum, Discussion Paper on Agricultural Biotechnology, Inside US Trade, 24 September 1999, pp21–23

13 The applicability of SPS to GM products is complex. SPS applies to organisms, but this key term is not defined in SPS. Cereal in a carton is not an organism, but the cut grain used to make the cereal is an organism. Seeds are organisms

14 But the risk that GM seeds would injure insects is probably not covered by SPS which omits many non-disease ecological risks

15 The WTO Secretariat has devised a good flow-chart showing how trade supervision is split between SPS and TBT, and how some regulations are not supervised

by either. See World Trade Organization, Sanitary and Phytosanitary Measures (WTO Agreement Series 4, 1998), pp15–16. Students of the SPS Agreement often get confused by thinking that SPS is designed to permit certain regulations, and thus regulations not permitted are prohibited. This is error.

16 Agreement on Technical Barriers to Trade, art 1.5
17 SPS Agreement, Annex A.1
18 Appellate Body Hormones Decision, paras 113–118
19 For a good discussion of the role of science in trade agreements, see David A Wirth (1994) 'The Role of Science in the Uruguay Round and NAFTA Trade Disciplines', *Cornell International Law Journal*, Vol 27
20 SPS Annex C, para 1(a) strengthens this discipline by requiring that SPS approval and inspection measures be 'completed without undue delay'. This provision has not yet been applied by a WTO panel
21 Appellate Body Agricultural Products Decision, para 84
22 See, eg 'Industry Presses US Government to Uphold Sound Science Rules', *Inside US Trade*, 23 April 1999, p7; 'Transatlantic Business Dialogue', Berlin Communiqué, 30 October 1999, p29 (urging governments to reaffirm the WTO's commitment to sound science criteria), available at http://www.tabd/com.recom/berlincomm.html
23 Agreement on Trade-Related Aspects of Intellectual Property Rights
24 General Agreement on Trade in Services, art VI:1. See also the Basic Telecommunications Reference paper which calls for the prevention of anti-competitiveness practices in telecom, at www.wto.org/wto/services/tel23.htm
25 SPS Annex A, para 4
26 Appellate Body Hormones Decision, para 187; Appellate Body Salmon Decision, paras 123–124
27 Appellate Body Hormones Decision, para 194
28 Appellate Body Salmon Decision, para 124
29 Appellate Body Hormones Decision, para 187; Appellate Body Salmon Decision, para 125
30 Appellate Body Hormones Decision, para 186
31 Appellate Body Salmon Decision, para 129
32 Appellate Body Hormones Decision, para 186; Appellate Body Salmon Decision, paras 124
33 Appellate Body Hormones Decision, para 206
34 Appellate Body Hormones Decision, paras 206–208
35 Appellate Body Hormones Decision, paras 186, 189, 193, 197, 253(L). It is interesting to note that in 1927 the Committee of Experts for the Progressive Codification of International Law suggested that the Permanent International Court of Justice develop a 'rule of reasonableness' for sanitary measures. League of Nations, Committee of Experts for the Progressive Codification of International Law, The Most-Favoured-Nation Clause, reprinted in *American Journal of International Law*, No 22, pp133, 149 (Supplement Special, 1928)
36 Appellate Body Hormones Decision, paras 196, 197, 200
37 Appellate Body Hormones Decision, para 198 (and notes therein). Actually, the rendition of Dr Lucier's testimony in the Appellate Body opinion is taken out

of context. What Lucier actually said is that the risk would be *between* zero and one in a million. EC Measures Concerning Meat and Meat Products (Hormones), Report of the Panel, Annex, paras 819, 826. So in ascribing more certainty to Lucier's testimony, the Appellate Body seems to reject it on the merits

38 See Alan O Sykes, 'Regulatory Protectionism and the Law of International Trade', No 66 *University of Chicago Law Review*, No 1, pp31–33 (1999)

39 Appellate Body Hormones Decision, para 177

40 The SPS Agreement makes clear that governments are permitted to determine their desired 'level' of health protection or, in other words, their acceptable level of risk. SPS Agreement, Annex A, para 5. Indeed, the Appellate Body has implied that a government can set a goal of 'zero risk' as its level of protection. Appellate Body Salmon Decision, para 125. But measures taken to achieve this goal would still have to meet all SPS disciplines

41 Appellate Body Salmon Decision, para 152

42 See Joost Pauwelyn, 'The WTO Agreement on Sanitary and Phytosanitary (SPS) Measures as Applied in the First Three SPS Disputes: EC – Hormones, Australia – Salmon and Japan – Varietals', *Journal of International Economic Law*, Vol 2, pp641, 654 (1999)

43 Appellate Body Salmon Decision, paras 161–178. The analysis involves an examination of 'warning signals' and 'other factors' which can only be summarized in this article

44 Appellate Body Salmon Decision, paras 172–173. In civic Republican-style language, the panel criticizes the Australian government for not explaining why the changes were made and justifying these changes in terms of SPS commitments. Australia – Measures Affecting the Importation of Salmon, Report of the Panel, paras 7.18, 8.154 and n425

45 Appellate Body Salmon Decision, paras 27, 171

46 Appellate Body Salmon Decision, paras 176–178

47 SPS Article 5.6, n3

48 Appellate Body Salmon Decision, para 206.

49 Appellate Body Agricultural Products Decision, paras 197–200

50 Appellate Body Agricultural Products Decision, paras 126, 130

51 In the Salmon case, the Appellate Body confirmed the panel's view that a violation of SPS Article 5.5 implied a violation of Article 2.3. Appellate Body Salmon Decision, paras 178, 240, 255

52 Some commentators have criticized the Appellate Body for making it so easy for governments to use a more stringent regulation than an international standard. For example, see Ryan David Thomas, 'Where's the Beef? Mad Cows and the Blight of the SPS Agreement', *Vanderbilt Journal of Transnational Law*, No 32, pp487, 507–516 (1999)

53 SPS Annex B, para 5 provides an obligation to notify other governments of a proposed regulation that would be below international standards, but only if the regulation would have a significant effect on trade

54 '27 Nations Seek Equivalence Status to Open U.S. Doors to Meat, Poultry', *World Food Regulation Review*, No 8, May 1999, p13

55 SPS art 8 and Annex C, para 1(a)
56 Japan – Measures Affecting Agricultural Products, Report of the Panel, para 8.58. Thus, Article 5.7 should not be thought of as an exception because that might imply that the defendant government would have the burden of proof
57 Appellate Body Agricultural Products Decision, paras 92–93
58 Rio Declaration on Environment and Development, 14 June 1992, Principle 15, reprinted in *International Legal Materials*, No 31, pp874, 879 (1992)
59 Quick, Reinhard and Bluthner, Andreas (1999) 'Has the Appellate Body Erred? An Appraisal and Criticism of the ruling in the WTO Hormones Case', *Journal of International Economic Law*, No 2, pp603, 625 (1999)
60 EC Measures Concerning Meat and Meat Products (Hormones), Report of the Panel, WT/DS26, para 8.157
61 Appellate Body Hormones Decision, paras 123–125
62 Appellate Body Hormones Decision, para 124
63 It might be argued that Australia gains by having the WTO free its regulatory system from encrusted special interests (ie salmon producers)
64 See generally Damien Geradin (1997) *Trade and the Environment. A Comparative Study of EC and US Law*, pp23–29, 37–39, 60–65, Cambridge University Press
65 For example, the World Wide Fund For Nature (WWF) has called for amending or interpreting the SPS and TBT Agreements to respect fully the Precautionary Principle. WWF, A Reform Agenda for the WTO Seattle Ministerial Conference, September 1999, p4. The European Commission brought up SPS reform at the failed WTO negotiations for a 'Clinton Round' in Seattle. 'EU Defends Link of AG to Other Parts of Seattle Declaration', *Inside US Trade*, 10 December 1999, pp1, 2
66 The earliest discussion this author has seen of the role of precaution in sanitary measures was by John Bell Condliffe in 1940. Condliffe explained that it is 'not a simple matter to determine when precautionary measures are unjustified and are, in fact, simply a method of indirect protectionism'. J B Condliffe (1940) *The Reconstruction of World Trade*, p199. The precautionary principle had its modern origin in the North Sea conferences of the 1980s. James Cameron and Julie Abouchar, 'The Precautionary Principle: A Fundamental Principle of Law and Policy for the Protection of the Global Environment', *Boston College International and Comparative Law Review*, No 14, pp1, 4–5
67 World Charter for Nature, 28 October 1982, para 11(b), reprinted in *International Legal Material*, No 22, p455 (1983)
68 Barton, Charmian (1998) 'The Status of the Precautionary Principle in Australia: Its Emergence in Legislation and as a Common Law Doctrine', *Harvard Environmental Law Review*, No 22, pp509, 516. Compare Separate Opinion of Judge Laing of the International Tribunal for the Law of the Sea in the Southern Bluefin Tuna Cases, at para 14. Judge Laing formulates the precautionary principle as: 'in the face of serious risk to ... the environment, scientific uncertainty or the absence of complete proof should not stand in the way of positive action to minimize risks or take actions of a conservatory, preventative or curative nature'.

69 Rio Declaration on Environment and Development, 14 June 1992, Principle 15, reprinted in *International Legal Materials*, No 31, pp874, 879 (1992)

70 Cameron, James (1999) 'The Precautionary Principle', in Gary P Sampson and W Bradnee Chambers (eds) *Trade, Environment, and the Millennium*, pp239, 241

71 Another question: Does it mean cost-effective to the producer, to the government, or to the whole economy?

72 European Commission, 'Guidelines on the Application of the Precautionary Principle', 17 October 1998, p9. It is interesting to note that in the context of food safety, the Government of Sweden has presented a formulation of the Precautionary Principle that does not include cost-benefit analysis, but does call for a 'proportionate' response. Codex Alimentarius Commission, Report of the 14th Session of the Codex Committee on General Principles, ALINORM 99/33A, April 1999, para 28, at ftp.fao.org/codex/ALINORM/al9933ae.pdf

73 von Moltke, Konrad (1999) 'The Dilemma of the Precautionary Principle in International Trade', 3 *Bridges* 3 (July–August), available at http://ictsd.org/English/BRIDGES3-6.pdf

74 See Jones, Wayne (1999) 'Weigh Up the Costs and Benefits', *OECD Observer*, No 216, March, p30

75 For discussion of the benefits of GM, see Morris, Julian (1999) 'Flawed campaign threatens world's poor: Environmentalists are wrong to oppose free trade in genetically modified organisms', *Financial Times*, 23 November 1999, p15; Shah, Mahendra and Strong, Maurice (1999) *Food in the 21st Century: from Science to Sustainable Agriculture,* pp36-39 (Consultative Group on International Agricultural Research) (available on CGIAR website)

76 WTO Secretariat, 'Trade and Environment', Special Studies 4 (1999), available on http://www.wto.org (hereinafter WTO Report), p13

77 *International Environmental Law and Policy*, 360–363 (David Hunter, James Saizman and Durwood Zaeike (eds) 1998)

78 This statement was drafted by a civil society conference, http://users.wantree.com.au/~rabbit/prec.htm. See Ronald Bailey, 'Precautionary Tale', *Reason*, April 1999, p37

79 Wallach and Sforza, *supra* note 2, pp54, 60

80 But see the observation by Pascal Lamy, the Trade Commissioner for the European Union. According to Lamy:

In the US they believe that if no risks have been proven about a product, it should be allowed. In the EU we believe something should not be authorized if there is a chance of risk.

'Parliament Yields in Spat with Prodi, But 'People's Party' Issues New Demands', *BNA Daily Report for Executives*, 3 September 1999, pA-9

81 See Terence P Stewart and David S Johanson, 'Policy in Flux: The European Union's Laws on Agricultural Biotechnology and their Effects on International Trade', *Drake Journal of Agricultural Law*, No 4, pp243, 285–292 (1999) (discussing the applicability of TBT and SPS to GM labelling)

82 See, eg Horlick, Gary N (1999) 'The World Trading System at the Crossroad of Science and Politics', in Jagdish Bhagwati (ed) *The Next Trade Negotiating Round: Examining the Agenda for Seattle*, pp257, 258

83 Shahin, Magda, 'Trade and Environment: How Real is the Debate?', in *Trade, Environment, and the Millennium, supra* note 70, pp35, 54
84 Consumers International, 'Consumer Rights and the Multilateral Trading System: What Needs to be done before a Millennium Round 9' (1999), available at http://www.oneworld.org/consumers/trade/index.html
85 UN Development Programme, Human Development Report 75 (1999)
86 'US, Canada Concerned About Increase in Labelling Measures Affecting GMOs', International Environmental Reporter, No 22 p525 (1999); Michiyo Nakamoto, 'Japan's food labels decision may fuel trade friction: Tokyo is not against genetically modified food, but is responding to consumer concerns', *Financial Times*, 16 September 1999, p4
87 US Trade Representative, National Trade Estimate Report on Foreign Trade Barriers 1999, p112. It is unclear whom the US Trade Representative means by the 'United States'. In 1999, a Gallup poll showed that 68 per cent of the public wants labelling of GM organisms, *even if* labelling leads to a higher price. See Scott Kilman, 'Biotech Scare Sweeps Europe, and Companies Wonder if US Is Next', *Wall Street Journal*, 7 October 1999, pAl
88 Mandatory labelling may also be unconstitutional in countries which have strong protections for freedom of speech. For example, in 1996, the Second Circuit ruled that Vermont's factual label requirement was unconstitutional in compelling the producer to disclose its use of recombinant bovine growth hormones. In the federal court's view, Vermont was wrong to assume that it had a substantial state interest in facilitating the public's right to know. International Dairy Foods Association v Amestoy, 93 F.3d 67, pp13–17 (westlaw pagination). It is interesting to note that the rights of free speech and a free press do not prevent US state laws to shield farmers and food companies from public criticism. See Melody Petersen, 'Farmers Right to Sue Grows, Raising Debate on Food Safety', *New York Times*, 1 June 1999, pA1
89 See GATT Article IX (marks of origin)
90 A recent WTO panel decision could suggest an additional reason for the WTO not to interfere with factual labels – namely, that a principal purpose of the WTO is to protect individuals and the market-place. See United States – Sections 301–310 of the Trade Act of 1974, WT/DS/152/R, 22 December 1999 (unadopted), para 7.86. This decision (on the topic of the US Trade Act of 1974) held that the US government was not violating the WTO. In reaching this judgement, the WTO panel expanded on a previous GATT ruling to voice a remarkable conclusion that 'The multilateral trade system is, per force, composed not only of States but also, indeed mostly, of individual economic operators'. Ibid paras 7.76, 7.84. A WTO oriented in favour of the individual and the market would be very unlikely to rule against factual labels
91 Cartagena Protocol on Biosafety, www.biodiv.org. For background on the new protocol, see *Earth Negotiations Bulletin*, 31 January 2000, http://www.iisd.ca/biodiv/
92 Ibid art 1
93 Ibid art 3(h). Not all organisms are living. For example, the protein prion that appears to cause BSE comes within the terms of SPS even though it is not a living organism

94 Ibid art 3(g)
95 Ibid art 5
96 Ibid arts 8, 10.1, 10.3(b), 15.2
97 Ibid art 10.6 (emphasis added). The Protocol does not identify this as the Precautionary Principle, but the stated objective of the Protocol alludes to Principle 15 of the Rio Declaration. Id art 1
98 Ibid art 11.4, 11.6, 14.4. Such decisions are required within 270 days following notification of the prospective export. Id art 11.1, 11.6
99 Ibid art 11.8
100 Ibid art 16.2
101 Ibid art 18.2
102 Ibid art 18.2(a)
103 Ibid art 16.2
104 Ibid art 34. Convention on Biological Diversity, art 27.3
105 SPS art 11.3 states that nothing shall impair the rights of members under other international agreements, including the right to resort to good offices or a dispute settlement mechanism. This provision could serve as a basis for deference by the WTO to an arbitral decision under CBD
106 Biosafety Protocol, arts 10.6, 11.8
107 Pascal Lamy, Address to Assembly of Consumers Associations in Europe, November 1999, http://europe.eu.int/comm/trade/speeches articles/spla05en.htm
108 See, eg Burgess, John (2000) 'Trade Rules Set on Food Genetics; Compromise Gained on Labeling Issue', *W. Post*, 30 January, pA1; Alden, Edward (2000) 'Greens and Free Traders Join to Cheer GM Crop Deal', *Financial Times*, 31 January, p11

13

Too Many Fishing Boats, Too Few Fish: Can Trade Laws Trim Subsidies and Restore the Balance in Global Fisheries?

Christopher D Stone

Introduction

The world's capture fisheries are being overexploited. A reduction in this pressure, allowing stocks to rebuild, would increase productivity and maximize revenues in the long run. Fisheries managers are utilizing an array of techniques, including restraints on time, place, gear and catch, to dampen the level of harvest. But the chronic over-hang of excess capital and labour undermine those efforts. There is no single remedy. However, subsidies are a crucial culprit. Fishing subsidies, estimated at tens of billions of US dollars annually worldwide, lure and shelter the excessive catch capacity. As a consequence, there is a growing movement, in a variety of fora, to call fishery subsidies and 'overcapacity' into question.

This chapter proposes that trade disciplines should be more aggressively used in the campaign to reduce the pressure on stocks. Fish products constitute one of the major components in world trade. Many government programmes designed to support fishers appear to violate existing trade laws. There are, of course, major barriers to any assault on practices as widespread and entrenched as fishing sub-sidies. But inroads have been made, or are in the offing, even in the farm sector. In the fishing sector, the potential support of resource and environmental constitu-encies brightens the prospect for using trade law as an instrument of reform.

Background

Across the world, fisheries, once imagined to be inexhaustible, arc showing signs of strain. More and more of the world's major fishing regions and fish stocks are listed as 'overfished' or 'depleted'.[1] The most highly prized stocks have been hardest hit.[2] As the most fecund areas collapse or decline, modern vessels, outfitted with high-tech devices for locating, catching and on-board processing, open up increas-ingly remote areas for exploitation. Meanwhile, many older, conventional vessels, not fitted for frontiers, redouble pressure inward, netting ever-smaller and less optimal prey.[3] Precincts of marine sanctuaries, in which stocks can hide and recover, have shrunk in response; all major trawlable shelves are being trawled.[4] At the same time, pollution, development and other pressures of human habitation assault coastal wetlands and mangrove areas, impairing their service as natural spawning grounds and nurseries for the replenishment of marine stocks.

Not all the data are dire. Since 1950, global fish production increased from 20 million to 110 million tons.[5] Over the past decade, a striking increase in aquaculture, which now amounts to about 19 per cent of the total world fish production, significantly augmented the modest over-all gains in capture fisheries.[6] Indeed, over the past 50 years, the increase in total fish harvest actually outpaced the increase in human population.[7]

Nonetheless, there is almost universal agreement that these facially positive statistics mask unsettling trends. The yield from marine capture fisheries (the dominant sector) shows signs of stagnation; further sustainable expansion is unlikely.[8] The fact that the level of effort has been expanding far faster than catch supports this pessimism.[9] Moreover, the figures obscure a, pronounced shift in catch quality. At the docks, species that were formerly throw-backs are replacing high-value species.[10] Five low-value species, only one of them eaten by humans (the rest being used for animal feed and fertilizer) account for the entire increase in catch since 1983.[11] Juveniles compose an increasing percentage of the harvest.[12] In addition, our brash invasion of deep sea spaces, ecosystems about which we know very little, has produced portents of collapse, with uncertain threats to the food web and biodiversity.[13] At the same time, increasing reports of high environmental costs and doubts about the long-term sustainability of many of the enterprises cloud the promise of aquaculture.[14]

The severity of the situation is uncertain. A full critique of global fisheries would require multiple perspectives. The prognosis shifts, depending on whether one adopts the economic perspective of *consumer satisfaction* (assuming tastes as a given and maximizing net revenue),[15] *food security* (maximizing a proxy for nutrition, such as protein per dollar of effort, over the longterm), *biodiversity* (maximizing a proxy for species or ecological diversity), or *regional development* (making special allowances for regions particularly dependent on fish for employment and food).

For example, from the economic perspective of consumer satisfaction, a catch that is constant in terms of tonnage and capture costs, but that sells for less on the market, is a setback. However, from the perspective of feeding the world's burgeoning populations, an increase in tonnage, even at some decline in market value, may be desirable, as long as it represents a sustainable expansion in protein. Alternatively, a protein maximizing strategy would presumably exploit the higher reserves of lower valued species that tend to be lower on the food web, rather than the more highly valued ('tastier') species, such as swordfish and tuna, that tend to be near the top of the food chain. Such a protein-maximizing strategy would presumably exploit the high reserves of lower value species as input to other foods (as fertilizer and 'feed') rather than as direct human fare.[16] On the other hand, if one resolves to move lower down the food chain to promote a strategy of protein maximization, one risks destabilizing keystone species and processes, thus impairing both biodiversity and productivity in unforeseen ways.

Hence, how one evaluates the global fishing situation depends on which of these objectives one adopts, and on judgements as to their interrelationship. But it is safe to say that no one is satisfied from any of these perspectives. Indeed, fishing is an area in which even resource optimists concede the need for significant reevaluation of policies.[17] The most provocative estimate remains this: FAO calculated that if fishing pressures relaxed to allow the rehabilitation of stocks, the catch of capture fishers could stabilize at a level 20 tonnes higher globally. That increase could add US$16 billion to gross revenues annually, and at a lower cost to the industry and environment.[18]

The Limitations of Conventional Fisheries Management Policies

The effort to manage fisheries has a long history and has utilized a wide array of techniques. Regulatory measures have included restrictions on quarry, locale, gear and seasons, and, more recently, experiments with tradable catch quotas.[19]

However, the root problem facing regulators has always been open access. Fishing grounds are unrestricted 'commons' areas, and the ownership of a fish is not allocated until the moment of capture. As a result, each fisher is indifferent to the costs that removal of the resource imposes on other members of the fleet, and investment in fishing proceeds to the point at which each fisher can no longer recover his own opportunity costs.[20] If there are too many vessels, the temptation to cheat on year-end catch rules is great. Hence, restraints on entry are crucial to regulators' success.

The recognition of coastal state jurisdiction over an adjacent 200-mile fishery zone[21] promised relief, inasmuch as the state gained the power to exclude foreign fleets, at least when there were no surplus stocks.[22] But efforts to exploit the potential of the managerial zones have been uneven and slow. Some nations that reduced pressure by excluding foreign vessels simply permitted local fleets to expand to replace or augment the void created by foreign fleet expulsion; virtual open access and its symptoms persist.[23]

Even where enclosure led to promulgation of a new bundle of regulations, the new rules have often proven inadequate and even perverse. For example, the shortening of seasons have commonly led to 'fishing Olympics'. Fishers simply attack with larger and ever more lethal vessels 'to get while the getting is good'. When the season ends, the added catch capacity is either laid up or redeployed to plunder another quick harvest somewhere else. Shortened seasons also produce bulges in production where smooth production would be optimal. Because fish spoil, most of the catch must be marketed as canned or frozen rather than as high-priced fresh fish.

Similarly, government imposed limits on vessels and gear have proven ineffectual or worse. Prohibiting the most efficient means of fishing simply raises unit costs without assuring a reduction in catch. Quotas (Total Allowable Catches (TACs)) have also proven flawed. Industry commonly pressures managers to set the TACs too high. Moreover, because of inadequate monitoring, the immediate effect of catch limits is to deter vessels from landing, or, more accurately, *re-*

porting any excess. It is widely assumed that a considerable quantity of excess catch is either thrown back (much of it to die)[24] or landed as contraband resources for the 'black' fish market.[25]

To cite these infirmities is not to dismiss fisheries zones and their managers. But even the successes are double-edged. For example, regulatory achievements, particularly limits to entry within the fisheries zones, may simply drive some vessels into the high seas areas to escape national regulatory reach. High seas catches, which constituted 5 per cent of the harvest in the 1970s, rose to 10 per cent in the 1980s.[26] Concern that plunderers of coastal waters might respond to the imposition of fisheries zones by turning their attentions to uncontrolled high seas areas produced several countermeasures, including resolutions against drift-netting,[27] the FAO Code of Good Practices,[28] and the UN Convention on Highly Migratory and Straddling Stocks.[29] Despite their worthy ambitions, the impact of these measures remains to be demonstrated.

'Overcapitalisation' and Excess Capacity

There is no single explanation for why fisheries management has not been more successful. Areas of overlapping jurisdiction and the high seas present special obstacles to multilateral cooperation. Even in areas of exclusive jurisdiction, inadequately understood non-anthropogenic variables, such as natural fluctuations in recruitment and temperature, frustrate proper management decisions. Regulatory measures, including catch limits, must pass through a gauntlet of attacks from entrenched fishing, shipbuilding and allied support industries. Once limits are declared, monitoring violations presents a further challenge.

While many factors thus conspire to frustrate efforts at fisheries management, it has become popular recently to focus attention on 'overcapitalization': too many vessels are chasing too few fish. There is some truth in the charge. But it is also misleading. While investment in vessels and other capital, such as port infrastructure and gear, may be specially problematic,[30] the excess is that of an *activity* – fishing – and not of *capital* alone. Industry pours labour, fuel and other inputs, in addition to capital, into fishing in excess of what is required to achieve the appropriate level of harvest.

This is not to say that reducing fleets and other capacity and input factors will solve the problems. On the contrary, the strengthening and extending of conventional fisheries management will continue to warrant the greatest effort. However, as long as the catch capacity (all inputs considered) far exceeds the optimal, those caught up in the overhang, particularly underemployed fishermen and owners of older, unprofitable vessels that have to struggle just to break even, will resist and subvert regulatory efforts. All too often, the politics of excess capacity translates into the disregard of science and the slackening of needed reforms.[31]

Theoretically, 'overcapacity' is a state in which *the value of inputs to fishing is greater than required for most efficiently achieving the desired level of fishing activity.* However, there is little consensus on what would constitute the 'right' capacity, or the 'right' level of inputs, against which excess should be measured. For instance, the safe catch level for any stock is always controversial and fluctuates from year to year. In the light of the uncertainties, it is not clear what level of fishing activity will net the 'right' catch. It is simply unclear what inputs, many of which have long investment periods, are economically warranted. Even if it is coherent to claim that the present harvest could be caught with one-half the fleet tonnage,[32] focusing on the *physical* capacity while disregarding *costs* is not sensible. Surely it is not desirable to keep every vessel out to sea until its holds are 100 per cent full if deploying a few more vessels, 90 per cent full would be cheaper.[33] The fact that newer vessels are considerably more efficient than their older competitors further complicates estimates of the necessary inputs.[34] Moreover, as in any industry, there must be some idling of capacity – creation of apparent 'excess' – in the normal displacement of outmoding investment.

The fact that fishing capacity is an artifact of regulation also complicates the definition of 'excess'. Artificially shortened seasons and other restrictions in catch per vessel increase the number of vessels and other capacity factors that arc 'needed'. It is unclear how much of the 'overcapacity' is an economically rational response to (suboptimal) regulation.[35] Some data suggest that the overbuilding has cusped and is undergoing, as one would expect, a degree of correction.[36]

The bottom line is that a direct estimate of the theoretically 'correct' capacity is elusive. There are too many uncertainties to identify the 'right' level of capacity to achieve the 'right' level of activity. Nonetheless, the allegations of widespread overcapacity have an undeniable basis. First, there is the inefficiency that inevitably results from the competition to reduce free access goods to ownership. Second, as indicated above, some of the fisheries regulations unintentionally elicit economically redundant investment and consequently compound the excess. Finally, the industry has been the historical beneficiary of public subsidy. Subsidization lowers private costs at public expense, thereby increasing the investment in fishing beyond the level that market signals would warrant.

Thus, features of the industry and its environment, and the government subsidies in particular, fairly support the allegations of widespread overcapacity, even though it is impossible to put a dollar or tonnage figure on that excess.[37] This is not to say that all government financial assistance programmes induce excess catch capacity or that they are all indefensible.[38] Moreover, given the present state of affairs, it is not clear that a mere withdrawal of catch-enhancing financial support would be an adequate response. Rehabilitation may require a more severe reduction in capacity, at least for a time period. Additional measures may be required to facilitate the disinvestment of relatively immobile capital and labour factors.[39] Nonetheless, a re-examination of fisheries subsidies, and the role they play in driving the dubious levels of harvest, is a key ingredient of reform.

Subsidies in Fishing

Gauging the amount of subsidies worldwide, or even on a nation-to-nation basis, is a formidable task. Many programmes are involved. In various places and at various times, financial assistance to the fishing industry has included grants, low-cost loans and loan guarantees for new vessel construction and repair, subsidies to support the purchase of new gear, support for construction of cold storage and processing plants, support for fish prices and fishermen's wages, and the provision of marine insurance, harbour maintenance and fuel discounts.

Observers standing outside government have attempted national or regional estimates of what it all comes to.[40] And some authoritative organizations have approached governments *directly* for the data. Most prominently, as early as the 1960s, and again in the 1970s, the Organisation for Economic Co-operation and Development (OECD) canvassed its members to prepare Reports on Financial Assistance to the Fishing Industry. The results, although now outdated in detail, convey a sense of the range of support measures. Combined with other studies, OECD's results leave no doubt that financial support for the fishing industries is widespread and massive.[41] In addition to the OECD, the WTO is *supposed* to be collecting contemporary data.[42] As of this date, however, the submissions have been paltry at best.[43]

All such direct efforts to acquire subsidy data are frustrated by the variety, magnitude and scope of subsidies, combined with the reluctance of governments to compile and come forward with fully comprehensive figures. This reluctance is not entirely a matter of the conventional concealment of data from outsiders. A subsidizing government may not know the crucial figures itself. Governments only partially budget, or do not budget at all, certain subsidies, such as the government's cost for a portfolio of loan guarantees. Other subsidies take the form of a general policy commitment to forgive government loans to firms that are failing.[44] US legislation has gone as far as to 'bail out' vessels seized by foreign nations for fishing infractions.[45] How is one to begin to monetize such risk-shifting supports, which may never make their way into government fisheries budgets but certainly affect the level of economic activity?

The FAO 'Special Chapter'

In default of a direct window into subsidies, item by item and government to government, the most ambitious and authoritative effort to identify subsidies is a 1993 study (literally special chapter), undertaken for the FAO. The FAO's attempt was indirect. Rather than query each government on its financial support, the author, Francis Christy, Jr, inferred the magnitude of government support through an industry profile that subtracted gross costs from gross revenues on a global basis. Employing 1989 data, Christy estimated gross revenues from marine fisheries worldwide at US$70 billion[46] and operating costs at US$92.2 billion.[47] This indicated an annual operating deficit of US$22 billion before accounting for capital costs. When the study added estimated capital costs (US$32 billion) to the estimated operating costs, it concluded that the global economy spent about US$124 billion to land US$70 billion worth of fish, an apparent $54 billion deficit. The widely reported inference was that the fishing industry was being subsidized US$54 billion a year.[48]

The US$54 billion figure is so startling as to arouse some scepticism. To begin with, the equation of deficits with subsidies is unwarranted unless no portion of the losses are being borne by firms.[49] Moreover, as the author is the first to acknowledge, there are major obstacles to constructing a reliable set of fisheries statistics.[50] In particular, the estimated revenues (US$70 billion) may be too low. Many catches simply go unreported because there are so many landing spots stretched across so lengthy a coastline in much of the world.[51] In addition, restrictions such as catch quotas and seasons provide the fishers that violate those regulations an incentive to under-report. By contrast, there are few incentives to over-report. Hence, one presumes that official reports systematically understate revenues from year to year. As a result, the actual fisheries revenue must be higher and the subsidy figures correspondingly lower than Christy's estimates. To illustrate, if 1989 costs were US$124 billion and the actual revenues US$100 billion, then the level of (largely subsidized) deficit would fall to US$24 billion.

Christy may also have overstated the subsidy for capital costs. He derived the US$32 billion figure by estimating the replacement value of the fleet (US$320 billion) and applying a 10 per cent return to impute an opportunity cost.[52] One might well question the propriety of using the costs of replacing an ageing fleet as the basis for valuing industry capital, particularly if we assume that the fleet is, or ought to be, in partial liquidation.[53] The *investment* in the fleet would be better represented by market value: the amount owners, many of whom hold ageing vessels, would actually receive on sale, an amount that captures expected cash flows from operation.[54] Hence, even if the presumed 10 per cent return to capital is accepted, the estimated asset value (US$320 billion), and the linked 'subsidy' both probably require downward revision.

On the other hand, it is important to note that the FAO did not address at least three major categories of subsidy, each of which would warrant an adjustment upward. The first category is government support through a wide variety of soft, unbudgeted commitments, such as relief for firms and fishers who fall on hard times.[55] Second are environmental externalities, including the ravaging of ecosystems and the deaths of non-targeted sea life. The fact that the price of the product does not include these social costs amounts to a 'subsidy' of the fishing industry from an economic point of view.[56] The third area includes unaccounted-for resource rents. Under an ideal resource policy, fishermen would pay a fee calculated to constrict the harvest to a level that maximized the stock's long-term value to the society. Some coastal nations presently confront fishers with such a charge in the form of taxes, licence charges or government-auctioned quotas.[57] However, governments 'subsidize' a fisher wherever the levy falls short of the optimal, which is always the case in the high seas beyond national jurisdiction.[58]

For all these reasons, FAO's well-publicized estimate of global subsidies could be off in either direction, depending upon how one resolves uncertainties both in data and in definition. But whether the actual figure is less or more than the FAO's US$54 billion, there is every reason to believe that the sum is positive and large enough to demand considerable policy attention.[59] We are not only taking too many fish to maintain long-term sustainability, we are paying an unnecessarily high price, both in terms of catch costs and natural resource capital, in the bargain.

Application of Trade Laws

Whatever the exact magnitude of fisheries subsidies, the threat they pose has not gone entirely unchallenged. The European Union (EU) instituted a policy as early as

1983 to cut back on subsidies for vessel construction.[60] The Working Group on Oceans of the Commission on Sustainable Development (CSD) formally urged governments to reduce subsidies to the fishing industry.[61] The Asia-Pacific Economic Cooperation (APEC) approved a four-year fisheries trade study that will address the subsidies issue.[62]

This chapter addresses the question of the role that trade laws could, and should play in challenging fisheries subsidization and relieving pressures on stocks. Of course, the primary and direct concern of trade disciplines is to eliminate distortions in trade law not to preserve resources. The fact that much of the motivation to reduce subsidization comes from resource and environment factions may suggest that the problem be addressed directly in fisheries management and other non-trade fora. Nonetheless, subsidization is a concern of trade law, and there is no reason why trade laws should manifest that concern with less vigilance in fisheries than in any other sector.

Fishing products constitute one of the major components of world trade, with a value of approximately US$50 billion[63] – over 11 per cent of the world trade in agriculture.[64] Among the developing countries, fish trade plays a particularly large and increasing role in garnering foreign exchange. As a group, the developing countries earned US$11 billion from non-domestic fish sales in 1993, nearly twice that of the next major crop (coffee) and dwarfing revenues from the other traditional cash crops of banana, rubber, tea, meat and rice.[65] China's self-pronounced plan to become a 'fishing superpower' includes the goal of exporting US$4 billion in captured fish products at the start of the 21st century.[66] Thus, trade and overfishing are linked. Those concerned with overfishing must consider whether trade law's anti-subsidy disciplines may not be a crucial part of the remedy.

Bringing Fish Within the Agricultural Agreement Framework

One major avenue of trade law has been blocked, at least temporarily. The recently concluded Uruguay Round Agreement on Agriculture (URAA), which aimed at progressively and substantially reducing agricultural subsidies, in general might have included fish and fisheries products. But proposals to do so failed to overcome the resistance of some major fishing nations. The final document expressly excludes fish products.[67] The unwillingness of the URAA negotiators to confront fish subsidies is regrettable and perhaps merits revisiting by the WTO Membership in the future.

The URAA establishes a framework for identifying and rolling back each country's Aggregate Measure of Support (AMS). Subsidies that have minimal effects on trade or production are exempt. The URAA does not explicitly *prohibit* unexempted subsidies. Instead, an aggrieved importing member may apply countervailing duties (CVDs), which are otherwise GATT-illegal, against the subsidizing country.[68]

Surely, one could justify the inclusion of fish within the broader URAA. Presumably, cross-elasticity of demand between fish and other agricultural products is relatively high; distortions in the trade of one affect the trade of others. Additionally, aquaculture and mariculture, which are the most dramatically surging sectors of fishing, resemble farming more closely than they do 'hunting'. Moreover, fishing communities, like farming communities, present politicians with concentrations of single industry voters who must be weaned from a long tradition of dependence on subsidies. Furthermore, the experience gained and foundation formed during the URAA negotiations might prove useful in working towards an agreement on fishing. Finally, the formulation and administration of rules applicable to both agriculture and fisheries would be efficient; the combined approach might even advance a sense of 'equal treatment' among traders in food products, and with it the willingness to comply with the WTO and its rulings.

On the other hand, those concerned about world fisheries have reason to be wary of tying the fate of fish subsidies to farm subsidies under the URAA. Despite an appearance of progress in the farm sector, it remains to be seen whether the URAA will have any real impact. The URAA is to be renegotiated starting in 1999. That process is certain to drag on for several years. To throw fish back into the negotiations will only ally the resistance of farmers with those of fishers. Moreover, the remedy under the URAA for non-exempt subsidies is limited to CVDs which must be instigated by an importer state whose domestic industry is injured by the subsidies.[69] Complaints and remedies under the Agreement on Subsidies and Countervailing Measures (SCM), the GATT's generally applicable anti-subsidy disciplines, are less restrictive. Thus, bringing fish subsidies under the default provisions of the general SCM has advantages over folding fish into the URAA. In fact, the URAA shields from challenge a number of programmes, such as export subsidies which would otherwise be vulnerable to SCM attack and exempts many farm programmes from attack until 2004 (the so-called 'peace clause').[70] In addition, while the URAA exempts certain environmental subsidies made 'as part of a well-defined environmental or conservation programme',[71] the exemptions are almost certainly narrower than those resource advocates would approve.[72]

Aside from the possible strategic disadvantages of bringing fish within the agricultural agreement, certain features of fishing warrant distinct treatment. For example, one might more readily exempt subsidies to enrich fishing grounds than one would 'green light' subsidies to enrich the soil. A supporter of the exemption for fisheries would reason that fishermen exploit common fishing grounds, the maintenance of which has public goods attributes, while farmers ordinarily work their own property on which they internalize the costs and benefits of inputs and activities. Also, differences between the modes of farming and fishing subsidies make the subsidization of fisheries more resistant to transparency and reform. For instance, agricultural subsidies typically take the form of schemes to protect specific crops through crop price support and tariffs. In contrast, a larger portion of fisheries' subsidies goes into infrastructure and inputs, such as fuel, vessels, gear and labour. Additionally, a subsidized fleet will often catch different fish in different seasons. This seasonal variation makes it difficult to identify whether a particular subsidy supports the catch of traded or untraded species.[73]

Countervailing Duties Under Domestic Trade Laws

Challenges to fish subsidies do not require that fish be included as agriculture products under the URAA. Trade in fish, like the trade of any other primary product, remains subject to the general body of trade law. For example, an importing nation could challenge an exporter's fish subsidies by using its own domestic legislation to impose countervailing duties.[74] At least two US cases illustrate this strategy. In 1986, the US International Trade Administration determined that imports of Canadian groundfish should be subject to a countervailing duty on the basis of a slew of subsidy programmes, including vessel assistance, investment tax credits, regional development and improvement loans, insurance premium prepayments, and loan guarantees.[75] In 1991, reacting to charges by US salmon farmers, the US International Trade Commission imposed an average 26 per cent tariff on imports of fresh Norwegian farmed salmon. The Commission based its action on a finding that the US industry suffered an injury that could be traced to Norway's low-cost loans to its salmon farmers and its industry specific payroll tax deduction. Norway appealed to the GATT, but in 1994 the GATT Committee on Subsidies and Countervailing Measures upheld the Panel's decision supporting the US.[76] Complaints from Scotland and other EU countries alleging subsidization and dumping in violation of WTO rules are currently prompting the European Commission (EC) to pressure Norway to limit support to its domestic salmon farming industry's production.[77]

Direct Challenges Through the World Trade Organization

The traditional remedy for an importing nation aggrieved by a subsidy was to institute its own 'countervailing actions' unilaterally. The penalized exporter could appeal the CVDs under the GATT. In contrast, the SCM provides alternative remedies within the WTO from the first instance. The importer can institute a traditional countervailing measure based on Article VI along with a challenge based on the strengthened Prohibited or Actionable Subsidy provisions of Parts II and III, respectively.[78]

To support a challenge to fishery subsidies under the SCM structure, a challenger would have to overcome a series of barriers. The complainant must show that (a) there was a 'subsidy' as defined in Article 1; that (b) the subsidy is *specific* as defined in Article 2; and that (c) the subsidy is either *prohibited* or *actionable* as distinct from *nonactionable*.[79] The complainant may also have to show that (d) a prima facie case of wrongful subsidization survives any exception or defence, such as a qualifying regional development programme.[80] The following discussion examines some of the most significant problems that can be expected to arise.

Subsidies
SCM's Article 1 defines subsidies to include any benefit-conferring 'form of income or price support'[81] and any benefit-conferring 'financial contributions by a government or any public body within the territory of a Member ie, where':

(i)   there are direct or potential (as in loan guarantees) transfers of funds; or
(ii) government revenue that is otherwise due is foregone or not collected;. . . or
(iii) a government provides goods or services other than general infrastructure; or
(iv) a government entrusts to a funding mechanism or ostensibly private body the supports illustrated in (i)–(iii).

Clear Subsidies

Past studies of industrial financial assistance record a slew of practices that would certainly constitute 'subsidies' in the Article 1 sense. Low-rate loans, loan guarantees or outright grants for the purchase, construction and repair of fishing vessels have probably been the most important such practices.[82] But Article 1 would also bring into question financial assistance ranging from price supports for fish products[83] and wages,[84] to grants to reduce prices of fishing gear and bait,[85] and to government purchases or subsidies for marine insurance[86] and fuel.[87] Article 1 might also cover harvest-reducing expenditures such as paying owners to scrap vessels[88] or to reduce their harvest to meet catch limitations.[89] These practices could be construed as benefit-conferring transfers of funds per (i) even if the payments are too irregular to be classed as 'income support'.[90]

Borderline Subsidies

The question of whether other support measures are 'subsidies' presents even more difficult issues of interpretation. These borderline measures include a host of expenditures that a government might want to classify as 'general infrastructure' and therefore not a 'subsidy' under Article I (iii). Port facilities and lighthouses probably escape 'subsidy' characterization on that basis. Other public works expenditures, such as artificial reefs and wetlands rehabilitation, are less plausibly 'general infrastructure'. They might still escape characterization as 'subsidies' nonetheless, on the grounds that they are outside 'goods or services' as those terms should be understood in Article 1, or alternatively, that they are 'non-specific' expenditures under the standards set forth in Article 2.[91]

Another shadowy but potentially significant area of subsidy involves governments' increasing practice of purchasing access rights to a foreign Exclusive Economic Zone (EEZ) on behalf of their distant-water fleets. Recall that with the establishment of fishing zones, each coastal nation has the legal authority to bar access and grant conditional entry. The EU pays approximately US$350 million annually to open developing countries' waters to EU members' fleets.[92] EU member countries co-finance most of these agreements.[93] Both payments certainly advantage EU fleets over competitors in product markets. Arguably, the EU payments and the individual nation's co-financing are 'subsidies' in the sense of 'providing goods or services'.[94]

A government's practice of rescuing failing fishing firms or 'bailing out' vessels that have been seized for fishing infractions are other illustrations of possible 'borderline' subsidization.[95] Such practices reduce the risks facing favoured enterprises and thus can convey potentially trade-distorting advantages. However, it is unclear whether the practice would qualify as a subsidy under SCM. Those nations that challenge such practices as a 'subsidy' would characterize it as a 'potential direct transfers of funds or liabilities'.[96] However, SCM uses 'loan guarantees' to illustrate a direct transfer.[97] That illustration suggests an intention to limit the provision to formal programmes offering ex ante assistance, as distinct from soft assurances of ex post rescue. The WTO will have to interpret various similar measures on a case-by-case basis.

'Implicit Subsidies'

'Implicit subsidies' constitute a third category of problematic subsidization. This group includes benefits that a nation confers on its industry not by transferring value, but by declining to impose arguably socially justifiable costs. For example, a nation that countenances lax legal standards or fails to collect resource rents endows its firms with a competitive advantage. Whether these failures constitute 'subsidies' under the trade laws is even more doubtful than in the case of 'borderline' subsidies. Nonetheless, 'implicit subsidies' raise issues too significant to ignore.

Consider first the issue of lax legal regimes. The argument has been made that where one nation's enforcement of environmental regulations falls below international standards or law, a nation that enforces the mandated standard, at higher cost to its industry should be allowed to impose a CVD on the imports of the lax state.[98] For example, the United Nations Convention on the Law of the Sea (UN-CLOS) requires each nation to determine the allowable catch in its EEZ in a manner calculated to prevent 'over-exploitation.'[99] A fish importer might allege that the exporter advantaged its domestic fleet by disregarding its obligation under UNCLOS. Arguably, over-exploitation creates a trade advantage by lowering costs and gaining markets in the short-term. Even if an importer could prove such a case, however, and demonstrate that its own coastal harvests were in compliance with UNCLOS and other relevant fisheries treaties, no trade law decisions have characterized as 'subsidization' the cost advantages gained by non-compliance with international environmental standards.[100] Should the issue arise under the SCM, the most likely analysis would be that the benefits conferred by lax enforcement would not meet the 'financial contributions' element of the SCM's definitions of subsidy.[101]

The issue of whether lax law enforcement can be construed as implicit subsidy is therefore currently dormant. But the SCM makes the question worth revisiting. Under the pre-Uruguay Round law, the complainant's *unilateral* initiation of CVDs was the predominant response to subsidies. This practice of unilateral response gave rise to the well-founded concern that importers might use charges of lax enforcement as a disguise for illicitly motivated restrictions on trade.[102] It is significant that under the new SCM framework and particularly in the context of the 'serious prejudice' actions discussed in Part II, Chapter 3 below, there is a larger role for *multilateral* dispute resolution. This greater opportunity for multilateral action means that the law can endorse a more robust definition of subsidy without running the risk of unilateral subterfuge.

We could simply require that all challenges based on implicit subsidies had to go directly to or through a WTO consultation or settlement panel process. The multilateral WTO procedures provide some assurance against the abuses of unilateral actions. At the least, the issue might be tabled for discussion before the Committee on Subsidies and Countervailing Measures (CSCM) or the Committee on Trade and the Environment (CTE).

The argument for challenging foregone resources rent as an implicit subsidy is also provocative. As suggested above, fishermen who withdraw resources from a common pool[103] should ideally pay a fee calculated to maximize the stock's long-term economic rent. The knowledge of fisheries dynamics is too shallow (for example, the 'natural' fluctuation of stocks is unknown) to confidently reckon the correct charge. Nonetheless, several coastal nations confront fishers with a rough proxy of optimal rent in the form of a license fee or tradable catch quota. It is difficult to judge whether the charges are below the optimal level, such that they might constitute a subsidy. In the Uruguay Rounds, the US suggested the simple test of whether the licence (or other right) was disposed of at public auction.[104] The price of an auctioned licence would provide the base-line for calculating an optimal rent. Presumably where the licence was not subject to auction, one could construct the amount of the subsidy from the payments received by nations that did auction comparable access rights.

In a trade context, the challenger would be a nation whose fishers paid the presumptively correct resource rent. The object of the challenge would be fishers with whom that nation is in competition and who took the resource for 'free' or at a discounted level'.[105] The challenger would argue, based on economic theory and the practice of some nations, that the inadequate charge was a 'revenue ... otherwise due [but] foregone' under SCM Article 1.1(ii), or that the government, by not charging, thereby 'provides goods or services' under Article 1.1 (iii). In an analogous situation under domestic law, the US successfully challenged Canada on its sales of softwood in the US where the producers allegedly paid inadequate stumpage charges.[106] Whether a WTO Dispute Settlement Panel (DSP) would accept a similarly broad reading remains an open question. However, developing norms of international law provide growing support for the argument. For example, the United Nations Convention on Biological Diversity (CBD) provides that 'Each Contracting Party shall, as far as possible and as appropriate, adopt economically and socially sound ... incentives for the conservation and sustainable use of components of biological diversity.[107] Failure to charge the 'true' resource rent, the argument would go, is a failure to adopt economically and socially sound policies. That argument would support an interpretation of non-collection as a 'revenue due' and a subsidy.

Prohibited Subsidies

Thus far, this chapter has only surveyed the different sorts of actions and inactions that might meet the SCM's definition of subsidy under the SCM, Part I. Not all subsidies are treated alike, however. Parts II, III and IV of the SCM make subsidies respectively 'prohibited', 'actionable', and 'non-actionable'.

Subsidies are absolutely prohibited where they are contingent upon (a) export performance or (b) the use of domestic over imported goods.[108] Such practices have certainly taken place in the fisheries context.[109] Whether they are currently widespread and significant remains to be, and should be, ascertained.[110]

Actionable Subsidies

Subsidies are actionable where one member causes injury to the domestic industry of another member, nullifies or impairs benefits to other members, or causes serious prejudice to the interests of another member. The 'serious prejudice' provisions are the most intriguing, because they reach not only subsidies that displace or impede imports into the market of the subsidizing member, but extend to subsidies that impede or displace exports into a third country market (6.3(b)), or lead to an increase in world market share in the subsidized product by the subsidizing member (6.3(d)).

Serious prejudice may be found to exist where:

(i)   the total *ad valorem* subsidization of a product exceeds 5 per cent;
(ii)   subsidies are paid to cover the operating losses sustained by an industry;
(iii) subsidies other than one-time measures are paid to an enterprise to cover operating losses; and
(iv)   there is direct forgiveness of debt and/or grants to cover debt repayment. (Article 6.1)

If one of the above elements exists the burden of proof shifts on to the subsidizer. Following the shift, serious prejudice may be found unless the subsidizing member demonstrates that it caused none of the effects enumerated in 6.3, such as the displacement of another member from the market of the subsidizing member or a third country market.[111]

While no government currently provides a breakdown of its financial support according to these categories, the literature includes numerous illustrations of fisheries assistance that could be pressed into each of the four 'serious prejudice' categories. However, the first of the triggers is almost certainly the most potent. On the face of the still untested language, it would appear that if any member's *total ad valorem* subsidization of a fish product exceeds 5 per cent, serious prejudice 'shall be deemed to exist'. Once 'deemed to exist', the subsidizing member has the burden to show that it did *not* impede any member's exports into the subsidizing member's market; did *not* displace another member's sales from third country markets; and did *not* increase the subsidizer's world market share.

Because the 5 per cent provision is entirely novel there is no case-law to clarify it. Thus, many issues of scope must be resolved. Annex IV contains the methodology for calculating whether the 5 per cent threshold has been breached. The methodology settles some questions,[112] while it raises others.[113] Notwithstanding the present ambiguities, the 5 per cent clause is certain to be of great interest for those wishing to challenge fish sector subsidies.

The other 'serious prejudice' clauses are also potentially far-reaching. Indeed, they are not subject to a 5 per cent threshold, but they similarly open important questions of scope. For instance, how does one demonstrate *industry operating losses* and *firm operating losses*. Many nations provide maritime insurance industry-wide; some governments pay firms directly for items such as fuel or exempt them from taxes. Do these payments fall within Article 6's 'serious prejudice' category on the grounds that if the firms had to bear these costs, they, or the industry as a whole, would operate at a loss? Hopefully, the CSCM or CTE will provide further guidance. Otherwise, case-law must clarify this area.

Non-Actionable Subsidies

Considering how little has been done to confront fisheries subsidies, it may appear premature to raise the possibility that an assault on subsidies might go too far. But such a prospect springs from the potential tension between those who are motivated by traditional trade distortion grounds and those who are motivated by resource and environmental concerns. Presumably both camps are allied against benefits that promote artificially high catch levels, such as vessel construction loans and grants. But the environmental and resource camp will want to carve out as non-actionable a class of allegedly 'good' subsidies, such as those aimed at enhancing stock productivity or at reducing catch pressure.

To illustrate this tension, imagine a government programme that trimmed fleet sizes by purchasing 'excess' vessels from owners, perhaps even sinking them where the wreckage would form an artificial fish-habitat. That programme appears prima facie defensible from an environmental or resource point of view. If there are fewer vessels there will he less catch and more fish. However, trade negotiators are apt to regard those, or any environmental and resource exceptions, warily. Arguably, a vessel repurchase or decommissioning programme props up the value of a firm's outworn vessels. Such a programme can provide a subterfuge for transferring wealth to the nation's fleet owners, thereby artificially lowering unit costs and potentially distorting trade. Hammering out which classes of subsidy should not be actionable (to 'green light' in trade law parlance) is inescapably controversial.

The negotiators of the Agricultural Agreement attempted to mediate this tension by providing a narrow exemption to the commitment to reduce subsidies for those, payments made 'as part of a well-defined environmental or conservation programme.[114] However, the exemption applies only so long as the programme has 'no, or at most minimal, trade distorting effects'.[115] Even when a programme meets that criterion, the exemption only applies to the payments for the extra costs or loss of income occasioned by complying with the government programme.[116]

The SCM as it stands is not appreciably more expansive. 'Green-lighted' subsidies are limited to certain payments for (1) research and development; (2) assistance to disadvantaged regions within the territory of a Member; and (3) assistance to promote adaptation of existing facilities to new environmental requirements imposed by law.' The parsimony of the SCM exemptions leaves in doubt, as a matter of trade law, the legal status of at least three major categories of 'subsidies': subsidies pursuant to international obligations, non-obligatory productivity-enhancing subsidies and catch-reducing subsidies. The following section examines those categories in that sequence.

Subsidies Pursuant to International Obligations

Nations expend an increasing portion of their fisheries budgets on measures that might be construed as compelled by international law. Possible sources of obligation include regional seas agreements,[118] the Convention on Biological Diversity,[119] UNCLOS,[120] and agreements on wetlands,[121] endangered species,[122] and straddling stocks.[123] The tension between the WTO agreements and Multilateral Environmental Agreements (MEAs) exemplifies the conflict in this area. Imagine a country that heavily subsidizes the building of artificial reefs, the improvement and development of coastal fishing grounds, expenditures for marine pollution control and perhaps various services that protect spawning and nursery areas and inhibit bio-invasion.[124] One can also imagine a trade complaint portraying such benefits as the 'provision of goods or services' that are 'specific' benefits to the fishing industry and thus potentially actionable subsidies under the SCM.[125] In response to such a charge, the subsidizer might invoke UNCLOS, Art 61, which obliges the coastal state to take measures 'designed to maintain or restore populations of harvested species at levels which can produce the maximum sustainable yield...'[126]

It is hard to believe that a nation that can portray its actions as honouring its obligations under UNCLOS should be vulnerable to trade charges under the SCM.[127] In fact, a nation so charged might claim that the SCM carried forward by implication the 'general exceptions' defences under GATT Article XX and that the measures mandated by UNCLOS were conclusively related 'to the conservation of exhaustible natural resources'.[128] In this manner, the WTO might resolve some of the apparent tension between trade law and resource conventions within existing frameworks. On the other hand, the uncertainty and potential for conflict warrant placing this issue on the diplomatic agenda for further discussion.

Non-obligatory Productivity-Enhancing Subsidies

In other cases, a government will provide subsidy benefits under a productivity-enhancing programme, but cannot plausibly characterize those benefits as *compelled* by an MEA or other international law obligations. For example, a nation's programme to construct fish-breeding reefs may go beyond what is understood as the true commitment of any relevant convention. Or there might be a convention that compels the action, but the nation undertaking the programme is not a party to it (the US is not a member of UNCLOS). Alternatively, the principle to which the nation points as justification, however admirable and broadly touted, may neither be formally embedded in any convention nor accepted broadly enough to be incorporated into customary international law ('soft').[129]

Those who support 'green-lighting' cannot rest their case on the argument that the subsidies increase food supplies per se. If that were sufficient, nations providing free fertilizers and fuel to their farmers could make the same argument. A special distinction in favour of fish subsidies would have to rely on the fact that the productivity of capture fisheries cannot be enhanced without a provision of public goods. Public goods in this context would include provisions to monitor and police conservation and pollution regulations, as well as to provide harvest-enhancing services, such as the improvement of fishing grounds and the construction of artificial reefs.[130]

On the other hand, even if the WTO acknowledges the legitimacy of a government providing these shared services, the 'green-lighting' advocate must explain why the expenses should be borne by the public at large, through the tax base, rather than shouldered on the fishers through user charges (as is done to some extent by New Zealand).[131]

Catch-reducing Subsidies

A final group of potentially controversial subsidies aims at a reduction in fishing. Examples include paying ship owners to decommission,[132] scrap[133] or temporarily lay up[134] their vessels. Some nations compensate fishers whose vessels have been docked due to catch limitations, presumably mitigating the pressure to cheat.[135] Some of these measures may be defended by bringing them under the headings discussed above, that is, as implemented pursuant to international obligations, or as non-obligatory product-enhancing subsidies. For example, a nation whose catch-limiting subsidies were challenged might depict them as furthering MEAs. It may characterise other subsidies as short-term efforts required for long-term productivity gains.

Nonetheless, subsidies that aim to decrease the pressure on stocks deserve distinct consideration. For one reason, when a nation provides support to limit the catch, the opportunities for trade-distortion are less apparent than when subsidization increases production. By reducing domestic supply, the nation's product prices should rise. This increases demand for other nations' products in its own market and, if the nation is an exporter, provides competitors an advantage in foreign markets. The basis on which another country would complain is uncertain.

A complainant would most likely argue that when elevated to a dependable national policy, the assurance of a vessel buy-back amounts to an *ex ante* risk-reducing (investment-inducing) benefit to the domestic fleet. The important policy question is whether the risks of abuse are significant enough to warrant a trade-law challenge to some catch-reducing programmes that many fishery managers regard as vital. In the analogous situation in the farming sector, where a government pays farmers to withdraw land from production, the Agricultural Agreement exempts 'resource retirement programmes' that meet certain requirements.[136] This is not an easy issue and represents further warrant for a sectoral study.

Conclusion

Global fisheries are ailing. There is no simple, and surely no single cure. For primary care we must look to fisheries management. But as long as investment in the harvesting sector remains excessive, the best-conceived management plans will be rejected, subverted or ignored. Fishing capacity must be reduced.

One cannot address overcapacity without confronting subsidization. National legislatures have shown little inclination to tackle subsidies voluntarily and unilaterally. The disease feeds on itself: the more subsidies, the more capacity; the more capacity, the fewer fish per unit effort; the lower the fishers' returns, the more intense the pressure for government relief.

A proposal to treat this malady with trade remedies may sound quixotic. Even with the new SCM, no one expects nations to abandon sectoral subsidies easily. Trade negotiators are still fighting tariffs and non-tariff barriers (NTBs), more traditional and 'easier' targets than fishing subsidies. Even when subsidies are called into question, those in fisheries have not excited much criticism until quite recently. Government assistance in many sectors, notably energy and agriculture, is probably comparable and sometimes worse.[137] Moreover, it is sobering to reflect upon the fact that the Agricultural Rounds, which refused to confront fish products, produced more text than commitment. Most of the support for applying trade-law disciplines to the fisheries trade comes from resource conservationists, not trade diplomats. Against this background, why should anyone hope to make more headway against fisheries subsidies?

Any progress will have to overcome strong resistance. Nonetheless, one should not dismiss the possibility of conscripting trade law into the fisheries campaign.

Fish are one of the world's major traded products. They have become a major export for developing countries. Moreover, even if agricultural subsidies are as steep, the subsidization of fishing is potentially more pernicious than the subsidization of farm products. There are many arguments against farm subsidies, but long-term impairment and the collapse of productivity are not usually among them. In addition, the potential alliance of powerful conservationist and environmental NGOs may make fishing subsidies more vulnerable than those in farming.

The question is not whether to amend trade laws to make fisheries subsidies challengeable. Many subsidies are in clear violation of the trade laws. In particular, the new SCM provides an untested, potentially far-reaching sword. A WTO member that exports fish could trigger the 'serious prejudice' provisions by showing that a subsidizing competitor impairs the challenger's access to the markets of the subsidizer or a third party. A test case would be welcome. Regardless of whether a member brings such a suit, the proposals for a sectoral study of fisheries trade should go forward. Indeed, the CTE, CSD, FAO and APEC all appear primed to examine subsidy-reduction and other capacity cutback measures.[138]

The case for confronting fisheries subsidies is clear. We are over-harvesting the earth's living marine resources. Much of the problem arises from excessive subsidies, particularly those that exacerbate catch levels. The elimination or confinement of these subsidies would not, in themselves, heal the world's fisheries. But it would relieve national budgets of perverse expenditures, ease the task of fisheries managers, remove distortions to trade, help to foster a larger, more valuable catch in the long-term and protect the environment. It is time to act.

Appendix 13.1
A Bioeconomic Model of Fisheries Subsidies

This appendix is intended to provide a relatively non-technical version of the classic bioeconomic analysis of an open-access fishery.[139] The size of a fish stock is a function of natural and anthropogenic factors. Each year, a number of juvenile fish are recruited into the stock and a number die through natural causes including predation, disease and age. A natural equilibrium population is reached when the stock (in weight) that is added by recruitment and growth is exactly offset by losses through mortality.

By fishing, humans increase the natural rate of mortality as a function of fishing effort.[140] This creates new equilibria at levels where withdrawals through catch are exactly replaced by natural additions. The catch at each equilibrium is represented by the inverted sustainable yield curve in Figure 13.1, each point corresponding to the potential catch, harvestable on a long-term annual basis for each level of effort. However, not all catches are of equal size. The peak, MSY, represents the maximum catch that can be harvested on a recurring basis. In the figure, the level of fishing effort E corresponds to the MSY. Any effort in excess of E will lead over time to a catch lesser than MSY.

Economic analysis is superimposed on the biological by accounting for the revenues and costs of fishing. Regarding revenues, price is here assumed to be invariant with output, so that the Sustained Yield Curve (in weight) can be identified with Total Sustainable Revenue (TSR)(in US dollars) – the revenues that could be earned on a recurring basis at each level of fishing effort. The peak of TSR – maximum revenues – equals the peak sustainable yield, MSY.

Costs are displayed in the form of a Total Costs Curve (TC).[141] MEY (for Maximum Efficient Yield) is the point on the TSR most in excess of TC. It is at MEY that the slopes of the TC and TSR curves are equal, signifying equality of marginal costs and benefits.[142] It is therefore the point of maximum rent – that is, the point at which the return to the resource is most in excess of normal profits. With some simplification, E* can be identified as the social optimal: the point of effort beyond which social benefits decline faster than social costs. Any effort in excess of E* is inefficient: resources put into the capturing fish at margins beyond this would yield greater benefit if diverted out of the fishery into other sectors.[143]

The dilemma in capture fisheries management stems from the fact that, as long as there are no barriers to entry, and fish are unowned until captured, effort will exceed E*. This follows from the fact that in the competition to catch fish, each would-be harvester internalizes only his 'private' costs of establishing ownership, such as incremental fuel and labour. There are other costs that are largely externalized. First, as the stock dwindles, the costs of capturing the marginal unit rises: the quarry being less dense, there is more water to filter or area to travel for each ton of catch. Second, congestion costs increase with effort. And third, because the fish are unowned until capture, each fisher externalizes all but a fraction of the asset-depleting cost his haul exacts from the fishery.[144] Cooperation among the fishers would retard the increased effort: as a group, they have a mutual interest in restraint. But each fisherman is a potential free-rider on the restraint of the others. With large numbers (assured by the open entry condition) cooperation is unachievable. As a consequence, fishing effort expands until the least efficient fishers are earning revenues just equal to their private opportunity costs (which equates with the level at which resource rents are thoroughly dissipated).[145] A is the point of equilibrium at which total revenue and total costs meet. Fishing effort persists to E_{open}, even though A represents both less revenue and higher costs than the effort at both EY and MSY.[146]

Several policy instruments have been developed to counteract this tendency towards excessive fishing. The manager can address *technical input* variables – for example, mandating larger mesh size so as to provide juveniles a longer time to grow. *Access* to the fish can be restricted, by locale or by season. Attempts can be made to limit *output,* from per vessel quotas to declaration of a Total Allowable Catch (TAC). The firms' cost functions can be addressed directly through *taxes* calculated to drive the level of effort back to E*.[147] And there has been experience with the establishment of *property rights* in the stock.[148] Essentially, ownership shares (labelled ITQs for Individual Tradable Quotas) are created in the TAC and allocated. Each share represents a market-transferable entitlement to a specified percentage of the TAC, backed by the power of government to exclude interlopers. The fact that each fisherman's catch is restricted bars the expansion of effort to the point where private marginal costs equal marginal revenues. Emphasis is shifted from maximization of revenue to the reduction of costs for a harvest equivalent to the

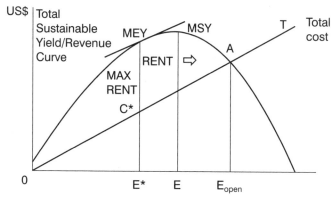

Figure 13.1 *Fishing effort*

TAC. Opportunities for cost reduction arise because a group of fishermen can combine effort to reach their joint ITQ ceilings at a lower aggregate cost than if they fished competitively. The cost-reducing combination can be achieved either through cooperation of rights-holders or via transfers, concentrating ITQs in a reduced number of efficient fishers – eg owners of high-cost vessels selling their rights to owners of low-cost vessels. Moreover, each fisherman holding such an investment has stronger incentive to internalize the long-term consequences of his activities than he does under conditions of free access. Any depletion of the asset works not merely to his contingent and fractional disadvantage (as one of many competing fishermen with a hope of capturing stock in future seasons) but more directly erodes his investment in his own 'property', his tradable share. Cooperation with managers is, if not assured, fostered.

There is a sizeable body of literature analysing and comparing each of these approaches and recording the difficulties of implementation. Here, it is only to be observed that whatever flaws may be identified in each strategy (the 'effectiveness' of many depend on their raising the unit costs of fishing, often perversely)[149] they each, separately or in combination, at least aim in the correct direction – namely, to reduce the level of catch from E_{open} back towards E^*.[150] The same cannot be said of all subsidies, however.

Cost-reducing Subsidies

Through subsidies, the government intervenes in this dynamic in one of three ways. The first and dominant subsidy strategy is to defray the costs of fishing inputs. Examples range from government funding for vessel construction to the purchase of foreign water 'access fees' and the provision of casualty and unemployment insurance. The slope and shape of the cost curve of an industry subject to cost-reducing subsidies will vary with the particular policy. But Figure 13.2 illustrates the effects with the line S_1, which represents costs to the industry net of subsidies received.

Costs borne by fishers decline, and thus the level of effort expands to E_{sub1}. The value of the stock is further reduced, and with sparser stocks, the costs per unit caught rise.[151]

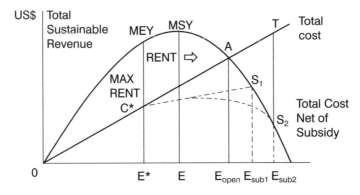

Figure 13.2 *Effect on fishing effort of cost reduction subsidies*

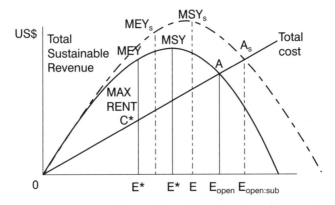

Figure 13.3 *Effect on fishing effort of stock-enhancement subsidies*

Worse, the 'relief' that the subsidies provide industry and labour may prove only temporary and self-defeating. Once the newly created (subsidized) 'rents' are in place, and efforts have expanded to the subsidized level, E_{sub1}, there is more aggregate investment in fishing but the returns are no better than before. This produces political pressure for the government to institute a new round of subsidies, moving the costs net-of-subsidies curve to S_2. If the lobbying prevails, effort extends even less efficiently, to E_{sub2}. The cost of subsidy to the government rises to $T - E_{sub2}$. And industry entreaties for further rounds of 'relief' are not quelled.

Stock-enhancement Subsidies

Rather than try to lower the cost of effort, other subsidies aim to expand the stock – for example, the improvement of grounds and the building of artificial shoals at public expense. The effect of these subsidies is to move MEY, MSY, etc to the right, as indicated in Figure 13.3 restrained and other management devices ineffective, the yield moves to the new points of rent dissipation and effort A_s and $E_{open:sub}$ respectively.

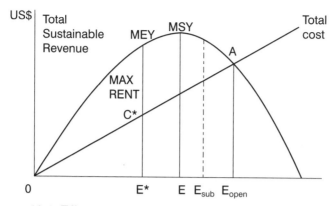

Figure 13.4 *Effect on fishing effort of effort-constraining subsidies*

Effort-constraining Subsidies

A third group of subsidies compensate fishers for reduction of effort. Such subsidies include compensation to fishers to keep vessels in port and the repurchase of 'excess' vessels.[152] The immediate effect (Figure 13.4) is to reduce effort E_{open} to a new E_{sub}. But this is not an economic equilibrium. Unless measures are taken to eliminate a rebound in other inputs (entry of new vessels, employment of more efficient gear, etc) the level of harvest can be expected to return to the rent-dissipating point A, associated with E_{open}.

Acknowledgements

The author would like to acknowledge the support and comments of the Global Environment and Trade Study (GETS), New Haven, Connecticut, Steven Charnovitz, Howard Chang, Michael Knoll, Mateo J Milazzo and Eric Talley in the preparation of this chapter.

Notes

1   United Nations Food and Agricultural Organization (FAO), 'The State of the World Fisheries and Aquaculture', pp8–11 (1995) (hereinafter SOFIA, 1995). In 1993, 60 per cent of the world's marine stocks on which data were available were classified as either 'fully to heavily exploited' (44 per cent) or 'overexploited' (16 per cent). Ibid p8. Another 6 per cent were characterized as 'depleted' and 3 per cent as in recovery from overfishing. Ibid. Categories are all based on conjectures as to maximum sustainable yield (MSY). See Appendix 13.1
2   Western Atlantic bluefin tuna have dwindled from 250,000 to 22,000 in two decades. They have been proposed for listing as an endangered species. Anne

Swardson, Net Losses: Fishing Decimating Oceans 'Unlimited' Bounty, *Washington Post*, 14 August 1994, pA1.

3   See Garcia, S (1986) 'Seasonal Trawling Bans can be Very Successful in Heavily Overfished Areas: The 'Cypress Effect,' *Fishbyte*, April 1986, pp7–8

4   Pauly, D and Christensen, V (1995) 'Primary Production Required to Sustain Global Fisheries' (letter), *Nature*, No 374, pp255, 257. The reference is to de facto sanctuaries as distinct from the few 'no-fishing' zones that arc legally mandated

5   Food and Agricultural Organization of the United Nations, 'Global Fishery Production in 1994 (visited on 24 May 1997): http://www.fau.org/waiccnt/faoinfo/fishery/catch/catch94a.htm (hereinafter FAO, Global Fisheries Production in 1994). The most recent data shows a continual inching up in all categories: marine, mariculture inland and aquaculture

6   FAO, 'Global Fishery Production 1994', Indeed, an astounding one quarter of the fish used for food (as opposed to fertilizer, etc) is now accounted for by fish farming. Food and Agriculture Organization of the United Nations, Fisheries Department. Projection of World Fishery Production in 2010) (visited on 24 May 1997) http://www.fao.org/waicent/faoinfo/fishery/highligli/2010.htm (hereinafter FAO, 'Fishery Production in 2010'). The shift towards aquaculture and mariculture is not a bad sign per se. To some extent it parallels the shift from foraging to agriculture, and reflects the relative strength of property rights over open access regimes. However, further study should examine whether the associated environmental costs of fish farming is higher than that caused by marginal capture fishing

7   FAO, 'Global Fishery Production in 1994', Figure 1 (indicating that between 1950 and 1994 rose from approximately 7kg/person to 14). Because an appreciable share of the catch spoils and because advances have been made over the past decades in fish handling, trends in per capita landings presumably understate advances in per capita availability to consumers

8   Of course, the prospects for expansion of yield on a sustainable basis will vary with the strength of management regimes that arise. The FAO's most recent pessimistic estimate for 2010 projects total production at 107 million metric tonnes (mmt), of which the capture sector will contribute 80mmt; its most recent optimistic estimate for 2010 projects total production of 144mmt of which the capture sector will contribute 105mmt. FAO, *Fishery Production in 2010*

9   Reference to technology-indexed fleet capacity illustrates this trend. For example, between 1970 and 1989 the registered tonnage of the major vessel fleet increased by 87 per cent, and, despite increased support of spotter planes, wider nets, factory and mother ships, the landings increased by only 46 per cent. S M Garcia and C Newton, *Current Situation, Trends and Prospects in World Capture Fisheries*, p19 and Table 3 (14–16 June 1994) (unpublished manuscript on file with *Ecology Law Quarterly*). When a 'technology coefficient' is introduced to make allowances for advances in technology, the decline per vessel (tonne) was more dramatic, from 6.4 to 2.1 tonnes of fish landed per gross tonne of registered vessel, Ibid Table 4

10 Nonetheless, between 1970 and 19S9 the value of capture sector landings increased more (107 per cent) than the increase in total landings (46 per cent). Ibid. The authors also report that revenue per gross registered ton increased from US$2100 to US$2300 over the same period. Ibid

11 'Fishing Crisis in World's Oceans: 90 Nations at UN Conference to Consider Limits, 1994', available in *Nexis,* World Library, Allnws file. However, tastes shift continuously, and a shift in fishing practices that led to food exploitation of 'lower' species could conceivably produce the same protein, tonne for tonne as the current mix of catch (discussed below)

12 See Garcia, *supra* note 3, p8

13 See William J Broad, 'Creatures of the Deep Find their Way in the Table', *New York Times,* 26 December 1995, pC1. (Deep seas fisheries already showing signs of collapse, with uncertain ramifications on food web)

14 See, eg Seth Mydans, 'Thai Shrimp Fanners Facing Ecologists' Fury', *New York Times,* 28 April 1996, pA3

15 Also economists and biologists have parted on the optimal level of fishing. Marine biologists have classically stressed maximum sustainable biological yield (MSBY). MSBY is the quantity that can be taken without depleting the stock. Because stocks are themselves subject to fluctuation, the amount would presumably not be constant from year to year. See A A Rosenberg et al, 'Achieving Sustainable Use of Renewable Resources', *Science,* No 263, p828 (1993). However, because the cost per unit of harvest lends to increase as the stock declines, the economically 'efficient' level of fishing (identified with maximum net revenues from the stock, MNR) is presumed to be lower than MSBY. See Appendix: Ross D Eckert, *The Enclosure of Ocean Resources,* Hoover Institute Press, p123 (1979); Mike Holden, *The Common Fisheries Policy,* Blackwell Science Inc, pp169–185 (1994)

16 To illustrate, a food security policy would presumably increase research into the commercial prospects of Antarctic krill, whose total weight, worldwide, has been estimated (at the high end) at 1.35 billion tonnes (five times the aggregate weight of all the humans on earth). Jane E Stevens, 'The Secret Lives of Krill: Dismantling the Myths of Southern Oceans', *Sea Frontiers,* 2 June 1995, pp26, 27. These reserves have thus far been exploited only at moderate levels. Ibid. Unless specially prepared, krill are unappetizing (their shells concentrate fluorides out of the sea) and if not processed within three hours are unfit for human consumption. Ibid p31. This means that their huge potential is principally as food stock. That is not to dismiss their significance for food security, however. Approximately 30 per cent of the world catch is used as meat much of it in aquaculture. FAO, Fishery Production in 1994, Figure 1. Fishmeal and oil amounted to an estimated 34.7 million metric tonnes in 1994. Ibid

17 See Kent Jeffreys, 'Rescuing the Oceans', in *The True State of the Planet,* p295 (Ronald Bailey, (ed) 1995). Income from marine fishing reportedly accounts for about 1 per cent of the global economy. Peter Weber, *Net Loss,* p6 (1994) (observing, however, that the effects are of the fishing industry vary depending on its local importance)

18 Food and Agriculture Organization of the United Nations, 'Marine Fisheries and the Law of the Sea: A Decade of Change', in *The State of Food and Agriculture 1992*, pp29–30 (1992) (hereinafter SOFIA, 1992) (using the 1989 global fisheries data). In the US, the Department of Commerce has estimated that rational fisheries management, including a rehabilitation permitting reduction in pressure, would increase domestic fishing revenues US$2.9 billion a year. US Department of Commerce, *National Oceanic and Atmospheric Administration. NOAA Strategic Plan: A Vision for 2005*, p89 (1996)
19 See Jeffreys, *supra* note 17, pp309–312
20 See Appendix 13.1
21 Third United Nations Conference on the Law of the Sea, UN Doc A/Conf.57/122, reprinted in Official Records Vol XVII, p151. Sales No E.84.V.3 (1984) (hereinafter UNCLOS)
22 Third United Nations Conference on the Law of the Sea. UN Doc A/Conf.62/122, reprinted in Official Records Vol XVII
23 For the most part the coastal states continued to treat their new resource as a free access good. Some of the distant water fleets refocused efforts to the high seas, while others negotiated entry into coastal Exclusive Economic Zones (EEZs). See Rory McLeod, Market Access Issues for the New Zealand Seafood Trade, p14 (New Zealand Fishing Industry Board, 1996). Giulio Pontecorvo, 'The Enclosure of the Marine Commons: Adjustment and Redistribution in World Fisheries', 12 *Marine Policy*, p361 (1988)
24 FAO does not estimate the mortality of cast-backs, which is a difficult figure to establish. SOFIA, 1995, p21
25 The extent of illegal fishing is, by its *very* nature, uncertain, but believed to be substantial It has been estimated that half the fish landed in England have been caught illegally. Richard North, 'The Madness that Threatens our Oceans', *Daily Mail*, 5 August 1994, available in *Nexis,* World Library, Allnws file. According to a report by the European Commission, monitoring for violations is ineffective, jeopardizing the future of the industry. See 'Fisheries: Member States Incapable of Controlling Fleets, Says Report', *European Report, European Information Services*, 20 March 1996, available in *Nexis,* World Library, Allwld file
26 SOFIA, 1995, p14. Also, many nations with a tradition in fishing and a heavily subsidized fishing fleet have managed to escape the dwindling stocks and toughening regulations by turning to the stocks of Africa and other less-regulated developing countries
27 See, eg Convention for the Prohibition of Fishing with Long Driftnets in the South Pacific (without Protocols), *opened for signature,* 23 November 1989, ILM No 29, p1454 (1990); Large-Scale Pelagic Driftnet Fishing and Its Impact on the Living Marine Resources of the World's Oceans and Seas, GA Res 225, UN GAOR. 44th Sess Supp No 49, 85th plen mtg, p147, UN Doc A//44/49 (1990); Large-Scale Pelagic Driftnet Fishing and Its Impact of the Living Marine Resources of the World's Oceans and Seas, GA Res 215, UN GAOR, 46th Sess Supp No 49, 79th plen mtg, p143, UN Doc A//46/49 (1992)

28 Food and Agriculture Organization of the United Nations, *Code of Conduct for Responsible Fisheries* (visited on 25 May 1997) http://www.fao.org/WAICENT/ faoinfo/fishery/agreem/codecond/codecon.htm

29 Draft Agreement for the Implementation of the Provisions of the United Nations Convention on the Law of the Sea of 10 December 1982 Relating to the Conservation and Management of Straddling Fish Stocks and Highly Migratory Fish Stocks. UN Conference on Straddling Fish Stocks and Highly Migratory fish Stocks, 6th Sess, p1, UN Doc A/Conf 164/33 (1995) (hereinafter Straddling Fish Stocks)

30 There may the justification for singling out excessive capital and regarding it even more warily than other excessive inputs. Much of fishing capital (one has only to think of vessels and port infrastructure) is specific to an industry and to a locale in some instances. Hence, once investments are made, each year there is pressure to turn the fleet out as long as operating costs (often subsidized, see *infra* Part I.B.) can be covered, whether the impact on the ever-fluctuating stock warrants the activity or not. Labour which suffers its own limited mobility in the form of dependent fishing communities, is far more complex. Any solution to the problems caused by overcapacity must address facilitating an exit of both capital and labour, such as by worker retraining. See Joshua John, 'Managing Redundancy in Overexploited Fisheries' (World Bank Discussion Papers, Fisheries Series No 24, 1994)

31 See McLeod, *supra* note 23, p21. Even the 'science', as represented by the estimates of safe catch levels by consultant scientists, has not been immune from the political pressures created by excessive capacity. See US Department of Commerce, *supra* note 18, p86

32 Christopher Newton, UN Food and Agriculture Organization, quoted in William D Moltanbano, Fishing for Solutions to Depletion of Seafood Stocks, *L A Times*, 11 March 1995, pA2

33 Eugene H Buck, CRS Report for Congress: Overcapitalization in the US Commercial Fishing Industry (Congressional Research Service, 1995) pp7–8 stating that:

> In reality, optimum fleet size to harvest the resource may necessitate certain 'inefficiencies' such as the capacity of Alaska fishermen to adjust to wide fluctuations in anticipated salmon runs or the ability of marginal fishermen to shift among various seasonal fisheries. The appropriate level of capital depends on a number of highly variable and unpredictable factors – natural oceanic and atmospheric conditions that significantly affect the numbers of fish available and can fluctuate substantially between seasons. Consequently, current population assessments as well as future predictions are often problematic. ... Without accurate population data it is difficult to assess industry efficiency at any given time and, therefore, to determine the extent of overcapitalization.

> In addition, small boats can reach stocks inaccessible to large boats, and viceversa

34 See McLeod, *supra* note 23, p13. New vessels enjoy a catching power ratio of 1.5:1 relative to older vessels of the same size. The ratio rises to 3:1 for larger

vessels. SOFIA, 1995, p23. FAO reports that some administrators require owners introducing new vessels to compensate owners of older vessels for their removal. Ibid

35 Buck, *supra* note 33, p8, points out that:

> Fishermen anticipate that Federal, State or regional public bodies will eventually impose some sort of access controls. Such anticipation may motivate some individuals to enter the industry prematurely. Others may be deterred from leaving ailing fisheries and moving into more profitable new fisheries for fear of being denied significant quota shares if access control is adopted for their traditional fishery

36 See Matteo J Milazzo. 'Reexamining Subsidies in World Fisheries 59–61' (May 1997) (unpublished manuscript on file with *Ecology Law Quarterly*) (examining Lloyd's of London data on the world's fleet). During the last five years (for which there is data), there has been a decline in new ship construction (gross tonnage added). The average age of vessels in the world fleet is now over 18 years, or roughly the useful life of a vessel. SOFIA, 1995, p19–20

37 Subsidization of operating costs, by artificially lowering the cost curve, shifts the supply curve and drives output beyond the efficient level. There is already a 'subsidizing' transfer of public wealth to each catcher and also presumptive overcapitalization where property rights are imperfectly established – wherever fish are, in effect, free access goods – more assets will be dedicated to harvesting than is efficient in the free-for-all competition. See Appendix 13.1

38 See *infra*, Part II, C.4

39 See John, *supra* note 30

40 For example, Canada's governmental support for the Atlantic fisheries alone has been estimated at C\$8 billion for the decade beginning in 1981. That is roughly equal to the value of the entire landed catch. William E Schrank (1995) 'Extended Fisheries Jurisdiction: Origin of the Current Crises in Atlantic Canada's Fisheries', *Marine Policy*, No 19, pp285, 291

41 See Organisation for Economic Co-operation and Development, Financial Support to the Fishing Industry of OECD Member Countries (1965) [hereinafter OECD 1965]: Organisation for Economic Co-operation and Development, Financial Support to the Fishing Industry of OECD Member Countries (1980) [hereinafter OECD 1980]. Between 1983 and 1990 European Economic Community (EEC) support for member fishers (independent of national government support) rose from US\$80 million to US\$580 million. SOFIA, 1992, p149. 20 per cent was for ship-building and renovation. Japan reported that in 1990 the credit balance to fisheries from government and commercial sectors combined was approximately US\$19 billion. Ibid, pp149–150

42 The provision for a Notification of Subsidies under the WTO Agreement on Subsidies and Countervailing Measures (SCM) [hereinafter SCM] applies to fisheries as well as other sectors. Office of the US Trade Representative. Executive Office of the President, 'Final Act Embodying the Results of the Uruguay Round of Multilateral Trade Negotiations, Agreement on Agriculture', Annex 1, MTN/FA II-A1A-3, p16 (15 December 1993). See also, Office of the US Trade

Representative, Executive Office of the President, 'Final Act embodying the Results of the Uruguay Round of Multilateral Trade Negotiations, Agreement on Subsidies and Countervailing Measures', MTN/FAV-13 p31 (15 December 1993)

43 There is no indication that the US has submitted any data

44 Japan has explicitly acknowledged what may be true of many countries: that the government financing system supports businesses in financial difficulty by assuming their liabilities. Indeed, 'the amount of liability taken over by the government has been substantial in recent years due to the severe economic status of the fishing industry'. SOFIA, 1992, p149

45 The Fisherman's Protective Act provides that should a foreign country seize or fine the owners of a US vessel for alleged infringement of domestic fishery management requirements, the US will, under certain circumstances, reimburse the fine fee or other direct charge paid to secure the vessel's release. See 22 USC §§1971–1973 (1997)

46 SOFIA, 1992, pp159–160

47 SOFIA, 1992, p145

48 In contrast to the many people who argue that the study demonstrates a US$54 billion 'subsidy', Christy more accurately states that his figure is a deficit, most of which subsidies are presumed to cover. Ibid. Thus, the subsidy may not cover all of the deficit diminishing fishers earnings

49 Christy, as distinct from many who cite the study, recognizes that his figure is a deficit, 'most of which' subsidies 'are presumed to cover', SOFIA, 1992, pp159–160. Some portion of the government underwritten losses are presumably recaptured in fees. See *supra* note 22

50 SOFIA, 1992, p146

51 Ibid. The FAO uses a presumed market value for each species to calculate estimated revenue. Ibid

52 Ibid

53 Nor should one assume that governments intend to replace retired capacity on a ton for ton (or even catch-capacity for catch-capacity) basis

54 The cash flow will of course vary with the level of subsidy

55 See *infra*, Part II, C.1.b

56 A full accounting for environmental losses, including values such as biodiversity that are not priced in markets, would require appeal to some contingent valuation technique. The estimated amount would inevitably be controversial. Nonetheless, in principle the subsidy is real and likely to be appreciable

57 For a comparison of the relative merits of control through landing taxes and merchantable quotas, see Terry Heaps and John F Helliwell (1995) 'The Taxation of Natural Resources', in Vol 1, Alan J Auerbach and Martin Feldstein, *Handbook of Public Economics*, pp430–440

58 See SOFIA, 1992, p151. Not making the firm pay the natural resource cost is an economic subsidy, but, as discussed below, is not necessarily a 'subsidy' under the SCM. Some commentators include protectionist measures as a fourth son of 'subsidy' untallied by the Special Chapter: around the world domestic fishing industries benefit from tariff and non-tariff barriers. As distinct from

pure subsidies, these measures benefit domestic sellers over importers (by taxing domestic consumers). The global effect may be to reduce fishing effort because they raise rather than lower prices to consumers

59 Milazzo, *supra* note 36, p86, estimates current global fisheries subsidies (of capacity and effort-enhancing character) from a low of US$11 billion to a high of US$21.5 billion

60 The history of the EC's restructuring is discussed in Holden, *supra* note 15, pp19–33. Guidance targets have been revised periodically but effective agreement remains elusive. See 'Fisheries Council Ministers Agree Five Year Plan to Save Fish Stocks', European Report, European Information Service, 16 April 1997, available in *Nexis*, World Library, Allwld file (discussing EU adoption of compromise proposal to cut fleet capacity up to 30 per cent, but indicating UK intention to resist implementation pending satisfactory resolution of quota jumping)

61 'Protection of the Oceans, All Kinds of Seas, Including Enclosed and Semi-enclosed Areas, and Coastal States and the Protection, Rational Use and Development of Their Living Resources: Report of the Secretary-General', UN ESCOR, Commission on Sustainable Development, 4th Sess, p13, UN Doc E/CN.17/1996/3 (1996)

62 'Summary Conclusions of the Seventh APEC Fisheries Working Group Meeting', Asia-Pacific Economic Cooperation Seventh Fisheries Working Group Meeting, Item 6.2 (29–31 May 1996) (photocopy on file with *Ecology Law Quarterly*)

63 SOFIA, 1995, p32

64 The 11 per cent figure is for 1990. See Garcia and Newton, *supra* note 9, p9, who also indicate that the value of fish trade increased at a faster rate than agriculture in general

65 SOFIA, 1995, p32 (reporting that developing countries as a group recorded an increasingly positive trade balance in fishery products, which reached US$13.4 billion in 1993)

66 See Wu Yunhe, 'China Christens Plan to Be a Fishing Superpower', China Daily, 16–22 June 1996, available in *Nexis*, World Library, Allnws file

67 URAA Annex 1, p16

68 URAA Art 5

69 Ibid

70 Ibid, Arts 1(f) and 13. See Paul C Rosenthal and Lynn E Duff, 'Reforming Global Trade in Agriculture', in *The World Trade Organization*, pp145, 170–172 (Terence P Stewart (ed) 1966)

71 Ibid. Annex 2, 12(1). See generally, Vinod Rege, 'GATT Law and Environment-Related Issues Affecting the Trade of Developing Countries', *Journal of World Trade*, June 1994, pp95, 154–155

72 See *infra* Part II, Chapter 4

73 A foundation for negotiating reform in agriculture was an OECD study of producer subsidy equivalents (PS) country by country and crop by crop. However, efforts to apply a comparable methodology to fish products run into enormous difficulties. McLeod *supra* note 23, pp30–31

74 For WTO members, domestic law measures, while available, are constrained by the disciplines of the Agreement on Subsidies and Countervailing Measures (SCM) Part V

75 Final Affirmative Countervailing Duly Determination, Certain Fresh Atlantic Groundfish From Canada, 51 Fed Reg 10.041. 10.041-42 (1986) (certain benefits held to constitute subsidies within the meaning of section 701 of the Tariff Act of 1930. 19 USCS §1671 (West. WESTLAW through P.L. 105-4, approved 3 March 1997). Warranting a CVD of 5.82 per cent *ad valorem*)

76 GATT Dispute Panel Report, adopted by the Committee on Subsidies and Countervailing Measures, United States – Imposition of Countervailing Duties on Imports of Chilled Atlantic Salmon from Norway, in 2 Handbook of WTO/GATT Dispute Settlement, p883 (1995) (4 December 1992)

77 'Fish Farming: A Promise of Halibut', *The Economist*, 31 August 1996, p50

78 The importing country has, however, to select one form of relief, either a countervailing duty or a countermeasure, SCM art 10, note 33. See also ibid, Art 4, 7

79 There is one caveat: a member may initiate article 9's consultation provisions if its domestic industry suffers serious adverse effects 'difficult to repair' in consequence of another member's programmes that are technically 'non-actionable' under art 8.2, Ibid, art 9.1

80 See Americo Beviglia Zampetti, 'The Uruguay Round Agreement on Subsidies', *Journal of World Trade*, December 1995, pp5, 13 14

81 SCM, art 1.1(a)(2), as those terms are defined in Article XVI of GATT 1994

82 In any challenge, the nation defending its practices might be able to show, for example, that the cost of its loan guarantee programme was not a subsidy considering the fees the nation collected and infrequency of defaults. I refer to grants to fishers for the purchase of loans, rather than grants direct to the ship-building industry. Support for the builders is more problematic because a complainant would have to show how much of the benefit to the builder was passed along as a benefit to the fisher

83 OECD, 1980, p12 (Canada); Ibid, p22 (Faeroe Islands)

84 Ibid, p100 (guaranteeing minimum weekly income for fishers in Norway)

85 Ibid, p103 (Norway)

86 See ibid, p46 (Greece)

87 The FAO has estimated that governments pay out US$5 billion annually in fuel subsidies alone. William D Montalbano, 'Fishing for Solutions to Depletion of Seafood Stocks', *L A Times*, 11 March 1995, pA2. A nation pursuing a policy of favouring fishers in the area of fuel payments might argue on either of two grounds that they are not subsidizing. First, where, as in the US, fuel benefits are as available to farmers and pleasure boat owners as to fishermen the benefits are not sufficiently 'specific'. Second, if the alleged subsidy takes the form of an exemption from taxes, and the tax funds go into a separate account for building and maintaining roads, it is not really a 'tax' but a 'user fee' that fishermen (and farmers) should not pay, since they traffic the waters (and farms), not the roads

88 See OECD, 1980, p57 (Italy): ibid p64 (offering low-interest loans for fleet reductions in Japan)

89 Ibid, p122–123
90 However, environmental and resource advocates may argue for special green-light approval of subsidies that increase productivity or relieve catch pressure. See *infra* Part II, Chapter 3
91 Only subsidies that are 'specific' to an enterprise, industry, or group of industries trigger the various remedies of the SCM. SCM Art 1.2. 2
92 House of Lords, Select Committee on the European Communities, 'Third Country Fisheries Agreements', Session 1996–97 (3rd Report), p5 (reporting that the EU spent more than 280 million ECU in 1996 for the rights to fish in non-EU waters other than by cash payment)
93 Milazzo, *supra* note 36, p24
94 Modes of compensating access other than by cash payment are harder, but not impossible, to fit into the mould of a legal subsidy. For example, some access is arranged on a trade-for-access basis in which a nation opens up its waters in return for preferential access for various of its own fish products. Milazzo estimates that the European Union (EU) funding alone for 'third party access agreements (including co-financing by members) probably amounts to at least US$500 million. Ibid. Since 1991, the US has paid the Pacific island states US$14 million annually on behalf of US tuna purse seiners. Ibid, p47. Japan is spending about US$200 million on distant water access and foreign fisheries 'assistance', one objective of which is to assure continued fishing rights in developing nations waters. Ibid, p45. From a trade perspective, all these payments are distorting. From a resource perspective, the payments are warranted only in the case that the fee paid covers the full cost of the harvest. Conversely, to the extent that the fee is less than the true resource cost, the payments not only distort trade, they are inefficient. Graciela Chichilnisky has forcefully demonstrated that free trade amplifies such inefficiencies that stem from inadequately defined properly rights. See Chichilnisky, 'Clobal Environment and North-South Trade', *American Economic Review*, No 84 p851 (1994). Milazzo raises serious concerns about the environmental and developmental consequences of these arrangements with cash-strapped nations, such as Mauritania. Milazzo, *supra* note 36, p42
95 See *supra* note 45 and accompanying text
96 SCM, Art 1.1(a)(1)(i)
97 Ibid
98 See Kenneth S Komoroski, 'The Failure of Governments to Regulate Industry: A Subsidy Under the GATT?', 10 *Houston Journal of International Law*, p189 (1988). As indicated in the text, no case decision has adopted this argument. Nonetheless, the author argues for keeping the possibility of a CVD open where a nation gains a competitive advantage by failure to live up to 'minimum international environmental standards' that have been 'affirmatively established' in international law through conventions or 'customary/normative principles'. Ibid, p209
99 UNCLOS, Art 61. At the present time, the language of many provisions in Multilateral Environmental Agreements (MEAs) touching living marine resources is probably too vague to determine that a member's lax actions constituted a violation. UNCLOS, Article 118, addressing living resources of the high seas, such

as tuna swimming beyond national EEZs, is representative in providing little more than that states should cooperate with each other

100 Rege, *supra* note 71, p157

101 Ibid. Rege notes that the current GATT definition of subsidy

> [M]akes it clear that, in order to constitute a subsidy, there should be a positive action by the government which directly or indirectly results in a financial contribution or benefits being conferred on recipients. The definition would not cover situations where it is alleged that the government has... failed to take action by adopting appropriate environmental standards

Ibid.

102 For scepticism about use of CVDs to achieve harmonization and a 'level playing field,' see Richard B Dagan and Michael S, Knoll. 'Duties to Offset Competitive Advantage', 10 *Maryland Journal of International Law and Trade,* pp273, 285–287 (1986) (stating that costs and values of clean environment vary considerably from country to country, and domestic industries may manipulate environmental sympathies to achieve competitive advantage)

103 This rationale would not apply to aquaculturists, as long as the aquaculture is not imposing untaxed costs

104 The US proposed that 'governmental provision of extraction rights for natural resources, so long as the right to extract or exploit the natural resource is so through an auction bidding process open to all parties' should not be actionable US also proposed that the provision of processed natural resource products by a government should not be considered an actionable subsidy so long as the natural resource product is offered to all parties on the same terms and conditions. Patrick J McDonough, 'Subsidies and Countervailing Measures', in 1 *The GATT Uruguay Round: A Negotiating History* (1986–1992) p903 and note 547 (Terence P Stewart (ed) 1993)

105 Nation A's failure to charge full resource costs to *its own fleet* provides a basis for alleging subsidization. There is less reason to suppose that A's failure to tax full costs to B's fleet provides a basis for an action.

106 Chapter 19 Canada–US Binational Review Panel Report, in the Matter of Certain Softwood Lumber Products from Canada, USA-92-1904-01, 13 T.T.R. 161 (6 May 1993)

107 Convention on Biological Diversity, 5 June 1992. Art 11, 31 ILM p818 (1992)

108 SCM, Art 3

109 For example, OECD, 1980, p91 identifies what would be suspect New Zealand loans and grants given to promote export of non-traditional species/products as well as incentive deductions for exports of certain species/fish products

110 SOFIA, 1995, pp262–266 (suggesting that low-income developing countries may have benefited from targeted export subsidies for agricultural products; those countries may use similar methods to give their fishers an advantage in the fish trade)

111 SCM, Art 6.2.

112 In determining the 5 per cent, the cost of support to the government, as distinct from benefits to the recipient, forms the numerator. The denominator

focuses on the recipient's sales. See SCM, Annex IV(2) (stating that 'in determining whether the overall rate of subsidization exceeds 5 per cent of the value of the product, the value of the product shall be calculated as the total value of the recipient firm's sales in the most recent twelve month period ...' SCM Annex 1V(3) adds that '[w]here the subsidy is tied to the production or sale of a given product, the value of the product shall be calculated as the total value of the recipient firm's sales of that product ...')

113 Among the questions raised are: firm definition: product definition; unallocated subsidies: and displacement controversies. Ibid. For instance, fishing cooperatives are intermediate units between government and firm in a number of countries, including Japan. Are they 'firms' for purposes of Annex IV? Assume a firm of member A receive only 3 per cent Article 1 non-exempt subsidy, but its high seas tuna operations arc subsidized 10 per cent. If the firm is exporting tuna to member B, does B have a serious prejudice complaint on the basis of tuna as the relevant product? Much of the support that could be regarded as trade distorting 'subsidies' are not allocated to firms in the best kept government records. Consider the costs of maintaining fishing grounds. Will allocating these costs to an exporting firm be part of the complainant's prima facie case? Finally, it is not clear how to handle complaints where the crux of B's objection is that A's subsidies are displacing B's firms from potential markets in C or A. If A's firms sell their high seas catches to C and those fleets are subsidized 3 per cent, is it significant (and a violation) that A's firms selling to C (all sales to C included) are being subsidized 15 per cent in toto?

114 URAA, Annex 2, 12(i) (specifying the basis for exemption of payments under agricultural programmes)

115 Ibid, Annex 2(1)

116 Ibid, Annex 2, 12(ii)

117 SCM, Art 8.2

118 See, eg Convention for the Protection of the Mediterranean Sea Against Pollution, 16 February 1976, 15 *ILM*, p290

119 See 31, *ILM*, p818

120 See *infra* note 98 and accompanying text

121 See, eg Convention on Wetlands of International Importance, 3 February 1971, 11 *ILM*, p963

122 See, eg Convention on International Trade in Endangered Species of Wild Fauna and Flora, 3 March 1973, 12 *ILM*, p1085

123 See eg UN Straddling Fishstocks Agreement

124 Fisheries Agency of Japan 1996 fiscal year budget includes about ¥32 billion for 'Coastal Fishing Grounds Development' and ¥17.6 billion for 'Shoreline Preservation', Fisheries Agency of Japan. 1996 Budget. US Department of State, Ref No 197465

125 SCM, Art 1(a)(1)(iii)

126 UNCLOS, Art 61(3)

127 Any such complaint would be brought by a nation alleging lost markets in a third country, and would most likely rely on 'serious prejudice'. The complainant would be in the awkward position of tracing the competitive disadvantage

its fishers suffered (fewer, more costly-to-catch fish) to its frugal failure to join the international convention the charged WTO member is raising as a shield

128 GATT, Art XX(g) provides a defence to actions brought under the GAIT 'measures relating to the conservation of exhaustible natural resources'. Art XX(b) defends measures 'necessary to protect ... plant life or health'. Strictly speaking, these measures are not part of the SCM which is a separate agreement; however. SCM, Art 32.1 enigmatically provides that 'no specific action against, a subsidy of another Member can be taken except in accordance with the GATT of 1994, as interpreted by this Agreement'. Whether an SCM subsidy has to meet GATT special defences remains an open question

129 International law accepts as 'law' a body of general practices even if they are not embossed in treaty among the parties. That body of law is referred to as 'customary law'. On that basis, some of UNCLOS's provisions may bind nations not party to UNCLOS. See Alexandre Kiss and Dinah Shelton, *International Environmental Law*, pp105–106 (1991)

130 There have been scattered experiments in privatization of reefs, See Jeffreys, *supra* note 17, pp319–321 (mentioning that some individuals and groups have treated reefs as private property, even in the absence of government recognition of a private property right)

131 McLeod, *supra* note 23, p88, reports that New Zealand policy is to charge the industry directly where costs of providing service for industry can he identified. In 1995 the government anticipates recovering US$34 million as full cost recovery for fisheries management services, detection of offences, research, etc. The New Zealand response appears to be correct. Why should a failure to mimic it not be considered a subsidy? One response might be that in this less than ideal world it is unrealistic to suppose that user charges will become universal; and that considering the nature of the resource, the plight of world fisheries and the exigencies of food supply, the trade laws ought not to inhibit fisheries managers from adopting the most promising tactics for stock enhancement, ie to provide the good from the public purse, as a second best solution

132 Holden, *supra* note 15, pp31, 33; OECD, 1980, p64, indicates compensation by Japan for 'fleet reduction'

133 OECD, 1980, p57 (Italy)

134 Ibid, p16 (Denmark)

135 Ibid, pp122–123 (Sweden)

136 URAA, Annex 2(10)

137 Worldwide, rice is subsidized 86 per cent, wheat, 48 per cent and beef 35 per cent. See Shailagh Murray (1996) 'Subsidies Shackle EU Competitivenss', *Wall Street Journal*, 28 October 1996, pA13. If one accepts Christy's estimates for fish, the worldwide level of subsidization was 77 per cent in 1989. See *supra* Part I.B.I. This article suggests that the estimate of a US$54 billion subsidy of a US$70 billion catch may be excessive. However, the catch of some species of fish must be subsidized at a level higher than the fisheries industry mean, perhaps at a level quite comparable to the levels of highly subsidized crops, and it is quite possible that the most highly subsidized fish catches are supported at a level comparable to the levels of highly subsidized crops

138 The issues might even be appropriate for consideration by the Trade Policy Review Mechanism (TPRM) (Annex 3) which, while 'not ... intended to serve as a basis for the enforcement of specific obligations under the Agreement'. TPRM A(1), may have broad, still-untapped powers to accommodate examination of trade-sustainability links. See International Institute for Sustainable Development (1996) 'The World Trade Organization and Sustainable Development: An Independent Assessment', pp37–38 (1996)

139 This figure, one of a style common in fisheries analyses is adapted from National Marine Fisheries Service (1996) 'Economic Status of US Fisheries', p6; the discussion of the basic model draws on that report and on Lee G Anderson (1986) *The Economics of Fisheries Management*

140 Effort is intended (not without conceptual and observational difficulties) to sum a basket of inputs that includes vessels, labour, gear, time spent fishing and even skill

141 In this model TC does not capture some social, including environmental costs, such as the existence value of non-commercial species, and the option value of biodiversity portfolios. If accounted for, these would raise the cost curve and move E^* to the left

142 See note 143

143 As my colleague Eric Talley points out the identification of marginal revenue and costs with *social* benefits and *social* costs is linked to the simplifying but improbable condition that price is independent of output, which eliminates considerations of consumer surplus that would flow from a larger catch at a reduced price. While the identification of E^* with the social ideal may be inexact, it is safe to assume that the true social ideal, with the condition of price independence relaxed, is less than E (in other words, the level sanctioned by economic theory is less than that sanctioned by biology), but not to the right of MSY. For a much more complex and technical analysis where prices are variant, see Anderson, *supra* note 139, pp74–83

144 Roughly, if there are 100 fishers in the fleet, and the removal of a marginal fish costs US$1 in terms of reduced asset value (which can be thought of as increased costs of fishing for the remaining fish increased probability of 'crash' of the resource, etc) the successful fisher, who realizes the full market costs of the fish, bears (in excess of his internalized incremental costs) only a contingent 1/100 share of the cost of its removal: the asset value decreased by US$1, but it 'costs' the catcher only his expected 1 cent

145 See Terry Heaps and John F Helliwell (1985) 'The Taxation of Natural Resources', in 1 Alan J Auerbach and Martin Feldstein, *Handbook of Public Economics*, p430

146 Andersen observes more comprehensively that 'A biological and economic equilibrium occurs if, at the existing level of effort, catch equals growth so the population will not change and at the same time revenue equals costs so the amount of effort will not change. If either of these conditions does not hold, then the population size or the level of effort will change', *supra* note 139, p31

147 See Andersen, *supra* note 139, pp219–231

148 More precisely, in the flow from the stock

149 For example, seasonal and per-vessel quota, by artificially restricting return on investment, are facially inefficient. A justification might be advanced for such measures, however, when imposed for a short-term only as a means of achieving equitable distribution in response to a sharp but temporary decline in stock abundance

150 ITOs also induce concentration of effort in vessels with the lowest long-term average costs

151 And government expenditures increase by the amount of the subsidy

152 As noted in the text, some such government programmes if adopted as a reliable government commitment, might be construed as cost-reduction subsidies

14

WTO Food and Agricultural Rules: Sustainable Agriculture and the Human Right to Food

Mark Ritchie and Kristin Dawkins

Introduction

As United States Department of Agriculture (USDA) Secretary Dan Glickman predicted, food and agriculture issues were a challenging and acrimonious item on the agenda at the World Trade Organization (WTO) Ministerial Meeting in Seattle. In a speech to the Center for Strategic and International Studies, Glickman argued that the intensity and sensitivity of agricultural issues is greater than in the past and that agricultural issues would be the dominant and most difficult issue in the Seattle Ministerial.[1] US Trade Representative Charlene Barshefsky certainly supported this view, asserting before Congress that agriculture would be at the 'heart' of the US agenda for future world trade talks.[2]

For anyone who followed the previous Uruguay Round of world trade negotiations, these comments might seem familiar. Contentious debate over agriculture trade rules is nothing new. From the very beginnings of the WTO's predecessor, the General Agreement on Tariffs and Trade (GATT),[3] agriculture has been a central and contentious issue. From the founding meeting in Havana in 1947 to the recently completed Uruguay Round,[4] food and agriculture issues have repeatedly disrupted the entire trade negotiation process.[5]

As a result, agricultural trade negotiations often give rise to poorly considered and unworkable outcomes. The final language in the Uruguay Round Agreement on Agriculture[6] (AoA) was cobbled together at the last minute, papering over differences in order to permit the conclusion of the negotiations on tariffs, banking, textiles and many other important sectors of the economy. In recognition of the unsatisfactory nature of the AoA, it was agreed that this would only be a temporary measure,[7] and negotiations on new commitments began in 2000, and will likely be accelerated as part of the Doha Development Agenda. These agriculture talks have, in effect, already begun and are considered to be part of what is called the 'built-in' agenda of the WTO. Negotiators know that they have to tackle this issue whether or not there is an agreement to begin a comprehensive new round of negotiations.[8]

One outcome of the last round of talks is that despite the signing of a 'peace clause'[9] designed to keep agricultural trade disputes to a minimum, there are more agriculture- and food-related trade disputes in the WTO than ever before. The US alone has recently filed 12 complaints in the WTO on agriculture issues, far exceeding the previous record.[10] One reason for the proliferation of disputes is that many of the new rules call for such dramatic changes that countries have been unable or reluctant to implement them. Chile, Hungary and the Philippines, for example, have announced that they will not be implementing certain rules and have asked the rest of the WTO members for formal exemptions.

The Chilean government, one of the most fervent proponents of radical liberalization in the Uruguay Round, is now arguing that they cannot live up to some of their WTO commitments because world commodity prices have fallen instead of risen as they had hoped. Chilean officials are saying that living up to current WTO obligations would destroy much of their agricultural economy, so they are begging for a waiver that would permit them to change or abandon their previous commitments. The director of the Chilean Ministry of Agriculture's international department, Sergio Ramos, has said that world 'markets have been so sporadic and have gone down quickly that our price band mechanism has been unable to cope'.[11]

Only a handful of countries have asked for formal permission to abandon or postpone commitments made in the agriculture agreement, but many others are also finding it difficult to comply – primarily due to the general collapse of international commodity prices since the end of the Uruguay Round. According to *The Economist*, commodity prices are lower than at any point in the 150 years they have been keeping records.[12] Countries totally dependent on commodity exports have much lower export revenues, which leads to a reduction in the food commodity imports that they are able to pay for, affecting their food security and further diminishing the global market, thus pushing global food prices down even lower.[13]

With crop and livestock prices at historic lows around the planet, many countries, including the US, are overtly or covertly abandoning their WTO commitments. In the US this year, family farmers are facing a crisis much like that of the mid-1980s due to exceptionally low farm-gate prices. Since the signing of the WTO agreement in December 1994, farm prices for most of the major commodities have fallen 30 per cent or more and agricultural bankers in the heart of family farm country see grim times for at least the next few years.[14] In response to this crisis, the US government has abandoned a number of the commitments made during the Uruguay Round agriculture talks, including promises to reduce government subsidies, to refrain from imposing import controls and to cut export subsidies.[15]

Perhaps most shocking is that US farm subsidies have continued to rise, not fall, as had been promised by AoA proponents. USDA Secretary Dan Glickman predicted 1999 would be 'the highest year on record in terms of direct payments to farmers by the government – $15.3 billion,'[16] nearly 50 per cent above US government direct payments to farmers at the height of the Uruguay Round. In 1990, for example, direct payments were around US$9 billion.[17] The US has also been imposing import controls in hopes of boosting prices for US farmers, including new restrictions on wheat gluten from Europe[18] and lamb from New Zealand.[19]

The most important deviation from the AoA commitments is in the area of export dumping or exporting goods at prices below their cost of production. The federal government, through a complex system of loan guarantees, deliberately sets domestic farm-gate prices at far below the cost of production for many commodities. Due to its large share of the global market, US prices for commodities tied to government loan rates have historically set the global market price for these commodities, as traders and processors jockey for supplies. Under the US system, the government takes grain as collateral for farmer loans that are set at below the cost of production. It then releases the collateralized grain to the domestic market at those low prices. Theoretically, the loan rate would establish the floor price, but recent events have caused prices to drop below the already low loan rates. As farmers struggle to stay in business they produce more commodities to maintain their net income and debt payments, adding to surpluses that further depress market prices. Increasing domestic supplies have caused the US government to double the amount of export subsidies it gives to companies to clear domestic markets while also increasing export dumping via so-called 'food aid'.[20] In the next year, the Clinton Administration is looking to use US$5.5 billion in export credits, an increase of more than 50 per cent, and to increase food aid shipments to more than 10 million tons, compared to the normal average of 3 million tons.

Notwithstanding the impassioned rhetoric of those who proclaimed that the Uruguay Round would mark the end for trade distorting farm programmes, protectionist import barriers and predatory export dumping, there is a long way to go to reach those goals. Indeed, current price and policy trends suggest that the chasm between reality and the purported free trade ideals may get larger.

Under pressure from Congress to classify US farm subsidies as emergency aid to exempt them from mandatory WTO notification requirements, Secretary Glickman has stated that he may not even formally report these payments to the WTO.[21] Farmers in Florida are asking the government to impose new import controls on a number of fresh fruits and vegetables in response to currency devaluations that they believe are being used to avoid tariffs. They argue that Mexico can simply devalue the peso by the same percentage as the tariff, nullifying the effect of the tariff in terms of net cost to US buyers, a move devastating to Florida producers.[22] On the export-dumping issue, the head of the USDA Agricultural Marketing Service, Tim Galvin, shocked analysts when he proposed that, in order to raise prices for US soybean farmers, the US government should buy and give away a major portion of next year's soybean crop.[23]

It comes as no surprise that the current agriculture trade rules are being abandoned or ignored since they were poorly constructed, internally contradictory and slated for renegotiations from the very beginning. While there is widespread dissatisfaction with the current WTO agriculture rules, analysis of what is wrong and how to fix it remains wildly divergent.

For example, some believe that current rules do not go far enough in opening other markets to US agriculture and that this is the cause of current low prices in the US.[24] Others argue that the Uruguay Round opened US markets to far too great a level of imports, resulting in competitive crops being dumped into the US market and a resulting plunge in domestic farm prices.[25] Others argue that the AoA failed to address adequately major trade distorting practices, like production subsidies and export dumping, resulting in a global market that is more chaotic than ever before. Although there are bitter disagreements over how to fix current agriculture trade rules, nearly everyone concurs that they must be either reformed or abandoned.

This chapter will not attempt to explain or describe the details of the agriculture agreement signed at Marrakesh as there are many excellent descriptive articles that have been published.[26] Likewise, this chapter will not attempt to predict the future impacts of the current AoA. Far too much time has been spent arguing over the predictions of computer models, none of which have come close to reality. We have chosen to focus this chapter on one impact of current WTO rules of agricultural trade – the increase in export dumping by grain corporations based in the US and on the impact of this dumping on two public policy concerns: sustainable agriculture and the human right to food security. The first section will look at the link between the current WTO agriculture trade rules and the increase in export dumping. Second, we will look at the impact of this dumping on efforts by farmers to move towards more sustainable farming practices. The third section will look at the impact of this dumping on food security in terms of the right to food in the United Nation's Universal Declaration of Human Rights.[27] The fourth section will look at how we might use forthcoming WTO ministerial decision to make positive changes in current WTO agriculture trade rules with regard to our two main themes, sustainable farming and food security. This section will look at the global political context for the ministerial agreement and how that might affect both the official agriculture negotiations and citizen efforts to win reforms. The fifth and final section details a set of recommendations for the kinds of changes in WTO rules that would help to encourage instead of discourage sustainable farming and food security.

WTO Agricultural Trade Rules: Enhancing Trade Volumes Through Export Dumping

The US and the European Union (EU) dominated the Uruguay Round of multilateral trade negotiations. They used this control to craft agricultural trade rules with their main objective being an increase in the volume of trade in food and fibre products by the major companies that were based inside their territories, many of which enjoy dominant positions globally.[28] US and EU negotiators made three important changes in WTO agricultural trade rules that served to promote this narrow interest. First, these trading companies found ways to lower the prices paid to farmers. The strength of family farm lobbies in both the US and in Europe had been strong enough in the past to win government support for setting the loan rate and, hence, domestic farm prices high enough to permit most farmers to stay in business most of the time. Supplemental payments are only needed from the government in particularly lean years. As long as internal prices were kept above world market prices there would be fewer imports and fewer exports. Domestically produced crops, from both the US and Europe, were more expensive on world markets and therefore less competitive than crops from Thailand or Argentina. To accomplish the corporate goal of lowering crop prices, new agriculture trade rules were developed requiring countries to bring domestic prices down to the lower world prices.[29]

Second, they did everything possible to reduce government subsidies,[30] including those that helped to keep a number of small and medium-sized farmers in business. Many farmers around the planet are supported in various ways that make it possible for them to continue producing for local markets, effectively shutting out import foods. New rules were drawn up to reduce subsidies to domestic producers in the hope that these reductions would push a number of farmers out of business and off their farms; their production would then be replaced by imported foods. In the context of a global market, this would mean, for example, more corn from the US going into Brazil and more sugar from Brazil coming into the US.

Third, US and EU negotiators worked hard to remove as many economic barriers[31] (import tariffs, export levies, etc) and non-economic barriers (such as health and safety regulations)[32] to trade. Their objection was that these barriers to imports and exports tended to raise the short-term price of internationally traded goods, potentially making them less price competitive than locally produced goods. Again, the basic objective is to increase the volume of imports and exports. At the same time, agribusiness lobbyists were working overtime to protect their clients' right to use government funds for export subsidies and credits. In this endeavour, they were also largely successful. While the Uruguay Round did result in some reduction in export subsidy expenditures,[33] a number of the most important export subsidy programmes, such as credit guarantees, were left untouched.[34]

US and EU negotiators successfully walked the tightrope of protecting export subsidies while cutting government support in other areas. The end result has been more or less as expected: increased volumes of production to try to make up in volume traded what was lost to lower prices and less government support – and thus increased export dumping. In spite of waves of financial and economic instability since the signing of the WTO agreement in Marrakesh, import and export volumes flowing through Europe and the US have risen due to lower prices and payments and to the reduction in regulatory controls on trade. In the US, for example, exports of our two largest crops, corn and soybeans, have risen in spite of global economic difficulties. Before the signing of the Marrakesh Agreement (1993–1994 market year) US corn exports were 1.328 million bushels compared to 1.504 million bushels during the 1997–1998 marketing year – an increase of over 10 per cent. For soybeans, US exports before Marrakesh were 589 million bushels compared to 870 million last year.[35]

Trade Volumes Rise Along With Export Dumping

This increase in the volume of US grain and oilseed exports in the face of global economic difficulty is due in part to an increase in export dumping by the US. This increase in dumping is due largely to three factors: (1) the setting of farm prices by the federal government at artificially and unrealistically low levels; (2) rising costs of production, causing an even greater gap between falling export prices and rising costs of production; and (3) the expansion of direct and indirect export subsidies. All three of these factors are closely linked to the implementation of current WTO rules, as discussed below.

In the US, the AoA was the guidebook for the rewriting the commodity sections of new federal farm legislation. This new law, ironically called the 'Freedom to Farm' bill, was designed to meet WTO agreements calling for lower US farm prices, resulting in a drop of around 25 per cent in the prices paid to US farmers. This legislated reduction brought prices below costs, resulting in export prices far below average costs of production.

Much of the agribusiness sector has been consolidated into literally a handful of global monopolies or near-monopolies since the signing of the Uruguay Round agreements in April 1994. While it is not yet possible to fully assess the wide spectrum of impacts of this degree of monopolistic control, it is evident that higher prices are being charged to farmers for inputs and lower prices paid to them for their production.[36] While concern about monopolistic behaviour is growing among producers in the US, the Clinton Administration has steadfastly refused to allow any discussion of anti-trust disciplines at the WTO. Perhaps the most obfuscatory but telling statement reflecting this refusal was made by Joel Klein, Assistant Attorney General for the Antitrust Division of the Justice Department, in a 30 June speech to an Organisation of Economic Co-operation and Development (OECD) conference on trade and competition: '[T]he relationship between international trade and international antitrust is so important, so complete, and so rapidly evolving that no one institution or series of bilateral or multilateral arrangements should be permitted to monopolize it'.[37]

The third element of the new trade rules that have contributed to export dumping are the provisions that essentially legitimized, for the very first time in history, the paying of export subsidies for grain and other farm commodities. GATT rules against dumping had prohibited the sale of goods at prices below the cost of production, including a return on investment and the cost of marketing: 'The contracting parties recognize that dumping by which products of one country are introduced into the commerce of another country at less than the normal value of the products, is to be condemned if it causes or threatens material injury to an established industry'.[38] However, under the new WTO rules, export subsidies are explicitly permitted and they are transferable between and among different crops and producers at the discretion of governments.[39] Under these rules, the US government can now move export subsidies from one crop to the next and be completely legal under the WTO. This means that when certain US internal prices are so low they do not need export subsidies to out-compete the production of other countries, the situation of US corn and soybeans at the moment, export subsidies formerly used for those crops can be transferred to other crops to help finance their dumping.

Impact of WTO-encouraged Export Dumping on Economically and Ecologically Sustainable Agriculture

Each of these three dumping policies – lowering of farm prices, encouraging monopoly, and the legitimizing of export subsidies – have had negative impacts on efforts to move US farming practices towards financial and ecological sustainability. For the purposes of this chapter, we define sustainable agriculture by four broadly accepted elements: (1) prices which cover the full cost of production, including environmental costs and fair income; (2) reduced dependence on chemical fertilizers and pesticides; (3) reduction of externalized ecological impacts through pollution prevention and cost internalization; and (4) greater reliance on the use of ecologically modem farming practices such as integrated pest management (IPM), crop rotations, no-till and reduced tillage systems, and other practices that reduce soil loss and contamination, cut air and water pollution, and avoid losses in habitat and biodiversity.

The farm crisis we face today speaks for itself in terms of economic sustainability. The price levels and support cuts facilitated by the WTO agreement have put most US farmers at risk of bankruptcy. A few statistics on the current crisis will provide some context. While it is not accurate to directly tie all aspects of the current crisis to the Uruguay Round Agreements, there are strong indications of its major role, especially in the lowering of farm prices. Since the signing of the Uruguay Round Agreements, wheat prices are down 42 per cent and corn prices are down 38 per cent.[40] In almost all regions of the North America, net farm income is down dramatically. In Illinois, Farm Business Management Association records in 1998 showed a drop to US$11,074 average farm income compared to the recent five-year average of US$31,000.[41] In the Red River Valley of North Dakota and Minnesota, farm income fell to US$20,600 in 1998 compared to US$37,000 in 1997.[42] On Prince Edward Island, in Canada, farm income is down to US$7.5 million after averaging US$43 million between 1990 and 1996.[43]

As farm prices fall, many producers respond by attempting to increase their yields. Some do this by ploughing up more land. Others do it by applying ever greater quantities of fertilizer and other chemicals. This intensification strategy is often harmful to the environment. Even the WTO itself has begun to acknowledge the negative ecological consequences of falling farm prices. A recent report of the official WTO Committee on Trade and Environment (CTE)[44] cited studies[45] acknowledging that farm price cuts in the North (US, Europe, etc) can result in an increase in the intensity of their chemical use and other inputs. These studies show that because most farmers are in debt, and therefore need to maintain their cashflow, they increase production through either intensification (more fertilizer and pesticides) or extensification (ploughing up new lands). Both of these responses are environmentally damaging, and both have been seen in the US since prices began to fall after the WTO-framed 'Freedom to Farm' bill of 1996. The most thorough analysis of the environmental impacts of agricultural trade liberalization, conducted by the North American Free Trade Agreement (NAFTA) Commission for Environmental Cooperation, includes a case study of corn (maize) that concludes that 'the differential pace and degree of reduction and elimination of tariffs and other trade barriers under NAFTA can have major impacts on production and consumption substitution in ways that are not optimal for economic efficiency or environmental enhancement'.[46]

The WTO rules have created a disincentive for ecological cost internalization at both the farm level and at the national level. Some approaches to more sustainable agriculture production do not involve great increases in costs, but some do – with economic implications for farmers. For example, the United Nations Food and Agriculture Organization (FAO) has found that for soya and other oil crops the internalization of environmental costs would result in the long term in 'marked increases of production costs of the major producers and exporters and affect their relative competitiveness and international market shares'.[47] Another example is the cost internalization mechanism called the 'polluter pays principle'.[48] Adding additional taxes to the cost of fertilizer or pesticides to help cover some of the costs of clean-up are facing stiff resistance as prices paid to farmers are being lowered by the trade regime. There have been some proposals to implement countervailing duties to offset externalized environmental costs,[49] but such duties are likely to be condemned as barriers to trade. WTO-led cuts in farm prices have put organic and other sustainable farmers at greater economic risk. Although the organic market in the US and Europe has been growing by 10–20 per cent annually,[50] – many organic producers are finding that current market prices are so low they are unable to get premium prices high enough to continue their organic production. For example, in 1994, the year that the AoA was signed, prices received by Minnesota soybean growers using organic methods was over US$21 dollars per bushel. This had declined to only US$8.00 per bushel in 1999, with predictions that prices would continue to decline.[51]

Impact of Export Dumping on the Human Right to Food Security

Ensuring an adequate, safe and affordable food supply is perhaps the oldest and most basic role of government. Throughout human history, local, regional and national governments have ensured a steady supply of basic foods by taking steps to eliminate or counteract supply (and therefore price) fluctuations related to unpredictable factors such as the weather, disease, pests and technology. The United Nations 'Universal Declaration of Human Rights' declared the right to food and to feed oneself as a central obligation of government along with protecting freedom of religion and the right to be free from torture. Over the years, governments have developed a broad range of policy tools, such as inventory management schemes, quantitative controls on import and export controls, cost-of-production price supports and government-held emergency food reserves to keep supply balanced with demand in order to keep prices within acceptable ranges, for both farmers and consumers.[52]

The AoA, however, included a large number of provisions specifically designed to limit the type and magnitude of government interventions allowed in the pursuit of stable prices for farmers and consumers. The resulting price volatility has been especially hard on poor countries, increasing the social and economic burden[53] of their governments and adding to their costs for food imports.[54] Perhaps the most important rules of the AoA in this regard were those that tended to increase export dumping and those that placed limits on the ability of individual countries to protect themselves from this dumping or other price destabilization actions. Many developing countries that rely on commodity exports for their foreign earnings have seen this income drop, reducing their pool of hard currency. Since the new Uruguay Round agreement severely limits governments' ability to control imports and exports through quantitative restrictions or tariffs, there is very little they can do except borrow more money or go without crucial imports, such as medicine or basic foods.

With new WTO rules limiting the ability of countries to control imports, local farmers are seeing the prices they receive fall to the lower world levels. This either bankrupts them, thus putting them out of farming and perhaps at hunger's door, or it means that they do not have any profit that they can use to re-invest for improving yields. In both cases, the right to food is being violated in both the short and long-term. Many of the more severely affected countries in the WTO, primarily members of the Least Developed Countries (LDC) group and the Net Food-Importing Developing Countries (NFIDC) group, have been calling on the international agencies to address the problems being created by the Uruguay Round. Analysis by the FAO since 1995 suggests that for all low-income food deficit countries, their food import bill will indeed be US$9.8 billion higher in the year 2000 than at the start of the Uruguay Round negotiations, of which US$3.6 billion – a 14 per cent increase – would be directly attributable to the Uruguay Round results.[55] The International Monetary Fund (IMF) disputed the FAO findings, however, on the grounds it overstated the degree of liberalization likely to occur from 1995–2000 and subsequently overstated the likely price changes. The IMF claimed the 1996 'food price spikes' were 'unrelated to the Round' and that 'declining stocks [predicted as an outcome of the Round] do not necessarily imply proportional declines in food aid'.[56] With this disagreement over price projections and their direct causes in hand, the WTO Committee on Agriculture decided in 1996 not to trigger the 'Marrakesh Decision',[57] which committed developed countries to provide compensation to low-income food deficit countries if they are adversely affected by higher food prices as a result the AoA.[58]

In an attempt to address this conflicting documentation on Uruguay Round specific food security impacts, the South Centre, an intergovernmental agency in Geneva that serves as a think-tank for its developing country members, has prepared a 27-point 'Checklist to Assist the Preparation of Country Experiences on the Impacts of the WTO Agreement on Agriculture' that gives some indication of the kinds of impacts they believe the WTO is having on their food supply and security.[59]

Using the WTO Agriculture Talks to Promote Economically and Ecologically Sustainable Agriculture

The key components of sustainable agriculture – adequate income, reduced dependency on chemicals, cost internalization and movement towards ecologically modern practices – are essential to the achievement of what is called 'multifunctional agriculture'. This concept recognizes that farmers provide many products and services to the whole society, beyond food and fibre. These functions include the maintenance of healthy land and clean water, soil fertility and genetic diversification, habitat preservation, carbon sequestration, flood control, employment, open space, beautiful vistas, recreation, renewal opportunities, and protected greenbelts and wildlife.

Sometimes referred to as 'public goods,' these positive non-commercial, services supplied by agriculture are rarely valued in the marketplace. Even the use of economic instruments to correct market failures towards sustainable development has traditionally focused on the negatives. For example, eco-taxation along the lines of the 'polluter pays principle' (PPP) has been proposed to bring pesticide prices up to their 'real' level[60] or to reduce nutrient surpluses.[61] Production of positive externalities, it is argued, should be rewarded according to a mirror of the PPP; some suggest this approach be called the 'provider gets principle' (PGP)[62] or, perhaps, the 'stewardship is rewarded principle' (SRP) or the 'pay for provision of public goods principle' (PPG). And a wide range of economic and policy instruments are available to reward the producers of multifunctional agriculture. These include subsidies, grants, tax concessions, technical assistance and improved access to markets through, for example, government procurement[63] – all of which can be applied at any level of government, including the local level.[64]

We believe that the application of basic economic and ecological criteria to new systems of multifunctional agriculture is the best way to re-create sustainable farming systems and rural communities. To accomplish this, we believe that the following changes need to be made to current WTO rules to support, instead of harm, economic and ecologically sustainable agriculture. Sustainable agriculture needs to be supported by WTO rules that include the following: (1) Phasing out export dumping; (2) banning of export subsidies; (3) global anti-trust measures that address a wide-range of anti-competitive business practices; (4) support for government assistance to farmers making the transition to more sustainable farming practices; (5) support for the development of multifunctional agriculture, including policies for rewarding farmers for the provision of green services to society that are transborder or global in nature; (6) consumer labelling and government procurement practices to encourage sustainable agriculture; (7) mechanisms for tariff and non-tariff measure adjustments in response to currency fluctuations; and (8) protection of national and regional supply and demand balancing mechanisms, including the use of quantitative import and export regulations and domestic supply management programmes.

Using the WTO Agricultural Talks to Promote the Human Right to Food Security

The United Nations Universal Declaration of Human Rights is fairly clear in its declaration of the centrality of food security as a fundamental human right. Article 25.1 states that 'Everyone has the right to a standard of living adequate for the health and well-being of himself and of his family, including food'. There is a growing concern among human rights leaders and activists around the planet about the growing number of human rights violations that may be directly attributable to the actions of global institutions, such as the World Bank, the IMF and the WTO. Over the past few years, non-governmental organizations (NGOs) from all over the world have been meeting to discuss the threats to food security posed by the current world trading system and to develop specific proposals for changes in WTO rules that would help to move the world trading system in ways that would tend to support instead of discourage food security.[65] A consensus seems to be forming around a package of seven major reforms. First, we need specific language in the WTO protecting the right of nations to take action to protect the most vulnerable people in their societies in times of economic crisis. For example, India has proposed that developing countries be allowed, under the AoA Article 20 on 'Non-Trade Concerns,' to implement agricultural and other policies to pursue food security objectives without facing AoA sanctions.[66] Other 'non-trade concerns', such as the relationship of agriculture to culture – in terms of cosmologies, rites of passage, social celebrations, family and community institutions, traditional clothing and cuisine, and innumerable other social norms – are also of significance. The use of government intervention to protect food security and cultural traditions should be respected by the WTO.

Second, the WTO should encourage countries to take measures to encourage domestic food production for domestic food consumption. The current WTO rules are based on the idea that nations will be better off if they 'import their food security'. This kind of ideological approach has been a disaster for many nations and has led to severe criticism of the WTO by nearly every development NGO and agency. WTO rules that make it a violation of trade rules to use government intervention to support local farmers must be replaced by new rules that enable countries to effectively address economic crisis facing family and peasant farming, in both North and South countries.[67] Some WTO members have already begun to make specific proposals along these lines.

Third, current WTO provisions that have encouraged nations to eliminate emergency food storage facilities and programmes should be repealed. Stocks of food held near centres of population in virtually every country are one of the most important components of any successful food security scheme. The elimination of many of these food reserves since the signing of the Marrakesh Agreement has resulted in huge price fluctuations and dangerously low levels of reserve food stocks on more than one occasion.[68]

Fourth, WTO rules should be changed to support greater diversity in food production systems. A key to food security is the maintenance of regionally diverse agricultural systems, often characterized by sustainable practices on a smaller scale. These include the maintenance of biological diversity, such as the cultivation of land races and vigorous communities of insects and microbial life on a healthy diversified farm.[69] Perhaps most importantly, food security depends upon access to food within a region, regardless of comparative advantage and market forces.

Fifth, more needs to be done to ensure that the WTO does not violate workers' rights to organize for collective bargaining and to receive wages that are adequate to maintain a healthy diet and standard of living. While half of the world's population still lives on the land, the other half are in or near cities and dependent on their earnings to buy food for their families. Employment and wages have fallen in many countries since the signing of the WTO agreement, yet there has been no reaction other than admonitions for 'staying the course' and experimenting with even more radical economic deregulation. WTO rules must accommodate other international guarantees of workers' rights in order to help address the problems of food insecurity facing many in our cities.

Sixth, global rules must advance local, state and national efforts to prevent or break-up monopolies in the food and agriculture sectors. The end result of all monopolies is higher costs and lower efficiency. Furthermore, great power can be wielded by whoever controls the food supply. While food has often been used as a weapon by corrupt political leaders, the controlling forces now are transnational corporations that in economic terms are bigger than most nations.

Seventh, there is a call for the creation of a working group or committee at the WTO on Trade and Food Security, along the lines of the current Committee on Trade and Environment (CTE). This is seen as the beginning of recognition by the WTO that their actions affect food security and that they have a responsibility, as members of the United Nations family of global institutions, to support the commitments to economic, social, cultural, civil, and political human rights detailed in the Universal Declaration of Human Rights.

Political Context of the Upcoming World Agricultural Trade Negotiations

In 1986, when the Uruguay Round began, negotiators assumed that their four-year schedule of global trade talks would be business as usual. Nobody outside the closed fraternity of trade negotiators knew anything about GATT, which meant that negotiations could go forward as they had in the past – without public input and without political oversight or approval at the end. Since most of the talks were in secret, no documents were released to the public.[70] At least in the beginning, the negotiators were correct in their assumption that there would be very little questioning of their actions, motivations or judgements.

Alongside these institutional barriers of secrecy was another factor that limited public participation or democratic assessment. Almost no family farmer, peasant or any other citizen organization on the planet had ever heard of GATT, except perhaps in passing, and none knew anything about the past actions, emerging debates or the potential implications. Ignorant citizens' groups were bliss as far as GATT negotiators and bureaucrats were concerned. Fortunately, public ignorance of the Uruguay Round was to be short-lived. Four key developments changed this political formula.

First, there was a revolution in global communications technology. The advent of faxes, email, the internet and cheap overseas long-distance calling greatly accelerated the spread of information around the globe. Cross-border connections and collaborations in the 1970s and early 1980s, such as the Nestlé Boycott and the gatherings of the United Nations Conference on Trade and Development (UNCTAD), which encouraged the engagement of NGOs, laid the groundwork for citizen groups – both North and South – to communicate, collaborate and share information on the new GATT round at a level never before imagined. The concerns of the handful of people who saw the importance of these talks could be easily, cheaply and widely communicated with activists, the media and opinion-leaders all over the world. With electronic communications, the 'voices crying out in the wilderness' could be heard around the planet. The daily news bulletin on the Uruguay Round, published by the Institute for Agriculture and Trade Policy, eventually reached tens of thousands of subscribers.[71]

Second, a new generation of global activists came of age. Thanks to prior campaigns, there already existed a network of sophisticated global thinkers, analysts and activists. Most were not previously familiar with GATT or trade per se, but as they tuned in electronically, they immediately understood the pattern. These people were already active in national and global networks working on issues such as poverty, hunger, environmental degradation and human rights and, as they understood the stakes, began to gather staff and resources with which to begin campaigning on GATT.[72]

Third, many GATT insiders failed to notice that the veil was being lifted. Negotiators were accustomed to secrecy and negotiating traditions outside the realm of normal democratic accountability – circumstances that were ripe for abuse. The kinds of proposals made, especially by the Reagan Administration,[73] were so radical and outrageous that it became easy to paint a picture of GATT as a monster (eg 'GATTzilla') aimed at destroying environmental laws, family farmers, poor people and all that was good. Corporate greed generated a sharp backlash.

Fourth, GATT extended into the realm of domestic politics. Many of the most extreme proposals had nothing to do with international trade rules, but were aimed instead at overturning domestic laws and regulations via the secretive process of trade negotiations. For example, the attempt (ultimately successful) by Presidents Reagan, Bush and Clinton to use the Uruguay Round to overturn US patent law engendered fierce opposition from small inventors who saw this change as a threat to their well-being.[74]

As part of the arrogance that characterized these negotiations, many of the key GATT negotiators embellished their speeches to favorite constituency groups with boasts and promises about what domestic laws they were going to get rid of via GATT. US Trade Representative Clayton Yeutter was one of the most public and vocal, promising chemical industry groups and others that he was using the Uruguay Round talks to overturn US environmental and consumer protection laws that he and President Reagan did not like. In an article purporting to balance trade and environmental interests, Yeutter said that 'we need to 'Gatt' the greens, not green the Gatt'.[75]

These four dynamics eventually led to the creation of a global campaign of local and national groups that began to knit together the information, analysis and political strategy needed to start bringing democratic review and input into the global trade negotiations process. The Uruguay Round (along with the debate over NAFTA) turned out to be the turning point in the development of an informed public debate about the institutions of global economics and finance, and about the dynamics of global policy-making.

Since the end of the Uruguay Round, these networks have continued to grow and to develop in knowledge, strength and experience. Many new groups have begun to follow trade issues as they discover that the WTO, the new name for GATT, is making rules that affect some aspect of their work. For example, many environmental organizations that ignored the Uruguay Round have become very involved as they have seen the WTO dispute settlement process resulting in attacks on basic environmental programs.[76]

The announcement by the White House that they planned to bring the next ministerial to the US and to use it to launch a new round of negotiations has touched off a flurry of new organizing efforts and preparations. It is clear from the initial response to the idea of a new round of talks that things will be very, very different this time. The following is a short list of some of the new conditions that will influence the next round of talks.

Public Awareness

During the Uruguay Round, GATT was almost completely unknown. The WTO is, however, relatively well known; many organizations are tracking its activities on a day-to-day basis. It is not yet as publicly recognized as the IMF or World Bank, but it is no longer the world's best kept secret. With the low cost of email, even the smallest organizations in the poorest countries have access to the latest WTO news 24 hours a day, seven days a week.

Accountability, Access, and Participation

Many local, national and international groups working on specific issues, such as hunger or human rights, now understand that there is a connection between their issue and trade. Many see how trade, trade rules and trade disputes affect their work, and they are active on trade and WTO issues. During the last round the number of groups who saw the connections was very small.

NGO–Government Cooperation

There is a new collaboration among NGOs and some governments, especially in the countries of the South. During the last round of talks, governments and NGOs did not see their mutual interest, but this has changed. Today, many NGOs are conducting training sessions for negotiators from the South, NGOs are serving on advisory committees and delegations, and there is a great deal of collaboration on the development of negotiating goals and objectives.

Transparency

In the Uruguay Round all documents were treated as state secrets. Other than the negotiators, the only people who could get their hands on even the most innocuous proposals and reports were corporate officials who could afford the thousands of dollars needed to subscribe to the exclusive 'insider' newsletters and bulletins.

Documents are now more readily available and many end up on the internet or on the WTO website. With the aid of foreign language translation software, it is now possible to make most documents available to most groups at no cost on a timely basis. In the Uruguay Round it was a struggle to find out what was going on and then to share this information. The danger in the next round of talks will be one of overload leading to paralysis, as the flow reaches 'drinking from a fire hose' proportions.

New Institutions, Networks and Coalitions

During the Uruguay Round there was no existing infrastructure for monitoring the talks, sharing information, drawing conclusions, setting objectives and priorities, or carrying out coordinated efforts. This time around it will be very, very different. For example, NGOs have a specific centre in Geneva, the International Centre for Trade and Sustainable Development,[77] that serves as an information source, liaison and 'temporary office' for NGOs working on WTO issues. There are regular meetings and conference calls among the most active groups on a global basis and many of constituency groups have developed a consensus on their own specific objectives for the next round of negotiations.

Informed Media

In the past only a tiny number of reporters covered trade and, for the most part, they were so close to the negotiators and the GATT secretariat that they lacked basic objectivity. This time around, all kinds of press – from food and lifestyle features to science and environment journals to daily newspapers to the major broadcast stations – are tuned into trade and the WTO. The Seattle Ministerial Meeting of 1999 and subsequent negotiations will be covered from a wide range of perspectives.

Reality vs Computer Projections

Much of the debate during the Uruguay Round centred on computer projections made by governments and intergovernmental organizations, such as the World Bank. Their computers claimed that 'all ships will rise' under the terms of the final agreement signed in Marrakesh, Morocco. It turns out that this was not true. This time around, the debate will include an assessment of what has already happened, the invalidity of the prior, and therefore future, computer projections, and the need to build in assessment, evaluation, and escape clauses in case future government and intergovernmental organization predictions continue to be unreliable.

Shift in Power

In the Uruguay Round, concerned groups could raise some issues, but had virtually no impact on the outcome. As a result, the rules of trade have few constraints or safety-nets. At the same time, a number of governments from Southern countries expressed grave reservations about where the talks were headed and the potential negative impact on their countries. In the end, both the governments of the South and the NGOs have been proven right – the Uruguay Round agreement has been bad for the environment, consumers and for food security in the South. Critics have been largely vindicated. In the US, this reality has led to a rethinking by many in Congress about the wisdom of blindly following the lead of the president on trade matters, as the 1998 defeat of 'fast track' negotiating authority demonstrated.

We have reached a new stage in the debate where the concerns of environmental, consumer, farm, labour, human rights and other groups have come together to form a powerful lobby. Many governments of the South are now providing the leadership to challenge the old assumptions. This new bloc of South country governments and NGOs from around the world could turn out to be the defining axis in the next talks.

New Models

In the past there were only a few models of successful global campaigning, such as the Nestlé boycott. Today, there is a wide array of models for citizen action at the global level. The veterans' groups that forced governments to agree to a land mines treaty that the veterans had formulated offers an inspired example. Environmental groups have successfully influenced the implementation of the Framework Convention on Climate Change and peasant communities are working to ensure that the Convention on Biological Diversity guarantees their rights to save seeds. The defeat of the Multilateral Agreement on Investment was a momentous victory for non-governmental activists worldwide. This next round of WTO talks will have these victories and models to draw on.

Positive Alternatives

During the last round of trade talks, citizens were largely marginalized. In the intervening years we have gained enough power to block a continuation of 'business as usual', but this is not enough. The crises in the world economy, ranging from disastrously low farm and commodity prices to unstable currencies and wild speculation caused by 'hot money' investments, have to be tackled at the global level as part of the next round of trade talks. In addition to defending themselves from attack, like those they suffered during the Uruguay Round, citizens' groups are beginning to prepare for using the next round to advance positive ideas.

The Political Challenge Ahead: Saving The WTO

All three Bretton Woods Institutions – the IMF, the World Bank and the WTO – are under fire both from the public at large and from politicians. There are specific recent instances that contribute to this political difficulty, such as the financial derivatives-generated and IMF-mishandled Asian financial crisis;[78] the ongoing inability of the World Bank to carry out its mission effectively;[79] and attacks on family farmers and environmental regulations by the WTO.[80] Beyond these specifics is a fundamental critique of the concepts and practices of neo-liberal economic theory and their collective support for anything promoted as globalization.

At the end of the day, how the public comes to view these institutions will reflect on much broader concepts, such as the rule of law in international affairs. If the WTO continues to be viewed as 'captured' by a narrow group of corporate interests and as promoting policies and practices that are bad for the environment, working people, farmers and consumers, it will continue to undermine general public support for the entire international system that was built up after the Second World War.

From 1995–1998, the Institute for Agriculture and Trade Policy organized a series of conferences on the 50th anniversaries of the founding of the major postwar global institutions, including the UN, World Bank, IMF, WTO, FAO and the Universal Declaration of Human Rights. These conferences featured the surviving founders of each institution and were held in the original sites of the founding conferences. At the conference held on the 50th anniversary of GATT, World Bank and IMF, there was an urgency expressed by many of the 30 founders and early leaders gathered. They were well aware of fading pubic support and growing political hostility to these institutions and quite frank in their assessments of the problems with the institutions at present and the needs for reform.[81] A theme that was repeated over and over was the need for the institutions to shift from defending the interests of a few favoured industries or companies towards supporting the broad aims and aspirations of society. With regard to the WTO, this advice seems precisely on target. A growing percentage of the public wants government agencies – at all levels – to be more responsive to the needs of the individuals and of the planet. Global institutions such as the WTO are no longer insulated or isolated as they were in the past. Their actions will be judged by their effect on the real world, not by computer projection of rosy futures or fidelity to any one particular economic theory or ideology.

The main issues explored in this chapter, sustainable agriculture and food security, are only two in a whole sea of concerns that people will be using to judge the WTO by in the future. In the next set of talks, WTO negotiators could resolve many of the problems created by the Uruguay Round. If they do so, it would help to restore the public trust that has been squandered by this institution. For those of us who believe passionately in the need for global cooperation and in the rule of law in international affairs, it is crucial that we help to move the WTO and other global institutions away from defending a few special interests, and in the direction of actively supporting the values and concerns of the vast majority of the public in every country of the world.

Notes

1   Agriculture Secretary Dan Glickman, Speech to the Center for Strategic and International Studies, 16 June 1999

2   See US, Japan To Present Tariff Proposals For New WTO Negotiations, *Inside US Trade*, 2 July 1999

3   General Agreement on Tariffs and Trade, opened for signature 30 October 1947, 61 UST A3, 55 UNTS 187 (hereinafter 'GATT')

4   Final Act Embodying the Results of the Uruguay Round of Trade Negotiations, 15 December 1994, 33 ILM1 [hereinafter 'WTO']

5   For a closer look at the agriculture debates at the founding meeting, see Burt Henningson, United States Agricultural Trade and Development Policy During World War II: The Role of the Office of Foreign Agricultural Relations (1981) (PhD Dissertation, University of Arkansas (Fayetteville)). For a look at the same theme in the most recent round, see Farms Talk May Kill GATT, *Christian Science Monitor*, 4 September 1988

6   Agreement on Agriculture, Final Act Embodying the Results of the Uruguay Round of Trade Negotiations, signed at Marrakesh, 15 April 1994, 33. ILM 1125 (hereinafter 'AoA')

7   See Agreement on Agriculture, art 1(f)

8   Print to the ministerial meeting in Seattle in November–December 1999, a number of nations called for the launching of a new round of comprehensive talks in order for these mandated agriculture talks to be folded into the larger discussion. For preparatory documents submitted for the ministerial, see http://www.wto.org/wto/minist/seatdocs.htm

9   See Agreement on Agriculture, art 13

10 See Ambassador Peter Scher, Testimony before the Senate Banking and Finance and Urban Affairs Committee, Subcommittee on International Trade and Finance (4 May 1999)

11 'Chile to Seek Waiver From WTO For Wider Agriculture Price Band', 16 *International Trade Rep.* 936 (1999)

12 'A Raw Deal for Commodities', *The Economist*, 17 April 1999, p75

13 See 'Some considerations concerning the availability of adequate supplies of basic foodstuffs from external sources to LDCs and NFIDCs', contribution from the United Nations Conference on Trade and Development to the World Trade Organization Committee on Agriculture, 17–18 November 1998

14 'Federal Reserve: Farmers Face Frim Financial Outlook', *Agricultural News*, 1 July 1999, pA1

15 See 'Glickman Rejects Criticism of US Farm Aid as Trade Protectionism', *Inside US Trade*, 29 January 1999, p14

16 'A Biotech Warrior Stresses Subtlety', *St Louis Post-Dispatch*, 6 June 1999, pA7

17 Agriculture Payments: Numbers of Individuals Receiving 1990 Deficiency Payments and the Amounts, United States General Accounting Office, 1992

18 See 'US Faces Two New WTO Panels on Wheat Gluten and 1916 AD Act', *Inside US Trade*, 30 July 1999

19 See 'Australia, New Zealand Fight US Safeguards on Lamb in WTO', *Inside US Trade*, 6 August 1999

20 See Elliot, Ian, 'French, Australian Officials want US Credits, Aid on Table', *Feedstuffs*, 28 June 1999, p21

21 See text: 'Combest Letter to Glickman on AMTA', *Inside US Trade*, 2 July 1999

22 See Kevin Hall (1999) 'Sector Wants Tariff Cuts Linked to Devaluations', *Journal of Commerce*, 10 June 10, p5; and Rosselle, Tracy (1999) 'Top Ag Official Meet in Florida to Hear Complaints', *The Packer*, 14 June 1999

23 'Soybean Buy Called Alternative To Subsidy', *Omaha World-Herald*, 17 March 1999

24 See Glickman, Dan (1999) 'US Approach to Agriculture in A New Round,' Remarks to XIX Meeting of the Cairns Group (28 August); and Avery, Dennis (1999) 'Asian Recovery Won't Help US Farmers', *Journal of Commerce*, 4 June, p7

25 See Swenson, Leland (1999) statement before US House of Representatives Committee on Agriculture, 23 June 1999; and 'Trade Policy Should Help, Not Hurt Farmers, Milk Matters', *Family Dairies USA*, 15 June p1

26 See Steinie, Jeffrey J (1995) note, 'The Problem Child of World Trade: Reform School for Agriculture', 4 *Minn J Global Trade* 333; Josling, Tim (1999) 'Reform of World Agricultural Trade: The Uruguay Round Outcome', paper for seminar on the WTO Agricultural Negotiations: the Lead up to Seattle (30 April); 'Focus on the WTO: Into the Future: (Part I) Getting Ready for WTO Agricultural Negotiations', 5 *Union Farmer Q.* 12 (1999); and Murphy, Sophia (1999) 'Trade and Food Security: An Assessment of the Uruguay Round Agreement on Agriculture'

27 United Nations Declaration of Human Rights, art 25.1, United Nations General Assembly, 3rd Sess, GA Res 217A, UN Doc A/810 (1948)

28 The top five international agribusiness corporations by 1998 revenues are US-based Philip Morris (US$57.8 billion), US-based Cargill (SU$51.4 billion), Switzerland-based Nestlé (US$49.5 billion), UK/Netherlands-based Unilever (US$44.9 billion) and US-based Procter & Gamble (US$37.6 billion) according to data compiled by A V Krebs, Director of the Corporate Agribusiness Research Project. See *The Forbes 500 Annual Directory*; *The Forbes Top 500 Private Corporations*; and *Forbes International 500 Companies* (1999)

29 See Agreement on Agriculture, art 6.1

30 See Agreement on Agriculture, arts 6, 7

31 See Agreement on Agriculture, art 4

32 See Agreement on Agriculture, art 14

33 See Agreement on Agriculture, arts 8, 9, 10, 11, 12

34 The US government is gearing up to keep these kinds of export subsidies off the negotiating table in the future. See 'US to Resist Efforts to Classify Agricultural Credit Guarantees as Subsidies', *BNA Daily Report to Executives*, 28 June 1999

35 See 'Crop Production and Market Data', *Doane's Agriculture Reports*, No 62, pp19–25

36 See Heffeman, William (1999) Consolidation in the Food and Agriculture System: Report to the National Farmers Union

37 Klein, Joel (1999) 'A Reality Check on Antitrust Rules in the World Trade Organization, and a Practical Way Forward on International Antitrust', speech to the Organisation for Economic Co-operation in Europe, 30 June 1999

38 General Agreement on Tariffs and Trade, art VI. 1

39 See Agreement on Agriculture, arts 8, 9, 10, 11

40 Price figures are from Ian Elliot, *supra* note 21

41 See Miller, Dan (1999) 'Illinois', *Progressive Farmer*, July, p18

42 See Miller, Dan (1999) 'North Dakota', *Progressive Farmer*, July, p19

43 See 'NFU Presents Brief on Farm Income Crisis', *Union Farmer Monthly*, May 1999, p7

44 WTO Committee on Trade and Environment, Environmental Benefits of Removing Trade Restrictions and Distortions: note by the Secretariat, WT/CTE/W/67 (7 November, 1997)

45 See, eg K Anderson and R Tyers, 'Disarray in World Food Markets: A Quantitative Assessment', Cambridge University Press (1992).

46 For a fully developed analysis of all of the impacts of trade liberalization on all aspects of sustainable agriculture, see Commission for Environmental Cooperation (CEC), Assessing Environmental Affects of the North American Free Trade Agreement (NAFTA): An Analytic Framework (Phase II) and Issues Studies (1999). This study by the NAFTA Commission for Environmental Cooperation traced four aspects of agriculture that affect the environment – production, management and technology; physical infrastructure; social organization; and government policy – and evaluated their respective impacts on the air, water, land and biodiversity. The analysis was concentrated on North America, but the conclusions about the interrelationships between changes in trade policies, impacts on farm prices and eventual environmental impacts are largely applicable to an analysis of similar issues with the WTO. The CEC looked more closely at two specific sectors – the production of corn (maize) in Mexico and beef feed-lots in the US and Canada

47 Possible Impacts of Environmental Regulations on the Cultivation, Processing and Trade in the Two Major Annual and Perennial Oil Crops, FAO, CCP: OF97/2 (1997)

48 See Recommendation on Guiding Principles Concerning Environmental Policies, OECD (26 May 1972); Rio Declaration on Environment and Development, UNCED, A/CONF.151/26 (12 August 1992)

49 See Plopchan, Jr, Thomas K (1992) Recognition and Countervailing Environmental Subsidies, *International Law*, No 26, p763 (1992)

50 See 'Organic: Growing into the 21st Century', Organic Farm Research Foundation, Santa Cruz, California (1999)

51 Interviews with staff at the Organic Growers and Buyers Association, New Brighton, Minnesota (May 1999)

52 See Sarris, Alexander (1998) Price and Income Variability, workshop on Emerging Trade Issues in Agriculture, OECD

53 See 'The Food Situation in the Least Developed and Net Food Importing Developing Countries', FAO paper presented to the WTO Committee on Agriculture (20–21 November 1997)

54 See Konandreas, Panos, Greenfield, Jim and Sharma, Ramesh (1998) 'The Continuation of the Reform Process in Agriculture: Developing Countries' Perspectives', paper presented to seminar on Latin America and the Caribbean in Face of the Furthering Process of Multilateral Agricultural Reforms (23–24 November, 1998)

55 See *The State of Food and Agriculture: Agricultural Trade, Entering a New Era?*, FAO Agricultural Series No 28, ISSN 0081-4539 (1995)

56 International Monetary Fund Working Paper, The Uruguay Round and Net Food Importers (1995)

57 Marrakesh Decision on Measures Concerning the Possible Negative Effects of the Reform Programme on Least-Developed and Net Food-Importing Developing Countries, see *supra*, note 4

58 See Fowler, Penny (1996) 'The Marrakesh Decision: Honouring the Commitment to Net Food-Importing Developing Countries', Catholic Institute for International Research Briefing (September)

59 South Centre, Checklist to Assist the Preparation of Country Experiences on the Impacts of the WTO Agreement on Agriculture: Food Security, Farmers and a Fair Place for the South, Institute for Agriculture and Trade Policy, Foundation Charles Leopold Mayer pour le Progres de l'Homme, Solagral (30 September – 4 October 1998)

60 See Pearce, David and Tinch, Robert (1998) 'The True Price Of Pesticides', in William Vorley and Kenney (eds) *Bugs in the System: Redesigning the Pesticide Industry for Sustainable Agriculture*, pp 50–93, Iowa State Press

61 See Ministry of Agriculture, Nature Management and Fisheries, the Netherlands, Policy Document on Manure and Ammonia, http:// www.minlnv.nl/intemational/policy/environ/

62 See Environmental Effects of Trade Liberalization in the Agricultural Sector, submission by Norway to the WTO Committee on Trade and Environment, WT/CTE/W/100 (8 January 1999)

63 See Gale, Robert J P and Barg, Stephan R (1995) 'The Greening Of Budgets: The Choice Of Governing Instrument', in Robert J P Gale, Stephan R Barg and Sandy Gillies (eds)

64 van Broekhuizen R, Klep, L, Oostindie, H and van der Ploeg, J D (1997) Renewing the Countryside (in author's possession)

65 For historical background of the problem of implementing food security as a human right, see Orin Kirshner, 'Human Rights Lost: A (Very) Short History of the Post-World War II Global Food and Agriculture Policy Regime', Institute for Agriculture and Trade Policy (15 May 1996). For a review of NGO activities in food security as a human right, see 'Needs vs. Rights and the Right to Food' http://www.iatp.org/iatpHR50. For discussion of the AoA and its impacts on food security, see International Workshop on WTO Agreement on Agriculture, Research and Information System for the Non-Aligned and Other Developing Countries, Institute for Agriculture and Trade Policy and ActionAid (1998); and see Washington, DC, meeting on the WTO Agreement on Agriculture: Food Security, Farmers and a Fair Place for the South, Institute for Agriculture and Trade Policy and Foundation Charles Leopold Mayer pour Ie Progres de l'Homme and Solagral (1998)

66 See 'Food Security: An Important Non-Trade Concern – An Informal Paper by India', *Third World Economics*, 15 February 1999, p15

67 See 'Japan to Stress Self-Sufficiency in Food at WTO Talks', *PF Today*, 17 June 1999

68 See Ritchie, Mark and Lehman, Karen (1996) 'Food Shortages, Sustainable Agriculture and Hunger: The Paradox of Higher World Market Prices for Grains', Institute for Agriculture and Trade Policy

69 For a discussion of the significance of the relationship between ecosystem health and biological diversity see Gretchen Daily, 'Nature's Services: Societal Dependence on Natural Ecosystems', (1997)

70 See, eg Plank, Rosine (1987) 'An Unofficial Description of How a GATT Panel Works and Does Not, 29 *Swiss Review of International Competition*, No 29, L 81

71 To consult these and other IATP bulletins, see http:// www.newsbulletin.org/

72 See Raghavan, (1990) 'Recolonization: GATT, the Uruguay Round and the Third World' (1990)

73 The Reagan Administration appointed a long-time executive of the Cargill company, one of the world's largest grain traders, to head the US delegation in the AoA talks. Members of the Multilateral Trade Negotiation Coalition that advised the US Trade Representative at that time included Cargill, Ralston-Purina, ADM, General Mills, General Foods, Continental Grain, RJR Nabisco and Con Agra. It is not surprising that the Uruguay Round results meet the needs of those corporations to a great extent, rather than sustainable agriculture or rural development in either the North or the South

74 See Moore, W John (1993) 'Reinventing Patents', *Natural Focus*, 20 March 1993, p694

75 Yeutter, Clayton (1992) 'Gatting the Greens – Environmentalists must live with trade', *Financial Times*, 2 September 1994, p14. For more examples of this tendency to use trade talks as a convenient and largely secretive way to overturn or undermine domestic laws and regulations, see Walter Russell Mead, 'Bushism Found', *Harper's Magazine*, February

76 See eg 'World Trade Organization and the Environment: Technical Statement by United States Environmental Organizations', addressed to Deputy US Trade Representative Susan G Esserman and the Environmental Protection Agency's Acting Deputy Administrator Peter D Robertson (16 July 1999). For more detailed discussion, see Daniel Esty, *Greening the GATT: Trade, Environment and the Future*, Institute for International Economics (1994); and Steve Chamovitz, Improving Environmental and Trade Governance', *International Environmental Affairs*, Winter 1995

77 International Centre for Trade and Sustainable Development. The Centre's weekly trade news digest, *Bridges*, may be consulted at http:// www.icstd.org

78 For perspective on the Asian financial crisis, see 'The Crisis in Context: An Interview with Dr. Michael Chossudovsky', *The Big Picture* (February 1999), I; Chakravarthi Raghavan, 'Asian crisis a major market failure, says UNCTAD', *South North Dev. Monitor* (2 February 1998); and Walden Bello, 'The End of a 'Miracle' Speculation, Foreign Capital Dependence and the Collapse of the Southeast Asian Economies', *Multinational Monitor*, January-February 1998, pp10-16

79 See Rich, Bruce (1998) 'The Smile on the Child's Face', Epilogue to *Mortgaging the Earth* (1998)

80 See Chamovitz, Steve (1999 'Addressing Environment and Labor in the WTO', remarks presented at the Conference on 'The Next Trade Negotiating Round: Examining the Agenda for Seattle,' (July 22, 1999); and Letter and Technical Statement from US Environmental Organizations, *supra* note 77.

81 For a selection of papers about the 1948 Bretton Woods conference and GATT's founders and early leaders, see, 'The Bretton Woods-GATT System: Retrospect and Prospect After Fifty Years', (Orin Kirshner (ed), 1996).

15

International Investment and Sustainability: Options for Regime Formation

Konrad von Moltke

The Need for an International Investment Regime to Achieve Sustainability

The character of international investment has been changing. Twenty years ago, most international investment was undertaken by a few large multinational corporations (MNCs) which sought to secure their raw material supplies or which were establishing a market presence with production or sales units in the early phases of globalization. Foreign investment was an important adjunct of trade rather than an independent economic activity. Today, most companies listed on Organisation of Economic Co-operation and Development (OECD) stock markets are technically MNCs, with investments and economic interests in more than one country.

It is a mistake to view foreign direct investment simply as an adjunct to trade. Capital is a scarce resource, particularly in developing countries. The efficient allocation of capital is critical to the achievement of economic growth and sustainable development. At present, capital is allocated in a fashion that is counterintuitive, with the largest flows converging on the most developed countries. Other things being equal, capital should be seeking out the highest returns, which should be available where capital is most urgently needed – in the developing world. High returns are available in those countries, but the uncertain risks involved in such investments still make them unattractive. One paramount task for an investment regime is to improve efficiency in the allocation of capital by reducing uncertainty.

There have been encouraging trends. By the end of the century, foreign direct investment was being undertaken by enterprises large and small with a wide range of concerns. The option of investing in another country has become a normal part of strategic growth plans for enterprises. Indeed, individual investors are now seeking investment opportunities outside their own currency region as a matter of course. Mutual funds make these kinds of investments available to small investors.

Investment flows have increased dramatically. For many developing countries, foreign direct investment has become the most important source of capital inflows, overtaking both official development assistance and the funds made available by multilateral development banks. In developing countries, between a third and a half of private corporate investment is undertaken by affiliates of foreign corporations.[1] Investment flows from OECD to non-OECD countries have finally become positive, with large outflows from more developed to less developed markets. Between OECD countries, traditionally the recipients of the largest amounts of foreign investment, the number of enterprises that participate and the range of projects being funded has grown dramatically.

The growing significance of foreign direct investment gives greater urgency to long-standing debates about the creation of an international regime for investments. Investment is not an act of nature. It represents a critical economic function of great social significance. It also has major implications for the prospects to achieve greater sustainability. Mature strong economies generate and sustain significant levels of investment, and policy intervention is necessary primarily to ensure that essential market disciplines are maintained.

An international investment regime is ultimately about efficiency and fairness. Insecure or severely distorted conditions of investment are factors of risk, which are reflected in expected rates of return. Countries perceived as representing a high risk will only be able to attract investment for projects that offer exceptional rates of return. Under such conditions, many important projects remain unfunded, and funds that are available are used in ways that are not as efficient as they could be. The lack of clear rules also creates an incentive for side-payments and corruption which exact an economic penalty on projects and investment flows.

Issues of fairness arise because of unequal power and conflicting goals of the various participants in investment. Investors from countries that are perceived as weak will fear for the security of their investments in foreign countries. At the same time, some governments are significantly weaker than many major corporations and may find it difficult to impose their legitimate priorities. At the very least, the effort required to defend less secure investments is itself a drag on investment and a source of economic inefficiency.

Investments are private transactions aimed at generating positive rates of return, but they can have far-reaching implications for the welfare of countries, including the prospects for sustainable development, the use and protection of natural resources, and the availability of jobs, incomes and economic security. It is the role of government to balance these sometimes conflicting public and private interests, either by promoting investment or by creating incentives to direct investment to certain activities or regions, or by maintaining a system of taxes and fees that contribute to public policy goals.

Governments have a wide range of interests in an international investment regime. Small countries with a large involvement in foreign investment – the Netherlands, Belgium and Switzerland in particular – and medium-sized countries whose prosperity depends on international trade and investment – France, the UK or Canada – all have an urgent interest in protecting their investors. The US has an interest in an investment regime primarily because the total amount of investment by its citizens is large, even though it is relatively much smaller than those of most other OECD countries. The US is also more readily able to protect investments made in other countries by its citizens.

Those concerned with sustainable development have a particular interest in an investment regime. Many current economic activities, in developed and developing countries alike, are known to be unsustainable. Frequently, alternatives are available, but they require investment. In other words, without investment there is no hope of achieving sustainability. With such an urgent need for investment, the move towards sustainability requires that scarce resources be used efficiently – and that the imperatives of sustainability are respected in the investment process. Indeed, it can be argued that an investment regime which does not actively promote sustainable development represents an important step back from the widely endorsed principles of sustainable development.

Despite these fairly clear reasons for developing an international investment regime, this goal has proven surprisingly elusive.

Antecedents of an International Investment Regime

Attempts to establish an international investment regime are characterized by significant levels of conflict. Initially this involved conflicts between developed and developing countries. More recently, the strongest critics of multilateral investment rules are to be found among the ranks of environmental and social policy groups. In practice these conflicts have made it virtually impossible to frame properly the issues and to engage in open sustained negotiations.

The United Nations Conference on Trade and Employment, held in Havana in 1948, included the encouragement of the international flow of capital for productive investment as one of the objectives of the proposed International Trade Organization.[2] That agreement failed to be ratified and the General Agreement on Tariffs and Trade (GATT) that took its place was much more narrowly focused on tariff reduction and trade liberalization. It was not until the Uruguay Round that investment issues arose in the trade regime. The Uruguay Round produced two Agreements that are relevant to investment: on Trade Related Investment Measures (TRIMs) and the General Agreement on Trade in Services (GATS) that entails significant investment provisions.

Throughout the Uruguay Round, most developing countries resisted the inclusion of investment issues in the GATT. Since then, however, attitudes of some developing countries to a comprehensive multilateral investment agreement within the World Trade Organization (WTO) or elsewhere have changed. The countries that have been most successful in attracting foreign direct investment (FDI) have shown a much greater willingness to embrace a regime based on the principles espoused by OECD countries.

In parallel to discussions in GATT, the World Bank maintained an active interest in FDI, since this represents a potential complement to its funding activities. In 1965, the World Bank created the International Centre for Settlement of Investment Disputes (ICSID),[3] and in 1985 followed this with the Multilateral Investment Guarantee Agency (MIGA).[4]

Most controversial, however, was the attempt by the UN Centre for Transnational Corporations (UNCTC) to draft a Code of Conduct on Transnational Corporations.

This was fiercely resisted by some developed countries, to the point that UNCTC itself was abolished, one of the few UN agencies ever to have suffered that fate. The UNCTC Code addresses a number of important issues, including the long-term nature of investments, the obligations of investors, the need for respect of national laws and several issues relating to environmental management. Nevertheless, it addressed these issues in a fashion which has served to polarize further the relationship between investors and the receiving countries. It does not reflect adequately the obligations already accepted by many developing countries in bilateral investment agreements. Moreover its focus on 'multinational corporations' no longer corresponds to the complex reality of FDI. It cannot be viewed as the basis for a multilateral regime, or even as setting the agenda for negotiations leading to such a regime.

A remarkable number of bilateral investment agreements have been concluded, presumably well over 1000. Recently, some bilateral trade agreements also incorporate investment provisions. Such agreements have typically been concluded between an OECD country and a developing country. It is reasonable to assume that the motivation of one party is to attract investment while the other is seeking additional protection for that investment.

The bilateral agreements are generally concluded on the basis of 'prototype' bilateral investment treaties which have been elaborated by a number of countries. A complete list of these prototypes is not available, but it must be presumed that the instrument that is ultimately used will reflect the relative power and interests of the two parties.[5]

Bilateral investment agreements include dispute settlement provisions, in accordance with generally accepted international legal practice. Most of these provisions draw in one way or another on the International Centre for Settlement of Investment Disputes (ICSID). Alternatively, they incorporate the Arbitration Rules for the United Nations Commission on International Trade Law (UNCITRAL).[6]

The common characteristic of these bilateral agreements is that they do not 'internationalize' the investment process. The agreements seek to utilize existing national law in a framework that is accessible to nationals of the other country. The international regime that is created is minimalist, lacking individuality or any institutional or organizational capabilities. ICSID or UNCITRAL provide dispute settlement services.

It is tempting to view multilateral efforts to establish an international investment regime as little more than extending bilateral agreements to the multilateral level. Such a view misses the essential institutional differences between a regime that draws on existing national law and one that seeks to create new international law. In practice, these are entirely different regimes.

Increasingly, regional trade agreements also include investment provisions and frequently it is possible at the regional level to create the necessary institutions to address the issues that this raises. The European Community incorporates elaborate investment rules, underpinned by a comprehensive institutional structure that is clearly capable of weighing conflicting priorities and making legitimate policy decisions based on such a process. Mercosur also contains investment provisions, albeit in a form that maintains tight state control over any international proceeding initiated by private persons. The North American Free Trade Agreement (NAFTA) has gone further than any other regional trade agreement in developing a set of specific rules for investment. It is based on the bilateral agreements developed by both Canada and the US.

NAFTA allows foreign investors to side-step procedural or public interest safeguards in favour of a non-transparent, secretive system of arbitration with no right of appeal. While common in purely commercial areas where money is the only issue, Chapter 11 is unprecedented in its reach into critical areas of public policy-making.[7]

The right to initiate cases is unfettered by any need for consent from the parties. The result is a growing and alarming strategic use of the provisions by investors to further private interests, often threatening environmental protection and other public policy goals. It is clear from the history of the use of Chapter 11 to date that this strategic tool will be employed both before and after regulations have been adopted. This has changed the investor-state provisions from their intended role as a defensive investor protection mechanism to an offensive strategic tool.

Initiating such suits is virtually cost-free for major companies, costing literally just a few thousand dollars to prepare a notice of intent to arbitrate that starts the process and produces privileged access. Absent clarity on how to interpret the provisions (What constitutes expropriation? What is meant by national treatment?), this is a modest cost to business with a large potential cost to government.

There might be less cause for concern about the dispute resolution mechanism if there were greater certainty about the scope and interpretation of the provisions on which it rules. The scope of the provisions is alarmingly broad; the definition of 'measures' subject to review includes both legally binding and non-binding acts, and even such things as court decisions. This leaves a wide range of measures open to potential challenge, certainly including environmental and other public welfare laws, regulations, policies or administrative actions.

The results are deeply troubling from an environmental perspective. Not only has NAFTA opened up new avenues for foreign investors to challenge virtually any environmental measure, but it has done so without any of the safeguards of domestic process: transparency, openness, review. NAFTA is a clear example of how an investment agreement that does not provide for the attainment of some public goods is not neutral but represents a step backward.

The Multilateral Agreement on Investment (MAI)

Following the conclusion of the Uruguay Round, the OECD economics ministers launched negotiations for a Multilateral Agreement on Investment (MAI), for which the OECD provided the forum even though the negotiations were considered an independent enterprise. The decision to begin negotiations did not attract much attention. Their purpose was to create a single multilateral framework for investment so as to fill gaps left by bilateral agreements.

To assess the MAI initiative in the OECD it is important to understand the role that the OECD has played in the evolving trade regime. It has traditionally been a forum in which the governments of developed countries could articulate an agenda and explore agreements and disagreements before taking the issues to the wider forum of the GATT. In this manner, the OECD has acted as an informal preparatory forum for recent GATT Rounds – certainly since developing countries formed a majority in the GATT/WTO – including the Uruguay Round. Presumably this tradition provides an important background to the Ministerial Council's decision to launch the MAI negotiations.

Given the difficulties that had been encountered in addressing the issue of investment in the GATT/WTO, there was clearly the intention to develop an instrument that would become the basis of a broader global investment regime. In recent years, the OECD has extended its reviews of foreign direct investment to countries outside the organization – for example, Ukraine, Chile, Argentina and Brazil.[8] A number of these countries sat in on the MAI negotiations. In addition, a series of meetings were organized in parallel to the MAI negotiations to consult with the governments of the 'dynamic economies of Asia and Latin America'.[9] In essence, this was a form of lobbying of governments by other governments, seeking to create a favourable basis for action on an international investment regime.

In the light of the OECD experience analysing foreign investment, its publications on the topic, successful conclusion of the Uruguay Round and the significant effort to include key developing countries, the MAI negotiations were perceived as the completion of a long process. Given the existence of numerous bilateral and regional agreements and the broad consensus on the underlying principles, at least among the participants in the negotiations, framing the MAI was seen by many as primarily a technical task, which could be completed fairly expeditiously.

The negotiations were conducted by a group of senior civil servants and were largely isolated from the regular business of the OECD and from public debate. In March 1998, following an unprecedented international campaign, triggered by environmental interests but supported by a wide range of groups that are sceptical about the processes of globalization and the distribution of its benefits, the MAI negotiations were put on a slower track, with no deadline. In October 1998, the process was abandoned entirely after France withdrew, mainly because it could not shield its cultural industries from the MAI rules. The newly installed German government also decided to press for 'social and ecological compatibility', which could not have been accommodated in the technical draft under consideration. The result is a lengthy, much bracketed text that did not do much more than articulate the principles of most favoured nation (MFN) and national treatment, proscribe performance requirements and provide for dispute resolution. In this regard, the text of the MAI mirrors quite closely the typical bilateral agreements on investment concluded by many OECD countries. It also reflects many of the investment provisions of NAFTA.

The MAI was institutionally stunted. Trying not to pre-empt a later transfer to the WTO or the creation of a separate entity for investment, the negotiators produced an institutional structure not unlike that of the original GATT, without a strong organizational base and with the narrowest of institutional resources. It is difficult to understand how the MAI negotiators could have failed to perceive the problems created for the GATT by its strange institutional structure, imposed by the need to circumvent the consent of the US Senate. Apart from the difficulties encountered in any attempt to amend the Agreement, without legal identity or a proper secretariat, the GATT remained a pawn of the member states. While this offered the advantage of avoiding conflicts with powerful member states, it entailed the drawback that broader international interests were never properly articulated. An investment agreement, with its inherent need to balance different policy priorities, can hardly be expected to survive without a strong advocate for the common interest underlying the regime.

In retrospect, launching the MAI negotiations as a technical process in the OECD without a clear political mandate can be seen to have been an error. By creating a negotiating process that was not integrated with the organizational structure of the OECD, the negotiators failed to perceive early warning signs. For example, an attempt by the OECD Environment Committee to engage the negotiators in debate was waved off. No thought was given to the problems that are likely to arise when bilateral agreements, which leave the parties in full control of the process, are turned into a multilateral agreement, which creates new international law and initiates a dynamic that must ultimately lead to new organizational structures.

The dangers of this process are illustrated by experience with the NAFTA Chapter 11 investment provisions, which reflect many of the assumptions underlying the MAI.[10] The difficulties that have arisen in NAFTA in relation to the investor–state dispute settlement process illustrate the dangers inherent in relying on an inappropriate institutional structure to balance private rights and public needs. Similar problems might have been expected under the MAI.

The assumption that the principles underlying the GATT/WTO system are also appropriate for an investment regime has never been questioned.[11] Even more seriously, the lessons from 50 years of struggling with the institutionally inadequate GATT appear not to have been learned. While the initial resistance to the MAI originated in environmental circles, it ultimately encountered a road-block because no major party endorsed it enthusiastically. Once countries began to focus on its implications, the number of reservations grew so large as to nullify the effectiveness of the agreement. In other words, the negotiations collapsed because the original approach was flawed.

In retrospect, the opposition to the MAI appears increasingly as the first event in a gathering movement to resist globalization. Followed quickly by the inability of the US Administration to obtain fast-track authority from Congress, an enormously damaging public dispute about the appointment of a new head of the WTO and the collapse of negotiations in Seattle, the failure of the MAI demonstrated the vulnerability of the institutions that have been created to guide the emergence of international markets. A common theme of each of these events is the attempt to continue down a well-trodden path at a time when the reality of international economic relations has changed beyond all recognition. While markets have been innovating at an extraordinary pace, governments appear to believe that the remedies of 50 years ago still provide answers to the challenges of international markets.

An International Investment Regime

An international regime for investments is the natural next step in the secular process of economic liberalization that was launched after the disaster of World War II and has now come to be known as 'globalization'. It is also essential to any move towards greater sustainability. There are several reasons why such an investment regime should be actively promoted.

- Without such a regime, many countries will continue to pay economic penalties as the risks of investment without adequate legal protections are factored into the expected rate of return.
- The efficiency gained by reducing such risks is one of the major justifications for an international investment regime.
- As in other economic regimes, increased efficiency can lead to greater sustainability but does not automatically do so.[12] At the very least, it creates opportunities for promoting greater sustainability.
- In a world replete with unsustainable infrastructure, only further investment holds the promise of constructive change in favour of greater sustainability.

Investment risks that are susceptible to being reduced by an agreement occur principally in relation to investments in poorer developing countries, which not only attract less investment but are expected to provide higher rates of return. All things being equal, capital should flow towards countries with low levels of existing investment, since these are likely to offer the greatest opportunities for new investment. All things are not, however, equal. In practice, investment flows are unequally divided and tend to favour a limited number of countries, among them the most highly developed ones. There are numerous reasons for this situation, but the existence of risks associated with insecurity of investments is certainly an important one.[13] Presumably, an international investment regime can contribute to reducing such disparities.

Along with efficiency gains, there is a range of critical issues relating to the broader social, political and environmental dimension of investment – in a word, sustainability. An international investment regime must balance these different considerations and do so in a continuing manner that responds to changing priorities over time. To perform this balancing function, the investment regime must be dynamic in nature.

The critical question is, therefore, what are the essential characteristics of an international investment regime? Only a clear answer to this question can guide the preliminary determinations for the necessary negotiations. Four principles are commonly identified as governing the 'extent and nature of liberalization' to be achieved in an international investment regime:[14]

- Right of establishment
- National treatment
- Non-discrimination or most favoured nation treatment (MFN)
- Transparency.

In addition, it is widely assumed that 'performance requirements' – that is, certain conditions imposed on investors by host countries, should be limited or outlawed. These four principles need to be examined from the perspective of sustainable development, the only universally accepted criterion for evaluating the broader social and political significance of such a regime. It appears that the principles of national treatment and MFN, the central principles of the GATT/WTO regime, will need to be balanced in the light of two further principles:

- Market disciplines
- Investor responsibility.

Moreover, in the light of experience with NAFTA it appears that the GATT/WTO dispute settlement system is inappropriate to the needs of an investment regime.

The goal of an investment agreement is to promote non-discrimination, which is also the goal of the trade regime. Yet to achieve this goal an investment agreement will need institutions that are different from those employed by the trade regime. The reason for this paradox lie in the nature of investment and in the requirements that this imposes on an investment regime.

The Time-frame of Investment

Trade in goods occurs within a limited time-frame. It is neither instantaneous nor very extended. Goods transactions are typically measured in days or months. Sales of certain major capital goods – aeroplanes, for example – may extend over several years. However, as the time-frame of the sale gets longer, the sale increasingly resembles an investment, involving leases, loans or even some form of ownership stake.

The significance of the temporal dimension of a sale lies in the social, economic and legal relationships that are established. The sale of goods creates a limited relationship expressed as a contract that specifies dates, conditions of delivery, prices and other relevant considerations. It may include warranties over an extended period of time, which are, however, strictly tied to the goods being traded. This is a relationship that is readily standardized. Indeed, many aspects of international trade in goods are by now highly standardized, including contracts of sale, payments procedures, deadlines and jurisdictional issues in case of dispute. Sales of like products are alike. It is increasingly possible to sell goods internationally over the telephone or the internet. Apart from warranties and possible service agreements, the legal relationship between buyer and seller is terminated on completion of the transaction.

Frequently the seller will seek to establish a longer term relationship based on certain characteristics of the goods being sold, the inclusion of property rights in the sale (for example licences), sales strategies or other methods. In most cases, however, the resulting relationship is a personal one between buyer and seller, and either party can terminate it without further consequences. It involves public goods marginally or not at all.

Trade in services represents a more complex relationship, extending over widely varying periods of time. Provision of services can be a one-off event or represent a continuing activity. Nevertheless, trade in services can be seen as roughly analogous to trade in goods, in the sense that the service can be defined in clear and explicit terms and expressed in the form of a contract between two private parties in different countries. Normally the service provider does not acquire any rights in the country of the client. The service provider may, however, travel to the country where the service is being provided and may require some infrastructure, which in turn represents an investment. For this reason, GATS includes a range of investment provisions.

The time-frame of investments, on the other hand is widely divergent. Purely financial transactions – portfolio investment in particular – can be extremely liquid, subject to purchase and sale almost instantaneously. The underlying social and legal relationship can be described as ephemeral.

Some investments are long-term, measured in years or even decades. The power plant that is built today may still be operational a century later – well beyond the time when it is fully depreciated – much modified but nevertheless in the same location and often utilizing the same fuel. The forest that is cut down today may not regenerate in 2000 years and the farm or the plantation that replaces it will transform the landscape in which it is located. It will be the object of changing crops and evolving practices from one year to the next.

An international investment regime that does not recognize the broader social dimensions of investment will contribute to the destruction of social and environmental values. It will defeat efforts to achieve greater sustainability. This is a claim that has frequently been made with respect to the entire process of 'globalization' and it is not always accurate. With regard to investment, however, the stakes are real. Constructing an international regime that is sensitive to a range of social, political and environmental variables linked to sustainability is a daunting task.

Economic Citizenship and the Right of Establishment

The social and legal relationship established by productive investments is different from that involved in the sale of goods and the operations of portfolio investment for the following reasons:

- Productive investments involve the purchase of open-ended contracts of an indeterminate duration.
- An investor acquires a range of rights and obligations in the country where the investment is located. These may include rights to real estate, emission rights to the environment, the right to contract with individuals and corporations and the right to undertake financial transactions.
- Some investments imply ancillary investments by public authorities – for example, for transportation, education and training, and for environmental services.
- An investor must accept obligations to respect the law of the jurisdiction(s) in which the investment occurs and to contribute to the community in which the investment is located – for example, by paying taxes.
- Investments require institutions to ensure fair administration of the law, to provide for the needs of employees.

Investment creates a complex system of rights and obligations, extending into an indefinite future that can best be described as a form of economic citizenship.

Viewed from a social and political perspective, trade in goods and the making of a productive investment have hardly anything in common. An international investment regime that serves the interests of all parties concerned must reflect these differences at all levels, in the principles it applies, in the institutions it employs and in the details of its provisions.

Investors must be able to invest in a jurisdiction as of right. If foreign investment is subject to some form of approval or licensing, this results in the creation of rents that must ultimately be borne by the investment and will impact the expected rate of return. In particular, government licensing schemes result in opportunities for side payments that are not accounted for but still need to be covered from the investment process itself.

The right of establishment is fundamental to creating the status of economic citizenship: the right to purchase and sell goods and real property, the right to enter into contracts, the right to apply for permits and authorizations, the right to manufacture, store, ship, export. All of these rights are subject to the law of the jurisdiction as a matter of course. In particular, the ability to obtain secure property rights is an essential aspect of any investment since these rights will be needed as security for loans and other transactions. Without clear property rights it can also become difficult to obtain insurance, which in turn will tend to raise the cost of investment or at the very least the expected rate of return. What is at issue for foreign investors is that they be put on an appropriate footing in comparison to domestic investors.

National Treatment

There are two aspects of environmental management that can be significant factors in determining what constitutes 'national treatment'. Facilities are rarely 'like' from an environmental perspective; and measures applied to otherwise 'like' facilities at different times are liable to be significantly different.

Environmental management is a dynamic activity, responding to growing knowledge concerning the environment and anthropogenic threats to it, as well as to changing perceptions concerning the seriousness of these threats. Moreover, environmental management is typically achieved through a 'package' of measures, involving standards, permits and licences on one hand and economic incentives on the other. In addition a complex structure of information and accountability, to management, to stockholders, to the authorities and to the public at large represents a critical element of enforcement. Environmental management is always institutionally rich. The underlying reason for this complex approach is the difficulty in producing desired results in the natural environment which responds to the laws of nature through policy measures, which can only affect social behaviour. Consequently, the operation of environmental policy is always and inevitably indirect and subject to a degree of imprecision. To compensate for this imprecision, governments have been forced to cumulate measures – command-and-control, incentives and informational obligations.

An added level of complexity derives from the continuous development of technologies designed to protect the environment. As these technologies become available, policy must adjust to reflect new capabilities.

Finally, the 'absorptive capacity' of the natural environment, such as it is, represents a scarce resource to which there are no precisely delimited property rights, entailing a complex allocation process involving both public and private interests. Later, 'like' facilities located in a watershed or within the distribution range of atmospheric pollutants, must take into account the existence of prior emitters – which must in turn be subjected to new conditions to make room for new sources.

To cite one example, environmental permits for installations as basic as coal-fired power plants, one of the oldest forms of power generation, can differ widely from one facility to the next. Moreover, countries approach the problems arising from the dynamic and complex character of environmental management differently. A comparison of permits for coal-fired power plants in the Netherlands and the Federal Republic of Germany in the early 1980s showed that each facility had specific characteristics arising from the technology employed, the characteristics of the fuel, existing emissions and shifting priorities of public policy, rendering comparisons virtually impossible. Moreover, administrative practice in the Netherlands allowed the continuous tightening of permits over many years; environmental management was, in fact, a continuous process of negotiation between the investor and the public authorities. In the Federal Republic of Germany much more weight was placed on long-term security of permits. New permits tended to be much more stringent – and much closer to the limits of current technologies – than in the Netherlands, but after several years the requirements in the Netherlands tended to be more onerous than in Germany.[15]

There is no intrinsic reason why it should be impossible to determine what 'like' treatment is under these circumstances. It is, however, a complex process which occurs continuously in all countries where equal treatment before the law is upheld. It is a demanding, continuous, dynamic process and raises questions about the institutional capabilities of an international regime. Certainly an international agreement that provides for investor–state dispute proceedings needs to be developed with caution, since it is liable to change in unpredictable ways the delicate balance which currently exists between investors and regulatory authorities within countries.[16]

Faced with the challenge of developing appropriate environmental standards, issuing permits and licences, and ensuring that all relevant measures have been complied with, environmental authorities in all countries are forced to engage in some form of selective enforcement. They must set priorities for enforcement action based on criteria such as the nature of the environmental threat, past history of a facility or public pressure. Under these circumstances, determining what represents 'national treatment' can be a challenge.

One of the paradoxes of the principle of national treatment when applied to investments is that it does not put foreign and domestic investors on an equal footing – as it does when applied to goods in trade. It provides foreign investors with rights not enjoyed by their domestic counterparts. In most countries, the grounds on which domestic actors can take a government to court are quite circumscribed. An international investment agreement, such as NAFTA, that gives private investors the right to initiate proceedings against host country governments establishes a new set of legal provisions for the benefit of foreign investors which are not available to domestic investors.

Most Favoured Nation Treatment (MFN)

It would seem axiomatic that MFN – the idea that benefits extended to investors of one country will be extended to investors from all countries party to the agreement – is a strong institution for an international investment regime that seeks to promote non-discrimination. Nevertheless, a number of issues concerning sustainability arise in this context as well, essentially reflecting the need to take a static institution and apply it in a dynamic manner. The potential conflict with the climate regime is fairly straightforward and is discussed below. Additionally, the need for selective enforcement actions makes the environmental and management practices of the country of origin of an investor a matter for reasonable concern. Finally, with growing international integration of product chains, effective responsibility for certain environmental, and labour, practices rests with the home country investor rather than with management in the host country. For example, the environmental practices of semi-conductor manufacture are largely determined by the purchaser, while the labour practices of some textile manufacture are subject to review by foreign buyers.[17]

The Framework Convention on Climate Change (FCCC) states:

> The Parties should protect the climate system for the benefit of present and future generations of humankind, on the basis of equity and in accordance with their common but differentiated responsibilities and respective capabilities. Accordingly, the developed country Parties should take the lead in combating climate change and the adverse effects thereof (Art. 4).

The notion of common but differentiated responsibilities and respective capabilities has caused a good deal of discussion. The existence of a list of countries in Annex 1, which have undertaken to limit their emissions of greenhouse gases, and the steady development of new institutions, such as Activities Implemented Jointly (AIJ) and the Clean Development Mechanism (CDM) launched by the Kyoto Protocol to the FCCC, introduce a range of new distinctions between countries, which are likely to result in distinctions between foreign investors. The result is a regime in which investments from developed countries in other Annex I countries may receive credits for reductions in greenhouse gas emissions, while 'like' investments from non-Annex I countries would not. Similarly, investments from Annex I countries in non-Annex I would be favoured under the CDM, while investments between non-Annex I countries would not.

Investment lies at the core of the climate regime which can, in fact, be described as an investment agreement. Combating climate change requires investments in climate-friendly technologies and implies obstacles to investment in technologies that are not climate-friendly. The climate regime has not developed to the point where its effects are predictable. Nevertheless, an international investment regime needs to respect the requirements of the climate regime.

As governments confront foreign investors – in particular investors from 'off-shore' investment countries – whose background is not or hardly known, it is not unreasonable to make certain distinctions based on the known requirements in the home market of the investor concerning environment and other factors of sustainability. An investment by a major enterprise from a country with rigorous environmental controls may attract different levels of scrutiny from comparable investments from other countries or investments from tax havens where there is no environmental activity at all.

The last thing an international investment agreement should do is to promote the investment equivalent of flags of convenience which play such a central role in rendering international shipping – and its environmental performance and respect for labour standards in particular – almost impossible to control properly. For example, in the provinces of coastal China problems with foreign direct investment relating to the use of ozone-depleting substances are encountered primarily when the investors come from Hong Kong or Taiwan. It is reasonable to seek particularly close control over their actions, whether or not this contravenes the principle of MFN. Similarly, it does not seem unreasonable to consider home country practices when awarding concessions to manage forests. For example, companies from Malaysia with a record of damaging forest practices have been acquiring forestry concessions in the countries of Africa and Latin America. A government concerned about the future of its forests could reasonably be expected to impose additional requirements on the granting of such concessions.[18]

It is not beyond the ingenuity of international negotiators to develop solutions to these issues, but they go beyond the declaration of MFN. They will presumably require some institutional mechanism to review apparently 'discriminatory' behaviour and to judge its acceptability. Such a procedure must, however, be prepared to face the issue of its legitimacy in balancing individual rights and public goods.

Investor Obligations

Investor responsibility has been the most important bone of contention in various attempts to address investment issues at an international level. The debate concerning investor responsibility was severely polarized in the 1970s and into the 1980s. The UNCTC Code of Conduct dealt primarily with host state rights and investor responsibility; the OECD approach focused on investor rights, outlawed performance requirements and relegated what remained in the area of investor responsibility to separate, less binding 'Guidelines'. In the 1990s, the OECD approach appeared to prevail, as numerous countries moved towards liberalization of their capital markets. This trend was most pronounced in some countries of Latin America, Chile and Argentina in particular.[19] Mercosur adopted two protocols for Intra-Zone and for Extra-Zone originated foreign direct investment (FDI), whose provisions appear to be largely consistent with the OECD Declaration and subsequent OECD instruments.[20] As a result, attitudes towards FDI have shifted in many Latin American countries and have left the OECD approach as the only one currently under active consideration.

In practice it is hard to see how an international investment agreement can be concluded which does not address investor responsibility. The major challenge is to identify the international dimension of this issue – that is, the aspect that requires some form of international action. Many of the difficulties to date have arisen from the attempt to codify internationally the action of private investors that should fall entirely under national jurisidiction.

The most basic of all responsibilities is to respect the laws and regulations of the host country. This simple statement requires some interpretation. Implementation of regulations is uneven in all countries, but more so in some than in others. Situations may arise where stringent regulations exist, for workers' health and safety and environmental protection in particular, but where respect for these regulations is sporadic at best. Are foreign investors expected to comply with local practice, or are they to be measured by a more stringent standard?

The answer to this question may lie in the nature of the investment. Where the output from foreign investment feeds into a product chain in which the foreign investor plays a dominant role – for example, in electronics, in forestry or in mining – the foreign investor should be held to the most stringent interpretation of the law. Where the output of foreign investment is absorbed locally – for example, in some food processing or for transport services or power generation – the standards to be applied are essentially local in character, subject to the need of a foreign investor to protect its good reputation, or a global brand. Where obligations are international in nature – for example, relating to stratospheric ozone depletion, climate change or biodiversity – foreign investors must meet these international obligations. The interpretation of obligations that are variable in nature requires a significant degree of institutional sophistication at the international level.

The issue of 'performance standards' has played an important role in the debate about international investment. These are obligations which may be linked to the approval of investment and which may differ, or seem to differ, from comparable requirements imposed on domestic investors. To the extent that certain foreign investors or their investments are different from domestic ones, there would seem to be no problem with imposing performance requirements on them which reflect their special status. In practice, however, using such differences to justify the imposition of standards is liable to give rise to serious conflicts within any investment regime, since effectively it transfers decision-making to the dispute settlement process.

The draft MAI takes a clear position on performance requirements: it is against them. It lists 11 different requirements that are outlawed. This list covers most of the issues commonly raised in connection with performance requirements. The implication of this provision is that governments will have to provide subsidies to investors if they want to impose performance requirements. It is also worth noting that governments may impose performance requirements on their nationals but would be prohibited from doing so for foreign investors.

Some difficulties arise from the hybrid character of most international investment agreements: they are agreements between states but they concern to a significant degree the actions of private parties, and in some instances create certain rights for these private parties. As agreements between states, international investment agreements can hardly impose direct obligations on private investors; yet the maintenance of market discipline, in particular between private actors, is an essential goal of an investment agreement. 'Performance requirements' were an attempt to articulate the kinds of requirements which international investors might reasonably be expected to meet.

In practice, performance requirements are a reflection of the fact that the investor is acquiring significant rights in the jurisdiction of investment and that it is consequently normal for a negotiation to occur between the investor and the public authorities where the investment is to occur. This negotiation can cover a large range of topics, such as the provision of infrastructure, the right to utilize scarce natural resources such as air and water, the need to protect biodiversity and wildlife, employment, community development and other issues. The relationship between the parties can reflect a large number of different situations, ranging from dominance on the part of the investor to dominance on the part of the public authorities. It is essential that these negotiations be fair and equitable and that their outcome properly reflect the needs and interests of all parties concerned. While this may sound simple, it is not easy to achieve, but prior determinations of what topics are negotiable – which is the effect of the list of outlawed performance requirements in the MAI – do not resolve the underlying dilemma.

The problem of performance requirements is exacerbated by the provisions of investment agreements, such as NAFTA Chapter 11 or the draft MAI concerning expropriation. Apart from the obvious strictures against direct expropriation without adequate compensation, there are also rules concerning indirect expropriation – that is, through the imposition of measures that have the same effect. This raises the issue of 'takings', which is extremely sensitive from an environmental perspective. There is some evidence that dispute panels are much more willing to view legitimate government measures as a 'taking', and therefore subject to compensation, than the jurisprudence in any national jurisdiction, even the US. From an environmental perspective it is essential that any international investment agreement specify that environmental measures taken in the public interest have a presumption of legitimacy and are not subject to compensation. Otherwise public authorities would end up having to pay for any environmental measures they decide on.

It would promote a solution to the dilemmas posed by investor obligations if a process could be developed that clearly identifies the international interest in this issue and restricts negotiation to them.

Transparency

Transparency is a critical institution of dynamic regimes. Because of the processes of change involved in such regimes and the continuing uncertainty about relevant facts and the identity of interested parties, dynamic regimes use transparency as an institution to ensure access to information and the participation of key actors, some of whom may not be known in advance. More static regimes can reasonably assume that all key parties are present or represented, and that all material information will be available through them. That assumption is inoperative in a more dynamic situation and transparency is the appropriate response.

'Transparency' is not a process that gives rights to persons in an arbitrary manner. Apart from the basic right to know and the obligation on members of the regime to be publicly accountable, actual participation can, and generally should, be made dependent on objective criteria.

The instruments for transparency are well established, beginning with ensuring that all operational documents are made publicly available in a prompt manner, ensuring that meetings are public unless there are strong reasons for the respect of confidentiality and providing avenues for persons outside the regime who may have an interest in outcomes to make their opinions heard for certain kinds of proceedings – dispute settlement in particular. Under no circumstances should an international investment regime be created that does not include strong provisions for transparency, together with specific rules designed to achieve this goal.

Dispute Settlement

The need for a dispute settlement process as part of any international investment regime is clear. Without such a process, it is unlikely to increase the calculability of risks to a significant degree. This dispute settlement process must, however, properly reflect the principles and the structures of the regime that is being created.

Each of the factors which establish the need for a dynamic investment regime – the long-term nature of investment and the consequent need to reflect change over time, the relationship between an investor and the investing country, and the difficulty of determining 'like circumstances' in an investment regime – also define characteristics of the dispute settlement process. It is not fortuitous that the issues that arise in developing a dispute settlement process for an investment regime are the same issues that have arisen in the confrontation between the (static) GATT/WTO system and the (dynamic) structures for environment and sustainability. The dispute settlement system for an investment regime must be open, accountable, capable of handling technical information and of balancing conflicting policy objectives. No such dispute settlement system exists yet at the international level, even though they exist at many other levels of governance, ranging from the US Supreme Court to rural magistrates in Central Europe.

It is risky, even irresponsible, to impose tasks on institutions that are unable to discharge them. The results can be devastating for the institutions in question, and highly unsatisfactory in substantive terms. Under NAFTA, the attempt to use the arbitration procedures of ICSD and UNCITRAL to review regulatory measures adopted by public authorities has resulted in a process that is dysfunctional and ultimately threatens the entire regime.[21]

The dispute settlement system of an investment agreement will typically be called on to adjudicate the rights of an individual investor in relation to the actions of some public authority. In many instances it will need to consider the circumstances of a specific project or investment and balance these against the broader public interest that may be affected by such a project. This represents a major institutional innovation. One solution could be to draw the courts of the host country into the process so that the international tribunal would address its conclusions to a domestic court with the appropriate competences and legitimacy. Of course, this does not resolve problems created by domestic courts that act in a manner that is contrary to the international legal obligations of the host country.

'Like' Investments

The central principle underlying an investment regime is that of 'non-discrimination'. In the GATT/WTO system, non-discrimination is achieved through MFN and national treatment, the central institutions of the GATT/WTO system.

The application of MFN and national treatment revolves around the word 'like', that is the obligation to treat 'like' products or investments equally. The difficulty arises from imposing an inflexible obligation in connection with an indeterminate term. The interpretation of the term 'like' represents in many ways the most serious conflict between the GATT/WTO regime and the requirements of sustainable development which make it necessary to distinguish between products produced sustainably and those produced unsustainably (for example, wood products from unsustainably harvested timber, or pond versus wild-caught shrimp, or possibly agricultural products employing genetically modified organisms from those not doing so). Thus far, the GATT/WTO has steadfastly, and incorrectly, maintained that products may not be distinguished by their mode of production.[22] GATT negotiators clearly recognized that a more determinate word (for example, 'identical' or 'same') would nullify the effectiveness of the central principles on which the multilateral trade regime rests. French and Spanish do not have a comparable word, so the translation renders 'like' as 'equivalent'. Equally, a less determinate word ('similar') would expose the regime to all kinds of arbitrary discrimination. Unfortunately, interpreters of the GATT have tended to emphasize the determinacy of the obligation over the need to interpret the indeterminate word 'like'.

If distinctions between 'like' products in international trade needed for ensuring greater sustainability of production have proved difficult to introduce, determining what are 'like' investments is sure to cause extraordinary difficulties. These difficulties are already reflected in the text of most existing investment agreements which refer not to 'like' investments but require MFN and national treatment 'in like circumstances'.

An interpretative note proposed in March 1998 by the chairman of the MAI negotiations takes a first step towards discussing the difficulties surrounding MFN and national treatment for investments:

> National treatment and most favoured nation treatment are relative standards requiring a comparison between treatment of a foreign investor and investments and treatment of domestic or third country investors and investments. Governments may have legitimate policy reasons to accord differential treatment to *different types* of investments. Similarly governments may have legitimate policy reasons to accord differential treatment as between domestic and foreign investors and their investments in certain circumstances, for example where needed to secure compliance with certain domestic laws that are not inconsistent with national treatment and most favoured nation treatment. The fact that a measure applied by a government has a different effect on an investment or investor of another Party would not in itself render the measure inconsistent with national treatment and most favoured nation treatment. The objective of 'in like circumstances' is to permit consideration of all relevant circumstances, including those relating to a foreign investor and its investments, in deciding to which domestic or third country investors they should appropriately be compared' (emphasis added).[23]

This text goes some of the way to identifying issues surrounding the concept of 'in like circumstances' in an investment agreement. It does not, however, address the issue of the interpretative process which is necessary to make these general observations effective. This process depends critically on the institutional capabilities of the international investment regime. An investment regime without an effective secretariat, with a dispute settlement process that relies on a changing group of arbitrators and without adequate public accountability is liable to find itself embroiled in conflict within a very short time. The experience of NAFTA – which has modest institutional capabilities – is illustrative in this regard.[24]

The interpretative note does not, however, adequately address the temporal dimension of investment: circumstances can change over time, but a productive investment will continue and consequently 'like circumstances' can involve a great deal of variation. One farm begins with growing corn, moves to genetically modified seed and ends up with an intensive hog-raising operation, while another converts to organic production and builds an internet business.

Institutional Capability

The controversy surrounding the draft MAI demonstrates the complexity of the issues that are at stake in an international investment regime. Even apparently self-evident issues, such as MFN, national treatment or the elimination of performance requirements will require much more careful consideration in a dynamic context. The reality of foreign direct investment has changed dramatically since the post-war era, since the elimination of fixed exchange rates and since the debt crisis of the 1980s. More changes are to be expected, with the move towards more sustainable forms of production and the huge investments that implies with the introduction of the euro and with the current crisis of international markets, particularly if the Japanese banking system continues to falter. Moreover, countries with ageing populations and capital surpluses will find that the only option to generate income for retirement-age people is through the investment of their capital surpluses in countries with younger populations.

These are issues quite unlike those addressed in the trade regime over the past 50 years. The process of the reduction and elimination of tariffs, the development of disciplines for non-tariff barriers and the inclusion of further sectors such as services and agriculture in the GATT/WTO system never required a rethinking of the core principles of the regime. Only the agreement on intellectual property rights has created a new structure of rights and obligations.

The GATT system was characterized by its institutional sparseness. The GATT itself could not be amended. Since the GATT secretariat was not an international organization, its functions were strictly limited. Implementation of the agreements under the GATT was multiunilateral – that is, it rested entirely with the countries involved, except in cases of conflict. Initially this unusual structure served the trade regime well since it was essentially a negotiating forum and breaches of the regime's disciplines could be tolerated as long as the general direction of trade liberalization was maintained. The dispute settlement process was central to the regime's success because it provided a slightly more dynamic source of interpretation than the sparse organizational structures.

It was not until the Uruguay Round that the institutional inadequacies of the GATT became so strong that a move was made to streamline the dispute settlement process and to draw together in a single organization, the WTO, the agreements which had proliferated with changing memberships under the GATT. The ensuing organization still has many of the characteristics of the GATT, in particular the unwieldy structure of councils and committees with unrestricted membership, the tendency to view all issues in terms of a negotiation and the use of dispute settlement as a principal means of implementation. Thus far, the WTO has proved no more adept than the GATT at addressing policy issues that require a balancing of conflicting goals, such as those relating to the environment. When all is said and done, the only priority that can be recognized is the need for trade liberalization.

An international investment regime deals with a much more complex agenda. It will need to be institutionally more sophisticated than the GATT/WTO system. One of the more surprising elements of the MAI text is the lack of attention to institutional needs. There appear to be a number of unarticulated assumptions concerning the appropriate institutional structure, derived from the GATT/WTO, which upon closer scrutiny turn out to be questionable. The MAI provides for a 'Parties Group', which resembles the GATT Council and the Contracting Parties of the GATT even more than the General Council of the WTO. It specifies that there will be a secretariat which has no independent functions whatsoever.[25] This makes it a more virtual organization than even the ICSID, which at least has a secretary-general who has certain specified, though modest, functions under the agreement.

The MAI is the first multilateral approach to investment that did not arise out of an existing organizational context, be it a regional trade agreement or the United Nations Centre on Transnational Corporations. It consequently had to create the entire institutional structure needed to address the complex, dynamic agenda of investment, since it had no implied organizational background, like the European Union, NAFTA, Mercosur, the United Nations – or the OECD for that matter. It reflected the assumption that the institutions that have served the trade regime would be adequate for an investment regime. Implicitly, the negotiators must have hoped that the two would one day be merged. It is doubtful whether that would have served either the needs of trade liberalization or the demands of international investment in a satisfactory manner.

Reflecting the heavy reliance on the trade regime for its institutional inspiration, the draft MAI relies on dispute settlement as a means of implementation. The dispute resolution procedures of the MAI, modelled on those of the WTO and those of bilateral investment agreements, assume that the future task of the investment regime will be to apply an essentially immutable set of principles. The evolution of international investment over the past 50 years and the necessary adjustment of public policy to go along with it, suggest that the principal task of the investment regime will be promoting the understanding of the processes of investment and the maintenance of essential market disciplines, such as rules governing competition and the environment, that are necessary to ensure that investment serves overarching goals of public policy. Above all, an investment regime must have the capability to moderate conflicting priorities, most notably private interests and public goods, in a manner that is widely accepted as legitimate

A Different Approach: A Framework Agreement on Investment

All the attempts to address investment at the international level have assumed that what is needed is a system of rules that must be applied, much as in the trade regime, by governments and reinforced through a dispute settlement process. This is a fundamentally static view of the investment process and its function in economic and social policy. It makes no provision for the dynamic aspects of an investment regime, nor does it reflect the complex legal and contractual relationships between investor and host country that characterize foreign direct investment. It does not provide for the necessary balancing of conflicting policy priorities, in particular between investment and sustainable development.

A better approach might draw some lessons from international environmental regimes which have faced the problem of addressing issues that evolve over time and consequently demand a dynamic international regime.

The approach that is now well established in environmental regimes is to begin with a framework agreement which establishes basic institutions, creates an organizational structure and defines a continuing process designed to achieve certain articulated aims. Since negotiators cannot know what measures will ultimately be needed, most multilateral environmental agreements are quite indeterminate as to the appropriate institutions that will be required. Over time, a body of evidence accumulates and additional measures can be adopted to ensure that the regime continues to move in the desired direction.

Conceivably, a framework agreement represents a better approach to addressing international investment policies. Such an agreement would outline a set of goals for the regime, including the goal of achieving sustainable development, as well as a process to explore the necessary steps towards those goals. The result would be an incremental regime, capable of responding to emerging needs and adapting to changing practices in international investment.

There is significant advantage in moving investment out of the organizations that have sought to address this issue thus far: the World Bank, the WTO, the United Nations Organization for Trade and Development and the OECD. Several decades of effort in these organizations have resulted in stalemate. After the collapse of the MAI negotiations, every attempt to launch a new process designed to produce an agreement on investment is liable to attract vigorous opposition. An approach that begins with modest steps and recognizes the tasks as incremental offers better chance for success.

The central challenge of any international investment regime will be to maintain a high level of predictability while retaining essential flexibility. In many ways, that resembles the dilemmas of the institutions that govern the monetary system. While they need to be highly stable and predictable over long periods of time, in moments of crisis they must act decisively even if this breaks with what appeared to be a well-established precedent. The challenge facing an international investment regime is not as daunting as that confronted by monetary authorities. Its purpose is, after all, to ensure the highest possible level of calculability of private economic risks in the investment process while ensuring that overriding goals of public policy – sustainability, human rights and the vitality of communities – are respected. That does not sound like a goal beyond the reach of international society as it has evolved over the past decades, but it is a goal that can only be attained if the investment regime reflects an adequate institutional base and the capability to balance conflicting goals of policy.

Before launching a major international negotiation, it is essential to identify the interest that will be served by this process and that cannot be achieved by lesser means, essentially an international interest. From the perspective of sustainable development, there is an urgent need for an investment regime that actually promotes environmentally sound and sustainable foreign direct investment. The current international structure, resting largely on bilateral investment treaties, does not meet this need.

It is important to recognize that bilateral agreements serve a useful purpose and can reasonably continue to do so. They have contributed to greater security of investment. What they have proved unable to accomplish is to achieve more even flows of investment, or at least flows that more properly reflect potential returns. A multilateral investment regime would need to contribute directly to this outcome if it is to provide added value beyond the current system.

In general, there are a number of international goods that require significant levels of investment. Ensuring greater calculability of investments in these sectors is certainly one of the goals of any international investment agreement. Among the goods not sufficiently served by current flows of foreign direct investment are certain environmental values, such as the prevention of global climate change or the promotion of more sustainable exploitation of natural resources, as well as development in the poorer countries. It makes sense to tie the availability of certain internationally guaranteed investor rights to the provision of such international goods. In other words, it may be desirable to introduce investor rights into agreements such as the UN Framework Convention on Climate Change or an international forestry agreement, should one ever be agreed. In this manner it would become possible to achieve the kind of balancing between private rights and public goods that lies at the heart of any broader investment agreement. It would also permit some experience to accumulate in a limited context where the public benefits are not in doubt, thereby bridging the time during which no global investment regime exists to promote security, responsibility and calculability.

The available options are limited to promote investments that are desirable from the perspective of sustainable development. In practice, governments have chosen to provide subsidies – for example, through the Global Environment Facility. Subsidies have certain undesirable characteristics: they perpetuate themselves and always entail the risk that necessary investments will not be made at all unless they are subsidized, even when they are economical without subsidy. Providing certain investor rights permits governments to improve the relationship between risk and return by lowering risk rather than increasing returns. That is an approach with few drawbacks that does not burden the public purse and represents a classic function of government as rule-maker.

It could be argued that a segmentation of the international investment regime is undesirable. After all, investment is a universal activity and in principle more investment is a broadly desirable goal of public policy. The problems associated with an international investment regime, outlined above, suggest, however, that it is necessary to find organizations that can provide the necessary balance between rights and obligations. By inserting new investor rights into regimes that pursue some other legitimate international policy goal – for example, the prevention of global climate change or the promotion of sustainable forest practices – it becomes possible to create this balance in a more limited context.

There is no public interest in providing additional international rights to investors who act in an environmentally irresponsible manner. Conversely, investors who act in accordance with international environmental requirements – for example, climate change or sustainable commodities production – have the right to expect the support of the international community. One of the most effective ways to provide this support and to create incentives for more sustainable investments is to introduce a system of rights for such investors. Such a system should serve to improve the risk/return relationship of sustainable investment just as surely as a subsidy would, but without the economic drawbacks of a subsidy, since it would be in conformity with the functions of government at all levels.

The goal of establishing a global investment agreement is currently out of reach. On one hand, the institutional development of international society has not progressed to the point where such a regime could be envisaged. On the other hand, public opinion in a number of key countries is strongly against a general investment agreement making it a politically delicate undertaking. Under these circumstances, a number of more modest practical steps can help to explore the real dimensions of this enterprise. A framework convention, together with investment provisions in certain sectoral agreements, is presumably a pragmatic way to proceed.

Notes

1   Fitzgerald, E V K et al (1998) 'The Development Implications of the Multilateral Agreement on Investment', a Report Commissioned by the Department for International Development (UK), Finance and Trade Policy Research Centre, University of Oxford (manuscript, March)

2   United Nations Conference on Trade and Employment, held at Havana, Cuba, from 21 November 1947 to 24 March 1948: *Final Act and Related Documents* (Lake Success, New York, Interim Commission for the International Trade Organization, 1948, p5) quoted in United Nations Centre on Transnational Corporations, UNCTC, *The Impact of Trade-related Investment Measures on Trade and Development,* United Nations, New York, 1991, p79

3   The World Bank, 'An Overview of ICSID', www.worldbank.org/html/extdr/icsid/html (2 January 1999), p1. Aron Broches (1985) 'The Experience of the International Centre for Settlement of Investment Disputes', in Seymour J Rubin and Richard W Nelson (eds) *International Investment Disputes: Avoidance and Settlement (Studies in Transnational Legal Policy No 20)*, West Publishing Co, St. Paul, MN, pp79–80

4   United Nations Conference on Trade and Development, *International Investment Instruments: S Compendium. Vol I: Multilateral Instruments*, United Nations, New York, 1996, piv

5   United Nations Conference on Trade and Development, *International Investment Instruments: S Compendium. Vol III: Regional Integration, Bilateral and Nongovernmental Instruments*, United Nations, New York, 1996, pp213–243

6   UNCITRAL is an organ of the UN General Assembly. Established in 1966, UNCITRAL's goal is to promote harmonization and unification of commercial law. It developed the Convention on the Recognition and Enforcement of Foreign Arbitral Awards, which entered into force 7 June 1959 (www.un.or.at/uncitral/english/texts/arbconc/58conv.htm – 3 January 1999). UNCITRAL has, by resolution of the General Assembly, established Arbitration Rules (www.un.or.at/uncitral/english/texts/arbconc/arbitrul.htm – 3 January 1999) and Conciliation Rules (www.un.or.at/uncitral/english/texts/arbconc/concirul.htm – 3 January 1999)

7   Mann, Howard and von Moltke, Konrad (1999) 'NAFTA's Chapter 11 and the Environment: Addressing the Impacts of the Investor-State Process', International Institute for Sustainable Development, Winnipeg. Available at http://www.iisd1.ca/trade. Konrad von Moltke and Howard Mann, 'Institutional Misappropriation', *International Environmental Agreements*, Vol 1 No 1 (autumn 2000)

8   Reviews of foreign investment are published by the OECD: Brazil (1998), Ukraine (1997), Chile (1997), Argentina (1997)

9   See, for example, OECD, *Foreign Direct Investment: OECD Countries and Dynamic Economies of Asia and Latin America*. OECD, Paris, 1995

10 See von Moltke and Mann, *supra* p7

11 See pp352–367 below

12 International Institute for Sustainable Development, *Trade and Sustainable Development Principles*, IISD, Winnipeg, 1994

13 See Schmidt, Helmut (1990) 'Facing One World: A report by an Independent Group on Financial Flows to Developing Countries', *International Environmental Affairs*, Vol 2, No 2 (spring), pp174–181

14 Ostry, Sylvia (1997) *A New Regime for Foreign Direct Investment*, Group of Thirty, Washington, DC, p11 (reordered).

15 von Moltke, Konrad, Boerwinkel, Fred, Meiners, Hubert (1985) *Rechtsvergleich deutsch-niederländischer Emissionsnormen zur Vermeidung von Luftverunreinigungen Teil 1: Bundesrepublik Deutschland; Teil 2: Niederlande; Teil 3: Tabellen. (Teil 1* also in Dutch: *Rechtsvergelijking van duits-nederlandse emissienormen ter bestrijding van luchtverontreiniging*), Institute for European Environmental Policy, Bonn.

16 See Mann, Howard and von Moltke, Konrad (fn7).

17 See von Moltke, Konrad et al (1998) *Global Product Chains: Northern Consumers, Southern Producers, and Sustainability,* (Environment and Trade 15), United Nations Environment Programme.

18 Sizer, Nigel and Plouvier, Dominiek (2000) *Increased Investment and Trade by Transnational Logging Companies in Africa, the Caribbean and the Pacific: Implications for the Sustainable Management and Conservation of Tropical Forests,* World Wide Fund For Nature, Bruxelles.

19 Agosin, Manuel R (1995) *Foreign Direct Investment in Latin America,* Inter-American Development Bank, Washington, DC.

20 Colombi, Pedro and Podrez, Javier 'Mercosur Protocols for Foreign Investment Promotion and Protection', in: OECD, *Investment Policies in Latin America and Multilateral Rules on Investment.* OECD, Paris, pp115–125

21 See Howard and Konrad von Moltke (fn 7)

22 For example, GATT 1994 stipulates: '... any advantage, favour, privilege or immunity granted by any contracting party to any product originating in or destined for any other country shall be accorded immediately and unconditionally to the like product originating in or destined for the territories of all other contracting parties'. (art 1.1) and 'The products of the territory of any contracting party imported into the territory of any contracting party shall not be subject, directly or indirectly, to internal taxes or other internal charges in excess of those applied, directly or indirectly, to like domestic products'. (art III.2) See Robert Howse and Donald Regan, 'The Product/Process Distinction – An Illusory Basis for Disciplining Unilateralism in Trade Policy' (January 2000 draft, available at http://www.wto.org)

23 'Environment and Labour in the MAI, Chairman's Proposals – March 1998' (updated 15 May 1998, http://www.oecd.org (25 August 1998)

24 See Mann, Howard and von Moltke, Konrad (fn 7)

25 'The Parties Group shall be assisted by a Secretariat'. (art XI.7)

16

How Intellectual Property Could be a Tool to Protect Traditional Knowlege

David R Downes

Introduction

The knowledge, innovations and practices of indigenous and local communities that are developed and passed on through traditional culture are closely linked to the conservation and sustainable use of biodiversity.[1] This 'traditional knowledge' is a valuable heritage for the communities and cultures that develop and maintain it, as well as for other societies and the world as a whole.[2] Traditional knowledge informs resource management systems and practices of resource use in many indigenous and traditional farming cultures, thus helping to prevent the extensive loss of biodiversity and the decline in biological resources associated with industrial patterns of resource use.[3] Traditional knowledge also comprises extensive familiarity with the practical uses of these resources as sources of medicine, foodstuffs and other goods.[4] As a result, this knowledge is itself a valuable resource not only for these communities but also for outsiders, including academic researchers, government agencies and commercial firms, both foreign and domestic.[5] Traditional knowledge has been used in many industries as a starting point for new product development, in sectors such as specialty food and beverages, pharmaceuticals, agriculture, horticulture, and personal care and cosmetics; and it remains a significant resource for many commercial research and development programs.[6]

Finally, traditional knowledge is important to its holders as an integral part of their cultural heritage, and, in this sense, its protection is important for ensuring the enjoyment of the right to maintain and take part in cultural life, as recognized under international human rights instruments,[7] as well as the emerging right to control and protect this traditional knowledge as a form of intellectual property, as recognized in the UN Draft Declaration on Indigenous Rights.

The value of such traditional knowledge is recognized in the Convention on Biological Diversity (CBD),[8] which has been ratified by over 170 countries. In particular Article 8(j) of the CBD establishes a general requirement that the parties to the Convention respect, preserve, and maintain such traditional knowledge; promote its wider application with the approval and involvement of its holders; and encourage the equitable sharing of the benefits from its use.[9] Governments have broad discretion as to the steps they take to implement this obligation.

Despite such official recognition of its importance, traditional knowledge is being lost at an alarming rate. The continuing loss of biodiversity, biological resources, and habitat erodes the physical matrix for traditional knowledge systems. At the same time, many in indigenous and local communities fear they are losing control of their remaining knowledge to outsiders that are appropriating its benefits. Intellectual property rights (IPRs), as one of the primary mechanisms used by the world's nations to allocate rights over knowledge, play a significant role in the relationship between indigenous and local communities, their knowledge and the other societies with which they interact. Many aspects of IPRs appear to be more or less neutral, but some aspects may, in fact, be contributing to the problem of knowledge loss, while others have the potential to help solve it.

Although IPRs currently provide limited incentives for the development or maintenance of knowledge within communities, some form of IPRs could be a valuable tool for communities to use to control their traditional knowledge and to gain a greater share of the benefits. The utility of IPRs in this respect might be enhanced through national-level modifications to existing IPRs or the creation of new categories of intellectual property rights specifically tailored to traditional knowledge (such new varieties are often referred to as *sui generis* rights). At the international and regional levels, a framework of laws, policies and programmes would be needed to support such modifications and to ensure their effective implementation within a global economy and trading system.

The Introduction to this chapter critiques the polarized international debate over IPRs and traditional knowledge in an effort to clarify the terms of discussion. The following section proposes five ways to explore the potential for using IPRs to help traditional knowledge holders benefit from their knowledge and thereby increase incentives for them to preserve it and the biodiversity to which it is related. Specifically, the next section argues that:

1 The 'life patenting' exception and *sui generis* clause under the Trade-related Aspects of Intellectual Property Rights (TRIPS) Agreement of the World Trade Organization (WTO) should be maintained, if not expanded, in order to make space for the modification or elaboration of rights that benefit indigenous and local communities.
2 The use of geographical indications or trademarks for products of indigenous and local communities' traditional knowledge should be explored.
3 A requirement that patent applicants should disclose elements of traditional knowledge incorporated within the patent, as well as the origin of genetic resources used in the invention, should be considered.
4 Other intellectual property-related concepts from both conventional and indigenous intellectual property systems – such as authors' moral rights – should be evaluated as models for protecting traditional knowledge.
5 Case studies on the impact of IPRs on the control and sharing of benefits from the specific uses of traditional knowledge and associated genetic resources should be analysed in order to identify benefits from traditional knowledge that are not being shared and to design mechanisms for increasing benefit sharing.

A Preliminary Critique of the
Current International Debate

There is a continuing controversy over the impacts of intellectual property systems on the traditional knowledge of indigenous and local communities.[10] Many indigenous peoples, representatives and commentators complain that existing intellectual property systems are inadequate to protect indigenous intellectual and cultural property rights.[11] Other critics argue that the existing systems encourage the erosion of indigenous traditional knowledge. In their view, existing systems, which are oriented around the concept of private ownership and individual invention, are inherently at odds with indigenous cultures, which emphasize collective creation and ownership of knowledge. Indeed, '[t]here is concern that IPR systems encourage the appropriation of [traditional knowledge] for commercial use without the fair sharing of benefits, or that they violate indigenous cultural precepts by encouraging the commodification of such knowledge'.[12]

On the other hand, advocates for conventional intellectual property systems argue that IPRs, as currently defined, create effective incentives for the innovative use of biodiversity, which in turn creates profits on which innovators can draw in negotiating benefit-sharing arrangements with the holders of traditional knowledge and biodiversity.

Discussion of these matters to date has often been hampered by the lack of an adequate base in intellectual property law and the concrete uses of traditional knowledge.[13] This section critiques a few of the many complex issues in this area in the hope of establishing a stronger foundation for future analysis and discussion.

Oversimplification Regarding Traditional Knowledge and Intellectual Property Rights (IPRs)

IPRs such as copyright and patent are legal mechanisms to encourage innovation – the creation and disclosure of new knowledge or new expressions. These rights are granted to a defined individual or group of individuals identified as the inventor or creator, although they can be transferred to another by sale or gift.

Traditional knowledge and practices, in contrast, are often handed down from generation to generation, and have no clearly identifiable individual inventor. Thus, it has been widely stated that IPRs are not suitable for traditional knowledge because they protect new knowledge that is created by individuals and do not recognize collective rights.[14]

The reality is, however, more complicated than these generalizations suggest. First, while it is true that many indigenous cultures appear to develop and transmit knowledge from generation to generation within a communal system, individuals in local or indigenous communities can distinguish themselves as informal creators or inventors, separate from the community.[15] They may be singled out for their efforts and praised as clever or scorned as peculiar.[16] Equally important, some indigenous or traditional societies are reported to recognize various types of intellectual property rights over knowledge, which may be held by individuals, families, lineages or communities.[17] Discussion of IPRs and traditional knowledge should draw more on the 'diversity and creativity of indigenous approaches to IPR issues'.[18] Finally, there are power and knowledge divisions among people in many communities. Thus, the sharing of benefits with a community as a whole is no guarantee that the people who are working to conserve traditional knowledge and associated biodiversity will gain the rewards they deserve for their efforts.

Second, some IPRs – in particular, geographical indications, and in some circumstances, trademarks – are, in fact, intended not to reward innovation, but rather to reward members of an established group or community for adhering to traditional practices of the community or group's culture. They are designed to reward goodwill and reputation created or built up by a group of producers over many years or even centuries. Geographical indications, in particular, could create economic rewards for producers who use traditional methods in the region where the product has been traditionally produced.[19]

Exclusive Focus on Market-based IPRs

IPRs are one of the mechanisms used to maintain the existing systems of knowledge and technology creation that is characteristic of capitalist industrialized societies. Most IPRs are market-oriented mechanisms aimed at ensuring that innovators gain a share of the economic benefits. Patents, for example, are useful only where there is a market for a product subject to the patent or other right, or for the product that is produced by the process subject to the patent. Geographic indicators are useful where consumers are willing to pay a premium on the market for products manufactured in the relevant region according to that region's traditional methods.

Yet there are exceptions to the rule that IPRs are market-based mechanisms. One example is the moral right of authors, which is protected under the law of a number of countries and recognized in international human rights law. Experience with the implementation of this and other non-market-based rights could be useful in developing models for the right to protect traditional knowledge, innovations and practices.[20]

Even more important, market-based mechanisms – whether they consist of IPRs or some other mechanism – are not the only incentives for encouraging the creation or maintenance of knowledge or practices. In fact, some kinds of knowledge, such as most scientific discoveries about qualities or the behaviour of the natural world, are excluded from IPR protection, and their use is kept in the public domain. Although changes are underway, especially in molecular biology and biotechnology, IPRs are not widely used incentives for basic research in most scientific fields.

Incentives other than IPRs that encourage information include recognition through publication, citation, academic tenure, prizes for academic achievement or demonstrations of skill in public competitions and awards of government grants for research.[21] These incentives generally involve competition, but they do not involve direct competition on the market for payment in return for knowledge produced. The history of Western-style science illustrates that these mechanisms have been effective.[22] A heavy emphasis on the role of IPRs in encouraging innovation is characteristic of the policy of industrialized countries, especially the US. In fact, some US trade officials argue that the strongest, broadest protection of IPRs is the best policy for society, without acknowledging the countervailing value of information in the public domain, free of private ownership and available for use by all, including innovators themselves. Thus, a few years ago Carla Hills, then US Trade Representative (USTR), called for the 'complete protection of intellectual property... [T]he higher the protection, the more ... [intellectual property] benefits developing countries.... [T]he more you protect intellectual property, [the more that] established firms are willing to pour more into research and development to try to address mankind's problems ...'.[23]

Despite such rhetoric, there is controversy even within the US over the proposed expansions of IPR advocated by US officials, including trade officials, at the behest of certain industrial sectors. US Administration proposals regarding copyright of digital information, for example, have been criticized as excessively favouring current large-scale owners of copyrights.[24] Similarly, it is argued that the expansion of IPRs to control digital reproduction of information may hinder freedom of speech.[25] At a 1996 World Intellectual Property Organization (WIPO) diplomatic conference in Geneva, the US was forced to abandon its support of a broad *sui generis* IPR for databases after a surge of domestic opposition from a combination of industrial groups, citizens' organizations, scientific researchers and libraries.

Moralistic and Absolute Language For and Against IPRs

Advocates on both sides of this debate have advanced their claims in moralistic terms. Arguably, there is a core of moral value to existing IPR systems. This reflects a widely held notion that a person has a moral right to control the product of his or her labour and creativity.[26]

Yet while intellectual property principles may have a moral core, there is no clear moral basis for the specific forms that IPRs have taken under existing regimes or could take under various proposals. Modern thinking on IPR systems is that they are socially agreed-upon incentives designed to encourage innovation as well as public disclosure of information about those innovations – at least in the case of patents in which the application is published once the patent is issued.[27] The precise outlines of an IPR are defined by striking a balance among various social goals. On one side, a private property right is conferred to reward a specific inventor's or creator's investment in research and development, and to encourage public disclosure of the invention or creative work. On the other hand, the right is limited in duration and subject to exceptions in order to maintain the public domain needed for a free flow of ideas and information for use by all inventors and creators. As one commentator noted, 'intellectual property rights are limited monopolies conferred in order to gain present and future public benefit; for the purpose of achieving those goals, the 'limitations' on the right are just as important as the grant of the right itself'.[28]

For instance, the Agreement on Trade-related Aspects of Intellectual Property Rights (TRIPS Agreement)[29] provides that WTO members must honour patents for a term of at least 20 years. As applied to the diverse economic systems and technological levels of development found in the 130-plus members of the WTO, this term may or may not strike the right balance between competing social goals in every case. It would be absurd to argue that this 20-year limit has a moral basis. No human rights would be violated if a country established a patent term of 18 years rather than 20. The duration of a patent merely reflects a balance between competing social interests, aimed at maximizing social welfare. It is impossible to deduce a single fair and equitable IPR system from the general human rights principles available to us. In sum, while categorical moral claims may be essential to the definition of an intellectual property system's core principles, the precise delineation of the parameters of a given type of intellectual property right should be an instrumentalist or utilitarian exercise.

During the Uruguay Round of negotiations under the General Agreement on Tariffs and Trade (GATT), certain US interests – such as the chemicals, pharmaceuticals and the entertainment industries – persuaded the US government to put IPR protection on the agenda. Initially, the grounds for including IPRs were far from obvious. Intellectual property had previously been considered primarily a domestic policy question to be decided according to a particular country's development needs. Thus, while some of the earliest multilateral agreements in international law concern intellectual property (such as the Paris and Berne Conventions), they imposed only limited uniformity upon countries.

Intellectual property fits awkwardly into the context of trade negotiations. Trade liberalization is about removing barriers to market competition, while intellectual property protections establish private rights to prevent market competition. The US found itself in the perverse position of arguing that the goal of trade liberalization necessitated trade restrictions in the form of import bans on products produced by unlicensed copiers of patented pharmaceuticals or copyrighted sound recordings. To help support this counterintuitive argument, US industry and government officials habitually employed the rhetorical device of branding foreign copiers of US technology as 'pirates'.

The 'piracy' slogan is misleading. Even in the U.S., a bastion of strong intellectual property rights, ordinary people do not consider copying IPR-protected items to be an outrage equivalent to the theft of physical property, let alone the kidnapping and robbery associated with the term 'piracy'.[30] As one well-known US commentator on intellectual property in digital information said, '[w]hen I give speeches [on software copying], I always ask how many people in the audience can honestly claim to have no unauthorized software on their hard disks. I've never seen more than 10 per cent of the hands go up'.[31]

A problematic result of industry efforts is that IPR policy in countries like the US is increasingly driven by trade policy, which seeks to maximize US-based industry's foreign earnings by maximizing its legal control over innovative technologies or entertainment products.[32] Industry rhetoric about piracy led to an understandable counter-attack by advocates for farmers' rights and interests of indigenous peoples and developing countries. They coined the term 'biopiracy' to describe the industrial practice of patenting products based in part upon traditional knowledge or genetic resources contained in traditional varieties, without providing compensation or recognition. These often-witty counter-attacks were useful in denying industry its effort to grab the moral high ground. Catalogues of alleged cases of biopiracy dramatized the importance of contributions of traditional knowledge and informal innovation by indigenous and local communities situated mainly in the developing world.[33]

However, an examination of specific cases in which traditional knowledge is commercialized reveals that it is not always easy to determine exactly the nature and extent of the inequity.[34] Imprecise references to the technical language and concepts of intellectual property law sometimes make it difficult to identify exactly what the practical problems are, and may unnecessarily alienate one interest group or another, such as industry, intellectual property experts, and indigenous and local organizations. These are the very groups that should cooperate, or at least negotiate, in order to define mechanisms for more effective sharing of benefits with the providers of traditional knowledge and genetic resources.

For instance, a patent that is properly granted does not generally cover already-existing knowledge. On the other hand, there are significant exceptions. One exception is that under the 'first-to-file' system that prevails in most of the world, the first inventor to file a patent application may obtain the patent even if another person achieved the invention earlier. Another exception, more relevant for indigenous concerns, is that in researching whether an invention is already part of the 'prior art' (in which case it would not satisfy the novelty requirement of patentability), a patent office does not necessarily perform a thorough survey of foreign literature in which descriptions of traditional knowledge appeared. Finally, a peculiarity of US patent law provides that prior art found outside US territory will be grounds for preventing patenting only where the prior art is embodied in written form. The result is that knowledge held in an oral tradition (as is the case with much traditional knowledge) may be vulnerable to patenting by outsiders.

Recommendations on Using Intellectual Property to Implement Article 8(j) of the Convention on Biological Diversity

Despite the continuing controversy, there are several areas where useful work could be done to enhance the sharing of benefits related to IPRs with indigenous and local communities. These include:

- the preservation of space under the TRIPS Agreement to develop modified or new forms of IPRs for traditional knowledge;
- the exploration of the potential application of certain IPRs to enhance benefit sharing;
- the disclosure of traditional knowledge and genetic resources used in a patented invention;
- the evaluation of non-market-based IPRs, such as authors' moral rights; as models for mechanisms to protect traditional knowledge; and
- carrying out case studies on existing uses of traditional knowledge and on sharing its benefits.

When considering these areas of inquiry, it is important to keep in mind the objectives that advocates for indigenous peoples and farming communities have articulated in this area:

- to ensure that a fair share of the benefits go to indigenous and local communities when others use the knowledge or resources that these communities have conserved, and to ensure that use is subject to the communities' prior informed consent;
- to ensure that the people of indigenous and local communities receive recognition for their contributions to universal knowledge and welfare;
- to help indigenous and local communities develop their own economic uses of their traditional knowledge and associated biological resources, consistent with traditions of sustainable use; and
- to protect the interests of indigenous and local communities with respect to their knowledge, innovations, and practices as defined under 8(j) of the CBD, as part of a broader goal of achieving protection of their cultural heritage.

As argued in the Introduction, moral claims help define core principles of an intellectual property system, but they are of little use in defining the detailed outlines of specific categories of intellectual property rights, which are better defined on an instrumentalist basis in order to maximize the desired combination of social goals. Thus, this chapter seeks to identify intellectual property mechanisms that could help indigenous and local communities to achieve the goals of Article 8(j): to maintain their traditional knowledge and gain a greater share of benefits from traditional knowledge and related biological resources. It does not, however, seek to determine whether such mechanisms would produce 'equitable' benefit sharing.

Indigenous and local communities seeking to use IPRs will likely face substantial practical obstacles. IPR systems generally involve complex procedures and legal concepts which result in the need for expensive legal assistance, as well as repeated communication with national or international government offices. To the extent that new IPR measures are employed to assist communities, financial and technical assistance and streamlined procedures, or other facilitating measures, will be needed. On the other hand, similar obstacles apply to at least some of the alternatives that have been offered, such as public sector funding of projects in indigenous and local communities. These could easily fall prey to the same problems of top-down design, inept grant selection and corruption that have plagued development assistance generally.

Maintain or Expand Life Patenting Exception and *Sui Generis* Clause under the Trade-related Aspects of Intellectual Property Rights (TRIPS) Agreement

Exploring ways for using IPRs to enhance benefits for traditional knowledge holders will require experimentation with variations and additions to the existing intellectual property system. To promote such experimentation, governments should maintain the flexibility provided in the TRIPS Agreement relating to life patenting. In particular, the exception should be maintained under Article 27.3(b) of the TRIPS Agreement which allows countries to exclude plants and animals from patenting and provides for the development of *sui generis* systems for plant variety protection. In fact, it might be useful to consider expanding the exception from patenting to cover micro-organisms. Maintaining this discretion is essential to preserve the flexibility needed to experiment with various approaches to the protection of traditional knowledge, and to allow for further evaluation of other complex ethical and socio-economic issues. In contrast, requiring all countries to recognize uniformly life patenting and mandating uniform systems of plant variety protection would block countries from gaining the experience needed to implement Article 8(j) of the CBD effectively.

As summarized by the CBD Secretariat in the background paper on IPRs for COP III, the TRIPS Agreement's current provisions on patenting: [require] countries to recognize patents on most products and processes, including pharmaceuticals, modified microorganisms, and 'microbiological processes'. (Article 27.3(b)). Furthermore, countries must protect plant varieties either through patents or an 'effective *sui generis* system' or both (ibid). The TRIPS Agreement leaves to each country's discretion whether to recognize patents on plants or animals or 'essentially biological [but not microbiological] processes for the production of plants or animals' (ibid). The provisions of Article 27.3(b) have been pending review since 1999, and will likely be accelerated as part Doha Development Agenda.[35] TRIPS 'provides developing countries with a five-year grace period to phase in most of the Agreement's requirements', while the least-developed countries 'have an eleven-year grace period for implementing most obligations'.[36]

Maintaining flexibility to implement Article 8(j) of the CBD is only one of several rationales for avoiding the expansion of patenting requirements under TRIPS.[37] First, the scope of biotechnology patents in countries with expansive patent coverage is frequently too broad. Such excessive breadth could stifle, rather than stimulate, productive innovation, by requiring future inventors to negotiate expensive licences to a multitude of previously patented research tools and substances needed to take further inventive steps. Concern about overboard patent claims is even growing in the US, a nation with arguably the most expansive patent system.[38] Even US industry groups have opposed some of the farthest extensions of patent rights sought in recent patent applications.[39] This suggests that other nations are well advised to take a 'wait-and-see' approach by which they can learn from the US experience, rather than rushing to adopt a policy whose benefits are unproven.

Second, governments may wish to avoid the expansion of IPRs in order to slow the flow of private investment into biotechnology until they have a proper regulatory framework in place to control its environmental impacts. If investment flows too quickly into this industry, there will be a vested interest against regulation and in favour of externalizing environmental costs. Thus, society as a whole, rather than the producers of biotechnology, will take on the risks. By definition, IPRs are designed to encourage private sector investment in technological development. Hence, avoiding the extension of IPRs to modified organisms remains a reasonable policy choice for countries until an effective bio-safety protocol is negotiated and enters into force, and until national regulations and institutions are in place at the national level.[40] This would be consistent with the CBD's precautionary approach and its requirement that parties protect against environmental impacts of genetically modified organisms and maintain economic incentives for conservation.

Third, governments need to maintain the power to regulate the use of IPRs so as to ensure that rights holders do not abuse their market power through anti-competitive actions. Members of the WTO may wish to define the types of measures needed to control anti-competitive abuses. The over-broad patent claims in biotechnology, and the continued blurring of the lines between invention and discovery in that sector, intensify the risk of anti-competitive effects. Until there is more clarity, a country would be acting reasonably by avoiding the extension of patenting to cover modified organisms. Fourth, while major trading nations are still applying unilateral pressure to force trading partners not only to meet TRIPS standards but to go beyond them, discussion of raising TRIPS standards would be inappropriate. This is a serious problem that disturbs the balance of trade-offs which persuaded developing countries to sign the Uruguay Round agreements. For instance, the US has threatened Argentina with trade sanctions on the grounds that Argentina's protection of IPRs is not strong enough. Yet some of the US demands would arguably have forced Argentina to implement stronger IPR protections than TRIPS requires. For example, the US complained that Argentina's new patent law delayed extension of patents to pharmaceuticals until the year 2000, even though developing countries do not have to phase-in patent protection of new product types under TRIPS until a total of ten years after TRIPS enters into force, well after 2000.

Finally, life patenting raises a number of other environmental, social and economic issues,[41] as well as significant ethical issues, for a range of people in different countries. Further public consideration is needed of the complex issues before the WTO adopts a blanket rule.

Explore the Development of Geographical Indications or Trademarks for Products of Indigenous and Local Communities' Traditional Knowledge

Geographical indications and trademarks, or *sui generis* analogies to them, could be valuable tools for indigenous and local communities seeking to gain economic benefits from their traditional knowledge or to prevent its objectionable commercial use by outsiders. To date, debate on IPRs and biodiversity has focused on patents and on plant breeders' rights. The potential value of geographical indications and trademarks warrants greater attention.[42] Trademarks are protected under the TRIPS Agreement, and may prove to be a useful tool for indigenous and local communities. A trademark is defined under TRIPS as '[a]ny sign, or any combination of signs, capable of distinguishing the goods or services of one undertaking from those of other undertakings ...'[43] WTO members are expected to provide for registration of trademarks. Where confusion is likely, the owner of a registered trademark has the exclusive right to prevent third parties from using similar signs for identical or similar goods. Indicators of geographic origin are especially suitable for use by indigenous and local communities since they are based on collective traditions and a collective decision-making process; they protect and reward traditions while allowing evolution; they emphasize the relationships between human cultures and their local land and environment; they are not freely transferable from one owner to another; and they can be maintained as long as the collective tradition is maintained.

Geographical indications are defined under the TRIPS Agreement as 'indications which identify a good – as originating in the territory of a [WTO] Member, or a region or locality in that territory, where a given quality, reputation or other characteristic of the good is essentially attributable to its geographical origin'.[44] WTO members must prohibit registration of trademarks that are misleading as to geographic origin. They must also provide legal procedures for interested parties to prevent competitors from placing designations on their products that mislead the public about their geographic origin.[45]

The TRIPS Agreement provides for additional protection of geographical indications for wine and spirits.[46] The obligations regarding geographical indications, however, are subject to a number of exceptions that may render them less effective as a means of protecting traditional knowledge.[47] The prime example of a system of geographic indications is found in France, where local products (*produits de terroir*) 'occupy a special niche in the present agricultural and foodstuffs sector of southern Europe,'[48] including France, Spain, Italy and Portugal. These products derive their value from a combination of environmental factors and cultural factors, in particular the traditional, collectively maintained techniques for production. France's Appellations d'Origine Contrôlée (AOC) is an especially comprehensive system of geographical indications for assuring the authenticity of such products. There are systems of AOCs for wines, cheeses and spirits,[49] as well as for some other products, such as walnuts and poultry.

The relevant law provides that 'the geographic name that constitutes the appellation of origin or any other similar name may not be used for any similar product... or for any other product or service as long as such a use is capable of altering or weakening the distinctiveness of the appellation of origin'.[50] While these controls are enforced at the national level – and to a lesser extent internationally through TRIPS – the regional producers themselves establish the rules of production through collective bodies that they control. While the production methods can evolve over time, there is a strong emphasis on tradition, with roots that are often centuries old.[51] One example of indigenous peoples' use of identification of origin as a tool to protect cultural forms and their use comes from the southwestern region of the US. There, artisans of several Native American tribes earn as much as US$800 million annually from commercial sales of arts and crafts. For instance, the distinctive styles of Pueblo pottery, silver jewellery and other items such as drums are well known. Styles and designs are considered a cultural heritage; in Zuni, a design may be the property of a certain family and no person outside that family has the right to use it. These indigenous communities were concerned that non-indigenous producers were using inauthentic methods to produce similar products that they passed off as indigenous traditional goods. In response, the state of New Mexico enacted the Indian Arts and Crafts Protection Law. The law places a duty on retailers of native arts and crafts to investigate whether goods are produced by indigenous persons by hand using natural materials. Only if a good passes this test can it be labelled as 'an authentic, Indian, hand-made piece'. Controversy continues because the law does not address whether goods are produced by traditional methods. Although this example is unrelated to biodiversity, it offers significant lessons for indigenous control of traditional knowledge.[52] Through such mechanisms, there may be opportunities to gain benefits from products of biological resources produced through traditional methods or based on traditional knowledge.[53]

As mentioned earlier, the TRIPS Agreement requires WTO members to provide for protection of geographical indications and trademarks. The creation of systems of geographical indications or the support of community efforts to use trademarks could bring economic rewards to communities seeking to market products based upon sustainable, traditional production practices. Geographical indications and trademarks benefit consumers by providing them with reliable information and assurances of authenticity.[54] They also respond to certain indigenous concerns more effectively than do other IPRs. In particular, rights to control trademarks and geographical indications can be maintained in perpetuity, and they do not confer a monopoly right over the use of certain information, but simply limit the class of people who can use a specific symbol. As noted above, geographical indications are different from patents and copyrights in that they are not specifically designed to reward innovation. Rather, they reward producers that are situated in a certain region and that follow production practices associated with that region and its culture and customs.

They are designed to reward goodwill and reputation created or built up by a group of producers over many years, and in some cases over centuries. In this sense, they can operate to maintain traditional knowledge and practices.

Geographical indications also lend themselves better to communal organization than do other IPRs. A producer qualifies to use a geographical indication according to its location and method of production. It is immaterial whether the producer is an individual, family, partnership, corporation, voluntary association or municipal corporation. Typically, the producers based in the relevant region work cooperatively to establish, maintain and enforce guidelines for production of the good, subject to the geographical indication.[55]

Geographical indications also accord with the emphasis that indigenous communities typically place upon their traditional ways of life, including their relationship with their ancestral lands, waters, and living ecosystems. As one expert on the French system of appellations of origin has explained:

An appellation of origin goes much further than a simple indication of... where a product is obtained or produced. [It also refers to] the further effects wrought upon a product by natural factors specific to the locality[,] such as micro-climate, soil formation, and so on[,] and also by specific human factors that pertain to the product[,] such as vinification procedure, pruning methods, maturation, and so on. The notion involves the interaction between these natural and human factors, specific and peculiar to the locality, which produces the distinctive quality or character of [that region's] product.[56] As a general matter, it has been argued that developing countries may find it in their interest to use geographical indications as a tool to help create and maintain both domestic and export markets for distinctive goods originating in their territory.[57] In fact, some developing countries are advocating stronger protection of geographical indications in current talks in the TRIPS Council.[58]

While geographical indications are categorized as a type of intellectual property under the TRIPS Agreement, they are more responsive to certain indigenous concerns than are patents, trademarks, and copyrights. Many indigenous representatives emphasize that their cultural heritage is 'inalienable', not to be freely bought or sold. Similarly, a geographical indication such as an AOC is not freely transferable. For instance, if an owner of a vineyard and winery qualified to use an AOC for the Medoc region of Bordeaux sells the business and land to another, the buyer will not be allowed to use the AOC without maintaining the required practices. The AOC can never be transferred outside the Medoc region. In addition, a producer that qualifies for an AOC does not thereby gain an unmitigated right to use it indefinitely. If the producer's practices fall below the defined standards, it may lose the right to use the certification mark.[59]

An initial practical step for interested indigenous and local representatives would be to survey industry and consumer groups regarding market demand for various types of indigenous products from different regions. An essential criterion for the utility of a geographical indication or trademark for a product is whether there is a significant market for that product. Also relevant is the degree of the threat of unauthorized imitations. The control of marks can be useful not only where the community seeks to market its products and deter unfair competition, but also where the community opposes commercialization of its culture and seeks to block the marketing of unauthorized products.

Another initial step could be to bring together representatives of communities whose products have significant market potential (identified through the survey above) with experts from (1) some of the principal national or regional systems of geographical indications, and (2) some of the indigenous systems for controlling marks, to indicate the authenticity of indigenous goods produced by traditional methods. Through a workshop or conference, these groups could collaborate to identify principles for systems for using geographical indications that are workable for indigenous and local communities. They could also explore the kinds of regional or international structures that may be needed to support such systems, keeping in mind models or options such as the Lisbon Agreement for the Protection of Appellations of Origin[60] or the talks underway in the TRIPS Council regarding a system within the WTO for international registration.

Consider Requiring Patent Applicants to Disclose Traditional Knowledge and Origin of Genetic Resources Used in the Invention

A number of commentators have proposed requiring or encouraging the disclosure in patent applications of the country and community of origin for genetic resources and of the informal knowledge used to develop the invention.[61] These disclosures might also include 'the certification of prior approval of the use by the source country or community'.[62] While disclosure of genetic resources goes to Article 15 of the CBD,[63] many plant genetic resources are developed through manipulation, experimentation and conservation by indigenous or local communities over many generations. Thus, they in fact embody 'knowledge, innovations and practices' of these communities and warrant protection under Article 8(j). In support of the view that such a disclosure requirement is feasible:

[t]here is evidence suggesting that such a step would in large part involve simply regularizing a practice that is already common in filing patent applications. One recent study reviewed over five hundred patent applications in which the invention involved the use of biological materials, such as materials derived from plants or animals; most were in the pharmaceutical field, with some in other fields such as cosmetics and pesticides. The applications reviewed came from a number of jurisdictions, including France, Germany, UK, Spain, the USA, and the European Patent Office. Of the applications involving plants, the country of origin was invariably mentioned unless the plant was widely distributed or well known (such as the lemon or rosemary). A number of applications also mentioned indigenous or traditional uses as prior art.[64]

Nevertheless, the proposal requires further study before it can be implemented.[65] In particular, key terms such as 'indigenous' and 'local communities' must be more clearly defined.[66] There have been proposals that the requirement of disclosure might be enforced by making it a condition of approval of an application and providing for the revocation of a patent where a disclosure was shown to be fraudulent. Such strong enforcement measures would necessitate a clear definition of key terms.

The patent disclosure issue should be addressed within the TRIPS Council, as the protection of traditional knowledge and genetic resources rights must be integrated with trade regulations, and especially with the implementation of the TRIPS Agreement, to be effective.[67] Eventually, the TRIPS Council should consider whether to incorporate the patent disclosure concept into an interpretation or amendment of the Agreement to be recommended to the WTO Governing Council. The World Intellectual Property Organization (WIPO) and the CBD Secretariat should be involved in the development of specific options, as well as in a cost-benefit analysis of requiring patent applicants to disclose the country and community of origin of genetic resources and the traditional knowledge used to develop an invention. The study should also consider how to define more clearly the role of traditional knowledge as prior art, in the light of cases such as the recently revoked US patent on turmeric.[68] It would be useful to review the extent to which the proposal might be implemented by a clarification or amendment of the requirements for explanation of 'background art' in patent applications under the European Patent Convention. The study should involve consultation with interested parties, and with indigenous peoples in particular.

Authors' Moral Rights and Other Models for Protecting Traditional Knowledge

One intellectual property concept that has received surprisingly little attention to date in the debate on traditional knowledge and intellectual property is the so-called authors' moral right, which is the right to be acknowledged as the source of a work and to protect its integrity. This right is recognized under the Berne Convention for the Protection of Literary and Artistic Works.[69] This concept could be a model for IPR measures that would enable communities to require recognition of the contribution of their traditional knowledge and associated resources to inventions and scientific research.[70] It has the particular attraction of being designed to protect non-market values'.

Related concepts are found in the UNESCO/WIPO Model Provisions for National Laws on the Protection of Expressions of Folklore Against Illicit Exploitation and Other Prejudicial Actions.[71] In addition, the concept that 'defensive publication' of inventions could reduce the risk of monopoly control over plant genetic resources has been mentioned as deserving consideration in the analogous area of traditional knowledge.[72]

Conduct Case Studies on the Impact of IPRs on the Control and Sharing of Benefits from Specific Uses of Traditional Knowledge and Associated Genetic Resources

Discussions of the impact of IPRs on the sharing of benefits from the commercial use of traditional knowledge and associated genetic resources could benefit from more fact-based analyses of specific cases. Intensive studies of specific cases would help parties and stakeholders to identify more precisely the actual role of IPRs. Thus, in Decision III/17, the Conference of Parties encouraged:

> [g]overnments, and relevant international and regional organizations, to conduct and communicate to the Executive Secretary, for dissemination through means such as the clearing-house mechanism, case studies of the impacts of intellectual property rights on the achievement of the Convention's objectives, including relationships between intellectual property rights and the knowledge, practices and innovations of indigenous and local communities embodying traditional lifestyles relevant for the conservation of biological diversity.[73]

These studies should be carried out in consultation with stakeholders, and, in particular, with indigenous peoples. They should also draw on relevant expertise, including intellectual property law and scientific disciplines.

What creates the inequity in the use of traditional knowledge of indigenous and local communities in developing patented inventions? This question is best answered through an analysis of case studies. First, cases will reveal specific instances of misappropriation or questionable distribution of benefits. While analysis may reveal that broad assertions (such as the notion that the neem tree[74] has been patented) are inaccurate, a finer-grained review may well reveal specific problems. The reported European Patent Office revocation of a particular neem-related patent and the US Patent and Trademark Office's (PTO's) revocation of a patent on the use of turmeric to heal wounds are two examples of the success of such an approach.[75]

Second, according to the value systems of many indigenous cultures, the use of traditional knowledge for private monetary gain is inherently objectionable. For example, knowledge of medicinal plants may be considered a sacred gift, which might be shared freely with the world, but which should not be exclusively controlled for sale at a profit. In contrast, today's increasingly privatized economies rely on a different theory. They tend to look to the public sector for basic research, and then seek to create incentives – principally IPRs – for the private sector to develop basic research findings into useful products for which consumers will pay. It remains to be seen whether this is the best strategy for maximizing public welfare over the long term in key sectors like agriculture, medicine and food. Third, while IPR systems may treat indigenous and Western knowledge alike in most cases, the systems operate as a whole to discriminate in effect against holders of informal knowledge as a group. For example, such knowledge holders or creators have limited access to the legal and technical expertise needed to navigate the patent system. Consistent with this limited access, corporations or individuals from developed countries own the large majority of patents worldwide. Developing countries account for only a small fraction of patents issued, and inhabitants of rural communities, especially indigenous peoples, are generally the least advantaged social groups in developing countries. As a result, industrial patents on products derived from traditional knowledge often pit a highly privileged group against one of the least privileged. Each of the following three case studies illustrates at least one of these themes.

Example 1: The Turmeric Patent
Turmeric is a spice long used in India as a flavouring and colourant in food, as well as an ingredient in medicines and cosmetics. It is derived from the root of *Curcuma longa*, a plant in the same family (Zingiberaceae) to which ginger belongs. It has a long history of uses in traditional medicine in many regions, including India.[76]

In 1995, the US Patent and Trademark Office (PTO) granted Patent No. 5,401.504 for the use of powdered turmeric to speed the healing of wounds. The patent was assigned to the University of Mississippi Medical Center. The Council of Scientific and Industrial Research (CIR) of India filed a challenge to the patent in October 1996. The CIR argued that the patent failed the legal requirement of novelty because the use of turmeric to heal wounds was a part of the prior art. CIR presented publications from India indicating that turmeric was a well-known folk remedy in India. In August 1997, the US Patent and Trademark Office rejected the patent, finding that it constituted prior art as represented by the Indian scientific publications. This case demonstrates the importance of documenting traditional knowledge, although access to the information must be structured in a way that ensures benefit sharing. The doctrine of 'prior art,' and the practice of reviewing it, should be adjusted to reduce the chance of success for non-novel patents like those involving turmeric.[77]

Example 2: The Ayahuasca Patent[78]
For centuries, shamans of indigenous tribes throughout the Amazon Basin have processed the bark of *Banisteriopsis caapi*, along with other rainforest plants, to produce a ceremonial drink known as 'ayahuasca' or 'yage'. The shamans use ayahuasca in religious and healing ceremonies to diagnose and treat illnesses, meet with spirits and divine the future. According to tradition, ayahuasca – which means 'vine of the soul' in the Quechua language – is prepared and administered only under the guidance of a shaman. Indigenous peoples have characterized the ayahuasca vine as a religious and cultural symbol analogous to the Christian cross or Eucharist.

On 17 June 1986, Loren S Miller, a US citizen, obtained US Plant Patent No. 5.751.[79] The patent granted Miller rights over a purported variety of *Banisteriopsis caapi*, which he dubbed 'Da Vine'. The patent was granted on the basis of Miller's claim that Da Vine represented a new and unique variety of *B caapi*. Miller stated in his patent application that he had obtained a cutting of the plant from a 'domestic garden in the Amazon rainforest of South America'.[80] Indigenous leaders of the Amazon learned of the patent in the mid-1990s and objected to it on the grounds that it enabled a private citizen to appropriate a plant that belongs to the sacred traditions of many indigenous peoples of the Amazon. In March 1999, the Center for International Environmental Law (CIEL) filed a request for re-examination of the patent with the US PTO on behalf of the Coordinating Body of Indigenous Organizations of the Amazon Basin (COICA) and the Coalition for Amazonian Peoples and their Environment (Amazon Coalition).[81]

At the same time, CIEL, COICA, and the Amazon Coalition asked the PTO to carry out a broader review of the impacts of its policies and procedures on traditional knowledge. In August 1999, the three groups filed detailed recommendations for changes to PTO procedures on prior art that would better protect traditional knowledge.[82]

In November 1999, the PTO issued a decision rejecting the patent claim. The PTO accepted the petitioners' arguments that the claimed plant variety was not distinctive or novel, but did not acknowledge the argument that the plant's religious value warranted an exception from patenting.[83] If the patent owner is unable to present evidence refuting the PTO's ruling, then the patent will be cancelled.

Example 3: Patents and the Neem Tree

For hundreds of years, rural people in India have used parts of the neem tree for a variety of uses ranging from toothpaste to pesticides. A number of corporations, both Indian and foreign, have taken patents on inventions employing materials derived from the neem tree in uses that often relate to traditional uses of neem.[84] For instance, a US company, WR Grace, has patented a number of inventions relating to the neem tree. One patent taken out by Grace in the US in 1990 covered a technique for improving the storage stability of neem seed extracts containing azadirachtin.[85] Another patent obtained by Grace in 1994 covered a storage-stable insecticidal composition including a neem seed that had increased stability.[86] The heightened stability of this preparation over traditional neem preparations presumably makes it more convenient for commercial distribution as well as on-farm use. Many of these patented inventions are different from traditional uses of neem. They apply only to the specified inventions, without interfering with Indian farmers' traditional practices. Contrary to some public declarations, there is no patent on the neem tree.[87] The 'seed itself – being a product of nature – is not patentable unless considerably modified'.[88] While the holders of a number of patents relating to neem drew on knowledge of traditional practices in India, the inventor in each case probably made use of many Western practices that are in the public domain, such as techniques for chemical analysis and the preparation of suspensions. The inventor most likely used these practices either because their patents had already expired or because they involved scientific knowledge that was not patentable. In other words, traditional and Western technologies in the public domain were exploited equally, without compensating the originators or their descendants.

However, it is possible that some of the patents were not novel because they not only drew upon, but consisted of, traditional knowledge. The range of neem-related patents should be examined and compared. As the turmeric example indicates, some of them may constitute prior art in the form of traditional knowledge, which should not have been patented. Indeed, the European Patent Office has reportedly disallowed one patent held by WR Grace on this ground.[89]

Conclusion

The implications of conventional intellectual property systems for traditional knowledge and biodiversity have been the subject of a polarized international debate. This chapter has sought to suggest some options by which indigenous peoples might work within the system, modify it, or adapt it so as to protect their knowledge and gain more benefits from its use. One option involves the possible use of geographical indications and trademarks to create market incentives for local and indigenous communities to produce traditional products based on their knowledge of sustainable uses of biological resources. Another involves the possible creation of non-market rights for indigenous and local communities to protect their traditional knowledge, looking to a precedent in the European concept of the author's moral rights. The chapter argues in favour of maintaining the flexibility found in the WTO's Agreement on Trade-related Aspects of Intellectual Property Rights, so that developing countries belonging to the WTO have the freedom to adopt intellectual property systems suited to the cultural and developmental needs of the indigenous and local communities within their borders. Finally, the chapter suggests some modifications or exceptions to patent rights that could respond to concerns of developing countries and indigenous groups about encroachment on their biological and cultural heritage.

In an economy that is increasingly global and knowledge-based, intellectual property regimes must adapt in response to the concerns of diverse and far-flung constituencies. To ensure that these regimes are effective and have legitimacy, intellectual property policy-makers should work with these constituencies to explore practical options like the ones discussed here.

Notes

1   The 1992 Convention on Biological Diversity defines biodiversity as 'the variability among living organisms from all sources, including, inter alia, terrestrial, marine and other aquatic ecosystems and the ecological complexes of which they are part; this includes diversity within species, between species and of ecosystems'. UN Conference on Environment and Development: Convention on Biological Diversity, 31 ILM 818 (1992), at art 2. This definition encompasses the diversity of life forms found in all of nature, as well as the genetic diversity of varieties and breeds of domesticated plants and animals. The Con-

vention recognizes biodiversity's role in 'maintaining life sustaining systems of the biosphere' and in 'meeting the food, health and other needs of the growing world population'. See ibid at Preamble.

2 Consistent with widespread usage, this article uses the abbreviated term 'traditional knowledge' to refer to the subject-matter of Article 8(j) of the Convention on Biological Diversity – ie 'knowledge, innovations and practices of indigenous and local communities embodying traditional lifestyles relevant for the conservation and sustainable use of biological diversity'. While 'traditional knowledge' is a convenient shorthand to refer to the complex of ideas embraced by Article 8(j), it is important to remember that indigenous knowledge systems do not just conserve knowledge but also innovate; they are evolving and dynamic, rather than static

3 See, eg Oldfield, M L and J B Alcom (1991) 'Conservation of Traditional Agroecosystems', in Oldfield, M L and Alcom, J B (eds) *Biodiversity: Culture, Conservation and Ecodevelopment*, Westview Press, pp37–58; Gary Nabhan (1989) *Enduring Seeds: Native American Agriculture and Wild Plant Conservation*, North Point Press (1989).

4 See Brush, Stephen B (1996) 'Whose Knowledge, Whose Genes, Whose Rights?' in Stephen B Brush and Doreen Stabinsky (eds) *Valuing Local Knowledge: Indigenous People and Intellectual Property Rights*, pp1–10

5 See, eg, Reid, Walter V et al(1993) 'A New Lease on Life', in Reid, Walter V et al (eds), *Biodiversity Prospecting: Using Genetic Resources for Sustainable Development*, pp1–52; Mark J Plotkin 'The Outlook for New Agricultural and Industrial Products from the Tropics', in *Biodiversity*, pp106–116

6 For a comprehensive survey of the range of products and sectors for which biodiversity is an important resource, see Kerry ten Kate and Sarah A Laird (1999) *The Commercial Use of Biodiversity*, Earthscan Publications (1999).

7 See, eg Article 27 of the Universal Declaration of Human Rights, GA res 217A (III), UN Doc A/810 p71 (1948); Article 15 of the International Covenant on Economic, Social and Cultural Rights, GA res 2200A (XXI), 21 UN GAOR Supp (No 16), p49, UN Doc A/6316 (1966), 993 UNTS3, entered into force 3 January 1976

8 UN Conference on Environment and Development: Convention on Biological Diversity, 31 ILM 818 (1992), available at http://www.biodiv.org (visited 1 April 2000)

9 Paragraph (j) of Article 8, *supra* note 2, provides that '[e]ach Contracting Party shall, as far as possible and as appropriate: (j) Subject to its national legislation, respect, preserve and maintain knowledge, innovations and practices of indigenous and local communities embodying traditional lifestyles relevant for the conservation and sustainable use of biological diversity and promote their wider application with the approval and involvement of the holders of such knowledge, innovations and practices and encourage the equitable sharing of the benefits arising from the utilization of such knowledge, innovations and practices'.

10 See United Nations Environment Programme, Convention on Biological Diversity, Conference of the Parties, The Impact of Intellectual Property Rights Systems on the Conservation and Sustainable Use of Biological Diversity and

on the Equitable Sharing of Benefits From Its Use: A Preliminary Study: note by Executive Secretary, pp32–33, UN Doc No UNEP/CBD/COP/3/22 (1996) [hereinafter The Impact of Intellectual Property Rights Systems], available at http://www.biodiv.org/cop3/index.html (visited 10 April 2000)

11 See, eg Mataatua Declaration on Cultural and Intellectual Property Rights of Indigenous Peoples (Commission on Human Rights, Sub-Commission on Prevention of Discrimination and Protection of Minorities, Working Group on Indigenous Populations, Geneva), Doc No E/CN.4/Sub.2/AC.4/1993/CRP.5

12 The Impact of Intellectual Property Rights Systems, *supra* note 10, p32

13 As the CBD Secretariat has noted, '[i]t appears ... that there has been little objective analysis of specific instances involving actual or potential impacts of IPR on the traditional knowledge or practices of indigenous or local communities'. Ibid, p34

14 See, eg Axt, Josephine et al (1993) *Biotechnology, Indigenous Peoples, and Intellectual Property Rights*, Washington, DC: Congressional Research Service, 58

15 See Gupta, Anil 'Building upon What the Poor Are Rich in: Honey Bee Network Linking Grassroots Innovations, Enterprise, Investments and Institutions', http://csf.Colorado.edu/sristi/papers/building.html (visited 10 April 2000)

16 Interview with Anil Gupta, Professor at the Indian Institute of Management and Coordinator of the Society for Research and Initiatives for Sustainable Technologies and Institutions (SRISTI), in Ahmedhabad, India (1 February 1999)

17 See Cleveland, David A and Murray, Stephen C (1997) 'The World's Crop Genetic Resources and the Rights of Indigenous Farmers', *Current Anthropology*, No 38, pp477,483–485

18 Downes, David R (1997) Comments on Rights of Indigenous Farmers in Crop Genetic Resources, *Current Anthropology*, No 38, pp498,499

19 See discussion *infra* Part III.B.

20 See discussion *infra* Part III.D.

21 See, eg Gupta, Anil 'Accessing biological diversity and associative knowledge system: can ethics influence equity?', (1995), available at http://csf.Colorado.edu/sristi/papers/equity.html (visited 9 April 2000)

22 See Brush, Stephen B (1996) 'Is Common Heritage Outmoded?', in Stephen B Brush and Doreen Stabinsky (eds) *Valuing Local Knowledge: Indigenous People and Intellectual Property Rights*, pp143–164. It will be important to explore non-market alternatives to IPR, such as scholarly standards for citation to information from people in indigenous and local communities. They are, however, beyond the scope of this chapter

23 Boyle, James (1996) *Shamans, Software, and Spleens: Law and the Construction of the Information Society*, p124

24 See Litman, Jessica (1996) 'Revising Copyright Law for the Information Age', *Oregon Law Review*, No 75, pp19, 47

25 Barlow, John Perry (1994) 'The Economy of Ideas: A framework for rethinking patents and copyrights in the Digital Age (Everything you know about intellectual property is wrong)', *Wired*, No 2

26 Thus, the United Nations Universal Declaration of Human Rights provides that '[e]veryone has the right to the protection of the moral and material interests

resulting from any scientific, literary or artistic production of which he is the author'. Universal Declaration of Human Rights, adopted 10 December 1948, GA res 217A (III), UN Doc No A/810, p27 (1948).

27 See Blakeney, Michael (1996) 'Trade-related Aspects of Intellectual Property Rights: A Concise Guide to the TRIPS Agreement', pp151–152 (1996)

28 Boyle, *supra* note 23, p138

29 Agreement on Trade-Related Aspects of Intellectual Property Rights, 15 April 1994, 33 ILM p81 (1994) [hereinafter TRIPS], available at http://www.wto.org/wto/legal/finalact.htm#GATT94 (visited 3 April 2000)

30 Boyle, *supra* note 23, p124. This social consensus is reflected in the law. For example, an inventor owns a patent for only twenty years, while an owner of physical property typically holds legal rights for a lifetime and has the right to designate an heir

31 Barlow, *supra* note 25

32 See Jaszi, Peter (1996) 'Caught in the Net of Copyright', *Oregon Law Review*, No 75, p299 (1996)

33 See, eg Rural Advancement Foundation International (RAFI), 1996 Biopiracy update: Bolivian Quinoa Claimed in US Patents Communiqué Updates, in RAFI Communiqué (30 December 1996), http://www.rafi.org/web/allpub-display.shtml?pfl=com-list-all.param (visited 13 April 2000); see also Rural Advancement Foundation International, Conserving Indigenous Knowledge: Integrating two systems of innovation (1994)

34 See *infra*, Part III.E

35 United Nations Environment Programme, The Convention on Biological Diversity and the Agreement on Trade-related Aspects of Intellectual Property Rights (TRIPS): Relationships and Synergies, Conference of the Parties to the Convention on Biological Diversity [hereinafter: Relationships and Synergies], 3rd Meeting, p26, UN Doc UNEP/CBD/COP/3/23 (5 October 1996), http://www.biodiv.org/cops3/index.html (visited 10 April 2000)

36 TRIPS, *supra* note 29, art 65.2, 66

37 For further discussion of public interest concerns regarding TRIPS, see David Downes and Matthew Stilwell, 'The 1999 WTO Review of Life Patenting Under TRIPS', revised Discussion Paper (November 1998), http://www.ciel.org/pubbaw.html (visited 10 April 2000)

38 See, eg Rebecca S Eisenberg, 'Genes, Patents, and Product Development', *Science*, No 257, p903 (1992); see also Rebecca S Eisenberg, 'Technology Transfer and the Genome Project: Problems with Patenting Research Tools', 5 *Risk: Health, Safety and Environment*, 163 (1994)

39 Eisenberg, Rebecca S (1992) 'Genes, Patents, and Product Development', *Science*, No 257, p903 (1992)

40 The effectiveness of such an indirect measure to reduce domestic investment may be limited in a global economy. A country's trading partners may choose to encourage greater investment in biotechnology and trade rules could place limits on the country's power to limit imported biotechnology products, although the recently concluded protocol to the CBD on biosafety should help to establish some minimum safety standards

41 See 'The Impact of Intellectual Property Rights Systems', *supra* note 10
42 Graham Dutfield, 'Can the TRIPS Agreement Protect Biological and Cultural Diversity?', pp20–23 (Biopolicy International Series, No 19, 1997)
43 TRIPS, *supra* note 29, art 22
44 Ibid art 22
45 Ibid art 23
46 Ibid art 24
47 Ibid art 15
48 See Berard, L and Marchenay, P (1996) 'Tradition, Regulation, and Intellectual Property: Local Agricultural Products and Foodstuffs in France' [hereinafter 'Tradition, Regulation, and Intellectual Property'], in Brush, Stephen B and Stabinsky, Doreen (eds) *Valuing Local Knowledge*, Island Press, pp230, 238
49 There are over 400 AOC designations for wines and 32 for cheeses. See ibid, pp230, 238
50 Louis Lorvellec (1996) 'You've Got to Fight for Your Right to Party: A Response to Professor Jim Chen', *Minnesota Journal of Global Trade*, No 5, pp65, 68, quoting Code de la Consommation, art L. 115-5, para 4
51 'Tradition, Regulation, and Intellectual Property', *supra* note 48
52 See Pinel, Sandra L and J Evans, Michael (1994) 'Tribal Sovereignty and the Control of Knowledge', in Tom Greaves (ed) *Intellectual Property Rights for Indigenous Peoples: A Source Book*
53 For a preliminary review of the potential in cases of products such as kava and basmati, see David R Downes and Sarah A Laird (1999) 'Innovative Mechanisms for Sharing Benefits of Biodiversity and Related Knowledge: Case Studies on Geographical Indications and Trademarks', http://www.ciel.org/pubbaw.html (visited 1 April 2000)
54 See Paul J Heald (1996) 'Trademarks and Geographical Indications: Exploring the Contours of the TRIPS Agreement', *Vanderbilt Journal of Transnational Law*, No 29 pp635, 655
55 'Tradition, Regulation, and Intellectual Property', *supra* note 48
56 Ralph S Brown (1994) 'New Wine in Old Bottles: The Protection of France's Wine Classification System Beyond Its Borders', 12 *Boston University International Law Journal*, pp472–473, quoting affidavit of Jerome Marie Patrick Louis Agostini, p6, as noted in Institut National des Appellations D'Origine v Vintners International Co, 958 F.2d 1574 (Fed Cir 1992)
57 Ibid, p471
58 See WTO, 'What's New: INTELLECTUAL PROPERTY: Council debates call to expand geographical indications protection', (28 March 2000), http://www.wto.org/wto/new/whatsnew.htm (describing call for expansion to other products of the higher level of protection currently given to geographical indications for wines and spirits, supported by countries such as Turkey, India, Pakistan, Mauritius, Sri Lanka, Egypt, and Cuba)
59 See Lorvellec, *supra* note 50, p65
60 Lisbon Agreement for the Protection of Appellations of Origin and their International Registration of 31 October 1958 (as revised at Stockholm on 14 July 1967 and as amended on 28 September 1979), WIPO Publication: No 264(E),

http://www.wipo.org/eng/main.htm (under Documents, Texts of WIPO-Administered treaties, Lisbon agreement) (visited 13 April 2000)

61 See Hendrickx, F et al (1994) 'Access to Genetic Resources: A Legal Analysis', in V Sanchez and C Juma (eds) *Biodiplomacy: Genetic Resources and International Relations*; M A Gollin (1993) 'An Intellectual Property Rights Framework for Biodiversity Prospecting', in W V Reid et al (eds) *Biodiversity Prospecting: Using Genetic Resources for Sustainable Development*. A detailed proposal can be found in Farhana Yamin (1995) *The Biodiversity Convention and Intellectual Property Rights*, Foundation for International Environmental Law and Development

62 'Relationships and Synergies', *supra* note 35; Hendrickx et al, *supra* note 61; see also Brendan Tobin (1997) *Protecting Collective Property Rights in Peru: The search for an interim solution*

63 A related proposal was advanced in July 1997 by the European Parliament, which amended a proposed directive on biotechnology inventions to require that applications for patents based upon material of human, plant or animal origin must state that the materials were obtained in a manner consistent with the laws of the country of origin and, for human materials, with the consent of the person from whom they were taken. This amendment was, however, rejected by the European Commission on the ground that it exceeded the European Union's obligations under the CBD

64 'Relationships and Synergies', *supra* note 35, Annex I

65 There should also be study of the relationship of such a disclosure requirement with the TRIPS Agreement. Article 29, 'Conditions on Patent Applicants', states that members 'shall' require that applicants disclose 'the invention in a manner sufficiently clear and complete for the invention to be carried out by a person skilled in the art'. TRIPS, *supra* note 29. Members also 'may' require disclosure of the best mode for carrying out the invention and information regarding foreign applications. Ibid.

66 For instance, are only local communities in developing countries covered? What about traditional knowledge that remains in regions of developed countries or countries with economies in transition from socialist to market systems?

67 See Thomas Cottier (1996) 'The New Global Technology Regime: The Impact of New Technologies on Multilateral Trade Regulation and Governance', *Chicago-Kent Law Review*, No 72, p415

68 See *infra*, Part III.E.1

69 The Berne Convention was established on 9 September 1886, entered into force on 5 December 1887 and is codified at 331 UNTS, p217

70 Cf Cathryn Berryman (1994), 'Toward More Universal Protection of Intangible Cultural Property', *Journal of Intellectual Property Law*, pp293, 293–333

71 Included as Appendix 10 in Dr Darrell A Posey (1996) 'Traditional Resource Rights: International Instruments for Protection and Compensation for Indigenous Peoples and Local Communities' IUCN – The World Conservation Union

72 See Crucible Group (1994) 'People, Plants and Patents: the impact of intellectual property on biodiversity, conservation, trade and rural society', The Crucible Group, pp78–79 (1994)

73 United Nations Environment Programme, The Biodiversity Agenda: Decisions from the Third Meeting of the Conference of the Parties to the Convention on Biological Diversity, Decision 111/17, UN Doc UNEP/CBD/COP/3/38 (4–15 November 1996), available at http://www.biodiv.org/ cop3/html/COP-3-3 8-Rep-e.htm (visited 13 April 2000)

74 See *infra* Part III.E.3

75 Ibid

76 See Dr Duke's Phytochemical and Ethnobotanical databases, http://www.ars-grin.gov/cgi-bin/duke(ethnobot.pl) (search using *Curcuma longa*) (visited 3 April 2000)

77 See Sanjay Kumar (1997) 'India wins Battle with USA over Turmeric Patent', *Lancet*, No 350, p724; US PTO Patent No 5.401.504

78 The description of this example is adapted from Glenn M Wiser (1999) 'PTO Rejection of the "Ayahuasca" Patent Claim: Background and Analysis', http:// www.ciel.org/ptorejection.html (visited 1 April 2000)

79 Plant patents are a special kind of US patent available under the Plant Patent Act (1998) 35 USC §§ pp161–165. Originally intended to protect the identification by growers of new fruit varieties they are available for novel and distinctive varieties of asexually reproduced plants not found in an uncultivated state

80 See US Plant Patent No 5.751 (17 June 1986)

81 For further information, see The Ayahuasca Patent Case, http://www.ciel.org/ ayahuascapatentcase.html (visited 1 April 2000)

82 See generally, 'Comments on Improving Identification of Prior Art: Recommendations on Traditional Knowledge Relating to Biological Diversity Submitted to the United States Patent and Trademark Office', (2 August 1999), available at http://ciel.org/identificationofpriorait.pdf (visited 12 April 2000)

83 A detailed analysis may be found in Glenn M Wiser (1999) PTO Rejection of the 'Ayahuasca' Patent Claim: Background and Analysis, http:// ciel.org.ptorejection.html (visited 1 April 2000)

84 See Gupta, Anil (1996) Patent on 'Neem': Will it deprive Indian farmers of right to use it?, http://csf.Colorado.edu/sristi/papers/patentonneem.html (visited 1 April 2000) [hereinafter Patent on 'Neem']

85 US Patent No 4.946.681

86 US Patent No 5.124.349

87 Patent on 'Neem', *supra* note 84

88 Ibid

89 See S Gopikrishna Warrier (1997) 'India: US Patent Part of Prior Art', Business Line, 30 October, p3; 'European Patent Office Disallows Patent on Neem Oil', Chemical Business Newsbase, 27 January 1998, available in LEXIS, Chemical Industry database

Index